THE NATIONAL TRUST

HANDBOOK

FOR MEMBERS AND VISITORS 2008

1 February 2008 to 31 January 2009

© 2008 The National Trust

Editor: Lucy Peel
Editorial assistance: Penny Shapland, Penny Clarke, Wendy Smith
Production: Peter Kraushaar, Graham Prichard
Art direction: Neil Eastell
Customer care: Alex Youel
Design: Mike Blacker, Cindy Edler (4643)
Database developers: Roger Shapland, Dave Buchanan
Maps: ©Maps in Minutes™ 2007. ©Crown Copyright, Ordnance Survey & Ordnance Survey Northern Ireland 2006 Permit No. NI 1675 & ©Government of Ireland, Ordnance Survey Ireland.
Origination by Zebra
Printed by St Ives, Peterborough
Printed on VGreen Silk and City Green made from 100 per cent post-consumer waste

NT LDS stock no: 73801/08
ISBN 978-0-7078-0406-4

Please keep this Handbook for reference, and record your membership number here:

Renewal month:

Photographic acknowledgements

National Trust Photographic Library photographers:
Mary Allwood, Matthew Antrobus, Peter Aprahamian, Rob Auckland, Bill Batten, Niall Benvie, Andrew Besley, Clive Boursnell, Michael Boys, Heather Bradshaw, Bernie Brown, Andrew Butler, Gavan Caldwell, Michael Caldwell, Colin Clarke, Vera Collingwood, Peter Cook, Michael Allwood-Coppin, Val Corbett, Joe Cornish, Derek Croucher, Bill Davis, David Dixon, Rod J. Edwards, Andreas von Einsiedel, Derek Forss, Geoffrey Frosh, Lee Frost, Dennis Gilbert, Jim Hallett, Ray Hallett, Geoff Hamilton, Jerry Harpur, Paul Harris, Mike Harry, Jo Haughton, Paul Hobson, Ross Hoddinott, Chris Holmes, Andrea Jones, Chris King, Roger Kinkead, David Kjaer, Andrew Lawson, David Levenson, Brian Lightfoot, Nadia Mackenzie, Leo Mason, Duncan McEwan, Nick Meers, Colin Molyneux, Andrew Montgomery, Geoff Morgan, Robert Morris, James Mortimer, David Noton, Alasdair Ogilvie, Hugh Palmer, Erik Pelham, Mike Read, Stephen Robson, David Sellman, Neil Campbell-Sharp, Ian Shaw, Steve Stephens, Colin Sturges, Robert Thrift, David Tipling, Rupert Truman, Paul Wakefield, John Walton, David Watson, Paul Watson, Tony West, Mike Wilkes, Emma Williams, Mike Williams, Jennie Woodcock.

Additional photographs supplied by: NT/Richard Bifield, E. Chambré Hardman Collection, NT/Ian Grafton, NT/Mike Hardy, NT/Fisheye Images, John Such/Scanair, NT/David Slade, NT/A Tryner, NT/Derek Wilbraham, www.scenicireland.com

Front cover: the north front of Speke Hall, Liverpool.
Title page, clockwise from top left: the Saloon, Coughton Court, Warwickshire; Acorn Bank Garden, Cumbria; scabious; detail of a parlour, Birmingham Back to Backs; Kingston Lacy, Dorset; Derwentwater, Cumbria; robin in winter.
Contents page, from top: barn owl; local produce at Wordsworth House, Cumbria; Patterson's Spade Mill, Co. Antrim; Tom Heights, Coniston.
Back cover: European river otter.

Contents

General information

Highlights for 2008	4
How to use this Handbook	8
What's new	10
Area maps	11
Making the most of your visits	370
Holidays with the National Trust	378
How you can help the National Trust	380
Making contact	382
National Trust membership	384
Membership application form	385
Your questions answered	387
County/administrative area index	389
Property & general index	395

Places to visit

South West	25
South & South East	109
London	169
East of England	181
East Midlands	213
West Midlands	235
North West	263
Yorkshire	295
North East	315
Wales	329
Northern Ireland	351

The National Trust cares for 707 miles (1,138 km) of coastline, 253,349 hectares (626,051 acres) of countryside,

Today the pressures of contemporary life mean that the values at the heart of the Trust's work are needed more than ever. The National Trust was founded more than a century ago to protect places of natural beauty and historic interest for ever, for everyone.

This year, in response to a demand for increased opening, and so that you can enjoy even more great days out, we have extended our opening season considerably. Most properties are now open from at least 1 March to 2 November. Some, of course, never close.

Here are just a few of the new highlights to look out for in 2008 – more reasons to make the most of your membership:

■ **Celebrations at Hardwick Hall** Commemorating the 400th anniversary of Bess of Hardwick's death, 2008 sees a host of special exhibitions planned throughout the year.

■ **Quarry Bank Mill** To celebrate Cheshire's Year of the Gardens 2008, the Trust will be opening its newly acquired 'secret' garden in spring.

■ **The Museum of Childhood** re-opens at Sudbury Hall following a £2.2 million refurbishment. The new museum offers a fun and fascinating look at childhood from the 19th century to the present day.

The National Trust is involved in promoting four key themes – all of them issues facing us today and relevant to the future sustainability of the organisation. These are cultural heritage, hidden nature, climate change and local food – so read on to find out more about how you can get involved.

Cultural heritage

The memories and stories associated with our properties and the people who lived there are all unique and deserve to be looked after. There's a chance to find out about what life was like for the paupers living in The Workhouse, Southwell, in the 19th century or, in stark contrast, the life of Bess of Hardwick, Elizabethan England's wealthiest woman who built Hardwick Hall. The range of properties the Trust cares for, from humble urban back to

backs to grand castles, wild stretches of coastline to archaeological sites and glorious gardens, means there is so much heritage out there just waiting for you to discover. The nation's heritage plays a part in all our lives, as it underpins our quality of life and contributes to our sense of national and local identity.

Hidden nature

Conserving nature, for the benefit of everyone, is at the heart of what the National Trust does and our properties are a great place to discover hidden nature. To help you find out more there are hundreds of special events held every year, from bat walks and bug safaris, to fungi forays and guided nature walks. There are plenty of ways you can get involved.

And new for 2008 is our very first Hidden Nature Week, with numerous events and competitions to encourage adults and children to discover and care for wildlife in their own environment. Visitors will also get the chance to see behind the scenes into birds' nests, bat roosts and otter holts, via new cameras which are being installed.

An oystercatcher nest with eggs on the shingle beach at Orford Ness

Produce for sale at Stourhead Farm Shop, Wiltshire. The farm shop is managed by two local Trust tenant farmers to provide the area with high quality, fresh produce

There are plenty of other places to see wildlife with the National Trust. Our traditional orchards, gardens, coastline and countryside are full of hidden nature – you just need to find it! To find out more about Hidden Nature Week and wildlife events visit www.nationaltrust.org.uk/hiddennature

Local food

However stunning and inspiring they are, the value of National Trust gardens goes way beyond the aesthetic. Over 50 working and ornamental kitchen gardens provide local and seasonal produce to our restaurants and tea-rooms. So why not visit and see the mouthwatering crops being grown, find inspiration for your garden at home and taste the produce yourself over lunch?

As well as getting a taste of heritage, visitors can learn about traditional food production and the importance of local and seasonal food through our Plot to Plate events. So, if you're keen to get back to basics and grow your own produce, then visit one of our kitchen gardens and pick up

some tips. Here are a couple of examples to get your taste buds going:

- **Sizergh Castle**, Cumbria: the kitchen garden grows soft fruits, including strawberries, raspberries, loganberries and redcurrants, which are used in recipes available in the new tea-room.

- **Clumber Park**, Nottinghamshire: the walled kitchen garden, constructed in 1772, covers four acres and has one of the longest glasshouses in National Trust ownership. Vines, figs and peaches are grown here and all produce is provided to the restaurant and also sold to visitors. The gardeners also hold special tasting days, when you can compare modern and traditional taste sensations.

If it's a shopping experience you are after, then why not try one of our regular farmers' markets selling delicious locally grown food? From Sissinghurst in Kent to the hugely popular Stourhead Estate in Wiltshire, we are working to promote local and seasonal food. Find out more by visiting our website.

15 houses and gardens, 149 registered museums, **127 factories, workshops and mines,**

28 castles, twelve lighthouses, two gold mines, 78 mills, 57 historic villages, 43 pubs and much else besides

Before and after views of rock ridges below the summit of Glyder Fawr, Snowdon. A climber stands between the rocks, showing the amount of snow in 1996, and a similar view, showing the lack of snow in 2006. From the climate change exhibition 'Exposed'

Climate change

The effects of climate change can be felt daily – whether it be something as mundane as having to mow the grass year round or profoundly more serious, such as tackling eroding coastlines and dealing with flooding.

Besides changing practices to adapt to the impact on our buildings, gardens, coast and countryside, the National Trust is committed to reducing its own environmental footprint and is taking many steps, both large and small, to help the environment. These steps may be something as high profile as supporting national campaigns (such as the anti-Stansted Airport expansion campaign), to something as simple as the launch of our environmentally friendly jute bag, which has been snapped up by members and visitors alike.

Yet as well as these key issues, our role as guardians of the nation's heritage remains unchanged. So whatever you're looking for – be it art and architecture, fun for the family, gardens and wildlife, or simply a pleasant walk through countryside or a cream tea with family or friends – this Handbook will help you plan some great days out.

Easy properties to get to without a car

Giant's Causeway (p.362)
On the North Antrim Coast Path, with buses from Coleraine and Ballycastle. In summer, the Causeway Rambler links the Giant's Causeway with Carrick-a-Rede.

Hardcastle Crags (p.305)
From Hebden Bridge you can walk along the river or catch a bus.

Lanhydrock (p.76)
Pleasant walk from Bodmin Parkway station. NCN3 runs past the entrance.

Osterley Park (p.176)
Follow the London Cycle Network, get the bus or tube.

Prior Park (p.90)
Regular public transport from the centre of Bath.

Quarry Bank Mill (p.285)
Easy access by train. Bus drops off at property.

Shropshire Hills (p.245)
Shropshire Hills Shuttle Bus runs to Carding Mill Valley and the Long Mynd (weekends and bank holidays between Easter and October).

Sutton Hoo (p.207)
Within easy reach of rail and bus services.

Treasurer's House (p.312)
City-centre house close to cycle routes. Good bus links from surrounding areas.

The Workhouse (p.234)
Good bus link between Nottingham and Newark on Trent.

Please remember – your membership card is always needed for free admission

Liverpool – European Capital of Culture 2008

If there's one place you should visit in 2008, it is Liverpool.

Liverpool is the European Capital of Culture in 2008 and a mouth-watering programme of events awaits for all tastes and ages throughout the year. Much of this programme is free, with a huge emphasis on the public participating and performing in events as the city aims to become 'the biggest stage in the world'.

Liverpool is also marking the year with the opening of several new venues, including the 10,600-seater Liverpool ECHO Arena. In addition the city is the venue for the 2008 National Trust AGM on 1 November.

Key highlights include:

18 April–10 August
Art in the Age of Steam The Walker art gallery hosts a unique exhibition featuring artists from Monet to Hopper, celebrating the power and impact of the railway on art.

30 May–31 August
Gustav Klimt The UK's first major retrospective of the work of the legendary Austrian artist will be at Tate Liverpool.

12 July–1 November 09
The Beat Goes On Showcasing Merseyside's world-shaping music scene, from the Cavern to Creamfields, at World Museum Liverpool.

For more information visit www.liverpool08.com

18–21 July The Tall Ships' Race 2008
A flotilla of more than 100 of some of the most beautiful vessels on the sea gather for a maritime spectacular on the River Mersey.

4 September and **2 October**
Sir Simon Rattle conducts the Berlin Philharmonic Orchestra and the Royal Liverpool Philharmonic Orchestra. Includes the world premiere of new work by Brett Dean.

2 October–11 January 09 Le Corbusier
The life and work of the most famous architect of the 20th century will feature in a new international exhibition at the Crypt in Liverpool's Metropolitan Cathedral.

The National Trust in Liverpool

2008 is also a great opportunity to visit the National Trust's Liverpool properties: 16th-century Speke Hall on the banks of the River Mersey; Mr Hardman's Photographic Studio – a complete time capsule of Liverpool life in the mid-20th century, containing superb examples of Hardman's unique photographic images; Mendips and 20 Forthlin Road, the childhood homes of John Lennon and Sir Paul McCartney; and the wonderful dune coastline at Formby just outside Liverpool, with its resident population of red squirrels and superb coastal walks.

Pitt Street, Liverpool, photographed by E. Chambré Hardman

The Handbook gives details of how you can visit National Trust properties, including opening arrangements for the period from the start of February 2008 to the end of January 2009, and available facilities. Property entries are arranged by area (see map on page 11) and are ordered alphabetically within each area. Maps for each area appear on pages 12 to 24, and these show properties with a charge for entry, together with a selection of coast and countryside places. Maps also show main population centres.

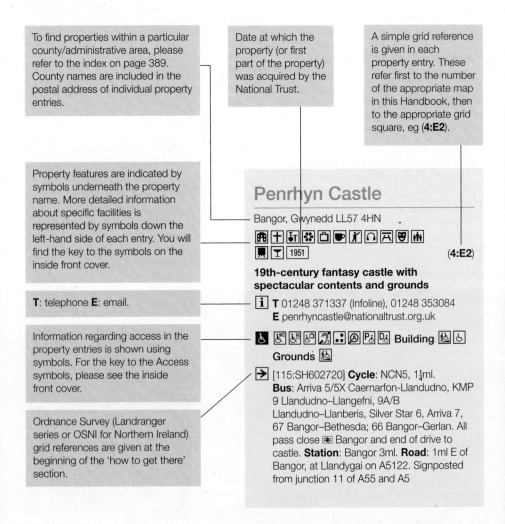

To find properties within a particular county/administrative area, please refer to the index on page 389. County names are included in the postal address of individual property entries.

Date at which the property (or first part of the property) was acquired by the National Trust.

A simple grid reference is given in each property entry. These refer first to the number of the appropriate map in this Handbook, then to the appropriate grid square, eg (**4:E2**).

Property features are indicated by symbols underneath the property name. More detailed information about specific facilities is represented by symbols down the left-hand side of each entry. You will find the key to the symbols on the inside front cover.

T: telephone **E**: email.

Information regarding access in the property entries is shown using symbols. For the key to the Access symbols, please see the inside front cover.

Ordnance Survey (Landranger series or OSNI for Northern Ireland) grid references are given at the beginning of the 'how to get there' section.

Penrhyn Castle

Bangor, Gwynedd LL57 4HN

1951 (**4:E2**)

19th-century fantasy castle with spectacular contents and grounds

T 01248 371337 (Infoline), 01248 353084
E penrhyncastle@nationaltrust.org.uk

Building Grounds

[115:SH602720] **Cycle**: NCN5, 1¼ml. **Bus**: Arriva 5/5X Caernarfon-Llandudno, KMP 9 Llandudno–Llangefni, 9A/B Llandudno–Llanberis, Silver Star 6, Arriva 7, 67 Bangor–Bethesda; 66 Bangor–Gerlan. All pass close Bangor and end of drive to castle. **Station**: Bangor 3ml. **Road**: 1ml E of Bangor, at Llandygai on A5122. Signposted from junction 11 of A55 and A5

Please remember – your membership card is always needed for free admission

Opening arrangements

The information is given in table format, intended to show at a glance when properties or parts of properties are open and when they are closed.

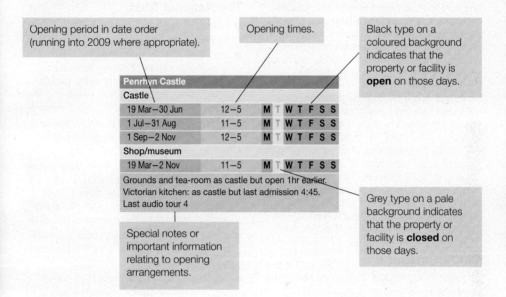

Opening period in date order (running into 2009 where appropriate).

Opening times.

Black type on a coloured background indicates that the property or facility is **open** on those days.

Penrhyn Castle									
Castle									
19 Mar–30 Jun	12–5	M	T	W	T	F	S	S
1 Jul–31 Aug	11–5	M	T	W	T	F	S	S
1 Sep–2 Nov	12–5	M	T	W	T	F	S	S
Shop/museum									
19 Mar–2 Nov	11–5	M	T	W	T	F	S	S

Grounds and tea-room as castle but open 1hr earlier.
Victorian kitchen: as castle but last admission 4:45.
Last audio tour 4

Special notes or important information relating to opening arrangements.

Grey type on a pale background indicates that the property or facility is **closed** on those days.

Please note the following points about this year's Handbook:

- areas are shown in hectares (1ha = 2.47 acres) with the acres equivalent in brackets. Short distances are shown in yards (1 yard = 0.91m); longer distances are measured in miles (ml). Heights are shown in metres (m).

- although opening times and arrangements vary considerably from place to place and from year to year, most houses will be open during the period 1 March to 2 November inclusive, usually on three or more days per week between about noon and 5pm.

  Please note that, unless otherwise stated in the property entry, last admission is 30 minutes before the stated closing time.

- we make every effort to ensure that property opening times and available facilities are as published, but very occasionally it is essential to change these at short notice. Always check the current Handbook for details and, if making a special journey, please telephone in advance for confirmation. You can also check our website **www.nationaltrust.org.uk**

- when telephoning a property, please remember that we can provide a better service if you call on a weekday morning, on a day when the property is open. Alternatively, call our Membership Department on 0844 800 1895, seven days a week (9–5:30 Monday to Friday, 9–4 at weekends and bank holidays).

Extra copies of *The National Trust Handbook* are available, while stocks last.

Car parking sticker

This year your car parking sticker can be found in this Handbook, lightly glued to a new bookmark which can also be easily removed. Your Handbook should fall open where the sticker and bookmark appear. For technical reasons the sticker in some copies will be on the back of the bookmark (and upside down) and in some on the front of the bookmark and the correct way up. If you need a replacement or additional sticker please contact the Membership Department (see p.382).

Please remember that the sticker is not a substitute for a valid membership card, which should continue to be shown to staff on request whenever you enter Trust properties and pay and display car parks. Please note that this year's Handbook now runs from 1 February 2008 to 31 January 2009 inclusive. This reflects the Trust's efforts to open its properties, or at least parts of them, significantly earlier in the year than before. In case of doubt, the 2008 Handbook is the definitive guide to opening arrangements.

Gift Aid on Entry

This year, most National Trust properties will be operating the Gift Aid on Entry scheme at their admission points. Where the scheme is operating, non-members are offered a choice between paying the standard admission price or paying the Gift Aid Admission, which includes a 10% voluntary donation. Gift Aid Admissions enable the National Trust to reclaim tax on the whole amount paid* – an extra 25% – potentially a very significant boost to property funds.

The admission prices shown on the National Trust's website, or from the Trust's Membership Department, are inclusive of the 10% voluntary donation where properties are operating the Gift Aid on Entry scheme, but both the standard admission price and the Gift Aid Admission will be displayed at the property and on our website.

Most National Trust members already pay their subscriptions using Gift Aid, helping the

* Gift Aid donations must be supported by a valid Gift Aid declaration, and a Gift Aid declaration can only cover donations made by an individual for him/herself or for him/herself and members of his/her family.

Trust to the tune of many millions of pounds every year at no extra cost to themselves. If you would like to know more about Gift Aid please contact the Membership Department on 0844 800 1895.

The National Trust:

● looks after special places for ever, for everyone.

● is a registered charity, founded in 1895, to look after places of historic interest or natural beauty permanently for the benefit of the nation across England, Wales and Northern Ireland.

● is independent of the Government and we receive no direct state grant or subsidy for our core work.

● one of Europe's leading conservation bodies, protecting through ownership, management and covenants 253,349 hectares (626,051 acres) of land of outstanding natural beauty and 707 miles (1,138 kilometres) of coastline.

● is dependent on the support of its 3.5 million members and its visitors, volunteers, partners and benefactors.

● is responsible for historic buildings dating from the Middle Ages to modern times, ancient monuments, gardens, landscape parks and farmland leased to over 1,000 tenant farmers.

● has the unique statutory power to declare land inalienable. Such land cannot be voluntarily sold, mortgaged or compulsorily purchased against the Trust's wishes without special parliamentary procedure. This special power means that protection by the Trust is for ever.

● spends all its income on the care and maintenance of the land and buildings in its protection, but cannot meet the cost of all its obligations and so is always in need of financial support.

● Our strategic aims 'to 2010 and beyond' are:
　– engaging supporters
　– improving our conservation and environmental performance
　– investing in our people
　– financing our future.

Please remember – your membership card is always needed for free admission

This key shows how England, Wales and Northern Ireland are divided into eleven areas for the purposes of this Handbook, and displayed on seven maps. The maps show those properties which have individual entries as well as many additional coast and countryside sites in the care of the National Trust.

In order to help with general orientation, the maps show main roads and population centres. However, the plotting of each site serves only as a guide to its location. (Full-scale maps can be purchased from National Trust shops.) Please note that some countryside properties, for example those in the Lake District, cover many thousands of hectares. In such cases the symbol is placed centrally as an indication of general location.

KEY:

Map **1** South West
Map **2** South and
       South East
       London
Map **3** East of England
       East Midlands
Map **4** Wales
       West Midlands
Map **5** Yorkshire
       North West (S)
Map **6** North West (N)
       North East
Map **7** Northern Ireland

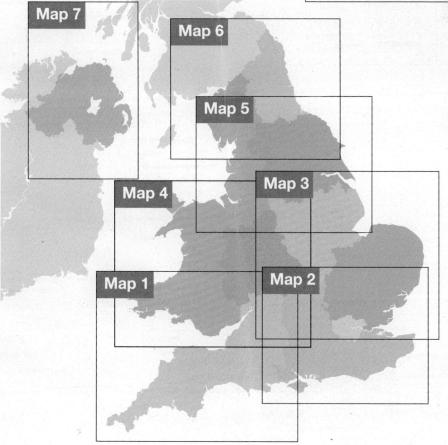

For general and membership enquiries, please telephone 0844 800 1895

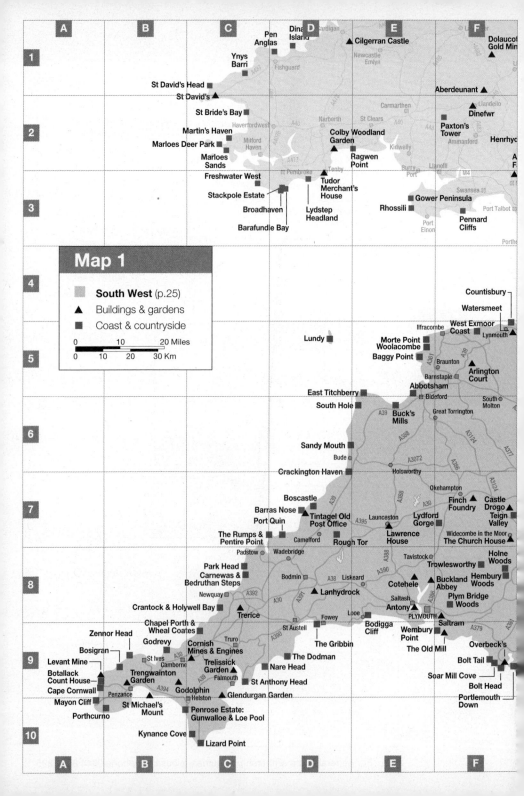

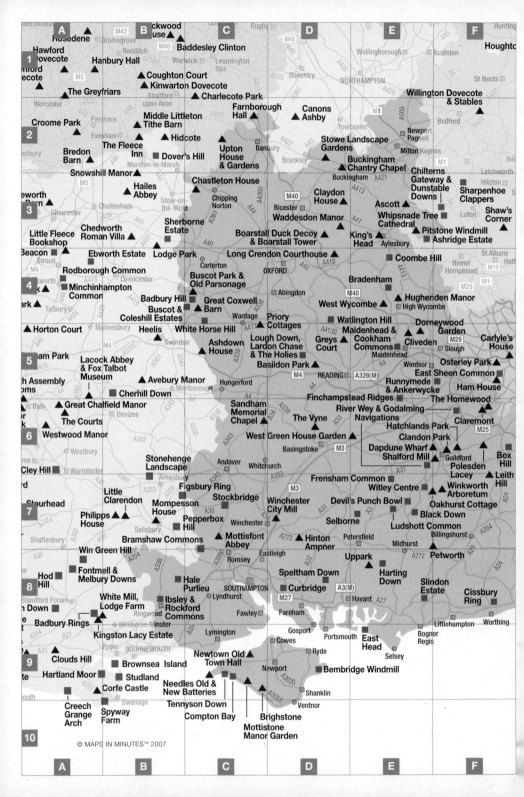

G **H** **I** **J** **K** **L**

on Mill

Wicken Fen

Mildenhall

Histon
Burwell
Newmarket

1

Bury St Edmunds
Theatre Royal

Saxmundham

Leiston
Aldeburgh

CAMBRIDGE
M11

Anglesey Abbey & Lode Mill

Ickworth

Stowmarket

Dunwich Heath Coast Centre & Beach

Woodbridge

Wimpole Hall & Home Farm

Melford Hall

Lavenham Guildhall

IPSWICH

Kyson Hill
Sutton Hoo

Orford Ness

2

Royston
Haverhill
Long Melford
Sudbury

Flatford: Bridge Cottage
Pin Mill

Felixstowe

Saffron Walden

Thorington Hall

Dedham Vale

Harwich

3

Stevenage

M11

Coggeshall: Paycocke's & Grange Barn

Colchester

Bourne Mill

A1(M)
Welwyn Garden City
Ware
Hertford

Bishop's Stortford
A120
Braintree
Witham
West Mersea

Clacton-on-Sea

Hatfield Forest

Hoddesdon
Harlow

Blake's Wood

Chelmsford
Maldon

Copt Hall Marshes

4

M25
M11

Danbury & Lingwood Commons

Northey Island

Burnham-on-Crouch

Rayleigh Mount

5

Fenton House
Sutton House

Brentwood
Rayleigh
Southend-on-Sea

2 Willow Road
George Inn
Eastbury Manor House
Rainham Hall

Basildon
Canvey Island

Roman Bath
Blewcoat School

Red House

Sheerness

St John's Jerusalem

6

Lindsey House
Morden Hall Park
Watermeads
Selsdon Wood

Owletts
Coldrum Long Barrow

Rochester

Whitstable
Herne Bay
Margate

Quebec House

Knole
Old Soar Manor

Maidstone

M2

Faversham
Canterbury

Ramsgate

Chartwell
Emmetts

Ightham Mote

Stoneacre

M20

Deal

Toys Hill

M23

Sprivers Garden

Ashford

South Foreland Lighthouse

7

Standen

Chiddingstone
Tunbridge Wells

Scotney Castle

Sissinghurst Castle Garden

M20
White Cliffs
Dover
Folkestone

Wakehurst Place

Tenterden

Smallhythe Place
Royal Military Canal

Hythe

Nymans

Sheffield Park Garden

Bateman's

Bodiam Castle
Lamb House

Rye
New Romney

8

Hurstpierpoint
Lewes

Battle

Hastings

Devil's Dyke
A27

Hailsham
Bexhill-on-Sea

Hove
Brighton

Monk's House
Alfriston Clergy House

Newhaven
Eastbourne

Frog Firle Farm

Birling Gap & Seven Sisters

9

Chyngton Farm

Crowlink

Map 2

South and South East (p.109)

London (p.169)

▲ Buildings & gardens

■ Coast & countryside

0   10   20 Miles

0   10   20   30 Km

10

G **H** **I** **J** **K** **L**

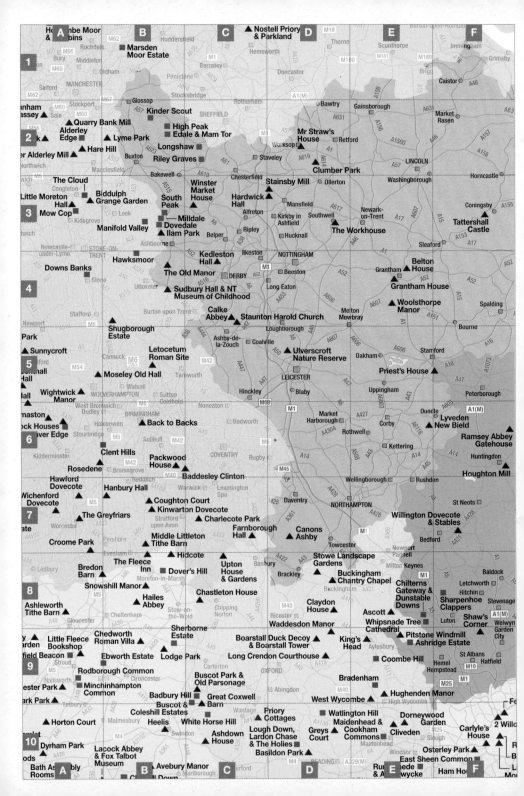

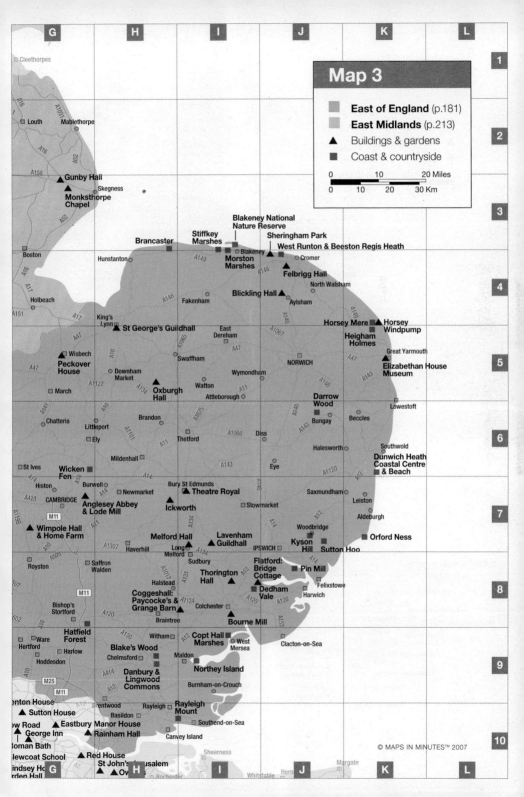

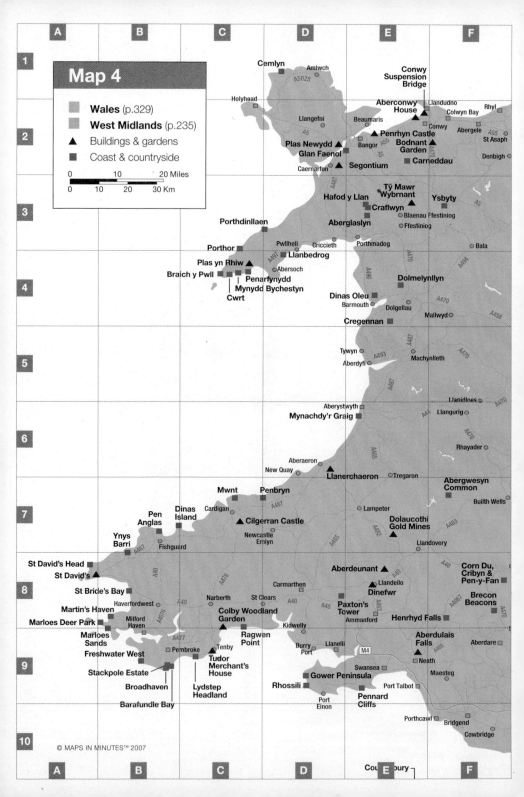

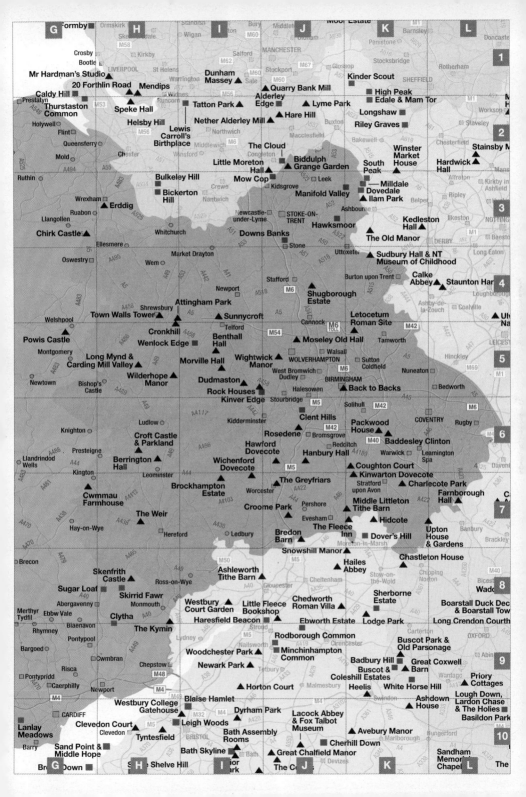

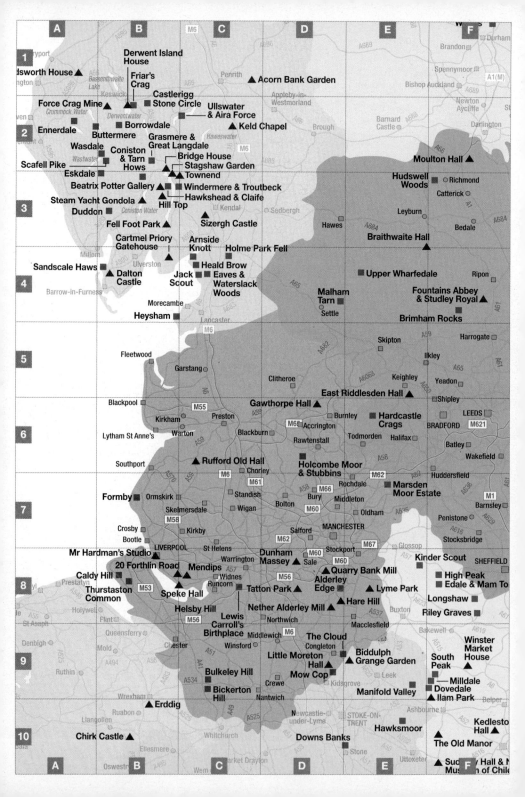

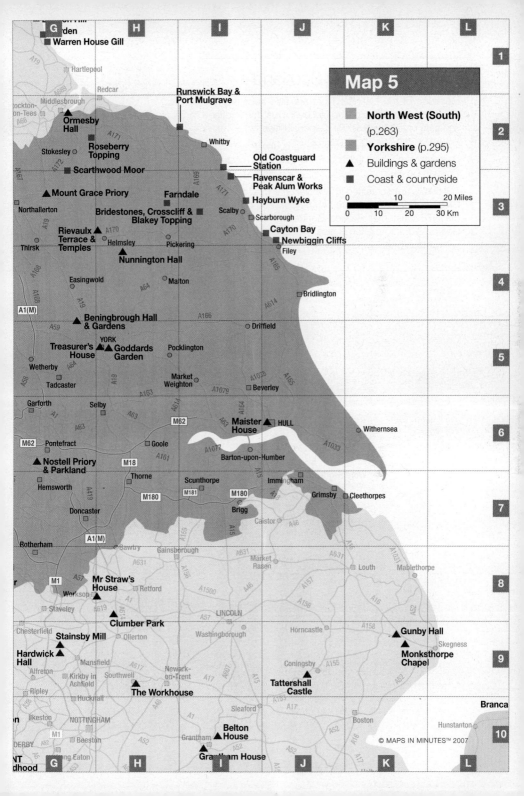

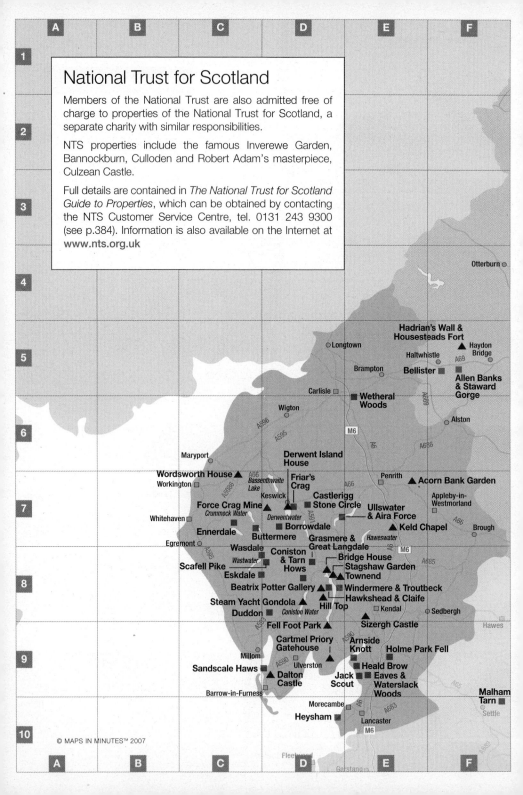

National Trust for Scotland

Members of the National Trust are also admitted free of charge to properties of the National Trust for Scotland, a separate charity with similar responsibilities.

NTS properties include the famous Inverewe Garden, Bannockburn, Culloden and Robert Adam's masterpiece, Culzean Castle.

Full details are contained in *The National Trust for Scotland Guide to Properties*, which can be obtained by contacting the NTS Customer Service Centre, tel. 0131 243 9300 (see p.384). Information is also available on the Internet at **www.nts.org.uk**

Otterburn

Hadrian's Wall & Housesteads Fort

Longtown

Haydon Bridge

Haltwhistle

Brampton

Bellister

Allen Banks & Staward Gorge

Carlisle

Wetheral Woods

Wigton

Alston

Maryport

Derwent Island House

Penrith

Acorn Bank Garden

Wordsworth House

Bassenthwaite Lake

Friar's Crag

Workington

Keswick

Castlerigg Stone Circle

Appleby-in-Westmorland

Force Crag Mine

Crummock Water

Derwentwater

Ullswater & Aira Force

Whitehaven

Borrowdale

Keld Chapel

Brough

Ennerdale

Buttermere

Grasmere & Great Langdale

Haweswater

Egremont

Wasdale

Coniston & Tarn Hows

Bridge House

Scafell Pike

Wastwater

Stagshaw Garden

Eskdale

Townend

Beatrix Potter Gallery

Windermere & Troutbeck

Steam Yacht Gondola

Hawkshead & Claife

Duddon

Hill Top

Coniston Water

Kendal

Sedbergh

Fell Foot Park

Sizergh Castle

Hawes

Cartmel Priory Gatehouse

Arnside Knott

Holme Park Fell

Millom

Ulverston

Heald Brow

Sandscale Haws

Dalton Castle

Jack Scout

Eaves & Waterslack Woods

Malham Tarn

Barrow-in-Furness

Morecambe

Settle

Heysham

Lancaster

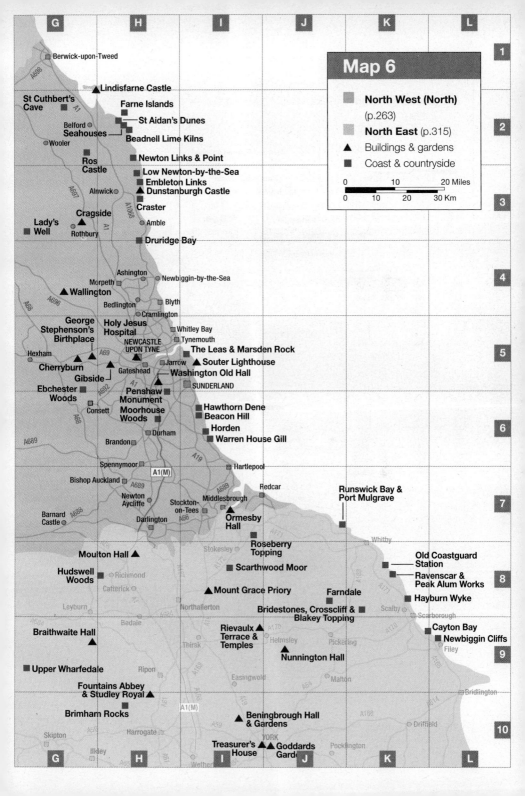

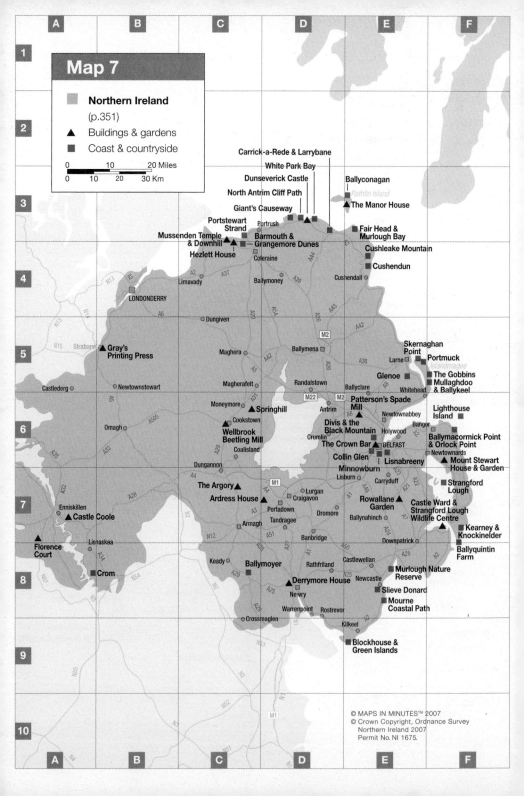

Ask most people what they love best about Devon and Cornwall, and it is likely that their answer would be: the coast. The glorious south-western coastline – so varied and distinctive, so unspoilt, so breathtakingly beautiful – exudes a powerful magnetism, drawing us back again and again for refreshment, relaxation and inspiration.

The Trust protects 366 miles (36 per cent) of the coastline of Devon and Cornwall, along with extensive areas of farmland, woodland and moorland. Wherever you are in the two counties, you are never more than 25 miles from the sea – from the great sandy beaches of the north coast, where the surf comes rolling in, from the high rocky headlands like a string of fortifications around the coast, from the weedy pools, coves and tidal inlets of the south coast. And around it all runs the incomparable South West Coast Path, at 630 miles the longest National Trail in the country, linking everywhere and providing unparalleled access on foot to all the lonely shores and soaring cliffs.

To the east, the region of Wessex is incredibly diverse. Spreading from Gloucestershire in the north, south through Somerset and Wiltshire, down to Dorset, it contains spectacular stretches of coastline, chalk downland, high moorland, historic landscapes and beautiful rolling countryside. The Cotswolds, in the north, boasts many lovely villages, some of which are partly owned by the Trust – which also owns uplands, farmland and ancient woodland. Altogether the Trust cares for more than 25,000 hectares (61,700 acres) of countryside in Wessex and welcomes an estimated 12 million visitors every year.

Surfing and sand

Among the popular spots in Devon and Cornwall are the surfing beaches of Godrevy and Chapel Porth; Kynance Cove on the Lizard, famous since Victorian times for its fantastic rocks and botanical rarities; Wembury, close to Plymouth Sound, with its rock pools and children's events; and Carnewas, overlooking the famous beauty spot of Bedruthan Steps.

Families flock to such glorious beaches as Woolacombe Sands, Holywell Bay and Crantock, Sandy Mouth and Duckpool on the north coast, and South Milton Sands, Porthcurno and Gunwalloe on the south.

In Dorset, the Purbeck Estate boasts one of Britain's best beaches, two National Nature Reserves and is home to the richest 10 square miles of wild flowers in the country.

The Jurassic Coast, a World Heritage Site, stretches all the way along the Dorset and East Devon coast, covering Purbeck, Burton Bradstock and Golden Cap, and Branscombe. Here lies a wonderfully varied landscape – ranging from heathland, dunes and a mile-long stretch of sand, to shingle and sandstone cliffs, perfect for picnics, walking and fossil hunting.

Above: **Golden Cap on the Jurassic Coast**
Left: **the glorious sandy beach of Woolacombe Sands**

Previous page: doorway at Cotehele, Cornwall (1:E8)

History – ancient, industrial and 20th-century

For those who like to delve a bit more deeply into the history of wherever they are, there are detailed leaflets available covering the Trust's coast and countryside (see page 30). In the old mining areas of Cornwall and West Devon, newly designated a World Heritage Site, you will find ruined engine houses now protected and preserved by the Trust; some of them, such as those at Botallack near St Just, clinging to the cliff edge just above the sea. In Botallack's Count House Workshop on

Right: sand sculpture at Kynance Cove
Below: Botallack near St Just
Below right: Parson Hawker's driftwood hut at Morwenstow

the clifftop you will find fascinating displays on the St Just coast's mining history.

There are many curious structures to be discovered and explored around the coasts of Devon and Cornwall, telling stories of this peninsula's colourful past – such as the military fortifications at Froward Point near Brixham and St Anthony Head near St Mawes, Parson Hawker's driftwood hut high on the cliffs at Morwenstow, the castellated coastguard lookout at Mayon Cliff above Sennen Cove, and the candy-striped 84ft-tall Gribbin daymark near Fowey.

West Dorset's historic landscape includes magnificent Iron Age hill forts, such as Hod Hill, Eggardon and Lambert's Castle, and make sure you don't miss North Somerset's Cheddar Cliffs. Cheddar, Britain's largest gorge, was carved by melt-water from the last Ice Age and has been forming and changing over the past 2 million years. Not far away you can experience the drama of Brean Down, which extends a mile and a half into the Bristol Channel and has truly breathtaking views, as well as abundant wildlife and fascinating history – including a Roman Temple, Napoleonic era fort and Second World War gun battery.

For information on coastal and countryside events held throughout the year, including surfing and sand sculpture competitions, treasure hunts, wildlife walks, barbecues and boat trips, go to the National Trust website or pick up a What's On guide to Devon and Cornwall.

www.nationaltrust.org.uk/coastandcountryside

Wildlife

The abundance of wildlife you will find on the Trust's coast and countryside sites in Devon and Cornwall bears witness to many years of pioneering nature conservation work. Try walking the Rosemergy and Bosigran cliffs near Zennor in West Penwith; between Bolt Head and Bolt Tail in South Devon; or from Kynance to Mullion on the Lizard, and appreciate the swathes of wild flowers which carpet the grazed clifftops in spring and summer.

That emblematic bird, the Cornish chough, has returned to breed in Cornwall at last, on the grazed cliffs of the Lizard. If you visit Lizard Point, be sure to stop by the Chough Watchpoint next door to the café, particularly at fledging time in the summer. On an old viaduct in Plym Bridge Woods, near Plymouth, you will find the observation post for the successful Peregrine Falcon Watch, set up to protect breeding falcons nearby (www.plym-peregrines.co.uk).

Above: peregrine falcon Below right: large blue butterfly Below: Rodborough Commons

The glorious rolling heathland on the Exmoor coast of North Devon, and in West Penwith and around Chapel Porth in Cornwall, provides a rich habitat for birds and insects. Ashclyst Forest on the Killerton Estate and Lydford Gorge are great spots for bats and butterflies (as are the Lanhydrock and Arlington estates), and there are numerous other sites, including areas of Dartmoor such as Hembury, where rare butterflies flourish under protective grazing regimes introduced by the Trust.

One high-summer sight not to be missed is the astonishing display of vivid arable flowers, such as poppies and corn marigolds, along with the wonderfully named Venus's looking-glass and weasel's snout, in the fields of West Pentire near Crantock in North Cornwall.

Some of the most important areas of chalk grassland in the country are found at Calstone, Cherhill Down and Whitesheet Hill in Wiltshire. Cherhill Down has a wide range of wildlife, including 25 varieties of breeding butterfly, while Fontmell and Melbury Downs in North Dorset are rich in flora and offer fantastic views.

One of Dorset's largest remaining expanses of heathland is on the Corfe Castle Estate on the Isle of Purbeck. This is an important breeding site for heathland birds as well as being home to sand lizards, snakes, dragonflies, grasshoppers, crickets, moths, beetles and butterflies.

At Minchinhampton and Rodborough Commons in Gloucestershire there are rare butterflies and wild flowers, including thirteen recorded species of orchid, while the large Holnicote Estate in Somerset boasts thirteen species of bat, and Collard Hill in the same county is home to the rare large blue butterfly.

As well as Studland, one of the richest areas for wildlife in Dorset is Brownsea Island in Poole Harbour. It boasts an immensely diverse range of wildlife and habitats over a very small area. It is also one of the few places in the country where there are still red squirrels.

Space for all to explore

The Trust has provided many specially adapted or graded paths and viewpoints around the coast, and inland too, so that some of the loveliest spots can be enjoyed by everyone, such as those at Glebe Cliff by Tintagel, Loe Pool near Helston, Snapes Point and Bolberry Down near Salcombe, Cadson Bury on the River Lynher near Callington, and Branscombe and Salcombe Hill near Sidmouth in East Devon.

Right: **Exmoor's Horner Wood** Below: **children at Dyrham** Bottom: **Sherborne Farm in the Cotswolds**

Discover Horner Wood, with its magnificent pollarded oaks and heathland grazed by red deer, or climb to Exmoor's highest point on Dunkery Beacon and enjoy the views along the coast. The Sherborne Estate, in the Cotswolds, is scattered with wonderful views, varied wildlife, water meadows and perfect picnic spots.

Or for somewhere really different, visit the Bath Skyline, a unique 6-mile walk around the outskirts of the city, through woodlands and wildflower meadows – a great retreat whether you want to picnic, fly kites or are just after some peace and quiet. Nearer Bristol discover Leigh Woods, a National Nature Reserve which contains numerous waymarked trails and hidden paths. It even has an all-ability special orienteering trail.

Further east, Burrow Mump in Somerset has stunning views across the Levels and Moors to the River Parrett and Glastonbury Tor. There are also 87 miles of footpaths, bridleways and cycle paths running across the beautiful Holnicote Estate – perfect for exploring the open moors and deep-sided valleys in the heart of Exmoor National Park.

Coast and countryside guides

To help you make the most of your time and to discover more about the places you visit, there are nearly 40 in-depth guide leaflets available covering the coast and countryside owned by the Trust in Devon and Cornwall. For a full list, please contact either the Cornwall or the Devon office. To buy specific Cornwall leaflets, contact the shop at Lanhydrock (01208 265952); for Devon leaflets contact the shop at Arlington Court (01271 851116).

Car parks in the West Country

The Trust owns numerous coastal car parks in Dorset, Devon and Cornwall, most of which are simply inconspicuous parking spots providing access to lovely remote coves, cliffs and headlands, undisturbed homes to a host of birds, bugs and butterflies. Some of the Trust's car parks are the gateways to more popular destinations, where you will find visitor facilities such as beach cafés and WCs.

Dorset					
Cogden, West Dorset	SY 503 883	Scabbacombe	SX 912 523	Botallack	SW 366 334
Stonebarrow Hill	SY 383 933	Man Sands	SX 913 531	Cape Cornwall	SW 353 318
Langdon Hill	SY 413 931	Salcombe Hill	SY 139 882	Bollowall	SW 354 314
Burton Bradstock	SY 491 888	Branscombe	SY 197 887	Porth Nanven (Cot Valley)	SW 358 308
Ringstead Bay	SY 760 822			Highburrow	
Spyway	SY 996 785	**Cornwall**		(Loe Bar west)	SW 635 249
		Morwenstow	SS 205 154	Penrose (Loe Pool west)	SW 639 259
Devon		Duckpool	SS 202 117	Degibna Chapel	
Barna Barrow,		Sandy Mouth	SS 203 100	(Loe Pool east)	SW 653 252
Countisbury	SS 753 497	Northcott Mouth	SS 204 084	Chyvarloe (Loe Bar east)	SW 653 235
Countisbury	SS 747 497	Strangles Beach	SX 134 952	Gunwalloe Church Cove	SW 660 207
Combe Park,		Glebe Cliff, Tintagel	SX 050 884	Predannack	SW 669 162
Hillsford Bridge	SS 740477	Port Quin	SW 972 805	Kynance Cove	SW 688 132
Woody Bay	SS 676 486	Lundy Bay	SW 953 796	Lizard Point	SW 703 116
Hunter's Inn,		Lead Mines, Pentireglaze	SW 942 799	Poltesco	SW 726 156
Heddon Valley	SS 655 481	Pentire Farm	SW 935 803	Bosveal (for Durgan)	SW 775 276
Trentishoe Down	SS 635 480	Park Head	SW 853 707	Trelissick	SW 836 397
Trentishoe Down	SS 628 479	Carnewas		St Anthony Head	SW 847 313
Torrs Walk, Ilfracombe	SS 511 475	(for Bedruthan Steps)	SW 850 690	Percuil	SW 858 342
Baggy Point, Croyde	SS 433 397	Crantock	SW 789 607	Porth Farm	
Brownsham, Hartland	SS 285 259	Treago Mill (for Polly Joke)	SW 778 601	(Towan Beach)	SW 867 329
East Titchberry, Hartland	SS 244 270	Holywell Bay	SW 767 586	Porthcurnick	SW 876 357
Wembury Beach	SX 517 484	St Agnes Beacon	SW 704 503	Pendower Beach	SW 897 384
Stoke	SX 556 465	Wheal Coates	SW 703 500	Carne Beach	SW 905 384
Ringmore	SX 649 457	Chapel Porth	SW 697 495	Nare Head	SW 922 380
South Milton Sands	SX 677 415	Basset's Cove	SW 638 440	Penare (Dodman Point)	SW 998 404
Bolberry Down	SX 689 384	Reskajeage Downs	SW 623 430	Lamledra (Vault Beach)	SW 011 411
East Soar	SX 713 376	Deadman's Cove	SW 625 432	Coombe Farm	SX 110 512
Snapes Point	SX 739 404	Derrick Cove	SW 620 429	Pencarrow Head	SX 150 513
Prawle Point	SX 775 354	Hudder Down	SW 612 428	Frogmore	SX 157 517
Little Dartmouth	SX 874 492	Hell's Mouth	SW 599 427	Lansallos	SX 174 518
Higher Brownstone	SX 905 510	Godrevy	SW 582 432	Hendersick	SX 236 520
Coleton Camp	SX 909 513	Carn Galver	SW 422 364	Bodigga	SX 273 543
		Levant	SW 368 345	Cotehele Quay	SX 424 682

All income from Trust pay & display car parks supports conservation work.

www.nationaltrust.org.uk/coastandcountryside

Neptune's Legacy

Morte Bay in North Devon

Drifts of pink thrift leading down to an azure sea; waves dramatically crashing against the rocks on a winter's day; the evocative mew of the gulls; the beams from numerous distant lighthouses sweeping across the sea – all reasons why the coast of Britain is loved and why, when I have the time, I want to walk the entire coast of Devon and Cornwall.

As the toe of England dips into the Western Approaches, about 36 per cent of the coast of the two counties – which measures 1,025 miles – is saved for the nation and lovingly looked after by numerous National Trust wardens and volunteers. The comprehensive ownership of the coast, and now some of the more tranquil river estuaries on the southern shores, is one of the greatest achievements of the National Trust – and one which brings many tourists to the region.

The first coastal property in England to come to the infant National Trust was Barras Nose, near Tintagel in North Cornwall, bought by public subscription in 1897. In North Devon, Miss Rosalie Chichester gave parts of Morte Point in memory of her parents in 1909; a generous gift which was followed by several others, culminating in her bequest of the Arlington Estate in 1949.

These two means of acquisition set the trend. In the 1920s and 1930s several places, such as Pentire Point and The Rumps, near Polzeath, and Bolt Head near Salcombe, were threatened by development and saved by many local subscribers. Memories of happy times spent at the seaside encouraged others to leave property or money as a memorial, particularly in the post-Second World War period. Lawrence Binyon's famous commemorative words: 'At the going down of the sun and in the morning, we will remember them,' were written looking out over the North Cornwall coast – a testimony to its timelessness and beauty.

In 1965 Enterprise Neptune was launched, and since then numerous properties have been acquired, saved and enhanced for the nation.

And still the task continues: with the shore establishment HMS Cambridge at Wembury near Plymouth, bought recently with the help of a successful public appeal and now miraculously restored, and St Agnes Head in Cornwall, which was acquired in 2006.

How can we help to preserve the coast for future generations to enjoy? Join the National Trust; become a volunteer warden; help to pick up marine debris and litter; and to quote a seaside postcard: 'Take only memories and leave only footprints.'

■ Jeremy Pearson, Curator

Barras Nose, near Tintagel

A La Ronde

Summer Lane, Exmouth, Devon EX8 5BD

 1991   (1:G7)

Quirky 18th-century house with fascinating interior decoration and collections

This unique sixteen-sided house, described by Lucinda Lambton as having 'a magical strangeness that one might dream of only as a child', was built for two spinster cousins, Jane and Mary Parminter, on their return from a grand tour of Europe in the late 18th century. It contains many objects and mementoes of their travels. The extraordinary interior decoration includes a feather frieze and a fragile shell-encrusted gallery, said to contain nearly 25,000 shells, which can be viewed in its entirety on closed-circuit television.

What's new in 2008 Parminter Walk, part of the original perimeter walk, is now reopen (uneven underfoot, stout footwear advisable)

⭐ Unsuitable for caravans/trailers due to narrow lanes and limited parking. Tel. in advance. Small and fragile rooms, so large/bulky bags need to be left in lockers at entrance and groups of 15+ must tel. in advance

ℹ️ **T** 01395 265514, 01395 255918 (shop), 01395 255912 (tea-room)
E alaronde@nationaltrust.org.uk

🎭 Family activities, exhibitions

🚶 Parminter Walk

♿ 🚾 👓 🅿️ **Building** 🏞️ **Grounds** 🏞️

🏠 NT shop. Plant sales

🍴 Mary-Jane tea-room (NT-approved concession)

A La Ronde								
House								
15 Mar–2 Nov	11–5	**M**	**T**	**W**	T	F	**S**	**S**
Shop/grounds								
15 Mar–2 Nov	10:30–5:30	**M**	**T**	**W**	T	F	**S**	**S**
Tea-room								
15 Mar–2 Nov	10:30–5	**M**	**T**	**W**	T	F	**S**	**S**

Due to the size and nature of the house, small delays may occur at busy times

A La Ronde: a unique sixteen-sided house

👶 Hip-carrying infant seats for loan. Children's quiz/trail. 'Touch and take' shell basket. Family activities

🎬 Suitable for school groups

➡️ [192:SY004834] **Foot**: East Devon Way borders property. South West Coast Path within ⅔ml. **Bus**: Stagecoach in Devon 57 Exeter–Exmouth to within ¼ml. **Station**: Lympstone Village (U) 1¼ml; Exmouth 2ml. **Road**: 2ml N of Exmouth on A376

🅿️ Free parking. Coaches must be booked

NT properties nearby
Branscombe, Killerton

Antony

Torpoint, Cornwall PL11 2QA

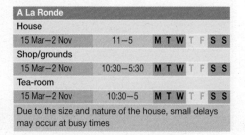 1961   (1:E8)

Superb early 18th-century mansion set in parkland and fine gardens

Faced in silver-grey Pentewan stone and flanked by colonnaded wings of mellow brick, this classically beautiful house is a beguiling mixture of the formal and informal, the venerable and the modern. Still very much the home of the Carew Pole family, it contains fine collections of paintings, furniture and textiles. The expansive grounds bordering the tidal Lynher estuary were landscaped by Repton and include a formal garden with topiary, a knot garden, modern sculptures and the National Collection of Daylilies. The woodland garden (owned by the Carew Pole Garden Trust) has outstanding

Antony								
House/garden								
24 Mar–29 May	1:30–5:30	M	**T**	**W**	**T**	F	S	S
1 Jun–31 Aug	1:30–5:30	M	**T**	**W**	**T**	F	S	**S**
2 Sep–30 Oct	1:30–5:30	M	**T**	**W**	**T**	F	S	S
Shop/restaurant								
As house	12:30–5:30							
Woodland garden								
1 Mar–30 Oct	11–5:30	M	**T**	**W**	**T**	F	**S**	**S**

Open BH Mons. Bath Pond House interior can only be seen by written application to the Property Manager, on days house is open

displays of rhododendrons, azaleas, magnolias and camellias (including the National Collection of *Camellia japonica*).

⭐ NT members free to woodland garden (not NT) only on days when house is open

ℹ️ **T** 01752 812191
E antony@nationaltrust.org.uk

Building ⬚⬚ Grounds ⬚➡️

💺 Restaurant (NT-approved concession) in east wing. Children's menu

👫 Baby-changing facilities. Baby back-carriers admitted. Hip-carrying infant seats for loan. Children's quiz/trail

➡️ [201:SX418564] **Cycle**: NCN27, 2ml.
Ferry: Torpoint 2ml. **Bus**: First 81/B/C from Plymouth (passing close ⯈ Plymouth), alight Great Park Estate, ¼ml. **Station**: Plymouth 6ml via vehicle ferry. **Road**: 6ml W of Plymouth via Torpoint car ferry, 2ml NW of Torpoint, N of A374, 16ml SE of Liskeard, 15ml E of Looe

🅿️ Free parking, 120yds

NT properties nearby
Cotehele, Saltram

Arlington Court and The National Trust's Carriage Collection

Arlington, nr Barnstaple, Devon EX31 4LP

🎟️🎟️✝️🎟️🎟️🎟️🎟️🎟️🎟️🎟️🎟️🎟️
🎟️🎟️🎟️🎟️🎟️ 1949 **(1:F5)**

Intimate and intriguing Regency house, set in extensive estate, and impressive collection of horse-drawn vehicles

Hidden in a wooded valley on the edge of Exmoor, the Arlington Estate houses numerous extraordinary collections, inside and out. The last owner, Miss Rosalie Chichester, developed

Arlington Court is an intimate and intriguing Regency house full of extraordinary collections

Unless indicated, last admission is always 30mins before closing time

Arlington Court

House & Carriage Collection		M	T	W	T	F	S	S
16 Mar–2 Nov	11–5	M	T	W	T	F	S	S
Shop/tea-room/garden/bat-cam								
2 Mar–9 Mar	12–4	M	T	W	T	F	S	S
16 Mar–29 Jun	10:30–5	M	T	W	T	F	S	S
30 Jun–31 Aug	10:30–5	M	T	W	T	F	S	S
1 Sep–2 Nov	10:30–5	M	T	W	T	F	S	S
7 Nov–21 Dec	11–4	M	T	W	T	F	S	S

Special guided tours 2 & 9 March, 12–3. Booking essential. Whole property open Sats of BH weekends. Other Sats in July & Aug, only garden, bat-cam, shop & tea-room open. Light refreshments only 2 Nov–16 Dec. Grounds open dawn–dusk, 1 Nov–31 Jan 09

a deer park and encouraged wildlife on her 1,125-hectare (2,700-acre) estate, which includes an ancient heronry, and today Arlington is recognised as being one of the top spots in Devon for wildlife (particularly famed for its rare lichens, as well as for bats, dormice, hares, otters and owls). You can even spy on the colony of lesser horseshoe bats roosting in the roof of the house, live, using the interactive 'bat-cam' (best time between May and August). The house is crowded with treasures to suit all interests, from model ships and rare 18th-century Beauvais tapestries to an amazing assortment of shells. The Stable Block is home to working horses and the Trust's internationally important collection of more than 50 horse-drawn carriages, from the grand state chariot to sombre hearse. If this whets your appetite for the elegant transport of the past, you can enjoy a horse-drawn carriage ride around the grounds. Back down to earth, you will find 12 hectares (30 acres) of informal pleasure grounds, including a formal Victorian garden, to explore, picnic or play in. The recently restored walled kitchen garden provides flowers for the house and produce for the tea-room.

What's new in 2008 Harnessing demonstrations at stables at 12 most days

⭐ Carriage rides available most days, weather permitting. Please tel. prior to visit to avoid disappointment. Voucher for drink in tea-room awarded to everyone arriving by bicycle. Pushchairs not admitted to house

ℹ️ **T** 01271 850296
E arlingtoncourt@nationaltrust.org.uk

🎭 Open-air theatre, activity workshops for children throughout the school holidays, Experience Carriage Driving days and craft and produce fairs

🚶 Range of waymarked walks around the estate

♿ 🚻 Building Grounds

🏠 NT shop. Plant sales

🍴 Old Kitchen tea-room (licensed) in the north wing of the house. Serves hot and cold meals and picnic food. Children's menu

👶 Baby-changing facilities. Front-carrying baby slings and hip-carrying infant seats for loan. Rain covers available. Children's play area. Children's activity workshops in school holidays. Children's I-Spy sheet, quiz and Tracker Packs

🏫 Suitable for school groups. Education room/centre

🐕 On short leads in gardens, grounds and Carriage Collection

➡️ [180:SS611405] **Bus:** TW Coaches 309 Barnstaple–Lynton (passing close ☒ Barnstaple), infrequent.
Station: Barnstaple 8ml. **Road:** 8ml N of Barnstaple on A39. Use A399 from South Molton if travelling from the east

🅿️ Free parking, 150yds. Coaches access car park at 2nd entrance. An area will be marked off if prior warning is given

NT properties nearby
Dunster Castle, Knightshayes Court, North Devon Coastline, Watersmeet

Ashleworth Tithe Barn

Ashleworth, Gloucestershire GL19 4JA

🏠 1956   (1:J2)

15th-century tithe barn

The barn, with its immense stone-tiled roof, is picturesquely located on the banks of the River Severn.

⭐ No WC

ℹ️ **T** 01452 814213
E ashleworth@nationaltrust.org.uk

For further information go to www.nationaltrust.org.uk

The stone circle at Avebury, Wiltshire, is a world heritage site

♿ Building ♿

➜ [162:SO818252] **Bus**: Swanbrook 351 Gloucester–Upton upon Severn (passing close Gloucester), alight Ashleworth ¼ml. **Station**: Gloucester 7ml. **Road**: 6ml N of Gloucester, 1¼ml E of Hartpury (A417), on W bank of Severn, SE of Ashleworth

P Parking (not NT) on the roadside

NT properties nearby
Bredon Barn, May Hill, Westbury Court Garden

Ashleworth Tithe Barn								
All year	9–6	**M**	**T**	**W**	**T**	**F**	**S**	**S**
Closes dusk if earlier. Other times by appointment								

Avebury

nr Marlborough, Wiltshire SN8 1RF

🏛 🚣 🏠 🗃 👤 🍴 ⛵ 👟

🚲 1943   (1:K4)

World-famous stone circle at the heart of a prehistoric landscape. Archaeological finds displayed in on-site museum

This internationally renowned stone circle, a World Heritage Site, partly encompasses the pretty village of Avebury. Many of the stones were re-erected in the 1930s by the archaeologist Alexander Keiller, who uncovered the true wonder of one of the most important megalithic monuments in Europe. You can walk right up to the stones and touch them, then watch an exciting interactive audio-visual display which brings their story, and that of the people who strove to uncover their past, alive. The Barn Gallery and the Stables Gallery house the museum, exhibiting many of the fascinating finds from all the local excavations. Another layer of history is provided by the buildings themselves: the dovecote is 16th-century, while the thatched threshing barn and stables are 17th-century. Nearby, the gentle rise of Windmill Hill, once the site of an important Neolithic settlement, has several well-preserved Bronze

Avebury								
Stone circle								
All year		**M**	**T**	**W**	**T**	**F**	**S**	**S**
Museum/galleries								
1 Feb–31 Mar	10–5	**M**	**T**	**W**	**T**	**F**	**S**	**S**
1 Apr–31 Oct	10–5	**M**	**T**	**W**	**T**	**F**	**S**	**S**
1 Nov–31 Jan 09	10–4	**M**	**T**	**W**	**T**	**F**	**S**	**S**
Circle restaurant								
1 Feb–31 Mar	10–5	**M**	**T**	**W**	**T**	**F**	**S**	**S**
1 Apr–31 Oct	10–5:30	**M**	**T**	**W**	**T**	**F**	**S**	**S**
1 Nov–31 Jan 09	11–3:30	**M**	**T**	**W**	**T**	**F**	**S**	**S**
Shop								
1 Feb–29 Feb	11–4	**M**	**T**	**W**	**T**	**F**	**S**	**S**
1 Mar–31 Mar	11–5	**M**	**T**	**W**	**T**	**F**	**S**	**S**
1 Apr–30 Sep	10–6	**M**	**T**	**W**	**T**	**F**	**S**	**S**
1 Oct–31 Oct	10–5	**M**	**T**	**W**	**T**	**F**	**S**	**S**
1 Nov–31 Jan 09	11–4	**M**	**T**	**W**	**T**	**F**	**S**	**S**
Closes dusk if earlier. Closed 24–26 Dec. Barn Gallery may close in very cold weather								

Age burial mounds and boasts commanding views. West of Avebury, the Iron Age earthwork of Oldbury Castle crowns Cherhill Down, along with the conspicuous Lansdowne Monument. With the spectacular folds of Calstone Coombes, this area of open downland provides wonderful walking.

What's new in 2008 Events to mark the 70th anniversary of the founding of the Alexander Keiller Museum

⭐ Please note that due to on-going conservation work some sections of the stone circle may be closed. Avebury stone circle is in the guardianship of English Heritage and managed on its behalf by the NT

ℹ️ **T** 01672 539250
E avebury@nationaltrust.org.uk

🕅 'Unravelling the story of the stone circle'. Booking essential

🛡️ Including family fun trails and activities, living history craft workshops, talks and tours

🚶 *Walking around Avebury* guide features six local walks; obtainable from property (£2.50 plus 50p p&p)

♿ [icons] **Grounds** [icon]

🛍️ In old Granary. Museum shop also sells books on archaeology

🍽️ The Circle Restaurant (licensed). The Trust's only vegetarian restaurant, specialising in vegan and gluten-free dishes, using organic and local products

👶 Baby-changing facilities. Pushchairs and baby back-carriers admitted. Family fun trails and activities

🎒 Suitable for school groups. Education room/centre. Hands-on activities

🐾 On leads in stone circle and estate

🚲 Ridgeway National Trail and NCN4 & 45 pass through property and are shared with walkers

➡️ [173:SU102699] **Foot**: Ridgeway National Trail. **Cycle**: NCN4 & 45. **Bus**: Stagecoach in Swindon 49 Swindon–Trowbridge; Wilts & Dorset 5, 6 Salisbury–Swindon. All pass close ➤ Swindon. **Station**: Pewsey 10ml; Swindon 11ml. **Road**: 6ml W of Marlborough, 1ml N of the Bath road (A4) on A4361 and B4003

For information regarding prices, see page 10

🅿️ Parking, 500yds, £5 (pay & display) located off A4361. NT and EH members free. Parking during the Summer Solstice in late June may be limited. Tel. estate office before travelling. Conditions of entry apply for the visitor car park

NT properties nearby
Heelis, Lacock Abbey, Stonehenge Landscape

Avebury Manor and Garden

nr Marlborough, Wiltshire SN8 1RF

[icons] 1991 (1:K4)

16th-century manor house with tranquil Edwardian garden

A much-altered house of monastic origin, the present buildings date from the early 16th century, with notable Queen Anne alterations and Edwardian renovation. The charming Edwardian garden was completely redesigned in the early 20th century and provided inspiration for Vita Sackville-West, a frequent visitor in the 1920s. Visitors can relax amidst the topiary and tranquil spaces of this delightful garden, which is contained within ancient walls and clipped box hedges, creating a series of outdoor 'rooms'. Some of the features are believed to be survivals of the original priory precinct.

⭐ The manor house is occupied and furnished by private leaseholders, who open a part of it to visitors. Due to restricted space guided tours operate and ticket numbers are limited. Tours run every 40 minutes from 2, last tour starting at 4:40. Following periods of prolonged wet weather it may be necessary to close the house and garden

ℹ️ **T** 01672 539250
E avebury@nationaltrust.org.uk

Avebury Manor and Garden								
House								
1 Apr–28 Oct	2–4:40	**M**	**T**	W	T	F	S	**S**
Garden								
31 Mar–28 Oct	11–5	**M**	**T**	W	T	**F**	**S**	**S**
Admission to house by timed ticket and guided tour (max. 12 per tour)								

🎦 House only

♿ 🚻 ⬚ 🅿 🅟 🅟 Building 🚶
Grounds ♿ ➡

🏠 In old Granary. Museum shop also sells books on archaeology

🍽 The Circle Restaurant (licensed). The Trust's only vegetarian restaurant, specialising in vegan and gluten-free dishes, using organic and local products

👪 House not suitable for young children

➡ [173:SU100699] **Foot**: Ridgeway National Trail. **Cycle**: NCN4 & 45. **Bus**: Stagecoach in Swindon 49 Swindon–Trowbridge; Wilts & Dorset 5, 6 Salisbury–Swindon. All pass close ⊠ Swindon. **Station**: Pewsey 10ml; Swindon 11ml. **Road**: 6ml W of Marlborough, 1ml N of the Bath road (A4) on A4361 and B4003

🅿 Parking, 600yds, £5 (pay & display). Located off A4361. NT and EH members free. Parking during the Summer Solstice 17–22 June will be very limited. Tel. estate office before travelling. Parking charge may vary

NT properties nearby
Heelis, Lacock Abbey, Stonehenge Landscape

Barrington Court

Barrington, nr Ilminster, Somerset TA19 0NQ

🏛 🗄 ❀ 🏠 🗄 🍽 🎡 🎭 👪 🎦 🚹
☂ 1907   (1:16)

Beautiful Jekyll-inspired gardens, working kitchen garden and Tudor manor house let to Stuart Interiors

Influenced by Gertrude Jekyll, this enchanting formal garden is laid out in a series of walled rooms which are awash with colour. The working stone-walled kitchen garden produces a variety of wonderful fruit and vegetables, which can be enjoyed in the restaurant, while the arboretum delights visitors with vivid autumn hues. The Tudor manor house was restored in the 1920s by the Lyle family and is currently let to Stuart Interiors as showrooms. Here visitors are treated to a rather different kind of visit, with the opportunity to purchase splendid antique or reproduction furniture.

What's new in 2008 Cider exhibition

⭐ Repairs planned to the Court House roof, which will involve outside scaffolding

ℹ **T** 01460 242614 (Infoline), 01460 241938
E barringtoncourt@nationaltrust.org.uk

Powder-blue Ceanothus 'Cascade' in full bloom overhanging a border of lavender at Barrington Court

⚑ Wide range of events. Please see website or tel. for details

⌖ Many public rights of way

♿ ⚿ ♨ ⌂ ⌖ ♿ ♿ Building ♿
Grounds ♿ ➡ ♿ ♿

⌂ NT shop. Plants and kitchen garden produce

⚫ Strode House Restaurant (licensed). Available for functions and Christmas lunches. Booking recommended. Corporate and private lunches weekdays in Nov and Dec (groups 25–50 only). Booking essential. Beagles café

♟ Baby-changing facilities. Pushchairs and baby back-carriers admitted. Hip-carrying infant seats for loan. Children's quiz/trail. Family activity packs

▮ Suitable for school groups

➜ [193:ST396182] **Cycle**: NCN30. **Bus**: First 632/3 Ilminster–Martock, with connections on 30A from Taunton. **Station**: Crewkerne 7ml. **Road**: in Barrington village, 5ml NE of Ilminster, on B3168. Signposted from A358 (Ilminster–Taunton) or A303 (Hayes End roundabout)

P Free parking, 30yds

NT properties nearby
Fyne Court, Lytes Cary Manor, Montacute House, Tintinhull Garden, Treasurer's House

Barrington Court									
House/garden/shop									
1 Mar–31 Mar	11–4:30	M	T	W	T	F	S	S
1 Apr–30 Sep	11–5	M	T	W	T	F	S	S
2 Oct–2 Nov	11–4:30	M	T	W	T	F	S	S
6 Dec–14 Dec	11–4	M	T	W	T	F	S	S
Restaurant									
1 Mar–30 Mar	11–4	M	T	W	T	F	S	S
31 Mar–30 Sep	12–3	M	T	W	T	F	S	S
29 Mar–28 Sep	12–5	M	T	W	T	F	S	S
2 Oct–2 Nov	11–4	M	T	W	T	F	S	S
6 Dec–14 Dec	11–4	M	T	W	T	F	S	S
Café									
29 Mar–30 Sep	11–5	M	T	W	T	F	S	S
4 Oct–26 Oct	11–4	M	T	W	T	F	S	S

1 April–30 Sept: restaurant open for lunches only weekdays, for lunches and teas weekends. Café may be closed in poor weather (Oct)

Bath Assembly Rooms

Bennett Street, Bath, Somerset BA1 2QH

♨ ⌂ ⚫ ⌖ ♩ ⚑ ♟ ▮ ♫ ⌕ 1931   **(1:J4)**

Elegant public rooms at the heart of fashionable 18th-century Bath life

Designed by John Wood the Younger in 1769, the Assembly Rooms were at the heart of fashionable Georgian society, and were the perfect venue for entertainment and socialising. Bombed in 1942, they were subsequently restored and now visitors can fully appreciate the magnificent rooms. The Rooms are now let to Bath & North East Somerset Council, which has its Fashion Museum on the lower ground floor.

★ Admission charge to Fashion Museum (inc. NT members)

ℹ **T** 01225 477789
E bathassemblyrooms@nationaltrust.org.uk

♩ 7 languages

⚑ Heritage Open Week, autumn half-term

♿ ⚿ ♨ ⌂ ♿ Building ♿ ♿ ♿
Grounds ♿

⚫ Assembly Rooms Café (not NT) in card room and formal garden. Open daily all year, available when rooms not in use for booked functions; tel. 01225 444477 for reservations

♟ Baby-changing facilities. Pushchairs admitted. Family activities during the summer holidays

▮ Suitable for school groups. Hands-on activities

➜ [156:ST749653] **Cycle**: NCN4, ¼ml. **Bus**: from ⊞ Bath Spa and surrounding areas. **Station**: Bath Spa ¾ml. **Road**: N of Milsom Street, E of the Circus

Bath Assembly Rooms								
1 Feb–29 Feb	11–5	M	T	W	T	F	S	S
1 Mar–31 Oct	11–6	M	T	W	T	F	S	S
1 Nov–31 Jan 09	11–5	M	T	W	T	F	S	S

Last admission 1hr before closing. Closed when in use for booked functions and 25/26 Dec. Access is guaranteed in Aug, but at other times visitors should tel. in advance

P Parking (not NT) (pay & display), charge inc. NT members. Street parking very limited, park & ride recommended

NT properties nearby
The Courts Garden, Dyrham Park, Great Chalfield Manor and Garden, Lacock Abbey, Leigh Woods, Prior Park, Tyntesfield, Westwood Manor

Blaise Hamlet

Henbury, Bristol BS10 7QY

🏠 🏡 👪 1943   (1:I3)

Nine rustic cottages around a green

A delightful hamlet of nine very different picturesque cottages in a wonderfully tranquil location. The hamlet was designed by John Nash in 1809 to accommodate Blaise Estate pensioners.

⭐ No WC

ℹ️ **T** 01275 461900
   E blaisehamlet@nationaltrust.org.uk

👪 Pushchairs admitted

➔ [172:ST559789] **Cycle**: NCN4, ¾ml. **Bus**: First 1 from ⮞ Bristol Temple Meads; also 43 from city centre. **Station**: Sea Mills 3ml; Filton Abbey Wood 3½ml. **Road**: 4ml N of central Bristol. Entrance on Hallen Road, W of Henbury village, just N of Weston Road (B4057)

A cottage in Blaise Hamlet, built in 1809

Blaise Hamlet							
All year	**M**	**T**	**W**	**T**	**F**	**S**	**S**

P No parking on site. Not suitable for coaches. Car parking on Hallen Road

NT properties nearby
Bath Assembly Rooms, Clevedon Court, Dyrham Park, Horton Court, Leigh Woods, Prior Park, Tyntesfield, Westbury College Gatehouse

Boscastle

Cornwall

🏰 🏡 📷 ☕ 👪 🚹 1955   (1:D7)

Picturesque harbour and village on the north Cornish coast

Much of the land in and around Boscastle is owned by the Trust. This includes the cliffs of Penally Point and Willapark, which guard the sinuous harbour entrance, Forrabury Stitches, high above the village and divided into ancient 'stitchmeal' cultivation plots, as well as large areas of woodland and meadow in the lovely Valency Valley.

What's new in 2008 National Trust café open in former pilchard cellar

ℹ️ **T** 01840 250353
   E boscastle@nationaltrust.org.uk

🚹 NT *Coast of Cornwall* leaflet 3 includes map and details of circular walks and information on local history, geology and wildlife

♿ 🚾 Grounds 🔣.

📷 NT shop

🍴 New café open in the lower harbour with outdoor tables in sheltered courtyard

👪 Children's quiz/trail

Boscastle							
All year		**M**	**T**	**W**	**T**	**F**	**S**	**S**
Shop/NT info								
11 Feb–2 Nov	10:30–5	**M**	**T**	**W**	**T**	**F**	**S**	**S**
3 Nov–30 Nov	10:30–4	M	T	W	**T**	**F**	**S**	**S**
27 Dec–2 Jan 09	10:30–4	**M**	**T**	**W**	**T**	**F**	**S**	**S**
Shop open later than 5 in high season								

Charges for National Trust members apply on some special event days

The picturesque harbour at Boscastle on the north Cornish coast

→ [190:SX097914] **Bus**: Western Greyhound 595 from Bude, 584/594 from Wadebridge (with connections on 555 at Wadebridge for ⊠ Bodmin Parkway). **Road**: 5ml N of Camelford, 3ml NE of Tintagel on B3263

P Parking (not NT) (pay & display), charge inc. NT members, 100yds

NT properties nearby
Tintagel Old Post Office

Bradley

Newton Abbot, Devon TQ12 6BN

[icons] 1938 (1:G8)

Delightful medieval manor house, set in woodland and meadows through which the River Lemon runs

Set in an area of 'wild space' on the outskirts of the market town of Newton Abbot, Bradley Manor is a charming, unspoilt historic house still lived in by the donor family. Predominantly 15th century, parts of the building date back to the 13th century and some original decoration survives from that time. This little-changed, relaxed family home contains a superb collection of furniture and paintings. The meadows and woodland surrounding it are a green haven for families.

★ No refreshments. No WC

i **T** 01803 843235
E bradley@nationaltrust.org.uk

☺ Shakespeare in the park, crafts

🚶 Woodland and meadow walks

[icons] **Building** [icon] **Grounds** [icons]

[icon] Hip-carrying infant seats for loan. Children's quiz/trail. Unpacked Tracker Packs

[icon] Suitable for school groups. 3D jigsaw model of house

[icon] Only in meadows and woodland surrounding manor

→ [202:SX848709] **Foot**: within easy walking distance of town along Totnes road. **Bus**: Stagecoach in Devon X64, Country Bus 176/7 from Newton Abbot (passing close ⊠ Newton Abbot). **Station**: Newton Abbot 1½ml. **Road**: drive gate (with small lodge) is ½ml from town centre on Totnes road (A381)

P Parking, 400yds. Free from 1:30. No coaches

NT properties nearby
Coleton Fishacre, Compton Castle, Greenway

Bradley								
1 Apr–30 Sep	2–5		M	**T**	**W**	**T**	F	S	S

1–31 Oct open weekdays by prior appointment only. Tel. at least one day in advance

Parking in National Trust car parks is free for members displaying stickers

Branscombe – The Old Bakery, Manor Mill and Forge

Branscombe, Seaton, Devon EX12 3DB

🔲❌🔟💺🚠🏠💷🚼🎖🚶 1965   (1:H7)

Charming vernacular buildings with mill and forge restored to working order

The Old Bakery is a stone-built and partially rendered building beneath thatch, which at the time of its closure as a business in 1987 was the last traditional working bakery in Devon. The old baking equipment has been preserved in the baking room and the rest of the building now serves as a tea-room. The water-powered Manor Mill probably supplied the flour for the bakery. The forge is open daily and the blacksmith sells the ironwork he produces.

⭐ WCs at bakery and village hall

ℹ️ **T** 01392 881691
E branscombe@nationaltrust.org.uk

🚶 Branscombe walks leaflet available

♿ 🚻

💷 Tea-room (NT-approved concession)

🚼 Pushchairs and baby back-carriers admitted. Family guide

🎖 Suitable for school groups. Live interpretation

🐕 On leads and only in garden and Old Bakery information room

➡️ [192:SY198887] **Foot**: South West Coast Path within ⅔ml. **Cycle**: public bridleway from Great Seaside to Beer gives shared access for cyclists. **Bus**: Axe Valley 899 Sidmouth– Seaton (connections from 🚉 Axminster or Honiton).

Branscombe									
Old Bakery									
19 Mar–2 Nov	11–5	M	T	**W**	**T**	**F**	**S**	**S**
Manor Mill									
23 Mar–29 Jun	2–5	M	T	W	T	F	**S**
2 Jul–31 Aug	2–5	M	T	**W**	T	F	**S**
7 Sep–26 Oct	2–5	M	T	W	T	F	**S**
Forge									
All year		**M**	**T**	**W**	**T**	**F**	**S**	**S**
Forge: tel. for details of opening times									

Station: Honiton 8ml. **Road**: in Branscombe village, off A3052

🅿 Free parking. Small NT car park adjacent to Forge, also car park adjacent to village hall; donations in well

NT properties nearby
A La Ronde, Loughwood Meeting House, Shute Barton

Brean Down

Brean, North Somerset

🔲🚠💷🚹🎖🚶 1954   (1:H4)

Promontory of land with dramatic cliffs and Victorian fort

One of the most striking landmarks of the Somerset coastline, Brean Down projects dramatically for over a mile into the Bristol Channel. It offers magnificent views for miles around and is rich in wildlife and history, making it an ideal place to explore. Palmerston Fort, built in 1865, provides a unique insight into Brean's past.

⭐ The cliffs are extremely steep. Please stay on the main paths, keep dogs on leads and wear suitable footwear. The beach (not NT) can be dangerous. The Fort and Down are reached by a steep climb from the car park. On most Sat and Sun afternoons from Easter to end Sept, volunteers open officers' quarters and gun magazines for visitors. Also open Mon, Wed and Fri during school holidays. Groups guided on request. No WC

ℹ️ **T** 01934 844518
E breandown@nationaltrust.org.uk

🚶 Circular walks leaflet

♿ 🚻 Building 🦽

💷 Brean Down Cove Café (not NT) by car park

🎖 Suitable for school groups. Small exhibition about Down and Fort in room opposite café entrance

🐕 On leads only

Brean Down							
All year	**M**	**T**	**W**	**T**	**F**	**S**	**S**

Dogs assisting visitors with disabilities are always welcome

→ [182:ST290590] **Bus**: First 112 Highbridge–
Weston-super-Mare (passing close ⊕
Highbridge and close ⊕ Weston-super-Mare),
alight Brean, 1¾ml. **Station**: Highbridge 8½ml.
Road: between Weston-super-Mare and
Burnham-on-Sea, 8ml from exit 22 of M5

P Parking, 200yds. NT members must display
cards. Situated at Brean Down Cove Café at
the bottom of Brean Down. The higher Down
is a steep climb from the car park and the Fort
is approx. 1½ml further

NT properties nearby
Cheddar Cliffs, Clevedon Court, Crook Peak,
Sand Point, Tyntesfield

Bredon Barn

Bredon, nr Tewkesbury, Worcestershire GL20 6EU

🏠 1951   **(1:K1)**

Large medieval threshing barn

The 14th-century barn is beautifully constructed
from local Cotswold stone and noted for its
dramatic aisled interior and unusual stone
chimney cowling.

⭐ No WC

ℹ️ **T** 01451 844752
   E bredonbarn@nationaltrust.org.uk

♿ Building 🔼

→ [150:SO919369] **Bus**: Astons 540/5
Evesham–Cheltenham (passing ⊕ Evesham).
Station: Pershore (U) 8½ml. **Road**: 3ml NE of
Tewkesbury, just N of B4080

P Parking very limited (land around barn not
NT). Access difficult – tight corners and
narrow lane to Barn. NT sign set back from
road

NT properties nearby
Ashleworth Tithe Barn, Croome Park, Hailes
Abbey, Snowshill Manor

Bredon Barn									
15 Mar–2 Nov	10–6		M	T	**W**	**T**	F	**S**	**S**
Closes dusk if earlier. All other times by appointment only									

Brownsea Island

Poole, Dorset BH13 7EE

➕🚻♨️🏛️🐾🏠🏢🍽️🔧🎭🏞️🔰
👫🎦🚶 1962   **(1:K7)**

**Peaceful island of woodland, wetland and
heath with a wide variety of wildlife,
famous for being the birthplace of
Scouting and Guiding**

Brownsea Island is dramatically located in Poole
Harbour, offering spectacular views across to
Studland, Old Harry Rocks and the Purbeck
Hills. This unspoilt setting offers an escape from
the noise and stress of modern life, making it a
great location for walks, picnics and exploring.
Thriving natural habitats, including woodlands,
heathland and lagoon, create a haven for wildlife
such as the rare red squirrel and a large variety
of birds and insects. Visitors to the island will be
fascinated by its rich history, including daffodil
farming, pottery works and acting as a decoy to
protect Poole in the Second World War. Robert
Baden-Powell held the first experimental
Scout camp here in 1907, and the island is now
known worldwide as the birthplace of Scouting
and Guiding.

What's new in 2008 Baden-Powell Outdoor
Centre open for school, Scouting and Guiding
groups. Includes Scout and Guide Heritage
Centre and facilities open to all visitors

⭐ Brownsea Island is only accessible by boat.
Ferry trips (not NT) depart from Poole Quay,
Sandbanks Jetty, Bournemouth Pier and
Swanage Pier

ℹ️ **T** 01202 707744
   E brownseaisland@nationaltrust.org.uk

🚶 Free guided walks every day – Introduction to
Brownsea Island. Group tours by
arrangement. Dorset Wildlife Trust reserve
self-guided trail and other tours

🎭 Programme of events, including family activity
days. Open-air theatre (tel. 01202 251987)

🚶 Walks for all abilities: woodland, heathland,
shoreline and clifftop. Self-guided trail leaflets,
including red squirrel and Baden-Powell trails

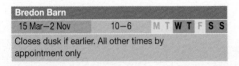 Building 🔼♿
 Grounds 🔼➡️

Please remember – your membership card is always needed for free admission

Brownsea Island		
15 Mar−18 Jul	10−5	M T W T F S S
19 Jul−31 Aug	10−6	M T W T F S S
1 Sep−27 Sep	10−5	M T W T F S S
28 Sep−2 Nov	10−4	M T W T F S S

Shop and Villano Café close 30mins before island. The island is open during the winter to booked groups only. Part of the island is leased to Dorset Wildlife Trust (tel. 01202 709445 for information). Brownsea Castle is not open to the public

NT shop (including red squirrel souvenirs and scouting souvenirs)

Villano Café near landing quay. Hot and cold refreshments, children's lunch boxes, ice-cream

Baby-changing facilities. Pushchairs and baby back-carriers admitted. Children's guide book. Children's quiz/trail. Family outdoor activity packs. Family activity days. All-terrain baby buggies for loan (booking advisable)

Suitable for school groups. Scout and Guide groups (day or residential). Education room/centre. Hands-on activities. Outdoor activity centre

A red squirrel at Brownsea Island

→ [195:SZ032878] In Poole Harbour. **Foot**: close to start/end of South West Coast Path at Shell Bay. **Ferry**: half-hourly boat service from 10 (not NT) from Poole Quay (tel. 01202 631828 or 01929 462383) and Sandbanks (tel. 01929 462383). Also service from Bournemouth and Swanage (tel. 01202 558550). Wheelchair users are advised to contact ferry operators. **Bus**: Wilts & Dorset 150 Bournemouth–Swanage, alight Sandbanks; 152 Poole–Sandbanks. Yellow Buses 12 Christchurch–Sandbanks, July–Aug only; also from surrounding areas to Poole Bridge, few min walk from Poole ferry. **Station**: Poole $\frac{1}{2}$ml to Poole Quay; Branksome or Parkstone, both $3\frac{1}{2}$ml to Sandbanks

NT properties nearby
Corfe Castle, Kingston Lacy, Studland Beach

Buckland Abbey

Yelverton, Devon PL20 6EY

1948 (1:E8)

700-year-old buildings, which were home to Elizabethan seafarers Drake and Grenville, set in the beautiful Tavy Valley

From 'matins and vespers' to swashbuckling tales of the sea, Buckland was the home of Cistercian monks and later the seafaring adventurers Grenville and Drake. Wander through the monastic Great Barn and newly created Elizabethan Garden to the Abbey itself with its exhibition galleries, interactive displays and costumes revealing the lives and stories of the people who changed the shape of the house

Buckland Abbey		
Estate/garden/restaurant/shop		
16 Feb−9 Mar	12:30−5	M T W T F **S S**
15 Mar−2 Nov	10:30−5:30	**M T W** T F **S S**
8 Nov−21 Dec	12−4	M T W T F **S S**
Abbey		
16 Feb−9 Mar	2−5	M T W T F **S S**
15 Mar−2 Nov	10:30−5:30	**M T W** T F **S S**
8 Nov−21 Dec	12−4	M T W T F **S S**

Admission by timed ticket at busy times. Last admission 45mins before closing

Unless indicated, last admission is always 30mins before closing time

Buckland Abbey, Devon: once a monastery, the house has many seafaring connections

and the fate of the country, and left their mark on the world. Treasures include Drake's Drum which, according to legend, will sound when England is in danger to summon Sir Francis Drake from his grave to save us. Beyond the house, discover meadows, orchards and woodland on the banks of the River Tavy on one of the estate walks, with the Letterbox Trail and Tracker Pack activities for all to enjoy.

What's new in 2008 Lecture lunch programme and guided tours for children in summer

⭐ The Abbey is presented in association with Plymouth City Museum

ℹ️ **T** 01822 853607
E bucklandabbey@nationaltrust.org.uk

🎭 Craft fairs 28/29 June, small entrance fee (inc. NT members) and 15/16 Nov. Medieval re-enactment. Moth and bat evenings. Family activities and Christmas events

🚶 Four waymarked walks through woodland and farmland, map available from reception; Letterbox Trail

♿ 🚻♿ ♿ 🔊 ⠿ Ⓟ Pↄ ♨ Building ♿♿ ♿
Grounds ♿ ➡️

🛍️ NT shop and plant sales. Independent craft workshops, usually open as Abbey. Woodturner (tel. 01364 631585) and countryside artist (tel. 01752 664096)

🍴 Guesthouse restaurant/tea-room (licensed) in the 13th-century Monks Guesthouse. Serving lunches, snacks and refreshments, March–Oct. Restricted menu, Nov-Feb. Open Dec for booked Christmas lunches. Children's menu

👶 Baby-changing and feeding facilities. Front-carrying baby slings and hip-carrying infant seats for loan. Children's quiz/trail. Parent and baby room. Guided tours for children in summer. Family activities

🏫 Suitable for school groups. Education room/centre. Live interpretation. Hands-on activities

➡️ [201:SX487667] **Cycle**: Drake's Trail, NCN27, 2ml. **Bus**: DAC 55 from Yelverton (with connections from 🚊 Plymouth) Mon–Sat; First 48 from Plymouth Suns. **Station**: Plymouth 11ml. **Road**: 6ml S of Tavistock, 11ml N of Plymouth: turn off A386 ¼ml S of Yelverton

🅿️ Free parking, 150yds

NT properties nearby
Antony, Castle Drogo, Cotehele, Lydford Gorge, Plym, Saltram

For further information go to www.nationaltrust.org.uk

Carnewas and Bedruthan Steps

nr Bedruthan, St Eval, Wadebridge, Cornwall
PL27 7UW

🚗🏠▣🏃🎞♿🏃👟 1930 (1:C8)

Dramatic coastline with views over massive rock stacks

This is one of the most popular destinations on the Cornish coast because of the spectacular clifftop view of rocks stretching into the distance across the sweep of Bedruthan beach (not NT). There are magnificent walks along the coast path between Carnewas and Park Head. The Trust has rebuilt the cliff staircase down to the beach, but it is **unsafe to bathe at any time** and visitors need to be aware of the risk of being cut off by the tide.

★ WC not always available

ℹ️ **T** 01637 860563
   E carnewas@nationaltrust.org.uk

👟 NT *Coast of Cornwall* leaflet 6 includes maps and details of circular walks and information on local history, geology and wildlife

♿ 🚻 Grounds 🐾

🏪 Shop and information centre

▣ Tea-room and garden (NT-approved concession) in Carnewas car park overlooking the coast

Bedruthan Steps looking towards Park Head promontory

Carnewas and Bedruthan Steps								
All year		M	T	W	T	F	S	S
Shop/info								
9 Feb–24 Feb	11–4	M	T	W	T	F	S	S
15 Mar–2 Nov	10:30–5	M	T	W	T	F	S	S
Tea-room								
9 Feb–20 Mar	11–5	M	T	W	T	F	S	S
21 Mar–30 Sep	10:30–5:30	M	T	W	T	F	S	S
1 Oct–16 Nov	11–5	M	T	W	T	F	S	S

Cliff staircase closed 1 Nov–31 Jan 09. Tea-room: limited opening in winter. Tel. 01637 860701 or 01841 540554 to check times

🚻 Children's quiz/trail

➔ [200:SW849692] **Foot**: ⅔ml of South West Coast Path on property. **Bus**: Western Greyhound 556 🚌 Newquay–Padstow. **Station**: Newquay 7ml. **Road**: just off B3276 from Newquay to Padstow, 6ml SW of Padstow

P Parking. Seasonal charge

NT properties nearby
Trerice

Castle Drogo

Drewsteignton, nr Exeter, Devon EX6 6PB

🏰✝❀🌳🏊🏠🏠▣🏃🎞🎭🚻
🎦👟🍴 1974 (1:F7)

The 'last castle to be built in England', set above the Teign Gorge with dramatic views over Dartmoor

What appears to be an ancient granite fortress overlooking the wilds of Dartmoor was actually the 20th-century home of self-made millionaire Julius Drewe. Employing the foremost architect of his age, Sir Edwin Lutyens, Drewe created an impressive family home – a bold statement that looks back to a romantic past, while heralding the modern era. Inside modern technology and family keepsakes – radios and gramophones, toys, dolls' houses, photographs and books – sit alongside 17th-century tapestries and inlaid tables. The servants' rooms are also fascinating and poignant. The beautiful formal garden, inspired by Gertrude Jekyll, makes a striking contrast to Dartmoor's ancient woodlands, which creep right up to the borders of the

The Teign Gorge and Castle Drogo: the 'last castle to be built in England'

grounds. Play a family game of croquet on the huge circular lawn, while younger children enjoy the play area nearby, then explore the estate and hike down through the wooded Teign Gorge to the rushing river far below.

What's new in 2008 Castle also open Tuesdays in school holidays (April–Oct)

⭐ The property is situated at a height of nearly 300 metres within Dartmoor National Park and can experience extreme weather conditions. Approach lane is narrow with tight corners. Appropriate clothing and footwear are recommended

ℹ️ **T** 01647 433306
E castledrogo@nationaltrust.org.uk

Castle Drogo									
1 Mar–9 Mar	11–4	M	T	W	T	F	**S**	**S**
15 Mar–23 Mar	11–5	**M**	T	**W**	**T**	**F**	**S**	**S**
24 Mar–20 Apr	11–5	**M**	T	**W**	**T**	**F**	**S**	**S**
21 Apr–25 May	11–5	**M**	T	**W**	**T**	**F**	**S**	**S**
26 May–1 Jun	11–5	**M**	T	**W**	**T**	**F**	**S**	**S**
2 Jun–20 Jul	11–5	**M**	T	**W**	**T**	**F**	**S**	**S**
21 Jul–31 Aug	11–5	**M**	T	**W**	**T**	**F**	**S**	**S**
1 Sep–25 Oct	11–5	**M**	T	**W**	**T**	**F**	**S**	**S**
26 Oct–2 Nov	11–4	**M**	T	**W**	**T**	**F**	**S**	**S**
29 Nov–14 Dec	12–4	M	T	W	T	F	**S**	**S**
18 Dec–22 Dec	12–4	**M**	T	**W**	**T**	**F**	**S**	**S**

Garden/shop/visitor centre/tea-room open 10:30 (11 between 29 Nov–22 Dec) and close 30mins after Castle. Closes dusk if earlier. Castle tea-room: as Castle & open in Dec for booked Christmas lunches and dinners. Tel. 01647 434131 for details

😈 From March–Dec inc. family trails and activities, walks, talks, art and craft workshops. Family event every day in school holidays (April–Oct)

🚶 Walks leaflet

♿ 🚻 🔣 🔣 ⋮⋮ 🔍 🅿 🔣 🔣 **Building** 🔣 🔣 **Grounds** 🔣 ➡️

📷 NT shop. Plant sales

🍽️ Castle tea-room in castle. Children's menu. Tea-room at visitor centre. Children's menu

👶 Baby-changing and feeding facilities. Baby back-carriers admitted. Hip-carrying infant seats for loan. Children's play area. Children's quiz/trail

🎭 Suitable for school groups. Live interpretation. Hands-on activities

🐕 On leads and only in car park and on estate walks

➡️ [191:SX721900] **Foot**: Two Moors Way. **Bus**: Stagecoach in Devon 172/173 Exeter–Moretonhampstead (passing ☒ Exeter Central) Mons–Sats. Carmel/First 274/9 from ☒ Okehampton, Suns & BHols May–Sept. **Station**: Yeoford (U) 8ml. **Road**: 5ml S of A30 Exeter–Okehampton. Take A382 Whiddon Down–Moretonhampstead road; turn off at Sandy Park

🅿️ Free parking, 400yds. Tight corners and narrow lanes

NT properties nearby
Finch Foundry, Fingle Bridge, Lydford Gorge, Parke Estate, Steps Bridge

For information regarding prices, see page 10

Chedworth Roman Villa

Yanworth, nr Cheltenham, Gloucestershire
GL54 3LJ

🏛 🏠 💷 🎦 🎧 🎴 🎭 🚼 ▣ 1924   **(1:K2)**

**Remains of one of Britain's largest
Romano-British villas set in the heart of
the Cotswolds**

The remains of one of the largest Roman villas in
Britain provide a fascinating insight into the
period. The site was discovered in 1864 by a
local gamekeeper and subsequently excavated.
Over a mile of walls survive along with beautiful
mosaics, two bathhouses, hypocausts, a water
shrine and latrine. Visitors to the museum will
discover artefacts from the villa, and an
audio-visual presentation brings history to life.

What's new in 2008 Hot drinks and light snacks
available at weekends and during school
holidays

ℹ️ **T** 01242 890256
   E chedworth@nationaltrust.org.uk

🎧 Adult and child version available from
   reception. Full interpretive guide to the villa's
   many exciting features (children free)

🎭 Living history events. Family trails

Detail of a mosaic in the dining room of Chedworth
Roman Villa, Gloucestershire, showing a drunken
satyr and a maenad

Chedworth Roman Villa									
1 Mar–16 Mar	11–4	M	T	W	T	F	S	S
18 Mar–2 Nov	10–5	M	T	W	T	F	S	S
4 Nov–16 Nov	10–4	M	T	W	T	F	S	S

Open BH Mons. See noticeboard for shop/tea tent
opening times

♿ 🚾 ♿ 🅿 ⠿ 🅿 🅳 Building 🅰 🅱
Grounds 🅻

🏠 Wide range of Roman and archaeological
   books, plus Roman-themed gifts and plants

☕ Light snacks and drinks for sale in shop. Tea
   tent serving hot drinks and sandwiches open
   at weekends and during school holidays

🚼 Baby-changing facilities. Pushchairs and baby
   back-carriers admitted. Children's guide.
   Children's quiz/trail. Family activity packs. Family
   trails. Activities for children in school holidays

▣ Suitable for school groups. Education
   room/centre. Live interpretation. Hands-on
   activities. Archaeological and living history
   activities for schools

➡️ [163:SP053135] **Station**: Cheltenham Spa
   9ml. **Road**: 3ml NW of Fossebridge on
   Cirencester–Northleach road (A429);
   approach from A429 via Yanworth or from
   A436 via Withington (coaches must approach
   from Fossebridge)

🅿 Two car parks: villa car park, 15yds from
   entrance. Overflow car park, April–Sept,
   250yds from entrance

NT properties nearby
Lodge Park and Sherborne Estate,
Snowshill Manor

The Church House

Widecombe in the Moor, Newton Abbot, Devon
TQ13 7TA

▣ 🏠 🚼 🧍 🐕 ✂ 1933   **(1:F7)**

**Fine two-storey granite building dating
from c.1540**

Originally a place where 'church ales' were held
in the 16th and 17th centuries ('ales' being
parish festivities raising funds for the church),
the building later became almshouses, a school

Many Trust properties are offering Gift Aid on Entry for non-members, see page 10

The Church House								
8 Feb–23 Dec	From 10:30*	M	T	W	T	F	S	S

Open to visitors when not in use as the village hall.
*Closing time of shop/information centre is dependent on the weather

and a workhouse, before becoming the village school again in 1875. It is now the village hall and is used regularly for village events. The adjacent Sexton's Cottage is a NT shop and Dartmoor National Park information point.

★ No WC, nearest in public car park

ℹ️ **T** 01364 621321
E churchhouse@nationaltrust.org.uk

♿ 🔲 D♿ Building 🏞 Grounds 🏞

🚼 Pushchairs admitted

➡️ [191:SX718768] In centre of Widecombe, N of Ashburton, W of Bovey Tracey. **Bus**: Country Bus/First 270/2 Newton Abbot–Totnes/ Tavistock; Carmel/Country Bus 274 from 🚉 Okehampton. Every Sun only, June–Sept only, but 270 runs daily Aug only. **Road**: on B3387 approx 12ml from A38, Bovey Tracey

🅿️ Parking (not NT), 100yds (pay & display)

NT properties nearby
Hembury, Holne Woods, Parke Estate

Clevedon Court

Tickenham Road, Clevedon, North Somerset
BS21 6QU

🏠 ❄️ 🍽 🚼 🎦 1961 (1:I4)

Outstanding 14th-century manor house and 18th-century terraced garden

Set in a beautifully landscaped terraced garden, the house was built by Sir John de Clevedon in c.1320, incorporating parts of a massive 13th-century tower and great hall. Much of the original building is still evident, although the Elizabethans made many alterations and additions. Home to the Elton family since 1709, visitors will see striking examples of Eltonware pottery and a fascinating collection of Nailsea glass.

★ The Elton family opens and manages the property for the NT

The Chapel, Clevedon Court, North Somerset

ℹ️ **T** 01275 872257
E clevedoncourt@nationaltrust.org.uk

♿ 🔲 👓 📷 P♿ D♿ Building 🏞 Grounds 🏞

☕ Tea-shop (not NT). Tel. property for opening dates

🚼 Children's guide. Children's quiz/trail

🏫 Suitable for school groups

➡️ [172:ST423716] **Bus**: First 362–364 from Bristol (passing 🚉 Nailsea & Backwell). **Station**: Yatton 3ml. **Road**: 1½ml E of Clevedon, on Bristol road (B3130), signposted from M5 exit 20

🅿️ Free parking, 50yds. Unsuitable for trailer caravans or motor caravans. Some parking 100yds E of entrance in cul-de-sac

NT properties nearby
Blaise Hamlet, Brean Down, Dyrham Park, Horton Court, Leigh Woods, Tyntesfield, Westbury College Gatehouse

Clevedon Court								
23 Mar–28 Sep	2–5	M	T	W	T	F	S	S

Open BH Mons. Car park opens at 1:15. Entry to house by timed ticket on busy days

For details of events go to www.nationaltrust.org.uk/events

Clouds Hill

Wareham, Dorset BH20 7NQ

🎫 🏠 🔳 🎨 🧍 1937   **(1:J7)**

The rural retreat of T. E. Lawrence

This tiny isolated brick and tile cottage in the heart of Dorset was the peaceful retreat of T. E. Lawrence ('Lawrence of Arabia'). The austere rooms are much as he left them and reflect his complex personality and close links with the Middle East, as detailed in a fascinating exhibition.

What's new in 2008 New trail through the rhododendrons to picnic spot on top of the hill

⭐ No WC

ℹ️ **T** 01929 405616
   E cloudshill@nationaltrust.org.uk

🧍 New trail to picnic spot on top of the hill

♿ 👓 **Building** 🏞️ **Grounds** 🏞️

🛍️ T. E. Lawrence books on sale

🖼️ Suitable for school groups

🐕 In the grounds on leads only

➡️ [194:SY824909] **Station**: Wool 3½ml; Moreton (U) 3½ml. **Road**: 9ml E of Dorchester, 1½ml E of Waddock crossroads (B3390), 4ml S of A35 Poole–Dorchester road, 1ml N of Bovington Tank Museum

Clouds Hill: T. E. Lawrence's rural retreat

Clouds Hill								
20 Mar–26 Oct	12–5	M	T	W	**T**	**F**	**S**	**S**

Open BH Mons. Closes at dusk if earlier; no electric light

🅿️ Free parking, 30yds. No coaches (only minibuses). No trailer caravans

NT properties nearby
Brownsea Island, Corfe Castle, Hardy Monument, Hardy's Cottage, Kingston Lacy, Max Gate

Coleridge Cottage

35 Lime Street, Nether Stowey, Bridgwater, Somerset TA5 1NQ

🎫 🧍 🖼️ 🧍 1909   **(1:H5)**

Home of the poet Samuel Taylor Coleridge

Discover the former home of Coleridge, who lived in the cottage for three years from 1797. It was here that he wrote *The Rime of the Ancient Mariner*, part of *Christabel, Frost at Midnight* and *Kubla Khan*. Mementoes of the poet can be seen here.

⭐ No WC, nearest WC at village library 500yds. The property is managed by Dunster Castle (01643 821314)

ℹ️ **T** 01278 732662
   E coleridgecottage@nationaltrust.org.uk

🧍 Coleridge Way starts at Coleridge Cottage

♿ 👓 🅰️ **Building** 🏞️

🖼️ Suitable for school groups

➡️ [181:ST191399] **Bus**: First 14 Bridgwater–Williton (passing close ➔ Bridgwater). **Station**: Bridgwater 8ml. **Road**: at W end of Lime Street, opposite Ancient Mariner pub, 8ml W of Bridgwater

🅿️ Parking (not NT), 500yds. Coach parking available by arrangement

NT properties nearby
Dunster Castle, Fyne Court, Holnicote Estate

Coleridge Cottage								
3 Apr–28 Sep	2–5	M	T	W	**T**	**F**	**S**	**S**

Open BH Mons & Easter

Charges for National Trust members apply on some special event days

Coleton Fishacre

Brownstone Road, Kingswear, Devon TQ6 0EQ

🀫 ❄ 🚗 🏠 🛏 ☕ 🎿 🎭 🎭 👪 🔲

🚶 | 1982 (1:G9)

Coleton Fishacre									
15 Mar–20 Jul	10:30–5	M	T	**W**	**T**	**F**	**S**	**S**
21 Jul–31 Aug	10:30–5	**M**	T	**W**	**T**	**F**	**S**	**S**
3 Sep–2 Nov	10:30–5	M	T	**W**	**T**	**F**	**S**	**S**
Open BH Mons								

A luxuriant garden by the sea, with an Arts & Crafts-style house, featuring Art Deco-influenced interiors

In this enchanting corner of South Devon, house, garden and sea meet in perfect harmony. Lose yourself in the magical garden, where viewpoints allow frequent enticing glimpses out over the sea and where tender plants from the Mediterranean, South Africa and New Zealand thrive. In this most evocative of holiday homes, built for Rupert D'Oyly Carte, there is true 1920s elegance. A light, joyful atmosphere fills the rooms and music plays, echoing the family's Gilbert and Sullivan connections.

⭐ The lane leading to Coleton Fishacre is narrow and can be busy. Use of passing places and reversing may be necessary. Members may prefer to visit on Friday or Saturday or from 2:30, when the property is quieter. Visitors wishing to walk the coast path are requested to park in Coleton Camp or Brownstone car parks

ℹ️ **T** 01803 752466
E coletonfishacre@nationaltrust.org.uk

🎿 Guided walk 2:15–3:15 every Fri (free). Other garden and house tours by arrangement or as advertised

🎭 Exhibition of local artwork in house. Music events in house and garden

🚶 Coastal walks on the surrounding Dart and Start Bay Estate. Please park in Coleton Camp or Brownstone car parks

♿ 🚻 ♿ ♿ ♿ ♿ P♿ D♿ Building 🏛♿ Grounds 🏛➡️

🛍 Selection of gifts, postcards and books. Plant sales: unusual shrubs and herbaceous plants

☕ Tea-room (NT-approved concession). Children's menu

👪 Baby-changing facilities. Hip-carrying infant seats for loan. Children's quiz/trail. Family activity packs

The holiday home of the D'Oyly Carte family, Coleton Fishacre has a light, joyful atmosphere

Parking in National Trust car parks is free for members displaying stickers

🎦 Hands-on activities

🐕 On leads only on surrounding NT land.
Dog crèche

➡ [202:SX910508] **Foot**: South West Coast
Path within ⅔ml. **Bus**: Stagecoach in Devon
120 Paignton–Kingswear; otherwise
Stagecoach in Devon 22/4 Brixham–
Kingswear (with connections from Paignton).
On all, alight ¾ml SW of Hillhead, 1½ml walk to
garden. **Station**: Paignton 8ml; Kingswear
(Paignton & Dartmouth Rly) 2¼ml by footpath,
2¾ml by road. **Road**: 3ml from Kingswear;
take Lower Ferry road, turn off at toll house
(take care in narrow lanes). Narrow entrance
and drive

Rolling hills provide an attractive backdrop to
Compton Castle's garden

P Free parking, 20yds. For visitors to house and
garden only. Coaches must book

NT properties nearby
Bradley, Compton Castle, Dart Estuary, Greenway

Compton Castle

Marldon, Paignton, Devon TQ3 1TA

🎦✝❄🏠🗄🎋👫🎦🚶 1951 (1:G8)

**Dramatic fortified manor house and small
formal garden**

Home to the Gilbert family for an almost unbroken
600 years, this imposing castle set against a
backdrop of rolling hills and orchards evokes a
bewitching mixture of romance and history. This is
the last truly fortified dwelling to be built in Devon,
and its extremely high curtain walls, symmetrical
towers and portcullis create an unforgettable
approach. Inside there are machicolations, spiral
staircases and squints, making Compton a place
of discovery and adventure for imaginative
children and adults alike.

What's new in 2008 Herb garden in the
inner courtyard

⭐ Credit cards not accepted

ℹ **T** 01803 843235
E comptoncastle@nationaltrust.org.uk

🚶 NGS garden day in June to include walks with
the gardener

♿ 🗺⠿🅿🅿 Building 🌿 Grounds 🔼➡

🛍 Table-top shop only – guidebooks, postcards
and plants

☕ Refreshments at Castle Barton restaurant
(not NT) from 10 (tel. 01803 873314).
No credit cards

👫 Baby-changing and feeding facilities. Baby
back-carriers admitted. Hip-carrying infant
seats for loan. Family guide. Children's
quiz/trail. Unpacked Tracker Packs

🎦 Suitable for school groups. Hands-on
activities. 3D model

➡ [202:SX865648] **Bus**: Stagecoach in Devon 7
🚂 Paignton–Marldon; 111/2 Dartmouth–
Torquay (passing 🚂 Totnes); 66 from
St Marychurch. On all alight Marldon, 1½ml.
Station: Torquay 3ml. Newton Abbot 6ml.
Road: at Compton, 5ml W of Torquay, 1½ml
N of Marldon. Signposted off A380 to
Marldon (not suitable for coaches) or turn
south from A381 Totnes road at Ipplepen –
2ml to Compton

P Free parking, 30yds. Additional parking at
Castle Barton opposite entrance, 100yds.
Access for coaches via Ipplepen, not
Marldon. Coaches may park at bus turning
area opposite, 125yds

NT properties nearby
Bradley, Coleton Fishacre, Greenway

Compton Castle							
2 Apr–30 Oct	11–5	M	T	W	T	F S S
Open BH Mons							

Dogs assisting visitors with disabilities are always welcome

Corfe Castle

The Square, Corfe Castle, Wareham, Dorset
BH20 5EZ

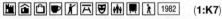 1982 (1:K7)

Thousand-year-old castle, an iconic survivor of the English Civil War, rising above the Isle of Purbeck

Corfe Castle		
1 Feb–31 Mar	10–5	**M T W T F S S**
1 Apr–30 Sep	10–6	**M T W T F S S**
1 Oct–31 Oct	10–5	**M T W T F S S**
1 Nov–31 Jan 09	10–4	**M T W T F S S**

Shop and tea-room close 5:30 April–Sept.
Closed 25, 26 Dec. High winds may cause closure of parts of grounds

One of Britain's most majestic ruins and once a controlling gateway through the Purbeck Hills, the castle boasts breathtaking views and several waymarked walks. Steeped in history, an interactive exhibition uncovers many stories of treachery and treason. Defended during the Civil War by the prudent and virtuous Lady Bankes, the castle fell, due to betrayal from within, and was subsequently destroyed by the Parliamentarians. Many fine Norman and early English features remain.

★ Extensive conservation work in progress, access may be restricted to certain areas of the castle. Please tel. or check website for information

i **T** 01929 481294 (Infoline), 01929 480921 (shop), 01929 480609 (Learning)
E corfecastle@nationaltrust.org.uk

Guided tours of castle often available, April–Oct

Living history, archaeology week, open-air theatre and cinema, school holiday activities, including family treasure trails

Corfe Common walks leaflet from NT shop

Grounds

In village square

Traditional tea-room (licensed) by castle entrance in village square. Children's menu

Baby-changing facilities. Pushchairs and baby back-carriers admitted. Family guide. Children's guide. Children's quiz/trail. School holiday activities inc. family treasure trails. Baby back-carriers for loan (small donation requested). Children must be accompanied by an adult within the castle

Suitable for school groups. Education room/centre. Hands-on activities. Interactive exhibition at Castle View

On leads only

[195:SY959824] **Bus**: Wilts & Dorset 142/3 Poole–Swanage (passing ⊠ Wareham). **Station**: Wareham 4½ml. Corfe Castle (Swanage Steam Railway) a few mins walk (park & ride from Norden Station). **Road**: on A351 Wareham–Swanage road

P Parking (pay & display) at Castle View, off A351 (800yds walk uphill to castle). NT members free. Norden park & ride (all-day parking, ½ml walk to castle) and West St (in village). Pay & display (neither NT)

NT properties nearby
Brownsea Island, Clouds Hill, Studland Beach

The majestic ruins of Corfe Castle in Dorset

Cornish Mines and Engines

Pool, nr Redruth, Cornwall TR15 3NP

⛏ 🏠 🎭 🎏 😷 🚻 🎒 🧍 1967 **(1:C9)**

Impressive beam engines and industrial heritage discovery centre

At the very centre of the Cornish Mining World Heritage Site, these two great beam engines sit preserved in their towering engine houses – a reminder of Cornwall's days as a world-famous centre of industry, engineering and innovation. Both engines were originally powered by high-pressure steam, introduced by local hero Richard Trevithick. One can still be seen in action, rotated by electricity, with the great beam rising and falling. The Discovery Centre gives you the whole dramatic story of Cornish mining, with an atmospheric film and static displays. Don't miss the experience of walking through the flue tunnel and the dizzying view up inside the 36m chimney stack.

⭐ Trevithick Cottage, once home to Richard Trevithick, is nearby at Penponds and open April to Oct, Wed 2–5, free (donations welcome)

ℹ️ **T** 01209 315027
E cornishmines@nationaltrust.org.uk

🧍 Self-guided site leaflet

♿ 🚾 📷 🖼 ⠿ 🅿️ P↓ **Building** ♿
Grounds ♿ ➡️

🚻 Baby-changing facilities. Pushchairs and baby back-carriers admitted. Children's quiz/trail

🎒 Suitable for school groups

➡️ [203:SW672415] **Cycle:** NCN3, ½ml.
Bus: from surrounding areas (some passing ⛟ Redruth). **Station:** Redruth 2ml; Camborne 2ml. **Road:** at Pool, 2ml W of Redruth on either side of A3047 midway between Redruth and Camborne. Site is signposted from A30 'Camborne East' junction. Industrial Discovery Centre at East Pool, behind Morrisons

Cornish Mines and Engines									
Centre/shop									
19 Mar–2 Nov	11–5		**M**	T	**W**	**T**	**F**	S	**S**

Nov to end Jan 09 by arrangement only; please tel. for details or to arrange group visits at any time of year

🅿️ Free parking (not NT), 25yds. Main car park is shared with Morrisons superstore

NT properties nearby
Glendurgan Garden, Godolphin, Godrevy, Trelissick Garden

Cotehele

St Dominick, nr Saltash, Cornwall PL12 6TA

🏰 🏠 ✝️ ⛏ ✳️ 🎎 🏛 🏠 🍴 🎭 🎏 😷 🚻 🎒 🧍 ⊤ 1947 **(1:E8)**

Tudor house with superb collections of textiles, armour and furniture, set in extensive grounds

In the woods above the tidal River Tamar nestles Cotehele, built by the Edgcumbes in Tudor times. It is a house of many stories, myths and legends. King George III and Queen Charlotte came to see Cotehele's ancient and romantic interior in 1789, and found it festooned with tapestries and adorned with textiles, arms and armour, pewter, brass and old oak furniture. Llittle has changed, and a visit to the old house is a magical experience. Outside, the terraces are formally planted, then beyond you can lose yourself in the jungle plantation of the valley garden, which includes a medieval stewpond and dovecote (complete with doves – a children's favourite). Climb to the top of the Prospect Tower, a three-sided 18th-century folly

Cotehele									
House									
15 Mar–2 Nov	11–4:30		**M**	**T**	**W**	**T**	F	**S**	**S**
Hall of House with garland									
24 Nov–23 Dec	11–4		**M**	**T**	**W**	**T**	**F**	**S**	**S**
Garden									
All year	10–dusk		**M**	**T**	**W**	**T**	**F**	**S**	**S**
Restaurant/shop/plants/gallery									
17 Feb–14 Mar	11–4		**M**	**T**	**W**	**T**	**F**	**S**	**S**
15 Mar–2 Nov	11–5		**M**	**T**	**W**	**T**	**F**	**S**	**S**
3 Nov–23 Dec	11–4:30		**M**	**T**	**W**	**T**	**F**	**S**	**S**
Edgcumbe Arms									
17 Feb–2 Nov	11–5		**M**	**T**	**W**	**T**	**F**	**S**	**S**

Open Good Fri. Barn Restaurant closed Fridays 21 March–31 Oct. Edgcumbe Arms closes at dusk if earlier than 5. Limited opening in Nov/Dec, tel. for details

Unless indicated, last admission is always 30mins before closing time

high above the house, and enjoy fantastic views, or seek out the tranquillity of the Upper Garden. Cotehele Quay on the river is home to the restored Tamar sailing barge, *Shamrock*, and gateway to the wider estate, with its abundant wildlife and evocative industrial ruins – all that remains of a rich industrial past.

What's new in 2008 Newly planted orchard of local fruit trees

i **T** 01579 351346, 01579 352711 (restaurant), 01579 352717 (tea-room), 01579 352713 (shop/plant sales) **E** cotehele@nationaltrust.org.uk

Full winter events programme

Estate walks leaflet available

Building Grounds

Plant sales. Gallery selling contemporary arts and crafts

Barn Restaurant (licensed). Children's menu. Edgcumbe Arms tea-room on Cotehele Quay. Children's menu

Queen Anne's Room, Cotehele, Cornwall

Baby-changing and feeding facilities. Hip-carrying infant seats for loan. Children's guide. Children's quiz/trail. Tracker Packs

Suitable for school groups. Education room/centre

Under close control on woodland walks

[201:SX422685] **Cycle**: NCN27, 8ml. Hilly route from Tavistock to Cotehele.
Ferry: Calstock can be reached from Plymouth by water (contact Plymouth Boat Cruises Ltd,. tel. 01752 822797) and from Calstock local river passenger ferry operates during summer subject to tides (tel. 01822 833331). **Bus**: First 190 Gunnislake–Callington (Suns, June–Sept only); DAC 79 Tavistock–Callington (passes Gunnislake) to within $1\frac{1}{4}$ml. **Station**: Calstock (U), $1\frac{1}{2}$ml (signposted from station). **Road**: on W bank of the Tamar, 1ml W of Calstock by steep footpath (6ml by road), 8ml SW of Tavistock, 14ml from Plymouth via Saltash Bridge; 2ml E of St Dominick, 4ml from Gunnislake (turn at St Ann's Chapel). Coaches only by prior arrangement

P Free parking. Parking charge on quay

NT properties nearby
Antony, Buckland Abbey, Lanhydrock, Lydford Gorge, Saltram

Cotehele Mill

St Dominick, nr Saltash, Cornwall PL12 6TA

1947   (1:E8)

Working watermill and workshops

A short level walk from Cotehele Quay, tucked away in the Morden Valley, the old mill is an atmospheric reminder of the recent past when corn was ground here for the local community. Flour is still produced in the traditional way and is on sale at the mill, and on Tuesdays and Thursdays you can see milling in action.
A range of outbuildings containing a collection of blacksmiths', carpenters', wheelwrights' and saddlers' tools is presented as workshops, giving an insight into the working lives of local craftsmen.

i **T** 01579 350606, 01579 351346 (property office) **E** cotehele@nationaltrust.org.uk

Cotehele Mill								
15 Mar–30 Sep	11–5	**M**	**T**	**W**	**T**	**F**	**S**	**S**
1 Oct–2 Nov	11–4:30	**M**	**T**	**W**	**T**	**F**	**S**	**S**

🎭 Guided tours at 3

♿ 🚻 ♿ **Building** 🏞 **Grounds** 🐕

♿ Pushchairs and baby back-carriers admitted. Children's quiz/trail

▦ Suitable for school groups

🐕 Under close control on woodland walk to mill. Not in mill buildings

➔ [201:SX417682] **Cycle**: NCN27, 8ml. Hilly route from Tavistock to Cotehele.
Ferry: Calstock can be reached from Plymouth by water (contact Plymouth Boat Cruises Ltd, tel. 01752 822797) and from Calstock local river passenger ferry operates during summer subject to tides (tel. 01822 833331). **Bus**: First 190 Gunnislake–Callington (Suns, June–Sept only); DAC 79 Tavistock–Callington (passes ⊠ Gunnislake) to within 1¼ml. **Station**: Calstock (U), 1½ml (signposted from station). **Road**: on W bank of the Tamar, 1ml W of Calstock by steep footpath (6ml by road), 8ml SW of Tavistock, 14ml from Plymouth via Saltash Bridge; 2ml E of St Dominick, 4ml from Gunnislake (turn at St Ann's Chapel). Coaches by prior arrangement only

🅿 There is no parking at the mill except by prior arrangement for visitors with disabilities. All other visitors must park at Cotehele Quay and walk ⅓ml through the woods. Do not forget your membership card!

NT properties nearby
Antony, Buckland Abbey, Lanhydrock, Lydford Gorge, Saltram

The Courts Garden

Holt, nr Bradford-on-Avon, Wiltshire BA14 6RR

❀ ☕ 🎭 🛡 ♿ ▦ 🚶 | 1943 | (1:J4)

Delightful English country garden

One of Wiltshire's best-kept secrets, this charming garden is full of variety and shows English country style at its best. The peaceful water gardens, with irises and lilies, and the beautiful herbaceous borders, complemented with surrounding topiary and ornaments, demonstrate an imaginative use of colour and planting. Stroll through the arboretum and enjoy the many wonderful species of tree and natural planting of spring bulbs.

What's new in 2008 Dye pond and lily pond re-lined to maintain water levels throughout the season

⭐ Please, no tripods or easels without prior consent. No ball games or picnics

ℹ **T** 01225 782875
E courtsgarden@nationaltrust.org.uk

🎭 By appointment at an additional charge

😊 See website for details

🚶 Walks leaflet available showing cross country route to Great Chalfield Manor and Garden

♿ 🚻 ♿ ⚲ 🔊 🅿 ♿ **Grounds** 🐕 ♿

🛒 Plant sales – small area at entrance

☕ Tea-room (NT-approved concession) on ground floor of house

♿ Pushchairs and baby back-carriers admitted. Children's quiz/trail

▦ Suitable for school groups

➔ [173:ST861618] **Cycle**: NCN4, 1¼ml.
Bus: First 237 Trowbridge–Melksham (passing close ⊠ Trowbridge).
Station: Bradford-on-Avon 2½ml; Trowbridge 3ml. **Road**: 3ml SW of Melksham, 2½ml E of Bradford-on-Avon, on S side of B3107. Follow signs to Holt

🅿 Free parking (not NT), 80yds. Parking in village hall car park opposite, on N side of B3107 (not for coaches)

NT properties nearby
Dyrham Park, Great Chalfield Manor and Garden, Lacock Abbey, Westwood Manor

The Courts Garden								
15 Mar–2 Nov	11–5:30	**M**	**T**	W	**T**	**F**	**S**	**S**
Tea-room open as garden. Out of season by appointment only								

Dunster Castle

Dunster, nr Minehead, Somerset TA24 6SL

[icons] 🛆 ❄ ♠ 🏠 𝑖 ⋂ 🗺 🛡 🚼 🖼

⊤ | 1976 | (1:G5)

Ancient castle with fine interiors and subtropical gardens

Dramatically sited on a wooded hill, a castle has existed here since at least Norman times, with an impressive medieval gatehouse and ruined tower giving a reminder of its turbulent history. Home of the Luttrell family for more than 600 years, the present building was remodelled in 1868–72 by Antony Salvin. The fine oak staircase and plasterwork ceiling he adapted can still be seen. Visitors can relax on the sunny sheltered terrace, which is home to a variety of subtropical plants and the National Collection of Strawberry Trees. Magnificent views over the Bristol Channel and a pleasant walk beside the River Avill add to the ambience.

What's new in 2008 Bat camera and ghostbusters' trail. New interpretation in the Morning Room

★ Castle closed for private functions on 6 & 27 June, 11 July and 12 Sept. Gardens and shop open as normal

ℹ️ **T** 01643 823004 (Infoline), 01643 821314
E dunstercastle@nationaltrust.org.uk

Dunster Castle										
Castle										
15 Mar–23 Jul	11–4:30	M	T	W	T		F	S	S
25 Jul–3 Sep	11–5	M	T	W	T		F	S	S
5 Sep–2 Nov	11–4:30	M	T	W	T		F	S	S
Garden/park										
1 Feb–14 Mar	11–4	M	T	W	T	F	S	S
15 Mar–2 Nov	10–5	M	T	W	T	F	S	S
3 Nov–31 Jan 09	11–4	M	T	W	T	F	S	S
Shop*										
15 Mar–24 Jul	10:30–5	M	T	W	T	F	S	S
25 Jul–4 Sep	10:30–5:30	M	T	W	T	F	S	S
5 Sep–2 Nov	10:30–5	M	T	W	T	F	S	S
3 Nov–31 Dec	11–4	M	T	W	T	F	S	S

Open Good Fri. Castle closed for private functions 6 & 27 June, 11 July and 12 Sept. Gardens and shop open as normal. Garden, park and shop closed 25/26 Dec. Shop closed Jan. *Shop short-term relocation, tel. to confirm opening times

For information regarding prices, see page 10

The marble chimney piece in the Drawing Room at Dunster Castle, installed by Salvin in the late 18th century

𝑖 'Attic and Basement' tours taking visitors to parts of the castle not normally on public view. Rooms are unfurnished. Tel. to book

🛡 Family events

♿ [icons] Building [icons] Grounds [icons]

🏠 NT shop. Plant sales

🚼 Baby-changing facilities. Baby back-carriers admitted. Front-carrying baby slings for loan. Family guide. Children's guide. Children's quiz/trail. Wheel-friendly route in gardens. Buggy park. Colouring sheets. Activity days. Ghostbusters' trail. Family events

🖼 Suitable for school groups. Live costumed interpretation. Adult study days

🐕 In park only on lead

➡ [181:SS995435] **Bus**: First 398 Tiverton–Minehead; also 28 Taunton–Minehead (passing ⊠ Taunton), alight Dunster Steep, ½ml. **Station**: Dunster (W Somerset Rly) 1ml. **Road**: in Dunster, 3ml SE of Minehead. NT car park approached direct from A39

🅿 Parking, 300yds

NT properties nearby
Arlington Court, Coleridge Cottage, Dunster Working Watermill, Holnicote Estate, Knightshayes Court

Dunster Working Watermill

Mill Lane, Dunster, nr Minehead, Somerset
TA24 6SW

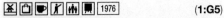 1976   **(1:G5)**

Fully restored watermill

A restored 18th-century watermill in a tranquil
riverside setting built on the site of a mill
mentioned in the Domesday Survey of 1086.

⭐ The mill is a private business and all visitors
inc. NT members pay the admission charge

ℹ️ **T** 01643 821759
  E dunstermill@nationaltrust.org.uk

♿ 🖼️ **Building** 🏔️

🏪 Selling mill flour, muesli and souvenirs (not NT)

🍽️ Riverside tea-room (not NT)

👪 Baby back-carriers admitted

🏫 Suitable for school groups

➡️ [181:SS995435] On River Avill, beneath
Castle Tor. **Foot**: approach via Mill Lane or
Castle Gardens. **Bus**: First 398 Tiverton–
Minehead; also 28 Taunton–Minehead
(passing 🚉 Taunton), alight Dunster Steep, ½ml.
Station: Dunster (W Somerset Steam Rly)
1ml. **Road**: in Dunster, 3ml SE of Minehead.
NT car park approached direct from A39

🅿️ Parking (not NT), 500yds. Alternative parking
in Dunster Castle NT car park, £2

NT properties nearby
Arlington Court, Coleridge Cottage, Dunster
Castle, Holnicote Estate

Dyrham Park

Dyrham, nr Bath, Gloucestershire SN14 8ER

🎭 🏃 1961   **(1:J4)**

**Spectacular late 17th-century mansion,
garden and deer park**

Set in a beautiful Gloucestershire valley and
surrounded by 110 hectares (274 acres) of
garden and rolling parkland, this grand baroque
house with spectacular sweeping views towards
Bristol, was designed by Talman for William
Blathwayt, Secretary at War during the reign of
William III. Lavish 17th-century collections
reflect the fashion for all things Dutch, including
splendid Delftware, paintings and furniture.
Later 18th-century additions include furniture by
Gillow and Linnell, and the Victorian domestic
quarters provide visitors with an intriguing
insight into life below stairs.

What's new in 2008 Ongoing West Garden
development – 'a contemporary garden with
echoes of the past'

⭐ Due to the fragile nature of their contents,
some rooms have very low light levels

ℹ️ **T** 0117 937 2501
  E dyrhampark@nationaltrust.org.uk

🎯 Park, garden and house walks and talks held
on weekdays during the season (not Good Fri
or BH Mons)

🎭 Tulipomania Festival 18–22 April. Family
activity days, winter lectures and workshops

🏃 Parkland walks available with map

Dunster Working Watermill									
Mill									
21 Mar–24 Mar	11–4:45	M	T	W	T	**F**	**S**	**S**	
1 Apr–31 May	11–4:45	**M**	**T**	**W**	**T**	F	**S**	**S**	
1 Jun–30 Sep	11–4:45	**M**	**T**	**W**	**T**	**F**	**S**	**S**	
1 Oct–29 Oct	11–4:45	**M**	**T**	**W**	**T**	F	**S**	**S**	
Tea-room									
As mill	10:30–4:45								

Open Good Fri: 10:30–4:45. Tea-room: may open
earlier at weekends; open at 9 on BHols

Dyrham Park									
House									
14 Mar–2 Nov	12–5	**M**	**T**	W	T	**F**	**S**	**S**	
Garden/shop/tea-room									
14 Mar–29 Jun	11–5	**M**	**T**	W	T	**F**	**S**	**S**	
30 Jun–31 Aug	11–5	**M**	**T**	**W**	**T**	**F**	**S**	**S**	
1 Sep–2 Nov	11–5	**M**	**T**	W	T	**F**	**S**	**S**	
8 Nov–14 Dec	11–4	M	T	W	T	F	**S**	**S**	
Park									
All year*	11–5:30	**M**	**T**	**W**	**T**	**F**	**S**	**S**	

Open BH Mons and Good Fri: 11–5. Last admission
1hr before closing. *Except 25 Dec

Many Trust properties are offering Gift Aid on Entry for non-members, see page 10

The east front of Dyrham Park on a beautiful sunny day

🚹 WC 🚻 ♿ •• 🅿️ 📷 Building 📖 ♿
Grounds 📖 ➡️

🏪 NT shop. Plant sales

🍽️ Courtyard tea-room (licensed) at main house. Children's menu. Kiosk (NT-approved concession) in tea-garden, serving hot drinks, sandwiches, ice-creams and snacks. Car park kiosk (NT-approved concession) for snacks and ice-creams

👶 Baby-changing facilities. Front-carrying baby slings and hip-carrying infant seats for loan. Children's guide. Children's quiz/trail. Children's activity packs. Family activity days

🏫 Suitable for school groups. Education room/centre. Hands-on activities. Adult study days. Guide leaflets to the house in several languages

🐕 Dog walking area close to main car park

➜ [172:ST743757] **Foot**: Cotswold Way passes property. **Cycle**: Avon and Wiltshire cycleways. **Bus**: special link from Queen's Square, ½ml 🚉 Bath Spa (tel. 0117 937 2501 for times). **Station**: Bath Spa 8ml. **Road**: 8ml N of Bath, 12ml E of Bristol; approached from Bath–Stroud road (A46), 2ml S of Tormarton interchange with M4, exit 18

🅿️ Free parking, 500yds

NT properties nearby
Bath Assembly Rooms, Clevedon Court, Lacock Abbey, Leigh Woods, Newark Park, Prior Park, Tyntesfield

Finch Foundry

Sticklepath, Okehampton, Devon EX20 2NW

🏠 🍴 🏪 🍽️ 🎭 🎪 😊 🚹 🏫 🧍 1994 (1:F7)

The last working water-powered forge in England

In the village of Sticklepath on the edge of Dartmoor you can discover the evocative sights and sounds of a 19th-century water-powered forge. See the three large waterwheels driving the huge tilt hammer and grindstone, and enjoy demonstrations throughout the day. The foundry used to make sickles, scythes and shovels for West Country farmers and miners. You will find a fascinating display of tools in the old grinding shop, and in the garden is a summerhouse that once belonged to Tom Pearse (of Widecombe Fair fame). Starting from the foundry there are waymarked walks along the River Taw and up on to Dartmoor.

ℹ️ **T** 01837 840046
E finchfoundry@nationaltrust.org.uk

🎭 Machinery demonstrations and talks throughout the day at quarter past each hour from 11:15–4:15

♿ 🚻 ♿ 👶 •• 📷 Building 📖 Grounds 📖
🏪 NT shop. Plant sales

Finch Foundry								
15 Mar–2 Nov	11–5	**M**	T	**W**	**T**	**F**	**S**	**S**

For details of events go to www.nationaltrust.org.uk/events

🍴 Tea-room. Children's menu

👪 Baby back-carriers admitted. Children's quiz/trail

🎒 Suitable for school groups. Teacher's resource pack available

🐕 Dogs welcome in all areas except tea-room, shop and foundry during demonstration

➡ [191:SX641940] In the centre of Sticklepath village. **Foot**: on the 180ml Tarka Trail. **Cycle**: on West Devon Cycle Route. **Bus**: Stagecoach in Devon X30, Western Greyhound 510, First X9 (Suns only), Exeter–Okehampton (passing close 🚆 Exeter Central) Carmel 179 Okehampton–Moretonhampstead. **Station**: Okehampton (Sun, June–Sept only) 4½ml. **Road**: 4ml E of Okehampton off A30

🅿 Free parking. Not suitable for coaches and high vehicles. Access is narrow and low

NT properties nearby
Castle Drogo, Lydford Gorge

Fyne Court

Broomfield, Bridgwater, Somerset TA5 2EQ

🚶 1967   (1:H5)

Nature reserve and visitor centre

The former pleasure grounds of the partly demolished home of the Crosse family, this nature reserve is now leased by Somerset Wildlife Trust. It is ideal for walks and discovering a wide variety of habitats.

What's new in 2008 Now the headquarters of the Quantock Hills Area of Outstanding Natural Beauty. Visit www.quantockhills.com

⭐ Only visitor centre and grounds open to visitors; buildings contain an education base for the Wildlife Trust. 8-hectare (20-acre) reserve managed by Somerset Wildlife Trust, remainder of estate by NT

Fyne Court									
1 Apr–31 Oct	9–6	M	T	W	T	F	S	S
1 Nov–31 Jan 09	9–5	M	T	W	T	F	S	S

Opens 10 Sat and Sun. Closes dusk if earlier. Tel. for shop and tea-room times

ℹ **T** 01823 652400 (Somerset Wildlife Trust) **E** fynecourt@nationaltrust.org.uk

𝄪 Tel. for details

♿ 🚾 Grounds ➡

🪴 Plant sales (not NT)

🍴 Tea-room (not NT)

👪 Baby-changing facilities. Pushchairs and baby back-carriers admitted

🎒 Suitable for school groups. Education centre. Hands-on activities. Booking essential

➡ [182:ST222321] 6ml N of Taunton; 6ml SW of Bridgwater. **Station**: Taunton 6ml; Bridgwater 6ml

🅿 Parking (not NT), 150yds

NT properties nearby
Beacon and Bicknoller Hills, Coleridge Cottage, Dunster Castle, Holnicote Estate

Glastonbury Tor

nr Glastonbury, Somerset

✚ 🚶 1933   (1:I5)

Prominent hill overlooking the Isle of Avalon, Glastonbury and the Somerset Levels

The dramatic and evocative Tor dominates the surrounding countryside and offers spectacular views over Somerset, Dorset and Wiltshire. At the summit of this very steep hill an excavation has revealed the plans of two superimposed churches of St Michael, of which only the 15th-century tower remains.

⭐ No WC

ℹ **T** 01985 843600 **E** glastonburytor@nationaltrust.org.uk

🐣 Easter trail and Apple Day

🚶 Public footpaths across the Tor

♿ Grounds

🐕 On leads only

Glastonbury Tor							
All year	M	T	W	T	F	S	S

Charges for National Trust members apply on some special event days

Glastonbury Tor, Somerset, with the 15th-century tower of St Michael at its summit

➡ [182/183:ST512386] **Foot**: short walk from the town centre, eastwards along A361. **Cycle**: NCN3. **Bus**: First 29 from ⊟ Taunton, 376 Bristol–Yeovil (passing ⊟ Bristol Temple Meads). All pass within ½ml of the Tor. **Road**: signposted from Glastonbury town centre, from where seasonal park & ride (not NT) operates

P No parking on site (except for orange or blue badge holders). Please use council-run park & ride from centre of Glastonbury from April to Sept, or park in free car park at Somerset Rural Life Museum, Abbey Farm, Glastonbury. Tel. 01458 831197 to confirm times available. Lower entrance to the Tor is approx. ⅓ml from museum car park

NT properties nearby
Collard Hill, Lytes Cary Manor, Polden Hills, Stourhead

Glendurgan Garden

Mawnan Smith, nr Falmouth, Cornwall TR11 5JZ

❋ 🏛 🏠 🗂 💷 🎭 🎋 🎦 🏃 1962   **(1:C9)**

Superb subtropical garden, with special interest for families

Described by the Fox family, who gave Glendurgan to the Trust, as 'a little peace [sic] of heaven on earth', the garden is a place of great beauty and tranquillity. Three valleys converge and drop towards the sparkling waters of the Helford River and the hamlet and beach at Durgan. The garden has many fine trees, rare and exotic plants from the four corners of the globe, outstanding spring displays of magnolias and camellias, plus carpets of wild flowers. Glendurgan has always been a magical place for children, with the baffling laurel maze, the Giant's Stride (rope swing), the beach and the recreated school house. It is an informal garden that all ages can enjoy. The house is privately occupied.

★ Ferry link to Durgan beach, from Helford Village, Helford Passage and Trebah Garden

i **T** 01326 250906 (during opening hours), 01872 862090 (out of hours), 01326 250247 (tea-room) **E** glendurgan@nationaltrust.org.uk

🎭 Series of garden events

🏃 *Coast of Cornwall* leaflet 16 (Helford River)

♿ 🚻 ♿ ♿ ♿ ♿ ♿ **Grounds** 🏞

🛍 NT shop. Plant sales

💷 Tea-room (NT-approved concession). Serving beverages, light lunches, snacks, cakes and ice-cream

Glendurgan Garden									
9 Feb–3 Aug	10:30–5:30	M	**T**	**W**	**T**	**F**	**S**	S
4 Aug–25 Aug	10:30–5:30	**M**	**T**	**W**	**T**	**F**	**S**	S
26 Aug–1 Nov	10:30–5:30	M	**T**	**W**	**T**	**F**	**S**	S
Open BH Mons. Closed Good Fri. Last admission 1hr before closing									

[📋] Baby-changing facilities. Pushchairs and baby back-carriers admitted. Giant's Stride (a pole with ropes to swing from) and maze

[📋] Suitable for school groups

→ [204:SW772277] **Foot**: South West Coast Path within ⅔ml. **Ferry**: service links Helford village, Helford Passage, Trebah beach and Durgan beach (for Glendurgan). Tel. 01326 250770. **Bus**: Truronian T4, 400 from Falmouth (passing close ⊠ Penmere). **Station**: Penmere (U) 4ml. **Road**: 4ml SW of Falmouth, ½ml SW of Mawnan Smith, on road to Helford Passage

[P] Free parking. Car park gates locked at 5:30

NT properties nearby
Trelissick Garden

Godolphin

Godolphin Cross, Helston, Cornwall TR13 9RE

[📋] [⅄] [2000] (1:B9)

Ancient and atmospheric house and garden set within an historic estate

At the heart of an historic estate, owned by the National Trust since 2000, lies one of Cornwall's most beautiful and romantic old houses. Newly acquired by the Trust, Godolphin was considered in the 17th century to be the most fashionable house in Cornwall. It was the springboard for the political ambitions of the illustrious Godolphin family, who had made their fortune from the rich mineral deposits on the estate. However, after 1710 no Godolphin lived here, and the house and estate were left to settle gently into the landscape. Centuries of benign neglect have given the house and garden and surrounding

Godolphin						
Estate						
All year	**M**	**T**	**W**	**T**	**F**	**S**	**S**

House and garden: at the time of going to print, arrangements for the opening of the garden and the house in 2008 have not been finalised. It is likely that access to the interior of the house will be limited whilst essential conservation work is carried out, but there will be some regular access to the garden and the house exterior. For up-to-date details, tel. 0844 800 1895 or visit www.nationaltrust.org.uk/godolphinhouse

estate buildings an extraordinarily haunting air of antiquity and peace, a fragile atmosphere that has been protected and nurtured through the 20th century by the Schofield family. Miraculously the garden has barely changed since the 14th and 16th centuries, with the latest fashions passing it by. It is so rare to discover a garden such as this, which has not been radically altered through the ages, and this is why it is considered to be one of the most important historic gardens in Europe. This garden is not about plants and flowers but about the unique surviving remains of a medieval pattern. There are many fascinating walks on the estate, which includes Godolphin Hill and more than 400 recorded archaeological features – ranging from Bronze Age enclosures to dramatic 19th-century mining remains. Godolphin is a distinct area within the 'Cornish Mining' World Heritage Site.

What's new in 2008 Newly acquired house and garden, reunifying the ancient estate

[★] Tel. 0844 800 1895 for details of house and garden admission

[ℹ] **T** 01736 762479 (estate)
 E godolphin@nationaltrust.org.uk

[⤢] Occasional guided walks on estate

[♨] See events leaflet or website

[⤢] Estate walks leaflet available

[♿] **Estate** [♿]

[📋] Pushchairs admitted to estate and garden

[📋] Estate suitable for school groups. Education room/centre. Some art/craft workshops for adult learners (booked groups only)

[🐕] On leads and only on estate

→ [203:SW599321] **Bus**: Truronian T20 Camborne–Helston (passing close ⊠ Camborne). **Station**: Camborne 9ml. **Road**: from Helston take A394 to Sithney Common, turn right on to B3302 and follow signs. From Hayle take B3302 through Leedstown. From W, take B3280 through Goldsithney

[P] Free parking. Coach access from Townshend

NT properties nearby
Glendurgan Garden, The Lizard, Penrose Estate, St Michael's Mount, Trelissick Garden, Trengwainton Garden

Dogs assisting visitors with disabilities are always welcome

Godrevy

Gwithian, nr Hayle, Cornwall

 1939 (1:B9)

High cliffs and sheltered coves with sandy beaches

The Trust owns all the coastline from Godrevy to Navax Point. The main beach below the summer car park connects to Gwithian Beach, forming an impressive sweep of unbroken sand around the edge of St Ives Bay. Away from the bustle of the beach, the coastal grasslands and heathland are rich with wild flowers and provide open access for miles of walking. Seals are a common sight, and guillemots, razorbills, fulmars and cormorants breed on the cliffs.

★ Please be aware of cliff edges, unstable cliffs and the state of the tide, and keep children supervised. WC not always available

ℹ️ **T** 01872 552412 (Area Warden)

🚶 NT *Coast of Cornwall* leaflet 9 includes details of walks

♿ 🚻 **Grounds** 🏛️

🍴 Ice-cream van. Godrevy Café (NT-approved concession) (licensed). Open main season and weekends/holidays all year. Tel. 01736 757999

🏫 Suitable for school groups

🐕 Seasonal restriction on beach, Easter to end Sept

➡️ [203:SW582430] **Bus**: Western Greyhound 340 from Penzance (passing close 🚉 St Erth and 🚉 Hayle). **Station**: Hayle 5ml. **Road**: just off the B3301 N of Gwithian village

🅿️ Charge for parking. Limited parking Nov–April

NT properties nearby
Cornish Mines and Engines, Godolphin, St Michael's Mount, Trengwainton Garden

Godrevy							
All year	M	T	W	T	F	S	S

Great Chalfield Manor and Garden

nr Melksham, Wiltshire SN12 8NH

🏛️➕✴️🚶♻️🏫🏫🚶 1943 (1:J4)

Charming 15th-century manor house with Arts & Crafts garden

A fine example of a medieval manor, complete with an upper moat, gatehouse and small parish church. Beautiful oriel windows and rooftop soldiers (*c*.1480) adorn the house, restored between 1905 and 1911 by Major R. Fuller – whose family still live here and manage the property on behalf of the Trust. The delightful gardens were designed by Alfred Parsons and feature terraces, gazebo and lily pond. Grass paths offer visitors romantic views across the spring-fed fishpond. The house and garden have featured in many tv and film productions, including *Persuasion* and *The Other Boleyn Girl*.

What's new in 2008 Recently renovated paths in rose garden

★ Great Chalfield Manor and Garden is administered for the NT by the tenant

ℹ️ **T** 01225 782239
E greatchalfieldmanor@nationaltrust.org.uk

🚶 Access to house is by guided tour only (numbers limited)

♻️ Garden open outside normal times for spring flowers, under National Gardens Scheme. Charity spring plant fair. Charge inc. NT members

Great Chalfield Manor and Garden								
Manor house								
30 Mar–2 Nov	*		M	**T**	**W**	**T**	F	S	**S**
Garden								
30 Mar–2 Nov	11–5		M	**T**	**W**	**T**	F	S	S
30 Mar–2 Nov	2–5		M	T	W	T	F	S	**S**

*Admission to manor house by guided tour. Tues–Thur: tours at 11:30, 12:15, 2:15, 3 & 3:45. Sun: tours at 2:15, 3 & 3:45. No booking for tours. Tours take 45mins and numbers are limited to 25. Visitors arriving during a tour can visit the adjoining parish church and garden first. Group visits are welcome on Fri & Sat (not BHols) by written arrangement with the tenant Mrs Robert Floyd. Charge applies

The west wing of the 15th-century Great Chalfield Manor, Wiltshire, seen from across the garden

Walks leaflet showing cross-country route to The Courts Garden

Building Grounds

Hip-carrying infant seats for loan

Suitable for school groups

→ [173:ST860631] **Foot**: pleasant 1ml walk by public footpath from The Courts Garden (NT), Holt. **Cycle**: NCN4. On the Wiltshire Cycleway. **Bus**: First 237 Trowbridge–Melksham (passing close Trowbridge), alight Holt, 1ml. **Station**: Bradford-on-Avon, 3ml. **Road**: 3ml SW of Melksham off B3107 via Broughton Gifford Common (follow sign for Broughton Gifford, take care in narrow lane). Coaches must approach from N (via Broughton Gifford); lanes from S too narrow

P Free parking, 100yds on grass verge outside manor gates

NT properties nearby
The Courts Garden, Dyrham Park, Lacock Abbey, Westwood Manor

Greenway

Greenway Road, Galmpton, nr Brixham, Devon
TQ5 0ES

2000 (1:G8)

Glorious woodland garden on the banks of the River Dart, with an atmosphere of romantic wilderness

This most nostalgic and magical of gardens, evoking a past world of long summer holidays and secret places waiting to be discovered, was described by previous owner Agatha Christie as 'the loveliest place in the world'. The beautiful garden is renowned for its rare half-hardy plants, underplanted with drifts of native wild flowers. Among the many corners to explore are a Victorian fernery, an exquisitely restored vinery and the enigmatic 'Raleigh's boathouse'.

Greenway			M	T	W	T	F	S	S
1 Mar–26 Oct	10:30–5				**W**	**T**	**F**	**S**	**S**

Barn Gallery: open as garden, showing modern contemporary art by local artists

Unless indicated, last admission is always 30mins before closing time

The magical woodland garden at Greenway has an atmosphere of romantic wilderness

Enjoy the adventure of arriving here by ferry and alighting at Greenway Quay, with dramatic views of the house from the river.

What's new in 2008 Open on Sundays for the first time. New footpath from Greenway Quay up to the garden. Exhibition 'Greenway, Another Chapter' (on the project to open the house in 2009); conservator's workshop open giving the opportunity to watch and even get involved in the cleaning and care of some of the many collections from the house

⭐ Greenway operates a traffic management system to reduce car impact on the local village. Whenever possible please travel by 'green ways' to Greenway. Ferries available from Dartmouth, Brixham and Torquay. Visitors travelling from Dittisham are encouraged to park in the Ham car park; however, we strongly recommend not using this route in July and August to avoid congestion

ℹ️ **T** 01803 842382 (Infoline), 01803 661903 (café) **E** greenway@nationaltrust.org.uk

🚶 'Meet the Gardener' guided walks. Details at reception

🎭 Lectures and workshops in the Barn Gallery. Garden days, plant fairs. Spring and autumn walks with lunch. Open-air theatre. Conservation talks and workshop

🚶 Walks through the estate link with the Dart Valley Trail, John Musgrave Trail, Greenway walk and Galmpton Village Walk. Details in reception. Please note that there is no parking for these walks at Greenway

♿ 🚻 🚾 🛗 📷 🔍 🅿️ **Grounds** ♿ ➡️

🛍️ NT shop with local crafts and produce, books and themed games. Plant sales

☕ Licensed café. Serves home-made light meals, locally produced seasonal and vegetarian food. Children's menu

👶 Baby-changing facilities. Pushchairs and baby back-carriers admitted. Children's quiz/trail. Children's activity packs. Tracker Packs

📖 Adult study days

🐕 On leads on main drive and café courtyard only. Not in garden. Walks on the estate, on leads near livestock

➡️ [202:SX876548] **Foot**: Dart Valley Trail from Kingswear or Dartmouth. Greenway Walk from Brixham. Village Walk from Galmpton. **Ferry**: enjoy a cruise on the River Dart from Dartmouth (use Dartmouth park & ride, bus service every 15mins, please allow at least 4hrs parking) and Dittisham. Sea/river link from Torquay and Brixham. Tel. Greenway Ferry and Quay Services (licensed operators to the NT) 01803 844010, www.greenwayferry.co.uk and www.rivierabelle.co.uk. Ferries available for individuals, groups and charters. NB: there is a steep walk uphill (800yds) from Greenway Quay to the garden. **Station**: Paignton 4½ml, Churston (Paignton & Dartmouth Steam Rly) 2ml. **Road**: there are no parking spaces on the narrow country lanes leading to Greenway. No brown signs; follow signs for Greenway Ferry/YHA

For further information go to www.nationaltrust.org.uk

Visit somewhere special today...

Baddesley Clinton (© NTPL/David Levenson)

... we're open early for you

In 2008, many National Trust properties will be opening earlier in the year than usual, giving you the perfect opportunity to make the most of spring and your membership. Check for details in your Handbook.

So come and enjoy today!

www.nationaltrust.org.uk

Bring history to life. Volunteer with us

Clandon Park (© NTPL/Stuart Cox)

People are the lifeblood of the National Trust and we're always on the lookout for volunteers with a special spark. You don't need vast knowledge, just a passion to inform, inspire and delight the millions of people who visit our properties every year.

To find out about the wide range of volunteering opportunities in our built and countryside properties, talk to a member of your local property team, read more on p.381, or visit our website **www.nationaltrust.org.uk/volunteer**

P Free parking, 550yds. Time limited on busy days. Mini coaches (25-seat max.) only and by prior arrangement. Greenway Quay: limited parking (not NT). Charges apply

NT properties nearby
Bradley, Coleton Fishacre, Compton Castle, Dart Estuary, Overbeck's

Hailes Abbey

nr Winchcombe, Cheltenham, Gloucestershire
GL54 5PB

[icons] 1937   **(1:K1)**

13th-century Cistercian abbey

Founded in 1246 and once a celebrated pilgrimage site, the abbey now lies in ruins. Remains of the dramatic cloister arches survive along with artefacts displayed in the museum.

★ Hailes Abbey is financed, managed and maintained by English Heritage. For further information tel. 0117 975 0700 (EH regional office) or visit www.english-heritage.org.uk/hailes

i **T** 01242 602398
E hailesabbey@nationaltrust.org.uk

♿ **:** Building

❑ EH shop in museum. Plant sales

♿ Ice-cream and soft drinks

♿ Baby-changing facilities

♿ Suitable for school groups

♿ On leads and only in grounds

→ [150:SP050300] **Foot**: Cotswold Way within ⅔ml. **Bus**: Castleways from Cheltenham, alight Didbrook, 1½ml, or more frequent to Greet, 1¾ml by footpath. **Station**: Cheltenham 10ml. **Road**: 2ml NE of Winchcombe, 1ml E of Broadway road (B4632, originally A46)

Hailes Abbey									
Site/museum									
21 Mar–30 Jun	10–5	M	T	W	T	F	S	S
1 Jul–31 Aug	10–6	M	T	W	T	F	S	S
1 Sep–30 Sep	10–5	M	T	W	T	F	S	S
1 Oct–31 Oct	10–4	M	T	W	T	F	S	S
Please confirm times with property									

P Free parking (not NT)

NT properties nearby
Hidcote Manor Garden, Snowshill Manor

Hardy Monument

Black Down, Portesham, Dorset

[icons] 1938   **(1:J7)**

Monument to Vice-Admiral Hardy

★ No WC. Car park not NT

i **T** 01297 561900
E hardymonument@nationaltrust.org.uk

→ From the B3157 Weymouth–Bridport road, turn off at Portesham; the road climbs steeply to a car park signposted 'Hardy Monument'

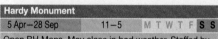

Hardy Monument								
5 Apr–28 Sep	11–5	M	T	W	T	F	S	S
Open BH Mons. May close in bad weather. Staffed by volunteers. Numbers at the top of the monument are limited. Children must be accompanied by an adult								

Hardy's Cottage

Higher Bockhampton, nr Dorchester, Dorset
DT2 8QJ

[icons] 1948   **(1:J7)**

Birthplace of novelist and poet Thomas Hardy

Thomas Hardy was born in 1840 in this small cob and thatch cottage and from here he would walk to school every day in Dorchester, three miles away. It was built by his great-grandfather and is little altered since the family left. The interior has been furnished by the NT (see also Max Gate). His early novels *Under the Greenwood Tree* and *Far from the Madding Crowd* were written here. It has a charming cottage garden.

★ No WC

i **T** 01305 262366
E hardyscottage@nationaltrust.org.uk

Hardy's Cottage								
23 Mar–30 Oct	11–5	M	T	W	T	F	S	S

& **:.** **⊘** **🅳** Building **🌳** Grounds **🏔** **➡**

🛍 Thomas Hardy's books, postcards and other items for sale

➔ [194:SY728925] **Station**: Dorchester South 4ml; Dorchester West (U) 4ml. **Road**: 3ml NE of Dorchester, ½ml S of A35. From Kingston Maurward roundabout follow signs to Stinsford and Higher Bockhampton

P Free parking (not NT). Cottage is 600yds walk through woods or lane from car park. Drop-off point by prior arrangement with Custodian

NT properties nearby
Clouds Hill, Hardy Monument, Max Gate

Heelis

Kemble Drive, Swindon, Wiltshire SN2 2NA

🏠 **🛗** **🛍** **☕** **🍴** **🚼** **⛱** **2005**   **(1:K3)**

Central office for the National Trust

An architectural gem, designed by Feilden Clegg Bradley Architects in 2005, the Trust's award-winning central office is a remarkable example of innovative and sustainable building construction. Timber from our woodlands and wool from Herdwick sheep grazed on Trust farmlands help make Heelis a unique working environment.

★ Heelis operates a green travel policy and, therefore, visitor parking facilities are limited and must be booked with reception. Admission to offices by booked guided tour only

ℹ **T** 01793 817400
   E heelisreception@nationaltrust.org.uk

🍴 Every Friday at 1, book with reception

& **🚾** **🅿** Building **🏔**

☕ Heelis café (licensed). Children's menu

🚼 Baby-changing facilities. Pushchairs and baby back-carriers admitted

Heelis									
All year	10–4	**M**	**T**	**W**	**T**	**F**	**S**	**S**	
Admission to offices by booked guided tour only. Shop/café open 10–5 Sat and 11–4 Sun & BHols. Facilities may also be open later at certain times of the year									

➔ [173:SU141850] **Bus**: Thamesdown Transport and Stagecoach, 13 & 14, alight Rodbourne Road, then 200yds.
Station: Swindon, ¾ml. **Road**: off B4289. Follow signs for McArthur Glen Retail Outlet. Park & ride from The Corps and Wroughton

P Parking (not NT), 100yds (pay & display). Additional car and coach parking at Outlet Centre North car park

NT properties nearby
Avebury, The Buscot and Coleshill Estates, Great Coxwell Barn, Lacock Abbey, White Horse Hill

Hidcote Manor Garden

Hidcote Bartrim, nr Chipping Campden, Gloucestershire GL55 6LR

✿ **🛍** **☕** **👕** **🚼** **🍴** **1947**   **(1:L1)**

Celebrated 20th-century garden in the beautiful north Cotswolds

Hidcote is one of England's great gardens. Designed and created by the horticulturist Major Lawrence Johnston in the Arts & Crafts style, it is made up of exquisite garden rooms, each possessing its own special character. Visitors will discover rare shrubs and trees, outstanding herbaceous borders and unusual plant species. The garden changes in harmony with the

Hidcote Manor Garden									
Garden									
15 Mar–30 Jun	10–6	**M**	**T**	**W**	T	**F**	**S**	**S**	
1 Jul–31 Aug	10–6	**M**	**T**	**W**	T	**F**	**S**	**S**	
1 Sep–1 Oct	10–6	**M**	**T**	**W**	T	F	**S**	**S**	
2 Oct–2 Nov	10–5	**M**	**T**	**W**	T	F	**S**	**S**	
Barn Café/plant sales/shop/ restaurant									
15 Mar–30 Jun	10–5	**M**	**T**	**W**	T	F	**S**	**S**	
1 Jul–31 Aug	10–5	**M**	**T**	**W**	T	**F**	**S**	**S**	
1 Sep–1 Oct	10–5	**M**	**T**	**W**	T	F	**S**	**S**	
2 Oct–2 Nov	10–4	**M**	**T**	**W**	T	F	**S**	**S**	
Barn Café/plant sales additional opening									
17 Apr–30 Jun	11–4	M	T	W	**T**	**F**	S	S	
1 Jul–31 Aug	11–4	M	T	W	**T**	**F**	S	S	
Shop/plant sales									
7 Nov–21 Dec	12–4	M	T	W	T	**F**	**S**	**S**	
Restaurant									
8 Nov–21 Dec	12–4	M	T	W	T	F	**S**	**S**	
Open Good Fri. Last admission 1hr before closing									

For information regarding prices, see page 10

The Pillar Garden, Hidcote Manor Garden

➔ [151:SP176429] **Cycle**: NCN5, 1¼ml.
Station: Honeybourne (U) 4½ml. **Road**: close
to village of Mickleton, 4ml NE of Chipping
Campden, 1ml E of B4632 (originally A46), off
B4081. Coaches are not permitted through
Chipping Campden High Street

🅿 Free parking, 100yds. Coaches must book –
space limited

NT properties nearby
Charlecote Park, Chastleton House, Dover's Hill,
Snowshill Manor, Upton House and Gardens

seasons, from vibrant spring bulbs to autumn's
glorious Red Border. Nestled in the Cotswolds
with sweeping views across the Vale of
Evesham, Hidcote is appealing all year round.

What's new in 2008 Work to restore Lawrence
Johnston's tennis court and reinstate the gable
end of the Plant House during the summer.
Further rejuvenation work along the Rock Bank,
including the Northern Scree

⭐ As the number of groups is limited per day,
group leaders should check with property
before booking transport. On BHols and fine
weekends garden is least crowded after 3

ℹ **T** 01386 438333
E hidcote@nationaltrust.org.uk

😃 Private evening tours, lecture lunches, open-
air theatre

🕴 Public footpaths leading from the car park,
including the Monarch's Way and
Cotswold Way

♿ 🚾 🧏 🔇 ⠿ 🅿 ♿ Building 🔽
Grounds ➡ 🎧

🏠 NT shop. Plant sales

🍽 Garden Restaurant (licensed) close to visitor
reception. Children's menu. Thatched Barn
Café close to car park

👶 Baby-changing facilities. Hip-carrying infant
seats for loan. Children's quiz/trail. Limited
access for pushchairs and prams

Holnicote Estate

Selworthy, Minehead, Somerset TA24 8TJ

✝ 🦆 🏛 🕴 🏠 🕴 🎏 🎮 ♿ 🕴
🚲 1944   **(1:G5)**

**Varied landscape of moorland, woods,
farms and coast, rich in wildlife**

The beautiful Holnicote Estate encompasses a
vast area of the Exmoor National Park, taking in
the high tors of Dunkery and Selworthy
Beacons, with breathtaking panoramic views. Its
traditional cottages and farms are grouped in
and around pretty villages and hamlets,
including Selworthy, Allerford, Bossington,
Horner and Luccombe. Offering 4ml of
spectacular coastline between Porlock Bay and
Minehead and over 100ml of footpaths through
enchanting rural landscapes, woods, moors,
farmland and villages, the Estate is a peaceful
escape from the hustle and bustle of everyday
living. Noted for its diversity of wildlife, many
rare species can be discovered in the Horner
and Dunkery Nature Reserve.

⭐ WCs at Bossington, Allerford, Selworthy
and Horner

ℹ **T** 01643 862452
E holnicote@nationaltrust.org.uk

Holnicote Estate									
Estate									
All year			**M**	**T**	**W**	**T**	**F**	**S**	**S**
Estate office									
All year	9–5		**M**	**T**	**W**	**T**	**F**	S	S
Estate office closed BHols and public hols									

Many Trust properties are offering Gift Aid on Entry for non-members, see page 10

[figure] *Holnicote Walks* leaflets available from estate office, Porlock visitor centre and Selworthy Periwinkle tea-rooms

[icons] Grounds

[icon] Suitable for school groups. Education room/centre. Hands-on activities. Adult study days

[icon] Dogs on leads

[icon] On Porlock family cycle route. Also waymarked adventurous mountain-bike trail

[icon] [181:SS920469] **Foot**: 3¾ml of South West Coast Path on property; Coleridge Way; Macmillan Way. **Bus**: Quantock 39 Minehead–Porlock, 300 Minehead–Lynmouth, alight Holnicote, then ½ml. **Station**: Minehead (West Somerset Rly) 5ml. **Road**: off A39 Minehead–Porlock, 3ml W of Minehead

[icon] Free parking. Large car parks with WCs at Selworthy, Bossington, Horner and Allerford. Others at North Hill, Dunkery, Webbers Post. Only Horner car park is suitable for coaches

NT properties nearby
Arlington Court, Beacon and Bicknoller Hills, Coleridge Cottage, Dunster Castle, Fyne Court, Knightshayes Court, Watersmeet

Horton Court

Horton, nr Chipping Sodbury, South Gloucestershire BS37 6QR   **(1:J3)**
Closed in 2008 due to refurbishment

Killerton

Broadclyst, Exeter, Devon EX5 3LE

[icons row] 1944   **(1:G6)**

Fine 18th-century house with costume collection, hillside garden and estate

Killerton house has a notably relaxed, welcoming and informal atmosphere. Visitors are often heard to remark that they could imagine living here: it feels so much like a real home. The house was built in 1778 for the Aclands, one of the oldest families in Devon, and you will find much here to bring generations of fascinating and dynamic Aclands to life. On the first floor, the Paulise de Bush collection of 18th- to 20th-century costume is displayed, with a different themed exhibition every year. Killerton house is beautifully positioned on the flanks of a hill, surrounded by its glorious garden

Farmland near Tivington: part of the Holnicote Estate in Somerset

and overlooking parkland. It also has an extensive agricultural and wooded estate. There are numerous waymarked circular walks, through a variety of habitats and landscapes. The garden is the great glory of Killerton. It was created in the 1770s by renowned nurseryman and landscape designer John Veitch, and features an abundance of rhododendrons, magnolias, herbaceous borders and rare trees, as well as an ice house and a rustic summerhouse (known as The Bear's Hut). There is a discovery centre near the stable courtyard and a packed programme of activities and events to enjoy all year round.

What's new in 2008 'Recollections: 30 years of costume at Killerton', an exhibition showing the gems of the Killerton collection

The Corridor, looking towards the original front door at Killerton, Devon

Killerton			M	T	W	T	F	S	S
House									
1 Mar–9 Mar	2–4		M	T	W	T	F	S	S
12 Mar–31 Jul	11–5		M	T	W	T	F	S	S
1 Aug–31 Aug	11–5		M	T	W	T	F	S	S
1 Sep–29 Sep	11–5		M	T	W	T	F	S	S
1 Oct–2 Nov	11–5		M	T	W	T	F	S	S
6 Dec–23 Dec	2–4		M	T	W	T	F	S	S
Park/garden									
All year	10:30–7		M	T	W	T	F	S	S
Restaurant									
As house	11–5								
Tea-room									
1 Feb–29 Feb	11–4		M	T	W	T	F	S	S
1 Mar–2 Nov	11–5:30		M	T	W	T	F	S	S
5 Nov–30 Nov	11–5		M	T	W	T	F	S	S
1 Dec–24 Dec	11–5		M	T	W	T	F	S	S
27 Dec–31 Dec	11–5		M	T	W	T	F	S	S
3 Jan–31 Jan 09	11–5		M	T	W	T	F	S	S
Shop/plant sales									
1 Feb–29 Feb	11–5		M	T	W	T	F	S	S
1 Mar–2 Nov	11–5:30		M	T	W	T	F	S	S
5 Nov–30 Nov	11–5		M	T	W	T	F	S	S
1 Dec–24 Dec	11–5		M	T	W	T	F	S	S
27 Dec–31 Dec	11–5		M	T	W	T	F	S	S
3 Jan–31 Jan 09	11–5		M	T	W	T	F	S	S

House open Mon 20 Oct (in half-term week). Tea-room closes 4:30 on Tues. Shop/plant sales close 5 when house closed, 3 on Christmas Eve. In winter shop and tea-room may not open in bad weather. Restaurant open as house 12 March–2 Nov and on selected dates in Dec for Christmas lunches, booking essential

⭐ Garden open every day of the year, including Christmas Day

ℹ️ **T** 01392 881345, 01392 881912 (shop), 01392 883133 (restaurant)
E killerton@nationaltrust.org.uk

Full events programme throughout year

Walks leaflet available for park and nearby Ashclyst forest. Orienteering course

Building **Grounds**

Quality plants grown on the property in peat-free compost

Licensed restaurant in house. Restaurant can be booked for special functions. Orchard tea-room (licensed) in stable block. Locally produced home-made food. Children's menu

Baby-changing and feeding facilities. Pushchairs and baby back-carriers admitted. Hip-carrying infant seats for loan. Children's play area. Children's quiz/trail. Family activities and discovery centre open in school holidays

Suitable for school groups. Education room/centre. Live interpretation. Award-winning Victorian programme. Orienteering courses. Learning Officer

Charges for National Trust members apply on some special event days

On leads and only in park

→ [192:SS973001] **Cycle**: NCN52.
Bus: Stagecoach in Devon 1/A/B Exeter–
Tiverton Parkway (passing close Exeter
Central), alight Killerton Turn ¾ml.
Station: Pinhoe (U), not Sun, 4½ml; Whimple
(U), 6ml; Exeter Central & St David's, both
7ml. **Road**: off Exeter–Cullompton road
(B3181); from M5 northbound, exit 30 via
Pinhoe and Broadclyst; from M5 southbound,
exit 28

P Free parking, 280yds

NT properties nearby
A La Ronde, Budlake Old Post Office Room,
Clyston Mill, Marker's Cottage,
Knightshayes Court

Killerton: Budlake Old Post Office Room

Broadclyst, Exeter, Devon EX5 3LW

1944   (1:G7)

Charming example of a 1950s Post Office Room with cottage garden

This small thatched cottage housed the village Post Office. Outside are a wash house, double-seated privy, pigsty and chicken house, 0.25-hectare (½-acre) garden with vegetable plot, cottage garden, herb and rose borders.

★ No refreshments or WC. Nearest WCs at Killerton. Footpath to Killerton along old carriage drive

i **T** 01392 881690
E budlakepostoffice@nationaltrust.org.uk

Building

Pushchairs and baby back-carriers admitted

On leads only in garden

→ [192:SS973001] **Cycle**: NCN52.
Bus: Stagecoach in Devon 1/A/B Exeter–
Tiverton Parkway (passing close Exeter
Central), alight Killerton Turn ¾ml.

Station: Pinhoe (U), not Sun, 4½ml; Whimple
(U), 6ml; Exeter Central & St David's, both
7ml. **Road**: off Exeter–Cullompton road
(B3181); from M5 northbound, exit 30 via
Pinhoe and Broadclyst; from M5 southbound,
exit 28

P Limited parking on site, 10yds.
Not suitable for coaches. Ample parking
at Killerton 800yds

NT properties nearby
Killerton, Clyston Mill, Marker's Cottage,
Knightshayes Court

Killerton: Clyston Mill

Broadclyst, Exeter, Devon EX5 3EW

1944   (1:G7)

Water-powered grain mill in working order

Dating back to the 19th century, Clyston Mill is in an idyllic setting by the River Clyst surrounded by farmland and orchards.

What's new in 2008 The mill will be producing flour this year. Please tel. to check dates of milling days

★ No refreshments or WC

i **T** 01392 462425
E clystonmill@nationaltrust.org.uk

Tours by arrangement

Short riverside walk

Building Grounds

Pushchairs and baby back-carriers admitted. Children's quiz/trail. Children need to be supervised – mill on three floors, steep narrow stairs

Suitable for school groups

→ [192:SX981973] **Cycle**: NCN52.
Bus: Stagecoach in Devon 1/A/B Exeter–
Tiverton Parkway (passing close Exeter
Central), alight Killerton Turn ¾ml.
Station: Pinhoe (U), not Sun, 4½ml; Whimple
(U), 6ml; Exeter Central & St David's, both
7ml. **Road**: off Exeter–Cullompton Road

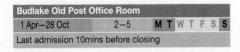

Budlake Old Post Office Room								
1 Apr–28 Oct	2–5	**M**	**T**	W	T	F	S	**S**
Last admission 10mins before closing								

Clyston Mill								
1 Apr–28 Oct	2–5	**M**	**T**	W	T	F	S	**S**

Parking in National Trust car parks is free for members displaying stickers

(B3181) in village of Broadclyst. Park in village car park, walk towards church and follow signs through churchyard

P Free parking (not NT), 450yds

NT properties nearby
Killerton, Budlake Old Post Office Room, Marker's Cottage, Knightshayes Court

Killerton: Marker's Cottage

Broadclyst, Exeter, Devon EX5 3HR

🏠 𝄞 ⟱ 1944 (1:G7)

Thatched medieval cob house with interesting interior

Constructed of cob (a mixture of clay and straw), the house contains a screen decorated with painted decorative 'grotesque' work and a landscape scene with St Andrew. In the garden is a cob summerhouse.

⭐ No WC

ℹ️ **T** 01392 461546
   E markerscottage@nationaltrust.org.uk

𝄞 Volunteers guide visitors around the property

♿ 🅳 Building ⟱ Grounds ♿
→ [192:SX985973] **Cycle**: NCN52.
Bus: Stagecoach in Devon 1/A/B Exeter–
🚉 Tiverton Parkway (passing close 🚉 Exeter Central). **Station**: Pinhoe (U), not Sun, 2½ml; Whimple (U), 4½ml; Exeter Central & St David's, both 6ml. **Road**: in village of Broadclyst. Park in village car park. Leaving car park by vehicle entrance, turn left, then right and turn right on to Townend. Marker's Cottage is second cottage on left

P Free parking (not NT), 250yds

NT properties nearby
Killerton, Budlake Old Post Office Room, Clyston Mill, Knightshayes Court

Marker's Cottage									
1 Apr–28 Oct		2–5	**M**	**T**	W	T	F	S	**S**

King John's Hunting Lodge

The Square, Axbridge, Somerset BS26 2AP

🏠 🅰️ 𝄞 📷 1968 (1:I4)

Wool-merchant's house of c.1500

The early Tudor timber-framed house provides a fascinating insight into local history.

⭐ The property is run as a local history museum by Axbridge and District Museum Trust, in co-operation with Sedgemoor District Council, Somerset County Museums Service and Axbridge Archaeological and Local History Society

ℹ️ **T** 01934 732012
   E kingjohns@nationaltrust.org.uk

𝄞 Occasional tours of historic Axbridge, start from the museum

♿ 🅳 Building ⟱
📷 In museum (not NT)
📷 Suitable for school groups
→ [182:ST431545] In the Square, on corner of High Street. **Bus**: First 126 Weston-super-Mare–Wells (passing close 🚉 Weston-super-Mare). **Station**: Worle (U) 8ml

P Parking (not NT), 100yds

NT properties nearby
Cheddar Cliffs, Clevedon Court, Prior Park, Tyntesfield

King John's Hunting Lodge								
21 Mar–30 Sep		1–4	**M**	**T**	**W**	**T**	**F**	**S**	**S**
Closed Oct–31 Jan 09: open first Sat of month to coincide with farmers' market, 10–4								

If you were fascinated on your visit to Killerton, you'll be sure to find inspiration at Castle Drogo too

Dogs assisting visitors with disabilities are always welcome

Kingston Lacy

Wimborne Minster, Dorset BH21 4EA

(1:K7)

Elegant country mansion with important collections, set in attractive formal gardens and extensive parkland

Home of the Bankes family for more than 300 years, this striking 17th-century house was radically altered in the 19th century by Sir Charles Barry. The house is noted for its lavish interiors, including William Bankes's dramatic Spanish Room, with its gilded leather walls. The family's collection of art is outstanding, with paintings by Rubens, Van Dyck, Titian and Brueghel as well as the largest private collection of Egyptian artefacts in the UK. This wonderfully eclectic experience continues outside. Take a stroll across the beautiful formal lawns towards the restored Japanese tea garden. There are several waymarked walks through the surrounding parkland, with its fine herd of North Devon cattle, and the 3,440-hectare (8,500-acre) estate – dominated by the botanically rich Iron Age hill fort of Badbury Rings, home to fourteen varieties of orchid.

North Devon cattle on the Kingston Lacy Estate

Kingston Lacy									
House		M	T	W	T	F	S	S
15 Mar–2 Nov	11–4			**W**	**T**	**F**	**S**	**S**
Garden/park								
2 Feb–9 Mar	10:30–4	M	T	W	T	F	**S**	**S**
15 Mar–2 Nov	10:30–6	**M**	**T**	**W**	**T**	**F**	**S**	**S**
7 Nov–21 Dec	10:30–4	M	T	W	T	**F**	**S**	**S**
Shop/restaurant								
2 Feb–9 Mar	10:30–4	M	T	W	T	F	**S**	**S**
15 Mar–2 Nov	10:30–5:30	**M**	**T**	**W**	**T**	**F**	**S**	**S**
7 Nov–21 Dec	10:30–4	M	T	W	T	**F**	**S**	**S**

Admission by timed ticket to house may operate on BH Suns & Mons. Open BH Mons. Last admission 4. Special snowdrop days in Jan/Feb

★ Point-to-point races are held at Badbury Rings on 24 Feb, 22 March and 12 April. On these days a charge is made for car parking. House may be semi-scaffolded in Sept and Oct. Some rooms may occasionally close early to prevent light damage

ⓘ **T** 01202 883402
E kingstonlacy@nationaltrust.org.uk

🚶 By arrangement outside normal hours

🎧 Virtual tour available with level access in the Egyptian Room

🎭 Garden and park events. Open-air theatre, concerts. Children's activity days. Carol concert. Farmers' markets

🚶 Waymarked park walks. Leaflet from reception

Please remember – your membership card is always needed for free admission

The Paved Garden at Knightshayes Court, Devon

🚹♿🚻👪🅿️🚜 Building 🏃
Grounds 👟♿

🛍️ NT shop. Plant sales

🍽️ Stables Restaurant (licensed) includes outside courtyard. Limited menu on Mon and Tues when house closed. Sunday roast lunches (beef is from Estate herd). Christmas lunches. Children's menu

👪 Baby-changing facilities. Front-carrying baby slings and hip-carrying infant seats for loan. Children's play area. Family activity packs. Children's activity days

🏫 Suitable for school groups. Live interpretation. Hands-on activities. Adult study days

🐕 On leads and only in park and on woodland walks

🚲 22ml of public bridleway with shared access for cyclists on the Estate (but not the park)

➡️ [195:ST980019] **Bus**: Wilts & Dorset 13 from Bournemouth, 3 from Poole (passing 🚉 Bournemouth & close 🚉 Poole), alight Wimborne Square for NT path, 2½ml. **Station**: Poole 8½ml. **Road**: on B3082 Blandford–Wimborne road, 1½ml W of Wimborne Minster

🅿️ Free parking. Charge at Badbury Rings on point-to-point race days

NT properties nearby
Brownsea Island, Corfe Castle, Hardy's Cottage, Max Gate, Mompesson House, White Mill

Knightshayes Court

Bolham, Tiverton, Devon EX16 7RQ

🏛️❄️🌳🏠🏺🛍️🚶🎪🎭👪🖼️
🚶🍽️ 1973   **(1:G6)**

Victorian country house with richly decorated interiors and garden with outstanding plant collection

When pioneer lace-maker John Heathcoat was chased out of Loughborough by the Luddites in 1816, his relocation to Tiverton led eventually to one of the finest surviving Gothic Revival houses being built in the lush landscape of mid Devon. In 1869 his grandson employed the architect and decorator William Burges – a passionate Gothic enthusiast – to build Knightshayes Court. He was an eccentric but inspired choice, responsible for a truly remarkable house and some extraordinary 'medieval' romantic interiors. The vast garden was the Heathcoat Amory family's great passion. They packed it with rare trees and shrubs creating the celebrated 'Garden

Knightshayes Court									
House									
16 Feb–24 Feb	11–4		M	T	W	T	F	S	S
15 Mar–2 Nov	11–5		M	T	W	T	F	S	S
Garden									
As house			M	T	W	T	F	S	S
Shop/plant centre/restaurant									
As house			M	T	W	T	F	S	S
6 Nov–9 Nov	11–5		M	T	W	T	F	S	S
13 Nov–21 Dec	11–4		M	T	W	T	F	S	S
Open Good Fri & weekends 1–9 March, 11–4									

Unless indicated, last admission is always 30mins before closing time

in the Wood', which includes a waterlily pond, amusing topiary and plenty of seasonal colour. The newly restored kitchen garden, now fully productive, supplies fresh organic vegetables and fruit to the licensed restaurant.

What's new in 2008 Secret Garden project now offers Tracker Packs. New discovery quizzes for the house

⭐ Access to some parts of the mansion and garden may be restricted during early spring and winter due to conservation work

ℹ️ **T** 01884 254665, 01884 257381 (reception), 01884 259010 (shop), 01884 259416 (restaurant) **E** knightshayes@nationaltrust.org.uk

🎭 Guided tours at weekends in Nov and Dec. Times and prices on request, inc. specialist plant nursery tours

🌷 Send sae for events leaflet

🚶 Leaflet showing current flowers and plants of interest. Updated monthly

♿ 🎨 📱 🔊 ⸬ 📷 📹 **Building** ♿ ♿

Grounds ♿ ➡️

🏛️ Gift shop. Well-stocked plant centre with many unusual plants (tel. 01884 243464)

🍽️ Stables Restaurant (licensed). In Oct opening hours may vary, although light refreshments are always available during opening hours. Children's menu

👶 Baby-changing facilities. Pushchairs and baby back-carriers admitted. Pushchairs for loan. Front-carrying baby slings for loan. Children's guide. Children's quiz/trail. Tracker Packs

🎒 Suitable for school groups. Education room/centre. Hands-on activities

🐕 On leads and only in facilities areas, woodland and park

➡️ [181:SS960151] **Cycle**: NCN3. **Bus**: First 398 Tiverton–Minehead, alight Bolham, then ¾ml. Otherwise Stagecoach in Devon 1 from 🚉 Tiverton Parkway; 55/A/B Exeter–Tiverton (passing close 🚉 Exeter Central), alighting Tiverton 1¾ml. **Station**: Tiverton Parkway 8ml. **Road**: 7ml from M5 exit 27 (A361); 2ml N of Tiverton; turn right off Tiverton–Bampton road (A396) at Bolham

🅿️ Free parking

NT properties nearby
Killerton, Budlake Old Post Office Room, Clyston Mill, Marker's Cottage

Lacock Abbey, Fox Talbot Museum and Village

Lacock, nr Chippenham, Wiltshire SN15 2LG

| 1944 | (1:K4)

Country house created out of a medieval abbey, former home of William Henry Fox Talbot, a pioneer of photography

The picturesque village, with its many lime-washed, half-timbered stone houses, dates from the 13th century and has been seen in many TV and film productions, including *Pride and Prejudice*, *Cranford Chronicles* and *Emma*. The Abbey is at the heart of the village and was founded in 1232 and converted into a country house c.1540. The atmospheric monastic rooms include medieval cloisters, a sacristy and chapter house and have survived largely intact. They have featured in two Harry Potter films, plus the recent *The Other Boleyn Girl*. The handsome 16th-century stable courtyard houses a clockhouse, brewery and bakehouse.

Lacock Abbey									
Museum									
23 Feb–2 Nov	11–5:30	**M**	**T**	**W**	**T**	**F**	**S**	**S**
8 Nov–21 Dec	11–4	M	T	W	T	F	**S**	**S**
3 Jan–31 Jan 09	11–4	M	T	W	T	F	**S**	**S**
Grounds/cloisters									
1 Mar–2 Nov	11–5:30	**M**	**T**	**W**	**T**	**F**	**S**	**S**
Abbey									
15 Mar–2 Nov	1–5:30	**M**	T	**W**	**T**	**F**	**S**	**S**
Shop									
23 Feb–14 Mar	11–4	**M**	**T**	**W**	**T**	**F**	**S**	**S**
15 Mar–2 Nov	10–5:30	**M**	**T**	**W**	**T**	**F**	**S**	**S**
3 Nov–31 Jan 09	11–4	**M**	**T**	**W**	**T**	**F**	**S**	**S**

Museum, Abbey & Grounds closed Good Fri, but High Street shop open. Museum (only) open winter weekends (11–4), but closed 22 Dec–2 Jan 09 inc. High Street shop closed 25, 26 Dec & 1 Jan 09. Admission by timed ticket to the Abbey may operate on BHol weekends and busy event days

The south corner of Lacock Abbey, with Sharington's Tower

The pioneering photographic achievements of William Henry Fox Talbot (1800-77), who invented the negative/positive process, can be experienced in the Fox Talbot Museum. His descendants gave the Abbey and village to the Trust in 1944. A stroll through the Abbey's Victorian woodland grounds reveals a stunning display of flowers in spring and magnificent trees, while the Botanic Garden reflects the plant collections of Fox Talbot – for whom botany was a lifelong scientific interest.

What's new in 2008 Holiday cottage due to open during 2008 season

⭐ Children's playground opposite Fox Talbot Museum maintained by Lacock Parish Council, not by NT

ℹ️ **T** 01249 730459
E lacockabbey@nationaltrust.org.uk

🚶 Tours of Abbey by appointment with the House Manager (tel. 01249 730227). Charge inc. NT members

🎭 See website for details of events. Garden open outside normal opening times for spring flowers under National Gardens Scheme

♿ 🚾🔊📷📷📷 **Building** ♿♿
Grounds 📷➡️📷

🏠 In village. Also museum shop (open times as museum)

☕ Tea-rooms, pubs, restaurant and bakery in the village. (Most owned by NT but leased and managed by tenants.)

👶 Baby-changing facilities. Baby back-carriers admitted. Children's guide. Children's quiz/trail. Hip-carrying infant seats for loan from the Abbey. Baby-changing facilities in Abbey WCs and Red Lion car park WCs. Children's play area (not NT) in village playing field (opposite visitor reception). No pushchairs in Abbey but can be left in hall

🏛️ Suitable for school groups. Education room/centre

➡️ [173:ST919684] **Foot**: surrounding network of footpaths inc. route beside Wilts & Berks Canal. **Cycle**: NCN4, 1ml. **Bus**: Faresaver 73 Melksham–Corsham, First 234 Chippenham–Frome (passing 🚉 Melksham and close 🚉 Chippenham and close 🚉 Trowbridge). **Station**: Melksham 3ml, Chippenham 3½ml. **Road**: 3ml S of Chippenham. M4 exit 17, signposted to Chippenham (A350). Follow signs for Lacock, leading to main car park

🅿️ Parking, 220yds (pay & display). NT members must display car sticker. No visitor parking on village streets

NT properties nearby
Avebury, The Courts Garden, Dyrham Park, Great Chalfield Manor and Garden, Prior Park, Westwood Manor

For general and membership enquiries, please telephone 0844 800 1895

The unpretentious interiors of Lanhydrock are furnished in typical high-Victorian style

Lanhydrock

Bodmin, Cornwall PL30 5AD

1953   (1:D8)

Magnificent late Victorian country house with extensive servants' quarters, gardens and wooded estate

Lanhydrock is the perfect historic country house and estate. Explore the high-Victorian interiors of this wealthy but unpretentious family home, and discover evidence of the Robartes family all around the house. Generations of the family have walked in the Long Gallery, contemplating historic events such as the English Civil War, Jacobite Rebellion or the First World War. The gatehouse and north wing (which houses the Long Gallery with its biblical plasterwork ceiling – chilldren enjoy spotting all the familiar stories and characters) are 17th century, while the rest of the house was restored after a fire in 1881, to include the latest advances in design and technology. There are 50 rooms to explore, with the servants' quarters and 'below stairs' being particularly evocative. The garden is firmly Victorian, with a magnificent collection of magnolias, camellias and rhododendrons, and is full of colour all year. Beyond you can follow numerous paths through woods and parkland down to the banks of the River Fowey, haunt of otters and kingfishers.

For information regarding prices, see page 10

★ 50 rooms are open to visitors, who should allow at least 2 hours to tour the house. Secure locker system for large bags. Church (adjacent to house): service every Sun 9:45

i T 01208 265950, 01208 265211 (estate) E lanhydrock@nationaltrust.org.uk

🔏 Guided garden tours on various days, weather permitting

♖ Including open-air concert in July

🚶 Estate walks leaflet available

♿ 🚻 📷 ⠿ 🅿️ Building 🔧 ↕ ♿ Grounds 🔧 ➡ 🚲

🏪 NT shop. Plant centre in car park

🍽 Servants' Hall restaurant (licensed) in main house. Children's menu. Stables snack bar in harness block

👶 Baby-changing and feeding facilities. Front-carrying baby slings and hip-carrying infant seats for loan. Children's play area. Children's guide. Children's quiz/trail. Pushchair for outdoor use for loan

🏫 Suitable for school groups. Education room/centre. Live interpretation. Hands-on activities

🐕 On leads and only in park and woods

Lanhydrock

House									
15 Mar–30 Sep	11–5:30	M	T	W	T	F	S	S	
1 Oct–2 Nov	11–5	M	T	W	T	F	S	S	
Garden									
All year	10–6	M	T	W	T	F	S	S	
Plant centre									
1 Mar–14 Mar	11–4	M	T	W	T	F	S	S	
15 Mar–30 Sep	11–5:30	M	T	W	T	F	S	S	
1 Oct–2 Nov	11–5	M	T	W	T	F	S	S	
Shop and refreshments									
2 Feb–3 Feb	11–4	M	T	W	T	F	S	S	
9 Feb–14 Mar	11–4	M	T	W	T	F	S	S	
15 Mar–30 Sep	11–5:30	M	T	W	T	F	S	S	
1 Oct–2 Nov	11–5	M	T	W	T	F	S	S	
3 Nov–24 Dec	11–4	M	T	W	T	F	S	S	
27 Dec–31 Dec	11–4	M	T	W	T	F	S	S	
3 Jan–31 Jan	11–4	M	T	W	T	F	S	S	

Open BH Mon & Mons in Aug. Refreshments: open 10:30 15 March–2 Nov. Shop and restaurant are inside the tariff area

→ [200:SX088636] **Cycle**: NCN3, runs past entrance. **Station**: Bodmin Parkway 1¾ml via original carriage-drive to house, signposted in station car park; 3ml by road. **Road**: 2½ml SE of Bodmin. Follow signposts from either A30, A38 Bodmin–Liskeard or take B3268 off A390 at Lostwithiel

P Free parking, 600yds

NT properties nearby
Trerice

Lawrence House

9 Castle Street, Launceston, Cornwall PL15 8BA

🏛 𝕏 🚼 ▦ 1964 (1:E7)

Beautiful Georgian town house

Built in 1753, Lawrence House was given to the Trust to help preserve the character of the street. It is now leased to Launceston Town Council and in use as a local museum and civic centre.

What's new in 2008 Display featuring recently restored watercolours by local architect Otto Peter

Lawrence House

31 Mar–26 Sep	10:30–4:30	M	T	W	T	F	S	S

Open evenings, weekends all year by appointment for groups or individuals for study

ℹ **T** 01566 773277
E lawrencehouse@nationaltrust.org.uk

𝕏 By arrangement with the Curator

♿ 🚾 ⠿ **Building** 🔨

🚼 Baby-changing and feeding facilities. Pushchairs and baby back-carriers admitted. Children's quiz/trail

▦ Suitable for school groups. Education room/centre. Hands-on activities

→ [201:SX330848] **Bus**: First 76/A from Plymouth (passing ⬛ Plymouth)

P Parking (not NT) (pay & display)

NT properties nearby
Cotehele

Levant Mine and Beam Engine

Trewellard, Pendeen, nr St Just, Cornwall TR19 7SX

🔧 🚂 🏠 𝕏 🖼 🚼 ▦ 𝕏 🐕 🍽 1967 (1:A9)

Unique steam-powered Cornish beam engine in action

The only Cornish beam engine anywhere in the world that is still in steam at a tin and copper mine, the famous Levant engine is housed in a small engine house on the edge of the cliffs. Restored after 60 idle years by a group of volunteers known as the 'Greasy Gang', it is a thrilling experience for young and old alike to see this old engine in action, with its evocative sounds and smells. You can take a short underground tour through the miners' dry tunnel, and the winding and pumping shafts are also on view, as is a restored electric winding engine. A film tells the story of Levant mine and the miners who worked here. A short walk along the cliffs will take you to Botallack Mine (NT), with its famous cliff-clinging engine houses and historical displays in the Count House Workshop; in the other direction is Geevor mine (not NT) and a mining museum.

What's new in 2008 Part of the Cornish Mining World Heritage Site

ℹ **T** 01736 786156
E levant@nationaltrust.org.uk

𝕏 Self-guided tour leaflet

Many Trust properties are offering Gift Aid on Entry for non-members, see page 10

Levant Beam Engine									
Steaming									
7 Mar–28 Mar	11–5	M	T	W	T	**F**	S	S	
2 Apr–30 May	11–5	M	T	**W**	T	**F**	S	S	
1 Jun–29 Jun	11–5	M	T	**W**	T	F	S	**S**	
1 Jul–30 Sep	11–5	M	**T**	W	T	F	S	**S**	
1 Oct–31 Oct	11–5	M	T	**W**	T	**F**	S	S	
Not steaming									
1 Feb–29 Feb	11–4	M	T	W	T	**F**	S	S	
7 Nov–30 Jan 09	11–4	M	T	W	T	**F**	S	S	
Open BH Suns & Mons									

 Building  Grounds

Small outlet for industrial/mining artefacts

Nearest refreshments (not NT) at Geevor mine or Pendeen village

Baby-changing facilities. Pushchairs and baby back-carriers admitted. Family activity trail

Suitable for school groups. Live interpretation

→ [203:SW368346] **Foot**: South West Coast Path passes entrance. **Bus**: First 17/A from Penzance. **Station**: Penzance 7ml. **Road**: 1ml W of Pendeen, on B3306 St Just–St Ives road

P Free parking, 100yds. Not suitable for coaches. Limited parking for coaches at Geevor mine, ½ml walk to Levant mine

NT properties nearby
Botallack Count House, St Michael's Mount, Trengwainton Garden

Little Clarendon

Dinton, Salisbury, Wiltshire SP3 5DZ

🏠 1940 (1:K5)

Late 15th-century stone house

★ No WC

ℹ **T** 01985 843600
E littleclarendon@nationaltrust.org.uk

→ ¼ml E of Dinton church, close to post office; take B3089 from Salisbury to Dinto

Little Clarendon									
24 March	2–5	**M**	T	W	T	F	S	S	
5 May	2–5	**M**	T	W	T	F	S	S	
26 May	2–5	**M**	T	W	T	F	S	S	
25 Aug	2–5	**M**	T	W	T	F	S	S	

The engine house at Levant Mine

Little Fleece Bookshop

Painswick, Gloucestershire GL6 6QQ

🏠 1942 (1:J2)

Traditional Cotswold house in the beautiful village of Painswick

A 17th-century building, originally part of a former inn and restored in an exemplary Arts & Crafts style in 1935. Although a private dwelling, Little Fleece trades as a bookshop during open hours.

What's new in 2008 Under new management. Michael MacCarthy has reopened as an antiquarian and second-hand bookshop specialising in art, gardens, architecture and local interest; also sells antiquarian prints

★ No WC, nearest in village

ℹ **T** 01452 812264
E littlefleece@nationaltrust.org.uk

Building

Pushchairs admitted

→ [162:SO868098] **Foot**: Cotswold Way within ⅔ml. **Bus**: Stagecoach in the Cotswolds 46 Nailsworth–Cheltenham Spa (passes close Stroud). **Station**: Stroud 4ml. **Road**: 3ml N of Stroud A46, 6ml SE of Gloucester B4073. Off main High Street, Painswick

P Large car park in village (not NT)

NT properties nearby
Haresfield Beacon, Rodborough Common, Stroud Commons, Woodchester Park

Little Fleece Bookshop
Variable. Contact the tenant for details

For details of events go to www.nationaltrust.org.uk/events

The Lizard and Kynance Cove

Cornwall

🏠 🚻 🎢 ♿ 🍽 🎣 👫 🎒 🧗 1935   (1:C10)

Dramatic and historic stretch of Cornish coast

The Lizard is the most southerly point of mainland Britain and the turning point of one of the busiest shipping lanes in the world. The coastline on either side offers dramatic cliff walks, masses of rare wild flowers and fascinating geological features. The area played a key role in the history of modern communications. Marconi's historic wireless experiments on The Lizard in 1901 are celebrated at the restored **Lizard Wireless Station**, Bass Point, and the **Marconi Centre** at Poldhu. Two miles north of Lizard Point lies Kynance Cove – white sand, turquoise water and islands of multicoloured serpentine rock with stacks and arches hidden amongst the towering cliffs – long considered one of the most beautiful places in Cornwall.

ℹ️ **T** 01326 561407 **E** lizard@nationaltrust.org.uk

🧗 NT *Coast of Cornwall* leaflet 14 includes maps and details of circular walks and information on local history, geology and wildlife

The Lizard								
All year		M	T	W	T	F	S	S

Tel. for opening times of Lizard Wireless Station and Marconi Centre

♿ ♿ Grounds ♿

🍽 Award-winning environmentally friendly café (NT-approved concession) at Kynance Cove beach. Ice-cream van at Kynance car park in July and Aug. Café on Lizard Point (not NT)

👫 Baby-changing facilities at Lizard Point car park WC and Kynance Cove WC

🎒 Suitable for school groups

🐕 Seasonal bans on some beaches, including Kynance

➡️ [203:SW688133] **Foot**: 3¾ml of South West Coast Path on property. **Bus**: Truronian T34 🚌 Redruth–Helston–Lizard, then to Kynance Cove 1½ml; to Lizard Point 1ml. **Road**: from Helston, A3083 to Lizard town

🅿️ NT car parks at Kynance and Lizard Point (charge Easter to Nov). Free parking in Lizard town, from where a footpath leads to Lizard Point. No caravans or trailers

NT properties nearby
Glendurgan Garden, Godolphin, St Michael's Mount

The lighthouse at the Lizard Peninsula sits on top of craggy cliffs

Charges for National Trust members apply on some special event days

Lodge Park and Sherborne Estate

Lodge Park, Aldsworth, nr Cheltenham, Gloucestershire GL54 3PP

🔔 ⊺ 1983   **(1:K2/L2)**

Rare 17th-century grandstand and Cotswold country estate

Lodge Park, situated on the picturesque Sherborne Estate in the Cotswolds, was created in 1634 by John 'Crump' Dutton and inspired by his passion for gambling, banqueting and entertaining. Until 1983 it was the home of Charles Dutton, 7th Lord Sherborne, and, when bequeathed, it was the first project undertaken by the Trust that relied totally on archaeological evidence. Visitors can now experience how the unique grandstand would have looked in the 17th century and enjoy the impressive views of the deer course and park, which was designed by Charles Bridgeman in the 1720s. Wonderful walks around the surrounding Sherborne Estate cover 1,650 hectares (4,000 acres) of beautiful rolling countryside, and include the restored and working water meadows and sweeping views of the River Windrush. The village of Sherborne is divided into two parts, with the East End exploiting the model village design of the mid 19th century, and the West End retaining many of the older buildings in the village.

What's new in 2008 Small National Trust shop, light refreshments and plant sales at Lodge Park

⭐ WC at Lodge Park only

ℹ️ **T** 01451 844130
     E lodgepark@nationaltrust.org.uk

🔨 Includes out-of-hours tours and walks

👹 17th- and 18th-century Living History displays

Lodge Park and Sherborne Estate							
Grandstand/Deer Park							
14 Mar–2 Nov	11–4	M T W T	**F**	**S**	**S**		
Sherborne Estate							
All year		**M T W T F S S**					

Grandstand open Easter Mon. Property occasionally closes for weddings. Please tel. to confirm opening times

♿ 👁️ 🔊 ♿ ♿ Building 🔁
🛍️ Small shop and plant sales

☕ Hot drinks and light refreshments available at Lodge Park. Post office & shop (not NT) in Sherborne village sells ice-cream and soft drinks. Open all year but closed Sat pm and all day Wed & Sun

👪 Pushchairs admitted. Children's quiz/trail. Tracker Packs

🐕 Under close control

➡️ [163:SP146123] **Bus**: Swanbrook 853 Oxford–Gloucester (passing ⮞ Gloucester and close ⮞ Oxford). 1½ml walk to Lodge Park from bus stop or 1ml Sherborne; also 833 Cheltenham–Northleach with booked connections for Sherborne (tel. 01452 423598). **Road**: 3ml E of Northleach; approach from A40 only

🅿️ Parking for estate walks at Ewe Pen Barn car park [163:SP158143] and water meadows [163:SP175154]. Donation of £1 welcome

NT properties nearby
Chastleton House, Chedworth Roman Villa, Hidcote Manor Garden, Snowshill Manor

Loughwood Meeting House

Dalwood, Axminster, Devon EX13 7DU

✝️ 👪 1969   **(1:H7)**

17th-century thatched Baptist meeting house

Around 1653 the Baptist congregation of the nearby village of Kilmington constructed this simple building dug into the hillside. They attended services here at the risk of imprisonment or transportation. The interior was fitted in the early 18th century.

⭐ No WC

ℹ️ **T** 01392 881691
     E loughwood@nationaltrust.org.uk

Loughwood Meeting House							
All year		**M T W T F S S**					

Services held twice yearly. Details at Meeting House

Parking in National Trust car parks is free for members displaying stickers

 Building

Pushchairs and baby back-carriers admitted. Family guide

→ [192/193:SY253993] **Bus**: Stagecoach in Devon 380 Axminster–Exeter (passing close ⊞ Axminster). **Station**: Axminster 2½ml. **Road**: 4ml W of Axminster; turn right on Axminster–Honiton road (A35), 1ml S of Dalwood, 1ml NW of Kilmington

P Small free car park, 20yds. Not suitable for coaches. Very narrow country lanes

NT properties nearby
Branscombe, Shute Barton

Lundy

Bristol Channel, Devon EX39 2LY

Old Light, Lundy, Devon

(1:D5)

Unspoilt island, home to a fascinating array of wildlife amidst dramatic scenery

Undisturbed by cars, the island encompasses a small village with an inn and Victorian church, and the 13th-century Marisco Castle. Of interest to nature-lovers are the variety of migratory seabirds, heathland and grassland habitats and the Lundy ponies. Designated the first Marine Conservation Area, Lundy offers opportunities for diving and seal watching.

★ The island is financed, administered and maintained by the Landmark Trust. Holiday cottages available to rent, tel. Infoline for details

i T 01271 863636 (Infoline)
E lundy@nationaltrust.org.uk

Building Grounds

Shop selling the famous Lundy stamps, souvenirs and postcards, plus general supplies and groceries

Marisco Tavern (not NT) (licensed) in the village. Children's menu

Baby-changing facilities. Pushchairs admitted. Family activity packs

Suitable for school groups. Education room/centre. Live interpretation. Hands-on activities

→ [180:SS130450] In the Bristol Channel 11ml N of Hartland Point, 25ml W of Ilfracombe, 30ml S of Tenby. **Cycle**: NCN31 (Bideford). **Ferry**: sea passages from Bideford or Ilfracombe according to tides up to four days a week, March to end Oct. Tel. Infoline for details. **Bus**: frequent services from ⊞ Barnstaple to Bideford or Ilfracombe. **Station**: Barnstaple: 8½ml to Bideford, 12ml to Ilfracombe

P Public parking at Bideford or Ilfracombe for ferries (pay & display)

NT properties nearby
Arlington Court, North Devon Coastline

Lundy							
1 Apr–31 Oct	M	T	W	T	F	S	S

Helicopter service from Hartland Point Nov to mid March, Mon & Fri only, for visitors staying on the island

Dogs assisting visitors with disabilities are always welcome

Lydford Gorge

The Stables, Lydford Gorge, Lydford,
nr Okehampton, Devon EX20 4BH

 1947   (1:F7)

The deepest gorge in the South West, with spectacular 30m waterfall

This lush oak-wooded steep-sided river gorge, with its fascinating history and many legends, can be explored through a variety of short or long walks. See the spectacular White Lady Waterfall, pass over the tumbling water at Tunnel Falls and watch the river bubble in the Devil's Cauldron. There's an abundance of wildlife to spot, including woodland birds, dragonflies darting above the river and trout swimming in the quieter stretches. A walk along a disued railway line will lead you to the bird hide; and you can enjoy a picnic in the orchard area or Pixie Glen.

★ Walking in the gorge is strenuous. It is extremely rugged, with uneven surfaces, slippery paths and vertical drops. Walking boots are essential. It is vital that children are supervised at all times. Unsuitable for visitors with heart complaints or walking difficulties and very young children

ℹ **T** 01822 820320, 01822 820441 (shop),
01822 822004 (tea-room)
E lydfordgorge@nationaltrust.org.uk

🎭 Seasonal walks. Children's activity days. Trails

🚶 1½ml and 3ml routes. Seasonal guided walks

The Main Walk through Lambhole Wood, Lydford Gorge, Devon

🏠 Shop and plant centre at main entrance. Small shop at waterfall entrance

🍽 Tea-rooms at both entrances to gorge, serving light lunches and delicious home-made cakes. Children's menu

👪 Baby-changing and feeding facilities. Baby back-carriers admitted. Front-carrying baby slings and baby back-carriers for loan. Children's play area. Children's activity days. Unsuitable for pushchairs due to uneven terrain and narrow paths

🎒 Suitable for school groups

🐕 On leads only

➡ [191/201:SX509845] **Foot**: as road directions or via Blackdown Moor from Mary Tavy. **Cycle**: NCN27 & 31. Property is close to three cycle routes: Devon Coast to Coast, West Devon Way and Plym Valley. **Bus**: First 86, 87 Plymouth–Barnstaple (passing close ▣ Plymouth); 187 ▣ Gunnislake– ▣ Okehampton, Sun, June to Sept only; bus stop at main entrance and waterfall entrance to gorge. **Road**: 7ml S of A30. Halfway between Okehampton and Tavistock, 1ml W off A386 opposite Dartmoor Inn; main entrance at W end of Lydford village; waterfall entrance near Manor Farm

P Free parking

NT properties nearby
Buckland Abbey, Castle Drogo, Cotehele, Finch Foundry

Lydford Gorge									
Gorge/shop/tea-room									
15 Feb–14 Mar	11–3:30	M	T	W	T	**F**	**S**	**S**	
15 Mar–5 Oct	10–5	**M**	**T**	**W**	**T**	**F**	**S**	**S**	
6 Oct–2 Nov	10–4	**M**	**T**	**W**	**T**	**F**	**S**	**S**	
Gorge/shop									
3 Nov–28 Dec	11–3:30	M	T	W	T	**F**	**S**	**S**	
Tea-room									
3 Nov–28 Dec	11–3:30	M	T	W	T	F	**S**	**S**	
Gorge (waterfall entrance only)									
29 Dec–31 Jan 09	11–3:30	**M**	**T**	**W**	**T**	**F**	**S**	**S**	
Please tel. for details of winter opening									

Please remember – your membership card is always needed for free admission

Lytes Cary Manor

nr Charlton Mackrell, Somerton,
Somerset TA11 7HU

🏠 ✝ ❖ ♨ 🏠 🎔 🎻 🎋 🎽 🏃

🖼 🧍 1949   (1:15)

Intimate manor house with Arts & Crafts-style garden

This intimate manor house was the former home of medieval herbalist Henry Lyte; here visitors can learn about his famous 16th-century plant directory, *Lytes Herbal*. The manor spans many years with its 14th-century chapel and 15th-century Great Hall. In the 20th century it was rescued from dereliction by Sir Walter Jenner, who refurbished the interiors in period style. Its Arts & Crafts-style garden is an intimate combination of outdoor rooms, topiary, statues and herbaceous borders. Explore the waymarked walks through the wider estate and riverside and uncover many features typical of farmed lowland England, including ancient hedges, rare arable weeds and farmland birds.

What's new in 2008 New estate walks as well as the existing River Walk now open all year round. Garden sundries sales area

ℹ️ **T** 01458 224471
   E lytescarymanor@nationaltrust.org.uk

🎻 Tel. to book

🎽 Spring plant fair 11 May. Family events in summer

Lytes Cary Manor							
15 Mar–2 Nov		11–5	**M**	**T**	**W**	T	F	S	S

Open BH Mons. Closes dusk if earlier. Estate open all year, dawn–dusk

🧍 Guided walks. Details from property

♿ 🖼 ⋮ P❖ D❖ Building 🔹 ♿ Grounds 🔹 Kiosk serving light refreshments

🎔 Kiosk serving light refreshments

🏃 Baby-changing facilities. Pushchairs admitted. Hip-carrying infant seats for loan. Children's quiz/trail. Family events in summer

🖼 Suitable for school groups

🐕 On leads and only in car park and estate walks

➜ [183:ST529269] **Bus**: First 376 Bristol–Yeovil (passing ☰ Bristol Temple Meads); 54/A/B/C Taunton–Yeovil (passing close ☰ Taunton). Both pass within ¾ml ☰ Yeovil Pen Mill. Alight Kingsdon, 1ml. **Station**: Yeovil Pen Mill 8½ml; Castle Cary 9ml; Yeovil Junction 10ml. **Road**: near village of Kingsdon, off A372. Signposted from Podimore Roundabout where A303 meets A37

P Free parking, 40yds. Coaches by prior arrangement only

NT properties nearby

Barrington Court, Montacute House, Priest's House, Stourhead, Tintinhull Garden, Treasurer's House

The intimate manor house of Lytes Cary

Max Gate

Alington Avenue, Dorchester, Dorset DT1 2AB

🏛 ✣ 🎗 🖼 1940   (1:J7)

Home of novelist and poet Thomas Hardy

Thomas Hardy designed the house and lived there for 43 years, from 1885 until his death in 1928. Here he wrote *Tess of the d'Urbervilles*, *Jude the Obscure* and *The Mayor of Casterbridge*, as well as much of his poetry. Visitors can see several pieces of his furniture.

⭐ No WC

ℹ **T** 01305 262538
   E maxgate@nationaltrust.org.uk

♿ ⣿ 🅐 Building 🦽

🖼 Suitable for school groups

➡ [194:SY704899] **Bus**: Coach House Travel 4 from town centre. **Station**: Dorchester South 1ml; Dorchester West (U) 1ml. **Road**: 1ml E of Dorchester. From Dorchester follow A352 Wareham road to roundabout named Max Gate (at junction of A35 Dorchester bypass). Turn left and left again into cul-de-sac outside the house

The Library at Mompesson House, Salisbury, Wiltshire

Max Gate								
26 Mar – 29 Sep	2–5	**M**	T	**W**	T	F	S	**S**

Only hall, dining and drawing rooms, and garden open. Private visits, tours and seminars for schools, colleges and literary societies, at other times, by appointment with the tenants, Mr and Mrs Andrew Leah

🅿 Free parking (not NT), 50yds

NT properties nearby
Cerne Abbas Giant, Clouds Hill, Hardy Monument, Hardy's Cottage

Mompesson House

The Close, Salisbury, Wiltshire SP1 2EL

🏛 ✣ 🍴 🏚 🖼 🍵 1952   (1:K5)

Elegant and spacious 18th-century house in the Cathedral Close

The house, featured in the award-winning film *Sense and Sensibility*, is a haven of peace in Salisbury's famous Cathedral Close. Its magnificent plasterwork, fine period furniture and graceful oak staircase are all part of the pleasure, and the Turnbull collection of 18th-century drinking glasses is of national importance. The delightful walled garden has a pergola and traditionally planted herbaceous borders.

ℹ **T** 01722 420980 (Infoline), 01722 335659
   E mompessonhouse@nationaltrust.org.uk

♿ 🆆 🎿 ⣿ 🅐 🅳 Building 🦽 Grounds 🧗

🛍 NT shop in High Street, 60yds. Tel. 01722 331884

🍵 Tea-room

🏃 Pushchairs and baby back-carriers admitted. Front-carrying baby slings and hip-carrying infant seats for loan. Children's guide. Children's quiz/trail

🖼 Suitable for school groups

➡ [184:SU142297] On N side of Choristers' Green in the Cathedral Close, near High Street Gate. **Bus**: from surrounding areas. **Station**: Salisbury ½ml

Mompesson House								
15 Mar – 2 Nov	11–5	**M**	**T**	**W**	T	F	**S**	**S**

Open Good Fri

The formal gardens at Montacute House are full of fine borders, roses and topiary

P Parking (not NT), 260yds in city centre (pay & display). Coach parking in Central Car Park. Coach drop-off point 100yds at St Ann's Gate

NT properties nearby
Mottisfont Abbey, Pepperbox, Philipps House and Dinton Park, Stourhead

Montacute House

Montacute, Somerset TA15 6XP

🏠 ❄️ 🍴 🏡 📷 💷 ✗ 🪑 🎭 👫 🖼️
📷 ⚹ 🍷 1931   (1:l6)

Magnificent Elizabethan Ham-stone house, incorporating National Portrait Gallery exhibition, garden and park

Montacute House is a magnificent, glittering mansion, built in the late 16th century for Sir Edward Phelips. Renaissance highlights include elegant chimneys, carved parapets, contemporary plasterwork and heraldic glass. On walking through the grand Long Gallery, the longest of its kind in Europe, visitors can admire more than 50 of the finest Tudor and Elizabethan portraits from the National Portrait Gallery collection. The splendid staterooms display a fine range of 17th- and 18th-century furniture and textiles, including beautiful samplers from the Goodhart collection. The fine formal gardens are perfect for an afternoon stroll and include an interesting collection of roses, topiary and mixed borders. Waymarked walks lead around the wider estate, which encompasses St Michael's Hill, the site of a Norman castle, and topped by an 18th-century lookout tower.

What's new in 2008 Wheelchair-accessible touch-screen computer on ground floor showing NPG collection. Civil weddings held in house

ℹ️ **T** 01935 823289
   E montacute@nationaltrust.org.uk

🚶 Many walks in park and estate to enjoy. Leaflet available

♿ 🚻 🪑 📷 👓 📷 P♿ Building 🪑♿
Grounds 🦽 ➡️

Montacute House								
House								
15 Mar–2 Nov	11–5	**M**	T	**W**	T	**F**	**S**	**S**
Garden/shop*								
1 Mar–14 Mar	11–4	M	T	**W**	**T**	**F**	**S**	**S**
15 Mar–2 Nov	11–6	**M**	T	**W**	**T**	**F**	**S**	**S**
5 Nov–21 Dec	11–4	M	T	**W**	**T**	**F**	**S**	**S**
Restaurant/café								
2 Mar–9 Mar	11–4	M	T	W	T	F	**S**	**S**
15 Mar–2 Nov	11–3	**M**	T	**W**	**T**	**F**	**S**	**S**
5 Nov–21 Dec	11–4	M	T	W	T	F	S	**S**
Park								
All year		**M**	**T**	**W**	**T**	**F**	**S**	**S**

*Shop closes 5:30 March–Nov. Restaurant closed on 1 & 8 March and Nov–Dec. Special opening of house for Mothers' Day, 2 March. Closes dusk if earlier

📷 NT shop. Plant sales

🍽 Licensed restaurant available for private bookings. Christmas lunches served Suns in Dec, booking recommended. Open weekdays for corporate and private lunches during Nov & Dec (groups 25–50 only), booking essential. Café

👪 Baby-changing facilities. Pushchairs and baby back-carriers admitted. Children's play area. Children's guide. Family trail. Garden activity packs. Family picnic area where children can run and play ball games

🔲 Suitable for school groups. Live interpretation

🐕 On leads and only in park

➜ [183/193:ST499172] **Foot**: Leyland Trail and Monarch Trail both pass through Montacute Park. **Cycle**: NCN30, passes Montacute village. **Bus**: South West Coaches 81 Yeovil Bus Station–South Petherton (passing within ¾ml 🚉 Yeovil Pen Mill). **Station**: Yeovil Pen Mill 5½ml; Yeovil Junction 7ml (bus to Yeovil Bus Station); Crewkerne 7ml. **Road**: in Montacute village, 4ml W of Yeovil, on S side of A3088, 3ml E of A303; signposted

🅿 Free parking. Limited parking for coaches

NT properties nearby
Barrington Court, Lytes Cary Manor, Priest's House, Stourhead, Tintinhull Garden, Treasurer's House

Newark Park

Ozleworth, Wotton-under-Edge, Gloucestershire
GL12 7PZ

🏃 1949   **(1:J3)**

Former Tudor hunting lodge later converted to fashionable home

An eclectic art collection can be enjoyed at this unusual and atmospheric house. It has a wild romantic garden with countryside walks and enjoys outstanding views.

What's new in 2008 Small gift shop. Croquet set for hire. 18th-century summerhouse restored

⭐ The property is lived in and has an interesting and warm atmosphere

For information regarding prices, see page 10

Newark Park was originally a hunting lodge

ℹ️ **T** 01793 817666 (Infoline), 01453 842644
E newarkpark@nationaltrust.org.uk

🎭 Open-air theatre production. Bat walks

🚶 Leaflet available

♿ ⠿ ♿ ♿ **Building** ♿ **Grounds** ♿

📷 Small gift shop

🍽 Self-service machine and ice-creams

👪 Baby back-carriers admitted. Family guide. Children's quiz/trail. Pushchairs on ground floor only

🔲 Suitable for school groups

🐕 On leads only in grounds

➜ [172:ST786934] **Foot**: Cotswold Way passes property. **Bus**: First 309, 310 Bristol–Dursley, alight Wotton-under-Edge, 1¾ml. Frequent services link 🚉 Bristol Temple Meads with the bus station. **Station**: Stroud 10ml. **Road**: 1½ml E of Wotton-under-Edge, 1¾ml S of junction of A4135 & B4058, follow signs for Ozleworth. House signposted from main road

Newark Park			M	T	W	T	F	S	S
19 Mar–29 May	11–5		M	T	**W**	T	F	S	S
1 Jun–2 Nov	11–5		M	T	**W**	T	F	**S**	**S**

Open BH Mons and Good Fri: 11–5. Closes dusk if earlier. Also open Easter Sat & Sun 11–5

P Free parking, 100yds. Coaches by prior arrangement only

NT properties nearby
Chedworth Roman Villa, Dyrham Park, Horton Court, Lodge Park and Sherborne Estate, Prior Park, Woodchester Park

The Old Mill

Wembury Beach, Wembury, Devon PL9 0HP

 1939   (1:F9)

Former mill house

A café is housed in the building, which stands on a small beach near the Yealm estuary.

What's new in 2008 New public access around Wembury Point

i **T** 01752 862314
   E oldmill@nationaltrust.org.uk

𝓚 Regular guided rock-pool rambles and other marine-related events are led by Devon Wildlife Trust wardens from Wembury Marine Centre (open Easter to end Sept); for details tel. 01752 862538

⚐ South West Coast Path runs through property

⚑ Café (NT-approved concession). Serving home-made cakes and light meals using local produce

⚐ Tracker Packs

⚐ On beach, 1 Oct–31 March only

→ [201:SX517484] **Foot**: South West Coast Path within ⅜ml. **Bus**: First 48 from ⊠ Plymouth, then ½ml. **Station**: Plymouth 10ml.
Road: at Wembury, off A379 E of Plymouth

P Parking. Charge applies. NT members must display cards

NT properties nearby
Overbeck's, Saltram

The Old Mill									
4 Apr–18 Jul	11:30–4:30	M	T	**W**	**T**	**F**	**S**	**S**
19 Jul–31 Aug	10:30–5	**M**	**T**	**W**	**T**	**F**	**S**	**S**
1 Sep–30 Sep	11:30–4:30	M	T	**W**	**T**	**F**	**S**	**S**

Also open Easter weekend 21–25 March and BH Mons. Limited winter opening, tel. 01752 862314 for details. May close early in bad weather

Overbeck's

Sharpitor, Salcombe, Devon TQ8 8LW

⌂ ✿ ⛟ ☐ ⚑ 𝓚 ⛶ ⚐ ⚑ ⚑ 1937   (1:F9)

Luxuriant coastal garden surrounding elegant Edwardian house with diverse collections

This beautiful garden offers spectacular views over the Salcombe estuary and surrounding coast. Run on organic principles, the 2.75-hectare (7-acre) garden has an intimate and informal atmosphere and is filled with rare and exotic plants, which flourish due to the sheltered microclimate. The inventor Otto Overbeck lived here until 1937, and the house contains his collections of curios, natural history and nautical artefacts, as well as his most peculiar invention, the 'Rejuvenator'.

What's new in 2008 New house trails for families. Series of circular guided walks. 'Animal' croquet. Open Bank Holiday Saturdays

★ WC not available when house is closed. No adapted WC. Grounds too steep for wheelchairs. Youth hostel on site (tel. 0870 770 6016). Special garden and tea-room opening at weekends during Feb half-term

Overbeck's									
Garden									
1 Feb–24 Feb	10–5	**M**	**T**	**W**	**T**	**F**	S	S
25 Feb–14 Mar	10–5	**M**	**T**	**W**	**T**	**F**	S	S
15 Mar–30 Jun	10–5	**M**	**T**	**W**	**T**	**F**	S	**S**
1 Jul–31 Aug	10–5	**M**	**T**	**W**	**T**	**F**	**S**	**S**
1 Sep–5 Oct	10–5	**M**	**T**	**W**	**T**	**F**	S	**S**
6 Nov–2 Nov	10–5	**M**	**T**	**W**	**T**	F	S	**S**
3 Nov–31 Jan 09	10–5	**M**	**T**	**W**	**T**	**F**	S	S
House/shop									
15 Mar–30 Jun	11–5	**M**	**T**	**W**	**T**	**F**	S	**S**
1 Jul–31 Aug	11–5	**M**	**T**	**W**	**T**	**F**	**S**	**S**
1 Sep–5 Oct	11–5	**M**	**T**	**W**	**T**	**F**	S	**S**
6 Oct–2 Nov	11–5	**M**	**T**	**W**	**T**	F	S	**S**

Open Sats of BH weekends. Tea-room open as house but 11–4:15, plus weekends 9–24 Feb (11–4). Garden closed 25 & 26 Dec & 1 Jan 09. Garden closes dusk if earlier than 5.

i **T** 01548 842893, 01548 845013 (shop), 01548 845014 (tea-room)
E overbecks@nationaltrust.org.uk

Out-of-hours tours on request

Circular coastal walks at Bolt Head and Tor Woods. South West Coast Path adjacent

Grounds

NT shop. Plant sales

Tea-room in converted billiard room. Children's menu

Baby-changing facilities. Pushchairs and baby back-carriers admitted. Family trails and hands-on activities. Single pushchairs only

Suitable for school groups

On leads only on coastal walks from car park

→ [202:SX728374] **Foot**: South West Coast Path within ⅜ml. **Ferry**: from Salcombe to South Sands, then ½ml strenuous walk (uphill). **Bus**: Stagecoach in Devon X64, Sun & BHol only; Tally Ho! 164, 606 from ≄ Totnes. From all alight Salcombe, 1½ml. **Road**: 1½ml SW of Salcombe, signposted from Malborough and Salcombe (narrow approach road). Roads leading to Overbeck's are steep and single track and not suitable for coaches over 25 seats or large vehicles

P Parking, 150yds. Charge applies to non-members. At peak times (weekends and school hols) the car park is reserved for visitors to the house and garden

NT properties nearby
Coleton Fishacre, Greenway, Saltram

Penrose Estate: Gunwalloe and Loe Pool

nr Helston, Cornwall TR13 0RD

1974 **(1:B10)**

Wooded country around Cornwall's largest natural lake and dramatic coastal scenery

At the heart of the Penrose Estate lies Loe Pool, a freshwater lake which meets the sea at the dramatic shingle bank of Loe Bar. Surrounding the Pool is a mix of rich farmland and woodland through which there are many paths, including the 5-mile circuit of the Pool itself. At Gunwalloe, two sandy coves lie either side of the 14th- and 15th-century church (not NT) and the valley reedbed provides a haven for birdlife.

i **T** 01326 561407
E southwestcornwall@nationaltrust.org.uk

Occasional guided walks

NT *Coast of Cornwall* leaflet 12 includes maps, details of walks and information on local history and wildlife

Grounds

Gunwalloe Beach Café (not NT)

Suitable for school groups. Penrose education and activity pack available for teachers. Education room at Chyvarloe basecamp

On leads only in landscape park at Penrose. Seasonal bans on one beach at Gunwalloe

Penrose Estate							
All year	M	T	W	T	F	S	S

Loe Pool, Cornwall, looking inland to a boathouse

🚲 Rough track from Helston to Loe Bar

➡️ [203:SW639259] **Foot**: South West Coast Path goes through property. **Bus**: First 2/2A, 🚂 Penzance–Falmouth to Porthleven. **Station**: Camborne 10ml to Porthleven. **Road**: Penrose Estate: 2ml SW of Helston on B3304 turn left, signposted Loe Bar, and left to car park. Gunwalloe: take A3083 from Helston and turn right 1ml past main RNAS Culdrose entrance

🅿️ Pay & display at Gunwalloe. Charge applies all year (NT members free). Free parking available at various sites around Penrose

NT properties nearby
Glendurgan Garden, Godolphin, The Lizard

Philipps House and Dinton Park

Dinton, Salisbury, Wiltshire SP3 5HH

🏠 🌳 🚶 1943   (1:K5)

Early 19th-century neo-Grecian house

An impressive collection of fine Regency furniture is housed on the ground floor of this neo-Grecian house, which was designed by Jeffry Wyatville in 1820 for William Wyndham. A variety of parkland walks can be enjoyed throughout the year.

⭐ No WC

ℹ️ **T** 01722 716663
E philippshouse@nationaltrust.org.uk

🚶 Various walks around the park start from the car park; leaflet from property (when open), or from the village shop/post office or NT shop in Salisbury

♿ 👓 Building 🏔️ Grounds 🏔️
🐕 In park only

Philipps House and Dinton Park									
House									
15 Mar–25 Oct	10–1	M	T	W	T	F	**S**	S
17 Mar–27 Oct	1–5	**M**	T	W	T	F	S	S
Park									
All year		M	T	W	T	F	S	S

➡️ [184:SU004319] **Bus**: Wilts & Dorset 25 from Salisbury (passing 🚂 Salisbury). Tourist Coaches 84 (Tisbury–Dinton). **Station**: Tisbury 5ml. **Road**: 9ml W of Salisbury, on N side of B3089; in Dinton take St Mary's Road at crossroads. Park in car park opposite cricket ground. House entrance 200yds further on left

🅿️ Free parking, 20yds. Visitors to house only should park at house. Visitors to park should at all times use St Mary's Road car park, from where walks begin

NT properties nearby
Little Clarendon, Mompesson House, Stonehenge Landscape, Stourhead

Priest's House

Muchelney, Langport, Somerset TA10 0DQ

🏠 🚶 🚲 1911   (1:I6)

Late medieval hall house in a picturesque village

Set in the picturesque village of Muchelney and little altered since the early 17th century, the house was built by the nearby Abbey (now run by EH) in 1308 for the parish priest. Interesting features include the Gothic doorway, magnificent double-height tracery windows and a massive 15th-century stone fireplace. The house is occupied and furnished by tenants.

⭐ No WC

ℹ️ **T** 01458 253771
E priestshouse@nationaltrust.org.uk

♿ 👓 🖼️ Building 🏔️

➡️ [193:ST429250] Muchelney is on the South Somerset Cycle Trail. **Bus**: First 54/A/B/C Yeovil Bus Station–Taunton (passing within ¾ml 🚂 Yeovil Pen Mill), alight Huish Episcopi, 1ml. **Road**: 1ml S of Langport

🅿️ No parking on site

NT properties nearby
Barrington Court, Lytes Cary Manor, Montacute House, Stembridge Tower Mill, Tintinhull Garden, Treasurer's House

Priest's House									
16 Mar–28 Sep	2–5	**M**	T	W	T	F	S	**S**
Admission by guided tour, last tour commences at 5									

Charges for National Trust members apply on some special event days

Prior Park Landscape Garden

Ralph Allen Drive, Bath, Somerset BA2 5AH

❄ 🎫 🏠 👙 🚻 🎭 🧍 🍷 1993   **(1:J4)**

Beautiful and intimate 18th-century landscape garden

One of only four Palladian bridges in the world can be crossed at Prior Park, which was created in the 18th century by local entrepreneur Ralph Allen, with advice from 'Capability' Brown and the poet Alexander Pope. The garden is set in a sweeping valley where visitors can enjoy magnificent views of Bath. Recent restoration of the 'Wilderness' has reinstated the Serpentine Lake, Cascade and Cabinet. A five-minute walk leads to the Bath Skyline, a six-mile circular route encompassing beautiful woodlands and meadows, an Iron Age hill fort, Roman settlements, 18th-century follies and spectacular views.

What's new in 2008 'Wilderness' restoration now complete; explore the Serpentine Lake, Cascade and Cabinet

⭐ Prior Park College, a school, operates from the mansion (not NT). Prior Park is a green tourism site; there is only disabled parking

ℹ️ **T** 01225 833422
    E priorpark@nationaltrust.org.uk

👙 Family trails and events. See website for details. Special-interest guided tours

🧍 Bath Skyline walk leaflet and map free from Prior Park visitor reception and NT website. No direct access from the Bath Skyline into the garden

♿ 🚾 ♿ ⠿ Ⓐ P♿ D♿ **Grounds** 🦽

🎫 Kiosk, Sat, Sun and BH Mons, March–Oct

🚻 Baby-changing facilities. Pushchairs and baby back-carriers admitted. Front-carrying baby slings and hip-carrying infant seats for loan. Children's quiz/trail. Family activity packs

Prior Park Landscape Garden								
1 Mar–31 Oct	11–5:30	**M**	T	**W**	**T**	**F**	**S**	**S**
1 Nov–31 Jan 09	11–dusk	M	T	W	T	F	**S**	**S**

Last admission 1hr before closing. Closed 25, 26 Dec & 1 Jan 09. Closes dusk if earlier than 5:30

🎭 Suitable for school groups. Live interpretation. Hands-on activities

🐕 Nov–31 Jan 09 only, on leads

➔ [172:ST760633] Prior Park is a green tourism site; there is only disabled car parking (please tel. to book), but public transport runs regularly (every 30mins) to and from the park. Please tel. for leaflet or download from the website. **Foot:** 1ml very steep uphill walk from railway station. To rear of railway station cross river, pass Widcombe shopping parade, turn right on to Prior Park Road at White Hart PH, proceed up steep hill, garden on left. Kennet & Avon canal path ¾ml. **Cycle:** NCN4, ¾ml. **Bus:** First 2 Bath–Combe Down. Park & ride services to town centre from Odd Down, Lansdown and Newbridge (daily) and Bath University (Sats). Please note that park & ride services do not go direct to garden. City Sightseeing Skyline Tour open-top tour bus runs to garden every 20mins in summer, every hour in winter (11–5). Pick up from railway station and Abbey. Half price to NT members. Due to major works at Bath Bus Station listings may change, please tel. for current transport information. **Station:** Bath Spa 1¼ml. **Road:** no brown signs

P Disabled parking only (please tel. to book)

NT properties nearby
Bath Assembly Rooms, Clevedon Court, The Courts Garden, Dyrham Park, Great Chalfield Manor and Garden, Lacock Abbey, Tyntesfield, Westwood Manor

St Anthony Head

Cornwall

🐕 🌊 🏠 🎫 🎭 🧍 🐕 1959   **(1:C9)**

Headland with fine views over Falmouth Bay

At the southernmost tip of the Roseland peninsula, St Anthony Head overlooks the spectacular entrance to one of the world's largest natural harbours – Carrick Roads and the Fal estuary. The starting point for a number of excellent coastal and sheltered creekside walks, the Head also bears newly revealed remains of a century of defensive fortifications.

Parking in National Trust car parks is free for members displaying stickers

A castle and church crown the summit of the iconic island of St Michael's Mount, Cornwall

i **T** 01872 862945
E stanthonyhead@nationaltrust.org.uk

NT *Coast of Cornwall* leaflet 18/19 includes maps and details of circular walks and information about local history, geology and wildlife

Grounds

Suitable for school groups. Adult study days

→ [204:SW847313] **Ferry**: Falmouth to St Mawes foot ferry (all year, but no Sun service in winter); St Mawes to Place (1ml from St Anthony Head along coast path), daily in summer only. **Bus**: Truronian T50 Truro–St Mawes, alight St Mawes for ferry to Place, or alight Portscatho, then 3ml. **Station**: Penmere, via ferry to St Mawes then to Place, 6ml. **Road**: S of St Mawes off A3078

P Parking

NT properties nearby
Trelissick Garden

St Anthony Head		
All year		M T W T F S S

St Michael's Mount

Marazion, nr Penzance, Cornwall TR17 OHS

1954 (1:B9)

Rocky island crowned by medieval church and castle, home to a living community

This iconic island rises gracefully to the church and castle at its summit. Accessible on foot at low tide across a causeway, at other times it is reached by a short evocative boat trip. The oldest

surviving buildings date from the 12th century, when a Benedictine priory was founded here. Following the English Civil War, the island was acquired by the St Aubyn family, who still live in the castle. In the intervening years many additions and alterations were made to convert it for use as a mansion house. Fascinating rooms from different eras include the mid 18th-century Gothick-style Blue Drawing Room.

What's new in 2008 Expanded programme of tours, talks and events

★ Sensible shoes are advisable as causeway and paths are cobbled and uneven. Steep climb to castle. Unsuitable for prams and pushchairs. Passages in the castle are narrow, so some delays may occur in the height of the season. Dogs are not allowed in the castle or grounds and there are no facilities or grassed areas for dogs on the island. Access by boat or causeway and all visits to St Michael's Mount are subject to favourable weather conditions

i **T** 01736 710507/01736 710265 (tide information/general enquiries), 01736 711067 (shop), 01736 710748 (restaurant)
E stmichaelsmount@nationaltrust.org.uk

Tours available of gardens. Please tel. for details

St Michael's Mount		
16 Mar–30 Jun	10:30–5	M T W T F S S
1 Jul–31 Aug	10:30–5:30	M T W T F S S
1 Sep–2 Nov	10:30–5	M T W T F S S

Last admission 45mins before castle closing time. Sufficient time should be allowed for travel from the mainland. Castle open during winter months for guided tours. Private garden open weekdays in May & June; Thur & Fri July–Oct. Special garden tours some evenings – see local information or website

Dogs assisting visitors with disabilities are always welcome

🎭 Including church services at 11:15 Suns, Whitsun–end Sept, Good Fri, Easter Sun and Christmas. Concert in Sept. Local bands play beside harbour most Suns July & Aug. Garden evenings with supper

♿ 🚻♿🔔⊡📷 Grounds 🦽

🏠 NT shop. Island shop (not NT). Plant sales

☕ The Sail Loft Restaurant (licensed). Menu features local seafood dishes. Children's menu. Island Café (not NT) (licensed)

🚼 Baby-changing facilities. Hip-carrying infant seats for loan. Children's quiz/trail

🎒 Suitable for school groups. Arrangements can be made for school or other groups during the winter months

➡ [203:SW515298] **Foot**: South West Coast Path within ⅝ml. **Cycle**: NCN3, ¾ml. **Bus**: First 2/A/B Penzance–Helston; 17B Penzance–St Ives. All pass ⊞ Penzance. **Station**: Penzance 3ml. **Road**: ½ml S of A394 at Marazion, from where there is access on foot over the causeway at low tide or, during summer months only, by ferry at high tide, if weather conditions favourable

🅿 Public car parks on mainland at Marazion opposite St Michael's Mount 400yds and 800yds (not NT, fee payable)

NT properties nearby
Godolphin, Trengwainton Garden

Saltram

Plympton, Plymouth, Devon PL7 1UH

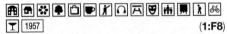

🍷 1957 **(1:F8)**

Magnificent Georgian house with opulent Robert Adam interiors, gardens, follies and landscaped parkland

Still a largely undiscovered treasure, and the result of centuries of sophistication and extravagance, Saltram is now the perfect family day out: close to Plymouth and yet in a world of its own. Home to the Parker family for nearly 300 years, the house with its original contents provides a fascinating insight into country estate life throughout the centuries. Fine Robert Adam interiors and beautiful collections bring the 'age of elegance' to life at Saltram. Learn about some of the fascinating characters and family stories, including the correspondence of Frances, the third Countess, with Jane Austen, and John, Lord Boringdon's, great friendship with Sir Joshua Reynolds. Explore the magnificent garden and romantic follies, and enjoy discovering many secluded spots throughout the landscape park and estate bordering the Plym estuary. For younger visitors there are children's activities rooms and a family trail to help you discover the secrets of Saltram, while the garden can be enjoyed with our family explorer packs.

Saltram in Devon has magnificent Robert Adam interiors

Please remember – your membership card is always needed for free admission

Saltram								
Park								
All year	Dawn−dusk	M	T	W	T	F	S	S
House								
21 Mar−2 Nov	12−4:30	M	T	W	T	F	S	S
Catering								
1 Feb−20 Mar	11−4	M	T	W	T	F	S	S
21 Mar−2 Nov	11−5	M	T	W	T	F	S	S
3 Nov−31 Jan 09	11−4	M	T	W	T	F	S	S
Shop/garden/gallery								
1 Feb−20 Mar	11−4	M	T	W	T	F	S	S
21 Mar−2 Nov	11−5	M	T	W	T	F	S	S
3 Nov−31 Jan 09	11−4	M	T	W	T	F	S	S

Admission by timed ticket. Open Good Fri. Last admission to house 45mins before closing. Shop/gallery/garden closed 24−26 Dec & 2 Jan 09. Catering closed 25 & 26 Dec. House opening date 21 March subject to completion of rewiring project. Tel. to confirm

What's new in 2008 Historic tack room in the stables will be open with information and a special display. Nature trail spotter sheet for the parkland

★ Occasional special events require NT members to pay for entry. Tel. for details. Opening date subject to completion of rewiring project on time

ℹ **T** 01752 333500
E saltram@nationaltrust.org.uk

🏃 Out-of-hours house tours available for groups, 10–11:30, Mon-Thurs inclusive. £10 (booking essential). Grounds: guided walks by arrangement

🎧 Available on request. These are especially suitable for visitors with sight difficulties

♥ Children's events, jazz picnic, open-air theatre, craft fairs, lecture lunches and Hallowe'en night

🏃 Extensive footpaths around the estate. Guided walks in grounds by arrangement

♿ 🚻 ... Building 🔼 🔽
Grounds 🔼 ➡️

🎁 Gift shop and plant centre in stables. Chapel Gallery in garden selling local arts and crafts

☕ Park Restaurant (licensed) in the stables. Occasional evening opening. Special events programme. Available for private hire/functions. Children's menu

🚼 Baby-changing facilities. Pushchairs for loan in house. Children's play area. Children's guide. Family house trail. Family garden explorer packs. Children's events

🏛 Suitable for school groups. Education room/centre. Hands-on activities. Adult study days

🐕 On leads on designated paths only, not in garden or grazed area of park

🚲 Many good cycle tracks in the parkland, part of NCN27

➡️ [201:SX520557] **Foot**: South West Coast Path within 4ml. **Cycle**: NCN27.
Bus: Plymouth Citybus 19, 20/A, 21/2, 50/1 from Plymouth, alight Marsh Mills, then ¾ml by footpath. **Station**: Plymouth 3½ml.
Road: 3½ml E of Plymouth city centre. Travelling south (from Exeter): leave A38, 3ml N of Plymouth. Exit is signed Plymouth City Centre/Plympton/Kingsbridge. At roundabout take centre lane, then 3rd exit for Plympton. Take right-hand lane and follow brown signs. Travelling north (from Liskeard): leave A38 at Plympton exit. At roundabout take first exit for Plympton, then as above

🅿 Free parking, 50yds

NT properties nearby
Antony, Buckland Abbey, Cotehele, Overbeck's

Shute Barton

Shute, nr Axminster, Devon EX13 7PT

🏠 🐕 🏃 🚻 1959 **(1:H7)**
Medieval manor house with later architectural features

★ No WC

ℹ **T** 01297 34692
E shutebarton@nationaltrust.org.uk

➡️ 3ml SW of Axminster, 2ml N of Colyton on Honiton−Colyton road (B3161)

Shute Barton								
5 Apr−27 Sep	2−5:30	M	T	W	T	F	S	S
1 Oct−29 Oct	2−5	M	T	W	T	F	S	S

Admission by guided tour. The house is tenanted; there is visitor access to most parts of the interior

Unless indicated, last admission is always 30mins before closing time

Snowshill Manor

Snowshill, nr Broadway, Gloucestershire
WR12 7JU

 1951 (1:K1)

Cotswold manor house with eclectic collection and Arts & Crafts-style garden

A traditional golden-yellow Cotswold manor house set in a delightful village high above the Vale of Evesham, Snowshill Manor is packed to the rafters with a spectacular collection of craftsmanship and design from across the globe. Charles Paget Wade amassed more than 22,000 items during his lifetime, creating an Aladdin's cave of unexpected delights. Outside, Wade created numerous 'outdoor rooms', as well as a series of terraces and ponds, each with their own character. The gardens have been run on organic principles since 1988 and are a haven of peace and tranquillity.

What's new in 2008 Children's turf maze and garden quiz, exhibition of photographs of Charles Wade's model village

⭐ The Wade Costume Collection is housed at Berrington Hall in Herefordshire and can be viewed there, by appointment only. Photography inside the house by written arrangement only

ℹ️ **T** 01386 852410
E snowshillmanor@nationaltrust.org.uk

🏃 Explorer tours taking in parts of the Manor and its collection not usually on display

😊 Children's activity days. Seasonal garden trails. Winter weekend warmer events

Some of the 'boneshaker' bicycles of 1870–85 in the Hundred Wheels Room at Snowshill Manor

♿ 🚻 Building 🦽
Grounds 🦽 ♿

📷 NT shop. Plant sales

☕ Licensed restaurant. Children's menu

👶 Baby-changing and feeding facilities. Front-carrying baby slings and hip-carrying infant seats for loan. Children's play area and maze. Children's quiz/trail. Tracker Packs. Children's activity days

➡️ [150:SP096339] **Foot**: Cotswold Way within ¾ml. **Bus**: Castleways, Evesham or Cheltenham–Broadway, then 2½ml uphill. **Station**: Station: Moreton-in-Marsh 7ml, Evesham 8ml. **Road**: 2½ml SW of Broadway; turn from A44 Broadway bypass into Broadway village; at green turn right uphill to Snowshill

🅿️ Free parking, 500yds. Walk from car park to manor and gardens along undulating country path. Transfer available

NT properties nearby
Chastleton House, Chedworth Roman Villa, Coughton Court, Hidcote Manor Garden, Lodge Park and Sherborne Estate

Snowshill Manor									
Manor									
19 Mar–2 Nov	12–5	M	T	**W**	**T**	**F**	**S**	**S**	
Garden									
19 Mar–2 Nov	11–5:30	M	T	**W**	**T**	**F**	**S**	**S**	
Shop/restaurant/grounds									
19 Mar–2 Nov	11–5:30	M	T	**W**	**T**	**F**	**S**	**S**	
8 Nov–14 Dec	12–4	M	T	W	T	F	**S**	**S**	

Admission by timed ticket at busy times. Tickets issued at reception on a first-come, first-served basis and cannot be booked in advance. Tickets often run out at peak times; please arrive early. Last admission: Manor 4:20; garden 5. Open BHols

For further information go to www.nationaltrust.org.uk

Stembridge Tower Mill

High Ham, Somerset TA10 9DJ

[✖] [1969] **(1:I5)**

The last remaining thatched windmill in England

[★] No WC

[i] **T** 01935 823289
E stembridgemill@nationaltrust.org.uk

[→] 2ml N of Langport, ½ml E of High Ham; take the Somerton road from Langport and follow High Ham signs. Take road opposite cemetery in High Ham. Mill is on right

Stembridge Tower Mill								
Outside viewing only*								
15 Mar–2 Nov	11–5	**M**	**T**	**W**	**T**	**F**	**S**	**S**

*Please respect privacy of holiday tenants in cottage. Possible to enter Mill Easter Mon, early May BH Mon and Aug BH Mon 11–5

Stoke-sub-Hamdon Priory

North Street, Stoke-sub-Hamdon, Somerset TA4 6QP

[⌂] [1946] **(1:I6)**

14th/15th-century farm buildings, formerly a priests' residence

The priests who lived here served the Chapel of St Nicholas (now destroyed). The Great Hall is open to visitors.

Stoke-sub-Hamdon Priory								
15 Mar–2 Nov	10–6	**M**	**T**	**W**	**T**	**F**	**S**	**S**

Closes dusk if earlier. Only Great Hall open

[★] No WC

[i] **T** 01935 823289
E stokehamdonpriory@nationaltrust.org.uk

[♿] **Grounds** [♿]

[→] [193:ST473175] **Bus**: South West Coaches 81 Yeovil Bus Station–South Petherton (passing within ¾ml [≋] Yeovil Pen Mill). **Station**: Crewkerne or Yeovil Pen Mill, both 7ml. **Road**: between A303 and A3088. 2ml W of Montacute between Yeovil and Ilminster

[P] No parking on site. Not suitable for coaches

NT properties nearby
Barrington Court, Lytes Cary Manor, Montacute House, Priest's House, Tintinhull Garden, Treasurer's House

Stonehenge Landscape

3/4 Stonehenge Cottages, King Barrows, Amesbury, Wiltshire SP4 7DD

[⌂][♿][🎧][🏛][■][🚶][🚲] [1927] **(1:K5)**

Ancient ceremonial landscape of great archaeological and wildlife interest

Within the Stonehenge World Heritage Site, the Trust owns and manages 850 hectares (2,100 acres) of downland surrounding the famous stone circle. Walking through the estate, visitors can discover other prehistoric monuments, including the Avenue, King Barrow Ridge, Winterbourne Stoke Barrows, the great henge of Durrington Walls and the Cursus, interpreted as a processional way. There is also a great diversity of wildlife.

Looking west from King Barrows Ridge over Stonehenge Down, Wiltshire

What's new in 2008 Improved landscape access

⭐ The stone circle is owned and administered by English Heritage (NT members admitted free). All grassland areas on the estate are designated NT open access and are open to everyone, but on foot only. Camping is not permitted anywhere on the estate. Please observe the NT byelaws. WC at the stone circle

ℹ️ **T** 01980 664780
E stonehenge@nationaltrust.org.uk

🎧 For the stone circle only. Available from the English Heritage kiosk

🚶 Much of the estate is available for visitors to explore on foot. Maps of accessible areas and self-guided walks leaflets can be obtained by contacting the property office. Guided walks for groups by arrangement

♿ 🅿️ **Grounds** ♿

🟥 Suitable for school groups

🐕 Under close control at all times

🚴 On byways and bridleways only

➡️ [184:SU120420] **Bus**: Wilts & Dorset 3 ⊠ Salisbury–Stonehenge. **Station**: Salisbury 9½ml. **Road**: Monument 2ml W of Amesbury, at junction of A303 & A344/A360

🅿️ Parking (not NT), 50yds. A charge may apply over the peak period June–Oct. NT members free

Stonehenge Landscape

NT land north of visitor centre open at all times, but small areas may be closed at the Summer Solstice (21 June) for up to two days

NT properties nearby

Avebury, Little Clarendon, Mompesson House, Philipps House and Dinton Park, Stourhead

Stourhead

Stourhead Estate Office, Stourton, Warminster, Wiltshire BA12 6QD

🏠🏛️✿🌳🥪🏚️🚽🎭🍴🚶🎧🌳🎭👥
🟥🚶🚴🔔🍷 1946   (1:J5)

World-famous 18th-century landscape garden and Palladian mansion

Lying in secluded privacy in its own valley, Stourhead is one of the finest landscape gardens in the world. Designed by Henry Hoare II as a place to entertain, the garden was laid out between 1741 and 1780. The magnificent lake is central to this iconic garden of classical temples and follies. Its lakeside paths and backdrop of colourful, rare and exotic trees reveal many beautifully contrived vistas, capturing the imagination of visitors for over two centuries.

Children playing under an Acer at Stourhead

Stourhead

Garden									
All year	9–7	**M**	**T**	**W**	**T**	**F**	**S**	**S**
House									
15 Mar–2 Nov	11:30–4:30	**M**	**T**	W	T	**F**	**S**	**S**
Tower									
15 Mar–2 Nov	11:30–4:30	**M**	**T**	**W**	**T**	**F**	**S**	**S**
Restaurant									
1 Mar–31 Mar	10–5	**M**	**T**	**W**	**T**	**F**	**S**	**S**
1 Apr–30 Sep	10–5:30	**M**	**T**	**W**	**T**	**F**	**S**	**S**
1 Oct–31 Oct	10–5	**M**	**T**	**W**	**T**	**F**	**S**	**S**
1 Nov–31 Jan 09	10:30–4	**M**	**T**	**W**	**T**	**F**	**S**	**S**
Shop									
1 Mar–31 Mar	10–5	**M**	**T**	**W**	**T**	**F**	**S**	**S**
1 Apr–30 Sep	10–6	**M**	**T**	**W**	**T**	**F**	**S**	**S**
1 Oct–31 Oct	10–5	**M**	**T**	**W**	**T**	**F**	**S**	**S**
1 Nov–31 Jan 09	10:30–4	**M**	**T**	**W**	**T**	**F**	**S**	**S**
Farm shop									
1 Apr–30 Sep	10–6	**M**	**T**	**W**	**T**	**F**	**S**	**S**
1 Oct–31 Jan 09	10–*	**M**	**T**	**W**	**T**	**F**	**S**	**S**

Garden, house and tower close dusk if earlier. Last admission to house and tower 4 (closing 4:30). Restaurant & shop closed 25 Dec. * Tel. for farm shop closing times

While the garden seasons change in beautiful succession, the majestic Palladian mansion, originally home to the Hoare family, houses a unique collection of Chippendale furniture, magnificent paintings and an exquisite Regency library. Waymarked walks can be enjoyed across the chalk downland and woodland of the wider estate, which is managed for nature conservation. Two Iron Age hill forts can be discovered, and from the top of King Alfred's Tower, a 50m-high red brick triangular folly, visitors will experience spectacular views across three counties.

What's new in 2008 Newly restored Pope's Cabinet plus exhibition giving a fascinating insight into the conservation work that has been done. Basement exhibition area opens with 'Servants' – revealing how people lived and worked on the estate. *Fête Champêtre*: 'A World of Entertainment'. A weekend celebration of global music and dance. 'Explorer' garden tour with state-of-the-art interactive guide

i T 01747 841152
 E stourhead@nationaltrust.org.uk

Available for garden

Programme of events throughout the year for children, families and adults, including free trails and drop-in activities

Five waymarked walks throughout countryside areas

Building Grounds

NT shop, plant centre and farm shop

Licensed restaurant serving fresh seasonal food. Children's menu. Private dining room max. 50 (must be booked). Refreshments and ice-cream in Spread Eagle courtyard during the summer. Spread Eagle Inn, open all year

Baby-changing facilities. Hip-carrying infant seats for loan in house. Children's guide. Family trails and activity packs. Pushchairs admitted to garden only. Children's activity area. Family and children's events

Suitable for school groups. Education room/centre. Hands-on activities. Adult study days

On short leads in landscape garden (1 Nov–31 Jan 09). Under close control all year on wider estate. Not admitted to house or King Alfred's Tower

Some access across estate on bridleways

→ [183:ST780340] **Cycle**: Wiltshire Cycle Way runs through estate. **Bus**: Wilts & Dorset 25/6 Salisbury–Hindon connecting with Wigglybus to Stourhead, Mon–Fri only; Wigglybus from ➔ Gillingham (meeting London train), Tues, Wed, Thur, Sat only (Wigglybus needs to be booked. Tel. 01747 861222); also Shaftesbury & District/Frome Minibuses 80 Frome–➔ Gillingham (Wed, Sat only); otherwise First 58 Shaftesbury–Wincanton (passing Gillingham) alight Zeals, 1¼ml. **Station**: Gillingham 6½ml; Bruton (U) 7ml. **Road**: at Stourton, off B3092, 3ml NW of Mere (A303), 8ml S of Frome (A361). King Alfred's Tower: 3½ml by road from Stourhead House

P Free parking, 400yds. Transfer by shuttle, throughout main season only, to house and garden entrances. King Alfred's Tower: designated parking 50yds

NT properties nearby
Barrington Court, Lytes Cary Manor, Mompesson House, Montacute House, Tintinhull Garden

Many Trust properties are offering Gift Aid on Entry for non-members, see page 10

Studland Beach and Nature Reserve

Purbeck Estate Office, Studland, Swanage,
Dorset BH19 3AX

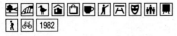

🚶 🚲 1982   **(1:K7)**

Vast area of sandy beaches and heathland

Glorious sandy beaches stretch continuously for
3 miles from South Haven Point to the chalk
cliffs of Handfast Point and Old Harry Rocks,
and include Shell Bay and a designated naturist
area. The heathland behind the beach is a haven
for many rare birds and native wildlife and is a
designated National Nature Reserve. Studland is
the richest 1,000 hectares (2,400 acres) for wild
flowers in Britain. There are several trails
through the sand dunes and woodlands,
including bird hides at Little Sea. Studland
Beach is just one highlight of the 3,200-hectare
(8,000-acre) Purbeck Estate cared for by the
National Trust.

⭐ WCs at Knoll Beach and Middle Beach. Shell
Bay WCs are composting

ℹ️ **T** 01929 450259
E studlandbeach@nationaltrust.org.uk

🔦 Guided tours of nature reserve by wardens

🎭 Family, winter and evening events

Studland Beach		M	T	W	T	F	S	S
Beach								
All year		M	T	W	T	F	S	S
Shop/café								
1 Mar–20 Mar	10–4*	M	T	W	T	F	S	S
21 Mar–29 Jun	9:30–5*	M	T	W	T	F	S	S
Shop								
30 Jun–1 Sep	9:30–6	M	T	W	T	F	S	S
Café								
30 Jun–1 Sep	9–7	M	T	W	T	F	S	S
Shop/café								
2 Sep–26 Oct	9:30–5	M	T	W	T	F	S	S
27 Oct–31 Jan 09	10–4*	M	T	W	T	F	S	S

*Shop/café closes 1hr later at weekends. Shop and
café open hours may be longer in fine weather and
shorter in poor weather. Visitor centre, shop and café
closed 25 & 26 Dec. **Car parks can be very full in
peak season**

🚶 Sand dunes trail and woodland walk leaflets
available

♿ 🚻 🚻 🚻 **Grounds** 🚻 🚻

🛍️ Located at Knoll Beach Visitor Centre and
seasonally at Middle Beach. NT range and
beach products

🍽️ Beach café (licensed) at Knoll Beach Visitor
Centre. Children's menu. Licensed café (not
NT) at Middle Beach. Fish restaurant (not NT)
(licensed) at Shell Bay

👶 Baby-changing facilities at all beach WCs.
Pushchairs for loan at Knoll Beach

🎒 Suitable for school groups. Education
room/centre. Adult study days

🐕 No restrictions 1 Oct–30 April. Knoll Beach &
Middle Beach: dogs on leads 1 May–27 June
and 8 Sept–30 Sept. No dogs allowed 28
June–7 Sept. Shell Bay & South Beach: dogs
on leads 1 May–30 Sept. Dogs permitted all
year on nature reserve, estate footpaths and
South West Coast Path (on a lead)

🚲 Cycling on bridleways across the Purbeck
Estate. Route booklet available from Visitor
Centre

➡️ [195:SZ036835] **Foot**: 5ml of South West
Coast Path on property. **Ferry**: car ferry from
Sandbanks, Poole, to Shell Bay. **Bus**: Wilts &
Dorset 150 Bournemouth–Swanage to Shell
Bay & Studland. Also 152 Poole–Sandbanks
(passing close ⓔ Parkstone); Yellow Buses 12
Christchurch–Sandbanks, July–Aug only, then
vehicle ferry from Sandbanks to Shell Bay.
Station: Branksome or Parkstone, both 3½ml
to Shell Bay or 6ml to Studland via vehicle
ferry

🅿️ Car parks at Shell Bay & South Beach (open
9–11), Knoll Beach & Middle Beach (open
9–8). Prices vary through the season. NT
members must show cards on entry

NT properties nearby
Brownsea Island, Clouds Hill, Corfe Castle,
Hardy's Cottage, Kingston Lacy, Max Gate

For details of events go to www.nationaltrust.org.uk/events

Tintagel Old Post Office

Fore Street, Tintagel, Cornwall PL34 0DB

🏠 ✿ 📷 👫 🎦 1903   **(1:D7)**

Tintagel Old Post Office									
15 Mar–30 Sep	11–5:30	**M**	**T**	**W**	**T**	**F**	**S**	**S**
1 Oct–2 Nov	11–4	**M**	**T**	**W**	**T**	**F**	**S**	**S**

One of the Trust's most delightful medieval buildings, enhanced by a cottage garden

Standing apart from its modern commercial neighbours on Tintagel's main street, this low-set 14th-century yeoman's farmhouse exudes charm and beckons the curious to explore. Inside, one room is restored to show how it looked when, for a brief time in the late 19th century, it was used as the local letter receiving station. The remaining rooms are furnished with local oak pieces and a good collection of samplers from the same period. Outside, the small enclosed cottage garden offers a tranquil haven away from the hustle and bustle of the busy village street.

⭐ WC in Trevena Square (not NT)

ℹ️ **T** 01840 770024
   E tintageloldpo@nationaltrust.org.uk

♿ 🚲 👓 🅰 Building 🌳 Grounds ♿

📷 NT shop. Plant sales

👫 Hip-carrying infant seat for loan. Children's quiz/trail. Pushchairs and backpacks can be left at entrance

🎦 Suitable for school groups

➡️ [200:SX056884] In centre of village.
   Foot: South West Coast Path within ⅔ml.
   Bus: Western Greyhound 524/5 from Bude, 584/594 from Wadebridge (with connections on 555 at Wadebridge from 🚂 Bodmin Parkway)

🅿️ No parking on site. Numerous pay & display car parks in village (not NT)

NT properties nearby
Barras Nose, Boscastle

Tintagel Old Post Office: a rare surviving example of Cornish domestic architecture

Charges for National Trust members apply on some special event days

Tintinhull Garden

Farm Street, Tintinhull, Yeovil, Somerset
BA22 8PZ

[icons] 1953   **(1:16)**

Delightful formal garden

Created last century around a 17th-century manor
house, this is one of the most harmonious small
gardens in Britain. It features secluded lawns,
small pools and colourful borders. There is also an
attractive kitchen garden and orchard to explore.

[i] **T** 01935 823289
   E tintinhull@nationaltrust.org.uk

[icons] Building [icons]

📷 Plant sales and guidebooks

🍵 Tea-room in courtyard. Light refreshments only

👪 Pushchairs and baby back-carriers admitted.
   Family activities

🎒 Suitable for school groups. Hands-on
   activities

➡️ [183:ST503198] **Bus**: First 52 Yeovil Bus
   Station–Martock (passing within ¾ml ⊠ Yeovil
   Pen Mill). **Station**: Yeovil Pen Mill 5¼ml; Yeovil
   Junction 7ml (bus to Yeovil Bus Station).
   Road: 5ml NW of Yeovil, ½ml S of A303, on
   E outskirts of Tintinhull. Follow road signs to
   Tintinhull village

Tintinhull Garden								
15 Mar–2 Nov		11–5	M	T	**W**	**T**	**F**	**S**	**S**
Closes dusk if earlier. Open BH Mons								

[P] Free parking, 150yds

NT properties nearby

Barrington Court, Lytes Cary Manor, Montacute
House, Priest's House, Stembridge Tower Mill,
Treasurer's House

Treasurer's House

Martock, Somerset TA12 6JL

[icon] 1971   **(1:16)**

Small medieval house

Medieval house with Great Hall, completed in
1293, and Solar Block containing an unusual
wall painting. There is also a kitchen, added in
the 15th century.

⭐ The house is occupied by tenants. Only the
   medieval hall, wall painting and kitchen are
   shown to visitors. No WC

[i] **T** 01935 825015
   E treasurersmartock@nationaltrust.org.uk

Treasurer's House								
16 Mar–28 Sep		2–5	**M**	**T**	W	T	F	**S**	**S**

Tintinhull Garden surrounds an elegant 17th-century manor house

Ferris's Cottage, Trelissick Garden, Cornwall

🦽 Building 🏞 Grounds 🦽

➡ [193:ST462191] **Bus**: First 52 Yeovil Bus Station–Martock (passing within ¾ml) ⊠ Yeovil Pen Mill). **Station**: Crewkerne 7½ml; Yeovil Pen Mill 8ml. **Road**: opposite church in middle of village; 1ml NW of A303 between Ilminster and Ilchester

🅿 Free parking (not NT), 400yds. Parking limited and unsuitable for trailer caravans

NT properties nearby
Barrington Court, Lytes Cary Manor, Montacute House, Priest's House, Stembridge Tower Mill, Tintinhull Garden

Trelissick Garden

Feock, nr Truro, Cornwall TR3 6QL

🌼 🌳 🦽 🏰 🏠 🏛 🍷 🎧 🎋 😃 👫
📕 🧍 🍸 1955   (1:C9)

Tranquil varied garden in fabulous position, with a superb collection of tender and exotic plants

This Cornish maritime garden is in an extraordinary position on a wooded peninsula. To the north it is embraced by Lamouth Creek, the winding estuary of the River Fal is to the east and to the south is Channels Creek and the great expanse of Carrick Roads. Trelissick is a magical place that will transport your imagination to days gone by. Throughout the year the 12-hectare (30-acre) garden is awash

with colour, while the park has breathtaking views down towards the sea. There is a fine Georgian stable block, a shop, gallery and restaurant (the house is not open to the public), and the whole estate is encircled with woods full of wonderful walks.

What's new in 2008 Crofters self-service restaurant, with additional open-air seating

⭐ Copeland China Collection, by courtesy of Mr and Mrs William Copeland, open Thur May and Sept, 2–4. Booking recommended, tel. 01872 864452. Joint ticket for garden and china collection £10.60, NT members £4. Fal River Links partnership ferries to Trelissick landing stage from Falmouth, Truro and St Mawes. Service operates May to Sept. Check with operators for times and disabled access

ℹ **T** 01872 862090, 01872 865515 (shop), 01872 863486 (catering)
E trelissick@nationaltrust.org.uk

😃 Theatrical, musical and winter events

🧍 NT *Coast of Cornwall* leaflet 17 – Trelissick woodland walks

Trelissick Garden		M	T	W	T	F	S	S
1 Feb–2 Nov	10:30–5:30	M	T	W	T	F	S	S
3 Nov–23 Dec	11–4	M	T	W	T	F	S	S
27 Dec–31 Dec	11–4	M	T	W	T	F	S	S
2 Jan–31 Jan 09	11–4	M	T	W	T	F	S	S
Woodland walks								
All year		M	T	W	T	F	S	S
Garden closes dusk if earlier								

Dogs assisting visitors with disabilities are always welcome

♿ ♿ ♿ ♿ ♿ ♿ ♿ ♿ Grounds ♿ ➤ ♿

📺 Shop, art gallery, Cornwall Crafts gallery. Plant sales

📺 Crofters restaurant (licensed). Last orders 30mins before closing. Children's menu. Ice-cream kiosk in car park, limited opening. Sunday lunches in Barn Function Room (licensed). Booking required, tel. 01872 863486. Also available for conferences and banquets

📺 Baby-changing facilities. Pushchairs and baby back-carriers admitted

📺 Suitable for school groups. Education room/centre

📺 Dogs on leads in the park and on woodland walks only; not allowed in the garden

➡ [204:SW837396] **Cycle**: NCN3. **Ferry**: link from Falmouth, Truro and St Mawes (see www.falriverlinks.co.uk). Enterprise boats 01326 374241, K&S Cruisers 01326 211056, Newman's Cruises/Tolverne Ferries 01872 580309. **Bus**: Truronian T16 from Truro (passing close ⛾ Truro). **Station**: Truro 5ml; Perranwell (U), 4ml. **Road**: 4ml S of Truro, on B3289 above King Harry Ferry

P Parking, 50yds, £3.50 (refunded on admission to garden)

NT properties nearby
Glendurgan Garden, Trerice

Detail of the Stream Garden at Trengwainton, Cornwall

Trengwainton Garden

Madron, nr Penzance, Cornwall TR20 8RZ

♿ ♿ ♿ ♿ ♿ ♿ ♿ ♿ ♿ 1961   **(1:B9)**

Sheltered garden with an abundance of exotic trees and shrubs

Intimately linked to the picturesque stream running the length of the garden, paths lead up to a terrace and summerhouses, from where there are splendid views across Mount's Bay to The Lizard. The walled gardens contain many rare and unusual species which are difficult to grow in the open anywhere else in the country. Kitchen garden crops are gradually being reintroduced into the productive area. Visitors can climb on to a raised platform to take in the scale of the walled gardens and their unique raised beds, built to the dimensions of Noah's Ark, as described in *The Bible*.

ℹ **T** 01736 363148, 01736 362297 (shop), 01736 331717 (tea-room)
E trengwainton@nationaltrust.org.uk

♿ By arrangement

♿ ♿ ♿ ♿ ♿ ♿ ♿ ♿ Grounds ♿ ➤

📺 NT shop. Plant sales

📺 Tea-room (NT-approved concession) adjacent to car park. Range of non-allergenic products. Children's menu

📺 Baby-changing facilities. Pushchairs and baby back-carriers admitted. Children's quiz/trail

📺 Suitable for school groups

📺 On leads only in garden, not tea-room garden

➡ [203:SW445315] **Foot**: footpath to the property from Penzance via Heamoor. **Cycle**: NCN3, 2½ml. **Bus**: First 17/A/B St Ives–St Just (passing ⛾ Penzance). **Station**: Penzance 2ml. **Road**: 2ml NW of Penzance, ½ml W of Heamoor off Penzance–Morvah road (B3312), ½ml off St Just road (A3071)

Trengwainton Garden								
Garden/shop								
10 Feb–2 Nov	10:30–5		**M**	**T**	**W**	**T**	F	S	**S**

Open Good Fri. Tea-room opens 10, last admission 15mins before closing

The Great Chamber, Trerice, Cornwall

P Free parking, 150yds

NT properties nearby
Godolphin, Levant Beam Engine,
St Michael's Mount

Trerice

Kestle Mill, nr Newquay, Cornwall TR8 4PG

T 1953 (1:C8)

Elizabethan manor house with fine interiors and delightful garden

A grand Elizabethan manor on a Cornish scale, Trerice remains little changed by the advances in building fashions over the centuries, thanks to long periods under absentee owners. Today the renowned stillness and tranquillity of Trerice, much prized by visitors, is occasionally pierced by the curious lilts of Tudor music or shouts of excitement from the Bowling Green (surely you will want to try a game of Kayling or Slapcock?), bringing back some of the bustle and noise that must have typified its time as a busy manor house.

i T 01637 875404
E trerice@nationaltrust.org.uk

Living history, children's craft activities, guided tours and lecture lunches

Building Grounds

NT shop. Plant sales

Tea-room (licensed) in Great Barn. Children's menu. Tea-garden (licensed)

Baby-changing and feeding facilities. Hip-carrying infant seats for loan. Children's quiz/trail. Children's craft activities

Suitable for school groups. Education room/centre. Live interpretation. Hands-on activities

Trerice								
House/shop								
9 Mar–2 Nov		11–5	M	T	W	T	F	S S

Tea-room & garden open 10:30. Tea-room: last serving 4:30. Garden, tea-room, shop & Great Hall open 6–7, 13–14, 20–21 Dec, 11–3, Sat & Sun

Unless indicated, last admission is always 30mins before closing time

The east front of Tyntesfield: a magical place, created by four generations of the Gibbs family

→ [200:SW841585] **Cycle**: NCN32.
Bus: Western Greyhound 527 ⊞ Newquay–
⊞ St Austell, alight Kestle Mill, ¾ml.
Station: Quintrell Downs (U), 1½ml.
Road: 3ml SE of Newquay via A392 and
A3058 signed from Quintrell Downs (turn
right at Kestle Mill), or signed from A30 at
Summercourt via A3058

P Free parking, 300yds. Coach access only via
Kestle Mill 1ml

NT properties nearby
Carnewas and Bedruthan Steps, Cornish Mines
and Engines, Lanhydrock, Trelissick Garden

Tyntesfield

Wraxall, North Somerset BS48 1NT

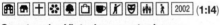 2002 (1:14)

**Spectacular Victorian country house
and grounds**

Tyntesfield, a glorious Gothic Revival
extravaganza, is a magical place, bristling with
towers and turrets, created by four generations
of the Gibbs family. Each generation left its mark
on Tyntesfield, and the house gives a unique
insight into the changing world of an English
country estate. Following the death of the
second Lord Wraxall, and a dramatic fundraising
campaign, Tyntesfield was saved by the nation,
for the nation. This exciting estate gives visitors
the chance to experience work in progress and
see the conservation building project in action.
Surrounding the house, the formal terraced
gardens lead down through rolling parkland
to the wonderful walled kitchen garden (still
in production).

What's new in 2008 Conservation work on the
house and estate buildings, funded from the
2006-2012 Heritage Lottery Fund Project

★ The project at Tyntesfield is still in the early
stages of development, but the property
offers a unique insight into the work needed
to conserve an estate. During 2008, visitors
will have the opportunity to experience the
conservation building work on the house and
on other buildings around the estate. This
work may, at times, result in limited access to
some parts of the property. Visitors can now
see all the ground-floor rooms. Facilities on-
site are temporary and basic while planning is
underway for new visitor facilities. Admission
to the house is by timed ticket for all visitors.
Tickets are issued at visitor reception on
arrival and cannot be booked. Entry to the
property and car park cannot be guaranteed
on busy days. Tel. Infoline for details

For further information go to www.nationaltrust.org.uk

ℹ️ **T** 0844 800 4986 (Infoline), 01275 461900
E tyntesfield@nationaltrust.org.uk

🏃 Out-of-hours house tours Wed & Sun at 10:15 only. Tel. 0871 527 1885

🎭 Including concerts and children's activities

🚶 Please ask at reception for details of walks

♿ 🚻 ⟁ ⬛ 🅿️ 🚌 Building 🔉 ♿
Grounds 🧏

🏪 Tyntesfield souvenirs, local Somerset produce and a plant centre with garden furniture

🍽️ Temporary kiosk serving light refreshments (no hot meals). Seating area in marquee

👶 Baby-changing facilities. Front-carrying baby slings and hip-carrying infant seats for loan. Children's quiz/trail. Family activity packs

🐕 Access restricted to some estate walks (not near the house or in gardens)

➡️ [172:ST506715] **Bus**: First 354 Bristol–Nailsea (drops on B3130 at bottom of drive). **Station**: Nailsea & Backwell 3½ml. **Road**: on B3128 at Wraxall. 7ml SW of Bristol; M5 southbound exit 19 via A369 (towards Bristol) and B3129. M5 Northbound exit 20, B3130 (towards Bristol), B3128

🅿️ Free parking. The car park is temporary, 1,000yds (transfer is available for those who prefer not to walk). Parking is limited and access to the car park cannot be guaranteed. Tight corners. One-way system

NT properties nearby
Blaise Hamlet, Clevedon Court, Dyrham Park, Leigh Woods, Prior Park

Tyntesfield									
House/chapel									
1 Mar–9 Mar	11–5	M	T	W	T	F	**S**	**S**	
15 Mar–2 Nov	11–5	**M**	**T**	**W**	T	F	**S**	**S**	
Gardens/visitor reception/shop/catering kiosk									
1 Mar–9 Mar	10:30–5:30	M	T	W	T	F	**S**	**S**	
15 Mar–2 Nov	10:30–5:30	**M**	**T**	**W**	T	F	**S**	**S**	
6 Dec–21 Dec	10–5	M	T	W	T	F	**S**	**S**	

Open Good Fri. Last admission to house 1hr before closing. Free flow entry by timed ticket. Entry cannot be guaranteed on busy days. Rooms may close for conservation work

Watersmeet

Watersmeet Road, Lynmouth, Devon EX35 6NT

🏠 🛶 🏞️ 🏠 🍴 🍽️ 🏃 👶 🚶 1996   (1:F5)

Dramatic river gorge and ancient woodlands near the rocky North Devon coast

A haven for wildlife, with waterfalls and excellent walking, where the lush valleys of the East Lyn and Hoar Oak Water tumble together. At the heart of this area sits Watersmeet House, a 19th-century fishing lodge, which is now an NT tea-room and tea-garden, shop and information point.

⭐ Property in deep gorge

ℹ️ **T** 01598 753348
E watersmeet@nationaltrust.org.uk

🏃 See local listings for guided walks on Watersmeet Estate

🚶 Walks leaflet from shop

♿ 🚻 🚌 Building 🔉 Grounds 🧏

🍽️ Tea-garden

👶 Baby-changing facilities. Children's quiz/trail

🐕 Including in the tea-garden

➡️ [180:SS744487] **Foot**: South West Coast Path within ⅔ml. **Bus**: TW Coaches 309, 310 from Barnstaple (passing close ⬛ Barnstaple), Quantock 300 from Minehead; Filers 300 from Ilfracombe. On all, alight Lynmouth, then walk through NT gorge. **Road**: 1½ml E of Lynmouth, in valley on E side of Lynmouth–Barnstaple road (A39)

🅿️ Parking (not NT), 500yds (pay & display). Free NT car parks at Combepark, Hillsford Bridge and Countisbury

NT properties nearby
Arlington Court, Dunster Castle, Holnicote Estate, West Exmoor Coast

Watersmeet								
Watersmeet								
All year		**M**	**T**	**W**	**T**	**F**	**S**	**S**
House								
15 Mar–31 Mar	10:30–4:30	**M**	**T**	**W**	**T**	**F**	**S**	**S**
1 Apr–30 Sep	10:30–5:30	**M**	**T**	**W**	**T**	**F**	**S**	**S**
1 Oct–2 Nov	10:30–4:30	**M**	**T**	**W**	**T**	**F**	**S**	**S**

West Exmoor Coast

Heddon Valley, Parracombe, Barnstaple, Devon
EX31 4PY

🐾 1963   **(1:F5)**

Towering cliffs, secluded coves and a beautiful wooded valley within Exmoor National Park

A favourite landscape of the Romantic poets and smugglers, with the Heddon Valley, Woody Bay and Hangman Hills to explore. This area offers spectacular coastal and woodland walks, as well as a NT information centre and gift shop in the Heddon Valley.

ℹ️ **T** 01598 763402
E heddonvalley@nationaltrust.org.uk

🦮 See local listings for guided walks on the local estate

🎭 See local listing for events throughout the year

🚶 Walks leaflet available from the National Trust shop and local tourist information centres

♿

🍦 Ice-cream kiosk in shop

👪 Children's activity packs. Tracker Packs. All-terrain pushchairs for loan

🏫 Suitable for school groups

➡️ [180:SS655481] **Foot**: South West Coast Path within ⅜ml. **Bus**: TW Coaches 309, 310 Barnstaple–Lynton (passing close ➤ Barnstaple), alight just N of Parracombe, then 2ml. **Road**: halfway between Combe Martin and Lynton, off A39 at Hunters Inn

🅿️ Parking, 50yds. Donations welcome

NT properties nearby
Arlington Court, Dunster Castle, Holnicote Estate, Watersmeet

West Exmoor Coast								
West Exmoor Coast								
All year		M	T	W	T	F	S	S
Heddon Valley Shop								
15 Mar–4 Jul	11–5	M	T	W	T	F	S	S
5 Jul–31 Aug	10:30–5:30	M	T	W	T	F	S	S
1 Sep–2 Nov	11–5	M	T	W	T	F	S	S

For information regarding prices, see page 10

West Pennard Court Barn

West Pennard, nr Glastonbury, Somerset
BA6 8LR

🏠 1938   **(1:I5)**

15th-century barn with an unusual roof

⭐ Access by key only – see opening arrangements. Upper floor of the barn is of compacted earth. The surroundings are pastures grazed by cows. In winter the ground is wet and soft – suitable footwear advised. No WC

ℹ️ **T** 01985 843600 (Regional office), 01458 850212
E westpennardcourtbarn@nationaltrust.org.uk

➡️ 3ml E of Glastonbury, 7ml S of Wells, 1½ml S of West Pennard (A361)

West Pennard Court Barn

Admission by appointment. Access by key, to be collected by arrangement with Mr P. H. Green, Court Barn Farm, West Bradley, Somerset. Tel. 01458 850212

Westbury College Gatehouse

College Road, Westbury-on-Trym, Bristol
BS9 3EH

🏠 👪 1907   **(1:I3)**

15th-century gatehouse

⭐ Access by key, Mon to Fri only – see opening arrangements. No WC

ℹ️ **T** 01275 461900
E westburycollege@nationaltrust.org.uk

➡️ 3ml N of the centre of Bristol

Westbury College Gatehouse

Access (Mon–Fri) by key to be collected by appointment from the Parish Office, Church Road, Westbury-on-Trym, Bristol BS9 4AG. Tel 0117 950 8644

The Parterre, Westbury Court Garden, Gloucestershire

Westbury Court Garden

Westbury-on-Severn, Gloucestershire GL14 1PD

❈ ◨ 🕇 ⎕ ⛨ 🚹 1967   **(1:J2)**

Dutch water garden – a rare and beautiful survival

Originally laid out between 1696 and 1705, this is the only restored Dutch water garden in the country. Visitors can explore canals, clipped hedges and working 17th-century vegetable plots and discover many old varieties of fruit trees.

What's new in 2008 New wall fruit trees and orchard trees planted in the winter

ℹ️ **T** 01452 760461
   E westburycourt@nationaltrust.org.uk

🕇 Evening guided tours (book at garden): 14 May, 11 June, 9 July, 6 Aug

😊 Easter Trail 21–24 March. Apple Day 18–19 Oct

♿ 🚾 ⠿ 📱 **Grounds** 🏛️

◨ Coffee machine. Hot and cold drinks

Westbury Court Garden									
12 Mar–30 Jun	10–5	M	T	**W**	**T**	**F**	**S**	**S**
1 Jul–31 Aug	10–5	**M**	**T**	**W**	**T**	**F**	**S**	**S**
1 Sep–26 Oct	10–5	M	T	**W**	**T**	**F**	**S**	**S**

Open BH Mons. Open other times of year by appointment

🚹 Pushchairs and baby back-carriers admitted. Family guide. Children's quiz/trail. Easter trail

➔ [162:SO718138] **Foot**: River Severn footpath runs from garden to river. **Bus**: Stagecoach in South Wales 73 🚃 Gloucester–Chepstow; Stagecoach in Wye & Dean 30/31 🚃 Gloucester–Coleford. **Station**: Gloucester 9ml. **Road**: 9ml SW of Gloucester on A48

🅿️ Free parking, 3yds

NT properties nearby
Ashleworth Tithe Barn, The Kymin, May Hill, The Weir

Westwood Manor

Bradford-on-Avon, Wiltshire BA15 2AF

🏛️ ✝ ❈ ▯ 🚹 1960   **(1:J4)**

15th-century stone manor house

The manor house, altered in the 17th century, has splendid late Gothic and Jacobean windows and ornate plasterwork. It contains a fine collection of exceptional period furniture, 17th- and 18th-century tapestries and needlework, as well as a number of important stringed musical instruments. Attractive views can be enjoyed from the modern topiary garden.

⭐ Westwood Manor is administered for the NT by the tenant. No WC

Many Trust properties are offering Gift Aid on Entry for non-members, see page 10

Westwood Manor

Westwood Manor								
23 Mar–30 Sep	2–5	M	**T**	**W**	T	F	S	**S**
Small groups at other times by written application with sae to the tenant								

i **T** 01225 863374
E westwoodmanor@nationaltrust.org.uk

♿ ⁝ Ⓜ Ⓝ **Building** Ⓟ **Grounds** Ⓟ

⛹ Hip-carrying infant seats for loan. Children's quiz/trail. House unsuitable for under-fives

➞ [173:ST812590] **Cycle**: NCN4, ¾ml.
Bus: Libra 94, Bodmans 96 ⚲ Bath–Trowbridge (passing close ⚲ Trowbridge).
Station: Avoncliff (U), 1ml; Bradford-on-Avon 1½ml. **Road**: 1½ml SW of Bradford-on-Avon, in Westwood village, beside the church; village signposted off Bradford-on-Avon to Rode road (B3109)

P Free parking, 90yds

NT properties nearby
The Courts Garden, Dyrham Park, Great Chalfield Manor and Garden, Lacock Abbey

White Mill

Sturminster Marshall, nr Wimborne, Dorset BH21 4BX

⚑ Ⓜ Ⓟ ⛹ ⚐ 1982   (1:K6)

Corn mill with original wooden machinery in a peaceful riverside setting

★ No WC, nearest at the Mill House

i **T** 01258 858051
E whitemill@nationaltrust.org.uk

➞ On the River Stour in the parish of Shapwick, close to Sturminster Marshall

White Mill								
22 Mar–2 Nov	12–5	M	T	W	T	F	**S**	**S**
Admission by guided tour. Open BH Mons: 12–5, last tour 4								

Woodchester Park

Nympsfield, nr Stroud, Gloucestershire GL10 3TS

⚑ ⁝ Ⓜ Ⓝ 1994   (1:J3)

Beautiful secluded Cotswold valley

The tranquil, wooded valley contains a 'lost landscape' – the remains of an 18th- and 19th-century landscape park with a chain of five lakes. Waymarked trails (steep in places) lead through picturesque scenery. An unfinished Victorian mansion (not NT) is open on specified days from Easter to October.

★ Address for correspondence for NT Woodchester Park: The Ebworth Centre, Ebworth Estate, The Camp, Stroud, Glos GL6 7ES. Woodchester mansion is not NT; for details, contact the Woodchester Mansion Trust, tel. 01453 861541.
WC not always available

i **T** 01452 814213
E woodchesterpark@nationaltrust.org.uk

Ⓜ Tours by arrangement

Ⓝ Contact warden for details

♿ **Grounds** Ⓟ

⛹ Under close control, on leads where requested

➞ [162:SO797012] **Foot**: Cotswold Way within ⅔ml. **Bus**: Ebley 35 Stoud–Nympsfield (passing close ⚲ Stroud). **Station**: Stroud 5ml. **Road**: 4ml SW of Stroud off B4066 Stroud–Dursley road

P Parking, £1.50 (pay & display). Accessible from Nympsfield road, 300yds from junction with B4066. Last admission to car park 1hr before dusk

NT properties nearby
Haresfield Beacon, Newark Park, Rodborough Common, Stroud Commons

Woodchester Park								
All year	9–dusk	M	T	W	T	F	S	S

While the South and South East is one of England's most densely populated and urbanised areas, it still boasts extensive and beautiful open spaces, as well as miles of dramatic coastline for visitors to enjoy. That so much has survived is due largely to the work of the National Trust, which over many decades has acquired and protected land threatened by development and insensitive use.

Ditchling Beacon in East Sussex

Countryside in Kent ranges from parts of the densely wooded Kentish Weald to the world-famous White Cliffs of Dover. In Sussex the Trust cares for large areas of the South Downs – ranging from the steep escarpment at Devil's Dyke to the highest point in East Sussex at Ditchling Beacon, as well as the dramatic coastline of the Seven Sisters.

Surrey offers steep chalk downland at Box Hill, lowland heath at the Devil's Punch Bowl, ancient woodland on Leith Hill and flower-rich meadows on the hillside at Denbies.

The Ashridge Estate, on the border of Buckinghamshire and Hertfordshire, is a vast area of magnificent Chilterns countryside, featuring woodlands, commons and fine chalk downland. These support a wide range of flora and fauna, and offer much for visitors to enjoy – from stimulating walks to gentle strolls. There are many perfect picnic spots and some of the best views in the

Above: **Royal Military Canal in Kent** Below: **the Ashridge Estate**

South East. Don't miss the new Discovery Room in the Visitor Centre, next to the Bridgewater Monument, where you can find out much more about the history and wildlife of this precious estate.

There are numerous places for peaceful walks alongside rivers and canals, which are partly owned by the National Trust. The Trust holds 3 miles of the Royal Military Canal between Appledore and Warehorne in Romney Marsh, Kent, which was built as a defence against Napoleonic invasion. While there are nearly 20 miles of pleasant waterside to enjoy beside the River Wey in Surrey. Find out about the history of the waterway and take part in events at Dapdune Wharf or enjoy a boat ride.

Previous page: Illusionist painting of books and papers, Mottisfont Abbey, Hampshire (2:C7)

The Slindon Estate in West Sussex

Watch wildlife in its natural habitat in the woods, heathland and countryside managed by the Trust. At Toys Hill, near Westerham in Kent, there are large stretches of woodland where you can observe birds and mammals and identify plants and trees. While in West Sussex, Devil's Dyke, and Harting Down, near Petersfield, are havens for downland flora and fauna. Take your binoculars and camera, leave the paths and go exploring.

Enjoy idyllic English scenery on a stroll through open downland on the Sussex coast. Birling Gap is the place to go for spectacular sea views of the South Coast's lesser-known white cliffs: The Seven Sisters, near Eastbourne in East Sussex. Of course there are also the iconic White Cliffs of Dover in Kent, and the nearby Victorian lighthouse and keeper's cottage of South Foreland, where there are wonderful walks and even more panoramic views. For beautiful sandy beaches and dunes go to East Head, near Chichester Harbour in West Sussex.

As well as grand mansions, the National Trust protects many small gems tucked away in quiet countryside. The Slindon Estate, 6 miles north of Bognor Regis on the A29 in West Sussex, includes 17th-century flint cottages in Slindon village, which are owned by the Trust. There is also a row

Above: marbled white butterfly
Below: East Head in West Sussex

of Trust houses in the beautiful village of Chiddingstone, near Edenbridge in Kent. These date from the 16th and 17th centuries and are made mainly of timber, with plaster or brick fillings. Other Trust buildings in the village include the post office and the Castle Inn.

In the picturesque village of Long Crendon, near Aylesbury in Buckinghamshire, the old Courthouse is a fine example of an early timber-frame building where manorial courts were held from the time of King Henry VIII to the end of the 19th century. Nearby is the Boarstall Duck Decoy, a rare example of a once common device to trap duck, and the intriguing Boarstall Tower, which has fascinating links with the English Civil War.

www.nationaltrust.org.uk/coastandcountryside

White Horse Hill,
Uffington

Above: fly agaric.
Right: Devil's Dyke
in Sussex Below
left: Coldrum Long
Barrow in Kent
Below right:
Bembridge Windmill
on the Isle of Wight

burial chamber. Cissbury Ring, near Worthing in Sussex, was the site of intensive flint-mining in the early Neolithic period. There are also remains of an Iron Age hill fort and Roman fortifications to be explored.

One of the most famous ancient landmarks in the country is at Uffington in Oxfordshire. The White Horse, which can be seen for miles around, has been the subject of discussion since the 17th century. Thought to date from the Iron Age, it is referred to in 12th-century written records, however no one knows exactly why or when it was created.

Saddlescombe Farm, near Devil's Dyke in Sussex, is open on certain days each year to give visitors the opportunity to discover this fascinating ancient downland farm, which has more than 1,000 years of history. The open days include tours of the 17th-century farm buildings, the surrounding downs and the walled garden. Booked tours for interested groups are available throughout the summer.

Reigate Fort, just off the M25 in Surrey, is newly opened to visitors. Built in 1898 as one of thirteen military installations stretching from the North Downs to Essex, the fort is still intact today – with magazine rooms, a tool store, firing step and casemates to explore. Visitors can see the exterior of the fort structures, while information boards show how the interiors looked. A guidebook, guided tours inside the buildings and special study days for groups are available. There is also a virtual picture gallery on the National Trust website.

Find out about ancient civilisations at Coldrum Long Barrow near Trottiscliffe in Kent, where the Trust owns a Neolithic

■ For details of the open days at Saddlescombe Farm, see the regional newsletter events list. For group tours, telephone 01273 857712.

■ For details of the guidebook, guided tours and study days at Reigate Fort, telephone 01342 843225.

Alfriston Clergy House

The Tye, Alfriston, Polegate, East Sussex
BN26 5TL

🏠 ✳️ 🏛️ 🍴 🎒 🎭 🚶 🖼️ 1896   (2:H8)

Medieval thatched cottage and picturesque garden

This 14th-century thatched Wealden 'hall house' was the first building to be acquired by the National Trust in 1896. It has an unusual chalk and sour milk floor, and its pretty cottage garden is in an idyllic setting beside Alfriston's parish church, with views across the meandering River Cuckmere.

⭐ No WC. Nearest in village car park

ℹ️ **T** 01323 870001
   E alfriston@nationaltrust.org.uk

🎭 Themed hunts held during school holidays. Themed family fun days throughout season

♿ 👓🔊 **Building** 🔎 **Grounds** ♿

👨‍👧 Pushchairs and baby back-carriers admitted. Children's quiz/trail

🖼️ Suitable for school groups

➡️ [189:TQ521029] **Foot**: South Downs Way within ⅔ml. **Cycle**: NCN2.

The herb garden, Alfriston Clergy House, East Sussex

Alfriston Clergy House									
1 Mar—9 Mar	11—4	M	T	W	T	F	S	S
15 Mar—26 Oct	10—5	**M**	T	**W**	**T**	F	**S**	**S**
27 Oct—21 Dec	11—4	**M**	T	**W**	**T**	F	**S**	**S**
Open Good Fri								

Bus: Countryliner 125 from Lewes, Renown 126 from Eastbourne & Seaford (pass close ➡ Lewes and Seaford), Cuckmere Valley Rambler bus, weekends only from Berwick. **Station**: Berwick (U) 2½ml. **Road**: 4ml NE of Seaford, just E of B2108, in Alfriston village, adjoining The Tye and St Andrew's Church

🅿️ Parking (not NT), 500yds at other end of village

NT properties nearby

Bateman's, Frog Firle Farm, Monk's House, Sheffield Park Garden

Ascott

Wing, nr Leighton Buzzard, Buckinghamshire
LU7 0PS

🏠 ✳️ 1949   (2:E3)

Jacobean house remodelled in the 19th century, with superb collections and gardens

Originally a half-timbered farmhouse, Ascott was bought in 1876 by the de Rothschild family and considerably transformed and enlarged. It now houses a quite exceptional collection of fine paintings, Oriental porcelain and English and French furniture. The extensive gardens are a mixture of the formal and natural, containing specimen trees and shrubs, as well as a herbaceous walk, lily pond, Dutch garden and remarkable topiary sundial.

ℹ️ **T** 01296 688242
   E ascott@nationaltrust.org.uk

Ascott									
25 Mar—27 Apr	2—6	M	**T**	**W**	**T**	**F**	**S**	**S**
29 Apr—24 Jul	2—6	M	**T**	**W**	**T**	F	**S**	**S**
29 Jul—12 Sep	2—6	M	**T**	**W**	**T**	**F**	**S**	**S**
Open BH Mons. Last admission 1hr before closing. Garden open in aid of NGS on Mons 5 May and 25 Aug (NT members pay on these days)									

Unless indicated, last admission is always 30mins before closing time

🚻 ♿🐕📶♿📷💧 Building 👶🚻
Grounds 👶➡️

➡️ [165:SP891230] **Bus**: Arriva X15 Aylesbury–
Milton Keynes (passing close 🚉 Aylesbury &
Leighton Buzzard). **Station**: Leighton
Buzzard 2ml. **Road**: ½ml E of Wing, 2ml SW
of Leighton Buzzard, on S side of A418

🅿️ Free parking, 220yds

NT properties nearby
Ashridge Estate, Claydon House

Ashdown House

Lambourn, Newbury, Berkshire RG17 8RE

 1956 **(2:C5)**

**Unusual Dutch-style house on the
Berkshire Downs**

There are spectacular views from the roof of this
highly distinctive house with beautiful walks in
the neighbouring Ashdown Woods.

⭐ Ashdown House is in the county of
Oxfordshire. Postal address as above.
No WC. The house is tenanted and access
is limited to the staircase and roof

ℹ️ **T** 01494 755569 (Infoline), 01793 762209
E ashdownhouse@nationaltrust.org.uk

♿ 📶📷💧 Building 👶 Grounds 👶

🐕 On leads and only in woodland

➡️ [174:SU282820] **Bus**: Thamesdown 47
Swindon–Lambourn, with connections from
Newbury (passing close 🚉 Swindon &
Newbury). **Road**: 2½ml S of Ashbury, 3½ml N
of Lambourn, on W side of B4000

🅿️ Free parking, 250yds. Not suitable for coaches

NT properties nearby
Avebury, Buscot Park, Great Coxwell Barn,
White Horse Hill

Ashdown House									
House/garden									
2 Apr–29 Oct	2–5	M	T	**W**	T	F	**S**	S
Woodland									
All year	Dawn–dusk	**M**	**T**	**W**	**T**	F	**S**	**S**
Admission by guided tour to house at 2:15, 3:15 & 4:15. Numbers limited									

Ashridge Estate

Visitor Centre, Moneybury Hill, Ringshall,
Berkhamsted, Hertfordshire HP4 1LX

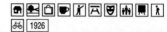
🚲 1926 **(2:E3)**

Vast area of open downland and woods

This magnificent and varied estate runs across
the borders of Herts and Bucks, along the main
ridge of the Chiltern Hills. There are 2,000
hectares (5,000 acres) of woodlands, commons
and chalk downland supporting a rich variety of
wildlife and offering splendid walks through
outstanding scenery. The area's focal point
is the Monument, erected in 1832 to the
Duke of Bridgewater. There are also spectacular
views from Ivinghoe Beacon, accessible from
Steps Hill.

What's new in 2008 Discovery Room with
aerial-view map, colourful wildlife murals and
hands-on interactive displays for children

⭐ WC not always available

ℹ️ **T** 01494 755557 (Infoline), 01442 851227
E ashridge@nationaltrust.org.uk

🏃 Programme of guided walks all year

😀 Children's workshops and activity days.
Guided walks

🚶 Extensive network of paths. Information about
self-guided walks available from the shop

♿ 🚻🚻♿📶📷💧 Grounds 👶➡️🦽

Ashridge Estate									
Estate									
All year		**M**	**T**	**W**	**T**	**F**	**S**	**S**
Visitor centre/shop									
15 Mar–21 Dec	12–5	**M**	**T**	**W**	**T**	**F**	**S**	**S**
Monument									
15 Mar–26 Oct	12–5	M	T	W	T	F	**S**	**S**
Tea-room									
1 Feb–29 Feb	10–5	M	**T**	**W**	**T**	**F**	**S**	**S**
15 Mar–21 Dec	10–5	**M**	**T**	**W**	**T**	**F**	**S**	**S**
31 Dec–31 Jan 09	10–4	M	**T**	**W**	**T**	**F**	**S**	**S**
Open BH Mons and Good Fri: 12–5. Monument: last admission 4:30. Monument also Mon–Fri by arrangement, weather permitting. Shop and tea-room close dusk if earlier than 5									

The Ashridge Estate supports a rich variety of wildlife

🍽 Licensed tea-room (NT-approved concession) in visitor centre. Children's menu

♿ Baby-changing facilities. Pushchairs and baby back-carriers admitted. Family activity packs. Children's workshops and activity days

🎒 Suitable for school groups. Education room/centre. Hands-on activities. Learn & Discover at the Ashridge Estate. Primary school programme

🐕 Under close control

🚲 Short stretch of permitted cycle path and 9ml of bridleways giving cyclists shared access

➡ [181:SP970131] **Foot**: 2¾ml of The Ridgeway on property. **Bus**: Monument: Arriva 30/31 from 🚃 Tring, alight Aldbury, ½ml. Beacon: Arriva 61 Aylesbury–Luton (passing close 🚃 Aylesbury and Luton); Centrebus 327 from Tring to Monument and Beacon, Suns May–Sept only. **Station**: Monument: Tring 1¾ml; Beacon: Cheddington 3½ml. **Road**: between Berkhamsted and Northchurch, and Ringshall and Dagnall, just off B4506

🅿 Free parking, 50yds

NT properties nearby
Chilterns Gateway Centre, Pitstone Windmill, Shaw's Corner, Whipsnade Tree Cathedral

Basildon Park

Lower Basildon, Reading, Berkshire RG8 9NR

🏠 ❄ 🌱 🏛 🍽 🎯 🎨 🛡 ♿ 🎒

🚶 🔔 🍴 1978 **(2:D5)**

18th-century country house set in extensive parkland

This beautiful Palladian mansion featured in the recent film adaptation of Jane Austen's *Pride and Prejudice*. It was built in 1776–83 by John Carr for Francis Sykes, who had made his fortune in India. The interior is notable for its original delicate plasterwork and elegant staircase, as well as for the unusual Octagon Room. The house fell on hard times early in the last century, but was rescued by Lord and Lady Iliffe, who restored it and filled it with fine pictures and furniture. The early 19th-century pleasure grounds are being restored, and there are waymarked trails through the parkland.

What's new in 2008 Children's trails

ℹ **T** 0118 984 3040
   E basildonpark@nationaltrust.org.uk

🎯 Morning guided tour: £4 members, £10 non-members. Tel. for prices of evening tour

🛡 Family events, lecture lunches, concerts

🚶 Leaflet with details of waymarked trails

♿ 🚻 🎨 🔊 ⬛ 🅿 **Building** 🦽🦽
Grounds 🦽

🍽 Licensed restaurant. Children's menu

♿ Baby-changing facilities. Front-carrying baby slings and hip-carrying infant seats for loan. Children's quiz/trail

Basildon Park									
House									
19 Mar–26 Oct	12–5	M	T	**W**	**T**	**F**	**S**	**S**
10 Dec–14 Dec	12–4	M	T	**W**	**T**	**F**	**S**	**S**
Shop									
19 Mar–26 Oct	11–5	M	T	**W**	**T**	**F**	**S**	**S**
29 Oct–21 Dec	12–4	M	T	**W**	**T**	**F**	**S**	**S**
10 Dec–14 Dec	11–5	M	T	**W**	**T**	**F**	**S**	**S**
Restaurant/grounds									
As house	11–5	M	T	**W**	**T**	**F**	**S**	**S**

Open BH Mons. House and shop close 7 on 12 Dec. Property closes at 4 on 15, 16 & 17 Aug for firework concerts

The elegant Octagon Room at Basildon Park in Berkshire

🏛 Suitable for school groups

🐕 On leads and only in park, woodland and grounds

→ [175:SU611782] **Bus**: Thames Travel 132 ▣ Reading–▣ Goring & Streatley.
Station: Pangbourne 2½ml; Goring & Streatley 3ml. **Road**: between Pangbourne and Streatley, 7ml NW of Reading, on W side of A329; leave M4 at exit 12 and follow A4 to Newbury, then brown NT signs to Pangbourne. If coming from Oxford take A34 ring road and leave at Henley/Reading junction, then turn right at roundabout for Wallingford bypass, cross river and take first left on to A329

🅿 Free parking, 400yds

NT properties nearby
Greys Court, The Vyne

Bateman's

Burwash, Etchingham, East Sussex TN19 7DS

🏛 🏠 ✖ ⬆ ✿ 🗄 ⬜ 🚪 😃 👫
🚶 [1940]   **(2:H7)**

Jacobean house, home of Rudyard Kipling

The interior of this beautiful 17th-century house, Rudyard Kipling's home from 1902 to 1936, reflects the author's strong associations with the East. There are many oriental rugs and artefacts, and most of the rooms – including his book-lined study – are much as Kipling left them.

For information regarding prices, see page 10

The delightful grounds run down to the small River Dudwell with its watermill, and contain roses, wild flowers, fruit and herbs. Kipling's Rolls-Royce is also on display.

What's new in 2008 Room information sheets in the house. Improved virtual tour

⭐ The garden is open free of charge in November and December. Shop and tea-room are open the same time as the garden during these months

ℹ️ **T** 01435 882302
   E batemans@nationaltrust.org.uk

😃 Family Fun days, Kipling literary days, Paint the garden. Easter Egg trails, Jungle Hunt trails, Hallowe'en trails

🚶 Garden and estate walks

♿ 🚾 🤱 ⠿ 📷 🅿 🐕 Building 🪜 ♿
Grounds 🏞 ➡

Bateman's									
House									
15 Mar–2 Nov	11–5		**M**	**T**	**W**	T	F	**S**	**S**
Garden/tea-room/shop									
1 Mar–9 Mar	11–4		M	T	W	T	F	**S**	**S**
15 Mar–2 Nov	11–5*		**M**	**T**	**W**	T	F	**S**	**S**
5 Nov–23 Dec	11–4		M	T	**W**	**T**	**F**	**S**	**S**

Open Good Fri: 11–5. The mill grinds corn most Weds and Sats at 2. ***Shop closes 5:30 March–Oct**. Shop, tea-room and garden open 22 and 23 Dec

🛍 NT shop with largest collection of Kipling books for sale in the area

🍽 Mulberry Tea-room (licensed). Children's menu

👶 Baby-changing facilities. Front-carrying baby slings and hip-carrying infant seats for loan. Children's guide. Children's quiz/trail

🐕 On leads and only in car park; dog crèche

➡ [199:TQ671238] **Bus**: Renown 318 Uckfield–🚆 Etchingham. **Station**: Etchingham 3ml. **Road**: ½ml S of Burwash. A265 W from Burwash, first turning on left

🅿 Free parking, 30yds. Coaches: tight left turn into first bay

NT properties nearby
Bodiam Castle, Scotney Castle, Sissinghurst Castle Garden

Bembridge Windmill

High Street, Bembridge, Isle of Wight PO35 5SQ

🏍 ⛴ 🛍 🍽 🎓 👶 🖼 🚶 1961 (2:D9)

Grade I listed windmill

Built *c*.1700, this stone-built tower with its wooden cap and machinery is the only surviving windmill on the island. Visitors can explore its four floors and also enjoy the wonderful views.

⭐ No WC

ℹ **T** 01983 873945
  E bembridgemill@nationaltrust.org.uk

Bembridge Windmill									
15 Mar–30 Jun	10–5	M	**T**	**W**	**T**	**F**	**S**	**S**
1 Jul–30 Sep	10–5	M	**T**	**W**	**T**	**F**	**S**	**S**
1 Oct–2 Nov	10–5	M	**T**	**W**	**T**	**F**	**S**	**S**

Closes dusk if earlier. Also open Easter Mon and both May BHol Mons

🎓 Conducted school groups and special visits March to end Oct (but not July or Aug), by written appointment

🚶 The Windmill is the starting point for the Culver trail

♿ 🔊 👓 Dₐ Building 🔧

🛍 Small shop in kiosk

🍽 Kiosk. Tea, coffee and ice-cream

👶 Children's quiz/trail

🖼 Suitable for school groups

➡ [196:SZ639874] **Cycle**: NCN67, ½ml. **Ferry**: Ryde (Wightlink Ltd) 6ml (tel. 0870 582 7744); E Cowes (Red Funnel) 13ml (tel. 0844 844 9988). **Bus**: Southern Vectis 14 from 🚆 Ryde Esplanade to within ½ml; 10 Newport–Sandown to within ¼ml. **Station**: Brading (U) 2ml by footpath. **Road**: ½ml S of Bembridge on B3395

🅿 Free parking (not NT), 100yds in lay-by

NT properties nearby
Brighstone Shop and Museum, Mottistone Manor Garden, The Needles Old Battery and New Battery, Newtown Old Town Hall

Bateman's, East Sussex, the former home of Rudyard Kipling

Boarstall Duck Decoy

Boarstall, nr Aylesbury, Buckinghamshire HP18 9UX

🦆🐾🎯🏠♿🎒🚶 1980 **(2:D3)**

Rare survival of a 17th-century duck decoy in working order, with a woodland nature trail and visitor centre

⭐ WC during opening hours

ℹ️ **T** 01844 237488
E boarstalldecoy@nationaltrust.org.uk

➡️ Midway between Bicester and Thame, 2ml W of Brill

Boarstall Duck Decoy								
5 Apr–25 Aug	10–4	M	T	W	T	F	**S**	**S**
9 Apr–20 Aug	3:30–6	M	T	**W**	T	F	S	S
Open BH Mons: 10–4								

Boarstall Tower

Boarstall, nr Aylesbury, Buckinghamshire HP18 9UX

🏰❄️🎯 1943 **(2:D3)**

14th-century moated gatehouse and gardens

ℹ️ **T** 01280 822850 (Mon–Fri)
E boarstalltower@nationaltrust.org.uk

➡️ Midway between Bicester and Thame, 2ml W of Brill

Boarstall Tower								
2 Apr–29 Oct	2–6	M	T	**W**	T	F	S	S
Open BHol weekends: Sat 11–4, Mon 2–6								

Bodiam Castle

Bodiam, nr Robertsbridge, East Sussex
TN32 5UA

🏰🦆🏠☕🎯🏛️🛡️♿🎒🚶🚂 1926 **(2:I7)**

Perfect example of a late medieval moated castle

One of the most famous and evocative castles in Britain, Bodiam was built in 1385, as both a defence and a comfortable home. The exterior is virtually complete and the ramparts rise dramatically above the moat. Enough of the interior survives to give an impression of castle life. There are spiral staircases and battlements to explore and wonderful views of the Rother Valley from the top of the towers. In the impressive gatehouse is the castle's original wooden portcullis, an extremely rare example of its kind.

What's new in 2008 Completely refurbished museum with new displays that put the castle in its context. New interpretation at the medieval harbour site

⭐ Bodiam Castle is often used by education groups in term time. The only WC is located in the car park, 400yds from the castle entrance

ℹ️ **T** 01580 830196
E bodiamcastle@nationaltrust.org.uk

🎯 Introductory talks on selected days during the summer

🛡️ For details send sae marked 'Events' or visit our website

Bodiam Castle, East Sussex, was built in 1385 as a defence as well as a comfortable home

Bodiam Castle

Castle

1 Feb—15 Feb	10:30—4	M	T	W	T	F	**S**	**S**
16 Feb—31 Oct	10:30—6	**M**	**T**	**W**	**T**	**F**	**S**	**S**
1 Nov—31 Jan 09	10:30—4	M	T	W	T	F	**S**	**S**

Shop/tea-room

1 Feb—15 Feb	10:30—4	M	T	W	T	F	**S**	**S**
16 Feb—31 Oct	10:30—5	**M**	**T**	**W**	**T**	**F**	**S**	**S**
1 Nov—24 Dec	10:30—4	M	T	**W**	**T**	**F**	**S**	**S**
27 Dec—31 Jan 09	10:30—4	M	T	W	T	F	**S**	**S**

Last admission into castle 1hr before closing. Castle closes dusk if earlier than stated. 30 & 31 Aug: historical re-enactment. Additional admission charge may apply

Sussex Border Path runs through estate

Building

Grounds

Wharf Tea-room. Book for private room with waitress service. Children's menu. Ice-cream kiosk open near castle during summer weekends and throughout Aug

Baby-changing facilities. Pushchairs and baby back-carriers admitted. Family guide. Children's activity packs

Suitable for school groups. Education room/centre. Live interpretation. Hands-on activities. Adult study days

On leads and only in grounds

→ [199:TQ785256] **Foot**: on the Sussex Border path. **Ferry**: Bodiam Ferry from Newenden Bridge (A28). **Bus**: Stagecoach in Hastings 349 ☒ Hastings–Hawkhurst. **Station**: Bodiam (Kent & E Sussex Rly) ¼ml; Robertsbridge 5ml. **Road**: 3ml S of Hawkhurst, 3ml E of A21 Hurst Green

P Parking, 400yds, £2. Coaches £5

NT properties nearby

Bateman's, Scotney Castle, Sissinghurst Castle Garden, Smallhythe Place

Take a walk at Box Hill and see the views of the South Downs

Box Hill

The Old Fort, Box Hill Road, Box Hill, Tadworth, Surrey KT20 7LB

1914 (2:F6)

Woodland and open down with wonderful views

An outstanding area of woodland and chalk downland, Box Hill has long been famous as a destination for day-trippers from London. Surprisingly extensive, it has much to offer the rambler and naturalist with many beautiful walks and views towards the South Downs. On the summit there is an information centre, shop, servery, ample car parking and a magnificent view.

What's new in 2008 Invasive scrub cleared to open up the views on the zig-zig road

i **T** 01306 885502
 E boxhill@nationaltrust.org.uk

Children's activities. Special Christmas shopping day 19 Dec. All welcome, especially visitors with disabilities

Short walk, nature walk, long walk, family fun trail, all with self-guided leaflets, 50p each

Building

Grounds

NT shop. Information about Box Hill obtainable

Servery. For snacks, hot and cold drinks and ice-cream. Ice-cream kiosk (not NT) in east car park

Box Hill

Box Hill		M	T	W	T	F	S	S
All year		**M**	**T**	**W**	**T**	**F**	**S**	**S**
Servery								
1 Feb—29 Mar	10—4	**M**	**T**	**W**	**T**	**F**	**S**	**S**
30 Mar—26 Oct	9—5	**M**	**T**	**W**	**T**	**F**	**S**	**S**
27 Oct—31 Jan 09	10—4	**M**	**T**	**W**	**T**	**F**	**S**	**S**
Shop/info centre								
1 Feb—29 Mar	11—4	**M**	**T**	**W**	**T**	**F**	**S**	**S**
30 Mar—26 Oct	11—5	**M**	**T**	**W**	**T**	**F**	**S**	**S**
27 Oct—31 Jan 09	11—4	**M**	**T**	**W**	**T**	**F**	**S**	**F**

Closes dusk if earlier. Shop, information centre and servery closed 25, 26 Dec & 1 Jan 09

Charges for National Trust members apply on some special event days

[icon] Baby-changing facilities. Pushchairs admitted. Children's quiz/trail

[icon] Suitable for school groups. Education room/centre

[icon] Under close control (where sheep grazing)

[icon] [187:TQ171519] **Foot**: 1ml of North Downs Way from Stepping Stones to South Scarp; 1ml of Thames Down link footpath at Mickleham Downs; 1ml from Dorking station (½ml from Box Hill station). Many rights of way lead to Box Hill summit. **Bus**: Sunray Travel 516 [icon] Leatherhead–Dorking to Box Hill village; Arriva 465 Kingston–Dorking to foot of Box Hill. In both cases 1½ml to summit. **Station**: Box Hill & Westhumble 1½ml. **Road**: 1ml N of Dorking, 2½ml S of Leatherhead on A24

[icon] Parking, £3 (pay & display). Coaches must not use zig-zag road from Burford Bridge on W side of hill as weight restriction applies, but should approach from E side of hill B2032 or B2033; car/coach parks at summit

NT properties nearby
Headley Heath, Leith Hill, Polesden Lacey, Ranmore Common

Bradenham Village

nr High Wycombe, Buckinghamshire

[icons] 1956   (2:E4)

Picturesque village in the Chiltern hills

The church and 17th-century manor house (not open) provide an impressive backdrop to the sloping village green. A network of paths provides easy access for walkers to explore the delightful surrounding countryside – which includes hills, farmland and classic Chilterns beech woods.

[icon] **T** 01494 755573
   E bradenham@nationaltrust.org.uk

[icon] Guided tours of manor garden

[icon] Grounds [icon]

[icon] Off-road cycling permitted on bridleways

Bradenham Village							
All year		M	T	W	T	F	S	S

[icon] [165:SU825970] **Station**: Saunderton 1ml. **Road**: 4ml NW of High Wycombe, off A4010

[icon] Parking at the village green

NT properties nearby
Hughenden Manor, West Wycombe Park

Brighstone Shop and Museum

North Street, Brighstone, Isle of Wight PO30 4AX

[icons] 1989   (2:C9)

The Island's only National Trust gift shop

Situated within a row of traditional cottages is the National Trust shop and village museum (run by the Brighstone Museum Trust), which depicts village life in the 19th century. The shop has a wide range of gifts and cards, including many local items.

[icon] Nearest WC in public car park, 100yds

[icon] **T** 01983 740689
   E brighstone@nationaltrust.org.uk

[icon] [icon] Building [icon]

[icon] Wide range of gifts and cards

[icon] Pushchairs admitted

[icon] [196:SZ428828] **Cycle**: NCN67, 100yds. **Ferry**: Yarmouth (Wightlink Ltd) 8ml (tel. 0870 582 7744); E Cowes (Red Funnel) 12ml (tel. 0844 844 9988). **Bus**: Southern Vectis 7 Newport–Alum Bay. **Road**: next to post office, just off B3399 in Brighstone

[icon] Free parking (not NT), 100yds

NT properties nearby
Bembridge Windmill, Mottistone Manor Garden, The Needles Old Battery and New Battery, Newtown Old Town Hall

Brighstone Shop and Museum								
1 Feb—20 Mar	10—1	M	T	W	T	F	S	S
21 Mar—23 May	10—4	M	T	W	T	F	S	S
24 May—27 Sep	10—5	M	T	W	T	F	S	S
25 May—28 Sep	12—5	M	T	W	T	F	S	S
29 Sep—21 Dec	10—4	M	T	W	T	F	S	S
22 Dec—31 Jan 09	10—1	M	T	W	T	F	S	S
Closed 25–28 Dec inc. and 1 Jan 09								

Buckingham Chantry Chapel

Market Hill, Buckingham, Buckinghamshire

✝ 1912   **(2:D2)**

15th-century chapel, restored by Gilbert Scott in 1875

⭐ Open by appointment only and available for hire. Contact tel. 01280 822850 for details. No WC

ℹ **T** 01280 822850
  E buckinghamchantry@nationaltrust.org.uk

➡ On Market Hill

Buckingham Chantry Chapel

Admission by appointment only. Tel. for details

Step Farm on the Buscot Estate, Oxfordshire

The Buscot and Coleshill Estates

Coleshill Estate Office, Coleshill, Swindon, Wiltshire SN6 7PT

🏠 ✖ ❋ ♿ 🏠 ♟ ☕ 🏃 🎭 🛡
🎒 🚶 1956   **(2:B4)**

Traditional agricultural estates with villages, farms and woodland

These estates on the western borders of Oxfordshire include the attractive, unspoilt villages of Buscot and Coleshill, each with a thriving village shop and tea-room. There are circular walks of differing lengths and a series of footpaths criss-crossing the estates.

⭐ Public WCs located in Coleshill estate office yard

ℹ **T** 01793 762209
  E buscotandcoleshill@nationaltrust.org.uk

🏃 Regular series of guided estate walks throughout the year

🚶 Walks leaflet available, 50p from Coleshill estate office

☕ Tea-room (not NT) in Buscot village shop. Shop/café (not NT) in Coleshill village

🎒 Suitable for school groups. Education room/centre

🐕 On leads only

➡ [SU239973] **Cycle**: NCN45, 10ml. Regional Route 40: Oxfordshire Cycleway.
  Bus: Stagecoach in Swindon 7 Swindon–Highworth (passing close ⊑ Swindon), alight Highworth then 2ml walk.
  Station: Swindon 10ml. **Road**: Coleshill village on B4019 between Faringdon and Highworth. Buscot village on A417 between Faringdon and Lechlade

🅿 Free car parks at Buscot village and Badbury Clump

NT properties nearby
Buscot Park, Great Coxwell Barn, White Horse Hill

The Buscot and Coleshill Estates

All year	M T W T F S S

Mill open 2nd Sun of the month: April to Oct, 2–5

Dogs assisting visitors with disabilities are always welcome

The Water Garden at Buscot Park, Oxfordshire, looking down the canal

Buscot Old Parsonage

Buscot, Faringdon, Oxfordshire SN7 8DQ

 1949 **(2:C4)**

Early 18th-century riverside house with small garden

⭐ No WC

ℹ️ **T** 01793 762209
E buscot@nationaltrust.org.uk

➡️ 2ml from Lechlade, 4ml from Faringdon on A417

Buscot Old Parsonage									
2 Apr—29 Oct	2—6	M	T	**W**	T	F	S	S

Admission by written appointment with the tenant.
Please mark envelope 'NT booking'

Buscot Park

Estate Office, Buscot Park, Faringdon, Oxfordshire SN7 8BU

 1949 **(2:C4)**

Neo-classical mansion with fine art and furniture collection, set in landscaped grounds

The late 18th-century house contains the fine paintings and furniture of The Faringdon Collection Trust. The grounds include various avenue walks, an Italianate water garden designed in the early 20th century by Harold Peto, and a large walled garden.

What's new in 2008 Induction-loop installed in tea-room and ticket office

⭐ This property is administered on behalf of the NT by Lord Faringdon, and the contents of the house are owned by The Faringdon Collection Trust. www.buscotpark.com

ℹ️ **T** 0845 345 3387 (Infoline), 01367 240786
E estbuscot@aol.com

🚶 Extensive walks in grounds

Building Grounds

🏷️ Occasional sales of plants surplus to garden requirements; also garden fruit, vegetables and flowers when in season (not NT)

☕ Licensed tea-room (not NT)

👶 Baby-changing facilities. Hip-carrying infant seats for loan

🐕 Only in the paddock

Buscot Park									
House/grounds/tea-room*									
21 Mar—26 Sep	2—6	M	T	**W**	**T**	**F**	S	S
See below	2—6	M	T	W	T	F	**S**	**S**
Grounds only									
24 Mar—30 Sep	2—6	**M**	**T**	W	T	F	S	S

Open BH Mons. Last admission to house 1hr before closing. House & grounds also open 2–6 (*tea-room 2:30–5:30) at weekends 22/23 March; 5/6, 19/20 April; 3/4, 10/11, 24/25 May; 14/15, 28/29 June; 12/13, 26/27 July; 9/10, 23/24 Aug; 13/14, 27/28 Sept

Please remember – your membership card is always needed for free admission

→ [163:SU239973] **Bus**: Stagecoach in Swindon 64, 74 Swindon–Fairford (both passing close ⇌ Swindon). On both, alight Lechlade, 2¾ml walk. **Road**: between Lechlade and Faringdon, on A417

P Free parking

NT properties nearby
The Buscot and Coleshill Estates, Great Coxwell Barn

Chartwell

Mapleton Road, Westerham, Kent TN16 1PS

🏠 ❄ 📷 🍵 🍴 🎭 🛡 ♿ 🚻 🧍

⛲ 1946   (2:G6)

Family home of Sir Winston Churchill

Bought by Sir Winston for its magnificent views over the Weald of Kent to Sussex, Chartwell was his home and the place from which he drew inspiration from 1924 until the end of his life. The rooms and gardens remain much as they were when he lived here, with pictures, books, maps and personal mementoes strongly evoking the career and wide-ranging interests of this great statesman. The terraced hillside gardens reflect the importance to Churchill of

Chartwell		M	T	W	T	F	S	S
House/garden								
15 Mar–29 Jun	11–5	M	T	**W**	**T**	**F**	**S**	**S**
1 Jul–31 Aug	11–5	M	**T**	**W**	**T**	**F**	**S**	**S**
3 Sep–2 Nov	11–5	M	T	**W**	**T**	**F**	**S**	**S**
Restaurant								
1 Feb–14 Mar	11–3	M	T	**W**	**T**	**F**	**S**	**S**
15 Mar–29 Jun	10:30–5	M	T	**W**	**T**	**F**	**S**	**S**
1 Jul–31 Aug	10:30–5	M	**T**	**W**	**T**	**F**	**S**	**S**
3 Sep–2 Nov	10:30–5	M	T	**W**	**T**	**F**	**S**	**S**
5 Nov–21 Dec	11–4	M	T	**W**	**T**	**F**	**S**	**S**
27 Dec–31 Jan 09	11–3	M	T	**W**	**T**	**F**	**S**	**S**
Shop/garden								
1 Feb–14 Mar	11–3	M	T	**W**	**T**	**F**	**S**	**S**
15 Mar–29 Jun*	11–5:30	M	T	**W**	**T**	**F**	**S**	**S**
1 Jul–31 Aug*	11–5:30	M	**T**	**W**	**T**	**F**	**S**	**S**
3 Sep–2 Nov*	11–5:30	M	T	**W**	**T**	**F**	**S**	**S**
5 Nov–21 Dec	11–4	M	T	**W**	**T**	**F**	**S**	**S**
27 Dec–31 Jan 09	11–3	M	T	**W**	**T**	**F**	**S**	**S**
Car park								
All year	9–5:30**	**M**	**T**	**W**	**T**	**F**	**S**	**S**

Admission by timed ticket to house, which should be purchased immediately on arrival but cannot be booked. Open BH Mons. Last admission 45mins before house closing. **Car park closes 5:30 (3:30 from 3 Nov–31 Jan 09) or dusk if earlier and is closed on 25 Dec. Garden open Nov–March, as above, weather and conditions permitting. *15 March–2 Nov garden closes 5

The dining room at Chartwell, Kent: the family home of Sir Winston Churchill

Unless indicated, last admission is always 30mins before closing time

the landscape and nature. They include the lakes he created, the water gardens where he fed his fish, Lady Churchill's Rose Garden and the Golden Rose Avenue – a Golden Wedding anniversary gift from their children which runs down the centre of the productive kitchen garden. Many of Sir Winston's paintings can be seen in the garden studio where talks are given most days about 'Painting as a Pastime'.

What's new in 2008 Specially commissioned portrait of Lady Soames, Winston and Clementine Churchill's youngest daughter, Mary. Late afternoon house tours on Thursdays (not bookable, not July and August)

⭐ Car park open for countryside access all year (except 25 Dec). Mansion being re-roofed late 2008. House less busy late afternoon

ℹ️ **T** 01732 866368 (Infoline), 01732 868381
E chartwell@nationaltrust.org.uk

🛡️ Lecture lunches, special tours, book signings, guided walks

🚶 Three waymarked walks

♿ 🚻 📷 ♿ Building ♿
Grounds ♿

🏠 NT shop with licence to sell alcohol. Plant sales

🍴 Licensed restaurant in car park. Children's menu. Dispatch Box kiosk next to restaurant

👶 Baby-changing facilities. Hip-carrying infant seats for loan. Children's quiz/trail

🏫 Suitable for school groups

🐕 On short leads in gardens

➜ [188:TQ455515] **Foot**: Greensand Way passes through car park. **Bus**: Metrobus 246 from Bromley North (passing ≋ Bromley South); Arriva 401 from Tunbridge Wells (passing ≋ Sevenoaks). Both Suns & BH Mons only. Otherwise Kent Passenger Services 238 ≋ Sevenoaks–Edenbridge (Wed only) or Surrey Connect 236 Westerham–East Grinstead (passing ≋ Edenbridge and ≋ Edenbridge Town), Mon–Fri only, to within ½ml. **Station**: Edenbridge (U) 4ml, Edenbridge Town 4½ml, Oxted 5ml, Sevenoaks 6½ml. **Road**: 2ml S of Westerham, fork left off B2026 after 1½ml; leave M25 at exit 5 or 6

🅿️ Parking, 250yds (pay & display). Year-round opening (except 25 Dec) for countryside access; gates locked at 5:30, March–Oct, 3:30 Nov–Feb 09. Coach park and disabled parking adjacent to main car park

NT properties nearby
Emmetts Garden, Ightham Mote, Knole, Quebec House, Toys Hill

Chastleton House

Chastleton, nr Moreton-in-Marsh, Oxfordshire GL56 0SU

🏛️ 🌸 🏠 🚶 🏠 👪 1991   (2:C3)

One of England's finest and most complete Jacobean houses

Chastleton House is filled not only with a mixture of rare and everyday objects, furniture and textiles collected since its completion in 1612, but also with the atmosphere of 400 years of continuous occupation by one family. The gardens have a typical Elizabethan and Jacobean layout, with a ring of fascinating topiary at their heart, and it was here in 1865 that the rules of modern croquet were codified. Since acquiring the property, the Trust has concentrated on conserving it rather than restoring it to a pristine state.

⭐ As Chastleton House is relatively fragile and the access roads are narrow, the number of visitors is restricted. Admission is by timed ticket, which can be reserved by contacting the property (Mon–Fri, 10–2) on 01608 674981 (booking line). No same day bookings. Visitors not booked are admitted on a first-come, first-served basis. No shop or tea-room

ℹ️ **T** 01494 755560 (Infoline), 01608 674355
E chastleton@nationaltrust.org.uk

🚶 Out-of-hours guided 'Private View' Wed mornings at 10, NT members £3, non-members £8

Chastleton House									
19 Mar–30 Sep	1–5	M	T	**W**	**T**	**F**	**S**	S
1 Oct–1 Nov	1–4	M	T	**W**	**T**	**F**	**S**	S

Admission by timed ticket, tel. property to book. Last admission 1hr before closing

The east front of Chastleton House, Oxfordshire, showing some of the fascinating topiary

🦽 🚻 🖼 ⛅ 🅰 🅿 🅳 Building 🔆 ♿

🚼 Pushchairs and baby back-carriers admitted. Hip-carrying infant seats for loan. Family activity packs

→ [163:SP248291] **Cycle**: cycles can be hired from Country Lanes at Moreton-in-Marsh station, Easter to 30 Sept (tel. 01608 650065). **Station**: Moreton-in-Marsh 4ml. **Road**: 6ml from Stow-on-the-Wold. Approach only from A436 between A44 (W of Chipping Norton) and Stow

🅿 Free parking, 270yds. Return walk to car park includes a short but steep hill. Sensible shoes recommended

NT properties nearby
Hidcote Manor Garden, Snowshill Manor, Stowe Landscape Gardens, Upton House and Gardens

Clandon Park

West Clandon, Guildford, Surrey GU4 7RQ

🏠 🐎 🔀 🏛 🍽 🎋 🚪 🛡 🚻
🔔 🍸 1956   (2:F6)

Grand 18th-century Palladian mansion

Clandon Park was built c.1730 for the 2nd Lord Onslow by the Venetian architect Giacomo Leoni. It is the most complete example of Leoni's work to survive – the most impressive room being the magnificent two-storeyed, white Marble Hall. The house is filled with a superb collection of 18th-century furniture, porcelain and textiles, acquired in the 1920s by the connoisseur Mrs Gubbay. The attractive gardens contain a grotto and sunken Dutch garden, and Clandon also boasts a Maori meeting house, brought back from New Zealand in 1892 by the 4th Earl of Onslow, who was Governor there. The Onslow family is unique in that it has provided three Speakers of the House of Commons.

For general and membership enquiries, please telephone 0844 800 1895

Clandon Park

Clandon Park									
House									
16 Mar–2 Nov	11–4:30	M	**T**	**W**	**T**	F	S	**S**	
Garden									
16 Mar–2 Nov	11–5	M	**T**	**W**	**T**	F	S	**S**	
Museum									
16 Mar–2 Nov	12–5	M	**T**	**W**	**T**	F	S	**S**	
Shop/restaurant									
2 Mar–9 Mar	12–4	M	T	W	T	F	S	**S**	
16 Mar–2 Nov	12–5*	M	**T**	**W**	**T**	F	S	**S**	
4 Nov–30 Nov	12–4	M	**T**	**W**	**T**	F	S	**S**	
1 Dec–23 Dec	12–4**	**M**	**T**	**W**	**T**	F	S	**S**	

Open BH Mons, Good Fri and Easter Sat. *Restaurant opens at 11. **Restaurant open 12–10 in Dec (booking essential)

⭐ The Queen's Royal Surrey Regiment Museum (tel. 01483 223419) is based at Clandon Park and open to visitors the same days as the house 12–5 (free entry)

ℹ️ T 01483 222482, 01483 222502 (Clandon Park Restaurant)
E clandonpark@nationaltrust.org.uk

🧑 Morning guided tours (Tues–Thur, extra charge) and introductory talks (free); booking essential

☺ Conservation demonstrations 2 & 9 March

♿ 🚻 🦽 🔉 🤳 ⠿ 🔍 Ⓟ Ⓓ
Building 🔋 ⬆ ♿ Grounds ♿

☕ Clandon Park Restaurant (NT-approved concession) (licensed). Booking essential for groups and during Dec. Children's menu

👪 Baby-changing facilities. Front-carrying baby slings and hip-carrying infant seats for loan. Children's quiz/trail. Pushchairs allowed in house Tues, Wed & Thur. Baby-feeding facilities; please ask staff

➡️ [186:TQ042512] **Bus**: Countryliner 478/9, Guildford–Epsom (passing ≋ Leatherhead and close ≋ Guildford); 463 Guildford–≋ Woking (passing ≋ Clandon); Arriva 36/7 from close ≋ Guildford, alight Park Lane roundabout, then ½ml walk to west gate of park. **Station**: Clandon 1ml. **Road**: at West Clandon on A247, 3ml E of Guildford; if using A3 follow signposts to Ripley to join A247 via B2215

For information regarding prices, see page 10

🅿 Free parking, 300yds

NT properties nearby
Box Hill, Claremont Landscape Garden, Hatchlands Park, Leith Hill, Polesden Lacey, River Wey and Dapdune Wharf, Shalford Mill

Claremont Landscape Garden

Portsmouth Road, Esher, Surrey KT10 9JG

🌼 🏠 🖥 🧑 🎭 👪 🎫 ⊤ 1949 (2:F6)

One of the first and finest gardens of the English Landscape style

Claremont is a beautiful garden surrounding a small lake and featuring an unusual grass amphitheatre. The garden's creation and development has involved great names in garden history, including Sir John Vanbrugh, Charles Bridgeman, William Kent and 'Capability' Brown. In 1726 it was described as 'the noblest of any in Europe' and the garden today is of national importance. Visitors walking round the lake will see the island and pavilion, grotto and many viewpoints and vistas. There are hidden features to enjoy as well as wider estate walks and a new children's play area.

What's new in 2008 Children's play area and family guide

⭐ No dogs April to Oct

Claremont Landscape Garden									
Garden									
1 Feb–31 Mar	10–5	M	**T**	**W**	**T**	**F**	**S**	**S**	
1 Apr–31 Oct	10–6	**M**	**T**	**W**	**T**	**F**	**S**	**S**	
1 Nov–31 Jan 09	10–5	M	**T**	**W**	**T**	**F**	**S**	**S**	
Shop/tea-room									
1 Feb–24 Feb	11–4	M	T	W	T	**F**	**S**	**S**	
25 Feb–31 Mar	11–4	M	T	**W**	**T**	**F**	**S**	**S**	
1 Apr–31 Oct	11–5	M	T	**W**	**T**	**F**	**S**	**S**	
1 Nov–21 Dec	11–4	M	T	**W**	**T**	**F**	**S**	**S**	
9 Jan–31 Jan 09	11–4	M	T	W	T	**F**	**S**	**S**	

Open all year (closed Mons 1 Nov–31 March). Closes dusk if earlier. Closed 25 Dec. Open 1 Jan 09 10–4. Belvedere Tower open first weekend each month April–Oct & New Year's Day. Late night openings 14, 21, 28 June until 9. Shop and tea-room close 1hr before garden, and may close early in bad weather

Claydon House

Middle Claydon, nr Buckingham,
Buckinghamshire MK18 2EY

🏠 ✝ ❖ 🔌 🍴 📷 🚹 🦊 🎭 🏛

📕 🚶 🚲 🔔 🍴 **1956**   **(2:D3)**

Splendid 18th-century English interiors in an idyllic country setting

Home of the Verney family for more than 400 years, the extraordinary interiors of Claydon House, built 1759-69, represent a veritable three-dimensional pattern book of 18th-century decorative styles. Outstanding features include the astonishingly lavish wood carving in the Chinese Room and the fine parquetry grand staircase. Claydon has strong associations with Florence Nightingale, who was sister-in-law to Sir Harry Verney. She was a regular visitor to the house, which contains many of her personal belongings. Claydon House is set within 21 hectares (52 acres) of unspoilt parkland with far-reaching views and lakeside walks. The courtyard contains small workshops and galleries, as well as a popular restaurant and tea-room (not NT). The private gardens are open to visitors at an additional charge (inc. NT members).

What's new in 2008 Exhibition of papers from the Verney archives focusing on 'Household Management' across four centuries

⭐ All Saints' Church (not NT) in the grounds is also open to the public

ℹ️ **T** 01494 755561 (Infoline), 01296 730349
   E claydon@nationaltrust.org.uk

🦊 Introductory talks and garden talks

🎭 Various events and family-friendly days

🚶 Permitted footpath (approx. 3ml) skirting lakes

♿ 🚻 🔆 🔍 📖 Building 🔆 ♿
Grounds 🔆 ➡️

The west front of Claydon House seen from across the lake

ℹ️ **T** 01372 467806
   E claremont@nationaltrust.org.uk

🦊 Tours 1st and 3rd Sat, 2nd Wed and last Sun of each month April to Oct. Starts 2 at entrance kiosk

🎭 Including children's activities during school holidays, lecture lunches and guided walks. Send sae for details

♿ 🚻 🔆 🔍 📖 Pⅈ Grounds ♿ ➡️

🍽 Licensed tea-room. Closed 18 & 19 Dec for Christmas lunches (booking essential). Children's menu

🚼 Baby-changing facilities. Pushchairs admitted. Children's quiz/trail. Children's play area. Family guide. Children's activities during school holidays

📕 Suitable for school groups

🐕 On short leads 1 Nov–31 March. No dogs April to Oct

➡️ [187:TQ128634] **Bus:** Travel London 515/A Kingston–Guildford (passing close ≋ Esher). **Station:** Esher 2ml; Hersham 2ml; Claygate 2ml. **Road:** 1ml S of centre of Esher, on E side of A307 (no access from Esher bypass)

Ⓟ Free parking at entrance

NT properties nearby
Clandon Park, Ham House and Garden, Hatchlands Park, The Homewood, Polesden Lacey, River Wey and Dapdune Wharf

Claydon House							
15 Mar–2 Nov	1–5*	**M**	**T**	**W**	T	**F**	**S**	**S**

Open Good Fri 1–5. *Closes dusk if earlier. Grounds, private garden (not NT – additional charge applies), shops & restaurants (not NT) 12–5. Special Christmas opening Dec 6/7, 13/14, 20/21 1–4

Many Trust properties are offering Gift Aid on Entry for non-members, see page 10

Art gallery, ceramics studio, stonemason, seasonal plant sales (all non NT). Second-hand bookshop

Carriage House Restaurant (not NT) (licensed) **privately owned**. Children's menu. Tea-room. Both open same days as house, 12–5:30. Tel. 01296 730004 for details

Baby-changing facilities. Front-carrying baby slings and hip-carrying infant seats for loan. Family guide. Children's guide. Children's quiz/trail. Family-friendly days

Suitable for school groups

On leads and only in park

On public rights of way only

[165:SP720253] **Foot**: Bernwood Jubilee Way. **Cycle**: NCN51. **Bus**: Arriva 17 from Aylesbury (passing close ⊠ Aylesbury). **Road**: in Middle Claydon 13ml NW of Aylesbury, 4ml SW of Winslow; signposted from A413 & A41 (M40 exit 9 12ml); entrance by N drive only

P Free parking

NT properties nearby
King's Head, Stowe Landscape Gardens, Waddesdon Manor

Cliveden

Taplow, Maidenhead, Buckinghamshire SL6 0JA

🏛 ❀ ♣ 🏠 🏚 ☕ ⛱ 🎭 👫 🎖 1942 **(2:E5)**

Magnificent formal gardens overlooking the River Thames, once the exclusive haunt of the rich and famous

With magnificent views across the River Thames, Cliveden was the glittering hub of society as the home of Waldorf and Nancy Astor in the early part of the 20th century, and later infamously associated with the 'Profumo Affair'. The spectacular estate, with a celebrated parterre, has a series of formal gardens, each with its own character, an outstanding collection of sculpture and statues from the ancient and modern worlds, as well as extensive woodland and riverside walks. The house is now let as a private hotel, part of which is open to visitors at limited times.

What's new in 2008 Major conservation work and replanting of parterre and Long Garden

⭐ No WC at woodlands

ℹ️ **T** 01494 755562 (Infoline), 01628 605069
E cliveden@nationaltrust.org.uk

Water Garden, Cliveden: just one of a series of formal gardens

Cliveden

Estate/garden										
1 Mar–26 Oct	11–6	**M**	**T**	**W**	**T**	**F**	**S**	**S**		
27 Oct–23 Dec	11–4	**M**	**T**	**W**	**T**	**F**	**S**	**S**		
House (part)/Octagon temple										
1 Apr–31 Oct	3–5:30	M	T	W	**T**	F	S	**S**		
Restaurant										
1 Mar–26 Oct	11–5	**M**	**T**	**W**	**T**	**F**	**S**	**S**		
27 Oct–2 Nov	11–4	**M**	**T**	**W**	**T**	**F**	**S**	**S**		
8 Nov–21 Dec	11–3	M	T	W	T	F	**S**	**S**		
Woodlands										
1 Mar–26 Oct	11–5:30	**M**	**T**	**W**	**T**	**F**	**S**	**S**		
27 Oct–23 Dec	11–4	**M**	**T**	**W**	**T**	**F**	**S**	**S**		
3 Jan–31 Jan 09	11–4	**M**	**T**	**W**	**T**	**F**	**S**	**S**		
Shop										
1 Mar–26 Oct	11–5:30	**M**	**T**	**W**	**T**	**F**	**S**	**S**		
27 Oct–23 Dec	11–4	**M**	**T**	**W**	**T**	**F**	**S**	**S**		

Admission to house is limited and by timed ticket only from Information Kiosk. Some areas of formal garden may be roped off when ground conditions are bad

Concerts, open-air theatre, children's theatre, seasonal guided walks

Building Grounds

Licensed restaurant. Children's menu. Kiosk in main car park

Baby-changing facilities. Children's guide. All-terrain buggies for hire. Family Garden Explorer Packs

Audio-visual guide in Gas Yard

Under close control and only in specified woodlands

→ [175:SU915851] **Bus**: no bus service. **Station**: Taplow (not Sun) 2½ml; Burnham 3ml. **Road**: 2ml N of Taplow; leave M4 at exit 7 on to A4, or M40 at exit 4 on to A404 to Marlow and follow brown signs. Entrance by main gates opposite Feathers Inn

P Free parking

NT properties nearby
Greys Court, Hughenden Manor, West Wycombe Park

Dorneywood Garden

Dorneywood, Burnham, Buckinghamshire
SL1 8PY

[1942] (2:E5)

1930s-style garden, with herbaceous borders, rose garden, cottage garden and lily pond

★ The upkeep of Dorneywood is paid for by the Dorneywood Trust, at no cost to the NT or public. Garden open by written appointment only on four days a year. Charge inc. NT members (goes to NGS). Write or email for tickets, giving at least two weeks' notice, to the Secretary, Dorneywood Trust, at above address

i T 01628 665361
E dorneywood@nationaltrust.org.uk

→ On Dorneywood Road, SW of Burnham Beeches, 1½ml N of Burnham village, 2ml E of Cliveden

Dorneywood Garden									
14 May	2–5	M	T	**W**	T	F	S	S	
28 May	2–5	M	T	**W**	T	F	S	S	
2 Jul	2–5	M	T	**W**	T	F	S	S	
26 Jul	2–5	M	T	W	T	F	**S**	S	

Admission by appointment

Emmetts Garden

Ide Hill, Sevenoaks, Kent TN14 6AY

[1965] (2:H6)

Interesting hillside garden with year-round features

Influenced by William Robinson, this delightful plantsman's garden was laid out in the late 19th century and contains many exotic and rare trees and shrubs from across the world. Explore the rose and rock gardens, and enjoy glorious shows of spring flowers and shrubs, followed by vibrant autumn colours. Its dramatic hilltop location means there are spectacular views.

What's new in 2008 Replacement 'Putto and Dolphin' statue on fountain in rose garden

i T 01732 751509 (Infoline), 01732 868381
E emmetts@nationaltrust.org.uk

Including family picnic day

Charges for National Trust members apply on some special event days

🚶 Weardale walk to Chartwell

♿ 🚻 🚹 👁 ‥ 🅿 🅿 ♨ **Grounds** 🅰 ➡

🛍 Tack Room shop. Plant sales

🍽 Stable Tea-room in former stable block

👶 Baby-changing facilities. Pushchairs and baby back-carriers admitted. Children's quiz/trail. Family picnic day

🏛 Suitable for school groups

🐕 On short leads only

➡ [188:TQ477524] **Foot**: from Ide Hill (½ml). Weardale walk from Chartwell (3ml) – guide leaflet available. **Bus**: New Enterprise 404 from Sevenoaks, Mon–Fri only, alight Ide Hill, 1½ml. **Station**: Sevenoaks 4¼ml; Penshurst (U) 5½ml. **Road**: 1½ml S of A25 on Sundridge to Ide Hill road, 1½ml N of Ide Hill off B2042, leave M25 exit 5, then 4ml

🅿 Free parking, 100yds

NT properties nearby
Chartwell, Ightham Mote, Knole, Quebec House, Toys Hill

Emmetts Garden									
Garden									
15 Mar–1 Jun	11–5	M	**T**	**W**	**T**	**F**	**S**	**S**	
4 Jun–29 Jun	11–5	M	T	**W**	**T**	**F**	**S**	**S**	
2 Jul–2 Nov	11–5	M	T	**W**	T	F	**S**	**S**	
Shop/tea-room									
As garden	11–4:30								
Open BH Mons. Last admission 45mins before closing									

Emmetts Garden: wonderful flowers and spectacular views

Great Coxwell Barn

Great Coxwell, Faringdon, Oxfordshire SN7 7LZ

🏠 🏛 1956   **(2:C4)**

13th-century stone barn

This large monastic barn has a stone-tiled roof and interesting timber structure.

⭐ No WC

ℹ️ **T** 01793 762209 (Coleshill Estate office)
   E greatcoxwellbarn@nationaltrust.org.uk

♿ ‥

🏛 Suitable for school groups

🐕 On leads only

➡ [163:SU269940] **Bus**: Stagecoach in Swindon 65/6 Swindon–Oxford (passing close � Swindon & passing � Oxford), alight Great Coxwell Turn, ¾ml. **Station**: Swindon 10ml. **Road**: 2ml SW of Faringdon between A420 and B4019

🅿 Limited parking in roadside lay-by

NT properties nearby
Ashdown House, Buscot Park, Coleshill Estate, including Badbury Hill, White Horse Hill

Great Coxwell Barn								
All year	Early–dusk	**M**	**T**	**W**	**T**	**F**	**S**	**S**

Greys Court

Rotherfield Greys, Henley-on-Thames, Oxfordshire RG9 4PG

🏠 🌼 🌳 🐾 🛍 🍽 🎋 🏡 🛡 👶
🚶 1969   **(2:D5)**

A picturesque house with tranquil walled gardens

Set amid rolling countryside, this enchanting place dates back to medieval times and has a serene and tranquil atmosphere. The gardens are designed as an inspirational series of outdoor areas through which you can stroll at your leisure, before enjoying a treat in the tea-room. If you are feeling a little more energetic, you can follow 'the Gentle Walk', a 30-minute circuit around the estate, created by the former owner Lady Brunner, for her husband.

Greys Court: a path through the inspirational gardens

⭐ **Please note that the house is closed until April 2009 for important reservicing and conservation work**. Gardens and tea-room remain open

ℹ **T** 01494 755564 (Infoline), 01491 628529
E greyscourt@nationaltrust.org.uk

🚶 Gardens only

🎭 Various events inc. guided walks, open-air theatre and music

🚶 Spectacular bluebells in the woods. Dogs welcome on the estate walk

♿ 🧒 📷 ⋯ 📷 Pd Dd **Grounds** ♿

📕 Book and card shop

🍴 Tea-room in Cromwellian stables. Light lunches and teas

🚼 Baby-changing facilities. Children's quiz/trail. Pushchairs in gardens only. Family explorer packs

Greys Court		M	T	W	T	F	S	S
22 Mar—27 Sep	12—5	M	T	W	T	F	S	S

Garden open in aid of NGS 17 May (charge inc. NT members)

🐕 In the car park and on the estate walk

➡ [175:SU725834] **Cycle**: on Oxfordshire cycleway. **Bus**: White's 145 from Henley-on-Thames town hall (½ml walk from ➤ Henley-on-Thames). Alight Greys Green and follow signed footpath to Greys Court (approx ¼ml). **Station**: Henley-on-Thames 3ml.
Road: W of Henley-on-Thames. From Nettlebed mini-roundabout on A4130 take B481 and property is signed to the left after approx. 3ml. There is also a direct (unsigned) route from Henley-on-Thames town centre. Follow signs to Badgemore Golf Club towards Peppard, approx 3ml out of Henley

🅿 Free parking, 220yds

NT properties nearby
Basildon Park, Cliveden, Hughenden Manor

Hatchlands Park

East Clandon, Guildford, Surrey GU4 7RT

🏠 🏡 ❄ 🌳 📷 🍴 ⛱ 🎭 🚼 🚶 1945   (2:F6)

18th-century mansion, with Adam interiors and collection of keyboard instruments, set in parkland

Built in the 1750s for Admiral Boscawen, hero of the Battle of Louisburg, the house contains the earliest recorded decorations by Robert Adam in an English country house – whose ceilings here appropriately feature nautical motifs. On display is the Cobbe Collection, the world's largest group of keyboard instruments associated with famous composers such as Purcell, J. C. Bach, Chopin, Mahler and Elgar. Hatchlands is set in a

Hatchlands Park								
Park walks								
23 Mar—30 Oct	11—6	M	T	W	T	F	S	S
House & garden								
23 Mar—31 Jul	2—5:30	M	T	W	T	F	S	S
1 Aug—31 Aug	2—5:30	M	T	W	T	F	S	S
2 Sep—30 Oct	2—5:30	M	T	W	T	F	S	S
Shop								
As house	1—5							
Restaurant								
As house	11—5							
Open BH Mons								

Dogs assisting visitors with disabilities are always welcome

The park at Hatchlands, Surrey, where there are many vistas to be enjoyed

beautiful 174-hectare (430-acre) park designed by Repton, with a variety of waymarked walks offering vistas of open parkland and views of the house. The woodlands are a haven for wildlife and there is a stunning wood, which is carpeted with bluebells from April to May.

i **T** 01483 222482
E hatchlands@nationaltrust.org.uk

Inc. Cobbe Collection Trust concerts, tel. 01483 211474 or see www.cobbecollection.co.uk

Building

Licensed tea-room (NT-approved concession). Busy for lunch on Wed concert days. Children's menu

Baby-changing facilities. Hip-carrying infant seats for loan. Children's quiz/trail. Tracker Packs

Under close control in designated parkland areas

→ [187:TQ063516] **Bus**: Countryliner 478/9 Guildford–Epsom (passing ≋ Leatherhead and close ≋ Guildford). **Station**: Clandon 2ml, Horsley 2½ml. **Road**: E of East Clandon, N of A246 Guildford–Leatherhead road

P Free parking, 300yds

NT properties nearby
Box Hill, Clandon Park, Leith Hill, Polesden Lacey, River Wey and Dapdune Wharf, Shalford Mill

Hindhead Commons and The Devil's Punch Bowl Café

London Road, Hindhead, Surrey GU26 6AB

1906 (2:E7)

The gateway to the Surrey Hills, with fine views

Take a walk through Hindhead Commons and see why this area of open heathland is classified as an Area of Outstanding Natural Beauty. Visitors can enjoy the stunning scenery of the Devil's Punch Bowl from a special viewpoint less than 50yds from the National Trust café.

i **T** 01428 683207 (Infoline), 01428 608771
E hindhead@nationaltrust.org.uk

Maps and local walks leaflets on sale

Grounds

Hindhead Commons									
Commons									
All year		M	T	W	T	F	S	S	
Café									
1 Feb–31 Mar	9–4	M	T	W	T	F	S	S	
1 Apr–31 Oct	9–5	M	T	W	T	F	S	S	
1 Nov–31 Jan 09	9–4	M	T	W	T	F	S	S	
Closed 25, 26 Dec and 1 Jan 09									

Please remember – your membership card is always needed for free admission

■ Devil's Punch Bowl Café. Hot and cold food available. Children's menu

👪 Baby-changing facilities

➜ [133:SU895356] Beside A3, at Hindhead, near crossroads with A287. **Bus**: Stagecoach in Hants & Surrey 18/19; 71 ≋ Haslemere–≋ Aldershot. **Station**: Haslemere 3ml

P Parking, £2 (pay & display). No lorries. Coach parties by arrangement

NT properties nearby
Ludshott Common, Oakhurst Cottage, Winkworth Arboretum, The Witley Centre

Hinton Ampner

Bramdean, nr Alresford, Hampshire SO24 0LA

🏠✻🏛■🎨👖🎋👪 1986 **(2:D7)**

Elegant country house with highly distinctive gardens

Best known for its fine gardens, Hinton Ampner is an elegant country house with an outstanding collection of furniture, paintings and *objets d'art*. The house was extensively remodelled after a traumatic fire in 1960 by its final owner, Ralph Dutton, 8th and last Lord Sherborne, who also created the gardens – widely acknowledged to be a masterpiece of 20th-century garden design. With their crisply manicured lawns and fine topiary, the gardens cleverly combine formal design with informal planting, and the gardeners are always on hand to talk to visitors. The walled garden, currently being turned back into a productive area, is a popular attraction with a thriving and extensive vegetable plot. Produce from the garden, when available, is on sale along with a wide range of plants.

What's new in 2008 Part of the upstairs of the property opening (Tues and Wed only)

Hinton Ampner								
Garden/tea-room/shop								
15 Mar–2 Nov	11—5	M	T	W	T	F	S	S
House								
15 Mar–2 Nov	12—5	M	T	W	T	F	S	S
Christmas: house/garden/tea-room/shop								
1 Dec–21 Dec	11—4	M	T	W	T	F	S	S
House open BH Mons and Good Fri 1–5. Last entry to garden 4:30. Last entry to house 4:45								

ℹ **T** 01962 771305
E hintonampner@nationaltrust.org.uk

♿ 🚻♿🅿️⋯🔊 **Building** ♿♿
Grounds ♿▶

🛍 NT shop. Plant sales

■ Small tea-room

👪 Baby-changing facilities. No baby-feeding facilities

➜ [185:SU597275] **Bus**: Stagecoach in Hampshire 67 Winchester–Petersfield (passing close ≋ Winchester & passing ≋ Petersfield). **Station**: Winchester 9ml, Alresford (Mid-Hants Railway) 4ml.
Road: on A272, 1ml W of Bramdean village, 8ml E of Winchester, leave M3 at exit 9 and follow signs to Petersfield

P Free parking. Special entrance for coaches. Map indicating where coaches can park sent with confirmation of booking

NT properties nearby
Mottisfont Abbey, Uppark House and Garden, The Vyne, Winchester City Mill

Part of the outstanding collection at Hinton Ampner

Unless indicated, last admission is always 30mins before closing time

The Homewood

Portsmouth Road, Esher, Surrey KT10 9JL

🏠 ✿ 1999   **(2:F6)**

20th-century Modernist house and garden

⭐ Administered and maintained on the Trust's behalf by a tenant. Please tel. for opening arrangements and prices. **Access is via minibus from Claremont Landscape Garden only**. No WC

ℹ️ **T** 01372 476424
    E thehomewood@nationaltrust.org.uk

➔ **Access is via minibus from Claremont Landscape Garden only**

Tel. for details. Panoramic photographs are available to see on www.nationaltrust.org.uk/homewood

Hughenden Manor

High Wycombe, Buckinghamshire HP14 4LA

🏠 ✿ 🌳 🍴 🏛️ 📷 ⚔️ 🔭 🎭 🏇
🏛️ 🚶 🚲 🍵 1947   **(2:E4)**

Country home of the Victorian statesman Benjamin Disraeli

Enjoy a glimpse into the private life of the most unlikely Victorian Prime Minister, Benjamin Disraeli, who lived here from 1848 until his death in 1881. Much of his furniture, books and pictures remain, as well as the recreated gardens based on the colourful designs of his wife, Mary Anne. Beautiful walks through the park and woodland surround this fascinating country home.

What's new in 2008 Two new audiotrails: German Forest and Top Secret Hughenden (about the Second World War)

⭐ Certain rooms have little electric light. Visitors wishing to make a close study of the interior of the house should avoid dull days early and late in the season

ℹ️ **T** 01494 755565 (Infoline), 01494 755573
    E hughenden@nationaltrust.org.uk

🏇 Manor tours at 11:30 (limited availability). Garden taster tours Wed–Fri, 11.30 & 2

🎧 Two new audiotrails: German Forest and Top Secret Hughenden (about the Second World War), £1

🎭 Programme of family-friendly events, inc. hands-on workshops and Discovery Days during school holidays

♿ 🚾 🦮 📖 👜 👓 📷 🅿️ 🎵 **Building** 🏛️ ♿
Grounds 🏛️

🍽️ The Stables Restaurant (licensed). Also available for Christmas lunches and winter events. Booked Christmas lunch and intro tour of manor available Thur and Fri, 6–21 Dec. Children's menu

👶 Baby-changing facilities. Hip-carrying infant seats for loan. Children's guide. Family activity packs. All-terrain outdoor buggy for loan. Family-friendly events, inc. hands-on workshops and Discovery Days during school holidays. Children's Tracker Packs

🏫 Suitable for school groups. Education room/centre. Live interpretation. Hands-on activities. Adult study days

🐕 Under close control in park and woodland

Hughenden Manor									
House									
1 Mar–2 Nov	1–5		M	T	**W**	**T**	**F**	**S**	**S**
6 Dec–21 Dec	12–3		**M**	T	W	T	F	**S**	**S**
Garden									
1 Mar–2 Nov	11–5		M	T	**W**	**T**	**F**	**S**	**S**
6 Dec–21 Dec	11–3:30		**M**	T	W	T	F	**S**	**S**
Park									
All year			**M**	**T**	**W**	**T**	**F**	**S**	**S**
Shop/restaurant									
1 Mar–2 Nov	11–5		M	T	**W**	**T**	**F**	**S**	**S**
Shop									
5 Nov–5 Dec	11–3:30		M	T	**W**	**T**	**F**	**S**	**S**
6 Dec–21 Dec	11–3:30		**M**	T	W	T	F	**S**	**S**
Restaurant									
5 Nov–5 Dec	11–3:30		M	T	W	T	F	**S**	**S**
6 Dec–21 Dec	11–3:30		**M**	T	W	T	F	**S**	**S**

Admission by timed ticket on Sun, BHols & other busy days. Open BH Mons. Last entry 4:30 or dusk if earlier. Manor tours at 11:30, limited availability. Walled garden open Thur and Fri. Garden taster tours Wed–Fri, 11.30 & 2. Occasional early closing for special events & weddings

For further information go to www.nationaltrust.org.uk

Hughenden Manor: the country home of Benjamin Disraeli

🚴 Bridleways running through the woodlands to nearby villages

➡ [165:SU866955] **Foot**: 1½ml from High Wycombe. **Bus**: Arriva 300 High Wycombe–Aylesbury (passing close ≋ High Wycombe). Note: Long and steep walk to house entrance. **Station**: High Wycombe 2ml. **Road**: 1½ml N of High Wycombe; on W side of the Great Missenden road (A4128)

🅿 Free parking, 200yds. Some waiting possible at peak times; parking space for only one coach; overflow car park 400yds

NT properties nearby
Claydon House, Cliveden, Waddesdon Manor, West Wycombe Park

Ightham Mote

Mote Road, Ivy Hatch, Sevenoaks, Kent TN15 0NT

🏛 ✝ ❀ 🛏 🏠 🗄 🖥 🛅 🎞 🛡 👫
🎥 🚶 🚴 1985   **(2:H6)**

Outstanding 14th-century moated manor house

Set in a Kentish sunken valley, Ightham Mote is a rare example of a moated medieval manor house, dating from 1320 with important later additions and alterations. It was the subject of the Trust's largest conservation project, begun in 1989 and completed in 2004 – an exhibition of which is in the visitor reception. Ightham Mote has many special features, including a Great Hall, Crypt, Tudor Chapel with a hand-painted ceiling and the private apartments of the American donor Charles Henry Robinson. However, one of its most enchanting features has to be the Grade I listed dog kennel, situated in the recently re-cobbled picturesque courtyard. Ightham Mote also offers some lovely gardens and water features with lakeside and woodland walks.

Ightham Mote									
House									
15 Mar–31 Oct	11–5	**M**	T	W	**T**	**F**	**S**	**S**	
1 Nov–21 Dec*	11–3	M	T	W	T	**F**	**S**	**S**	
Estate									
All year	Dawn–dusk	**M**	**T**	**W**	**T**	**F**	**S**	**S**	
Shop/restaurant**/**garden**									
15 Mar–2 Nov	10:30–5	**M**	T	W	**T**	**F**	**S**	**S**	
8 Nov–21 Dec	11–3	M	T	W	**T**	**F**	**S**	**S**	

Restaurant open for occasional themed evenings and for booked functions. Please tel. 01732 811314 for opening times of Mote Restaurant and 01732 811203 for shop opening times outside normal property hours. Booking at Mote Restaurant advised winter & evenings. **Except when function ongoing. Closed Jan 09. Mote Restaurant is available for wedding receptions. Shop/restaurant/partial gardens open 14 Feb–14 Mar 11–3, Thurs–Sun, except during restaurant functions when refreshment kiosk will open. *Partial gardens/courtyard & ground floor access Nov/Dec weekends, 11–3. Great Hall dressed for Christmas during Dec

What's new in 2008 Now open every Saturday. Guided tours to South Lake by arrangement. Partial gardens/courtyard and ground floor access (Nov/Dec, weekends, 11–3). Special reduced charge for winter weekends. Great Hall dressed for Christmas

[i] **T** 01732 811145 (Infoline), 01732 810378
E ighthammote@nationaltrust.org.uk

[ ] Regular free introductory talks, garden and tower tours

[ ] Family activities and lecture lunches

[ ] Three waymarked self-guided walks on surrounding estate – leaflet obtainable from visitor reception. Regular guided walks

[ ] Building [ ][ ] Grounds [ ][ ]

[ ] Plant sales

[ ] Mote Restaurant (licensed) adjacent to visitor reception. Children's menu. Refreshment kiosk in walled car park open on busy days

[ ] Baby-changing and feeding facilities. Front-carrying baby slings and hip-carrying infant seats for loan. Children's quiz/trail. Family activity packs. Family activities

[ ] Suitable for school groups. Education room. Hands-on activities. Adult study days

[ ] On estate walks only

[ ] On surrounding bridleways and roads on 223-hectare (550-acre) estate

[→] [188:TQ584535] Between Sevenoaks and Borough Green 1¾ml S of A25. **Bus:** New Enterprise 404 from ₴ Sevenoaks, calls Wed only, or on other days alight Ivy Hatch, ¾ml; Autocar 222 Tonbridge–₴ Borough Green, alight Fairlawne, ½ml (footpath); otherwise Arriva 306/8 ₴ Sevenoaks–Gravesend (passing ₴ Borough Green), alight Ightham Common, 1½ml. **Station:** Borough Green & Wrotham 3ml; Hildenborough 4ml; Sevenoaks 6ml. **Road:** 6ml N of Tonbridge on A227; 6ml S of Sevenoaks on A25; 16ml W of Maidstone on A20/A25

[P] Free parking, 200yds

NT properties nearby
Chartwell, Knole, Old Soar Manor, Toys Hill

The formal garden at Ightham Mote

King's Head

King's Head Passage, Market Square, Aylesbury,
Buckinghamshire HP20 2RW

 1925   (2:E3)

Ancient coaching inn

Set in the heart of this historic market town, the
King's Head is one of England's best preserved
coaching inns. Dating back to 1455, the building
has many fascinating architectural features –
including stained glass windows, exposed
wattle and daub and the original stabling for the
inn. Around the central cobbled courtyard there
is the town's Tourist Information Centre, a
thriving second-hand bookshop, coffee shop in
the Great Hall and various small retail outlets.
The award-winning Farmers' Bar is now run by
the local Chiltern Brewery.

What's new in 2008 Visitor reception and coffee
shop now open

⭐ The King's Head has full conference facilities.
Tel. for details or a brochure

ℹ️ **T** 01296 381501
   E kingshead@nationaltrust.org.uk

🎭 Aylesbury town festivals, art exhibitions

♿ 🚾 🅿️ **Building** 🏞️ **Grounds** 🏚️

☕ Farmers' Bar (not NT) (licensed). Lunches
provided by the Chiltern Brewery. Coffee shop

👪 Baby-changing facilities. Pushchairs and baby
back-carriers admitted

🏫 Suitable for school groups. Education room/
centre. Hands-on activities. Adult study days

➡️ [165:SP818138] At top of Market Square.
Access through cobbled lane. **Bus**: from
surrounding areas. **Station**: Aylesbury 400yds

🅿️ No parking on site. Car parks in town centre
(not NT)

King's Head									
Visitor reception									
All year	9–4	M	T	W	T	F	S	S	
Great Hall/bookshop									
All year	10:30–4	M	T	W	T	F	S	S	
Farmers' Bar									
All year	Licensing hours	M	T	W	T	F	S	S	
Closed BH Mons. Tours available Wed, Fri, Sat at 2									

NT properties nearby
Boarstall Duck Decoy, Boarstall Tower, Long
Crendon Courthouse

Knole

Sevenoaks, Kent TN15 0RP

🏛️ ❄️ ♣️ 📷 ☕ 🍴 🎭 👪 🎦 🚶
🚲 1946   (2:H6)

History and grandeur in the heart of Kent. Birthplace of novelist and poet Vita Sackville-West

Set within a glorious deer park, Knole appears
much like a small village when viewed from a
distance. It is a complex and beautiful house,
which has links with kings, queens and nobility,
as well as literary connections with Vita
Sackville-West and Virginia Woolf. Thirteen
superb state rooms are laid out much as they
were in the 18th century, to impress visitors with
the wealth and standing of the Sackville family
(who still live at Knole today). The house boasts
a world-renowned collection of Royal Stuart
furniture, paintings by Gainsborough, Van Dyck
and Reynolds, as well as important 17th-century
tapestries. The 404-hectare (1,000-acre) deer
park surrounding the house is a Site of Special
Scientific Interest.

What's new in 2008 Renewed interpretation on
the conservation of the historically unique
James II bed

Knole									
Park/shop/tea-room									
1 Mar–9 Mar	11–4	M	T	W	T	F	S	S	
House									
15 Mar–2 Nov	12–4	M	T	W	T	F	S	S	
Shop/tea-room									
15 Mar–2 Nov	10:30–5	M	T	W	T	F	S	S	
Christmas shop/tea-room									
5 Nov–21 Dec	11–4	M	T	W	T	F	S	S	
Garden									
2 Apr–22 Oct	11–4	M	T	W	T	F	S	S	
House, shop and tea-room also open Tues, 29 July–2 Sept and BH Mons. Park open daily for pedestrians. Vehicles admitted only when house is open. Garden (by courtesy of Lord Sackville): please note limited opening. **Great Hall open 1–9 Mar 11–2, Sat/Sun**									

Knole has links with kings, queens and nobility, as well as important literary connections

⭐ Please do not feed the deer; they can be dangerous. In order to protect Knole's fragile and rare textiles, light of all kinds is carefully controlled. This restricts opening hours of the show rooms – last entry 3:30. **There is no wheelchair access beyond the Great Hall**

[i] **T** 01732 450608 (Infoline), 01732 462100
E knole@nationaltrust.org.uk

🚶 Guided tours take place while house is closed to the public (booking required)

🎭 Educational family days in Aug. Exclusive evening candlelit tours in summer and autumn (tel. for details). Carol concerts in the Great Hall. Lord Sackville's Christmas lecture

🚶 Deer park has pedestrian access all year round

♿ 🚻 ♿ 🎨 ⠿ 📷 🅿 ♿ Building 🔽🔽
Grounds ♿

🛍 NT shop. Also open during events. Christmas shop open Wed–Sun (Nov and Dec). Annual plant sale, tel. for details

🍴 Brewhouse Tea-room (licensed). Also open Nov and Dec (Wed–Sun). Children's menu

👶 Baby-changing and feeding facilities. Front-carrying baby slings and hip-carrying infant seats for loan. Children's quiz/trail. Family activity packs

🏫 Suitable for school groups. Education room. Hands-on activities

🐕 On leads and in park only

🚲 Cycling permitted on roads and tracks

➡ [188:TQ532543] **Foot**: park entrance at south end of Sevenoaks town centre, opposite St Nicholas' church. **Bus**: from surrounding area to Sevenoaks, ¾ml walk. **Station**: Sevenoaks 1½ml. **Road**: leave M25 at exit 5 (A21). Park entrance in Sevenoaks town centre off A225 Tonbridge Road (opposite St Nicholas' church)

🅿 Parking, 60yds, £2.50. Park only open to vehicles from 10:30 when house open. When house closed parking available in nearby town centre. Park open to vehicles in winter when shop and tea-room open. Park gates locked at 6

NT properties nearby
Chartwell, Emmetts Garden, Ightham Mote, Toys Hill

Lamb House

West Street, Rye, East Sussex TN31 7ES

🏠 ❄ 1950 　　　　　　　　　　　(2:J8)
Fine brick-fronted house with literary associations

⭐ Administered and largely maintained on the Trust's behalf by a tenant. No WC

[i] **T** 01580 762334
E lambhouse@nationaltrust.org.uk

➡ In West Street, facing W end of church

Lamb House									
20 Mar—25 Oct	2—6	M	T	W	**T**	F	S	S

Leith Hill

c/o Mark Cottage, Leith Hill Lane, Holmbury
St Mary, Dorking, Surrey RH5 6LY

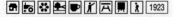 1923   (2:F7)

**Woodland, parkland, farmland and open
heath with Leith Hill Tower commanding
extensive views**

The highest point in south-east England, the hill
is crowned by an 18th-century Gothic tower,
with panoramic views north to London and
south to the English Channel. There are
colourful displays of rhododendrons and
bluebells in May and June. Rugged countryside
provides exhilarating walking in woodland and
over heathland and farmland.

What's new in 2008 Extended panoramic views
from the tower and surroundings

⭐ No WC. Henman base camp (hostel for
recreational, corporate and conservation
working groups), tel. 01306 711777 for
details. Etherley Farm Campsite. Tel. 01306
621423 for details

ℹ️ **T** 01306 711777
E leithhill@nationaltrust.org.uk

🚶 Guided walks throughout the year

🚶 Two circular trails – guide available from
dispenser, £1

♿ Tower 🔼 Grounds 🔼

🍴 Servery (not NT) at Leith Hill Tower. Light
refreshments when tower open. May close
early in bad weather

🏛 Suitable for school groups. Information room
and telescope in the tower

Leith Hill									
Tower									
2 Feb–29 Mar	10–3:30	M	T	W	T	F	**S**	**S**	
30 Mar–27 Jul	10–5	M	T	W	T	**F**	**S**	**S**	
2 Aug–31 Aug	10–5	M	T	**W**	T	**F**	**S**	**S**	
6 Sep–25 Oct	10–5	M	T	W	T	**F**	**S**	**S**	
26 Oct–31 Jan 09	10–3:30	M	T	W	T	F	**S**	**S**	
Wood/estate									
All year		**M**	**T**	**W**	**T**	**F**	**S**	**S**	

Open BHols. Closed 25 Dec (tower). Last tickets sold
30mins before closing time

🐕 Under close control in Rhododendron Wood

➡️ [187:TQ139432] **Foot**: comprehensive
network of rights of way including the
Greensand Way National Trail. **Cycle**: many
rights of way lead to the tower. **Bus**: Arriva 21
Guildford–Dorking (passing close ≋ Guildford
and passing ≋ Chilworth and Dorking), alight
Holmbury St Mary, 2½ml. **Station**: Holmwood
(U), not Sun, 2½ml; Dorking 5½ml. **Road**: 1ml
SW of Coldharbour A29/B2126

🅿️ Free parking in designated areas along road
at foot of the hill, some steep gradients to the
tower. No direct vehicle access to summit.
Rhododendron Wood £2 per car.

NT properties nearby
Box Hill, Clandon Park, Hatchlands Park,
Polesden Lacey, Ranmore Common

Long Crendon
Courthouse

Long Crendon, Aylesbury, Buckinghamshire
HP18 9AN

🏛 1900   (2:D4)

**Early 15th-century building set in idyllic
village**

Set in an attractive and unspoilt village, this
building is a fine example of early timber-frame
construction. Manorial courts were held here
from the reign of Henry V until Victorian times.
The ground floor (now tenanted) was the village
poor house.

What's new in 2008 Exhibition of village history
opening

⭐ The stairs at Long Crendon are extremely
steep. No WC

ℹ️ **T** 01280 822850
E longcrendon@nationaltrust.org.uk

♿ Building 🔼

Long Crendon Courthouse								
Upper floor only								
5 Apr–28 Sep	11–6	M	T	.W	T	F	**S**	**S**
9 Apr–24 Sep	2–6	M	T	**W**	T	F	S	S
Open BH Mons: 11–6								

Charges for National Trust members apply on some special event days

[165:SP698091] Next to the parish church at the end of High Street. **Bus**: Arriva 261, Aylesbury–Oxford (passing ⊠ Haddenham & Thame Parkway). **Station**: Haddenham & Thame Parkway 2ml by footpath, 4ml by road. **Road**: 2ml N of Thame, via B4011

P Limited on-street parking (not NT)

NT properties nearby
Boarstall Duck Decoy, Boarstall Tower, Claydon House, King's Head, Stowe Landscape Gardens, Waddesdon Manor

Monk's House

Rodmell, Lewes, East Sussex BN7 3HF

🏠 ✸ 🖼 [1980]   (2:G8)
Country retreat of the novelist Virginia Woolf

⭐ Administered and largely maintained on the Trust's behalf by a tenant

ℹ️ **T** 01323 870001
E monkshouse@nationaltrust.org.uk

→ From A27 SW of Lewes, follow signs for Kingston and then Rodmell village, where turn left at Abergavenny Arms pub, then ½ml

Monk's House								
2 Apr–29 Oct	2–5:30	M	T	**W**	T	**F**	**S**	S

Mottisfont Abbey Garden, House and Estate

Mottisfont, nr Romsey, Hampshire SO51 0LP

🏠 🖼 ✸ 🍽 🛏 🍴 🚻 🏛 🎁 🖼 🛡 ♿ 🖼
🚶 🔔 🍵 [1957]   (2:C7)

Historic house set in atmospheric gardens and grounds in the River Test Valley

This handsome house, built on the 12th-century remains of an Augustinian priory, stands amid sweeping lawns next to the River Test, immortalised by F. M. Halford, the father of modern fly fishing. Plump brown trout wallow in its fast-flowing, clear waters and the tranquil lawns alongside are dotted with majestic plane trees. Mottisfont's famous walled gardens house the National Collection of Old-fashioned Roses

The Long Gallery at Mottisfont Abbey in Hampshire

(at their best in June), which are a pleasure to visit at any time of the year. The house contains a stunning drawing room, decorated in the *trompe l'oeil* style by Rex Whistler in 1938, as well as Derek Hill's collection of early 20th-century art. The wider estate includes much of Mottisfont village and surrounding farmland and woods.

What's new in 2008 Refurbished Old Dining Room, as laid out originally by Mrs Russell (the donor of Mottisfont) who was known for her fine taste and patronage of the best artists of the mid 20th century

Mottisfont Abbey								
Garden/shop/Kitchen Café								
1 Mar–3 Apr	11–5	M	T	W	T	F	S	S
5 Apr–20 Apr	11–5	M	T	W	T	F	S	S
21 Apr–25 May	11–5	M	T	W	T	F	S	S
26 May–30 May	11–5	M	T	W	T	F	S	S
31 May–22 Jun	11–8	M	T	W	T	F	S	S
23 Jun–30 Oct	11–5	M	T	W	T	F	S	S
1 Nov–21 Dec	11–4	M	T	W	T	F	S	S
House								
1 Mar–3 Apr	11–5	M	T	W	T	F	S	S
5 Apr–20 Apr	11–5	M	T	W	T	F	S	S
21 Apr–25 May	11–5	M	T	W	T	F	S	S
26 May–22 Jun	11–5	M	T	W	T	F	S	S
23 Jun–30 Oct	11–5	M	T	W	T	F	S	S

Open Good Fri & Hallowe'en. Café last orders 5 in June. Garden closes 5 on Suns in June. Car park gates close 6, except June. Access to some show rooms in house may be restricted when functions are taking place. Please tel. in advance

★ From 31 May to 22 June, when the old-fashioned roses are in bloom, the gardens are open seven days a week, from 11 to 8. Weekends are extremely busy and weekday and/or evening visits are recommended (especially evenings to enjoy the scent of the roses)

ℹ️ **T** 01794 341220 (Infoline), 01794 340757
E mottisfontabbey@nationaltrust.org.uk

🎭 Open-air theatre, art exhibitions, seasonal events and family activities

🚶 7ml estate path (leaflet £1), access from main car park (open 9–6)

♿ 🚻 ... **Building** ... **Grounds** ... ➡️

🎁 NT shop. Second-hand bookshop. Rare and unusual plant sales. Rose sales, Easter–June

🍴 Kitchen Café (licensed) at east entrance to house. Children's menu. Kiosk outside rose garden at selected times

👪 Baby-changing facilities. Pushchairs admitted. Hip-carrying infant seats for loan. Children's quiz/trail. Family activity packs. Highchairs available in Kitchen Café

🎞️ Live interpretation. Film about the estate and rose garden

🐕 Dogs are welcome in car park and on estate walk

➡️ [185:SU327270] In Test Valley between Romsey and Stockbridge. **Foot**: situated on Hampshire's long distance path, Testway. Clarendon Way passes 2ml to the N. **Cycle**: on Testway. **Station**: Dunbridge (U) ¾ml. **Road**: signposted off A3057 Romsey to Stockbridge, 4½ml N of Romsey. Also signposted off B3087 Romsey to Broughton

🅿️ Free parking

NT properties nearby
Hinton Ampner, Mompesson House, Winchester City Mill

Mottistone Manor Garden

Mottistone, Isle of Wight PO30 4EA

❄️ ... 1965   (2:C9)

20th-century 'Mediterranean' garden with views to the sea

This magical garden, planted to allow for climate change with colourful borders, shrub-filled banks and grassy terraces, is set in a sheltered valley with distant views to the sea and surrounds an Elizabethan manor house (not open). There are delightful walks on to the downs across the adjoining Mottistone Estate.

What's new in 2008 Family explorer packs

ℹ️ **T** 01983 741302
E mottistonemanor@nationaltrust.org.uk

The magical Mottistone Manor Garden is set in a valley with distant sea views

Mottistone Manor Garden

15 Mar–2 Nov	11–5:30	M	T	W	T	F	S	S

Closes dusk if earlier. House open BH Mon 26 May only, 2–5:30. Guided tours for NT members on that day, 10–12. Additional charges apply

Open-air concerts

Many trails across surrounding estate

Grounds

Plant sales plus small gift shop

Tea-garden (NT-approved concession) serving hot and cold snacks

Baby-changing facilities. Pushchairs and baby back-carriers admitted. Children's quiz/trail

On leads only

→ [196:SZ406838] **Foot**: 1ml N of coastal path; 1ml S of Tennyson Trail. **Cycle**: NCN67. On the 'Round the Island' cycle route. **Ferry**: Yarmouth (Wightlink Ltd) 6ml (tel. 0870 582 7744); E Cowes (Red Funnel) 12ml (tel. 0844 844 9988). **Bus**: Southern Vectis 7 Newport–Alum Bay. **Road**: at Mottistone, between Brighstone and Brook on B3399

P Free parking, 50yds

NT properties nearby
Bembridge Windmill, Brighstone Shop and Museum, The Needles Old Battery and New Battery, Newtown Old Town Hall

The Needles Old Battery and New Battery

West High Down, Alum Bay, Isle of Wight
PO39 0JH

 1975   (2:C9)

Victorian coastal defence and secret rocket testing site perched high above the Needles Rocks

The Old Battery, built in 1862 following the threat of a French invasion, is a spectacularly sited fort containing exhibitions about its involvement in both World Wars. Two original gun barrels are displayed in the parade ground and a tunnel leads to a searchlight emplacement perched above the Needles Rocks. The New

The spectacularly sited Needles and yachts

Battery is on a separate site further up the headland and contains an exhibition on Britain's secret rocket testing programme during the Cold War.

What's new in 2008 Exhibition at the New Battery about the part the site played in the race for space

★ No vehicular access to either Battery (visitors with disabilities by arrangement). The Old Battery has a number of steep paths and uneven surfaces. Access to the tunnel is via a narrow spiral staircase. WCs are available for visitors to the Old Battery. The New Battery has uneven surfaces and steps down to the exhibition rooms. There is no WC at the New Battery. The route from the Old Battery up to the New Battery is steep

i **T** 01983 754772
   E needlesoldbattery@nationaltrust.org.uk

Building   Grounds

Shop at Needles Old Battery

The Needles Old Battery and New Battery								
Tea-room								
1 Feb–9 Mar	11–3	M	T	W	T	F	**S**	**S**
Battery/tea-room								
15 Mar–29 Jun	10:30–5	M	**T**	**W**	**T**	**F**	**S**	**S**
1 Jul–31 Aug	10:30–5	**M**	**T**	**W**	**T**	**F**	**S**	**S**
1 Sep–2 Nov	10:30–5	M	**T**	**W**	**T**	**F**	**S**	**S**
Tea-room								
8 Nov–14 Dec	11–3	M	T	W	T	F	**S**	**S**
10 Jan–31 Jan 09	11–3	M	T	W	T	F	**S**	**S**
The Needles New Battery								
15 Mar–2 Nov	11–4	M	**T**	W	**T**	F	**S**	**S**

Also open Easter Mon and May BHols. Property closes in high winds: tel. on day of visit to check

📖 Tea-room at Needles Old Battery serving home-made food

👪 Baby-changing and feeding facilities. Pushchairs and baby back-carriers admitted. Family activity packs. Family explorer packs 'A Soldier's Watch'

🏛 Suitable for school groups. Tours by NT guide (booking required, charge applies)

🐕 On leads only

➡ [196:SZ300848] **Foot**: access is on foot only from Alum Bay ¾ml along a well-surfaced private road, Highdown NT car park 2ml, Freshwater Bay 3½ml. **Cycle**: NCN67, ½ml. Round the Island route. **Ferry**: Yarmouth (Wightlink Ltd) 5ml (tel. 0870 582 7744); E Cowes (Red Funnel) 16ml (tel. 0844 844 9988). **Bus**: Southern Vectis 7 Newport–Alum Bay then ¾ml, or Southern Vectis 'Needles Tour' from Yarmouth (15 March–Oct only). **Road**: Alum Bay W of Freshwater Bay (B3322)

🅿 No parking on site. Parking Alum Bay (not NT; minimum £3), or in Freshwater Bay (IOW Council) or Highdown car park SZ325856 (NT) and walk over Downs

NT properties nearby
Bembridge Windmill, Brighstone Shop and Museum, Mottistone Manor Garden, Newtown Old Town Hall, Tennyson Down

Newtown Old Town Hall

Newtown, Newport, Isle of Wight PO30 4PA

🏛 🚶 👪 🏛 🧍 1933   **(2:C9)**

17th-century town hall with no town but a fascinating history

The small, now tranquil, village of Newtown once sent two members to Parliament and the Town Hall was the setting for often turbulent elections. This historic building contains an exhibition depicting the exploits of 'Ferguson's Gang' – a mysterious group of anonymous benefactors.

What's new in 2008 Regular art exhibitions

⭐ No WC, nearest WC in car park

ℹ **T** 01983 531785
   E oldtownhall@nationaltrust.org.uk

Newtown Old Town Hall							
15 Mar–29 Jun	2–5	**M**	**T**	**W**	**T**	F	S	S
30 Jun–31 Aug	2–5	**M**	**T**	**W**	**T**	F	S	S
1 Sep–22 Oct	2–5	**M**	**T**	**W**	**T**	F	S	S

Last admission 15mins before closing. Open Good Fri and Easter Sat. Closes dusk if earlier than 5

🚶 By written appointment

🧍 Footpaths lead to adjacent estuary and National Nature Reserve (tel. 01983 531622)

♿ 🚻 ♿ ♿ ♿ Building ♿

👪 Baby back-carriers admitted. Children's quiz/trail. Pushchairs admitted if visitor numbers allow

🏛 Suitable for school groups

➡ [196:SZ424905] **Cycle**: NCN67, ½ml. **Ferry**: Yarmouth (Wightlink Ltd) 5ml (tel. 0870 582 7744); E Cowes (Red Funnel) 11ml (tel. 0844 844 9988). **Bus**: Wightbus 35 from Newport; otherwise Southern Vectis 7 Newport–Yarmouth, alight Barton's Corner, 1ml. **Road**: Newtown is between Newport and Yarmouth, 1ml N of A3054

🅿 Free parking, 15yds. Not suitable for coaches

NT properties nearby
Bembridge Windmill, Brighstone Shop and Museum, Mottistone Manor Garden, The Needles Old Battery and New Battery

Nymans

Handcross, nr Haywards Heath, West Sussex RH17 6EB

🏛 🏠 ♿ ♿ 🏠 ♿ 📖 🚶 🎧 🎭 ♿
👪 🏛 🧍 🍴 1954   **(2:G7)**

Outstanding 20th-century garden with a collection of rare and important plants, set around a romantic house and ruins in a beautiful wooded estate

The Nymans Estate is the achievement of three generations of the Messel family. Created in the 20th century it is one of the great gardens of the Sussex Weald, internationally known for its beauty, atmosphere and collection of rare and important plants. There are wonderful views over the Sussex countryside towards the

Unless indicated, last admission is always 30mins before closing time

Spring in the Walled Garden, Nymans, West Sussex

South Downs. Rooms on the ground floor of the house are displayed largely as the family would have used them in the early part of the 20th century. The ruins, left by a fire in 1947, form a romantic backdrop to the garden. The 110 hectares (275 acres) of woodland include walks, a conifer avenue and the lake.

What's new in 2008 Restored sunken rock garden, rose garden and arboretum. 16th-century painting returns to Nymans House after five years' conservation. Guided walks. Family Tracker Packs. Composting demonstration area. Sustainable gardening trail

Nymans									
Garden/shop/restaurant									
2 Feb–16 Mar	10–4	M	T	**W**	**T**	**F**	**S**	**S**
19 Mar–2 Nov	10–5	M	T	**W**	**T**	**F**	**S**	**S**
5 Nov–31 Jan 09	10–4	M	T	**W**	**T**	**F**	**S**	**S**
House									
19 Mar–2 Nov	11–4	M	T	**W**	**T**	**F**	**S**	**S**

Property closes at dusk if earlier. Last admission to house 3:45. Restaurant closes 30mins before property. Open BH Mons. Shop open daily in Dec. Christmas lunches in restaurant Tues-Sun. Closed 25/26 Dec and 1 Jan 09

T 01444 405250
E nymans@nationaltrust.org.uk

Guided tours of the garden. Tel. for details

Audio guide available from reception

Summer theatre, lecture lunches and workshops, Easter trail, family discovery days, woodland weeks, Chinese and Chilean weeks, summer soirées, croquet, Head Gardener and other themed walks

Woodland walks leaflet available. Themed garden walks, including sustainable gardening and plant hunters' trails

Building Grounds

NT shop. Plant centre

Licensed restaurant. Christmas lunches Dec (booking required). Children's menu. Kiosk open on sunny days. Open-air seating

Baby-changing facilities. Pushchairs and baby back-carriers admitted to garden. Children's activity area in restaurant. Family trails. Family Tracker Packs

Unless indicated, last admission is always 30mins before closing time

[×] Suitable for school groups

[×] In Nymans Woods only

→ [187:TQ265294] **Bus**: Metrobus 273 Brighton–Crawley, 271 Haywards Heath–Crawley. Both pass [≋] Crawley. **Station**: Balcombe 4½ml; Crawley 5½ml. **Road**: on B2114 at Handcross, 4½ml S of Crawley, just off London–Brighton M23/A23

[P] Free parking. Space for three coaches only

NT properties nearby
Devil's Dyke, Sheffield Park Garden, Standen, Wakehurst Place

Oakhurst Cottage

Hambledon, nr Godalming, Surrey GU8 4HF

[×] 1952   **(2:E7)**

Small 16th-century timber-framed cottage

Restored and furnished as a simple labourer's dwelling, the cottage contains fascinating artefacts reflecting four centuries of continual occupation. The delightful garden contains typical Victorian plants.

[★] No WC

[i] **T** 01483 208477
   E oakhurstcottage@nationaltrust.org.uk

[×] [∴] [P×] [D×]

→ [186:SU965380] **Bus**: Countryliner 503 from Godalming (Wed only); otherwise Stagecoach in Hants & Surrey 71 Guildford–Hindhead (passes close [≋] Godalming), alight Lane End 1ml. **Station**: Witley 1½ml. **Road**: off A283 between Wormley and Chiddingfold

[P] Parking (not NT), 200yds outside post office

NT properties nearby
Petworth House and Park, Winkworth Arboretum, The Witley Centre

Oakhurst Cottage							
26 Mar–26 Oct	2–5	M	T	**W**	T	F	**S** **S**

Admission by guided tour and appointment only. Open BH Mons: 2–5. Please book at least 24 hours in advance

Old Soar Manor

Plaxtol, Borough Green, Kent TN15 0QX

[×] 1947   **(2:H6)**

Remains of a late 13th-century knight's dwelling

This is all that is left of the manor house of c.1290 which stood until the 18th century. The solar chamber over a barrel-vaulted undercroft was once inhabited by a medieval knight.

[★] No WC

[i] **T** 01732 811145 (Infoline), 01732 810378
   E oldsoarmanor@nationaltrust.org.uk

[×] Building [×]

→ [188:TQ619541] **Bus**: Autocar 222 [≋] Tonbridge–[≋] Borough Green; New Enterprise 404 from [≋] Sevenoaks. On both alight E end of Plaxtol, then ¾ml by footpath. **Station**: Borough Green & Wrotham 2½ml. **Road**: 2ml S of Borough Green (A25); approached via A227 and Plaxtol; narrow lane

[P] No parking on site. Not suitable for coaches

NT properties nearby
Chartwell, Ightham Mote, Knole, Toys Hill

Old Soar Manor							
7 Apr–28 Sep	10–6	**M**	**T**	**W**	**T**	F	**S** **S**

Owletts

The Street, Cobham, Gravesend, Kent DA12 3AP

[×] [×] 1938   **(2:H5)**

Red-brick Charles II house with interesting garden

[★] Owletts is occupied as a family home and is administered and maintained on the Trust's behalf by a descendant of the donor. No WC

[i] **T** 01372 453401
   E owletts@nationaltrust.org.uk

→ 1ml S of A2 at W end of village, at junction of roads from Dartford and Sole Street

Owletts							
27 Mar–25 Oct	2–5:30	M	T	**W**	T	F	**S** **S**

Petworth House and Park

Petworth, West Sussex GU28 0AE

Y 1947   (2:E7)

Magnificent country house and park with an internationally important art collection

The vast late 17th-century mansion is set in a beautiful 283-hectare (700-acre) deer park, landscaped by 'Capability' Brown and immortalised in Turner's paintings. The house contains the Trust's finest collection of pictures, with numerous works by Turner, Van Dyck, Reynolds and Blake, as well as ancient and neo-classical sculpture, fine furniture and carvings by Grinling Gibbons. The Servants' Quarters contain fascinating kitchens (including a splendid copper *batterie de cuisine* of more than 1,000 pieces) and other service rooms. On weekdays additional rooms in the house are open to visitors by kind permission of Lord and Lady Egremont.

What's new in 2008 Completed restoration of Matthew Brettingham's 18th-century Ionic Rotunda in the Pleasure Grounds

i **T** 01798 343929 (Infoline), 01798 342207
E petworth@nationaltrust.org.uk

10-minute 'Welcome to Petworth' introductory talks on the house and grounds on weekdays when house is open (subject to availability)

Available in English, German and French

Concerts, open-air theatre, family events, living history events, lecture lunches and Christmas events. Send sae for details

Pleasure Grounds: spring and autumn guided walks

Family portraits and Turner paintings in the Carved Room, Petworth, West Sussex

Building Park

NT shop. Plant sales

Licensed restaurant. Mother's Day and Christmas lunches by arrangement. Children's menu

Baby-changing facilities. Pushchairs admitted. Children's quiz/trail. Children's Tracker Packs

Suitable for school groups. Education room/centre. Hands-on activities. Adult study days

Under close control and only in park, not in Pleasure Grounds

→ [197:SU976218] **Bus**: Stagecoach in the South Downs 1 Worthing–Midhurst (passing ≥ Pulborough); Compass 76 Horsham–Petworth (passing ≥ Horsham).
Station: Pulborough 5¼ml. **Road**: in centre of Petworth (A272/A283); house and park car parks on A283; pedestrian access from Petworth town and A272. No vehicles in park

P Parking, 700yds. Coaches can drop off at Church Lodge entrance and park in house car park. There is a £2 parking charge for Petworth Park car park for non-members

NT properties nearby
Black Down, Oakhurst Cottage, Uppark House and Garden, Winkworth Arboretum

Petworth House and Park									
House									
15 Mar–5 Nov	11–5	**M**	**T**	**W**	T	F	**S**	**S**	
Shop/restaurant/Pleasure Grounds									
1 Mar–12 Mar	11–4	**M**	**T**	**W**	T	F	**S**	**S**	
15 Mar–5 Nov	11–5	**M**	**T**	**W**	T	F	**S**	**S**	
12 Nov–29 Nov	10–3:30	M	T	**W**	**T**	**F**	**S**	S	
4 Dec–21 Dec	10–3:30	M	T	**W**	**T**	**F**	**S**	**S**	

Open Good Fri. **Please note**: extra rooms shown weekdays from 1 (not BH Mons) as follows. Mon: White and Gold Room and White Library. Tues/Wed: three bedrooms on first floor

For information regarding prices, see page 10

Pitstone Windmill

Ivinghoe, Buckinghamshire

[✕] [▮] 1937 **(2:E3)**

Example of the earliest form of windmill

⭐ No WC

ℹ️ **T** 01442 851227
   E pitstonemill@nationaltrust.org.uk

➔ ½ml S of Ivinghoe, 3ml NE of Tring, just W of B488

Pitstone Windmill									
1 Jun—31 Aug	2:30—6	M	T	W	T	F	S	**S**

Open BHols. Due to staffing restrictions, property may not open as publicised. Please tel. in advance

Polesden Lacey

Great Bookham, nr Dorking, Surrey RH5 6BD

[icons] [🏃] 1942 **(2:F6)**

Regency country house with renowned Edwardian interiors and gardens, set in beautiful downland countryside

This Regency house is in an exceptional setting on the Surrey Hills and enjoys stunning views. The house was remodelled in 1906-09 by the Hon. Mrs Ronald Greville, a well-known Edwardian hostess. Her collections of fine paintings, furniture, porcelain and silver are displayed in the reception rooms and galleries, as they were at the time of her celebrated house parties. There are also extensive grounds, a

Polesden Lacey									
House									
15 Mar—25 Oct	11—5	M	T	**W**	**T**	**F**	**S**	**S**
26 Oct—2 Nov	11—4	M	T	**W**	**T**	**F**	**S**	**S**
Garden/tea-room									
1 Feb—15 Feb*	11—4	**M**	**T**	**W**	**T**	**F**	**S**	**S**
16 Feb—25 Oct	11—5	**M**	**T**	**W**	**T**	**F**	**S**	**S**
26 Oct—23 Dec*	11—4	**M**	**T**	**W**	**T**	**F**	**S**	**S**
2 Jan—31 Jan 09	11—4	**M**	**T**	**W**	**T**	**F**	**S**	**S**
Shop									
1 Feb—15 Feb*	11—4	**M**	**T**	**W**	**T**	**F**	**S**	**S**
16 Feb—25 Oct**	11—5	**M**	**T**	**W**	**T**	**F**	**S**	**S**
26 Oct—30 Nov*	11—4	**M**	**T**	**W**	**T**	**F**	**S**	**S**
1 Dec—23 Dec	11—4	**M**	**T**	**W**	**T**	**F**	**S**	**S**
2 Jan—31 Jan 09**	11—4	**M**	**T**	**W**	**T**	**F**	**S**	**S**

Open BH Mons. Garden closes dusk if earlier. *Garden, tea-room and shop closed 5 Feb & 19 Nov for staff training. Garden, tea-room and shop closed 24 Dec–1 Jan 09 inc. **Shop closed 16–17 June & 5–6 Jan 09 for stocktaking

beautiful walled rose garden, lawns and landscape walks for visitors to enjoy. Once the home of poet and playwright Richard Brinsley Sheridan, Polesden Lacey was the venue for the honeymoon of the future King George VI and Queen Elizabeth in 1923.

What's new in 2008 New car park and refurbished visitor facilities

ℹ️ **T** 01372 452048
   E polesdenlacey@nationaltrust.org.uk

🏃 Garden tours by volunteer guides on most days when the house is open. Special tours of the house for booked groups only at an additional charge

Polesden Lacey: Regency house extensively remodelled during the Edwardian period

☻ Events include the Polesden Lacey Festival: an open-air theatre and music festival

🧍 Guided walks

♿ 🚻 ♿ ♿ ·· 📷 ♿ ♿ Building ♿ ♿
Grounds ♿ ➡ ♿ ♿

🛍 NT shop. Plant sales

🍽 Licensed tea-room in stable block. Booked Christmas lunches throughout Dec

♿ Baby-changing facilities. Front-carrying baby slings and hip-carrying infant seats for loan. Children's play area. Children's quiz/trail. Family activity packs. Tracker Packs

🐕 On leads in designated parts of the grounds and car park. Under close control on landscape walks, estate and farmland

➡ [187:TQ136522] **Foot**: North Downs Way within ⅔ml. **Bus**: Arriva 465 ⇆ Dorking– ⇆ Surbiton, alight near Great Bookham, 1½ml. **Station**: Boxhill & Westhumble 2ml; Dorking 4ml. **Road**: 5ml NW of Dorking, 2ml S of Great Bookham, off A246 Leatherhead– Guildford road

🅿 Parking, 200yds (pay & display), 7:30–dusk, £2.50. Fee redeemable against purchases over £10 in shop or tea-room or NT membership taken out at Polesden Lacey. Car parking free 1–23 Dec

NT properties nearby
Box Hill, Clandon Park, Claremont Landscape Garden, Hatchlands Park, River Wey and Dapdune Wharf

Priory Cottages

1 Mill Street, Steventon, Abingdon, Oxfordshire OX13 6SP

🏠 🧍 1939   **(2:C5)**

Former monastic buildings, now converted into two houses

⭐ No WC

ℹ **T** 01793 762209
   E priorycottages@nationaltrust.org.uk

Priory Cottages								
2 Apr–24 Sep	2–6	M	T	**W**	T	F	S	S
Admission by written appointment with the tenant								

Quebec House

Quebec Square, Westerham, Kent TN16 1TD

🏠 🧍 ☻ ♿ 🖼 1918   **(2:G6)**

Childhood home of General James Wolfe, victor of the Battle of Quebec (1759)

This Grade I-listed gabled house in the beautiful village of Westerham has features of significant architectural and historical interest. It has 16th-century origins and was extended and changed in the 18th and 20th centuries. Quebec House was the childhood home of General James Wolfe and contains family and military memorabilia. The old coach house contains an exhibition about the Battle of Quebec (1759).

ℹ **T** 01732 866368 (Infoline), 01732 868381
   E quebechouse@nationaltrust.org.uk

♿ 🚻 ·· 📷 ♿ Building ♿ Grounds ♿

♿ Family trails

🖼 Suitable for school groups

➡ [187:TQ449541] **Bus**: Metrobus 246 from ⇆ Bromley North (passing ⇆ Bromley South); Arriva 401 from ⇆ Sevenoaks (also ⇆ Tunbridge Wells Suns). **Station**: Sevenoaks 4ml; Oxted 4ml. **Road**: at E end of village, on N side of A25, facing junction with B2026 Edenbridge road. M25 exit 5 or 6

🅿 Parking (not NT), 200yds to E of Quebec House on A25. Visitors should then follow footpath beside A25 to house

NT properties nearby
Chartwell, Emmetts Garden, Ightham Mote, Knole, Toys Hill

Quebec House								
15 Mar–2 Nov	1–5	M	T	**W**	**T**	**F**	**S**	**S**
Garden/exhibition								
15 Mar–2 Nov	12–5	M	T	**W**	**T**	**F**	**S**	**S**
Open BH Mons								

If Polesden fired your family's imagination, you will all enjoy exploring Nymans too

River Wey and Godalming Navigations and Dapdune Wharf

River Wey and Dapdune Wharf								
15 Mar–2 Nov	11–5	M	T	W	T	F	S	S

River trips 11–4 (conditions permitting). Access to towpath during daylight hours all year

Navigations Office and Dapdune Wharf, Wharf Road, Guildford, Surrey GU1 4RR

🖼️🛠️💺🏠💼🎭🎪🛡️👫🎒🚶

🚲 ☕ 1964   (2:F6)

Tranquil waterway running for nearly 20 miles through the heart of Surrey

The Wey was one of the first British rivers to be made navigable, and opened to barge traffic in 1653. This $15\frac{1}{2}$-mile waterway linked Guildford to Weybridge on the Thames, and then to London. The Godalming Navigations, opened in 1764, enabled barges to work a further 4 miles upriver. The award-winning visitor centre at Dapdune Wharf in Guildford tells the story of the Navigations and the people who lived and worked on them through interactive exhibitions. Visitors can see where the huge Wey barges were built and climb aboard *Reliance*, one of the last surviving barges. Boat trips are available.

ℹ️ T 01483 561389
   E riverwey@nationaltrust.org.uk

🏃 Tours of Dapdune Wharf and guided walks along the towpath by arrangement

The River Wey Navigations: a tranquil waterway

🎭 Programme of events

🏃 Year-round guided walks programme

♿ 🚽 ♿ ♿ •• 🅿️ Grounds 🔊

🏠 Small shop at Dapdune Wharf

☕ Small tea-room at Dapdune Wharf

👫 Pushchairs admitted. Children's quiz/trail. Baby-changing facilities at Dapdune Wharf

🎒 Suitable for school groups. Education room/centre. Hands-on activities

🐕 On leads at Dapdune Wharf and lock areas; elsewhere under control

🚲 Cyclists welcome, but the towpath is very narrow and cyclists are asked to give way to other users and to dismount in lock areas

➡️ [186:SU993502] **River**: visiting craft can enter from the Thames at Shepperton or slipways at Guildford or Pyrford. Visitor moorings available at Dapdune Wharf and along towpath side of Navigations. **Foot**: North Downs Way crosses Navigations south of Guildford. Easy access from town centre on foot via towpath. **Bus**: Arriva 28 Guildford–Woking, Stagecoach Hants & Surrey 20 Guildford–Aldershot, Arriva 4 Guildford–Park Barn (cricket ground, 100yds). **Station**: 🚉 Addlestone, Byfleet & New Haw, Guildford, Farncombe & Godalming all close to the Navigations. **Road**: Dapdune Wharf is on Wharf Road to rear of Surrey County Cricket Ground, off Woodbridge Rd (A322), Guildford. Access to rest of Navigations from A3 & M25

🅿️ Free parking, 10yds at Dapdune Wharf. Parking for the Navigations available in Godalming town centre, Catteshall Road bridge. Dapdune Wharf: Bowers Lane (Guildford), Send village, Newark Lane (B367), Pyrford Lock and New Haw Lock

NT properties nearby
Clandon Park, Claremont Landscape Garden, Hatchlands Park, Polesden Lacey, Shalford Mill, Winkworth Arboretum

Charges for National Trust members apply on some special event days

Runnymede

Runnymede Estate Office, North Lodge, Windsor Road, Old Windsor, Berkshire SL4 2JL

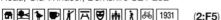 1931   (2:F5)

Riverside site of the sealing of Magna Carta

Runnymede is an attractive area of riverside meadows, grassland and broadleaved woodland, rich in flora and fauna, and with a network of pleasant footpaths. It was on this site, in 1215, that King John sealed Magna Carta, an event commemorated by the American Bar Association Memorial. The John F. Kennedy Memorial and various memorial trees are indicative of the area's importance in world history. Also here are the Fairhaven Lodges and Kiosks, designed by Lutyens, one of which is now an art gallery.

What's new in 2008 Art gallery with exhibitions and art courses throughout the year. Tel. 0845 200 8453 or visit www.1215art.com

★ (Runnymede is in the county of Surrey. Postal address as above.) The information given below relates to the Runnymede side of the river. WC only available when tea-room is open, tel. 01784 477110. No barbecues

ℹ **T** 01784 432891
E runnymede@nationaltrust.org.uk

🎭 Guided walks throughout the year

🚶 Three waymarked paths and network of footpaths; information/map guide available

♿ 🦽 •• 🅰 **Grounds** 🏔

The river meadows at Runnymede, Surrey

Runnymede	
All year	**M T W T F S S**

Grass riverside car park: April–30 Sept, daily when ground conditions allow, 10–7. Tea-room car park (hard-standing): April–30 Sept, 9–7; Oct–31 March, 9–5; closes dusk if earlier. Closed 24, 25 & 26 Dec. 1 Jan 09: open 11–3 (brunch menu only)

🍽 Magna Carta Tea-room (not NT)

🚼 Pushchairs admitted

🐕 On leads near livestock

🚲 Cycling permitted on Thames Path. NCN4 nearby

➡ [176:TQ007720] **Foot**: 1¼ml of Thames Path on property. **Bus**: Ankerwycke: Ashford Coaches 305 Staines–🚉 Wraysbury, also First 60 🚉 Slough–🚉 Wraysbury, alight Magna Carta Lane. Runnymede; 1½ml from Memorials: First 41 🚉 Egham–Old Windsor, alight 'Bells of Ouzeley'. **Station**: Egham ½ml from Runnymede, 1½ml from Memorials; Wraysbury 1ml from Ankerwycke. **Road**: Runnymede: on the Thames, 2ml W of Runnymede Bridge, on S side of A308 (M25, exit 13), 6ml E of Windsor. Ankerwycke: 3ml E of Windsor, 2ml W of Staines off B376 Staines to Wraysbury road, 1½ml from M25 (exit 13)

🅿 Parking (pay & display). Limited space for coaches on hard-standing, grass surface car park closed when wet

NT properties nearby
Cliveden, Osterley Park and House, River Wey and Dapdune Wharf

St John's Jerusalem

Sutton-at-Hone, Dartford, Kent DA4 9HQ

✚ ❖ 1943 (2:H5)

Tranquil garden and 13th-century chapel

⭐ Occupied as a private residence, maintained and managed by a tenant on the Trust's behalf. Access is to the chapel and garden only

ℹ **T** 01732 810378
E stjohnsjerusalem@nationaltrust.org.uk

➡ 3ml S of Dartford at Sutton-at-Hone

St John's Jerusalem									
2 Apr—24 Sep	2–6	M	T	**W**	T	F	S	S
1 Oct—29 Oct	2–4	M	T	**W**	T	F	S	S

Sandham Memorial Chapel

Harts Lane, Burghclere, nr Newbury, Hampshire RG20 9JT

✚ ❖ 🏠 👤 🎟 🛡 👫 🖼 1947 (2:C6)

Chapel containing Stanley Spencer's visionary paintings

Set amid pleasant countryside, this modest red-brick building houses an unexpected treasure – an outstanding series of wall paintings by Stanley Spencer. Inspired by his experiences during the First World War, and influenced by Giotto's Arena Chapel in Padua, the remarkable paintings are peppered with highly personal and unexpected detail. The work, which took six years to complete, is one of Spencer's finest achievements.

⭐ As there is no lighting in the chapel, it is best to view the paintings on a bright day. Groups by arrangement only to avoid delay. No WC, facilities nearby in pub (not NT), tel. 01635 278251

Sandham Memorial Chapel									
5 Mar—30 Mar	11–3	M	T	**W**	T	F	S	S
2 Apr—28 Sep	11–5	M	T	**W**	T	F	S	S
1 Oct—31 Oct	11–3	M	T	**W**	T	F	S	S
1 Nov—21 Dec	11–3	M	T	W	T	F	**S**	**S**

Open BH Mons: 11–5. Open other times by appointment

ℹ **T** 01635 278394
E sandham@nationaltrust.org.uk

♿ 🖼 👓 🏠 **Building** 🏞 **Grounds** 🏛

🏠 Stanley Spencer books on sale

🍴 Refreshments at Carpenter's Arms (not NT), 100yds 11–11. Tel. 01635 278251

👫 Pushchairs and baby back-carriers admitted. Children's quiz/trail

🖼 Suitable for school groups. Talks available. Out-of-hours visits available on request

🐕 In grounds on leads only

➡ [174:SU463608] **Bus**: Cango C21/2 'demand-responsive' service from Newbury. Book on 0845 602 4135. **Station**: Newbury 4ml. **Road**: 4ml S of Newbury, ½ml E of A34. From M4, follow A34, then brown signs. From A339 (Basingstoke to Newbury) follow brown signs and white NT signs

🅿 No parking on site. Parking in lay-by opposite chapel

NT properties nearby
Basildon Park, The Vyne

Scotney Castle

Lamberhurst, Tunbridge Wells, Kent TN3 8JN

🏰 🖼 🔊 ❖ ♿ ♿ 🏠 🍴 🎟 🎧 🏠
🛡 👫 🐕 1970 (2:I7)

Victorian country house set in one of England's most romantic gardens surrounded by a beautiful wooded estate

Scotney Castle was home to the Hussey family from the late 18th century and in 1835 Edward Hussey III, who took the Picturesque style as his inspiration, commissioned eminent architect Anthony Salvin to design a new country house in an Elizabethan style. The celebrated gardens, designed around the ruins of a 14th-century moated castle, feature spectacular displays of rhododendrons, azaleas and kalmia in May and June, wisteria and roses rambling over the ruins in summer, and trees and ferns providing rich colour in autumn. There are fine walks through the estate, with its parkland, woodland, hop farm and wonderful vistas and views. The house is opening in stages over the next five years,

Dogs assisting visitors with disabilities are always welcome

Romantic ruins at
Scotney Castle in Kent

with selected rooms open at the moment.
Visitors will be able to discover the different
styles of each room which show how a house
can be changed to accommodate three
generations of a family alongside modern living.

★ Designated one of the 'Seven Wonders of the
Weald'

ℹ️ **T** 01892 893820 (Infoline), 01892 893868
E scotneycastle@nationaltrust.org.uk

🦮 By arrangement and subject to availability

🛡️ Throughout the season

🧍 Estate walks guide on sale at garden entrance
and shop

♿ 🚻 ♿ 🔑 ⋮ 🅿️ ⬇️ House 🏔️
Grounds 🏔️ ➡️ ♿

🛍️ NT shop. Plant sales

☕ Light refreshments available in Walled Garden

Scotney Castle										
Garden/shop/catering										
1 Mar–9 Mar	11–4:30	M	T	W	T	F	**S**	**S**		
12 Mar–2 Nov	11–5:30	M	T	**W**	**T**	**F**	**S**	**S**		
8 Nov–21 Dec	11–4	M	T	W	T	F	**S**	**S**		
House										
12 Mar–2 Nov	11–5	M	T	**W**	**T**	**F**	**S**	**S**		
Estate walks										
All year		**M**	**T**	**W**	**T**	**F**	**S**	**S**		

Open BH Mons & Good Fri. Last admission 1hr before
closing. Closes dusk if earlier. House timed tickets

👶 Baby-changing facilities. Pushchairs admitted
to garden. Baby carriers available for loan.
Children's quiz/trail

➡️ [188:TQ688353] **Foot**: links to local footpath
network. **Cycle**: NCN18, 3ml. **Bus**: Arriva
256 Tunbridge Wells–Wadhurst (passing
🚉 Tunbridge Wells), alight Lamberhurst
Green, 1ml. **Station**: Wadhurst 5½ml.
Road: 1ml S of Lamberhurst off A21

🅿️ Parking, 130yds

NT properties nearby
Bateman's, Bodiam Castle, Sissinghurst Castle
Garden

Shalford Mill

Shalford, nr Guildford, Surrey GU4 8BS

🍴 ⬆️ 🦮 🎦 1932   (2:E6)

18th-century watermill with well-preserved
machinery

★ No WC. Regular guided tours. No parking

ℹ️ **T** 01483 561389
E shalfordmill@nationaltrust.org.uk

➡️ 1½ml S of Guildford on A281 opposite
Seahorse Inn

Shalford Mill									
16 Mar–2 Nov	11–5	M	T	**W**	T	F	S	**S**	

Guided tours for groups by prior arrangement, except
Wed & Sun

Please remember – your membership card is always needed for free admission

Sheffield Park Garden

Sheffield Park, East Sussex TN22 3QX

❀ ♨ 🏛 🏃 🎨 🐕 👪 🖼 🚶 1954   (2:G7)

Internationally renowned landscape garden and parkland

This magnificent informal landscape garden was laid out in the 18th century by 'Capability' Brown and further developed in the early years of the 20th century by its owner, Arthur G. Soames. The original four lakes form the centrepiece. There are dramatic shows of daffodils and bluebells in spring, and the rhododendrons and azaleas are spectacular in early summer. Autumn brings stunning colours from the many rare trees and shrubs, and winter walks can be enjoyed in this garden for all seasons.

★ Access to parkland limited to guided walks only

ℹ️ **T** 01825 790231
   E sheffieldpark@nationaltrust.org.uk

🎭 Events programme throughout the year

♿ 🚻 🚻 🅿️ 🚲 ◦◦ 🔄 🅿️ **Building** 🏛🔄
Grounds 🏛 ➡ 🚲

🛍 NT shop. Plant sales

☕ Tea-room (not NT) adjoins car park

Sheffield Park Garden										
2 Feb—2 Mar	10:30—4	M	T	W	T	F	**S**	**S**
4 Mar—4 May	10:30—5:30	M	**T**	**W**	**T**	F	**S**	**S**
5 May—1 Jun	10:30—5:30	**M**	**T**	**W**	**T**	F	**S**	**S**
3 Jun—5 Oct	10:30—5:30	M	**T**	**W**	**T**	F	**S**	**S**
6 Oct—2 Nov	10:30—5:30	**M**	**T**	**W**	**T**	F	**S**	**S**
4 Nov—31 Dec	10:30—4	M	**T**	**W**	**T**	F	**S**	**S**
3 Jan—31 Jan 09	10:30—4	M	T	W	T	F	**S**	**S**

Open BH Mons. Closed 23–26 Dec. Last admission 1hr before closing time or dusk if earlier

👪 Baby-changing facilities. Pushchairs and baby back-carriers admitted. Children's quiz/trail. Family activity packs. All-terrain pushchair and back carriers available

🖼 Suitable for school groups

➜ [198:TQ415240] **Bus**: Bluebell Rly link 473 from East Grinstead to Kingscote, then train to Sheffield Park; Countyliner 121 from Lewes (passing close ⬛ Lewes) (Sat only); 246 from Uckfield (Mon, Wed, Fri only). **Station**: Sheffield Park (Bluebell Rly) ¾ml; Uckfield 6ml; Haywards Heath 7ml. **Road**: midway between East Grinstead and Lewes, 5ml NW of Uckfield, on E side of A275 (between A272 & A22)

🅿️ Free parking

NT properties nearby
The Devil's Dyke, Nymans, Standen, Wakehurst Place

Autumn at Sheffield Park Garden, East Sussex

Unless indicated, last admission is always 30mins before closing time

Sissinghurst Castle Garden

Sissinghurst, nr Cranbrook, Kent TN17 2AB

1967 (2:17)

One of the world's most celebrated gardens, the creation of Vita Sackville-West and her husband Sir Harold Nicolson

This internationally renowned garden was developed by Vita Sackville-West and Sir Harold Nicolson around the surviving parts of an Elizabethan mansion. It comprises small enclosed compartments, with colour throughout the season, resulting in an intimate and romantic atmosphere. The library and study, where Vita worked, are open to visitors.

What's new in 2008 Guidebook by Adam Nicolson

★ The library and Vita Sackville-West's study are open 15 March–12 October

ℹ️ **T** 01580 710701 (Infoline), 01580 710700
  E sissinghurst@nationaltrust.org.uk

👹 Pond dipping, estate and garden tours, bat watch, painting, photography and family events throughout the season

🚶 Woodland & lake walks open all year. Free. Leaflet available

Tulips at Sissinghurst Castle Garden, Kent

♿ 🚻 ♿ ♿ ♿ ♿ ♿ P♿ ♿ **Building** ♿ ♿
Grounds ♿ ➡️

🛍️ NT shop. Plant sales

🍽️ Licensed restaurant. Christmas menu end Nov/Dec. Coffee shop near car park serving light refreshments, outside seating

👶 Baby-changing facilities. Baby back-carriers for loan. Children's quiz/trail. Children's activity packs. No pushchairs admitted in the garden as paths are narrow and uneven. Ball games etc not allowed in garden. Pond dipping. Family events throughout season

🏫 Suitable for school groups. Hands-on activities. Adult study days. Adult education in association with University of Kent

🚴 Cycling on local lanes and bridlepaths

➡️ [188:TQ810380] **Foot**: from Sissinghurst village, past church to footpath on left, signposted to garden. Path can get muddy. **Cycle**: NCN18, 8ml. **Bus**: special link from Staplehurst to garden, Tues, Fri, Sun & BHols only (tel. property); connecting bus to Smallhythe Place, otherwise Arriva 5 Maidstone–Hawkhurst (passing ⛁ Staplehurst), alight Sissinghurst, 1¼ml. **Station**: Staplehurst 5½ml. **Road**: 2ml NE of Cranbrook, 1ml E of Sissinghurst village on Biddenden Road, off A262

Sissinghurst Castle Garden									
Garden									
15 Mar–2 Nov	11–6:30	M	T	W	T	F	S	S	
Shop									
1 Mar–14 Mar	11–3	M	T	W	T	F	S	S	
15 Mar–2 Nov	11–5:30	M	T	W	T	F	S	S	
3 Nov–23 Dec	10:30–4:30	M	T	W	T	F	S	S	
Restaurant									
1 Mar–14 Mar	11–3	M	T	W	T	F	S	S	
15 Mar–26 Oct	10:30–5:30	M	T	W	T	F	S	S	
27 Oct–23 Dec	11–4	M	T	W	T	F	S	S	
Coffee shop									
1 Feb–24 Feb	11–4	M	T	W	T	F	S	S	
15 Mar–2 Nov	11–5	M	T	W	T	F	S	S	

Closes dusk if earlier. **Garden, shop and restaurant open from 10 at weekends and BHols**. Last admission 1hr before closing or dusk if earlier. Plant shop open 12–5:30

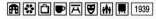 Parking, 315yds, £2

NT properties nearby
Bateman's, Bodiam Castle, Scotney Castle,
Smallhythe Place, Stoneacre

Smallhythe Place

Smallhythe, Tenterden, Kent TN30 7NG

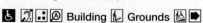 1939 (2:17)

Ellen Terry's early 16th-century house and cottage gardens

The half-timbered house, built in the early 16th century when Smallhythe was a thriving shipbuilding yard, was the home of the Victorian actress Ellen Terry from 1899 to 1928 and contains her fascinating theatre collection. The cottage grounds include her rose garden, orchard, nuttery, a wonderful display of wild flowers and the Barn Theatre, which holds exhibitions and regular performances of plays, music and talks.

What's new in 2008 Café open all season

⭐ Special bus link from Sissinghurst. Tel. for details

ℹ️ **T** 01580 762334
E smallhytheplace@nationaltrust.org.uk

🎭 Including indoor and open-air theatre

♿ 📷 👓 🖼️ Building 🌿 Grounds 🦽 ➡️

Ellen Terry's bedroom at Smallhythe Place, Kent

Smallhythe Place									
1 Mar–9 Mar	11–5	M	T	W	T	F	**S**	**S**
15 Mar–26 Oct	11–5	**M**	**T**	**W**	T	F	**S**	**S**
Café									
As house	12–4								

Open Good Fri. Last admission 4:30 or dusk if earlier

📷 Small collection of souvenirs. Occasional sales of plants from the garden

🍴 Small café (licensed) serving hot and cold drinks, alcoholic drinks and small snacks including ice-cream. Refreshments, including full meals, also available at Chapel Down Winery (not NT), 500yds from property

👨‍👧 Children's quiz/trail. Children's activity packs. Tracker Packs. Children must be accompanied by an adult

🏫 Suitable for school groups

🐕 In the grounds

➡️ [189:TQ893300] **Bus**: Coastal Coaches 312 🚌 Rye–Tenterden. **Station**: Rye 8ml; Appledore 8ml; Headcorn 10ml. **Road**: 2ml S of Tenterden, on E side of Rye road (B2082)

🅿️ Free parking (not NT), 50yds. Coaches park at Chapel Down Winery, 500yds

NT properties nearby
Bodiam Castle, Lamb House, Scotney Castle, Sissinghurst Castle Garden

South Foreland Lighthouse

The Front, St Margaret's Bay, Dover, Kent CT15 6HP

🏠 1989 (2:K6)

Fascinating and distinctive Victorian lighthouse

A striking landmark on the White Cliffs of Dover, this beautiful and historic building was the first to display an electrically powered signal and was used in experiments by Faraday and Marconi. Today, visitors can climb to the top of the lighthouse and enjoy views across east Kent and the Channel.

What's new in 2008 Regular children's events

i T 01304 852463
E southforeland@nationaltrust.org.uk

All visitors guided or accompanied in the tower. Out-of-hours tours by arrangement; guided walks to the lighthouse from the White Cliffs Visitor Centre, Mar–Oct

Children's activities

On Saxon Shore Way. Public footpaths in all directions. See White Cliffs of Dover

Building **Grounds**

Basic shop on ground floor

Bottled water and confectionery available from shop

Pushchairs and baby back-carriers admitted. Children's quiz/trail. Children's events. Pushchairs on ground floor (reception) only due to stairs

Suitable for school groups. Group activity pack

In the grounds

→ [179:TR359433] **No vehicular access**. **Foot**: on public footpaths 2½ml from Dover, 1ml from St Margarets. **Cycle**: NCN1, ½ml. **Bus**: Stagecoach in E Kent Diamond 15; Canterbury–Dover–Deal, alight Bay Hill then 1ml (via Lighthouse Road). **Station**: Martin Mill 2½ml; Dover Priory 4½ml by footpath

P No parking on site. Drivers should park at White Cliffs of Dover (NT) and walk along clifftops to lighthouse (approx. 2ml) or park at St Margaret's village/bay (approx. 1ml) and walk from there. Visitors with walking difficulties should tel. the property

NT properties nearby
The White Cliffs of Dover

South Foreland Lighthouse		M	T	W	T	F	S	S
14 Mar–3 Apr	11–5:30	M	T	W	T	F	S	S
4 Apr–24 Apr	11–5:30	M	T	W	T	F	S	S
25 Apr–22 May	11–5:30	M	T	W	T	F	S	S
23 May–5 Jun	11–5:30	M	T	W	T	F	S	S
6 Jun–17 Jul	11–5:30	M	T	W	T	F	S	S
18 Jul–11 Sep	11–5:30	M	T	W	T	F	S	S
12 Sep–29 Sep	11–5:30	M	T	W	T	F	S	S
17 Oct–27 Oct	11–5:30	M	T	W	T	F	S	S

Admission by guided tour, last tour 5. Open by arrangement during closed period for booked groups only

Sprivers Garden

Horsmonden, Kent TN12 8DR

1966   (2:H7)

Small 18th-century-style formal garden with nearby woodland walk

Occupied as a private residence, administered and maintained on the Trust's behalf by a tenant. No access to the house. No WC

i T 01892 893868
E sprivers@nationaltrust.org.uk

→ 3ml N of Lamberhurst on B2162

Sprivers Garden		M	T	W	T	F	S	S
8 June	2–5	M	T	W	T	F	S	**S**
11 June	2–5	M	T	**W**	T	F	S	S
14 June	2–5	M	T	W	T	F	**S**	**S**

Woodland walk (outside garden) open all year

Standen

West Hoathly Road, East Grinstead, West Sussex RH19 4NE

1973   (2:G7)

Arts & Crafts family home with Morris & Co. interiors, set in a beautiful hillside garden

Philip Webb, friend of William Morris, designed this family house in the 1890s. A showpiece of the Arts & Crafts Movement, it is decorated throughout with Morris carpets, fabrics and wallpapers, complemented by contemporary paintings, ceramics, embroidery and furniture. The house retains its original electric light fittings. The beautiful garden gives fine views over the Sussex countryside and there are delightful woodland walks set in the AONB of the High Weald.

Standen		M	T	W	T	F	S	S
1 Mar–9 Mar*	11–4:30	M	T	W	T	F	**S**	**S**
15 Mar–20 Jul*	11–4:30	M	T	**W**	**T**	**F**	**S**	**S**
21 Jul–31 Aug*	11–4:30	**M**	**T**	**W**	**T**	**F**	**S**	**S**
3 Sep–2 Nov*	11–4:30	M	T	**W**	**T**	**F**	**S**	**S**
8 Nov–21 Dec	11–3	M	T	W	T	F	**S**	**S**

Open BH Mons. Some queueing on approach to property may occur on BHols. *Shop/restaurant close at 5 & garden at 5:30

For information regarding prices, see page 10

Standen: Arts & Crafts Movement showpiece

⭐ Some exterior decoration may take place during 2008. Access to parts of the garden may be restricted during periods of bad weather. Only selected show rooms in house will be open outside the main visiting season and conservation work may be taking place

ℹ️ **T** 01342 323029
   E standen@nationaltrust.org.uk

🎭 Study days & demonstrations. Exhibitions. Craft workshops. Guided walks. Family activities

🚶 Nature walks through the Standen Estate: leaflets available from ticket office

♿ 🚻 🦽 ⚫ Ⓐ Pⱼ Dⱼ **Building** 🏛️ 🛗
Grounds 🏛️ ➡️

🛍️ Shop specialises in Arts & Crafts Movement merchandise. Licensed, selling local beers and wines. Plant sales

🍽️ The Barn Restaurant (licensed). Offers variety of hot and cold dishes. Reservations not possible. Children's menu

👶 Baby-changing facilities. Front-carrying baby slings and hip-carrying infant seats for loan. Family activities. Family activity packs. Children's quiz/trails

🎒 Suitable for school groups. Hands-on activities. Adult study days. Arts & Crafts resource room

🐕 On leads and only in designated areas; under close control on woodland walks

➡️ [187:TQ389356] **Cycle**: NCN21, 1¼ml. **Bus**: Bluebell Rly link 473 from 🚉 East Grinstead (tel. property for details); Metrobus 84 🚉 East Grinstead–Crawley (passing 🚉 Three Bridges), alight at approach road just north of Saint Hill, ½ml, or at Saint Hill, then ¾ml by footpath. **Station**: East Grinstead 2ml; Kingscote (Bluebell Rly) 2ml. **Road**: 2ml S of East Grinstead, signposted from town centre and B2110 (Turners Hill Road)

🅿️ Free parking, 200yds

NT properties nearby
Nymans, Sheffield Park Garden, Toys Hill, Wakehurst Place

Stoneacre

Otham, Maidstone, Kent ME15 8RS

🏚️ ❄️ 1928   (2:16)

15th-century half-timbered yeoman's house and harmonious garden

⭐ Occupied as a private residence, administered and maintained on the Trust's behalf by a tenant. Not suitable for coaches. No WC

ℹ️ **T** 01622 862871
   E stoneacre@nationaltrust.org.uk

➡️ At N end of Otham village, 3ml SE of Maidstone, 1ml S of A20

Stoneacre								
22 Mar–4 Oct	11–6	M	T	W	T	F	**S**	S
Open BH Mons. Last admission 1hr before closing								

Many Trust properties are offering Gift Aid on Entry for non-members, see page 10

Stowe Landscape Gardens

Buckingham, Buckinghamshire MK18 5DQ

🖼️🌸🦆🏠🍴🔨🗄️🎭👫🎦🚶

🔔 📶 1990   **(2:D2)**

Breathtakingly beautiful landscape gardens

A beautiful creation of the 18th century, Stowe is one of Europe's foremost landscape gardens. Hidden amongst spectacular vistas and vast open spaces are more then 40 monuments and temples, each with its own special significance. Visitors can also take a tour of Stowe House (not NT) or explore the 300 hectares (750 acres) of surrounding historic parkland. Stowe is the perfect setting for a family picnic or for those seeking peace and tranquillity, with walks and trails for all to enjoy. With the changing seasons, continuing restoration and a calendar of events for all the family, each visit provides something new.

What's new in 2008 Redesigned welcome leaflet with new map. Several reinstated statues

⭐ House (not NT), charge inc. NT members. Visitors to the gardens should allow plenty of time because of the extensive areas. Stowe House is used by Stowe School and opened to the public by Stowe House Preservation Trust. Tel. 01280 818166 for details or see www.shpt.org for opening times

Stowe Landscape Gardens									
5 Jan–2 Mar	10:30–4	M	T	W	T	F	**S**	**S**
5 Mar–2 Nov	10:30–5:30	M	T	**W**	**T**	**F**	**S**	**S**
8 Nov–31 Jan 09	10:30–4	M	T	W	T	F	**S**	**S**
Shop								
5 Jan–2 Mar	10:30–4	M	T	W	T	F	**S**	**S**
5 Mar–2 Nov	10:30–5:30	M	T	**W**	**T**	**F**	**S**	**S**
5 Nov–19 Dec	11–3	M	T	**W**	**T**	**F**	S	S
8 Nov–31 Jan 09	10:30–4	M	T	W	T	F	**S**	**S**
Tea-room								
5 Jan–2 Mar	10:30–3:30	M	T	W	T	F	**S**	**S**
5 Mar–2 Nov	10:30–5	M	T	**W**	**T**	**F**	**S**	**S**
8 Nov–31 Jan 09	10:30–3:30	M	T	W	T	F	**S**	**S**
Parkland								
All year	Dawn–dusk	**M**	**T**	**W**	**T**	**F**	**S**	**S**

Open BH Mons. Last admission 1½hr before closing. Gardens closed Sat 24 May

ℹ️ **T** 01494 755568 (Infoline), 01280 822850, 01280 818166 (House – not NT)
E stowegarden@nationaltrust.org.uk

🔨 Guided tours in gardens at 11 & 2 most days

🎭 Wide range of family events and activities. For details see website

🚶 Series of garden trails explore different areas and the stories behind Stowe Landscape Gardens

♿ 🚻 ♿ 🐕 🅿️ 🅿️ 🅳️ Building ♿
Grounds ♿ ➡️ ♿

The Palladian bridge at Stowe Landscape Gardens, Buckinghamshire

🗄 Well-stocked shop offers variety of NT products as well as plants and outdoor garden gifts

☕ Tea-room 80yds from visitor reception. Children's menu

👶 Baby-changing and feeding facilities. Pushchairs and baby back-carriers admitted. Children's quiz/trail. Children's activity packs

📖 Suitable for school groups. Live interpretation. Hands-on activities

🐕 On leads only

➔ [152:SP665366] **Foot**: 3ml from Buckingham along Stowe Avenue and through park.
Bus: Stagecoach Express X5 Cambridge–Oxford (passing ≅ Milton Keynes Central & Bicester North); Jeffs 32 from Milton Keynes (passing close ≅ Milton Keynes Central); Arriva 66 from Aylesbury (passing close ≅ Aylesbury). On all, alight Buckingham, then 3ml on foot. **Station**: Bicester North 9ml.
Road: 3ml NW of Buckingham via Stowe Avenue, off A422 Buckingham–Banbury road. Motorway access from M40 (exits 9 to 11) and M1 (exits 13 or 15a)

🅿 Free parking, 200yds

NT properties nearby
Canons Ashby House, Claydon House, King's Head, Waddesdon Manor

Uppark House and Garden

South Harting, Petersfield, West Sussex GU31 5QR

⊤ 1954   **(2:E8)**

Uppark: a tranquil and intimate 18th-century house

This gem on the South Downs, rescued after a major fire in 1989, houses an elegant Georgian interior with a famous Grand Tour collection which includes paintings, furniture and ceramics. An 18th-century doll's-house, with original contents, is one of the highlights. The complete servants' quarters in the basement are shown as they were in Victorian days when H. G. Wells' mother was housekeeper. The beautiful and peaceful garden is now fully restored in the early 19th-century Picturesque style, in a downland and woodland setting.

The Butler's Pantry at Uppark, West Sussex

What's new in 2008 Interpretation of people and place

⭐ Open on Good Friday

ℹ **T** 01730 825857 (Infoline), 01730 825415
    E uppark@nationaltrust.org.uk

🎭 Free garden history tour at 2:30, first Thur of month (April–Oct) and every Thur in July and Aug

🎒 School holiday trails and activities. Spring and autumn lecture lunches. Christmas events

🚶 Woodland walk

♿ 🚽 ♿ ♿ ∴ @ 🅿 🏢 Building ♿ ♿
Grounds ♿ ➡

🗄 NT shop. Plant sales

☕ Licensed restaurant. Children's menu

👶 Baby-changing facilities. Hip-carrying infant seats for loan. Children's quiz/trail. Children's activity packs. Children's ball games area

Uppark House and Garden								
House								
16 Mar–30 Oct	12:30–4:30	**M**	**T**	**W**	**T**	F	S	**S**
Part of house								
6 Dec–11 Dec	11–3	**M**	**T**	**W**	**T**	F	S	**S**
Garden/shop/restaurant								
16 Mar–30 Oct	11:30–5	**M**	**T**	**W**	**T**	F	S	**S**
30 Nov–18 Dec	11–3:30	**M**	**T**	**W**	**T**	F	S	**S**

Open Good Fri. BH Mons & BH Suns: Garden/shop/restaurant open 11–5 & house 11:30–4:30. Garden tours 1st Thur of each month and every Thur in July/Aug. Print Room open 1st Mon of each month, times as house

Charges for National Trust members apply on some special event days

The Oak Gallery, The Vyne, Hampshire: a treasure trove of history

On leads and only on Woodland Walk

[197:SU775177] **Foot**: South Downs Way within ⅔ml. **Bus**: Countryliner 54 Petersfield–Chichester (bus stop is 500yds from property, via a steep hill). **Station**: Petersfield 5½ml. **Road**: 5ml SE of Petersfield on B2146, 1½ml S of South Harting

Free parking, 300yds

NT properties nearby
Harting Down and Beacon Hill, Hinton Ampner, Petworth House and Park

The Vyne

Sherborne St John, Basingstoke, Hampshire RG24 9HL

1956   (2:D6)

A 16th-century house and estate and a treasure trove of history

Originally built as a great Tudor 'power house', The Vyne was visited by King Henry VIII on at least three occasions and was later home to the Chute family for more than 350 years. Dramatic improvements and changes over the centuries have made The Vyne a fascinating microcosm of changing fads and fashions over five centuries. The house is filled with the original family collection – an eclectic mix of fine furniture, portraits, textiles and sculpture. The attractive gardens and grounds feature an ornamental lake, one of the earliest summerhouses in England and woodland walks. A newly developed wetlands area, with new bird hide, attracts a wide diversity of wildlife.

What's new in 2008 As part of the ongoing restoration of The Vyne's walled garden, the new glass house will be open, plus recently reinstated vegetable plots

No ball games or picnics in the grounds

T 01256 883858
E thevyne@nationaltrust.org.uk

Guided tours of house arranged for groups (25-50) by appointment only 17 March–29 Oct: Mon, Tues & Wed 11–12

🎭 Open-air theatre, family events and lecture lunches. Extra value days – 1st & 2nd Mon of each month, excl. BHols

🧍 Woodland, parkland and wetland walks and trails

🅿 🎫♿♿♿♿·· ♿ Ⓟ♿ Building ♿♿
Grounds ♿

📷 NT shop. Plant sales

🍺 Brewhouse (licensed) adjacent to house. Kiosk in tea-garden open at busy times

👪 Baby-changing and feeding facilities. Hip-carrying infant seats for loan. Children's quiz/trail. Tracker Packs

🏫 Suitable for school groups

➔ [175/186:SU639576] **Cycle**: NCN23, 1ml. **Bus**: Stagecoach in Hampshire 45 from Basingstoke (passing ⊠ Basingstoke). No Sun service. **Station**: Bramley 2½ml; Basingstoke 4ml. **Road**: 4ml N of Basingstoke between Bramley and Sherborne St John. From Basingstoke Ring Road A339, follow North Hampshire Hospital signs until property signs. Follow A340 Aldermaston Road towards Tadley. Right turn into Morgaston Road. Right turn into car park

🅿 Free parking, 40yds. ½ml walk through gardens from visitor reception to house entrance

NT properties nearby
Basildon Park, Sandham Memorial Chapel

The Vyne										
House										
15 Mar–2 Nov	11–5		M	T	W	T	F	**S**	**S**	
17 Mar–29 Oct	1–5		**M**	**T**	**W**	T	F	S	S	
Grounds/shop/restaurant										
2 Feb–9 Mar	11–5		M	T	W	T	F	**S**	**S**	
15 Mar–2 Nov	11–5		**M**	**T**	**W**	T	F	**S**	**S**	
Shop/restaurant										
6 Nov–21 Dec	11–3		M	T	W	**T**	**F**	**S**	**S**	

Open Good Fri and BHol Mons: 11–5 (inc. house). Guided tours of house for groups (25–50) by appointment only 17 March–29 Oct: Mon, Tues & Wed 11–12. During busy periods timed tickets may be issued for entry to house

Waddesdon Manor

Waddesdon, nr Aylesbury, Buckinghamshire HP18 0JH

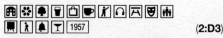

🏠🌸♦🚽📷🍽🎷🎶🎵🏹♿👪
🏫🧍🔔⧖ 1957   **(2:D3)**

Magnificent house and grounds in the style of a 16th-century French château

Waddesdon Manor was built between 1874 and 1889 for Baron Ferdinand de Rothschild to entertain his guests and display his vast collection of 18th-century French decorative arts. The furniture, Savonnerie carpets and Sèvres porcelain rank in importance with those in the Metropolitan Museum in New York and the Louvre in Paris. Outstanding are the portraits by Gainsborough and Reynolds, works by 17th-century Dutch and Flemish masters, and a spectacular silver dinner service made for George III. The extensive wine cellars can be visited. Waddesdon has one of the finest Victorian gardens in Britain, renowned for its seasonal displays, statuary and restored

Waddesdon Manor										
Gardens/shops/restaurants										
2 Feb–16 Mar	10–5		M	T	W	T	F	**S**	**S**	
19 Mar–23 Dec	10–5		M	T	**W**	**T**	**F**	**S**	**S**	
27 Dec–31 Dec	10–5		**M**	**T**	**W**	T	F	**S**	**S**	
3 Jan–31 Jan 09	10–5		M	T	W	T	F	**S**	**S**	
House										
19 Mar–26 Oct	12–4		M	T	**W**	**T**	**F**	S	S	
19 Mar–26 Oct	11–4		M	T	W	T	F	**S**	**S**	
Christmas season in house										
12 Nov–23 Dec	12–4		M	T	**W**	**T**	**F**	S	S	
12 Nov–23 Dec	11–4		M	T	W	T	F	**S**	**S**	
22 Dec–23 Dec	12–4		**M**	**T**	W	T	F	S	S	
Bachelors' wing										
19 Mar–26 Oct	12–4		M	T	**W**	**T**	**F**	S	S	
Coffee bar										
19 Mar–23 Dec	11–5		M	T	**W**	**T**	**F**	**S**	**S**	
Summerhouse										
19 Mar–26 Oct	11–5		M	T	**W**	**T**	**F**	**S**	**S**	

Admission by timed ticket only, inc. NT members. Open BH Mons. Last admission 1hr before closing. Sculpture in garden uncovered week before Easter, weather permitting. Bachelors' Wing: space limited and entry cannot be guaranteed. Coffee bar & summerhouse open weather permitting

Dogs assisting visitors with disabilities are always welcome

The colourful parterre at the south front of Waddesdon Manor, Buckinghamshire

pleasure garden. There is a rose garden, and the rococo-style aviary, newly painted and gilded, houses a splendid collection of exotic birds. Look out for changing displays in the refurbished Coach House and the Woodland Playground.

What's new in 2008 House displays on shopping in the 18th century. Exhibition of Rothschild autochromes in the Coach House

⭐ All visitors (inc. NT members) require timed tickets to enter the house, available from the ticket office. Last recommended admission to house 2:30. 28 & 29 July 'MAD about Waddesdon' festival, special admission prices apply (inc. NT members)

ℹ️ T 01296 653211 (Infoline), 01296 653226
E waddesdonmanor@nationaltrust.org.uk

🚶 Guided walks around the garden

🎧 Adult and family audio tours of the house, £2. Includes free child audio tour

🎭 Special interest days, children's activities, wine tastings, music evenings, garden workshops, floodlit opening, Christmas events. Manor Restaurant monthly evening openings

🚶 Wildlife interpretation trail

♿ 🚻🚼♿🔎📷ⓐ P↕ D↕ Building ♿♿
Grounds ♿➡️

🛍️ Gift and wine shops. Wine warehouse. Plant centre

🍽️ Manor Restaurant (not NT) (licensed). Open for breakfast, lunch and tea. Full Rothschild wine list. Children's menu. Stables Restaurant (not NT) (licensed) 800yds downhill from Manor. Buggy transfer available. Simple fresh food. Children's menu. Summerhouse kiosk in the gardens and coffee bar kiosk in shop courtyard – both open in good weather for alfresco snacks

👶 Baby-changing and feeding facilities. Front-carrying baby slings and hip-carrying infant seats for loan. Woodland playground and wildlife interpretation trail. Children's quiz/trail. Aviary. Children welcome in house under supervision. House tours for children during the school hols. Admission free for children in Aug

📖 Live interpretation. Adult study days. Audio-visual presentations

➡️ [165:SP740169] **Bus:** Arriva 16 from Aylesbury (passing close ≔ Aylesbury). **Station:** Aylesbury 6ml; Haddenham & Thame Parkway 9ml. **Road:** access via Waddesdon village, 6ml NW of Aylesbury on A41; M40 (westbound) exit 6 or 7 via Thame & Long Crendon or M40 (eastbound) exit 9 via Bicester

🅿️ Free parking

NT properties nearby
Claydon House, Cliveden, Hughenden Manor, King's Head, Stowe Landscape Gardens

Please remember – your membership card is always needed for free admission

Wakehurst Place

Ardingly, nr Haywards Heath, West Sussex
RH17 6TN

1964   (2:G7)

Kew's 'country garden', with plants from across the world

The 120 hectares (300 acres) at Wakehurst Place include walled gardens, water gardens, a wetland conservation area, woodland, lakes and ponds. Four National Collections, rare and exotic plants from the Himalayas and the southern hemisphere, and the Millennium Seed Bank are among the highlights.

What's new in 2008 Enhanced schools' and adult learning progammes. New home-cooked dishes. Wider range at plant centre

★ **Wakehurst Place is funded, administered and maintained by the Royal Botanic Gardens, Kew**. The Wellcome Trust Millennium Building, adjacent to Wakehurst Place, aims to house seeds from 10% of the world's flora by 2009 to save species from extinction in the wild. Enjoy the Millennium Seed Bank interactive public exhibition in the Orange Room and follow the journey of a seed from identification and collection, to drying and cold storage in the massive underground vaults. The mansion in the grounds is used principally for educational visits. Two rooms only are open to visitors

Wakehurst Place, West Sussex

Wakehurst Place			
Garden			
1 Mar–31 Oct	10–6		M T W T F S S
1 Nov–31 Jan 09	10–4:30		M T W T F S S
Restaurant			
All year			M T W T F S S

Closed 24/25 Dec. Shops closed on Easter Day. Catering not affected. Restaurant, shop and Seed Café open 10. Mansion, Seed Bank and restaurant close 1hr before garden. Shop trading restricted on Sun

i **T** 01444 894066 (Infoline), 01444 894000
E wakehurst@kew.org

Guided tours daily

Bluebell weekends, autumn colour festival, Christmas festivities, including regular family events all year and activities for younger visitors in Feb, May and Oct half-term hols

Numerous signed walks

Building

Grounds

Garden and gift shop (RBG Kew Enterprises). Plant sales open all year

The Stables & Tack Room Restaurant (not NT) (licensed) adjacent to mansion. Children's menu. Seed Café (not NT) at visitor centre. Further 56 covers outside on veranda

Baby-changing facilities. Pushchairs and baby back-carriers admitted. Family guide. Children's quiz/trail

Suitable for school groups. Education room/centre. Live interpretation. Hands-on activities. Adult study days

→ [187:TQ339314] **Foot**: footpath from Balcombe (5ml). **Bus**: Metrobus 81/82 Haywards Heath–Crawley, passing ≋ Haywards Heath and Three Bridges. **Station**: Haywards Heath 6ml; East Grinstead 6½ml; Horsted Keynes (Bluebell Rly) 3¾ml. **Road**: on B2028, 1½ml N of Ardingly; S of Turners Hill. From M23 exit 10, take A264 towards East Grinstead

P Parking (not NT) charges may apply, 400yds. For garden visitors only

NT properties nearby
Nymans, Sheffield Park Garden, Standen

Unless indicated, last admission is always 30mins before closing time

West Green House Garden

West Green, Hartley Wintney, Hampshire RG27 8JB

⚜ 🏠 🍽 🚼 1957   (2:D6)

Celebrated garden with an intriguing collection of follies

The delightful series of walled gardens, voted one of the UK's top 50 gardens, surrounds a charming 18th-century house. The largest features herbaceous beds with wonderful colour combinations and a superb ornamental kitchen garden. The Nymphaeum is fully restored with water steps and Italianate planting. The Lake Field and its follies and lake are now open but may, from time to time, be closed due to dampness. Restoration work is ongoing and, at the discretion of the lessee, restrictions are frequently necessary for the development and protection of the garden.

⭐ The property is let by the NT and the house is not open to visitors. The lessee has kindly agreed to the opening of the gardens and is responsible for all arrangements and facilities. There are limited visitor facilities. **Entry free to NT members on Wed & Sat only**

ℹ️ **T** 01252 844611
   E westgreenhouse@nationaltrust.org.uk

♿ 🦽🔊 **Grounds** 🦽

🏠 Gift shop (not NT). Plant sales

🍽 Tea-room (not NT). Lunches and teas

🚼 Pushchairs admitted

➔ [175:SU745564] **Bus:** Stagecoach in Hampshire 200 Basingstoke–Camberley (passing ☒ Winchfield, Blackwater and Camberley), alight Phoenix Green, 1ml. **Station:** Winchfield 2ml. **Road:** 1ml W of Hartley Wintney, 10ml NE of Basingstoke, 1ml N of A30

🅿 Free parking. Coaches must park on the gravel car park before the gates and must not let passengers alight in the lane

NT properties nearby
Basildon Park, Sandham Memorial Chapel, The Vyne

West Green House Garden							
14 May–10 Aug	11–4:30	M	T	**W**	T	F	**S** **S**
Open BH Mons							

West Wycombe Park

West Wycombe, Buckinghamshire HP14 3AJ

🏛 ⚜ ♠ 🚶 🚶 1943   (2:E4)

Perfectly preserved rococo landscape garden, surrounding a neo-classical mansion

The fine landscape garden was created in the mid 18th century by Sir Francis Dashwood, founder of the Dilettanti Society and the Hellfire Club. The house is among the most theatrical and Italianate in England, its façades formed as classical temples. The interior has Palmyrene ceilings and decoration, with pictures, furniture and sculpture dating from the time of Sir Francis. The lavishly decorated house has featured in many recent films and television series, including *The Importance of Being Earnest* and *Vanity Fair*.

⭐ The West Wycombe Caves and adjacent café are privately owned and NT members must pay admission fees. No picnics or dogs in park

ℹ️ **T** 01494 755571 (Infoline), 01494 513569
   E westwycombe@nationaltrust.org.uk

West Wycombe Park, Buckinghamshire

West Wycombe Park							
Grounds only							
1 Apr–29 May	2–6	**M**	**T**	**W**	**T**	F	S	S
House/grounds							
1 Jun–31 Aug	2–6	**M**	**T**	**W**	**T**	F	S	S

Admission by guided tour on weekdays, tours every 20mins (approx). Last admission 45mins before closing

🚶 Tours of house on weekdays. Tours of grounds by written arrangement

🚶 Circular walks leaflet available from post office, newsagent and Hughenden estate office

♿ 🅿 🔧 📷 🅿 Building 🅿🅿 Grounds 🅿

➡ [175:SU828947] **Foot:** circular walk links West Wycombe with Bradenham and Hughenden Manor. **Bus:** Arriva 340–2 High Wycombe–Stokenchurch; Red Rose 275 High Wycombe–Oxford (all pass close ⊞ High Wycombe). **Station:** High Wycombe 2½ml. **Road:** 2ml W of High Wycombe. At W end of West Wycombe, S of the Oxford road (A40)

🅿 Free parking, 250yds

NT properties nearby
Cliveden, Hughenden Manor, West Wycombe Village

West Wycombe Village and Hill

West Wycombe, Buckinghamshire

🏠 ✝ 🏛 🏋 🍴 🍽 🎋 🖼 🚶 🐕 1934 **(2:E4)**

Chilterns village with buildings spanning several hundred years

The village is rare in its architecture, with cottages and inns dating from the 16th to 18th centuries. The hill, with its fine views, is surmounted by an Iron Age hill fort and is part of the original landscape design of West Wycombe Park. It is now the site of a church and the Dashwood Mausoleum.

⭐ The church, mausoleum and caves do not belong to the NT. WCs in village

ℹ **T** 01494 755573
E westwycombe@nationaltrust.org.uk

A view of a row of houses at West Wycombe Village, Buckinghamshire, which comprises examples from the 16th to 18th centuries

🚶 Leaflets obtainable from village store (50/51 High St) and newsagent (36/37 High St): Village architectural trail and West Wycombe, Bradenham & Hughenden circular walks

♿ Grounds 🅿

🍽 Refreshments at garden centre and village pubs (not NT)

🔲 Suitable for school groups

➡ [175:SU828946] 2ml W of High Wycombe, on both sides of A40. **Bus:** Arriva 340–2 High Wycombe–Stokenchurch; Red Rose 275 High Wycombe–Oxford (all pass close ⊞ High Wycombe). **Station:** High Wycombe 2½ml. **Road:** 2ml W of High Wycombe. At W end of West Wycombe, S of the Oxford road (A40)

🅿 Free parking at top of hill and in village. Single track lane to top of hill. Height restrictions apply in village car park. Car park on hill locked at dusk

NT properties nearby
Cliveden, Hughenden Manor, West Wycombe Park

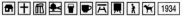

West Wycombe Village							
All year		**M**	**T**	**W**	**T**	**F**	**S**	**S**

The White Cliffs of Dover

Langdon Cliffs, Upper Road, Dover, Kent
CT16 1HJ

 1968

(2:K7)

Magnificent coastal site overlooking the English Channel

The White Cliffs of Dover are internationally famous. The Visitor Centre has spectacular views and introduces the visitor to 5 miles of coast and countryside through imaginative displays and interpretation. Much of the chalk downland along the clifftops is a Site of Special Scientific Interest, Area of Outstanding Natural Beauty and Heritage Coast, with interesting flora and fauna, and the Visitor Centre is an excellent place for watching the world's busiest shipping lanes.

What's new in 2008 Interpretation panels, children's challenges and walks leaflets

☆ WC only available when centre is open. Car parking fee applies

ℹ️ T 01304 202756
E whitecliffs@nationaltrust.org.uk

🎭 Guided walks from White Cliffs, including to South Foreland Lighthouse (2ml), April–Oct

😊 Plant Fair, children's activities and Apple Fayre

🚶 On public footpaths, towards St Margaret's and Deal. Self-guided and guided walks around property, and long distance footpath – Saxon Shore Way

The White Cliffs of Dover Visitor Centre with Dover Castle in the background

The White Cliffs of Dover									
Visitor Centre									
1 Feb–29 Feb	11–4	**M**	**T**	**W**	**T**	**F**	**S**	**S**	
1 Mar–31 Oct	10–5	**M**	**T**	**W**	**T**	**F**	**S**	**S**	
1 Nov–31 Jan 09	11–4	**M**	**T**	**W**	**T**	**F**	**S**	**S**	
Car park									
1 Feb–29 Feb	8–5	**M**	**T**	**W**	**T**	**F**	**S**	**S**	
1 Mar–31 Oct	8–6	**M**	**T**	**W**	**T**	**F**	**S**	**S**	
1 Nov–31 Jan 09	8–5	**M**	**T**	**W**	**T**	**F**	**S**	**S**	

Car park closed 24–25 Dec. Visitor Centre open July and Aug until 6 at weekends, closed 24–26 Dec

♿ 🚻 ♿ ♿ 👁 🔍 Building ♿ ♿
Grounds ♿

🎁 Range of souvenirs and gifts

☕ Coffee shop in Visitor Centre. Range of drinks, ice-cream, snacks and light lunches to eat in or take away. Children's menu

🚼 Baby-changing facilities. Pushchairs and baby back-carriers admitted. Baby back-carriers for loan. Children's quiz/trail. Children's activity packs. Tracker Packs

🎨 Suitable for school groups

🐕 Under close control at all times (stock grazing)

🚲 Cycling strictly prohibited along the White Cliffs

➡️ [138:TR336422] **Foot**: signed pathways from the port, station and town centre. Located on the Saxon Shore Way path. **Cycle**: NCN1. **Ferry**: signed route from Dover ferry terminal. **Bus**: Stagecoach in E Kent Diamond 15 Canterbury–Dover–Deal, alight Castle Hill then 1ml (via Upper Road). **Station**: Dover Priory 2½ml. **Road**: from A2/A258 Duke of York roundabout, take A258 towards Dover town centre, 1ml turn left into Upper Road, ¾ml turn right into entrance. From A20 straight ahead at first four roundabouts and left at second set of lights. Turn right at next lights. After ½ml turn right into Upper Road, follow for ¾ml turn right into entrance

🅿️ Parking, 100yds. Charge collected at gate. Disabled badge holders £1.50, car £2.50, motorhomes £3, coaches £5, annual season ticket £25. Not suitable for caravans

NT properties nearby
Bockhill Farm, Kingsdown Leas, St Margaret's Leas, South Foreland Lighthouse

For information regarding prices, see page 10

Winchester City Mill

Bridge Street, Winchester, Hampshire SO23 OEJ

[icons] 1929 (2:D7)

Working watermill in the heart of Winchester

Spanning the River Itchen, this water-powered corn mill was first recorded in the Domesday survey of 1086. Rebuilt in 1744, it remained in use until the turn of the last century and has now been restored to full working order. The waterwheel and machinery turn daily throughout the season and there is something to interest everyone, including awe-inspiring mill races, hands-on activities for children, a video presentation and displays about the river and its wildlife.

What's new in 2008 Current CCTV footage of nocturnal otter activity in the river

⭐ No WC available for public use at the Mill

ℹ **T** 01962 870057
E winchestercitymill@nationaltrust.org.uk

🚶 Tours by arrangement

😊 Holiday activities for children. Regular flour milling demonstrations

🚶 Winnall Moors walks leaflet

♿ [icons] Building

🏠 Well-stocked gift shop

👪 Pushchairs and baby back-carriers admitted. Children's quiz/trail. Holiday activities for children

🏫 Suitable for school groups. Education room/centre. Hands-on activities. Partnership with Hampshire & Isle of Wight Wildlife Trust with displays about the River Itchen

➡ [185:SU487294] At foot of High Street, beside City Bridge. **Foot**: South Downs Way, King's Way, Itchen Way, Three Castles Path, Clarendon Way – all pass through or terminate at Winchester. **Bus**: from surrounding areas. **Station**: Winchester 1ml

🅿 No parking on site. Parking at Chesil car park. Park & ride to Winchester from M3, exit 10

NT properties nearby
Hinton Ampner, Mottisfont Abbey

Winkworth Arboretum

Hascombe Road, Godalming, Surrey GU8 4AD

[icons] 1952 (2:F7)

Tranquil hillside woodland with sweeping views

Established in the 20th century, this hillside arboretum now contains more than 1,000 different shrubs and trees, many of them rare. The most impressive displays are in spring, with magnolias, bluebells and azaleas, and autumn, when the colour of the foliage is stunning. In the summer it is an ideal place for family days out and picnics.

ℹ **T** 01483 208477
E winkwortharboretum@nationaltrust.org.uk

😊 'Plant of the month', Family Fun Day and other seasonal events

Winchester City Mill									
16 Feb–24 Feb	11–4:30	M	T	W	T	F	S	S
5 Mar–6 Apr	11–5	M	T	W	T	F	S	S
7 Apr–20 Apr	11–5	M	T	W	T	F	S	S
23 Apr–25 May	11–5	M	T	W	T	F	S	S
26 May–1 Jun	11–5	M	T	W	T	F	S	S
4 Jun–13 Jul	11–5	M	T	W	T	F	S	S
14 Jul–7 Sep	11–5	M	T	W	T	F	S	S
10 Sep–26 Oct	11–5	M	T	W	T	F	S	S
27 Oct–24 Dec	11–4:30	M	T	W	T	F	S	S
1 Jan 09	11–4	M	T	W	T	F	S	S
Open BH Mons								

Winkworth Arboretum									
Arboretum									
All year	Dawn–dusk	M	T	W	T	F	S	S
Shop/tea-room									
1 Feb–29 Feb	11–4	M	T	W	T	F	S	S
1 Mar–18 Mar	11–4	M	T	W	T	F	S	S
21 Mar–18 Nov	11–5	M	T	W	T	F	S	S
25 Nov–16 Dec	11–5	M	T	W	T	F	S	S
6 Jan–31 Jan 09	11–4	M	T	W	T	F	S	S
Shop & tea-room open BH Mons 11–5. Arboretum may be closed in bad weather (especially in high winds)									

Many Trust properties are offering Gift Aid on Entry for non-members, see page 10

Bluebells at Winkworth Arboretum, Surrey: a tranquil woodland with sweeping views

[figure] Walks leaflet available. Tree guide listing 200 species

[figures] Grounds [figures]

[figure] Tea-room. Children's menu

[figure] Baby-changing facilities. Pushchairs and baby back-carriers admitted. Children's quiz/trail. Family Fun Day

[figure] Suitable for school groups

[figure] On leads only

[figure] [169/170/186:SU990412] **Bus:** Arriva 42/44 Guildford–Cranleigh (passing close [station] Godalming). **Station:** Godalming 2ml. **Road:** near Hascombe, 2ml SE of Godalming on E side of B2130

[figure] Free parking, 100yds

NT properties nearby
Clandon Park, Hindhead Commons, Oakhurst Cottage, River Wey and Dapdune Wharf, The Witley Centre

The Witley Centre

Witley, Godalming, Surrey GU8 5QA

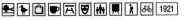 1921   **(2:E7)**

Countryside visitor and education centre

At the heart of Witley Common, a fascinating mix of woodland and heath, the purpose-built centre houses a countryside exhibition and provides a venue for school groups and children's holiday activities.

[figure] **T** 01428 683207
E witleycentre@nationaltrust.org.uk

[figure] Fun days and children's holiday events

[figure] Selection of walks leaflets available at shop

[figures] **Building** [figures] **Grounds** [figure]

[figure] Small shop with limited range of souvenirs

[figure] Ice-cream and soft drinks

[figure] Pushchairs admitted. Children's quiz/trail. Fun days and children's holiday events

[figure] Suitable for school groups. Education room/centre

[figure] Under close control

[figure] Cycling on bridleway around commons

[figure] [186:SU930410] **Bus:** Stagecoach in Hants & Surrey 70 Guildford–Midhurst, 71 Guildford–Haslemere (both passing close [station] Godalming & passing [station] Haslemere). **Station:** Milford 2ml. **Road:** 7ml SW of Guildford between London–Portsmouth A3 and A286 roads, 1ml SW of Milford

[figure] Free parking, 100yds

NT properties nearby
Black Down, Frensham Common, Hindhead Commons, Ludshott Common, Oakhurst Cottage, Winkworth Arboretum

The Witley Centre								
Centre								
4 Mar–29 Oct	11–4	**M**	**T**	**W**	**T**	**F**	S	S
Common								
All year		**M**	**T**	**W**	**T**	**F**	**S**	**S**

For details of events go to www.nationaltrust.org.uk/events

London

Several National Trust properties, which now fall within the Greater London area, would once have been set in open countryside. Large estates such as Osterley Park – originally created to entertain wealthy guests away from the hotbed of the city – now provide vital green lungs in the midst of surburbia. Similarly Sutton House in Hackney was originally part of a small village, yet is now in the heart of a densely populated urban area – ideally placed for carrying out the Trust's work with local communities and inner city schools.

Despite being one of the world's major conurbations, London still contains many green and relatively tranquil areas. The Trust has played an important role in securing several fragments of the city's once extensive common land for present and future generations to enjoy.

An unexpected jewel in Middlesex is Osterley Park House, which is surrounded by 145 hectares (359 acres) of park and farmland. The 18th-century mansion was designed in 1761 by Robert Adam, the leading architect and interior designer of his day, and the interiors are as dazzling and impressive now as they were when built. The park surrounding the mansion is a much-loved local amenity, and a major project is now underway to restore the gardens to their former 18th-century splendour.

In the midst of a densely built-up area of South West London lies an unexpected oasis. Morden Hall Park is a picturesque and historic park with meadows, waterways and lovely old buildings.

Above: **Sutton House**
Right and below:
Morden Hall Park

There is also an impressive rose garden (with more than 2,000 rose bushes). Whether you are looking for a safe haven for a stroll or a jog, a great spot for a picnic or a pleasant day out with the family, Morden Hall Park is well worth a visit.

Both Morden Hall Park and Osterley Park are particularly recommended for visitors with walking difficulties. Morden Hall Park has very accessible paths through the rose garden and along the river, while Osterley Park has many routes – around the lake and wider estate – that are suitable for wheelchair users.

Previous page: detail of entrance hall at Osterley Park, Middlesex (2:F5)

Blewcoat School Gift Shop

23 Caxton Street, Westminster, London SW1H 0PY

🏠 🖼 1954 **(2:G5)**

Early 18th-century school for the poor, now the National Trust's London shop

Built in 1709 at the expense of a local brewer and used as a school until 1926, this small and elegant building is now the National Trust's London gift shop.

⭐ No WC

ℹ️ **T** 020 7222 2877
E blewcoat@nationaltrust.org.uk

♿ 📷 Building 🔊

➡️ [176:TQ295794] Near the junction of Caxton Street and Buckingham Gate. **Foot**: Thames Path within ⅔ml. **Cycle**: NCN4, ¾ml.
Bus: Frequent local services (tel. 020 7222 1234). **Station**: Victoria ¼ml.
Underground: St James's Park (District & Circle Lines) 100yds

🅿️ No parking on site

NT properties nearby
Carlyle's House

Blewcoat School Gift Shop		M	T	W	T	F	S	S
All Year	10–5:30	**M**	**T**	**W**	**T**	**F**	S	S
27 Mar–18 Dec	10–7	M	T	W	**T**	F	S	S
15 Nov–20 Dec	10–4	M	T	W	T	F	**S**	**S**
Closed BH Mons and Good Fri								

Carlyle's House

24 Cheyne Row, Chelsea, London SW3 5HL

🏠 ✳️ 🎎 🎭 🖼 📷 1936 **(2:F5)**

The home of a Victorian celebrity couple

In 1834 Thomas Carlyle, a struggling Scottish writer, and Jane, his clever ambitious wife, rented this modest but roomy terraced house in the then unfashionable village of Chelsea. Within a few years the house had become a favourite gathering place of the literary world, including Dickens, Tennyson and Browning. Explore the Carlyles' home – preserved in 1895 as London's

Thomas Carlyle's House became London's first literary shrine

first literary shrine – and see the kitchen, dining room, drawing room, bedroom and Carlyle's intriguing soundproofed study, all with original contents. There is also a small garden. Then explore the surrounding streets and discover where many other famous writers, artists and composers lived.

ℹ️ **T** 020 7352 7087
E carlyleshouse@nationaltrust.org.uk

🎭 Talks

♿ 📷 👓 Building 🔊

🖼 Suitable for school groups. Booked school groups welcome: Wed, Thur & Fri between 10 and 1. Max 15

➡️ [176:TQ272777] Off Chelsea Embankment between Albert and Battersea Bridges. NT sign on corner of Cheyne Row. Or via Kings Rd and Oakley St. NT sign on corner of Upper Cheyne Row. **Foot**: Thames Path within ⅔ml.
Cycle: NCN4. **Bus**: frequent local services (tel. 020 7222 1234). **Underground**: Sloane Square (District & Circle Lines) or South Kensington (Piccadilly, District & Circle Lines) 1ml. **Station**: Victoria 1½ml

🅿️ No parking on site. Very limited street parking at pay & display meters nearby

NT properties nearby
Fenton House, Ham House and Garden, Morden Hall Park, Sutton House, 2 Willow Road

Carlyle's House		M	T	W	T	F	S	S
12 Mar–24 Oct	2–5	M	T	**W**	**T**	**F**	S	S
15 Mar–2 Nov	11–5	M	T	W	T	F	**S**	**S**
Open BH Mons: 11–5								

Unless indicated, last admission is always 30mins before closing time

Eastbury Manor House

Eastbury Square, Barking   IG11 9SN

🏠 ✳ 🗄 🍽 🍴 🎪 🎭 👬 🎦 🔊 1918   (2:G5)

Elizabethan merchant's house and gardens

An important example of a medium-sized brick-built Elizabethan manor house, the building is architecturally distinguished and well preserved, with notable early 17th-century wall paintings. The house is rumoured to have connections with the Gunpowder Treason Plot. 'Bee boles' can be seen in the walled garden. The property is managed by the London Borough of Barking and Dagenham.

⭐ House open 1st & 2nd Sat of month all year. Further to the award of a grant from the Heritage Lottery Fund, building work is expected to commence early 2008 to improve access and interpretation of the house: some areas will therefore be inaccessible to visitors. Please check www.barking-dagenham.gov.uk

ℹ️ **T** 020 8724 1002
E eastburymanor@nationaltrust.org.uk
W www.barking-dagenham.gov.uk

🍴 Guided tours available when open to the public on Mon and Tues and the first and second Sat of each month. Costumed guided tours on the first Sat of each month. Candlelit tours on the last Tues of each month

😊 Family days, heritage days, evening events

♿ 🚾 ♿ 🅿 🎧 👓 Building 🔼📶🔽
Grounds 🔼

🗄 The Old Buttery gift shop (not NT) sells a variety of traditional gifts and souvenirs, as well as books and publications

🍽 Garden tea-room (not NT) in house. In good weather, refreshments can be taken in kitchen garden. Hot and cold drinks, sandwiches and snacks

👬 Baby-changing facilities. Pushchairs admitted. Children's activities on Family Days and during school holidays

🔊 Suitable for school groups. Education room/centre

🐕 On leads and only in garden

Eastbury Manor House									
House									
All year	10–4	**M**	**T**	W	T	F	S	S	
Tea-room/shop									
As house	10–3:30								

Closed BH Mons. Last admission 45mins before closing. Closed 29 & 30 Dec. House open 1st & 2nd Sat of month all year

➡️ [177:TQ457838] In Eastbury Square, 500yds walk S from Upney station (follow brown signs). **Cycle**: LCN15 ¾ml. Upney Lane local cycle route links LCN15 to property. **Bus**: TfL 62, 287, 368 ➡ Barking–Rainham/Chadwell Heath. **Station**: Barking, then one stop on District Line to Upney ¼ml. **Underground**: Upney (District Line). **Road**: ½ml N of A13, 2ml E of A406, just off A123 Ripple Road

🅿 Free street parking for cars and coaches in Eastbury Square, adjacent

NT properties nearby
Rainham Hall, Sutton House

Fenton House

Hampstead Grove, Hampstead, London NW3 6SP

🏠 ✳ 🍴 👓 👬 🔊 🐕 1952   (2:G4)

Handsome 17th-century merchant's house with walled garden

Set in the winding streets of Hampstead village, this late 17th-century house contains an outstanding collection of porcelain, 17th-century needlework pictures and Georgian furniture, and the Benton Fletcher collection of early keyboard instruments, most of which are in working order. The delightful walled garden includes fine displays of roses, an orchard and a working kitchen garden.

What's new in 2008 Collection of English paintings and drawings bequeathed to Fenton House by the late actor Peter Barkworth. New loan of paintings by Sir William Nicholson

Fenton House									
1 Mar–16 Mar	2–5	M	T	W	T	F	**S**	**S**	
19 Mar–31 Oct	2–5	M	T	**W**	**T**	**F**	**S**	**S**	
22 Mar–2 Nov	11–5	M	T	W	T	F	**S**	**S**	

Open BH Mons and Good Fri: 11–5

The productive vegetable garden at Fenton House, Hampstead

⭐ For audition to use the early keyboard instruments, apply in writing one month in advance to the Curator of Instruments, c/o Fenton House

ℹ️ **T** 01494 755563 (Infoline), 020 7435 3471
E fentonhouse@nationaltrust.org.uk

🎭 Demonstration tours (max. 20) of instruments by the Curator. Send sae or go to events website for details

♥ Garden Easter Trail, summer concerts, costume exhibition and Apple Day

🚶 Self-guided walks leaflet 50p

♿ 🔲 👓 🅰️ **Building** 🌿 **Grounds** ♿

👶 Baby-changing facilities. Front-carrying baby slings for loan. Children's quiz/trail

🏫 Suitable for school groups

➡️ [176:TQ262860] Visitors' entrance on W side of Hampstead Grove. **Bus**: frequent local services (tel. 020 7222 1234).
Station: Hampstead Heath 1ml.
Underground: Hampstead (Northern Line) 300yds

🅿️ No parking on site

NT properties nearby
Sutton House, 2 Willow Road

George Inn

The George Inn Yard, 77 Borough High Street, Southwark, London SE1 1NH

🏠 🍺 🍽️ 👨‍👩‍👧 1937 **(2:G5)**

Last remaining galleried inn in London

Famous as a coaching inn during the 17th century and mentioned by Dickens in *Little Dorrit*, the George Inn is now leased to a private company and still in use as a public house.

ℹ️ **T** 020 7407 2056
E georgeinn@nationaltrust.org.uk

🍽️ Licensed restaurant (not NT)

👨‍👩‍👧 Children admitted subject to normal licensing regulations

🐕 On leads and only in courtyard

➡️ [176:TQ326801] On E side of Borough High St, near London Bridge Station.
Cycle: NCN4, $\frac{1}{4}$ml. **Bus**: frequent local services (tel. 020 7222 1234).
Station: London Bridge 🚉 & Underground (Northern & Jubilee lines)

NT properties nearby
Carlyle's House, Sutton House

George Inn								
All year		Licensing hrs	M	T	W	T	F	S S

Ham House and Garden

Ham Street, Ham, Richmond-upon-Thames
TW10 7RS

T 1948 (2:F5)

Unique 17th-century house with sumptuous interiors, original collections and partially restored formal gardens

One of a series of grand houses and palaces alongside the River Thames, Ham House and Garden is an unusually complete survival of the 17th century, where time appears to have stood still. Rich in history and atmosphere, Ham House was largely created by the charismatic Duchess of Lauderdale, who was deeply embroiled in the politics of the English Civil War and subsequent restoration of the monarchy. As a sumptuous statement of wealth and power, Ham was built to impress in its day and continues to do so today. With lavish interiors, unique historical features and unusual 17th-century gardens, Ham is a treasure trove waiting to be discovered. Its collections of art, textiles and furniture are outstanding, while its outbuildings – including an ice house, a dairy, with unusual cast iron 'cows' legs', and the

Ham House and Garden									
House									
15 Mar–2 Nov	12–4	**M**	**T**	**W**	T	F	**S**	**S**	
Garden									
All year	11–6	**M**	**T**	**W**	T	F	**S**	**S**	
Shop/café									
2 Feb–9 Mar	11–3:30	M	T	W	T	F	**S**	**S**	
15 Mar–2 Nov	11–5:30	**M**	**T**	**W**	T	F	**S**	**S**	
8 Nov–21 Dec	11–3:30	M	T	W	T	F	**S**	**S**	
Café									
3 Jan–31 Jan 09	11–3:30	M	T	W	T	F	**S**	**S**	

Open Good Fri: house 12–4; garden 11–6. Garden: closes at dusk if earlier; closed 25, 26 Dec & 1 Jan 09. Special Christmas openings in Dec for garden/shop/café. Christmas lunches

earliest known purpose-built still house (the 17th-century equivalent of an in-house pharmacy) – are intriguing. The gardens are a rare example of 17th-century design and are currently being restored.

What's new in 2008 The original 17th-century gates have been reinstated

★ No barbecues

i T 020 8940 1950
E hamhouse@nationaltrust.org.uk

The south front of Ham House seen from the Wilderness

📷 Free guided garden tours Weds 2 & 3 (dates as house, no booking necessary) and on selected Sats (please confirm in advance). Ghost tours, behind-the-scenes and treasures of the stores tours throughout year. Contact property or website for details (booking essential)

🎭 Open-air theatre, special guided tours, Christmas carol concerts and special openings

🚶 Local walks leaflet available from property

♿ 🅿️🖼️🎨👓📷🅿️ Building 🖼️↕️♿
Grounds 🖼️➡️♿

🎁 NT gifts, local arts and crafts, wide selection of books and plants grown in peat-free compost

🍴 Orangery Café (licensed). Children's menu

👶 Baby-changing facilities. Front-carrying baby slings and hip-carrying infant seats for loan. Children's quiz/trail. Children's activity packs. Tracker Packs

🎒 Suitable for school groups. Education room/centre. Hands-on activities

➡️ [176:TQ172732] On S bank of Thames, W of A307, between Richmond and Kingston; Ham gate exit of Richmond Park. **Foot**: Thames Path passes main entrance. 1½ml from Richmond, 3ml from Kingston. **Cycle**: NCN4. Ferry access from Twickenham.
Ferry: seasonal foot/bike ferry across River Thames from Twickenham towpath (by Marble Hill House–EH) to Ham House. **Bus**: TfL 371 Richmond–Kingston, alight Royal Oak pub, Ham Street, then ½ml walk. 65 Ealing Broadway–Kingston, alight Ham Polo Ground, Petersham Rd, ¾ml walk along historic avenues (both pass ≒ Richmond and Kingston). Also K5 Morden–Ham, alight Dukes Avenue, then 1ml walk (tel. 020 7222 1234). **Station and Underground**: Richmond 1½ml by footpath, 2ml by road. **Station**: Kingston 2ml.
Road: on S bank of the Thames, W of A307, between Richmond and Kingston; Ham gate exit of Richmond Park, readily accessible from M3, M4 and M25

🅿️ Free parking (not NT), 400yds

NT properties nearby
Carlyle's House, Claremont Landscape Garden, Morden Hall Park, Osterley Park and House

Lindsey House

99/100 Cheyne Walk, Chelsea, London
SW10 0DQ   **(2:G5)**
The property will only open on 13 September, 1–4, as part of London Open House Weekend

Morden Hall Park

Morden Hall Road, Morden SM4 5JD

🏠🍴🎁❀👜🚶🐕🅿️📷📖🖼️
🎭👥🎞️🚶♿ 1942   **(2:G5)**

Green oasis in the heart of suburbia

With its refreshing wide open spaces and tranquil, meandering river, Morden Hall Park is a rare public commodity in South West London. The attractive rose gardens, wild meadows and wetlands rich in wildlife, add up to a delightful haven in the midst of a densely built-up area. Visitors can stroll along the river to the site of two watermills which were used until 1922 to grind snuff, and explore other historic estate buildings now used by a range of local artisans. The original walled kitchen garden now houses a newly refurbished riverside café and gift shop, as well as a large, independently run garden centre.

What's new in 2008 Snuff Mill with new features, information and interactive displays. New refreshment kiosk. Second-hand bookshop

ℹ️ **T** 020 8545 6850
   E mordenhallpark@nationaltrust.org.uk

Morden Hall Park									
Park									
All year	8–6		**M**	**T**	**W**	**T**	**F**	**S**	**S**
Shop/café									
All year	10–5		**M**	**T**	**W**	**T**	**F**	**S**	**S**
Kiosk									
5 Apr–26 Oct	11–5		M	T	W	T	F	**S**	**S**
Second-hand bookshop									
5 Apr–26 Oct	12–4		M	T	W	T	F	**S**	**S**

Car park by café, shop and garden centre closes at 6. Shop and café closed 25, 26 Dec & 1 Jan 09. Rose garden and estate buildings area open 8–6. Snuff Mill Environmental Education Centre open first Sun of April–Oct, 12–4. Kiosk also open every day during school hols, April–Oct 11–5 (unless the weather is bad)

Many Trust properties are offering Gift Aid on Entry for non-members, see page 10

[icon] Guided tours by arrangement

[icon] Discovery days 3rd Sun each month from April to Oct and children's activities every Thur during school holidays. Programme of walks and workshops for adults

[icon] Various walks throughout the year. Tel. for details

[icons] Building [icons] Grounds [icons]

[icon] NT shop. Garden centre run by Capital Gardens plc as NT tenants (tel. 020 8646 3002). Second-hand bookshop

[icon] Riverside café. Children's menu. Refreshment kiosk in rose garden (open weekends and school hols)

[icon] Baby-changing facilities

[icon] Suitable for school groups. Education room/centre

[icon] On leads around buildings and rose garden; under close control elsewhere

[icon] Wandle Trail, from Croydon to Wandsworth, runs through the park

[icon] [176:TQ261684] Near Morden town centre. **Foot**: Wandle Trail from Carshalton or Wandsworth. **Cycle**: NCN22, route passes through park. **Bus**: frequent from surrounding areas (tel. 020 7222 1234). **Station**: Tramlink to Phipps Bridge stop, on park boundary ½ml. **Underground**: Morden (Northern Line) 500yds to park, 800yds to café & shop. **Road**: off A24, and A297 S of Wimbledon, N of Sutton

[icon] Free parking, 25yds

NT properties nearby
Claremont Landscape Garden, Ham House and Garden

Listening to a storyteller in a meadow at Morden Hall Park

Osterley Park and House

Jersey Road, Isleworth, Middlesex TW7 4RB

[icons] [1949] (2:F5)

Magnificent neo-classical house with fine Adam interiors, landscape park and 18th-century gardens

In 1761 the founders of Child's Bank commissioned Robert Adam to transform a Tudor mansion into an elegant neo-classical villa. This was their house in the country, created for entertainment and to impress friends and business associates. Today the spectacular interiors contain one of Britain's most complete examples of Adam's work. The magnificent 16th-century stable block survives largely intact. The house is set in extensive park and farmland, complete with 18th-century gardens and neo-classical garden buildings.

What's new in 2008 Garden and park restoration project continues with new examples of Georgian planting. 29 Oct–2 Nov Osterley Park House Conservation in Action Week

[icon] Please contact property to check operating times of mobility vehicles and transfer service. No barbecues, fires or gazebos. 19 & 20 July 'Osterley through the Ages' event, garden entry via ticket only (inc. NT members)

Osterley Park and House		M	T	W	T	F	S	S
House/Jersey Galleries								
12 Mar–2 Nov	1–4:30	M	T	**W**	**T**	**F**	**S**	**S**
6 Dec–21 Dec	12:30–3:30	M	T	W	T	F	**S**	**S**
Shop								
12 Mar–2 Nov	12:30–5	M	T	**W**	**T**	**F**	**S**	**S**
5 Nov–21 Dec	12–4	M	T	**W**	**T**	**F**	**S**	**S**
Tea-room								
12 Mar–2 Nov	11–5	M	T	**W**	**T**	**F**	**S**	**S**
5 Nov–21 Dec	12–4	M	T	**W**	**T**	**F**	**S**	**S**
Park								
1 Feb–29 Mar	8–6	**M**	**T**	**W**	**T**	**F**	**S**	**S**
30 Mar–25 Oct	8–7:30	**M**	**T**	**W**	**T**	**F**	**S**	**S**
26 Oct–31 Jan 09	8–6	**M**	**T**	**W**	**T**	**F**	**S**	**S**
Garden								
12 Mar–2 Nov	11–5	M	T	**W**	**T**	**F**	**S**	**S**

Open Good Fri & BH Mons. Car park closed 25 & 26 Dec. Garden open to 7 1st Thur in April–Oct

For details of events go to www.nationaltrust.org.uk/events

The elegant portico of Osterley Park House

☐ **Suitable for school groups. Education room/centre. Hands-on activities

☐ On leads only in park, unless indicated

☐ Cycling in park only with shared access

☐ [176:TQ146780] **Cycle**: links to London cycle network. **Bus**: TfL H28 Hayes–Hounslow–Osterley, H91 Hounslow–Hammersmith to within $\frac{1}{2}$ml. **Station**: Isleworth 1$\frac{1}{2}$ml. **Underground**: Osterley (Piccadilly Line), turn left on leaving station, $\frac{1}{2}$ml. **Road**: on A4 between Hammersmith and Hounslow. Follow brown tourist signs on A4 between Gillette Corner and Osterley underground station; from W M4, exit 3 then follow A312/A4 towards central London. Main gates at junction with Thornbury and Jersey roads

☐ Parking, 400yds, £3.50. Coach-parking free. Car park open as park

NT properties nearby
Ham House and Garden

☐ **T** 01494 755566 (Infoline), 020 8232 5050
E osterley@nationaltrust.org.uk

☐ Including guided walks, tours and family activities

☐ Free leaflet features a map of walks in the park. Estate guide (£1) features walks around the park and garden

☐ ☐ ☐ ☐ ☐ ☐ ☐ ☐ ☐ **Building** ☐ ☐
Grounds ☐ ☐ ☐

☐ NT gift shop

☐ The Stables Tea-room & Garden (licensed). Children's menu

☐ Baby-changing facilities. Front-carrying baby slings and hip-carrying infant seats for loan. Children's guide. Tracker Packs. Pushchairs admitted when visitor numbers allow

Rainham Hall

The Broadway, Rainham, Havering RM13 9YN

☐ ☐ ☐ ☐ ☐ 1949 (2:H5)

A charming and peaceful Georgian house and simple garden

Built in 1729 by Captain John Harle, who dealt in fine building materials. His house, which is unfurnished and awaiting conservation work, was a showcase for the high quality materials he sold. The simple garden has some surprising features.

What's new in 2008 Open-air theatre. Check website for details

☐ No WC

☐ **T** 020 7799 4552
E rainhamhall@nationaltrust.org.uk

☐ Short guided tours

☐ Open day events to coincide with the Rainham Christmas Fair and May Day activities. Open-air theatre

Rainham Hall									
5 Apr–25 Oct		2–5	M	T	W	T	F	**S**	**S**
Open BH Mons									

Charges for National Trust members apply on some special event days

→ [177:TQ521821] **Bus**: frequent local services (tel. 020 7222 1234). **Station**: Rainham, 200yds. **Road**: 5ml E of Barking. Just S of the church

P Limited parking (disabled only) on site. Free parking (not NT–Tesco), 300yds

NT properties nearby
Eastbury Manor House, Red House, Sutton House

Red House

Red House Lane, Bexleyheath DA6 8JF

 2003   **(2:H5)**

Unique home of William Morris – artist, craftsman and socialist

Red House is of enormous international significance in the history of domestic architecture and garden design. The only house commissioned by William Morris, it was designed and built in 1859 by his friend and colleague, architect Philip Webb. It was Webb's first house and was strongly influenced by Gothic medieval architecture. It is constructed with the emphasis on natural materials – warm red brick is set under a steep red-tiled roof – and there are numerous original features, including some items of fixed furniture designed by Morris and Webb, as well as wall paintings and stained glass by Edward Burne-Jones. Originally surrounded by orchards and countryside,

Red House							
1 Mar–21 Dec		11–4:45	M T	**W T F S S**

Admission by booked guided tour with limited free flow entry after 3:30. Tel. for details

Red House is now in suburbia, although visitors can still enjoy the peaceful garden which inspired some of Morris's later work.

What's new in 2008 Early stables now open to the public. New documents exhibition room, displaying a letter from Webb to Morris found under the floorboards. Embroidered panel of Aphrodite, designed by William Morris, in Dining Room. Picnics by arrangement

★ When the property was acquired by the NT from private owners in 2003 it was opened for visitors to see it as it was. Research has now begun to reveal more about the house as originally created by Webb and Morris and, as time goes on, more features and items are displayed. No WC

i **T** 020 8304 9878 (Bookings 9:30–1:30, Tues–Sat) **E** redhouse@nationaltrust.org.uk

Daily tours. Special tours by arrangement

Autumn Apple Day

Building **Grounds**

Small shop selling books and items related to the Arts & Crafts Movement and the house. Plant sales when available

The peaceful garden at Red House, Bexleyheath

Tea-room serving selection of light refreshments

Children's quiz

Suitable for school groups

[177:TQ481750] **Bus**: frequent local services. **Station**: ⊠ Bexleyheath, ¾ml. **Road**: off A221 Bexleyheath. Visitors will be advised how to reach the property when booking

No parking at property. Parking is at Danson Park (approx. 1ml). Parking charge at weekends and BHols

NT properties nearby
Ightham Mote, Knole, Rainham Hall

'Roman' Bath

5 Strand Lane, London WC2

 1948 (2:G5)

Remains of a bath – possibly Roman

The Bath is administered and maintained by Westminster City Council. No WC

T 020 8232 5050
E romanbath@nationaltrust.org.uk

Just W of Aldwych station (now closed), approach via Surrey Street

'Roman' Bath								
2 Apr–24 Sep	1–5	M	T	**W**	T	F	S	S

Admission by appointment only with Westminster CC (24-hrs notice) during office hours. Bath visible through window from pathway all year

Sutton House

2 & 4 Homerton High Street, Hackney, London E9 6JQ

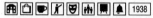 1938 (2:G4)

A Tudor house surviving in the heart of an East London community

Sutton House was built in 1535 by a prominent courtier of Henry VIII, Sir Ralph Sadleir. The house retains much of the atmosphere and character of a Tudor house despite some alterations by later occupants who included a succession of merchants, Huguenot silkweavers

The Great Chamber, Sutton House, Hackney

and Victorian schoolmistresses. Visitors will see oak-panelled rooms, original carved fireplaces, wall decorations and the charming internal courtyard, as well as a Tudor kitchen and intimate Georgian and Victorian rooms. An attractive exhibition tells the history of the house and its many occupants.

T 020 8986 2264
E suttonhouse@nationaltrust.org.uk

Tours 1st Sun of each month at 3

Including monthly family days, Hallowe'en ghost tours, Christmas carol concerts and Black History Month activities

Building

NT shop. Good selection of inexpensive gifts and local history books

Brick Place Café (NT-approved concession) (licensed)

Sutton House								
Historic rooms								
1 Feb–21 Dec	12:30–4:30	M	T	W	**T**	**F**	**S**	**S**
Art gallery/shop/café-bar								
1 Feb–21 Dec	12–4:30	M	T	W	**T**	**F**	**S**	**S**

Open BH Mons. Closed Good Fri. Sutton House is a lively property in regular use by local community groups. The rooms will always be open as advertised, but please tel. in advance if you would like to visit the property during a quiet time

Unless indicated, last admission is always 30mins before closing time

Baby-changing facilities. Children's quiz/trail. Family activity packs

🖼 Suitable for school groups. Live interpretation. Hands-on activities. Adult study days

→ [176:TQ352851] At the corner of Isabella Road and Homerton High Street.
Cycle: NCN1, 1¼ml. **Bus**: frequent local services (tel. 020 7222 1234).
Station: Hackney Central ¼ml; Hackney Downs ½ml

P No parking on site. Metered parking on adjacent streets

NT properties nearby
Fenton House, 2 Willow Road

2 Willow Road

Hampstead, London NW3 1TH

🏠 👤 🎭 1994   **(2:G5)**

Unique and influential Modernist home from 1939

This fascinating house was designed by the Modernist architect Ernö Goldfinger and occupied as his family home for more than 40 years. Alongside the collection of modern art, which includes works by Henry Moore, Max Ernst and Bridget Riley, are personal possessions and furniture designed by Goldfinger himself. The attention to detail and design in this intimate house is surprising and enlightening and it still looks modern today.

What's new in 2008 Earlier opening times on Sat with an extra tour at 11. Timed entry for non-guided viewing, 3–5 when busy

⭐ No WC, local pub allows visitors to use facilities

ℹ **T** 01494 755570 (Infoline), 020 7435 6166
E 2willowroad@nationaltrust.org.uk

2 Willow Road								
1 Mar–29 Nov	11–5	M	T	W	T	F	**S**	S
20 Mar–31 Oct	12–5	M	T	W	**T**	**F**	S	S

Entry by timed tour only at 12, 1 & 2 (plus 11 on Sats). Places on tours limited and available on a first-come first-served basis on the day. Non-guided viewing 3–5 with timed entry when busy. Introductory film shown at regular intervals

The elegant, light-filled landing at 2 Willow Road

👤 Tours at 12, 1 & 2 (plus 11 on Sat)

🎭 Guided walks, evening events, British Sign Language-interpreted walks and tours, please contact the house

♿ 🔲 ⠿ 🅰 Building 🔲 🔲
 Children's quiz/trail

→ [176:TQ270858] On corner of Willow Road and Downshire Hill. **Foot**: from Hampstead underground, left down High Street and first left down Flask Walk (pedestrianised). Turn right at the end into Willow Road.
Bus: frequent local services (tel. 020 7222 1234). **Station**: Hampstead Heath ¼ml.
Underground: Hampstead (Northern Line) ½ml

P No parking on site. Limited on-street parking. East Heath Road municipal car park, 100yds, open intermittently

NT properties nearby
Fenton House

East of
England

The East of England is a region characterised by wide expanses of open countryside, huge skies and sweeping views.

The Trust cares for 11,000 hectares (27,000 acres) of land, of which almost half supports such a rich biological diversity that these areas are designated Sites of Special Scientific Interest.

In Norfolk, Trust land includes the highest point in the county at West Runton, as well as the beautiful historic landscape and woodland at Sheringham Park.

On the edge of Norfolk's famous Broads is Horsey Mere, where the Trust owns more than 800 hectares (1,900 acres) of marshland, marrams and farmland. Nearby is the beautiful 'island' reserve of Heigham Holmes, where cranes returned to breed in 1982.

At Sutton Hoo you can get close to one of the most fascinating archaeological sites in this country's history, and enjoy walks over rare lowland heath along the River Deben. While on the Essex/Suffolk border, at the heart of 'Constable Country', Bridge Cottage is the perfect starting point for an inspiring walk into the beautiful Dedham Vale.

Many excellent walks are also to be had on Dunstable Downs in Bedfordshire, which command outstanding views over the Vale of Aylesbury and along the Chiltern Ridge.

Besides stunning scenery, the region is also proud of its strong culinary traditions and, wherever possible, our restaurants and tea-rooms serve local, seasonal and regional produce – not only providing the very best for visitors, but supporting the local economy.

At Wimpole Hall, rare breed meat from Home Farm and crops from the Walled Garden are available in the restaurant. While at Felbrigg Hall, fruit from the Walled Garden is made into more than 4,000 desserts for visitors to the estate, every year!

Elsewhere, herbs and flowers from the garden flavour and decorate meals at Oxburgh Hall and Peckover House, while Anglesey Abbey and Houghton Mill grind their own flour and use it in baking. So if you want to try the very best regional recipes, home cooked and made from the finest local ingredients, enjoy a meal at one of the Trust's excellent restaurants.

Sheringham Park

Above: **Sutton Hoo**
Left: **Houghton Mill**
Below: **Wimpole Home Farm**

Previous page: visitors at Houghton Mill, Cambridgeshire (3:F6)

Right: **Northey Island**

Above: **common seal** Right: **Dunwich Heath** Below: **Wicken Fen**

Abundant wildlife

There are splendid birdwatching opportunities throughout the East of England.

The North Norfolk coast, as well as being home to several major colonies of common and grey seals, hosts more than 3,000 pairs of breeding Sandwich terns in the summer, while in the autumn and winter thousands of waders and waterfowl descend upon the marshes of Blakeney Freshes. The Trust maintains this delicate natural habitat for the benefit of future generations, successfully balancing access with conservation.

Wicken Fen National Nature Reserve in Cambridgeshire is a haven for rare wildlife and virtually the last remnant of the extensive fenland that once covered much of the East of England.

Further down the coast in Suffolk is Orford Ness, the secret military test site which is now an internationally important nature reserve and vital habitat for rare species, such as the little tern.

Natural habitats in this area include Dunwich Heath, a surviving fragment of the sandy heaths locally known as the Sandlings. The heath, adjacent to the RSPB's reserve at Minsmere, is where the rare Dartford warbler returned to this part of the country, and is now home to a strong breeding population.

There are good birdwatching opportunities too, on the Essex coast, especially on the reserve of Northey Island in the Blackwater Estuary and at Copt Hall Marshes (visitors require a permit to visit Northey Island. Tel. the Warden on 01621 853142).

Magnificent walks and ancient woodland

As well as spectacular houses, the Blickling, Felbrigg, Ickworth and Wimpole estates offer wonderful walks through their breathtaking parkland.

For walks on the wilder side it is hard to beat Dunstable Downs in Bedfordshire. Climb to the top of the whaleback chalk downland and enjoy widespread views in every direction – over the Vale of Aylesbury and along the Chiltern Ridge. At the northern end of the Chiltern Hills discover a stunning variety of flora and fauna on the Sundon Hills, Moleskin and Markham, Sharpenhoe Clappers and Smithcombe Hills.

www.nationaltrust.org.uk/coastandcountryside

Hatfield Forest, near Bishop's Stortford – a 400-hectare (1,000-acre) Royal Hunting Forest – was created by Henry I in the 11th century. It remains largely unaltered and contains more than 900 ancient pollarded trees, some over 1,200 years old. However, just a mile down the road is Stansted Airport, where expansion plans could mean planes will fly directly over the forest and traffic will increase enormously, destroying 1,000 years of peace and tranquillity and threatening a fragile ecosystem with destructive pollution.

Help the National Trust to oppose the expansion of Stansted by visiting www.nationaltrust.org.uk/hatfieldforest and signing our online petition. By contrast, the 40 hectares (99 acres) of ancient woodland at Blakes Wood, near Chelmsford, is tranquil and secluded all year round.

Treats for all the family

In the south of the region the Trust cares for an outstanding Arts & Crafts house, home to one of the greatest literary figures of the 20th century. Shaw's Corner in Hertfordshire offers a rare glimpse into the life and work of George Bernard Shaw, and if you have never seen a real Oscar before, this is the place to go.

Above: **Blickling Hall, Gardens and Park, Norfolk**
Below: **Hatfield Forest** Bottom: **sailing organised by Brancaster Millennium Activity Centre**

In Suffolk, you can find out more about the exceptional children's author Beatrix Potter. The creator of characters such as Jemima Puddleduck and Peter Rabbit was a regular visitor to Melford Hall; and original sketches and curiosities are displayed there to enthral children of all ages.

Children will also enjoy the special play areas at many of our properties, including Blickling, Ickworth, Sutton Hoo and Wimpole Home Farm. Indeed, a visit to the Home Farm – with its rare breed animals, goats, rabbits, pigs and special lambing days – is a must for every family with younger children.

At Wicken Fen children can take part in hands-on learning at one of Britain's oldest nature reserves. For some serious family excitement visit Brancaster Millennium Activity Centre, which runs activity weeks throughout the year.

Kayaking, sailing, orienteering – there's plenty to keep the children occupied. Parents can join in or go off on their own adventures, confident that their offspring are safe in the hands of fully qualified and highly experienced instructors.

www.nationaltrust.org.uk/coastandcountryside

Anglesey Abbey, Gardens and Lode Mill

Quy Road, Lode, Cambridge, Cambridgeshire
CB25 9EJ

🏠 ✖ ♿ 🖻 🍴 ⓘ 🛡 👬 🛍 ⏲ 1966 (3:G7)

Jacobean-style country house with collection of treasures, set in fine formal and informal gardens with a working watermill

Behind its Jacobean-style exterior Anglesey Abbey is a vision of the golden age of English country house living, created by the first Lord Fairhaven and his brother from 1926 to 1966. It is a treasure trove of sumptuous furnishings, fine books and works of art, as well as a collection of French and English clocks. Life revolved around horse racing and shooting, and weekend guests enjoyed the height of 1930s luxury. As you move outside, examine the 12th-century gargoyles of the original priory and see if you can find the 20th-century additions added by Lord Fairhaven and his brother in 1939. This is a mere taste of Anglesey's statuary – there are more than 100 pieces of classical sculpture in the formal and landscape gardens. Be sure to explore the wildflower meadows and the Hoe Fen Wildlife Discovery area as well as the attractive Winter Garden, with its stunning year-round displays of colour. A mill at Anglesey was listed in the Domesday Book and the present watermill, Lode Mill, dates from the 18th century. Restored in

Anglesey Abbey										
Winter Garden										
1 Feb–16 Mar	10:30–4:30	M	T	**W**	**T**	**F**	**S**	**S**
5 Nov–21 Dec	10:30–4:30	M	T	**W**	**T**	**F**	**S**	**S**
31 Dec–31 Jan 09	10:30–4:30	M	T	**W**	**T**	**F**	**S**	**S**
House										
19 Mar–2 Nov	1–5	M	T	**W**	**T**	**F**	**S**	**S**
Garden										
19 Mar–2 Nov	10:30–5:30	M	T	**W**	**T**	**F**	**S**	**S**
Lode Mill										
As Winter Garden	11–3:30	M	T	**W**	**T**	**F**	**S**	**S**
19 Mar–2 Nov	1–5	M	T	**W**	**T**	**F**	**S**	**S**
Restaurant/shop/plants										
As gardens*		M	T	**W**	**T**	**F**	**S**	**S**

Open BHol Mon and Good Fri. The Gallery: 19 Nov–18 Jan 09: Wed–Sun 11–3:30. Snowdrop seasons: 16 Jan–17 Feb & 21 Jan–22 Feb 09 (days & times as Winter Garden). Summer late openings: restaurant & gardens only, 5 Jun–1 Aug, Thu & Fri until 9. NGS days: Sun 22 June & Sun 24 Aug (on these days entry proceeds go to charity. NT members are asked to make a donation). *Winter Garden/garden

1982, it is in full working order. Come and feel the power of water in action on the first and third Saturdays of every month (subject to water levels).

What's new in 2008 Visitor centre including catering at Redwoods, shop and plant centre, WCs and the Robinson Room for learning and functions

ℹ **T** 01223 810080
E angleseyabbey@nationaltrust.org.uk

The Coade stone caryatids on the Cross Avenue, Anglesey Abbey, Gardens and Lode Mill, Cambridgeshire

Unless indicated, last admission is always 30mins before closing time

New programme of tours. Tel. for details

Send sae for details

Building Grounds

NT shop with many local goods. Plant sales. Second-hand bookshop (opening later in season)

Redwoods restaurant (licensed). Serving traditional Cambridgeshire dishes reflecting the property, using locally sourced and seasonal produce. Children's menu

Baby-changing facilities. Hip-carrying infant seats for loan. Children's quiz/trail. Tracker Packs. Pushchairs admitted to gardens only

Suitable for school groups. Education room/centre

[154:TL533622] **Foot**: Harcamlow Way from Cambridge. **Cycle**: NCN51, 1¼ml. **Bus**: Stagecoach in Cambridge 10 from Cambridge (frequent services link Cambridge and bus station). **Station**: Cambridge 6ml. **Road**: 6ml NE of Cambridge on B1102. Signposted from A14, junction 35

P Free parking, 50yds

NT properties nearby
Houghton Mill, Ickworth House, Park and Gardens, Wicken Fen National Nature Reserve, Wimpole Hall, Wimpole Home Farm

Blakeney National Nature Reserve

Norfolk Coast Office, Friary Farm, Cley Road, Blakeney, Norfolk NR25 7NW

 1912 (3:13)

An extensive area of saltmarsh, vegetated shingle, dunes and grazing marsh

Blakeney National Nature Reserve is an iconic coastal reserve, well known for its internationally important seabirds and overwintering wildfowl and waders. It is also home to an increasing number of seals (both Common and Grey), at Blakeney Point. The reserve is an amazing place to see a huge range of important coastal habitats and species and covers an area of

The Lifeboat House on Blakeney Point

1,097 hectares (2,711 acres) at Blakeney Point, Blakeney Freshes, Blakeney Marshes, Morston Marshes and Stiffkey Marshes. The information centre at Morston Quay gives visitors the opportunity to understand more about this dynamic coastal environment.

What's new in 2008 New interpretation displays at Morston Quay Information Centre and the Lifeboat House on Blakeney Point as part of the 'GEESE' project. New interpretation boards at Stiffkey, Morston and Blakeney on marine awareness and Blakeney Harbour. Dog policy being revised, please contact for details

★ WCs at Blakeney Point closed Sept–April. Local authority maintained WCs at Morston Quay and Blakeney Quay

i **T** 01263 740241
E blakeneypoint@nationaltrust.org.uk

For school and special interest groups (small charge) by arrangement

The Peddars Way and Norfolk Coast Path passes through the reserve

Tea-room (NT-approved concession) at Morston Quay. No tea-room at Blakeney Point

Suitable for school groups

Dog policy being revised. Please visit website, email or tel. for details

Regional route 30 runs along ridge above the coast

Blakeney National Nature Reserve						
All year	M T W T F S S					

Tea-room and information centre at Morston Quay open according to tides and weather

→ [133:TG000460] **Foot**: Norfolk Coast Path passes property. **Cycle**: regional route 30 runs along ridge above the coast. **Ferry**: ferries (not NT) to Blakeney Point. **Bus**: Norfolk Green Coast Hopper 36 ⬛ Sheringham–Hunstanton. **Station**: Sheringham (U) 8ml. **Road**: Morston Quay, Blakeney and Cley are all off A149 Cromer–Hunstanton road

P Parking at Morston Quay, £2.50 all day (pay & display). Parking also at Blakeney Quay (administered by Blakeney Parish Council). All quayside car parks liable to flooding

NT properties nearby
Brancaster, Felbrigg Hall, Garden and Park, Sheringham Park

Blickling Hall, Gardens and Park

Blickling, Norwich, Norfolk NR11 6NF

1940   (3:J4)

Magnificent Jacobean house with gardens and park

Built in the early 17th century, Blickling is one of England's great Jacobean houses. The spectacular Long Gallery houses one of the finest private collections of rare books in England, and you can view fine Mortlake tapestries, intricate plasterwork ceilings, an excellent collection of furniture and paintings, as well as the newly restored 19th-century Hungerford Pollen painted ceiling. The glorious gardens are beautiful all year round – with thousands of spring bulbs, swathes of bluebells, vibrant summer borders and rich autumn colours. It really is a garden for all seasons and, with its 18th-century Orangery, secret garden and woodland dell, there is plenty to discover. The Hall is set in an historic park with miles of beautiful woodland and lakeside walks – it even has a pyramid-shaped Mausoleum.

What's new in 2008 Restoration of the kitchen and service areas. Learn about life downstairs in the 1930s and hear stories by the actual people who lived and worked at Blickling. Handling collection available

★ RAF Museum in Harness Room. Croquet available. Coarse fishing on lake (July–31 Jan 09), day tickets available. Second-hand bookshop

ℹ **T** 01263 738030
E blickling@nationaltrust.org.uk

🏃 Taster tours of house: 11:30 on most house open days, excluding BH weekends (additional charge, inc. NT members). Garden tours at 2 on most garden open days (additional charge, inc. NT members). Guided estate walks (approx. 3ml), twice a month: free

🛡 Including open-air concerts and theatre, guided walks, themed family and restaurant events. Leaflet available

Aerial view of Blickling Hall, Norfolk: one of England's great Jacobean houses

Blickling Hall, Gardens and Park

House										
15 Mar—27 Jul	11–5	M	T	**W**	**T**	**F**	**S**	**S**
28 Jul—31 Aug	11–5	**M**	T	**W**	**T**	**F**	**S**	**S**
1 Sep—2 Nov	11–5	M	T	**W**	**T**	**F**	**S**	**S**
Garden/shop/restaurant/bookshop								
1 Feb—14 Mar	11–4	M	T	W	**T**	**F**	**S**	**S**
15 Mar—27 Jul	10:15–5:15	M	T	**W**	**T**	**F**	**S**	**S**
28 Jul—31 Aug	10:15–5:15	**M**	T	**W**	**T**	**F**	**S**	**S**
1 Sep—2 Nov	10:15–5:15	M	T	**W**	**T**	**F**	**S**	**S**
3 Nov—31 Jan 09	11–4	M	T	W	**T**	**F**	**S**	**S**
Park								
All year	Dawn—dusk	**M**	**T**	**W**	**T**	**F**	**S**	**S**
Plant centre								
15 Mar—2 Nov	10:15–5:15	M	T	**W**	**T**	**F**	**S**	**S**
Cycle hire								
21 Mar—2 Nov	10:15–5	M	T	W	T	F	**S**	**S**

Open BH Mons: Easter–Aug inc. During local school
hols (Easter–Oct inc.), all facilities (inc. cycle hire) open
Wed–Mon inc. Closed 25 & 26 Dec

Extensive network of footpaths around the
estate including three waymarked walks.
Links to Weavers' Way and Marriott's Way
(long-distance paths)

Building

Grounds

NT shop and plant sales. Second-hand
bookshop in Lothian Barn

Restaurant (licensed) and courtyard café
(licensed) serving local seasonal produce.
Children's menu. Functions and weddings
catered for in private suite of rooms

Baby-changing facilities. Front-carrying baby
slings and hip-carrying infant seats for loan.
Children's play area. Family guide. Children's
quiz/trail. Family activity packs

Suitable for school groups

On leads in park and woods

Cycle hire centre in orchard picnic area. Map
available of routes. Bridleways on property
give shared use for cyclists

→ [133:TG178286] **Foot:** Weavers' Way from
Great Yarmouth & Cromer (Aylsham, 2ml).
Cycle: permitted path alongside Bure Valley
Rly, ✴ Wroxham–Aylsham. **Bus:** Anglian 711
from Salhouse (passing ✴ Hoveton &

Wroxham) Mon–Fri only (24hrs notice
required); otherwise Sanders 4, 41/3/4,
First/Norfolk Green X5 Norwich–Holt (passing
close ✴ Norwich), alight Aylsham 1½ml.
Station: Aylsham (Bure Valley Rly from ✴
Hoveton & Wroxham) 1¾ml; N Walsham (U)
8ml. **Road:** 1½ml NW of Aylsham on B1354.
Signposted off A140 Norwich (15ml N) to
Cromer (10ml S) road

P Parking, 400yds, £2

NT properties nearby
Felbrigg Hall, Garden and Park, Sheringham Park

Bourne Mill

Bourne Road, Colchester, Essex CO2 8RT

1936   (3:I8)

Picturesque watermill with working waterwheel

Parking limited. No WC

i **T** 01206 572422
  E bournemill@nationaltrust.org.uk

→ 1ml S of centre of Colchester, in Bourne
  Road, off the Mersea Road (B1025)

Bourne Mill									
1 Jun—29 Jun	2–5	M	T	W	T	F	S	**S**
1 Jul—31 Aug	2–5	M	**T**	W	T	F	S	**S**
Open Easter & May BH Suns & Mons								

Brancaster

Brancaster Millennium Activity Centre, Dial House,
Brancaster Staithe, King's Lynn, Norfolk
PE31 8BW

1923   (3:H3)

Extensive coastal area famous for wild birds

Extensive coastal area around the fishing village
of Brancaster Staithe. As well as the site of the
Roman fort of Branodunum and Scolt Head
Island (to which there is a private ferry service),
there are tidal mud and sandflats and
saltmarshes to explore. For those who prefer a
more structured visit, there is the well-resourced
Brancaster Millennium Activity Centre, which
offers residential and day courses for families,
adults and school groups. The centre also

For information regarding prices, see page 10

Brancaster
All year   M T W T F S S

delivers its innovative Energy Busters Outreach Programme, exploring ways to reduce carbon footprints with primary school age children.

What's new in 2008 The construction of a new fishing quay at Brancaster Staithe and associated interpretation on the local fishing industry, funded by Department of the Environment, Food and Rural Affairs, East of England Development Agency and King's Lynn and West Norfolk Borough Council

⭐ A private ferry runs from Burnham Overy Staithe (weather permitting) taking visitors to the internationally important Scolt Head Island National Nature Reserve, managed by Natural England (tel. 01485 210515). Scolt Head NNR is an important breeding site for four species of tern, oystercatcher and ringed plover. Please note that it can be dangerous to walk over the saltmarsh and sandflats, especially at low tide. Ferry, tel. 01485 210456. No WC, local authority maintained WC at Beach Road, Brancaster

ℹ️ **T** 01485 210719
E brancaster@nationaltrust.org.uk

Family fun weeks and activity days for children in school hols

♿ Grounds

Chilterns Gateway Centre at Dunstable Downs

Family fun weeks and activity days for children in school hols

Suitable for school groups. Education room/centre. Brancaster Millennium Activity Centre is suitable for residential school groups. Adult study days

Under control at all times on the beach; not on Scolt Head Island mid April–mid Aug. Dog-free area on Brancaster Beach, W of golf clubhouse May–Sept

Activity centre offers group cycling activities; all staff trained in cycle group leadership. 'Start Cycling' scheme organised for groups

➡️ [132:TF800450] **Foot**: Norfolk Coast Path passes property. **Cycle**: NCN1, runs along ridge above the coast. **Bus**: Norfolk Green Coast Hopper 36 ➔ Sheringham–Hunstanton. **Road**: Brancaster Staithe is halfway between Wells and Hunstanton on A149 coast road

P Parking (not NT) at public car park at Beach Road, Brancaster (charge inc. NT members). Limited parking at the Staithe

NT properties nearby
Blakeney National Nature Reserve

Chilterns Gateway Centre, Dunstable Downs and Whipsnade Estate

Dunstable Road, Whipsnade, Bedfordshire
LU6 2GY

🅿️ 🏛️ ♿ 🏠 ☕ 🍴 🎭 🎭 ♿ 👪 🎯 🚶

🚲 ☂️ 1928   (3:E8)

Extensive chalk and grassland Area of Outstanding Natural Beauty

Commanding outstanding views over the Vale of Aylesbury and along the Chiltern Ridge, this is a kite-flying hotspot and the ideal place to watch gliders soar over the glorious landscape. Set within 206 hectares (510 acres) of grassland and farmland, this prime walking country is home to a wealth of wildlife. Plan your route in the comfort of our visitor centre, then visit our family-friendly café before exploring the gift shop, which sells an excellent range of kites.

Many Trust properties are offering Gift Aid on Entry for non-members, see page 10

Chilterns Gateway Centre

Downs			
All year		M T W T F S S	

Centre			
1 Feb–17 Mar	10–4	M T W T F S S	
18 Mar–28 Oct	10–5	M T W T F S S	
29 Oct–31 Jan 09	10–4	M T W T F S S	

Chilterns Gateway Centre closed 24/25 Dec. Closes dusk if earlier in winter

What's new in 2008 Surfaced path linking Dunstable to the Chilterns Gateway Centre

⭐ The Centre is owned by Bedfordshire County Council and managed by the NT. Open daily (except 24/25 Dec) 10–5 (later, locally advertised times may apply in the summer)

ℹ️ **T** 01582 500920
E dunstabledowns@nationaltrust.org.uk

By appointment (if staffing availability permits)

Large selection of Downs-based circular walks leaflets available from Centre

♿ 🚻 Building Grounds

🏠 NT gift shop with large range of kites

☕ Café serving range of local produce, including the famous Bedfordshire Clanger

Baby-changing facilities. Pushchairs and baby back-carriers admitted

Suitable for school groups. Booking essential

Under close control, on leads near livestock

🚲 Public bridleway giving cyclists shared access. Route is part of Icknield Trail

➡️ [165/166:TL002189] **Foot**: footpaths from West Street and Tring Road, Dunstable.
Cycle: bridleway from West Street, Dunstable, and Whipsnade. **Bus**: Arriva 60 from Luton, Centrebus 327 from ≞ Hemel Hempstead and Red Rose 343 from ≞ St Albans, all Suns only; otherwise Arriva 61 Aylesbury–≞ Luton to within 1½ml.
Station: Luton 7ml. Luton Airport Parkway 7ml. **Road**: Dunstable Downs & car parks: on B4541 W of Dunstable. Whipsnade Estate: car parks at Whipsnade crossroads (Whipsnade Heath)–junction of B4541 & B4540. Whipsnade Tree Cathedral B4540 (off village green)

🅿️ Parking off B4540, Bison Hill and B4541 Dunstable Downs, and at Whipsnade Tree Cathedral and Crossroads. £1 charge on Dunstable Downs. Space for one coach only at Dunstable (no other coach facilities), booking essential. Car park adjacent to the Gateway Centre open 8–6 all year, or dusk if earlier

NT properties nearby
Ascott, Ashridge Estate, Shaw's Corner, Whipsnade Tree Cathedral

Coggeshall Grange Barn

Grange Hill, Coggeshall, Colchester, Essex
CO6 1RE

🏠 🛖 🛡️ 👪 1989 (3:18)

13th-century monastic barn

With a beautiful cathedral-like interior, majestic Coggeshall Grange Barn was originally part of a Cistercian monastery and is one of the oldest surviving timber-framed buildings in Europe. After years of agricultural use, the barn fell into disrepair but was saved from demolition and lovingly restored in the 1980s. It now houses a small collection of farm carts and local historic exhibits. Prior to its restoration, the barn was used as a film set for Southwark's Tabard Inn in Pier Paolo Pasolini's 1972 film version of Chaucer's *The Canterbury Tales*.

ℹ️ **T** 01376 562226
E coggeshall@nationaltrust.org.uk

🛡️ Craft fairs, theatre

♿ 🚻 Building Grounds

Pushchairs and baby back-carriers admitted. Children's quiz/trail

➡️ [168:TL848223] **Foot**: Essex Way long-distance footpath passes the barn.
Bus: First 70 Colchester–Braintree (passing close ≞ Marks Tey). **Station**: Kelvedon 2½ml.
Road: signposted off A120 Coggeshall bypass; ¼ml S from centre of Coggeshall, on B1024

Coggeshall Grange Barn

23 Mar–12 Oct	2–5	M T W **T** F S S	
Open BH Mons			

[P] Parking, 20yds. Only available during barn opening times

NT properties nearby
Bourne Mill, Hatfield Forest, Paycocke's

Dunwich Heath: Coastal Centre and Beach

Dunwich, Saxmundham, Suffolk IP17 3DJ

🔨🏛️🖐️🏠⏚☕𝒳🎴🛡️🚻🎭
🚶♿🍵 1968   **(3:K6)**

Coastal lowland heath, sandy cliffs and beach, rich in wildlife

Within an AONB and offering many excellent walks, the area is a remnant of the once extensive Sandlings heaths, with open tracts of heather and gorse, shady woods, sandy cliffs and beach. It is an important nature conservation area and home to scarce species such as the Dartford warbler and ant-lion.

What's new in 2008 Children's trail for children up to eight. 'Red Earth' project, May to September, an arts-based, coastal project with sculptures, events and interaction

⭐ Kite-flying restricted to beach only. Parking restrictions may operate at times of extreme fire risk. Cycling and horse riding on bridleway only

Dunwich Heath									
2 Feb–2 Mar	Dawn–dusk	M	T	W	T	F	S	S
13 Feb–17 Feb		M	T	**W**	T	F	**S**	**S**
5 Mar–20 Jul		M	T	**W**	T	F	**S**	**S**
24 Mar–30 Mar		**M**	**T**	**W**	**T**	F	**S**	**S**
26 May–1 Jun		**M**	**T**	**W**	**T**	F	**S**	**S**
21 Jul–14 Sep		**M**	**T**	**W**	**T**	F	**S**	**S**
17 Sep–21 Dec		M	T	**W**	T	F	**S**	**S**
27 Dec–28 Dec		M	T	W	T	F	**S**	**S**
31 Dec–4 Jan 09		M	T	**W**	**T**	F	**S**	**S**
10 Jan–31 Jan 09		M	T	W	T	F	**S**	**S**

Open BH Mons. Heath: open dawn–dusk. Coastguard Cottages: shop & tea-room open from 10. Closing times vary

[i] **T** 01728 648501
E dunwichheath@nationaltrust.org.uk

[𝒳] For details see property information boards and events leaflet

[🎭] Annual events programme, inc. 'Red Earth' project, an arts-based, coastal project with sculptures, events and interaction May–Sept

[🚶] Good network of walks. Three waymarked trails with map and information in guidebook

♿ 🚻📷Pⓙ🏛️ **Building** 🏛️♿
Grounds 🏛️➡️🚶

[📷] Gift shop in Coastguard Cottages

[☕] Licensed tea-room in Coastguard Cottages. Children's menu. Kiosk outside

Enjoying the sandy beach at Dunwich Heath, Suffolk. The area is home to some rare species

📶 Pushchairs and baby back-carriers admitted. Front-carrying baby slings for loan. Children's play area

🏛 Suitable for school groups. Education room/centre. Hands-on activities. Specialising in coastal processes and issues

🐕 Dog-free area on beach

🚴 On bridleways

➡ [156:TM476685] **Foot**: Suffolk Coast and Heaths Path and Sandlings Walk. Detailed maps on sale. **Cycle**: on Suffolk coastal cycle route. **Bus**: Coastlink from 🚉 Darsham & Saxmundham. Book only on 01728 833526. **Station**: Darsham (U) 6ml. **Road**: 1ml S of Dunwich, signposted from A12. From Westledon/Dunwich road, 1ml before Dunwich village turn right into Minsmere road. Then 1ml to Dunwich Heath

🅿 Parking, 150yds (pay & display). Cars £4, caravans/large vans £5, motorcycles £3, coaches £30 (unless booked to use tea-room), limited to three coaches

NT properties nearby
Flatford: Bridge Cottage, Orford Ness National Nature Reserve, Sutton Hoo

Elizabethan House Museum

4 South Quay, Great Yarmouth, Norfolk NR30 2QH

🏛 📷 🎫 🛡 📶 🏛 1943   (3:K5)

Small but delightful treasury of 16th-century domestic history

Step back in time at this beautiful 16th-century quayside house. Experience the lives of the people who lived here from Tudor to Victorian times. Find out what it was like to work in the kitchen and scullery through hands-on activities, and explore the differences between 'upstairs and downstairs' in Victorian life. There are Tudor costumes to try on, an activity-packed toy room and you can investigate the Conspiracy Room, where the execution of Charles I is said to have been planned. After the hive of activity inside this beautiful merchant's house, you can pause for a moment of peace in the small but delightful walled garden.

Elizabethan House Museum			
1 Apr–31 Oct*	10–5	**M T W T F** S S	
*Open 1:15–5 Sat & Sun			

What's new in 2008 Civil War display featuring locally excavated coin hoard

⭐ The house is leased to Norfolk Museums and Archaeology Service

ℹ **T** 01493 855746
E elizabethanhouse@nationaltrust.org.uk

🎫 Guided tours for ten or more people. Charges on application – must be booked

🛡 Events during school holidays. Tel. for details

♿ 🔽 🔍 ⠿ **Building** ♿

📶 Pushchairs and baby back-carriers admitted

🏛 Suitable for school groups. Guide available in French and German

➡ [134:TG523073] On Great Yarmouth's historic South Quay. **Foot**: level walk from railway station along North Quay on to South Quay. **Cycle**: regional route 30 Great Yarmouth–Cromer. **Bus**: local services, plus services from surrounding areas. **Station**: Great Yarmouth ½ml. **Road**: from A47 take town centre signs, then follow brown Historic South Quay signs. From A12 follow brown signs

🅿 No parking on site. Pay & display car park behind house run by the Borough Council. Spaces may not always be available

NT properties nearby
Horsey Windpump

Felbrigg Hall, Garden and Park

Felbrigg, Norwich, Norfolk NR11 8PR

🏛 🏠 ✝ ❄ 🌸 🍴 🏠 🏠 ☕ 🌳 🛡
📶 🏛 🎫 🚴 🍴 1969   (3:J4)

One of the most elegant country houses in East Anglia

A house of surprising contrasts, Felbrigg was built both before and after the English Civil War, and behind the sumptuous Stuart architecture lies a fascinating history. In the 19th century

The Gothic-style library at Felbrigg Hall, Norfolk: one of the most elegant country houses in East Anglia

Felbrigg was almost lost to the shopping sprees of rackety 'Mad Windham', but was rescued when it passed to the Ketton-Cremer family in 1923, who restored it to its former glory. Explore the imposing Georgian Drawing Room and Gothic-style library, then investigate the kitchen, with its collection of beautiful kitchen implements and shining array of copperware. Outside, Felbrigg is a gardener's delight, with a decorative and productive walled garden, Victorian pleasure garden and rolling landscape park – with a lake and 200 hectares (520 acres) of woods to walk through on waymarked trails.

What's new in 2008 New displays – 'Unseen Felbrigg'

i **T** 01263 837444
E felbrigg@nationaltrust.org.uk

Send sae for events leaflet

Waymarked walks to church, lake and woods

Building
Grounds

NT shop. Second-hand bookshop. Plant sales

Carriage restaurant (licensed). Children's menu. Turret tea-room (licensed). Occasionally only Carriage restaurant or Turret tea-room may be open. Booking advisable for restaurant

Felbrigg Hall, Garden and Park									
House									
1 Mar–2 Nov	11–5	**M**	**T**	**W**	T	F	**S**	**S**	
Gardens									
1 Mar–26 Oct	11–5	**M**	**T**	**W**	T	F	**S**	**S**	
26 May–1 Jun	11–5	**M**	**T**	**W**	**T**	**F**	**S**	**S**	
21 Jul–31 Aug	11–5	**M**	**T**	**W**	**T**	**F**	**S**	**S**	
27 Oct–2 Nov	11–5	**M**	**T**	**W**	**T**	**F**	**S**	**S**	
27 Dec–31 Dec	11–4	**M**	**T**	**W**	T	F	**S**	**S**	
Shop/refreshments/bookshop/plant sales									
1 Mar–2 Nov	As gardens	**M**	**T**	**W**	T	F	**S**	**S**	
3 Nov–14 Dec	11–4	M	T	W	**T**	**F**	**S**	**S**	
27 Dec–31 Dec	11–4	**M**	**T**	**W**	T	F	**S**	**S**	
5 Jan–31 Jan 09	11–4	M	T	W	T	**F**	**S**	**S**	
Estate walks									
All year	Dawn–dusk	**M**	**T**	**W**	**T**	**F**	**S**	**S**	
Open BH Mons and Good Fri. Timed tickets may be in operation 11–1									

Dogs assisting visitors with disabilities are always welcome

👶 Baby-changing facilities. Front-carrying baby slings and hip-carrying infant seats for loan. Children's guide

🎪 Suitable for school groups

🐕 On leads in parkland when stock grazing. Under close control in woodland

🚲 Regional route 30 runs through the park

➡ [133:TG193394] **Foot**: Weavers' Way runs through property. **Cycle**: Regional Route 30, Great Yarmouth–Wells. **Station**: Cromer (U) or Roughton Road (U), both 2½ml. **Road**: nr Felbrigg village, 2ml SW of Cromer; entrance off B1436, signposted from A148 and A140

🅿 Parking, 100yds, £2

NT properties nearby
Blakeney National Nature Reserve, Blickling Hall, Gardens and Park, Sheringham Park

Flatford: Bridge Cottage

Flatford, East Bergholt, Suffolk CO7 6UL

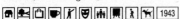 1943   (3:I8)

Beautiful 16th-century thatched cottage

In the heart of the beautiful Dedham Vale, the charming hamlet of Flatford is the location for some of John Constable's most famous pastoral paintings. You can find out more about Constable from the exhibition in the thatched cottage. Just upstream from Flatford Mill there is a beautiful riverside tea-garden and a shop at Bridge Cottage, as well as boats available for hire to explore the River Stour.

⭐ Flatford Mill, Valley Farm and Willy Lott's House are leased to the Field Studies Council, which runs arts-based courses for all age groups. For information on courses tel. 01206 298283. There is no general public access to these buildings, but the Field Studies Council will arrange tours for groups. Car park is not NT

ℹ **T** 01206 298260
E flatfordbridgecottage@nationaltrust.org.uk

🚶 Guided walks, including out-of-season walks, visiting sites of Constable's paintings in the Dedham Vale

🎭 Annual open day for Valley Farmhouse in Sept

🚶 Two waymarked walks at Flatford

Flatford: Bridge Cottage

Flatford: Bridge Cottage									
2 Feb–24 Feb	11–3:30	M	T	W	T	F	S	S
1 Mar–30 Apr	11–5	M	T	**W**	**T**	**F**	**S**	**S**
1 May–28 Sep	10:30–5:30	**M**	**T**	**W**	**T**	**F**	**S**	**S**
1 Oct–31 Oct	11–4	**M**	**T**	**W**	**T**	**F**	**S**	**S**
1 Nov–21 Dec	11–3:30	M	**T**	**W**	**T**	**F**	**S**	**S**
3 Jan–31 Jan 09	11–3:30	M	T	W	T	F	**S**	**S**

Open BH Mons. Property may close early in winter if weather is bad (Oct–Jan 08 inc.)

♿ 🚾 👥 📷 🅿 Building 🏛 ♿
Grounds 🏛 ♿

🛍 NT shop with a range of Constable-related books and gifts

🍴 Tea-room next to Bridge Cottage. Kiosk open during busy periods for ice-cream and snacks

👶 Pushchairs and baby back-carriers admitted. Front-carrying baby slings for loan

🎪 Suitable for school groups. Tours for school groups can be arranged on a theme of Constable's paintings at Flatford

➡ [168:TM077332] ½ml S of East Bergholt. **Foot**: accessible from East Bergholt, Dedham and Manningtree. **Bus**: Network Colchester 93 Ipswich–Colchester (passing ≋ Ipswich and close ≋ Colchester Town), Mon–Sat alight E Bergholt, ¾ml. **Station**: Manningtree 1¾ml by footpath, 3½ml by road. **Road**: on N bank of Stour, 1ml S of East Bergholt (B1070)

🅿 Parking (not NT), 200yds (pay & display), charge inc. NT members

NT properties nearby
Bourne Mill, Dedham Vale, The Suffolk Estuaries: Pin Mill and Kyson Hill, Thorington Hall

Hatfield Forest

Takeley, nr Bishop's Stortford, Hertfordshire CM22 6NE

🎪 1924   (3:G8)

Ancient royal hunting forest

Step back into the Middle Ages in the unique area of ancient coppiced and pollarded trees that is Hatfield Forest. Very little has changed since Henry I claimed this forested landscape in the early 12th century. This is a place of great historical and ecological importance, supporting rare and specialised wildlife – from deer to the smallest minibeast. Learn about the countryside, wildlife, art and history of this very special landscape in the Discovery Room. There are miles of excellent walks and nature trails to explore and fishing on the lake; there are even traditional woodland products for sale.

What's new in 2008 New interpretation at the site of the Doodle Oak. Wildlife and environment groups for young children (Acorns and Twiglets). Tel. 01279 870447 for details

⭐ There are no admission charges for this property, although a car park charge does apply. The Shell House is restored and open to visitors at weekends; exhibition in Discovery Room by the lake, explaining the history, management and wildlife of the Forest

ℹ️ **T** 01279 874040 (Infoline), 01279 870678 **E** hatfieldforest@nationaltrust.org.uk

🏃 Specialist interest walks and tours tailor-made to your requirements (booking essential). Tel. for details

Hatfield Forest: SSSI and National Nature Reserve

Hatfield Forest									
All Year	Dawn–dusk	**M**	**T**	**W**	**T**	**F**	**S**	**S**
Refreshments									
21 Mar–31 Oct	10–4:30	**M**	**T**	**W**	**T**	**F**	**S**	**S**
1 Nov–31 Jan 09	10–3:30	M	T	W	T	F	**S**	**S**

Refreshments available daily in school hols: summer 10–6; winter 10–3:30

🎭 Open-air theatre and concerts, including Woodfest (yearly celebration of woodland and associated activities). Father Christmas events. Wildlife-associated activities and walks. Send sae or visit NT website for details

🚶 Three trail guides available

♿ 🚻 ♿ 🅿️ **Grounds** ♿ ➡️ ♿

📷 Guides and postcards available from the entrance kiosk, Shell House and Discovery Room. Annual book sale

☕ Lakeside Café (not NT) (licensed) in lake area within forest. Serving home-made cakes and sandwiches. Local produce. Children's menu

👶 Baby-changing and feeding facilities. Pushchairs admitted. Children's quiz/trail. Wildlife and environment groups for young children. Father Christmas events

🏫 Suitable for school groups. Adult study days

🐕 On leads near livestock and around lake. Dog-free area near lake. Dog training workshops available through property

🚲 Several miles of grass track suitable for cycling. Cyclists excluded from area of lake, gravel pit and on boardwalk

➡️ [167:TL547203] **Foot**: Flitch Way from Braintree. Three Forests Way and Forest Way pass through the forest. **Cycle**: Flitch Way. **Bus**: Village Link 7 🚉 Bishop's Stortford–🚉 Elsenham, alight Takeley Street (Green Man), then ½ml. **Station**: Stansted Airport 3ml. **Road**: from M11 exit 8, take B1256 towards Takeley. Signposted from B1256

🅿️ Parking. 21 March–31 Oct & Suns all year. 10–5 or dusk if earlier. Cars £4.50, minibuses £6.50, coaches £25, school coaches £10

NT properties nearby
Blake's Wood, Bourne Mill, Coggeshall Grange Barn, Danbury and Lingwood Commons, Paycocke's, Wimpole Hall, Wimpole Home Farm

Unless indicated, last admission is always 30mins before closing time

Horsey Windpump

Horsey, Great Yarmouth, Norfolk NR29 4EF

🎦 ⚓ 🏠 🏠 💻 ✗ 🎭 👬
📷 🕴 1948   (3:K4)

Imposing five-storey drainage windpump

Striking windpump surrounded by internationally important wildlife habitats in the Broads National Park. The windpump offers stunning views of Horsey Mere and across the broadland landscape to the coast. The Horsey Estate is of exceptional nature conservation interest, notably for breeding birds and wintering wildfowl.

What's new in 2008 Wheelchair accessible nature garden adjacent to car park to be opened in June 2008

⭐ The Horsey Estate was acquired by the NT in 1948 from the Buxton family, who continue to manage the Horsey Estate with nature conservation as a priority. NT WCs open March–Oct, as shop/tea-room

ℹ️ **T** 01263 740241
E horseywindpump@nationaltrust.org.uk

✗ For school groups and special interest groups (small charge)

🕴 Waymarked circular walks, leaflet available

♿ 🚾 ♿ ♿ 📖 🅿 **Building** 🔔
Grounds 🔔

🏠 Small NT shop at the Staithe Stores, close to windpump

💻 Light refreshments and ice-creams available at the Staithe Stores, close to windpump

👬 Baby-changing facilities

📷 Suitable for school groups

Horsey Windpump									
1 Mar–23 Mar	10–4:30	M	T	W	T	F	**S**	**S**
24 Mar–6 Apr	10–4:30	**M**	**T**	**W**	**T**	**F**	**S**	**S**
7 Apr–25 May	10–4:30	M	T	**W**	**T**	**F**	**S**	**S**
26 May–31 Aug	10–4:30	**M**	**T**	**W**	**T**	**F**	**S**	**S**
1 Sep–26 Oct	10–4:30	M	T	**W**	**T**	**F**	**S**	**S**
27 Oct–2 Nov	10–4:30	**M**	**T**	**W**	**T**	**F**	**S**	**S**

Open Good Fri; BH Mons: 24 Mar, 5 May, 26 May & 25 Aug

🐕 On leads near livestock. Under close control elsewhere

➡️ [134:TG457223] **Cycle**: Regional Route 30, Great Yarmouth–Wells. **Bus**: First 1/A/B Lowestoft–Martham (passing close 🚂 Great Yarmouth), alight W Somerton School, 1¾ml. **Station**: Acle (U) 10ml. **Road**: 15ml N of Great Yarmouth on B1159; 4ml NE of Martham

🅿️ Parking, 50yds. 50p up to 1 hour, £1.50 for 4 hours or £2.50 all day (pay & display). Open dawn to dusk. Access difficult for coaches

NT properties nearby
Elizabethan House Museum

Houghton Mill

Houghton, nr Huntingdon, Cambridgeshire PE28 2AZ

🎦 🚻 💻 ✗ 📷 👬 📷 🕴 ♿ 1939   (3:F6)

Imposing 18th-century watermill

Full of hands-on exhibits for all the family, and with most of its machinery still intact, this five-storey weatherboarded mill is the last working watermill on the Great Ouse. Today wheat is still for sale, ground by a pair of millstones on Sundays and Bank Holiday Mondays. Close by, some parts of the river are so clear you can see fish darting about and you may even be lucky enough to spot a heron or a kingfisher. Across from the mill island, the river meadows offer marvellous walks under the willows.

Houghton Mill									
Mill/bookshop									
22 Mar–26 Apr	11–5	M	T	W	T	F	**S**	**S**
23 Mar–27 Apr	1–5	M	T	W	T	F	S	**S**
3 May–27 Sep	11–5	M	T	W	T	F	**S**	**S**
28 Apr–28 Sep	1–5	**M**	**T**	**W**	T	F	S	S
4 Oct–25 Oct	11–5	M	T	W	T	F	**S**	**S**
5 Oct–26 Oct	1–5	M	T	W	T	F	S	**S**
Tea-room									
As mill	11–5							
Walks/car park									
All year	9–6	**M**	**T**	**W**	**T**	**F**	**S**	**S**

Open BH Mons and Good Fri: mill 1–5; tea-room 11–5. Caravan and campsite open March–Oct. Groups and school parties at other times by arrangement with Property Manager

Houghton Mill: still functioning

What's new in 2008 Virtual Tour. Interactive model of water use in the landscape

⭐ Milling demonstrations subject to river level

ℹ️ **T** 01480 301494
E houghtonmill@nationaltrust.org.uk

🚶 Starting point for circular walks; maps available to buy

♿ 🚻 🏠 ◽◽ 🅿 **Building** 🏞️ **Grounds** ➡️

🍽️ Tea-room. Delightful riverside setting

🚼 Baby-changing facilities. Children's quiz/trail

🏫 Suitable for school groups. Hands-on activities

🐕 On leads and only in grounds

🚲 Through riverside meadows

➡️ [153:TL282720] **Foot**: Ouse Valley Way from Huntingdon. **Cycle**: NCN51 from Huntingdon. **Bus**: Huntingdon & District 555, Whippet 1A, from Huntingdon (passing close ➡ Huntingdon). **Station**: Huntingdon 3½ml. **Road**: in village of Houghton, signposted off A1123 Huntingdon to St Ives

🅿️ Parking, 20yds, £1.50 (pay & display). No access for large coaches (drop off in village square)

NT properties nearby
Anglesey Abbey, Peckover House and Garden, Ramsey Abbey Gatehouse, Wicken Fen National Nature Reserve, Wimpole Hall

Ickworth House, Park and Gardens

The Rotunda, Horringer, Bury St Edmunds, Suffolk IP29 5QE

🏰 🚍 ✳️ 🌳 🏠 ☕ 🍴 🏕️ 🎭 🚻 🏫
🚶 🚲 🔔 🍷 1956   (3:H7)

A Georgian Italianate palace in an idyllic English landscape

Ickworth's huge central Rotunda, flanked by two massive wings, dominates this eccentric house built by the equally eccentric 4th Earl of Bristol, who dreamed of creating an Italianate palace within an English landscape. It houses important collections of paintings (including work by Velázquez and Titian) and fine family portraits (several by Gainsborough), as well as Huguenot and ambassadorial silver and Regency furniture. The fabulous State Rooms were only used by the family on special occasions and are as

Ickworth House, Park and Gardens										
House										
15 Mar–30 Sep	1–5	M	T	W	T		F	S	S	
1 Oct–2 Nov	1–4:30	M	T	W	T		F	S	S	
Park										
All year	8–8	M	T	W	T		F	S	S	
Italianate Garden										
1 Mar–14 Mar	11–4	M	T	W	T		F	S	S	
15 Mar–2 Nov	10–5	M	T	W	T		F	S	S	
3 Nov–31 Jan 09	11–4	M	T	W	T		F	S	S	
Shop/restaurant										
1 Mar–14 Mar	11–4	M	T	W	T		F	S	S	
15 Mar–2 Nov	10–5	M	T	W	T		F	S	S	
3 Nov–31 Jan 09	11–4	M	T	W	T		F	S	S	

Park, gardens, shop and restaurant open daily during Suffolk CC school hols. Open all BHol Mons, Good Fri and the 1 Jan 09. Property closed 24, 25, 26 Dec. Park closes dusk if earlier than 8. Italianate Garden closes dusk if earlier than 5

For general and membership enquiries, please telephone 0844 800 1895

The south front at Ickworth, Suffolk, showing the huge central rotunda

pristine and awe-inspiring today as they were when orginally created. Today, the West Wing contains visitor, conference, banqueting and wedding facilities, while the East Wing is now The Ickworth Hotel. Wooded Pleasure Grounds provide a shady and delightful contrast to the formality of the Italianate Garden. Beyond there are 729 hectares (1,800 acres) of idyllic parkland, including a vineyard and dense woodland offering miles of walks. For the more adventurous, a family cycle route, 'trim trail' and challenging play area offer opportunities to burn off some more energy.

⭐ Ickworth offers conference, banqueting and wedding facilities in the West Wing (Sodexho Prestige) tel. 01284 735957 (ickworth.house@sodexho-uk.com). For The Ickworth Hotel tel. 01284 735350

ℹ️ **T** 01284 735270
E ickworth@nationaltrust.org.uk

🚶 House mini tours each day except Wed & Thur during open season at 12:15: £2.75 per person (inc. NT members). House admission extra

🎭 Themed restaurant events/meals, concerts, plays, school holiday and family activities, country life events. Event hamper service available. Please tel. Sodexho Prestige

🚶 Waymarked walks in park and woodland. Lengths vary from 1¼ml to 7ml. All terrains

🦽 ♿ 🚻 ⓦ ⚬ 🅿 House ♿ West Wing ♿ Grounds ♿ ➡ ♿

🛍 Plant sales and garden products

☕ West Wing Restaurant (NT-approved concession) (licensed) serving Ickworth Estate wines. Morning, lunchtime and afternoon menus, hot and cold meals, drinks. Kiosk (NT-approved concession) in visitor car park. Hot and cold drinks, ice-cream, snacks

👪 Baby-changing and feeding facilities. Front-carrying baby slings and hip-carrying infant seats for loan. Children's play area. Children's guide. Children's quiz/trail. Family activity packs. All-terrain pushchair available for outdoor use. Family 'trim trail' in woods

🏫 Suitable for school groups. Education room/centre. Hands-on activities. Live interpretation. Learning Officer. Adult study days

🐕 On leads

🚲 Family cycle route (2½ml), various surfaces with some steep gradients; helmets and adult supervision advised

➡️ [155:TL810610] **Foot**: 4½ml via footpaths from Bury St Edmunds. **Bus**: Burtons 344/5 Bury St Edmunds–Haverhill (passing close ⊠ Bury St Edmunds). **Station**: Bury St Edmunds 3ml. **Road**: in Horringer, 3ml SW of Bury St Edmunds on W side of A143

🅿 Free parking, 200yds

NT properties nearby
Anglesey Abbey, Lavenham Guildhall, Melford Hall, Theatre Royal, Bury St Edmunds

For information regarding prices, see page 10

Lavenham: The Guildhall of Corpus Christi

Market Place, Lavenham, Sudbury, Suffolk
CO10 9QZ

🐾 🏠 💷 🎭 👫 🗾 🏃 1951   (3:17)

Tudor building in the heart of the remarkably preserved medieval village of Lavenham

One of the finest preserved timer-framed buildings in Britain, the Guildhall is at the centre of what was once the 14th richest town in England. Built c.1530, it was one of the last buildings to be erected before the cloth economy crashed. Fascinating exhibitions give you an insight into local history and traditional farming practices, as well as the area's medieval cloth industry, while the dressing-up box will delight all children! Be sure to explore the tranquil walled garden, where there are traditional dye plants which produce colours that are bright even for today.

What's new in 2008 New programme of events. Tel. for details

ℹ️ **T** 01787 247646
E lavenhamguildhall@nationaltrust.org.uk

🎭 Talks, lecture lunches and craft demonstrations. Family fun days

🏃 Blue-badge guided walks around Lavenham village, £3

♿ 🦽 🐕 🖼 ⋮⋮ 📷 🎧 Building 🏛
Grounds 🏛

Lavenham Guildhall

Guildhall

8 Mar–31 Mar	11–4		M	T	**W**	**T**	**F**	**S**	**S**
1 Apr–2 Nov	11–5		**M**	**T**	**W**	**T**	**F**	**S**	**S**
8 Nov–30 Nov	11–4		M	T	W	T	F	**S**	**S**

Shop/tea-room

			M	T	W	T	F	S	S
As Guildhall									
1 Nov–21 Dec	11–4		M	T	W	**T**	**F**	**S**	**S**

Shop

3 Jan–31 Jan 09	11–4		M	T	W	T	F	**S**	**S**

Open BH Mons. Closed Good Fri. Parts of the building may be closed occasionally for community use. Tea-room open BH Mons

🏠 Gift shop with range of local products

💷 Tea-room serving light lunches and home-made produce. Children's menu

👫 Baby back-carriers admitted. Hip-carrying infant seats for loan. Children's quiz/trail. Dressing-up clothes. Family fun days

🖼 Suitable for school groups

➡️ [155:TL916493] **Foot**: 'railway walk' links Lavenham with Long Melford. **Cycle**: South Suffolk Cycle Route A1. **Bus**: Chambers 753 Bury St Edmunds–Colchester (passes close ➡ Bury St Edmunds and ➡ Sudbury). **Station**: Sudbury (U) 7ml. **Road**: A1141 and B1071

🅿️ Free parking (not NT), 10yds

NT properties nearby
Ickworth House, Park and Gardens, Melford Hall, Theatre Royal, Bury St Edmunds

Lavenham: The Guildhall of Corpus Christi contains fascinating exhibitions

Melford Hall

Long Melford, Sudbury, Suffolk CO10 9AA

[1960]   (3:17)

A fine mellow red-brick Tudor mansion

At first sight, the thrusting turrets and elegant Elizabethan banqueting house of Melford Hall look very much as they did when Elizabeth I visited with 2,000 courtiers in 1578. Inside the Hall, as well as a fine panelled banqueting hall, Regency, Georgian and Victorian rooms chart the tastes of the Hyde Parkers – who have lived here since 1786. A naval family, the house is filled with reminders of the family's history, including fine nautical paintings and even plunder looted from a Spanish ship in 1762. As well as being one of the earliest country houses in Britain to have central heating, Melford also boasts a family connection with Beatrix Potter, who sketched here on her visits, and the house is home to the original Jemima Puddleduck doll. Outside, the remains of an ancient deer park form part of 52 hectares (130 acres) of parkland surrounding Edwardian-style gardens.

What's new in 2008 New interpretation displays and local craft demonstrations. Refreshment facilities and a small selection of NT gifts

[i] **T** 01787 376395 (Infoline),
01787 379228
E melford@nationaltrust.org.uk

Programme of events throughout the season for all ages

1ml circular walk through park

Building

Grounds

Second-hand bookshop and plant sales area at South Gatelodge

Light refreshments only

Baby-changing facilities. Hip-carrying infant seats and baby sling for loan. Family trail

Suitable for school groups

On leads and only in car park and park walk

→ [155:TL867462] **Foot**: 'railway walk' linking Long Melford with Lavenham, 4ml.
Bus: Beestons/Chambers/Felix various services, Mon–Sat from Sudbury; Chambers 753, Mon–Sat Bury St Edmunds–Colchester; Network Colchester 90C, Sun Haverhill–Ipswich (passes ▤ Ipswich). All pass close ▤ Sudbury.
Station: Sudbury (U) 4ml. **Road**: in Long Melford off A134, 14ml S of Bury St Edmunds, 3ml N of Sudbury

[P] Free parking, 200yds. Access for coaches and other large vehicles by gated entrance 100yds north of main entrance (signed)

NT properties nearby
Flatford: Bridge Cottage, Ickworth House, Park and Gardens, Lavenham Guildhall, Theatre Royal, Bury St Edmunds

Orford Ness National Nature Reserve

Quay Office, Orford Quay, Orford, Woodbridge, Suffolk IP12 2NU

[1993]   (3:K7)

Internationally important nature reserve, with a fascinating 20th-century military history

The largest vegetated shingle spit in Europe, the Reserve contains a variety of habitats including shingle, saltmarsh, mudflat, brackish lagoons and grazing marsh. It provides an important location for breeding and passage birds as well as for the coastal shingle flora and wildlife, including a large number of nationally rare species. The Ness was a secret military test site

Melford Hall									
22 Mar–30 Mar	1:30–5	M	T	**W**	T	F	S	S
5 Apr–27 Apr	1:30–5	M	T	W	T	F	**S**	**S**
1 May–28 Sep	1:30–5	M	T	**W**	**T**	F	**S**	**S**
4 Oct–26 Oct	1:30–5	M	T	W	T	F	**S**	**S**
Open BH Mons								

Orford Ness National Nature Reserve								
22 Mar–28 Jun	M	T	W	T	F	**S**	S
1 Jul–27 Sep	M	**T**	**W**	**T**	F	**S**	S
4 Oct–25 Oct	M	T	W	T	F	**S**	S

The only access is by NT ferry from Orford Quay, with boats crossing regularly to the Ness between 10 & 2 only, the last ferry leaving the Ness at 5

For details of events go to www.nationaltrust.org.uk/events

Orford Ness, Suffolk: a haven for shingle flora

from 1913 until the mid-1980s. Visitors follow a 5½ml route, which can be walked in total or in part (the full walk involves walking on shingle). Other walks (approx. 3ml) are open seasonally.

⭐ Charge for ferry (inc. NT members). Access around the site is on foot only, but tractor-drawn trailer tours operate first Sat of the month July–Sept, booking essential. Some military buildings (eg 'pagodas') accessible only on guided events. No dogs or cycles

ℹ️ **T** 01728 648024 (Infoline), 01394 450900
E orfordness@nationaltrust.org.uk

🏃 Natural history, military history and general interest

🛡️ Working lighthouse visit – joint NT and Trinity House event. Wildtrack Working Holidays. Tel. 0870 429 2429 for details. Marine Conservation Society Beachwatch – coastal survey and clean up. Tel. 01394 450900 after July for details

🚶 Illustrated trail guide covering three available walks and children's quiz/trail for sale

♿ 🚾 **Grounds** 🔼 ▶️

👪 Pushchairs and baby back-carriers admitted. Access involves a boat crossing. All pushchairs etc must be suitable for lifting on to a boat and up and down steps

➡️ [169:TM425495] **Foot**: Suffolk Coastal Path runs nearby on mainland via Orford Quay. **Cycle**: NCN1, 1ml. No cycle parking. **Ferry**: access only via ferry *Octavia*. See 'opening arrangements'. **Bus**: County Travel/Gemini 160/1 from Woodbridge (passing 🚆 Melton). **Station**: Wickham Market 8ml. **Road**: access from Orford Quay, Orford town 10ml E of A12 (B1094/1095), 12ml NE of Woodbridge B1152/1084

🅿️ Parking (not NT), 150yds (pay & display), charge inc. NT members. Located in Quay Street

NT properties nearby
Dunwich Heath, The Suffolk Estuaries: Pin Mill and Kyson Hill, Sutton Hoo

Oxburgh Hall, Garden and Estate •

Oxborough, King's Lynn, Norfolk PE33 9PS

🏛️✝️✿🏚️☕🏃🏛️🛡️👪🏭
🚶 ⊤ 1952   (3:H5)

15th-century moated manor house

Oxburgh's secret doors and priest's hole make this a house of mystery and history. Step back in time through the magnificent Tudor gatehouse into the dangerous world of Tudor politics. Home to the Bedingfeld family since 1482, this stunning red-brick house charts their precarious history from medieval austerity to neo-Gothic Victorian comfort. As well as beautiful early Mortlake tapestries in the Queen's Room, Oxburgh houses beautiful embroidery by both Mary Queen of Scots and the famous Bess of Hardwick. Panoramic views from the roof look out over the Victorian French parterre, walled orchard, kitchen garden and a Catholic chapel. There are quizzes, trails and dressing-up clothes to try on, and the woodland is full of walks.

What's new in 2008 Priest's hole interpretation with visual displays. External tours of the hall and grounds with guides in Tudor costume during school holidays. Period headwear and costumes available to try on in the Armoury. As seen in David Dimbleby's *How We Built Britain*

ℹ️ **T** 01366 328258
E oxburghhall@nationaltrust.org.uk

Charges for National Trust members apply on some special event days

Oxburgh Hall is a house of mystery, with secret doors and a priest's hole

🏃 Regular garden tours and winter woodland tours. External tours of the hall and grounds. Gatehouse show rooms open weekends Jan to March. Out-of-hours tours by arrangement. Tel. for details

🎭 Open-air theatre. Children's events. Musical events. Living history. Lecture lunches. Christmas events

Oxburgh Hall, Garden and Estate									
House		M	T	W	T	F	S	S	
15 Mar–30 Jul	1–5	**M**	**T**	**W**	T	F	**S**	**S**	
31 Jul–31 Aug	1–5	**M**	**T**	**W**	**T**	**F**	**S**	**S**	
1 Sep–1 Oct	1–5	**M**	**T**	**W**	T	F	**S**	**S**	
4 Oct–2 Nov	1–4	**M**	**T**	**W**	T	F	**S**	**S**	
Garden/tea-room/shop									
2 Feb–9 Mar	11–4	M	T	W	T	F	**S**	**S**	
15 Mar–30 Jul	11–5	**M**	**T**	**W**	T	F	**S**	**S**	
31 Jul–31 Aug	11–5	**M**	**T**	**W**	**T**	**F**	**S**	**S**	
1 Sep–1 Oct	11–5	**M**	**T**	**W**	T	F	**S**	**S**	
4 Oct–2 Nov	11–4	**M**	**T**	**W**	T	F	**S**	**S**	
8 Nov–21 Dec	11–4	M	T	W	T	F	**S**	**S**	
3 Jan–31 Jan 09	11–4	M	T	W	T	F	**S**	**S**	

Open BH Mons and Good Fri: 11–5 (inc. house).
Gatehouse open for tours Sat & Sun 10–31 Jan 09.
Tel. for times

🚶 Woodland Explorer trail

♿ 🚻🦯🖼️🎨♿♿ **Building** 🖼️🦽
Grounds 🖼️➡️

🛍️ NT shop. Plant sales. Gun room – second-hand bookshop during season

☕ Licensed tea-room in Old Kitchen. Children's menu

🚼 Baby-changing facilities. Front-carrying baby slings and hip-carrying infant seats for loan. Children's guide. Children's quiz/trail

🎒 Suitable for school groups. Live interpretation and hands-on activities. Adult study day

➜ [143:TF742012] **Station**: Downham Market 10ml. **Road**: at Oxborough, 7ml SW of Swaffham on S side of Stoke Ferry road; 3ml from A134 at Stoke Ferry

🅿 Free parking

NT properties nearby
Peckover House and Garden, St George's Guildhall

Paycocke's

West Street, Coggeshall, Colchester, Essex
CO6 1NS

 1924 (3:I8)

Fine late Gothic merchant's house

With its unusually intricate panelling and
woodcarving, Paycocke's shows the wealth of
the area generated by the 15th- and 16th-
century wool trade. Examine the examples of
the famous Coggeshall lace displayed in the
house and explore the peaceful cottage garden.

⭐ Groups (10+) must book in advance with the
tenant. Children must be accompanied by an
adult. No WC, nearest WC in village centre –
400yds

ℹ️ **T** 01376 561305
E paycockes@nationaltrust.org.uk

♿ ⠿ Building Grounds

👪 Pushchairs admitted

➡️ [168:TL848225] **Foot**: close to Essex Way.
Bus: First 70 Colchester–Braintree (passing
≋ Marks Tey). **Station**: Kelvedon 2½ml.
Road: 5½ml E of Braintree. Signposted off
A120. On S side of West Street, 400yds from
centre of Coggeshall, on road to Braintree
next to the Fleece Inn

🅿️ Parking (not NT) at Grange Barn (½ml) until 5

NT properties nearby
Bourne Mill, Coggeshall Grange Barn, Flatford:
Bridge Cottage, Hatfield Forest

Paycocke's								
23 Mar–12 Oct	2–5	**M**	**T**	**W**	T	F	S	**S**
Open BH Mons								

The street façade of Paycocke's in Coggeshall, Essex

Peckover House and Garden

North Brink, Wisbech, Cambridgeshire PE13 1JR

🔔 🍴 1943 (3:G5)

**Elegant Georgian town house with
wonderful walled garden**

Explore the fascinating home of the Peckovers,
the Quaker banking family who lived here for
150 years. This is a hands-on house with a
'Cabinet of Curiosities', dressing-up clothes for
children of all ages, and three floors revealing
the lives of both the family and their servants.
Built c.1722, this is one of England's finest
townhouses with superb rococo plaster and
wood decorations. Outside, discover the hidden
wonders of the 0.8 hectares (2 acres) of
beautiful Victorian garden, with its orangery,
summerhouse, roses, fernery and manicured
croquet lawn, as well as a 17th-century
thatched barn and Georgian stables. There are
stunning displays of daffodils, narcissi and tulips
in spring and roses in summer.

What's new in 2008 2008 is the 60th (diamond)
jubilee of NT ownership of Peckover House.
Special events will be held to celebrate this
anniversary. Restored propagation house and
Victorian fernery now open. Virtual tour of the
show rooms available

⭐ For car parking follow signs to Chapel Road
car park and walk from there (250yds). Note:
visitors will find the birthplace (not NT) of
Octavia Hill, who co-founded the NT in 1895,
is within walking distance of Peckover House.
Tel. 01945 476358 for opening times

ℹ️ **T** 01945 583463
E peckover@nationaltrust.org.uk

🎭 Behind the Scenes – special guided tours one
weekend a month

Peckover House and Garden								
House/shop/bookshop								
15 Mar–2 Nov	1–4:30	**M**	**T**	**W**	T	F	**S**	**S**
Garden/restaurant								
15 Mar–2 Nov	12–5	**M**	**T**	**W**	T	F	**S**	**S**
Open BH Mons and Good Fri: 12–5. Also open 3 & 4 July for Wisbech Rose Fair								

The Dining Room at Peckover House, Cambridgeshire

Ramsey Abbey Gatehouse

Abbey School, Ramsey, Huntingdon, Cambridgeshire PE17 1DH

🏠 👬 1952 (3:F6)

Remains of a former Benedictine abbey

⭐ Property is on school grounds – please respect school security arrangements. Exterior can be seen all year, but interior open on selected days only. No WC

ℹ️ **T** 01480 301494
E ramseyabbey@nationaltrust.org.uk

➡️ At SE edge of Ramsey, at point where Chatteris road leaves B1096, 10ml SE of Peterborough

Ramsey Abbey Gatehouse
Please tel. for information about open days

🎭 Send sae for details

♿ 🚾 ♿ 🦽 ⠿ 🅰️ 📷 Building 🔆🔲 Grounds 🦽➡️🔲

🏠 NT shop. Plant sales. Second-hand bookshop

🍽️ Licensed tea-room in Reed Barn

👬 Baby-changing facilities. Front-carrying baby slings and hip-carrying infant seats for loan

🎒 Suitable for school groups. Hands-on activities. 'Upstairs downstairs' education package

➡️ [143:TF458097] **Foot**: from Chapel Road car park walk up passageway to left of Wisbech Arms public house, turn right by river. Peckover House is 100yds on right.
Cycle: NCN1, ¼ml. **Bus**: First X1
🚂 Peterborough–Lowestoft; X1 and Norfolk Green 46 from King's Lynn (passing close 🚂 King's Lynn). **Station**: March 9½ml.
Road: W of Wisbech town centre on N bank of River Nene (B1441)

🅿️ Free parking (not NT), 350yds

NT properties nearby
Houghton Mill, Oxburgh Hall, Garden and Estate, St George's Guildhall

Rayleigh Mount

Rayleigh, Essex

🎎 🏠 🎭 🐕 1923 (3:I10)

Norman motte and bailey remains

Dating from the earliest days after the Norman Conquest, Rayleigh Mount still commands sweeping views across the Crouch Valley, just as it did when Sweyn of Essex built the first defences. Display boards explain the main points of interest and many kinds of wildlife can be seen in this haven in the middle of Rayleigh town centre.

What's new in 2008 Views of the Mount and new exhibition on the history of Rayleigh in the adjacent windmill (owned by Rochford District Council. Tel. 01702 318120 for details)

⭐ No WC, nearest WC in Mill Hall

ℹ️ **T** 01284 747500
E rayleighmount@nationaltrust.org.uk

Rayleigh Mount								
Summer	7–6	**M**	**T**	**W**	**T**	**F**	**S**	**S**
Winter	7–5	**M**	**T**	**W**	**T**	**F**	**S**	**S**

The Mount closes 2 Sats and other opening times may vary. Tel. for details

Please remember – your membership card is always needed for free admission

🎭 Guided tours most summer Sat afternoons

🎭 Open-air theatre in July

♿ ⓐ

➔ [178:TQ805909] 100yds from High Street, next to Mill Hall car park. **Bus**: from surrounding areas. **Station**: Rayleigh 200yds. **Road**: 6ml NW of Southend (A129)

🅿 Parking (not NT) (pay & display), charge inc. NT members

NT properties nearby
Blake's Wood, Danbury and Lingwood Commons, Northey Island

St George's Guildhall

29 King Street, King's Lynn, Norfolk PE30 1HA

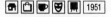 1951   **(3:H5)**

England's largest surviving medieval Guildhall

The building is now converted into a theatre and arthouse cinema and also houses several art galleries. Many interesting features survive.

ℹ **T** 01553 765565
    E stgeorgesguildhall@nationaltrust.org.uk

🎭 Theatre, film, music, comedy and King's Lynn Festival, performances, workshops and art exhibitions

♿ Building 🔎 Grounds 🔍

🏠 Crafts, Christmas shop from mid Nov (not NT)

🍽 Riverside restaurant (not NT) serves lunch and dinner Mon–Sat. Crofters Café (not NT), 9:30–5 Mon–Sat

🎒 Suitable for school groups

➔ [132:TF616202] On W side of King Street close to the Tuesday Market Place.
Cycle: NCN1, ¼ml. **Bus**: from surrounding area. **Station**: King's Lynn ½ml

St George's Guildhall								
All year			**M**	**T**	**W**	**T**	**F**	S S

Closed Good Fri, BH Mons, 24 Dec to 1st Mon in Jan 09. Tel. for opening dates and times for Guildhall. The Guildhall is not usually open on days when there are performances in the theatre. Tel. box office, open Mon–Fri 10–2, for details

🅿 Parking (not NT) (pay & display)

NT properties nearby
Oxburgh Hall, Garden and Estate, Peckover House and Garden

Shaw's Corner

Ayot St Lawrence, nr Welwyn, Hertfordshire AL6 9BX

🏠 ❊ 🏠 🚪 🎭 🚻 🎒 1944   **(3:F9)**

Home of famous Irish playwright G. B. Shaw

Built in 1902 and home to George Bernard Shaw for more than 40 years, Shaw's Corner is an Arts & Crafts house which is much as he left it. The clothes in Shaw's wardrobe, the typewriter, glasses and dictionary in his study and the collection of hats in the hall, as well as the 1938 Oscar for *Pygmalion*, give you the sense Shaw has just left the room. Hidden away in the garden is the hut in which Shaw wrote his best known works. The hut revolved to catch the sun, and the electric heater and telephone meant that Shaw could work here in all weathers. Surrounding it the orchard, flower meadow, rose dell and densely planted herbaceous beds create a vigorous, quintessentially English garden, richly stocked with pre-1950s plants.

What's new in 2008 New events programme

⭐ Access roads very narrow

ℹ **T** 01438 829221 (Infoline), 01438 820307
    E shawscorner@nationaltrust.org.uk

🎭 Events throughout the season, inc. open-air theatre during the summer

♿ 🚗 ⠿ ⓐ 🅿 Building 🔎 ♿ Grounds 🔍

🏠 Ice-cream, cold drinks, plants and second-hand books on sale

🚻 Front-carrying baby slings and hip-carrying infant seats for loan. Family activity packs

Shaw's Corner								
House								
15 Mar–2 Nov	1–5	M T	**W**	**T**	**F**	**S**	**S**	
Garden								
15 Mar–2 Nov	12–5:30	M T	**W**	**T**	**F**	**S**	**S**	

Open BH Mons and Good Fri. May close earlier when evening events occur

Unless indicated, last admission is always 30mins before closing time

🔥 Suitable for school groups

🐕 On leads and only in car park

➡️ [166:TL194167] **Cycle**: NCN12, 1ml.
Bus: Centrebus 304/Harpenden Taxis 904
from 🚆 St Albans, Suns April–Oct only;
otherwise Centrebus 304 🚆 St Albans–
Hitchin, alight Gustardwood, 1¼ml.
Station: Welwyn North 4½ml; Harpenden 5ml.
Road: in the village of Ayot St Lawrence.
A1(M) exit 4 or M1 exit 10. Signposted
from B653 Welwyn Garden City–Luton
road near Wheathampstead. Also from B656
at Codicote

🅿️ Free parking, 30yds. Small car park not
suitable for very large vehicles

NT properties nearby
Ashridge Estate, Chilterns Gateway Centre,
Pitstone Windmill, Wimpole Hall,
Wimpole Home Farm

Sheringham Park

Visitor Centre, Wood Farm, Upper Sheringham,
Norfolk NR26 8TL

🚶 🚲 1987   (3:J4)

Spectacular landscape park and woodland garden

Fabulous displays of rhododendrons and
azaleas from mid May to June, as well as a
gazebo and viewing towers with stunning
coastal vistas, make Sheringham one of the
finest examples of landscape design in the
country. Discover more about this outstanding
example of Humphry Repton's design legacy,
then stroll along the miles of beautiful paths
through the park and woodland. If your passion
is steam you can walk to the North Norfolk
Railway station at Weybourne, where there are
regular steamings.

ℹ️ **T** 01263 820550
E sheringhampark@nationaltrust.org.uk

🎪 Variety of wildlife and countryside events for all
plus children and family fun

🚶 Tree trail guide and waymarked walks

♿ 🖥️ 🦽 🔍 🗄️ ⚅ 📷 🅿️ 🚆 Building 🦽 🦽
Grounds 🏞️ ➡️ 🦽

🛍️ Limited range of goods. Plant sales

🍴 Refreshment kiosk with outdoor seating
(some under cover)

🚼 Baby-changing and feeding facilities.
Pushchairs and baby back-carriers admitted

🔥 Suitable for school groups. Education
room/centre. Learning Officer

🐕 On leads only near livestock and visitor
facilities

🚲 Cycle friendly. Some restrictions during
rhododendron season

➡️ [133:TG135420] **Foot**: Norfolk Coast Path
passes through property. **Cycle**: regional
route 30 1½ml S of property. **Bus**: Sanders 4,
4¼, First/Norfolk Green X5 Norwich–Holt
(passing close 🚆 Norwich), alight main
entrance; Norfolk Green X5/6 Cromer-
Fakenham, alight Upper Sheringham.
All pass 🚆 Sheringham. **Station**: Sheringham
(U) 2ml. **Road**: 2ml SW of Sheringham, 5ml
W of Cromer, 6ml E of Holt. Main entrance
at junction of A148 Cromer–Holt road
and B1157

🅿️ Parking, 60yds, £4 (pay & display). Coaches
(please advise for May/June visits) free

NT properties nearby
Beeston Regis Heath, Blickling Hall, Gardens
and Park, Felbrigg Hall, Garden and Park,
West Runton

Sheringham Park									
Park									
All year	Dawn–dusk	M	T	W	T	F	S	S
Visitor centre									
1 Feb–14 Mar	11–4	M	T	W	T	F	**S**	**S**
15 Mar–30 Sep	10–5	**M**	**T**	**W**	**T**	**F**	**S**	**S**
1 Oct–31 Oct	10–5	M	T	**W**	**T**	**F**	**S**	**S**
1 Nov–31 Jan 09	11–4	M	T	W	T	F	**S**	**S**

Refreshment kiosk opens at 11. Sheringham Hall is
privately occupied. April–Sept: limited access by
written appointment with the leaseholder. Visitor centre
& kiosk open every day in local Oct half-term hol

Sutton Hoo

Tranmer House, Sutton Hoo, Woodbridge,
Suffolk IP12 3DJ

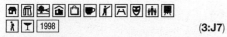

| 📖 | 1998 | (3:J7)

Awe-inspiring Anglo-Saxon royal burial site

Amazingly missed by grave robbers and left undisturbed for 1,300 years, Sutton Hoo provides clues to what has been called 'page one of English history'. Excavations in 1939 uncovered the incredible ship-burial of an Anglo-Saxon warrior king, including the iconic Sutton Hoo helmet, weapons and priceless royal treasure – all discovered when Edith Pretty hired Basil Brown to investigate some mysterious mounds of earth on her land! Incredible insights into Britain's history are offered by the fascinating Sutton Hoo exhibition, where a full-size reconstruction of the burial chamber and grave goods reveal the importance of the great Anglo-Saxon king buried here. One of Britain's most important and atmospheric archaeological sites, Sutton Hoo is set in a 99-hectare (245-acre) estate which offers estuary views and winding walks. There are beautiful displays of snowdrops, bluebells and daffodils in spring, and breathtaking rhododendrons in early summer.

What's new in 2008 Exhibition on the Anglo-Saxon kingdom of East Anglia, featuring artefacts loaned from the British Museum and leading museums in Suffolk and Norfolk (15 March-2 November)

The Exhibition Hall at Sutton Hoo, Suffolk

ℹ **T** 01394 389700
E suttonhoo@nationaltrust.org.uk

🎫 Guided tours of the Anglo-Saxon royal burial site most days. Weekly 'Amazing Artefacts' exhibition talk

🎭 Anglo-Saxon themed events. Wildlife/nature walks. Exclusive behind-the-scenes tours. Open-air theatre. Family events, children's activities and trails. Live interpreters on special event days

🚶 Varied woodland and heathland walks, with estuary views. Beautiful displays of snowdrops, bluebells and daffodils in spring, rhododendrons in early summer. Rare Suffolk Sandlings heathland

♿ 🚾 ♿ ♿ ♿ ♿ ♿ ♿ ♿ **Building** ♿ ♿
Grounds ♿ ➡ ♿

🏬 Gift shop selling locally produced ranges as well as jewellery, ceramics and children's gifts based on Sutton Hoo artefacts. Seasonal plant sale

🍴 Licensed restaurant serving local, seasonal food. Outdoor terrace with seating. Children's menu. Ice-cream kiosk in summer

Sutton Hoo		M	T	W	T	F	S	S
1 Feb–8 Feb	11–4						S	S
9 Feb–17 Feb	11–4	M	T	W	T	F	S	S
18 Feb–18 Mar	11–4						S	S
19 Mar–6 Apr	10:30–5	M	T	W	T	F	S	S
7 Apr–20 May	10:30–5			W	T	F	S	S
21 May–1 Jun	10:30–5	M	T	W	T	F	S	S
2 Jun–24 Jun	10:30–5			W	T	F	S	S
25 Jun–31 Aug	10:30–5	M	T	W	T	F	S	S
1 Sep–21 Oct	10:30–5			W	T	F	S	S
22 Oct–2 Nov	10:30–5	M	T	W	T	F	S	S
3 Nov–31 Jan 09	11–4						S	S

Open BH Mons. Estate walks open daily all year 9–6 (except for certain Thur, Nov–Jan 09 inc.)

👶 Baby-changing and feeding facilities. Pushchairs and baby back-carriers admitted. Children's play area. Children's quiz/trail. Dressing-up box in exhibition hall. Family events. Children's activities

🏫 Suitable for school groups. Education room/centre. Hands-on activities. Adult study days

🐕 On leads only. No entry to buildings or burial ground

➔ [169:TM288487] **Foot**: entrance to Sutton Hoo 1¼ml from Melton station. **Bus**: Ipswich Buses 71/3 Ipswich–Bawdsey (passing ≋ Melton). **Station**: Melton 1¼ml, Woodbridge 3ml. **Road**: on B1083 Melton–Bawdsey. Follow signs from A12 N of Woodbridge

🅿 Parking, 30yds. Car park (pay & display when exhibition closed). Motorcycle parking area, cycle racks and free pannier lockers

NT properties nearby
Dunwich Heath, Flatford: Bridge Cottage, Ickworth House, Park and Gardens, Orford Ness National Nature Reserve

Theatre Royal, Bury St Edmunds

Westgate Street, Bury St Edmunds, Suffolk
IP33 1QR

🐕 💬 🎭 🏫 | 1974 | (3:17)

The only surviving Regency playhouse in Britain

Built in 1819 by architect William Wilkins, the Theatre Royal in Bury St Edmunds was one of the most sophisticated, elegant and modern playhouses of its age. It has been undergoing restoration since 2005 and reopened in September 2007. The painted 'sky' ceiling, intimate auditorium and handsome façade make this a beautiful little theatre in which to imagine yourself back in the pre-Victorian era. A favourite venue for audiences and performers alike, with year-round drama, music, dance and comedy.

What's new in 2008 Now fully reopened following major restoration and development

For information regarding prices, see page 10

Open all year (apart from during performances) for visitors wishing to view the building. You are strongly advised to tel. for details

⭐ For full Theatre Royal information please visit www.theatreroyal.org

ℹ **T** 01284 769505
E theatreroyal@nationaltrust.org.uk

🎫 Tours available throughout the year. Booking strongly advised. Please note that due to the demands of the Theatre's performance schedule, it is not always possible for tours to take place. You are strongly advised to check in advance with the box office

🎭 Year-round programme of drama, music, comedy and dance

♿ 🚻 ♿ **Building** ♿

💬 Restaurant and bar facilities available 2hrs before most performances

🏫 Suitable for school groups

➔ [155:TL856637] **Bus**: from surrounding areas. **Station**: Bury St Edmunds ¾ml. **Road**: on Westgate Street on S side of A134 from Sudbury (one-way system)

🅿 Limited parking in Westgate Street. Nearest car park in Swan Lane (546yds)

NT properties nearby
Ickworth House, Park and Gardens, Lavenham Guildhall, Melford Hall

Thorington Hall

Stoke by Nayland, Suffolk CO6 4SS

🏠 | 1940 | (3:18)

Rambling Suffolk farmhouse built around 1600

⭐ Refurbishment work is planned throughout 2008 so visiting is restricted to the open day in September

ℹ **T** 01284 747500
E thoringtonhall@nationaltrust.org.uk

➔ 2ml SE of Stoke by Nayland

Open on Sat during Heritage Open Day period in Sept

Whipsnade Tree Cathedral

Trustees c/o Chapel Farm, Whipsnade, Dunstable, Bedfordshire LU6 2LL

🏃 🎭 🏛 🚶 1960   **(3:E8)**

Trees, hedges and shrubs planted in the form of a medieval cathedral

Surrounded by grassland and wild flowers, this incredible place was created after the First World War in a spirit of 'faith, hope and reconciliation'. Take your time wandering the grass avenues between the trees and hedges that form the chancel, nave, transepts, chapels and cloisters. Covering an area of 3.82 hectares (9.5 acres), the Tree Cathedral is not consecrated ground but welcomes everyone to discover its special sense of peace.

★ The property is owned by the NT and administered by the Trustees of Whipsnade Tree Cathedral Fund. No WC, nearest at Dunstable Downs 1½ml, not always open

ℹ **T** 01582 872406
   E whipsnadetc@nationaltrust.org.uk

🏃 Tours by arrangement

🎭 The annual interdenominational service is held on 15 June at 3

🚶 Whipsnade circular walk – information from the Chilterns Gateway Centre. Icknield Way footpath passes the Tree Cathedral

♿ **Grounds** 🧗

🏛 Suitable for school groups

🐕 Under close control

➡ [165/166:TL008180] **Foot**: on Icknield Way & Chiltern Way. **Bus**: Centrebus X31 ➦ Luton–➦ Hemel Hempstead. Also the following Sunday services: Arriva 60 from Luton (passing close ➦ Hemel Hempstead); Red Rose 161 from Aylesbury (passing close ➦ Aylesbury); Centrebus 327 from ➦ Hemel Hempstead and 343 from ➦ St Albans. **Station**: Cheddington 6ml; Luton 8ml. Hemel Hempstead 10ml. **Road**: 4ml S of Dunstable, off B4540

🅿 Free parking (spaces limited). Signposted off B4540

Whipsnade Tree Cathedral							
All year	M	T	W	T	F	S	S
Car park locked at 7, April–Oct; 5, Nov–end Jan 09							

NT properties nearby
Ascott, Ashridge Estate, Chilterns Gateway Centre, Shaw's Corner

Wicken Fen National Nature Reserve

Lode Lane, Wicken, Ely, Cambridgeshire CB7 5XP

🍴 🏃 🐾 📷 💷 🏃 🌳 🎭 🏛 🏛
🚶 🚲 🍵 1899   **(3:G6)**

One of Britain's oldest nature reserves and home to the Wicken Vision Project

An ancient fenland landscape and internationally renowned wetland site, Wicken Fen is home to the Wicken Vision Project, the Trust's most ambitious landscape-scale habitat restoration project. Explore one of England's most diverse wetland sites boasting more than 7,000 species of wildlife including otters, water voles and tree sparrows. Wicken Fen offers a mosaic of wetland habitats making sightings of raptors such as harriers, owls and kestrels commonplace. Konik ponies and Highland cattle can be seen grazing the reserve all year round and White Park cattle graze near the visitor centre from April to October. A raised boardwalk makes this rare and unique wildlife haven accessible and enjoyable for all, all year round.

What's new in 2008 Displays of reed, sedge and peat – set beside Wicken Lode, Boat House and Fen Cottage – tell the story of Wicken Fen's social history before the onset of industrial-scale fenland drainage

Wicken Fen National Nature Reserve								
11 Feb–17 Feb	10–5	M	T	W	T	F	S	S
18 Feb–23 Mar	10–5	M	T	W	T	F	S	S
24 Mar–31 Oct	10–5	M	T	W	T	F	S	S
1 Nov–31 Jan 09	10–4:30	M	T	W	T	F	S	S
Fen Cottage								
30 Mar–19 Oct	2–5	M	T	W	T	F	S	**S**

Café closed on Tues, 1 Nov–31 Jan 09. Reserve: closed 25 Dec. Some paths closed in very wet weather. Fen Cottage (showing the way of life c.1900) open BH Mons

Many Trust properties are offering Gift Aid on Entry for non-members, see page 10

i **T** 01353 720274
E wickenfen@nationaltrust.org.uk

⌖ Tours by arrangement. See events leaflet for details

☺ Including walks and talks, family events, craft workshops and boat trips

⚐ Boardwalk and nature trails interpreted through guides on sale in the Visitor Centre

♿ ▨▨▨▨▨▨ Building **▨▨**
Grounds **▨**

⬚ Books and gifts in Visitor Centre. Binoculars for hire

⬛ Café adjacent to Visitor Centre. Hot and cold drinks and home-made cakes and biscuits. Children's menu

♟ Baby-changing and feeding facilities. Pushchairs and baby back-carriers admitted. Children's quiz/trail. Children's activities in Visitor Centre. Family events throughout year. Boardwalk suitable for pushchairs

▦ Suitable for school groups. Education room/centre. Adult study days. Wren Building available to hire (suitable for training courses and adult education)

⌖ On leads only

⚲ Cycle routes are being developed across the Vision Project areas. Cycle tours of the Wicken Vision Area available on request

Numerous lush green paths cross Wicken Fen

➜ [154:TL563705] **Cycle**: NCN11 from Ely.
Bus: Stagecoach in Cambridge 12 from Cambridge, Ely & Newmarket, alight Soham High Street, 3ml, or X9, 9 Cambridge–Ely, alight Stretham, 6ml. All pass ⬛ Ely.
Station: Ely 9ml. **Road**: S of Wicken (A1123), 3ml W of Soham (A142), 9ml S of Ely, 17ml NE of Cambridge via A10

P Parking, 120yds, £2

NT properties nearby
Anglesey Abbey, Ickworth House, Park and Gardens, Wimpole Hall, Wimpole Home Farm

Willington Dovecote and Stables

Willington, nr Bedford, Bedfordshire

▨ ⌖ ♟ 1914 **(3:F7)**

Distinctive 16th-century stable and stone dovecote

★ No WC

i **T** 01480 301494
E willingtondovecote@nationaltrust.org.uk

➜ 4ml E of Bedford, just N of the Sandy road (A603)

Willington Dovecote and Stables							
1 Apr–30 Sep	**M**	**T**	**W**	**T**	**F**	**S**	**S**

Admission by written or telephone appointment with the Voluntary Custodian, Mrs J. Endersby, 21 Chapel Lane, Willington MK44 3QG. Tel. 01234 838278. Also open on the last Sun afternoon of the month (April–Sept inc.), 10–5

Wimpole Hall

Arrington, Royston, Cambridgeshire SG8 0BW

▨ ▨ ✝ ❖ ⬛ ⬚ ▨ ⌖ ▨ ▨
♟ ▦ ⌖ ▨ ⊤ 1976 **(3:G7)**

Magnificent Georgian house, part of the grandest working estate in Cambridgeshire. Includes a working rare breeds farm

Magnificent Wimpole Hall was originally built in 1640 but was much added to and altered in the following centuries. Its exquisite interiors were designed by many celebrated architects, including Gibbs, Soane and Flitcroft. Explore the fascinating servants' quarters and imagine the work needed to keep such a house running smoothly. Wimpole's famous walled kitchen garden produces delicious fresh fruit and vegetables for the restaurant, including 50 varieties of tomato! Marvel at the restored glasshouse, designed by Sir John Soane: the height of 19th-century sophistication. As well as colourful formal parterres and informal Pleasure Grounds, on either side of the formal grand avenue the sweeping landscaped parkland has a Gothic tower to discover, a Chinese bridge and tranquil serpentine lakes. In spring thousands of daffodils add to the delightful vistas.

What's new in 2008 Document Room opens displaying a selection of architectural drawings from Wimpole's famous archives. Virtual tour for those unable to access the Hall

★ Wimpole Home Farm also on site: working rare breeds farm with children's play area and activites. See separate entry

ℹ️ **T** 01223 206000
E wimpolehall@nationaltrust.org.uk

🔧 Out-of-hours tours by arrangement. Free garden tours on selected weekdays, June and Sept (subject to availability)

Wimpole Hall, Cambridgeshire

🎭 Concerts, open-air theatre, craft fair, family activity days, Living History events, lecture lunches. Tomato Weekend, Victorian Christmas

🚶 Walks leaflet available, £1

♿ 🚻 ... ... **Building** ... ...
Grounds ... ▶️ ...

🛍️ NT shop, farm shop, toyshop, second-hand bookshop. Plant sales

🍴 Old Rectory Restaurant (licensed). Children's menu. Stable Kitchen in stable block

👶 Baby-changing facilities. Front-carrying baby slings and hip-carrying infant seats for loan. Children's guide. Children's quiz/trail

📷 Extensive schools programme. Live interpretation. Hands-on activities. Lecture Lunches. Discovery Walks

🐕 On leads and only in park

Wimpole Hall								
Park								
All year	Dawn–dusk	M	T	W	T	F	S	S
Hall/bookshop								
15 Mar–16 Jul	1–5	M	T	W	T	F	S	S
19 Jul–31 Aug	1–5	M	T	W	T	F	S	S
1 Sep–29 Oct	1–5	M	T	W	T	F	S	S
2 Nov–30 Nov	1–4	M	T	W	T	F	S	S
Garden/shop/restaurant								
2 Feb–12 Mar	11–4	M	T	W	T	F	S	S
15 Mar–16 Jul	10:30–5	M	T	W	T	F	S	S
19 Jul–31 Aug	10:30–5	M	T	W	T	F	S	S
1 Sep–29 Oct	10:30–5	M	T	W	T	F	S	S
1 Nov–23 Dec	11–4	M	T	W	T	F	S	S
27 Dec–1 Jan 09	11–4	M	T	W	T	F	S	S
3 Jan–31 Jan 09	11–4	M	T	W	T	F	S	S
Gallery								
As garden	1–5							

Open BH Mons 10:30–5 (Hall 11–5) and Good Fri 10:30–5 (Hall 1–5). Closed every Fri except Good Fri. Hall, farm & garden open Sat–Thur during local school hols (Hall closed in Feb half-term)

Don't forget to visit Wimpole Home Farm. See overleaf

Charges for National Trust members apply on some special event days

➔ [154:TL336510] **Foot**: Wimpole Way from Cambridge, Harcamlow Way. **Cycle**: NT-permitted cycle path to main entrance from Orwell junction on A603. **Bus**: Whippet 75 from Cambridge (frequent services link ⊠ Cambridge and bus station). Alight Arrington, then a 1ml walk. **Station**: Shepreth 5ml. Taxi rank at Royston station 8ml. No services at Shepreth. **Road**: 8ml SW of Cambridge (A603), 6ml N of Royston (A1198)

🅿 Parking, 200yds, £2

NT properties nearby
Anglesey Abbey, Houghton Mill, Wicken Fen National Nature Reserve, Wimpole Home Farm

Wimpole Home Farm

Wimpole Hall, Arrington, Royston, Cambridgeshire SG8 0BW

 1976   (3:G7)

The largest rare breeds centre in East Anglia – part of the grandest working estate in Cambridgeshire

Wimpole Home Farm is a working farm consisting of historical thatched farm buildings and a modern farmyard. Get to know the wide range of rare breed sheep, goats, cattle, pigs and horses, and enjoy the daily milking demonstration and animal bath time in the summer. Be sure to take part in our many farm activities – from Shire horse wagon rides to collecting eggs and grooming the donkeys. A model farm, Wimpole was built in 1794 by Sir John Soane, at a time of great agricultural improvement. The Great Barn is home to displays explaining traditional methods of farming and a strangely fascinating collection of old farm tools. Hidden among the trees, an adventure playground for older children and a special area, including pedal tractors, for younger children make this an active day out for the whole family.

What's new in 2008 Stockman tours on Sats in June and Sept

⭐ Members pay half price to enter the farm in support of the rare breeds conservation programme

ℹ **T** 01223 206000
E wimpolefarm@nationaltrust.org.uk

🧍 Stockman tours, Sats in June and Sept (limited availability, tel. for details)

🎭 Spring lambing and family fun days throughout the year. Shearing and woolcraft days

♿ 🚾 🦽 🐾 Ⓟ P♿ D♿ **Building** 🦽 ♿ **Grounds** 🦽 ⚲

☕ Farm Kitchen serving light refreshments and hot meals. Children's menu. Groups can be accepted at the Old Rectory Restaurant

🚼 Baby-changing and feeding facilities. Pushchairs and baby back-carriers admitted. Children's play area. Children's guide. Children's quiz/trail. Special children's corner

🎦 Suitable for school groups. Live interpretation. Hands-on activities. Heavy horse driving courses

➔ [154:TL336510] **Foot**: Wimpole Way from Cambridge, Harcamlow Way. **Cycle**: NT-permitted cycle path to main entrance from Orwell junction on A603. **Bus**: Whippet 75 from Cambridge (frequent services link ⊠ Cambridge and bus station). Alight Arrington, then a 1ml walk. **Station**: Shepreth 5ml. Taxi rank at Royston station 8ml. No services at Shepreth. **Road**: 8ml SW of Cambridge (A603), 6ml N of Royston (A1198)

🅿 Parking, 500yds

NT properties nearby
Anglesey Abbey, Houghton Mill, Wicken Fen National Nature Reserve, Wimpole Hall

Wimpole Home Farm									
2 Feb–12 Mar	11–4	M	T	W	T	F	S	S
15 Mar–16 Jul	10:30–5	**M**	**T**	**W**	T	F	**S**	**S**
19 Jul–31 Aug	10:30–5	**M**	**T**	**W**	T	F	**S**	**S**
1 Sep–29 Oct	10:30–5	**M**	**T**	**W**	T	F	**S**	**S**
2 Nov–21 Dec	11–4	M	T	W	T	F	**S**	**S**
27 Dec–1 Jan 09	11–4	**M**	**T**	**W**	T	F	**S**	**S**
3 Jan–31 Jan 09	11–4	M	T	W	T	F	**S**	**S**

Open BH Mons and Good Fri: 10:30–5. Closed every Fri except Good Fri. Open Sat–Thurs during local school hols

East Midlands

Enjoy the diverse scenery of the East Midlands – from the breathtaking landscape of the Peak District to the peaceful woods and open heath of Clumber Park in Nottinghamshire. Within the Peak District National Park the National Trust cares for landmark features such as Kinder Scout and Dovedale. The high moorland of the High Peak, the magnificent expanse of heather moors on the Longshaw Estate and the secluded dales of the South Peak are just waiting to be explored.

Kinder Scout

There are walks and trails suitable for every ability in the Peak District. You may want to go on a leisurely walk around Ilam Park or try to reach the top of Mam Tor, where you will be rewarded with amazing views. Why not follow one of our guided walks and find out more about the area from one of our knowledgeable guides?

If a member of your party uses a wheelchair, then the Manifold Track in the South Peak is accessible to wheelchairs and there is an excellent pathway in Dovedale up to the Stepping Stones. There are also pathways suitable for wheelchairs at Clumber Park – and you can even hire a powered vehicle or wheelchair for your visit.

The Peak District is renowned for its scenery. There is natural drama everywhere – from the hidden limestone dales, imposing rock features and disappearing rivers of the South Peak to Winnats Pass, an impressive mile-long gorge in the High Peak.

Our historic houses are set among stately parkland with numerous historic features and wildlife to spot, and trails to explore. Among the most notable is the park at Calke Abbey, which is a National Nature Reserve. Why not go on a mini-adventure and see the deer or find the tree that is an incredible 900 years old? There are many paths around the park to enjoy, including three suggested walks in our Park Guide, as well as Tracker Pack activities to keep younger visitors happy and occupied.

In Lincolnshire, at Belton House, visitors can enjoy the magnificent landscaped park with its majestic deer herd. Within the park you can also see Bellmount Tower and the restored boathouse.

With picturesque parkland, peaceful woodlands, open heath and a serpentine lake at its heart, Clumber Park has more than enough space for you to explore and relax with family and friends. There are more than 20 miles of open tracks and footpaths on the 1,500-hectare (3,800-acre) estate – ideal for a gentle stroll, more vigorous hike, or you could decide to explore by bicycle.

Left and above:
Dovedale Below:
Mam Tor

Previous page: detail of the Parlour at Mr Straw's House, Nottinghamshire (3:D2)

Above and right:
Calke Abbey

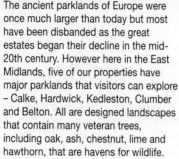

The ancient parklands of Europe were once much larger than today but most have been disbanded as the great estates began their decline in the mid-20th century. However here in the East Midlands, five of our properties have major parklands that visitors can explore – Calke, Hardwick, Kedleston, Clumber and Belton. All are designed landscapes that contain many veteran trees, including oak, ash, chestnut, lime and hawthorn, that are havens for wildlife.

Many of the ancient oaks in these parklands are giants, up to 10 yards in girth and ranging up to an estimated 1,000 years old. Clearly these old trees have witnessed much in the passing of time. So important are these wooded parklands that parts of them have special protection and have been notified as Sites of Special Scientific Interest, while Calke Park is also a National Nature Reserve.

These magnificent trees have great intrinsic beauty, as well as providing homes for insects, birds, fungi, mosses, lichens and small mammals. Many different animals and plants will use a tree during the various stages of its life as holes and crevices develop and the heartwood slowly decays, providing homes and food.

However, as the number of ancient trees has declined, so too has the wildlife that depends on them. One such victim is the very rare oak polypore fungus, which can now only be found at eighteen sites in the UK, including Calke and Kedleston.

Above: polypore
fungus Below:
Calke Park

Traditional values and methods are used to manage ancient trees and ensure that they remain havens for wildlife. This includes leaving piles of wood and fallen branches for invertebrates to live on, and using low-density grazing methods with sheep and cattle to manage the grassland. We are also working to ensure that the woodlands will be there for future generations by planting new trees. These will replace the older trees when they eventually die.

The parklands are open most days to explore. They are welcoming places, where visitors can savour peace and tranquillity and get close to wildlife.

To help you discover these special places why not follow a self-guided walk in one of our 'Park Guides', join a guided walk or find out about getting involved in some conservation volunteer work?

■ Carl Hawke, Regional Nature Conservation Advisor

Year-round pleasure

Whatever the time of year, there's always something to do in the countryside. Take a look at the *Discover Your Peak District* leaflet for suggested walks and events to enjoy – you can hunt for butterflies or listen to fantastical tales! In the autumn and winter many National Trust houses close their doors, yet the parks and countryside are always open for you to enjoy and explore.

Belton House

Grantham, Lincolnshire NG32 2LS

🏠 🐎 ✝ ❖ ♠ 🏛 📷 🚹 🎭
🚻 🏛 🔔 🍴 1984   (3:E4)

17th-century country house with magnificent interiors, beautiful gardens and extensive parkland

This fine example of Restoration architecture was built in 1685-88 for 'Young' Sir John Brownlow and recently featured in the BBC's adaptation of *Jane Eyre*. Enjoy stunning rooms displayed in 17th-century, Regency, Victorian and 1930s style, with fine furnishings, tapestries, paintings and Grinling Gibbons wood carvings. Outside, the tranquil gardens, richly planted Orangery and wonderful lakeside walks are a delight to explore.

What's new in 2008 Restored boathouse and new play equipment in adventure playground

[i] **T** 01476 566116
E belton@nationaltrust.org.uk

🚶 Guided tours in house 1st Wed in month (excluding school holidays)

🎭 Horse trials, Spitfire Prom, Easter and Hallowe'en trails, Upstairs Downstairs tours, Family Fun weekends and Christmas activities

♿ 🚾 ♿ 🔄 ⓶ ∴ 📷 🎧 🖼 **Building** 🔄 ♿
Grounds 🔄 ➡ 🚶

📷 Plant shop and garden sales

Enjoying the Italian Garden at Belton House, Lincolnshire

Belton House									
House									
1 Mar–14 Mar	12:30–4	M	T	W	T	F	**S**	**S**
15 Mar–2 Nov	12:30–5	M	T	**W**	**T**	**F**	**S**	**S**
Garden/park/shop/restaurant									
2 Feb–14 Mar	12–4	M	T	W	T	F	**S**	**S**
15 Mar–30 Jun	11–5	M	T	**W**	**T**	**F**	**S**	**S**
1 Jul–7 Sep	11–5	**M**	**T**	**W**	**T**	**F**	**S**	**S**
8 Sep–2 Nov	11–5	M	T	**W**	**T**	**F**	**S**	**S**
3 Nov–21 Dec	12–4	M	T	W	T	**F**	**S**	**S**
26 Dec–4 Jan 09	12–4	**M**	**T**	**W**	**T**	**F**	**S**	**S**
Adventure playground									
15 Mar–30 Jun	11–5:30	M	T	**W**	**T**	**F**	**S**	**S**
1 Jul–7 Sep	10:30–5:30	**M**	**T**	**W**	**T**	**F**	**S**	**S**
8 Sep–2 Nov	11–5:30	M	T	**W**	**T**	**F**	**S**	**S**

Garden & park open 10:30, 1 July–7 Sept, close 5:30, 15 March–2 Nov. Bellmount Woods: open daily, access from separate car park. Bellmount Tower: open occasionally. Tel. for details. House may close early in poor light conditions. Adventure playground may close in adverse weather conditions. Garden, park, shop, restaurant, adventure playground open daily during school hols, 15 March–2 Nov

🍴 The Stables Restaurant (licensed). Main meals 12–2. Children's menu. Ice-cream kiosk in adventure playground, weekends and school holidays 2–4:30. Coffee shop open weekends and peak periods for snacks and ice-creams

🚻 Baby-changing facilities. Pushchairs admitted. Front-carrying baby slings and hip-carrying infant seats for loan. Children's play area. Children's quiz/trails. Activity room in house; Belton Discovery Centre. Extensive outdoor adventure playground with under-6s 'corral'; miniature train rides in summer

🖼 Suitable for school groups. Live interpretation. Hands-on activities. Adult study days

🐕 On leads and only in parkland

➡ [130:SK930395] **Bus**: Stagecoach in Lincolnshire 1 Grantham–Lincoln; Centrebus 609 Grantham–Sleaford (both pass close ➔ Grantham). **Station**: Grantham 3ml. **Road**: 3ml NE of Grantham on A607 Grantham–Lincoln road, easily reached and signposted from A1

P Free parking, 250yds

NT properties nearby
Grantham House, Tattershall Castle, Woolsthorpe Manor, The Workhouse, Southwell

Please remember – your membership card is always needed for free admission

Calke Abbey

Ticknall, Derby, Derbyshire DE73 7LE

🏠🏡✝🐄❋🍴🏡🏡🎁💷🧍
🎭🛡🚻📷🧍🍽 1985   (3:C4)

A country house, park and garden where time has stood still

Calke Abbey is a unique house, completed in 1704. The house has been preserved as it was found in the 1980s, giving visitors a chance to explore a period when great country houses struggled to survive. It tells the story of an eccentric family who amassed a huge collection of hidden treasures, including an 18th-century silk bed. Why not end your visit along the cellars and servants' tunnel and then explore the stableyards? In the walled gardens, explore the Orangery, the flower and kitchen gardens and the unique Auricula Theatre. Take a walk around Calke Park, a National Nature Reserve, where you can see roaming deer and a 1,000-year-old oak tree.

What's new in 2008 New display in museum room, family garden trail and Tracker Packs

⭐ All visitors (inc. NT members) require a house and garden (or garden only) ticket from visitor reception. At busy times these will be timed tickets. Delays in entry to the house are possible at BHols. One-way system operates in the park; access only via Ticknall entrance

ℹ **T** 01332 863822
E calkeabbey@nationaltrust.org.uk

Detail of the gardener's bothy at Calke Abbey, Derbyshire

Calke Abbey									
House									
1 Mar–9 Mar	12:30–5	M	T	W	T	F	S	S	
15 Mar–2 Nov	12:30–5	M	T	W	T	F	S	S	
Garden/stables									
1 Mar–9 Mar	11–5	M	T	W	T	F	S	S	
15 Mar–2 Nov	11–5	M	T	W	T	F	S	S	
3 Jul–5 Sep	11–5	M	T	W	T	F	S	S	
Restaurant/shop									
1 Feb–12 Mar	11–4	M	T	W	T	F	S	S	
15 Mar–2 Nov	10:30–5	M	T	W	T	F	S	S	
21 Mar–18 Apr	10:30–5	M	T	W	T	F	S	S	
3 Jul–5 Sep	10:30–5	M	T	W	T	F	S	S	
3 Nov–3 Dec	11–4	M	T	W	T	F	S	S	
4 Dec–21 Dec	11–4	M	T	W	T	F	S	S	
5 Jan–31 Jan 09	11–4	M	T	W	T	F	S	S	
Calke Park/National Nature Reserve									
All year	Dawn–dusk	M	T	W	T	F	S	S	
House and garden open Good Fri									

🛡 Numerous events, from Family Fun days to guided walks and talks

🧍 Park guide avaiable showing different circular walks

♿🚾🧍♿🚪👓🅿 Building ♿♿
Grounds ♿➡

🏠 NT shop. Plant sales

🍽 Licensed restaurant. Children's menu. Coffee shop kiosk open busy afternoons

🧑‍🍼 Baby-changing facilities. Front-carrying baby slings and hip-carrying infant seats for loan. Children's quiz/trail. Family activity packs. Children's play area. Family activities and events. Family Tracker Packs

🏛 Suitable for school groups. Live interpretation. Education room/centre. Learning and Events Officer

🐕 On leads and only in park

➡ [128:SK367226] **Bus**: Arriva 69 East Midlands Airport–Swadlincote (with connections from 🚆 Derby on Arriva 68A/B at Melbourne), alight Ticknall, then 1½ml walk through park to house. **Station**: Derby 9½ml; Burton-on-Trent 10ml. **Road**: 10ml S of Derby, on A514 at Ticknall between Swadlincote and Melbourne. Access from M42/A42 exit 13 and A50 Derby South

Unless indicated, last admission is always 30mins before closing time

P Parking, £3.80 (refunded on admission to house & garden when open). Height of arch at Middle Lodge 3.6m

NT properties nearby
Kedleston Hall, Staunton Harold Church, Sudbury Hall and the National Trust Museum of Childhood

Canons Ashby House

Canons Ashby, Daventry, Northamptonshire NN11 3SD

1981   (3:D7)

Tranquil Elizabethan manor house set in beautiful gardens

Canons Ashby has been the home of the Dryden family since it was first built, and has survived almost unaltered since c.1710. It is a romantic property, with every inch – from the stone-flagged kitchen and dairy to the intimate interiors with their fascinating wall paintings and delicate Jacobean plasterwork – steeped in atmosphere. The house sits among beautiful gardens, where you can enjoy colourful herbaceous borders, an orchard featuring varieties of fruit tree from the 16th century and a surprisingly grand church – all that remains of the 12th-century Augustinian priory from which the house takes its name.

The south front, Canons Ashby House, Northamptonshire

Canons Ashby House										
House										
1 Mar–14 Mar	1–5	M	T	W	T	F	**S**	**S**
15 Mar–30 Sep	1–5	**M**	**T**	**W**	T	F	**S**	**S**
1 Oct–2 Nov	1–4	**M**	**T**	**W**	T	F	**S**	**S**
6 Dec–21 Dec	12–4	M	T	W	T	F	**S**	**S**
Gardens/park/church										
1 Mar–14 Mar	11–5:30	M	T	W	T	F	**S**	**S**
15 Mar–30 Sep	11–5:30	**M**	**T**	**W**	T	F	**S**	**S**
1 Oct–2 Nov	11–4:30	**M**	**T**	**W**	T	F	**S**	**S**
8 Nov–21 Dec	11–4	M	T	W	T	F	**S**	**S**
Shop/tea-room										
1 Mar–14 Mar	12–5	M	T	W	T	F	**S**	**S**
15 Mar–30 Sep	12–5	**M**	**T**	**W**	T	F	**S**	**S**
1 Oct–2 Nov	12–4	**M**	**T**	**W**	T	F	**S**	**S**
8 Nov–21 Dec	12–4	M	T	W	T	F	**S**	**S**

Open Good Fri: 1–5. Closes dusk if earlier. Tea-room open 11 (15 Mar–30 Sept)

What's new in 2008 See the start of work on the gardens to restore their Victorian splendour

i T 01327 860044 (Infoline), 01327 861900
E canonsashby@nationaltrust.org.uk

Monthly behind-the-scenes tours

Step Back in Time weekend, Christmas market, Shakespeare in the Park

Building Grounds

Vegetable labels in the kitchen garden at Clumber Park, Nottinghamshire

🗃 Gift shop and large second-hand bookshop

🍽 Cottage Garden tea-room. Light lunches. Children's menu

👫 Baby-changing facilities. Pushchairs and baby back-carriers admitted (except on busy days). Front-carrying baby slings for loan. Children's quizzes. Family Tracker Pack

📷 Suitable for school groups. Live interpretation. Teachers' Resource book

🐕 On leads and only in Home Paddock and car park

→ [152:SP577506] **Cycle**: NCN70.
Bus: occasional service from Banbury, taxi bus from Weedon Lois (not Sun).
Station: Banbury 10ml. **Road**: easy access from either M40 exit 11, or M1 exit 16. From M1 take A45 (Daventry) and at Weedon crossroads turn left on to A5; 3ml S turn right on to unclassified road through Litchborough and Adstone. From M40 at Banbury take A422 (Brackley) and after 2ml turn left on to B4525; after 3ml turn left on to unclassified road signposted to property

P Free parking, 200yds

NT properties nearby
Farnborough Hall, Stowe Landscape Gardens, Upton House and Gardens

Clumber Park

The Estate Office, Clumber Park, Worksop, Nottinghamshire S80 3AZ

🏠 ✝ ✿ 🌳 ♿ 🛏 ☕ 🍴 🎧 🎭 🎡 🎭
👫 🖼 🚶 🚲 🍷 1946   **(3:D2)**

Extensive area of parkland, including peaceful woods, open heath and farmland

The park comprises 1,500 hectares (3,800 acres), including peaceful woods, open heath and rolling farmland, with a superb serpentine lake at its heart and the longest avenue of lime trees in Europe. Part of Nottinghamshire's famed 'Dukeries', Clumber was formerly home to the Dukes of Newcastle. The house was demolished in 1938, but many fascinating features of the estate remain, including an outstanding Gothic Revival chapel and Walled Kitchen Garden, with spectacular glasshouses, growing old varieties of vegetables.

What's new in 2008 Extended area of cultivation in Walled Kitchen Garden and new interpretation

⭐ Park closed 16 Aug (concert day) and 25 Dec

ℹ **T** 01909 544917 (Infoline), 01909 476592
E clumberpark@nationaltrust.org.uk

🎧 Walled Kitchen Garden

🎭 Open-air concerts, theatre and special events throughout the year. Leaflet from Estate Office

Clumber Park								
Park								
All year	Dawn—dusk	M	T	W	T	F	S	S
Kitchen garden								
29 Mar—28 Sep	10—6	M	T	W	T	F	**S**	**S**
31 Mar—26 Sep	10—5	**M**	**T**	**W**	**T**	**F**	S	S
4 Oct—26 Oct	11—4	M	T	W	T	F	**S**	**S**
Shop/restaurant/plant sales								
31 Mar—26 Oct	10—6	M	T	W	T	F	**S**	**S**
31 Mar—24 Oct	10—5	**M**	**T**	**W**	**T**	**F**	S	S
27 Oct—31 Jan 09	10—4	**M**	**T**	**W**	**T**	**F**	**S**	**S**

Main facilities open BH Mons, closed 25 Dec. Chapel: open as shop but closed Feb/Apr for cleaning. Cycle hire: open as shop except Oct–31 Jan 09, when open weekends and school hols only. Interpretation centre: open all year. 183-berth caravan site: run by Caravan Club; open to non-members (tel. 01909 484758)

For general and membership enquiries, please telephone 0844 800 1895

🏃 Held throughout the year. Leaflet from estate office

♿ 🚻🛗🏷️🔊🎧🅿️🅿️ Chapel 🏷️♿
Grounds 🏷️➡️🚲

🛍️ NT shop. Plant sales

🍽️ Licensed restaurant. Children's menu during school holidays. Muniment Room and Duke's Study within restaurant available for private hire. Kiosk serving simple food during peak periods

👶 Baby-changing and feeding facilities. Children's quiz/trail. Cycles with child carriers or buggies available; parkland ideal for family activities. Family Tracker Pack

🖼️ Suitable for school groups. Hands-on activities. Adult study days. Learning Officer

🐕 Welcome in park. Must be on leads in Pleasure Ground and grazing areas

🚲 Cycle hire available April–Sept, daily; Oct to March, Sat & Sun and school holidays. Opens 10, variable closing. £5.70 for 2hrs, ID essential. Free helmet hire. Tandems, child seats, trailer bikes and trikes available. Waymarked cycle routes. Cycle orienteering

➡️ [120:SK625745] **Cycle**: NCN6.
Bus: Stagecoach in Bassetlaw 233 from Nottingham, First 25 from Rotherham, Suns only; otherwise Stagecoach in Bassetlaw 33 Worksop–Nottingham (passing close ☒ Worksop), alight Carburton, ¾ml.
Station: Worksop 4½ml; Retford 6½ml. **Road**: 4½ml SE of Worksop, 6½ml SW of Retford, 1ml from A1/A57, 11ml from M1 exit 30

The Lime Avenue at Clumber Park, Derbyshire. This avenue, the longest of its kind in Europe, was planted in 1840 by the 4th Duke of Newcastle

🅿️ Throughout the park. Main parking, 200yds from visitor facilities

NT properties nearby
Hardwick Hall, Mr Straw's House, The Workhouse, Southwell

Grantham House

Castlegate, Grantham, Lincolnshire NG31 6SS

🏛️🌸🍽️🏃🎭 1944 (3:E4)

Handsome town house, with architectural features from various eras and walled riverside garden

ℹ️ **T** 01909 486411
E granthamhouse@nationaltrust.org.uk

➡️ Immediately E of St Wulfram's church, Grantham

Grantham House									
6 Aug–28 Aug	2–5	M	T	**W**	**T**	F	S	S

Garden only 1st Sun of each month April–Nov. Admission at other times by arrangement. Tel. 01909 486411

Gunby Hall

Gunby, nr Spilsby, Lincolnshire PE23 5SS

🏛️🏠🏃🎭👶 1944 (3:G3)

Fine red-brick house, dating from 1700, with Victorian walled gardens

ℹ️ **T** 07870 758876
E gunbyhall@nationaltrust.org.uk

➡️ 2½ml NW of Burgh le Marsh, 7ml W of Skegness on S side of A158 (access off roundabout)

Gunby Hall									
House/garden									
4 Jun–27 Aug	2–5	M	T	W	T	F	S	S
Garden only									
2 Apr–28 May	2–5	M	T	**W**	T	F	S	S
3 Jun–28 Aug	2–5	M	**T**	**W**	**T**	F	S	S
3 Sep–25 Sep	2–5	M	T	**W**	**T**	F	S	S

The garden is also open on Tues & Thurs in April & May by written appointment to Dr and Mrs R. M. Ayres, Gunby Hall, Gunby, nr Spilsby, Lincolnshire PE23 5SS

For information regarding prices, see page 10

Gunby Hall Estate: Monksthorpe Chapel

Monksthorpe, nr Spilsby, Lincolnshire PE23 5PP

⊞ 🗺 🛡 ♿ 👹 2000   **(3:G3)**

Remote late 17th-century Baptist chapel

ℹ️ **T** 01909 486411
   E monksthorpe@nationaltrust.org.uk

➔ From A158 in Candlesby, turn off main road
   opposite Royal Oak pub, following signs to
   Monksthorpe. Follow road for about 1½ml
   and turn left. After 50yds turn left at dead
   end sign. Parking is on the left at entrance
   to avenue

Monksthorpe Chapel									
27 Mar–27 Sep	2–5	M	T	**W**	**T**	F	S	S

Chapel open and stewarded on some Sats: 5 April,
3 May, 7 June, 5 July (craft fair), 2 Aug, 6 Sept.
Services on Sats: 19 April, 17 May, 21 June, 19 July,
16 Aug, 20 Sept, 11 Oct (harvest service), 13 Dec
(carol service). Admission by key, obtained from Gunby
(£10 deposit required)

Hardwick Hall

Doe Lea, Chesterfield, Derbyshire S44 5QJ

🏚 🍴 🎨 ♣ 🎣 🏠 🛡 🏺 🔔 🌳 👹 ♿ 🚹 🎽 🏛 ☂ 1959   **(3:D3)**

One of Britain's greatest and most complete Elizabethan houses

Spectacular Hardwick Hall was built by Bess of
Hardwick, Elizabethan England's second richest
woman, and has survived almost unchanged.
Inside the atmospheric Hall you can see
Europe's finest collection of 16th- and 17th-
century embroideries and tapestries. The award-
winning 'Threads of Time' exhibition tells visitors
the story of Bess and the collections in the Hall.
Tranquil walled courtyards enclose the fragrant
restored herb garden, orchards and lawns. In
the historic parkland you can explore the Stone
Centre and learn about the traditional craft of
stonemasonry, enjoy the walks and trails and
see rare breeds of cattle and sheep. In the
grounds you can also visit the remains of
Hardwick Old Hall, which Bess continued to use
after her new house was built.

What's new in 2008 To commemorate the 400th
anniversary of the death of Bess of Hardwick a
series of special events will take place throughout
the year and a tapestry designed and produced
by our volunteers will be on display. Conservation
tours of Hall at 11 on Wed, Thur, Sat and Sun
(£2 donation towards conservation work)

⭐ The ruins of Hardwick Old Hall in the grounds
   are owned by the NT and administered by
   English Heritage (01246 850431)

ℹ️ **T** 01246 850430
   E hardwickhall@nationaltrust.org.uk

𝕏 Conservation tours of Hall 11 on Wed, Thur,
   Sat and Sun. Bookable at the Gatehouse on
   the day. £2 donation for conservation projects

🎧 For Tobit Table Carpet Room

👹 Themed activities to commemorate the 400th
   anniversary of the death of Bess of Hardwick

🚶 Guided walks through park and at Park Farm
   throughout the year

♿ 🚻 ♿ ⠿ 🅿️ 📶 Building 🏛 ♿
Grounds 🏛 ➡️

Hardwick Hall									
Hall									
1 Mar–2 Nov	12–4:30	M	T	**W**	**T**	F	**S**	**S**
6 Dec–21 Dec	12–4:30	M	T	W	T	F	**S**	**S**
Hall tours									
1 Mar–2 Nov	11–12	M	T	**W**	**T**	**F**	**S**	**S**
Garden									
1 Mar–2 Nov	11–5:30	M	T	**W**	**T**	**F**	**S**	**S**
6 Dec–21 Dec	11–5:30	M	T	W	T	**F**	**S**	**S**
Parkland gates									
All year	8–6	**M**	**T**	**W**	**T**	**F**	**S**	**S**
Old Hall (EH)									
21 Mar–30 Sep	11–5:30	M	T	**W**	**T**	F	**S**	**S**
1 Oct–31 Oct	11–5	M	T	**W**	**T**	F	**S**	**S**
Shop/restaurant									
1 Mar–2 Nov	11–5	M	T	**W**	**T**	F	**S**	**S**
Stone Centre									
1 Mar–2 Nov	11–4	M	T	**W**	**T**	F	**S**	**S**
6 Dec–21 Dec	11–4	M	T	W	T	F	**S**	**S**
Kiosk									
1 Mar–2 Nov	10–4:30	**M**	**T**	**W**	**T**	**F**	**S**	**S**

Open BH Mons and Good Fri: 12–4:30. Kiosk open
between Christmas and New Year. Park gates shut 6 in
summer, at dusk in winter

Many Trust properties are offering Gift Aid on Entry for non-members, see page 10

🛍 Hardwick souvenirs. 400th anniversary commemorative gifts

☕ Licensed restaurant serving hot food until 2:30. Menu includes meat reared on estate. Children's menu. Kiosk in main car park serving light refreshments

👶 Baby-changing and feeding facilities. Front-carrying baby slings and hip-carrying infant seats for loan. Children's quiz/trail. Reins for loan

🖼 Suitable for school groups

🐕 On leads and only in park and car park

🚲 Cycles permitted on parkland roads

➜ [120:SK463638] **Foot**: Rowthorne Trail; Teversal Trail. **Bus**: Pronto Chesterfield–Nottingham, alight Glapwell 'Young Vanish', then 1½ml. **Station**: Chesterfield 8ml. **Road**: Road: 6½ml W of Mansfield, 9½ml SE of Chesterfield; approach from M1 (exit 29) via A6175. Note: a one-way traffic system operates in the park; access only via Stainsby Mill entrance (leave M1 exit 29, follow brown signs), exit only via Hardwick Inn

🅿 Parking, 100yds, £2. Ponds parking, £2 (pay & display)

NT properties nearby
Clumber Park, Kedleston Hall, Stainsby Mill, Mr Straw's House, The Workhouse, Southwell

High Peak Estate

High Peak Estate Office, Edale End, Hope Valley, Derbyshire S33 6RF

🏛 🛗 🎎 🛍 🏠 🛡 👶 🖼 🚶 1936   (3:B2)

Vast area of outstanding walking country

The High Peak stretches from the heather-clad moors of Park Hall to the gritstone of Derwent Edge, and from the peat bogs of Bleaklow to the limestone crags of Winnats Pass. The wild Pennine moorlands are of international importance for their populations of breeding birds, including golden plover, merlin and red grouse. Sites of particular interest include Mam Tor, with its spectacular views, landslip and prehistoric settlement; Odin Mine, one of the oldest lead mines in Derbyshire; and the unspoilt valley of Snake Pass. Kinder Scout,

where the Mass Trespass of 1932 took place, is the highest point for 50 miles. The Trust also owns several farms in the beautiful Edale Valley. A major woodland restoration project (in partnership with the Forestry Commission) is under way in the recently acquired Alport Valley.

What's new in 2008 New Moorland Visitor Centre at Edale village, run by the Peak District National Park

⭐ No WC, available in adjacent villages: Hayfield, Castleton, Edale, Hope. Also at visitor centres/car parks at Heatherdene and Fairholmes nr Ladybower, Edale, Castleton

ℹ **T** 01433 670368
E highpeakestate@nationaltrust.org.uk

📖 Contact the property for a free leaflet

🚶 Walks leaflets available

👶 Children's guide

🖼 Suitable for school groups. Live interpretation. Hands-on activities. Teachers' Pack avaliable

🐕 Please keep dogs on leads March–July

➜ [110:SK100855] **Foot**: Pennine Way passes through property. **Bus**: frequent from surrounding areas to Castleton.
Station: Edale is 1½ml from Dale Head, 2ml from Lee Barn and 3ml from Edale End; Chinley is 3ml from South Head Farm; Hope is 3ml from Edale End. **Road**: estate covers area N & S of A57 on Sheffield side of Snake Top, E of Hayfield and W of Castleton

🅿 Many free car parks (not NT) in area. Also pay & display (not NT) at Edale, Castleton, Bowden Bridge and Hayfield. NT pay & display at Mam Nick (SK123833)

NT properties nearby
Ilam Park, Longshaw Estate, Lyme Park, Marsden Moor Estate

High Peak Estate							
All year		**M**	**T**	**W**	**T**	**F**	**S S**

Open and unrestricted access for walkers all year to moorland, subject to occasional management closures (advertised locally). Access to farmland is via public rights of way and permitted paths. Five information shelters open all year: Lee Barn (110:SK096855) on Pennine Way near Jacob's Ladder; Dalehead (110: SK101843) in Edale; South Head Farm (SK060854) at Kinder; Edale End (SK161864) between Edale and Hope; Grindle Barns above Ladybower Reservoir (SK189895)

Ilam Park

Ilam, Ashbourne, Derbyshire DE6 2AZ

❄ ♠ ♨ 🏠 🍴 🍷 🎭 🎪 🌿 👶

🎬 🚶 1934

(3:B3)

Beautiful area of open park and woodland

Set beside the River Manifold, Ilam Park's spectacular setting offers a chance to explore the limestone area of the Peak District. Enjoy the outstanding views towards Dovedale National Nature Reserve, part of the South Peak Estate, or use it as a base to explore the beautiful White Peak area. It's also a great place to while away an afternoon relaxing in the tea-room or browsing in the shop. Explore the National Trust's visitor centre and see changing exhibitions and an interactive display about the geology of the area. Enjoy the wonderful limestone scenery, rich daleside grasslands and important ash woodlands of the South Peak Estate. There are lovely walks around Ilam Park, through Dovedale and around Wetton Mill in the Manifold Valley.

What's new in 2008 'Jackson's Geology', a new touchscreen interpretation explaining the geology of the White Peak through the eyes of Dr Jackson, a pioneer in the study of the area

⭐ Postal address: South Peak Estate Office, Home Farm, Ilam, Ashbourne, Derbyshire DE6 2AZ

Ilam Park										
Park										
All year		**M**	**T**	**W**	**T**	**F**	**S**	**S**		
Shop/tea-room										
1 Feb–29 Feb	11–4	M	T	W	T	F	**S**	**S**		
1 Mar–29 Jun	11–5	**M**	T	W	T	F	**S**	**S**		
30 Jun–31 Aug	11–5	**M**	**T**	**W**	**T**	**F**	**S**	**S**		
1 Sep–31 Oct	11–5	**M**	**T**	W	T	**F**	**S**	**S**		
1 Nov–21 Dec	11–4	M	T	W	T	F	**S**	**S**		
3 Jan–31 Jan 09	11–4	M	T	W	T	F	**S**	**S**		

Hall is let to YHA and not open. Note: small caravan site run by NT (basic facilities) open to Caravan Club/NT members Mar–Oct (tel. caravan site booking office in season or estate office Nov–Feb)

ℹ️ **T** 01335 350503
E ilampark@nationaltrust.org.uk

🎭 Including guided walks with wildlife and history themes

🚶 Walks information available from visitor centre/shop

♿ 🚻 🔤 ⠿ 🅰 🅿 **Grounds** ♿

🛍 NT shop and plant sales

🍽 Manifold Tea-room. Children's menu

👶 Baby-changing and feeding facilities. Pushchairs and baby back-carriers admitted. Family & children's guides. Children's quiz/trail

🎒 Suitable for school groups. Education room/ centre. Hands-on activities. Adult study days

Ilam Park, Derbyshire, lies beside the River Manifold and has outstanding views

Charges for National Trust members apply on some special event days

🐕 On leads only

➡️ [119:SK132507] 4½ml NW of Ashbourne. **Cycle**: NCN68, 2ml. **Bus**: Glovers 443, TM Travel 202 from Ashbourne, Thur, Sat, Sun only, with connections from Derby; otherwise Bowers 442 ➤ Buxton–Ashbourne, alight Thorpe, 2ml

🅿️ Parking, 75yds (pay & display). Coaches by prior arrangement only

NT properties nearby
Biddulph Grange Garden, Kedleston Hall, Longshaw Estate, South Peak Estate, inc. Dovedale & Hamps & Manifold Valleys, Sudbury Hall and the National Trust Museum of Childhood

Kedleston Hall										
House/church										
1 Mar–2 Nov	12–5	M	T	W	T	F	S	S		
Garden										
1 Mar–2 Nov	10–6	M	T	W	T	F	S	S		
Park										
1 Mar–2 Nov	10–6	M	T	W	T	F	S	S		
3 Nov–31 Jan 09	10–4	M	T	W	T	F	S	S		
Shop/restaurant										
1 Mar–2 Nov*	11–5	M	T	W	T	F	S	S		
3 Nov–31 Jan 09	11–3	M	T	W	T	F	S	S		

Open Good Fri. Church opens at 11. Park: occasional day restrictions may apply in Dec/Jan 09. Closed 25/26 Dec. Last entry to hall 4:15. 25min introductory tour of hall at 11. *24 July–29 Aug open 12–4 Thur/Fri

Kedleston Hall

Derby, Derbyshire DE22 5JH

🏛️ ✝️ ♣️ 🦽 📷 🛍️ 🍴 🎫 🛡️ 👫 🖼️
🚶 🚲 🔔 ☕ 1987   (3:C4)

18th-century mansion with Adam interiors, Pleasure Ground and parkland

Take a trip back to the 1760s, when wealth and power enabled the creation of this outstanding house and beautiful landscape park. Designed to impress and amaze visitors, Kedleston was built between 1759 and 1765 for the Curzon family, who have lived in the area since the 12th century. Experience the most complete and least-altered sequence of Robert Adam interiors in England, with magnificent State Rooms and a fine collection of paintings and sculpture. The recently redeveloped Eastern Museum is full of fascinating objects collected by Lord Curzon when he was Viceroy of India (1899-1905). Four different walks allow you to explore the 330 hectares (820 acres) of historic parkland, with a beautiful series of lakes and cascades. Enjoy the garden, which has been restored to an 18th-century Pleasure Ground, and visit All Saints' Church (owned by the Churches Conservation Trust) which is all that remains of the medieval village of Kedleston.

North front of the outstanding 18th-century Kedleston Hall in Derbyshire

Parking in National Trust car parks is free for members displaying stickers

What's new in 2008 Explore with our new park leaflet and enjoy the family Tracker Packs (available from reception). A virtual tour of the State Rooms is now available in a ground floor, accessible room

★ All visitors, inc. NT members, must obtain ticket from visitor reception in main car park on arrival

ℹ️ **T** 01332 842191
E kedlestonhall@nationaltrust.org.uk

🚶 Occasional complimentary tours of gardens, stables and fishing rooms. Introductory talk by 18th-century costumed housekeeper most days. Out-of-hours tours of hall, garden, estate buildings and park available for booked groups at an additional charge (inc. NT members)

🎭 Throughout the year; leaflet available

🚶 Wilderness Walk, Lakeside Walk and long/short walks plus unrestricted access to rest of park. Leaflets from reception

♿ 🚻 Building Grounds ➡️

🛍️ NT shop. Plant sales

🍴 Licensed restaurant. Hot food served until 2:30. Children's menu

👶 Baby-changing facilities. Pushchairs admitted. Hip-carrying infant seats for loan. Children's guide. Children's quiz/trail. Tracker Pack

🏫 Suitable for school groups. Teachers' pack

🐕 On leads and only in park. Allowed on Wilderness and Lakeside Walks, not on long/short walks

🚲 Cycling permitted on parkland roads

➡️ [128:SK312403] **Bus**: Arriva 109 ⊞ Derby–Ashbourne, calls at the Hall weekends only, otherwise alight the Smithy, then 1ml. **Station**: Duffield (U) 3½ml; Derby 5½ml. **Road**: all traffic should aim for Markeaton roundabout where A52 intersects with A38 (do NOT follow A52). Follow brown signs on A38 (N), take exit from A38 (N) and then along Kedleston Road

🅿️ Free parking, 200yds. Non-members must pay admission fee to property to use car park

NT properties nearby
Calke Abbey, Ilam Park, Sudbury Hall and the National Trust Museum of Childhood

Longshaw Estate

Sheffield, Derbyshire S11 7TZ

(3:C2)

Excellent walking country with ancient woods and tumbled rocks

Walk through the maze of quiet paths and woods or hunt out some of the unusual sites of Longshaw's industrial past. The Visitor Centre is the ideal starting point for your visit.

What's new in 2008 Moorland Discovery Centre for use by education groups (includes meeting facilities). New visitor guide

ℹ️ **T** 01433 637904
E longshaw@nationaltrust.org.uk

🎭 School holiday family activities and other seasonal events throughout the year, including Christmas celebrations

🚶 Walks leaflet and guidebook available from shop

♿ 🚻 Building Grounds ➡️

🛍️ NT shop in visitor centre. Christmas tree sales in main car park in Dec; tel. for details

🍴 Tea-room at visitor centre. Children's menu

👶 Baby-changing facilities. Pushchairs and baby back-carriers admitted. Children's quiz/trail. Family activities in school hols

🏫 Suitable for school groups. Education room/centre

🐕 On leads only, not in visitor centre

Longshaw Estate								
Estate								
All year		M	T	W	T	F	S	S
Visitor centre/shop								
1 Feb–6 Apr	10:30–4	M	T	W	T	F	**S**	**S**
7 Apr–20 Apr	10:30–5	**M**	**T**	**W**	**T**	**F**	**S**	**S**
21 Apr–27 Jul	10:30–5	M	T	**W**	**T**	**F**	**S**	**S**
28 Jul–7 Sep	10:30–5	**M**	**T**	**W**	**T**	**F**	**S**	**S**
8 Sep–26 Oct	10:30–5	M	T	**W**	**T**	**F**	**S**	**S**
27 Oct–31 Jan 09	10:30–4	M	T	W	T	F	**S**	**S**
Open BH Mons. Lodge is not open. Extended opening 17–30 Dec, tel. 01433 637904 for details								

Dogs assisting visitors with disabilities are always welcome

→ [110/119:SK266800] **Bus**: First 240 Sheffield–Bakewell (passing ≋ Grindleford); 272 Sheffield–Castleton (passing ≋ Hathersage); TM Travel 65 Sheffied–Buxton (passing ≋ Grindleford). All pass close ≋ Sheffield. **Station**: Grindleford (U) 2ml (1ml to visitor centre, 100yds to Padley Gorge). **Road**: 7½ml from Sheffield, next to A625 Sheffield–Hathersage road; Woodcroft car park is off B6055, 200yds S of junction with A625

P Parking (pay & display). Car parks for estate at Haywood [110/119: SK256778], Wooden Pole [110/119: SK267790] and Woodcroft [110/119: SK267802]. Car parks not accessible to coaches, which should park on roadsides

NT properties nearby
Hardwick Hall, High Peak Estate, Ilam Park, Stainsby Mill

Lyveden New Bield

nr Oundle, Peterborough, Northamptonshire
PE8 5AT

🏠✝❄️🐾🎁☕🚶🎪🎭👶 🎖️🚶🚲🍷 1922 **(3:E6)**

Intriguing Elizabethan lodge and moated garden

Set in the heart of rural Northamptonshire, Lyveden is a remarkable survival of the Elizabethan age. Begun by Sir Thomas Tresham to symbolise his Catholic faith, Lyveden remains incomplete and virtually unaltered since work stopped on his death in 1605. Discover the mysterious garden lodge and explore the Elizabethan garden with spiral mounts, terracing and canals. Wander through the new orchard, containing many old varieties of apples and pears, or explore the Lyveden Way, a circular path through beautiful meadows, wooodland and villages.

What's new in 2008 New walks linking to Rockingham Forest

Lyveden New Bield		M	T	W	T	F	S	S
1 Feb–1 Dec	11–4	M	T	W	T	F	**S**	**S**
15 Mar–2 Nov	10:30–5	M	T	**W**	**T**	**F**	**S**	**S**
1 Aug–30 Aug	10:30–5	**M**	**T**	**W**	**T**	**F**	**S**	**S**
Open BH Mons. Good Fri: 10:30–5									

★ As featured in BBC series *Hidden Gardens*. Accompanied children free

i **T** 01832 205358
E lyvedennewbield@nationaltrust.org.uk

🚶 Lyveden Way: 9ml circular walk between Lyveden and Wadenhoe

♿ 🚾 ⑊ P♿ **Building** 🏛️ **Grounds** 🏞️

🎁 Small selection of gifts

☕ Ice-cream, confectionery, hot and cold drinks sold in shop

👶 Baby-changing facilities. Pushchairs and baby back-carriers admitted. Family guide

🎒 Suitable for school groups

🐾 On leads only

🚲 Lyveden to Wadenhoe is a bridleway suitable for cycles

→ [141:SP983853] **Bus**: Stagecoach in Northants X4 ≋ Northampton–≋ Peterborough; alight Lower Benefield, 2ml by bridlepath; 8 Kettering Corby, alight Brigstock, 2½ml. Both pass close ≋ Kettering. **Station**: Kettering 10ml. **Road**: 4ml SW of Oundle via A427, 3ml E of Brigstock, leading off A6116

P Free parking, 100yds

NT properties nearby
Canons Ashby House, Houghton Mill

Lyveden New Bield, Northamptonshire

The Old Manor

Norbury, Ashbourne, Derbyshire DE6 2ED

🏠 ✤ 🚶 👬 🎦 1987   **(3:B4)**

Low, stone-built medieval hall

Built between the 13th and 15th centuries, the hall's architectural features include a rare king post, medieval fireplace, a Tudor door and some 17th-century Flemish glass. The delightful gardens include a parterre herb garden.

ℹ️ **T** 01283 585337
E oldmanor@nationaltrust.org.uk

♿ 📷 ☷ 🔷 **Building** 🌳 **Grounds** 🏞

👬 Baby back-carriers admitted

🎦 Suitable for school groups

➡️ [128:SK125424] 4ml from Ashbourne; 9ml from Sudbury Hall. **Foot:** Norbury village is clearly signposted from A515. 2½ml walk to Norbury Church. **Bus:** D & G 409 Uttoxeter–Ashbourne, alight Ellastone, ¾ml. **Station:** Uttoxeter (U) 7½ml

🅿️ No designated car park. Coaches must drop passengers at top of drive

NT properties nearby
Ilam Park, Kedleston Hall, Sudbury Hall and the National Trust Museum of Childhood

The Old Manor		M T W T F S S
4 Apr–11 Oct	10–1	M T W T **F** S S
4 Apr–11 Oct	2–5	M T W T F **S** S

Property is tenanted and visits only available during opening hours. Organised groups should book by tel. 01283 585337. Visitors will be guided around the hall and gardens

Priest's House

Easton on the Hill, nr Stamford, Northamptonshire PE9 3LS

🏠 1966   **(3:E5)**

Small pre-Reformation stone building

Of interest for its architecture, the house also contains a small museum illustrating past village life.

What's new in 2008 New interpretation

ℹ️ **T** 01780 762619
E priestshouse2@nationaltrust.org.uk

♿ **Building** 🏠

➡️ [141:TF009045] **Bus:** Blands 180 from Stamford (passing close ➡ Stamford), alight Easton, ½ml. **Station:** Stamford 2ml. **Road:** approx. 2ml SW of Stamford off A43

🅿️ Ample roadside parking (not NT)

NT properties nearby
Lyveden New Bield, Woolsthorpe Manor

Priest's House		M T W T F S **S**
6 Jul–31 Aug	2:30–4:30	M T W T F S **S**

Unmanned. Also open by appointment daily throughout the year. Names of keyholders on property noticeboard. Appointments for groups may be made through local representative Mr Paul Way, 39 Church St, Easton on the Hill, Stamford PE9 3LL

Stainsby Mill: Hardwick Estate

Doe Lea, Chesterfield, Derbyshire S44 5QJ

✖️ 🚶 🎦 ♿ 👬 🎦 🚶 1976   **(3:D3)**

Impressive fully functioning water-powered flour mill

With newly reconstructed 1849–50 machinery, the mill is in full working order and gives a vivid evocation of the workplace of a 19th-century miller. Flour is ground regularly and is for sale throughout the season.

⭐ No WC, nearest at Hardwick Hall car park

ℹ️ **T** 01246 850430 (Hardwick Hall)
E stainsbymill@nationaltrust.org.uk

🚶 On request at the mill. Out-of-hours tours, contact Hardwick Hall

🛡 National Mills Day

Stainsby Mill		M T W T F S S
1 Mar–1 Jul	10–4	M T **W T** F **S S**
2 Jul–4 Sep	10–4	M T **W T F** **S S**
5 Sep–2 Nov	10–4	M T **W T** F **S S**
6 Dec–21 Dec	10–4	M T W T F **S S**

Open BH Mons and Good Fri. Open 1 Jan 09

Unless indicated, last admission is always 30mins before closing time

Contact Hardwick Hall for details of estate walks

Building Grounds

NT shop at Hardwick Hall. Flour and souvenirs sold at mill

Refreshments available at Hardwick Hall

Baby back-carriers admitted. Front-carrying baby slings available for loan. Children's quiz

Suitable for school groups. Live interpretation. Learning Officer

On leads and only in park

[120:SK455653] **Foot:** Rowthorne Trail and Teversal Trail nearby. **Bus:** Pronto Chesterfield–Nottingham, alight Glapwell 'Young Vanish', then 1½ml walk. **Station:** Chesterfield 7ml. **Road:** from M1 exit 29 take A6175 signposted to Clay Cross, then first left and left again to Stainsby Mill

Free parking (not NT). Limited car/coach parking area

NT properties nearby
Clumber Park, Hardwick Hall, Kedleston Hall, Mr Straw's House, The Workhouse, Southwell

Staunton Harold Church								
22 Mar–2 Nov	1–4:30	M	T	W	T	F	S	S
4 Jun–29 Aug	1–4:30	M	T	**W**	**T**	**F**	**S**	**S**
Open BH Mons and Good Fri								

Building

Refreshments available at Ferrers Centre and garden centre nearby (not NT)

Pushchairs admitted

Suitable for school groups

[128:SK380209] **Cycle:** NCN6, 2½ml. **Bus:** Arriva 68/A/B Derby–Melbourne (passing close ≥ Derby), alight Melbourne, 3ml; 69 East Midlands Airport–Swadlincote, alight Melbourne or Ticknall via Calke Park, both 3ml. **Road:** 5ml NE of Ashby-de-la-Zouch, W of B587. Access from M42/A42 exit 13

Free parking (not NT), 400yds next to rear of the garden centre (by courtesy of the owner). Entrance indicated by brown signs – anvil symbol

NT properties nearby
Calke Abbey, Kedleston Hall, Sudbury Hall and the National Trust Museum of Childhood

Staunton Harold Church

Staunton Harold, Ashby-de-la-Zouch, Leicestershire LE65 1RW

 1954 (3:C4)

Imposing church built in 1653, with fine panelled interior

Set in attractive parkland, this is one of the few churches built between the outbreak of the English Civil War and the restoration of the monarchy, representing an open act of defiance to Cromwell's Puritan regime by its creator, Sir Robert Shirley. The interior retains its original 17th-century cushions, carved woodwork and painted ceilings.

A one-way system operates on the estate; coaches follow alternative brown sign route. WCs (not NT) 500yds

T 01332 863822 (Calke Abbey)
E calkeabbey@nationaltrust.org.uk

Mr Straw's House

7 Blyth Grove, Worksop, Nottinghamshire S81 0JG

1990 (3:D2)

A 1920s house captured in time

Step back in time to the 1920s and find out how a grocer's family lived. This ordinary semi-detached house was the home of the Straw family, who threw nothing away for more than 60 years and lived without many of the modern comforts we take for granted. Photos, letters, Victorian furniture

Mr Straw's House								
15 Mar–1 Nov	11–5	M	**T**	**W**	**T**	**F**	**S**	S

Admission by timed ticket only for all visitors (inc. NT members), which must be booked in advance. All bookings by tel. or letter (with sae) to Custodian. On quiet days a same-day tel. call is often sufficient. Last admission 4. Closed Good Fri. Due to its location in residential area, property is closed on BHols as a courtesy to neighbours

The family living room in Mr Straw's House, Worksop in Nottinghamshire

and household objects can still be seen exactly where their owners left them. Explore all three floors of this award-winning visitor attraction and find out more about the Straw family from the introductory video and annual exhibition.

What's new in 2008 Annual exhibition, including a display of items not normally on view to the public

⭐ Blyth Grove is a private road; there is no access without advance booking. There is a car park with picnic area for visitors opposite the house. Please come to reception at 5 Blyth Grove at your allotted time

ℹ **T** 01909 482380
E mrstrawshouse@nationaltrust.org.uk

🛡 Guided tours. Behind-the-scenes tours. Rag rug days. Tasting-the-past days. The Friends group provides tea and cakes in the orchard 1st Sat of the month

♿ ⠿ ♿ Building 🛗

👪 Children's quiz/trail

🏛 Suitable for school groups. Hands-on activities. Teachers' resource pack

➡ [120:SK592802] **Cycle**: NCN6, ¾ml.
Bus: from surrounding areas.
Station: Worksop ½ml. **Road**: follow signs for Bassetlaw Hospital and Blyth Road (B6045). Blyth Grove is a small private road off B6045, just south of Bassetlaw Hospital A&E entrance. House signposted with black and white signs at the bottom of Blyth Grove

P Free parking, 30yds

NT properties nearby
Clumber Park, Hardwick Hall, Stainsby Mill, The Workhouse, Southwell

Sudbury Hall and the National Trust Museum of Childhood

Sudbury, Ashbourne, Derbyshire DE6 5HT

🏠🏠🔆🏠💼🍴🎧🎪🐗👪
🏛🚲🔔🍸 1967 (3:B4)

Late 17th-century house with sumptuous interiors and the Museum of Childhood, where you can take a fresh look at childhood

Sudbury Hall, which featured in the BBC's *Pride and Prejudice* and *Jane Eyre*, is a grand 17th-century family home. Experience the richly decorated interiors, including woodcarving by Grinling Gibbons, and the Great Staircase, which is one of the most elaborate of its kind in any English house. There's also another world to discover below stairs in the 1930s kitchen, before you enjoy a walk around the naturalised garden, by the lake and boathouse. Housed in the 19th-century service wing of Sudbury Hall, the Museum contains fascinating displays about children from the 19th century onwards. There are chimney climbs for adventurous 'sweep-sized' youngsters, a Victorian schoolroom and a fine collection of toys, games and dolls. The Museum traces the fascinating experience of childhood over the past 200 years. Find something for everyone in the eight new themed galleries, including captivating object displays, exciting activities for the whole family, personal histories, archive film, temporary exhibitions and lots, lots more.

For general and membership enquiries, please telephone 0844 800 1895

North front, Sudbury Hall, Derbyshire: home of the National Trust Museum of Childhood

What's new in 2008 The Museum of Childhood is opening its doors for the first time in spring, after a £2.2 million redevelopment project. In the Hall children can discover the 'Lords and Ladies dressing-up box' and the family character cards. In the garden visitors can enjoy new environmental and wildlife activities and garden tours (by appointment)

⭐ **The opening date of the Museum of Childhood is not confirmed. Tel. the Infoline for details in early 2008. When the Museum has opened it will have the same opening times as the tea-room & shop**

Sudbury Hall and the NT Museum of Childhood*										
Hall										
21 Mar–2 Nov	1–5	M	T	**W**	**T**	**F**	**S**	**S**
Tea-room/shop										
21 Mar–27 Jul	11–5	M	T	**W**	**T**	**F**	**S**	**S**
28 Jul–7 Sep	11–5	**M**	**T**	**W**	**T**	**F**	**S**	**S**
10 Sep–2 Nov	11–5	M	T	**W**	**T**	**F**	**S**	**S**
8 Nov–21 Dec	10:30–3:30	M	T	W	T	F	**S**	**S**
Christmas event in the Museum										
6 Dec–21 Dec	10:30–3:30	M	T	W	T	F	**S**	**S**
Grounds										
15 Mar–21 Dec	10:30–5	**M**	**T**	**W**	**T**	**F**	**S**	**S**

*For the Museum of Childhood opening details see **Important Notes above table.** Open BH Mons & Good Fri. Hall may close dusk if earlier than 5. Daily tours 11–12. School visits/taster tours at 11 & 12

For information regarding prices, see page 10

ℹ️ **T** 01283 585305 (Infoline), 01283 585337
E sudburyhall@nationaltrust.org.uk

🚶 Guided and specialist tours of Hall. Behind-the-scenes tours. Evening and morning tours by arrangement. Please note that this season there will no guided tours in the Museum of Childhood

🎧 Museum of Childhood – various AV and audio experiences

🎭 Family activities every weekend and school holidays

♿

Building 🔖🔖 Museum of Childhood 🔖🔖 Grounds 🔖

🏪 Museum shop in stableyard, with toys, children's goods and home-made fudge. Gift shop selling wide range of products

☕ The Coach House tea-room (licensed). Children's menu

👶 Baby-changing and feeding facilities. Front-carrying baby slings and hip-carrying infant seats, reins and indoor buggies for loan. Children's guide. Children's quiz/trail. Children's activity packs. Family activities

🎟️ Suitable for school groups. Live interpretation. Hands-on activities. Adult study days

➔ [128:SK158322] **Cycle**: cycleway from Uttoxeter to Doveridge, then road to property. **Bus**: Arriva 1 Burton on Trent–Uttoxeter (passing ≥ Tutbury & Hatton and close ≥ Burton on Trent). **Station**: Tutbury & Hatton (U) 5ml. **Road**: 6ml E of Uttoxeter at junction of A50 Derby–Stoke and A515 Ashbourne

P Free parking, 500yds

NT properties nearby
Calke Abbey, Ilam Park, Kedleston Hall, The Old Manor

Tattershall Castle

Tattershall, Lincoln, Lincolnshire LN4 4LR

🖼🏠📷📷🎧🎭👪🖼🎨🚶

🔔 1925   **(3:F3)**

Medieval castle rising dramatically above the Lincolnshire countryside

Explore the six floors of this red-brick medieval castle built by Ralph Cromwell, Lord Treasurer of England and one of the most powerful men in the country. Let the audio guide create a picture of what life was like at Tattershall Castle in the 15th century. Climb the 150 steps from the basement to the battlements and enjoy the magnificent views of the Lincolnshire countryside, then explore the grounds, moats and bridges.

ℹ️ **T** 01526 342543
E tattershallcastle@nationaltrust.org.uk

🎭 Including family days and concerts

🚶 Leaflet on walk around Tattershall village available from shop

♿ 🚻 📷 🎨 👓 P♿ Building 🏛♿ ♿
Grounds 🏛

Tattershall Castle								
1 Mar–14 Mar	12–4	M	T	W	T	F	**S**	**S**
15 Mar–1 Oct	11–5:30	**M**	**T**	**W**	T	F	**S**	**S**
4 Oct–2 Nov	11–4	**M**	**T**	**W**	T	F	**S**	**S**
3 Nov–16 Dec	12–4	M	T	W	T	F	**S**	**S**

Open Good Fri: 11–5:30. Last audio guide issued 1¼hrs before closing. NB: castle opens 1 on Sats when weddings are being held (except July/Aug)

📷 Hot and cold drinks and ice-cream available in shop. Seating area in exhibition room above shop

🏼 Baby-changing facilities. Pushchairs and baby back-carriers admitted. Children's guide. Children's quiz/trail. Family days

🖼 Suitable for school groups. Live interpretation. Hands-on activities

➔ [122:TF211575] **Cycle**: Hull to Harwich cycle route passes within 1ml. **Bus**: Brylaine 5 Lincoln–Boston (passing close ≥ Lincoln and Boston). **Station**: Ruskington (U) 10ml. **Road**: on S side of A153, 15ml NE of Sleaford; 10ml SW of Horncastle

P Free parking, 150yds. Coaches must reverse into parking area

NT properties nearby
Belton House, Grantham House, Gunby Hall, Monksthorpe Chapel

Tattershall Castle, Lincolnshire: six floors to explore

Many Trust properties are offering Gift Aid on Entry for non-members, see page 10

Ulverscroft Nature Reserve

nr Loughborough, Leicestershire

🕭 1945   **(3:D5)**

Reserve in the care of the Leicestershire and Rutland Wildlife Trust

Part of the ancient forest of Charnwood, Ulverscroft is especially beautiful in spring during the bluebell season.

⭐ No WC

ℹ️ **T** 01909 486411
   E ulverscroft@nationaltrust.org.uk

♿ Grounds 📶

➡️ [129:SK493118] 6ml SW of Loughborough. **Bus**: Arriva X2, 28A/B, 217/8 Leicester–Swadlincote (passing close ⇌ Leicester), to within 1ml. **Station**: Barrow upon Soar 7ml, Loughborough 7½ml.

🅿️ Roadside parking only

NT properties nearby
Calke Abbey, Staunton Harold Church

> **Ulverscroft Nature Reserve**
> Access by permit only from The Secretary, Leicestershire & Rutland Wildlife Trust, Brocks Hill Environment Centre, Washbrook Lane, Oadby, Leics LE2 5JJ. Tel. 0116 272 0444

Winster Market House

Main Street, Winster, nr Matlock, Derbyshire DE4 2DJ

🏠 🎒 1906   **(3:C3)**

Late 17th- or early 18th-century market house

The restored building is a reminder of when cheese and cattle fairs were a prominent feature of local life. The Trust's first acquisition in the Peak District, it now houses an information room, with interpretation panels and scale model of Winster village.

> **Winster Market House**
> | 1 Mar–31 Oct | Times vary | **M** | **T** | **W** | **T** | **F** | **S** | **S** |

⭐ No WC, public WC in side street nearby. Postal address: Home Farm, Ilam Ashbourne, Derbyshire DE6 2AZ

ℹ️ **T** 01335 350503
   E winstermarkethouse@nationaltrust.org.uk

♿ ⠿ Building 📶

🎒 Suitable for school groups

➡️ [119:SK241606] **Cycle**: NCN67, 3ml. **Bus**: Hulley's 172 Matlock–Bakewell (passing close ⇌ Matlock). **Station**: Matlock (U) 4ml. **Road**: 4ml W of Matlock on S side of B5057 in main street of Winster

🅿️ No parking on site

NT properties nearby
Hardwick Hall, Ilam Park, Kedleston Hall, Longshaw Estate, South Peak Estate, inc. Dovedale & Hamps & Manifold Valleys

Woolsthorpe Manor

Water Lane, Woolsthorpe by Colsterworth, nr Grantham, Lincolnshire NG33 5PD

🏠🎒❋🖥️💼📷🎭🛋️👨‍👩‍👧‍👦🎒

🕭 1943   **(3:E4)**

Birthplace and family home of Sir Isaac Newton

This modest 17th-century Lincolnshire manor house was the birthplace and family home of one of the world's most famous scientists. Instead of running the family sheep farm as a young man, Newton developed his remarkable work about light and gravity here. Visit the famous apple tree, discover Newton's ideas in the hands-on Science Discovery Centre and enjoy the short film. Explore the orchards, farmyard and paddocks and say hello to the rare breed Lincoln Longwool sheep.

The Wet Kitchen, Woolsthorpe Manor, Lincolnshire

What's new in 2008 Try on new costumes in the Byre activity room

⭐ Postal address: Woolsthorpe Manor, 23 Newton Way, Woolsthorpe by Colsterworth, nr Grantham NG33 5NR

ℹ **T** 01476 860338
E woolsthorpemanor@nationaltrust.org.uk

📷 Summer exhibition, family events and children's activities

🚶 Village walk from property. Leaflets available at ticket desk

♿ Building 🏞️ Grounds 🏛️

🏠 Small shop

🍴 Drinks and snacks in the Science Centre

👶 Baby-changing facilities. Baby back-carriers available for loan. Children's activities and quiz. Children's costumes. Family events

🎒 Suitable for school groups. Activity room. Hands-on activities. Live interpretation (please ask when booking). Hands-on interactive Science Centre

→ [130:SK924244] **Bus**: Centrebus 608 Grantham–South Witham (passes close ⭐ Grantham). **Station**: Grantham 7ml. **Road**: 7ml S of Grantham, ½ml NW of Colsterworth, 1ml W of A1 (not to be confused with Woolsthorpe near Belvoir). Leave A1 at Colsterworth roundabout via B676, at second crossroads turn right, then first left into Water Lane for car park

🅿 Free parking, 50yds. Groups must book in advance as parking for coaches is limited

NT properties nearby
Belton House, Grantham House, Tattershall Castle

Woolsthorpe Manor										
1 Mar–23 Mar	1–5	M	T	W	T	F	**S**	**S**
26 Mar–29 Jun	1–5	M	T	**W**	**T**	**F**	**S**	**S**
2 Jul–31 Aug	1–5	M	T	**W**	**T**	**F**	S	S
2 Jul–31 Aug	11–5	M	T	W	T	F	**S**	**S**
3 Sep–28 Sep	1–5	M	T	**W**	**T**	**F**	**S**	**S**
4 Oct–26 Oct	1–5	M	T	W	T	F	**S**	**S**
Open BH Mons and Good Fri								

Charges for National Trust members apply on some special event days

The Workhouse, Southwell

Upton Road, Southwell, Nottinghamshire NG25 0PT

🏠 👤 🎧 🖼 🎭 🏃 🖼 [2002]   (3:D3)

Atmospheric 19th-century workhouse

Explore the most complete workhouse in existence and immerse yourself in the unique atmosphere as the audio guide (based on archive records) brings the 19th-century inhabitants back to life. Find out about poverty through the years with the help of the interactive displays, then meet the Reverend Becher, the founder of The Workhouse, in the introductory film. Discover the segregated work yards, day rooms, dormitories, master's quarters and cellars, then see the recreated working 19th-century garden and food the paupers would have eaten.

What's new in 2008 Time Travel Tour and storytelling club

⭐ Groups welcome but please book in advance. Limited refreshments on site; food available in local villages

ℹ **T** 01636 817250
E theworkhouse@nationaltrust.org.uk

🏃 Tours run on selected summer evenings and throughout the open season

🎧 Included in the admission

🎭 Arts and social exhibitions. Special events programme throughout the season

♿ 🚾 ♿ 👁 📷 Ⓟ♿ Ⓓ♿ Building 🏛♿
Grounds 🏛 ➡

The Workhouse, Southwell										
1 Mar–16 Mar	11–4	M	T	W	T	F	**S**	**S**
17 Mar–31 Mar	11–4	M	T	**W**	**T**	**F**	**S**	**S**
1 Apr–30 Sep	12–5	M	T	**W**	**T**	**F**	**S**	**S**
1 Oct–2 Nov	11–4	M	T	W	T	F	**S**	**S**
Tours								
2 Aug–31 Aug	11–12	M	T	**W**	**T**	**F**	**S**	**S**

Open BH Mons and Good Fri. Last admission 1hr before closing. 2–31 Aug guided tours at 11 (except 25 Aug when open at 11, but no tours)

🏃 Baby-changing facilities. Pushchairs admitted. Hip-carrying infant seats for loan. Children's quiz/trail. 'Master's Punishment' game to play. Regular family events

🖼 Suitable for school groups. Live interpretation. Hands-on activities. Adult study days. Resource centre available

🐕 On leads only in grounds

➡ [120:SK712543] **Foot**: Robin Hood Trail goes past The Workhouse. **Cycle**: National Byway (Heritage Cycle Route). **Bus**: Nottingham City Transport 100/1 🚉 Newark North Gate–Nottingham; Stagecoach in Mansfield 29/A Newark–Mansfield (passing 🚉 Fiskerton). All pass 🚉 Newark Castle. **Station**: Fiskerton (U) 2ml, Newark North Gate 7½ml. **Road**: 13ml from Nottingham on A612 and 8ml from Newark on A617 and A612

Ⓟ Free parking, 200yds

NT properties nearby
Belton House, Clumber Park, Hardwick Hall, Mr Straw's House, Tattershall Castle, Woolsthorpe Manor

The Workhouse at Southwell is the most complete workhouse in existence

West Midlands

The West Midlands region has a wonderful mixture of outstanding natural beauty coupled with the urban bustle of Birmingham. It includes the two most rural counties in England, Shropshire and Herefordshire. The range of landscapes is unbeatable in variety, from the rugged uplands of the Shropshire Hills to the pure beauty of the rolling shires of Shakespeare Country and the North Cotswolds.

In Shropshire, the National Trust owns more than 2,800 hectares (7,000 acres) of some of the most breathtaking countryside in England. The Long Mynd, or 'Long Mountain', is a Site of Special Scientific Interest and offers excellent walking. An ancient track, the Portway, runs along the top of the great ridge which extends for 10 miles and is home to a wide range of upland flora and fauna. Savour the stunning views across the Shropshire and Cheshire plains, and the Black Mountains. Wenlock Edge is a rare and special landscape stretching for 19 miles through Shropshire. The thickly wooded limestone escarpment offers dramatic views, meandering paths, historic

Right: the Clent Hills

quarries and limekilns, as well as rare flowers, mammals, birds and insects.

The National Trust conserves and cares for some of the most beautiful landscapes in the region. Kinver Edge and the Clent Hills – only 12 miles from Birmingham – provide a contrasting landscape to the city and a welcome respite from the bustle of urban life.

Above and below: **the Long Mynd**

Previous page: visitors enjoying the garden at Baddesley Clinton, Warwickshire (4:K6)

Above: the Brockhampton Estate Right: bluebells at Hawksmoor Nature Reserve Below: Spanish chestnut trees at Croft Castle and Parkland

In Herefordshire, the Trust protects nearly 2,000 hectares (5,000 acres) of parkland and countryside, including the Brockhampton Estate. This historic ancient farmland and woodland is traditionally managed and has unbeatable rolling vistas looking towards the Malvern Hills.

Travel north-east to Staffordshire and you will find some of the finest scenery in the Staffordshire Peak District, including lowland heath at Downs Banks, near Stone, and ancient woodland at Hawksmoor Nature Reserve, in the Churnet Valley.

At Croft Castle and Parkland, near Leominster, the Spanish chestnut trees form a renowned avenue stretching for just over half a mile to the west of the castle. The tale of the chestnuts' origins suggests that the nuts came from the wrecks of the Spanish Armada in 1592, making some of the trees more than 400 years old.

www.nationaltrust.org.uk/coastandcountryside

At the Clent Hills, south-west of Birmingham, enjoy more than 180 hectares (445 acres) of stunning woodland and heathland rising to higher than 300 metres. There are miles and miles of footpaths, bridleways and trails for you and your family to explore.

Parkland

Bring a picnic and enjoy an unforgettable day out at one of our stately parkland properties. Forest walks in dappled sunlight, guided walks and nature trails and a range of super events for all to enjoy. Why not bring the family and visit Croome Park. Croome was 'Capability' Brown's first complete landscape, and there are miles of walks through lakeside gardens, views of the Malvern Hills as well as of the elegant park buildings.

At Attingham Park near Shrewsbury, enjoy the landscape designed by Humphry Repton. There are woodland walks and trails along the River Tern and through the deer park, with picturesque views of the Wrekin and Shropshire Hills – perfect places to relax and unwind.

Above: Croome Park was 'Capability' Brown's first complete landscape Below: Attingham Park

Look out for our leaflets and information boards at the properties or go to www.nationaltrust.org.uk

www.nationaltrust.org.uk/coastandcountryside

Attingham Park, built in 1785, is one of the greatest country houses in Shropshire

Attingham Park

Shrewsbury, Shropshire SY4 4TP

⟦1947⟧ (4:H4)

Elegant 18th-century mansion with Regency interiors and deer park

Attingham Park, built in 1785 to the design of George Steuart with alterations by John Nash, was in continuous ownership by eight generations of the Berwick family and exemplifies the changing fortunes of the English country house estate. One of the greatest country houses in Shropshire, it contains important collections of Regency furniture, Grand Tour paintings and ambassadorial silver. The large working estate and deer park, landscaped by Humphry Repton, is an area of great natural beauty. Set alongside the rivers Severn and Tern, there are numerous attractive walks and views over to the Shropshire Hills.

What's new in 2008 Attingham Re-discovered: a major interiors restoration programme. The mansion is now open on Thursdays from late March to October. The shop (including plant centre) is open every day

⭐ In situ restoration ongoing within various parts of the mansion

ℹ️ **T** 01743 708123 (Infoline), 01743 708162
E attingham@nationaltrust.org.uk

🚶 Free costumed guided tours of the house from 11, except BHols. Out-of-hours tours: £10 per head (inc. NT members). Programme of guided estate walks. Specialist house tours in Nov, Dec & Jan 09 (Sat/Sun) Tel. for details

🛡️ Family friendly events daily in local school holidays plus annual favourites including plant, food and frost fairs

♿ 🚻 Building Grounds

🏪 NT shop. Plant sales

🍴 Licensed tea-room catering for specialist diets. Children's menu. Kiosk in stableyard

👶 Baby-changing facilities. Front-carrying baby slings and hip-carrying infant seats for loan. Children's play area. Children's quiz/trail. Family activity packs. Children's activity packs. Family activity room in the house. Children's house quiz

🏫 Suitable for school groups. Indoor and outdoor programmes. Education room/centre. Live interpretation. Hands-on activities

Attingham Park										
Park/shop/reception										
1 Feb–12 Mar	9–4	M	T	W	T	F	S	S		
13 Mar–31 Oct	9–6	M	T	W	T	F	S	S		
1 Nov–31 Jan 09	9–4	M	T	W	T	F	S	S		
House										
1 Mar–9 Mar	1–4	M	T	W	T	F	S	S		
13 Mar–26 Oct	1–5:30	M	T	W	T	F	S	S		
27 Oct–2 Nov	1–4	M	T	W	T	F	S	S		
House tours										
As house	11–1									
Tea-room										
1 Mar–9 Mar	10:30–4	M	T	W	T	F	S	S		
13 Mar–26 Oct	10:30–5	M	T	W	T	F	S	S		
27 Oct–2 Nov	10:30–4	M	T	W	T	F	S	S		
8 Nov–31 Jan 09	10:30–4	M	T	W	T	F	S	S		
Carriage House Kiosk										
15 Mar–2 Nov	10:30–5	M	T	W	T	F	S	S		

Open BH Mons and Good Fri 11–5:30. Last admission 1hr before closing. Special house openings 'behind-the-scenes': 27 Oct–2 Nov. Christmas openings: 13/14 & 20/21 Dec. Tea-room: open 9–17 Feb & 27 Dec–4 Jan 09, 10:30–4. Closed 25 Dec

Unless indicated, last admission is always 30mins before closing time

🐕 On leads from car park through visitor reception, play area, deer park and in immediate vicinity of house

➔ [126:SJ550099] **Cycle**: NCN81. Leaflet on cycling from Shrewsbury station to Attingham available. **Bus**: Arriva 81, 96 Shrewsbury–Telford (passing close ≋ Shrewsbury & Telford Central). **Station**: Shrewsbury 5ml. **Road**: 4ml SE of Shrewsbury, on N side of B4380 in Atcham village

🅿 Free parking, 25yds

NT properties nearby
Attingham Park Estate: Cronkhill, Benthall Hall, Carding Mill Valley and the Shropshire Hills, Dudmaston, Moseley Old Hall, Powis Castle, Sunnycroft

Attingham Park Estate: Cronkhill

Atcham, Shrewsbury, Shropshire SY5 6JP

🏠 👭 1947   (4:H5)

First and best-known example of John Nash's Italianate villa designs, built in 1805

⭐ Visitors are reminded that the contents of the property belong to the tenants and should not be touched

ℹ **T** 01743 708123 (Infoline), 01743 708162
   E cronkhill@nationaltrust.org.uk

➔ From Attingham take road to Cross Houses; Cronkhill is on the right

Attingham Park Estate: Cronkhill
Open Sun: 23, 30 March, 18, 25 May, 24, 31 Aug 11–4

Baddesley Clinton

Rising Lane, Baddesley Clinton Village, Knowle, Solihull, West Midlands B93 0DQ

🏠✝️✳️🍴🏠🍴🎨🏞️🛡️👭🌐
🚶🚲🍴 1980   (4:K6)

Picturesque medieval moated manor house and garden

This atmospheric house dates from the 15th century and was the home of the Ferrers family for 500 years. The house and interiors reflect its heyday in the Elizabethan era, when it was a haven for persecuted Catholics – there are three priest's holes. There is a delightful garden with stewponds and a romantic lake and nature walk.

ℹ **T** 01564 783294
   E baddesleyclinton@nationaltrust.org.uk

🎨 Wed, Thur evenings by appointment. Supper can be included

👹 Easter trail for families. 'Hands on the Past' living history. Coffee lectures

♿ 🚽 🎨 👓 🅿 Building 🏠 ♿
Grounds 🏠 ➡️

🏠 NT shop. Second-hand bookshop. Plant sales

🍴 The Barn Restaurant (licensed). Children's menu

Baddesley Clinton								
House								
9 Feb–2 Nov	11–5	M	T	**W**	**T**	**F**	**S**	**S**
Grounds/shop/restaurant								
9 Feb–2 Nov	11–5	M	T	**W**	**T**	**F**	**S**	**S**
5 Nov–21 Dec	11–4	M	T	**W**	**T**	**F**	**S**	**S**
Admission by timed ticket to house; visitors may then stay until house closes if they wish. Open BH Mons								

The picturesque medieval moated manor house of Baddesley Clinton, Warwickshire

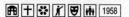 Baby-changing facilities. Front-carrying baby slings and hip-carrying infant seats for loan. Children's guide. Quiz/trail. Family Easter trail

▇ Suitable for school groups. Live interpretation. Hands-on activities

&⊙ 1½ml public bridleway giving shared access for cyclists

➔ [139:SP199723] **Foot**: Heart of England Way passes close. **Station**: Lapworth (U), 2ml; Birmingham International 9ml. **Road**: ¾ml W of A4141 Warwick–Birmingham road, at Chadwick End, 7½ml NW of Warwick, 6ml S of M42 exit 5; 15ml SE of central Birmingham

P Free parking, 50yds

NT properties nearby
Birmingham Back to Backs, Charlecote Park, Clent Hills, Hanbury Hall, Packwood House

Benthall Hall

Broseley, Shropshire TF12 5RX

🏠 ✛ ✸ 🏃 ♥ 🚼 [1958]   **(4:15)**

Handsome 16th-century house and restored garden

Situated on a plateau above the gorge of the River Severn, this fine stone house has mullioned and transomed windows and a stunning interior with carved oak staircase, decorated plaster ceilings and oak panelling. There is an intimate and carefully restored plantsman's garden, old kitchen garden and interesting Restoration church.

★ Benthall Hall is the home of Edward and Sally Benthall

i **T** 01952 882159
   E benthall@nationaltrust.org.uk

♥ Church services alternate Suns; visitors welcome

👤 🔳 ∷ 🔲 🔲 Building 🏔 Grounds 🏔

🚼 Pushchairs admitted. Children's quiz/trail

Benthall Hall								
25 Mar–25 Jun	2–5:30	M	**T**	**W**	T	F	S	S
1 Jul–30 Sep	2–5:30	M	**T**	**W**	T	F	S	**S**
Open BH Suns and Mons. Gardens open 1:30								

Yew trees in the garden at Benthall Hall, Shropshire

➔ [127:SJ658025] **Bus**: Arriva 9, 39, 99 Telford/Wellington–Bridgnorth, alight Broseley, 1ml (pass close ➶ Telford Central). **Station**: Telford Central 7½ml. **Road**: 1ml NW of Broseley (B4375), 4ml NE of Much Wenlock, 1ml SW of Ironbridge

P Free parking, 100yds. Only one coach at a time

NT properties nearby
Attingham Park, Dudmaston, Kinver Edge and the Rock Houses, Morville Hall, Moseley Old Hall, Sunnycroft, Wightwick Manor

Berrington Hall

nr Leominster, Herefordshire HR6 0DW

🏠 ✸ 🏛 🗂 🔲 🏃 🔲 ♥ 🚼 ▇
🏃 🍴 [1957]   **(4:H6)**

Neo-classical mansion with fine interiors, set in landscape grounds

Beautifully sited above a wide valley with sweeping views to the Brecon Beacons, this elegant Henry Holland house was built in the late 18th century and is set in parkland designed by 'Capability' Brown. The imposing external appearance belies a surprisingly delicate interior, with beautifully decorated ceilings and a

A view of the stableblock from the interior of the courtyard at Berrington Hall

spectacular staircase hall. There are wonderful collections of furniture and paintings, as well as a nursery, Victorian laundry and Georgian dairy. One room has a display of costumes from the collection of Charles Paget Wade of Snowshill Manor. The attractive walled garden contains an historic collection of local apple trees.

What's new in 2008 New children's guide

★ Not all of the costume collection is displayed, but can be viewed by appointment. Please write to the property

ℹ️ **T** 01568 615721
E berrington@nationaltrust.org.uk

Berrington Hall										
Below stairs/garden/shop/tea-room		M	T	W	T	F	S	S
2 Feb – 24 Feb	11 – 4	M	T	W	T	F	**S**	**S**
11 Feb – 13 Feb	11 – 4	**M**	**T**	**W**	T	F	S	S
1 Mar – 16 Mar	11 – 5	M	T	W	T	F	**S**	**S**
17 Mar – 2 Nov	11 – 5	**M**	**T**	**W**	T	F	**S**	**S**
6 Dec – 21 Dec	12 – 4:30	M	T	W	T	F	**S**	**S**
Park walk								
1 Mar – 16 Mar	11 – 5	M	T	W	T	F	**S**	**S**
17 Mar – 2 Nov	11 – 5	**M**	**T**	**W**	T	F	**S**	**S**
6 Dec – 21 Dec	12 – 4:30	M	T	W	T	F	**S**	**S**
House								
1 Mar – 16 Mar	1 – 5	M	T	W	T	F	**S**	**S**
17 Mar – 2 Nov	1 – 5	**M**	**T**	**W**	T	F	**S**	**S**
House tours								
As house	11 – 1							

Open Good Fri. Parkland: access restricted 1 Mar–16 June (due to nesting birds). Park Walk: closed 2 & 3 Aug. House ground floor only open 6/7 Dec

For information regarding prices, see page 10

🏃 Daily taster tours of the house 11:15–12:30. Daily below-stairs tours. Regular garden and park tours during summer

🎭 Easter trail. Second World War weekend in June. Apple weekend in Sept

🚶 Park walks open March to Dec. Access to parkland restricted 1 March–16 June (due to nesting birds)

♿ 🚾 ♿ ⠿ 🅿️ Building ♿ ♿ Grounds ♿ ➡️ ♿

🛍️ NT shop. Plant sales

☕ Licensed tea-room

👶 Baby-changing facilities. Front-carrying baby slings and hip-carrying infant seats for loan. Children's play area. Children's quiz/trail. Family activity packs. Easter trail

🎒 Suitable for school groups. Hands-on activities. Adult study days

➡️ [137:SO510637] **Bus**: Lugg Valley/Whittle 492 Ludlow–Hereford (passing close 🚆 Ludlow & Leominster), alight Luston, 2ml. **Station**: Leominster (U) 4ml. **Road**: 3ml N of Leominster, 7ml S of Ludlow on W side of A49

🅿️ Free parking, 30yds. Coaches: entry and exit via Luston/Eye Lane only (the B4361 off the A49). Tight turn into drive. No entry or exit for coaches directly from/to A49. Local area map on request

NT properties nearby
Brockhampton Estate, Croft Castle and Parkland, The Weir

Biddulph Grange Garden

Grange Road, Biddulph, Staffordshire ST8 7SD

⚹ 🏛 🍴 🍵 📷 👥 👪 1988   **(4:J2)**

A rare and exciting survival of a high Victorian garden

Designed in the mid-19th century by James Bateman to display specimens from his extensive and wide-ranging plant collection, the garden is set out in a series of connected 'compartments'. Visitors are taken on a sensory journey of discovery through tunnels and pathways to individual gardens inspired by countries around the world – from the tranquillity of a Chinese garden or an Egyptian Court to a formal Italian garden.

What's new in 2008 Refurbished woodland terrace area and joint ticket with Little Moreton Hall

⭐ There are many steps throughout the garden, tea-room, WCs and buildings

ℹ️ **T** 01782 517999
E biddulphgrange@nationaltrust.org.uk

🎫 Booked guided tours in groups of 10+, at 10 on Wed, Thur & Fri; A charge will apply (inc. NT members)

Inside the Chinese temple in Biddulph Grange Garden

Biddulph Grange Garden									
1 Mar–9 Mar	11–4	M	T	W	T	F	**S**	**S**
15 Mar–2 Nov	11–5	M	T	**W**	**T**	**F**	**S**	**S**
8 Nov–21 Dec	11–3	M	T	W	T	F	**S**	**S**

Open BH Mons. Closes dusk if earlier. Tea-room last orders 4:30; winter menu in Nov and Dec. Tel. for details

👥 Lunchtime talks and themed event days. Send sae for details

♿ 🚻 📷 👓 🅿️ Building 📷 Grounds 📷

🏛 NT shop. Plant sales

🍴 Tea-room. Children's menu

👪 Baby-changing facilities. Pushchairs admitted. Children's quiz/trail. Access for pushchairs is difficult

➡️ [118:SJ895591] **Bus:** Bakers 99 from Congleton (passing ➤ Congleton). **Station:** Congleton 2½ml. **Road:** ½ml N of Biddulph, 3½ml SE of Congleton, 7ml N of Stoke-on-Trent. Access from A527 (Tunstall–Congleton road). Entrance on Grange Road

🅿️ Free parking, 50yds

NT properties nearby
Little Moreton Hall

Birmingham Back to Backs

50-54 Inge Street/55–63 Hurst Street, Birmingham, West Midlands B5 4TE

🏛 ⬆️ 🏠 🎫 👥 👪 ▮ 🍷 2004   **(4:J5)**

Carefully restored 19th-century courtyard of working people's houses

Birmingham's last surviving court of back-to-back housing has now been fully restored by the Birmingham Conservation Trust and the National Trust. Thousands of houses like these were built, literally back to back, around courtyards, for the rapidly increasing population of Britain's expanding industrial towns. The story of the site is told through the experiences of the people who lived and worked here. Visitors move through four different periods, from 1840 to the 1970s. The design of each interior reflects the varied cultures, religions and professions of the families who made their homes here.

Birmingham Back to Backs

2 Feb – 23 Dec	10–5	M	**T**	**W**	**T**	**F**	**S**	**S**

Admission by timed ticket and guided tour only. Open BH Mons but closed on Tues following BH Mons. Please note: during term time property will normally be closed for use by school groups on Tues, Wed and Thur mornings. **Closed 1–7 Sept**

What's new in 2008 New events and on-site interpretation as part of the Whose Story? project

⭐ **Visiting the Back to Backs is by guided tour only**. Advance booking is strongly advised. Booking line open Tues–Fri, 10–4

ℹ️ **T** 0121 666 7671 (booking line), 0121 622 2442 (office)
E backtobacks@nationaltrust.org.uk

😊 Family learning events in summer and Easter school hols. Second World War-themed week in May. July fête. Christmas celebrations

♿ 🚻 🅿️ 🚗 📷 📷 📷 Building 📷

Everyday items at the Birmingham Back to Backs

🍬 Sweet shop

👫 Family learning events

🖼️ Suitable for school groups. Live interpretation. Hands-on activities

➔ [139:SP071861] **Foot**: in the centre of Birmingham next to the Hippodrome Theatre, within easy walking distance of bus and railway stations. Follow signs for Hippodrome Theatre. **Cycle**: NCN5. **Bus**: from surrounding areas. **Station**: Birmingham New Street ¼ml

🅿️ No parking on site. Nearest parking in Arcadian Centre, Bromsgrove Street

NT properties nearby
Baddesley Clinton, Charlecote Park, Clent Hills, Hanbury Hall, Kinver Edge and the Rock Houses, Moseley Old Hall, Packwood House, Wightwick Manor

Brockhampton Estate

Greenfields, Bringsty, nr Bromyard, Herefordshire WR6 5TB

🏠 ✝️ 🔥 ❄️ 🌳 🛶 🏠 📷 📷 🚶
🏠 📷 👫 📷 🚶 ☂️ 1946 **(4:17)**

Traditionally farmed estate and medieval manor house

At the heart of the Estate lies Lower Brockhampton, a romantic timber-framed manor house dating back to the late 1300s. The house is surrounded by a moat and is entered via a charming timber-framed gatehouse. Brockhampton was bequeathed to the National Trust in 1946 and is made up of 400 hectares (1,000 acres) of farmland and 280 hectares (700 acres) of mixed woodland. The Estate is home to a rich variety of wildlife, including dormice, buzzards and ravens. There are miles of meandering walks through the park and woodland, featuring oaks, beech and fascinating sculptures. There is also an interesting ruined chapel.

What's new in 2008 The Gatehouse has reopened. New nature trail at Lower Brockhampton

ℹ️ **T** 01885 488099 (Infoline), 01885 482077
E brockhampton@nationaltrust.org.uk

For details of events go to www.nationaltrust.org.uk/events

Brockhampton Estate

Estate parkland & woodland		M	T	W	T	F	S	S
All year	Dawn—dusk	M	T	W	T	F	S	S
House								
1 Mar—16 Mar	12—4	M	T	W	T	F	S	S
19 Mar—30 Mar	12—4	M	T	W	T	F	S	S
2 Apr—28 Sep	12—5	M	T	W	T	F	S	S
1 Oct—2 Nov	12—4	M	T	W	T	F	S	S
Guided tour								
As house	11—12	M	T	W	T	F	S	S
Tea-room								
As house								
11 Feb—17 Feb	11—4	M	T	W	T	F	S	S
1 Jul—31 Aug	11—5	M	T	W	T	F	S	S
8 Nov—28 Dec	11—4	M	T	W	T	F	S	S

Open BH Mons. Good Fri: 12–5. Last orders in tea-room 30mins before house closes

Guided tour of orchards, courtyard, chapel and house at Lower Brockhampton, 11–12 (dates as house opening)

Easter trails, moat dipping and bug hunts, bat walks, guided walks, re-enactment weekends, Hallowe'en events and Christmas fairs

Woodland and park walks from estate car park. Leaflets available

Building

Grounds

Local produce and crafts in the Granary Shop at Lower Brockhampton. Plant sales

Old Apple Store tea-room in estate car park. Light lunches and cream teas using local produce. Cakes are baked by farm tenants

Baby-changing facilities. Pushchairs and baby back-carriers admitted. Children's quiz/trail. Children's activity packs. Easter trails. Moat dipping and bug hunts. Nursery rhyme walk and family room

Suitable for school groups. Education room/centre. Hands-on activities

In woods and parkland, on leads

[149:SO682546] **Bus**: First/Bromyard Omnibus 419/420 Worcester–Hereford (passing ≊ Worcester Foregate Street & close Hereford). **Road**: 2ml E of Bromyard on Worcester road (A44); house reached by a narrow road through 1½ml of woods & park

There are miles of walks on the Brockhampton Estate

P Parking, 50yds & 1½ml

NT properties nearby
Berrington Hall, Croft Castle and Parkland, Croome Park, The Greyfriars, The Weir

Carding Mill Valley and the Shropshire Hills

Chalet Pavilion, Carding Mill Valley, Church Stretton, Shropshire SY6 6JG

1979 (4:H5)

Extensive and beautiful area of upland heath

This popular area, with excellent facilities for all, includes part of the Long Mynd, with stunning views across the Shropshire and Cheshire plains and Black Mountains. This is excellent walking country with much of interest to the naturalist; the Chalet Pavilion in Carding Mill Valley offers information about the area, as well as a tea-room and shop.

What's new in 2008 Many events of interest to walkers, families and others

For further information visit www.shropshirehills.info or www.cardingmillvalley.co.uk

Charges for National Trust members apply on some special event days

Carding Mill Valley and the Shropshire Hills								
Heathland								
All year		M	T	W	T	F	S	S
Tea-room/shop								
11 Feb–31 Mar	11–4	M	T	W	T	F	S	S
1 Apr–2 Nov	11–5	M	T	W	T	F	S	S
3 Nov–30 Nov	11–4	M	T	W	T	F	S	S
6 Dec–31 Jan 09	11–4	M	T	W	T	F	S	S

WC: open 9–7 summer; 9–4 winter. Tea-room and shop: closed 17 June & 20–25 Dec, open 27 Dec–4 Jan 09 (weather dependent)

ℹ️ **T** 01694 723068
E cardingmill@nationaltrust.org.uk

Holiday activities

Sensible footwear required

Building Grounds

NT shop. Plants sales

Chalet Pavilion Carding Mill Valley. Can be booked for functions. Children's menu

Baby-changing facilities. Pushchairs and baby back-carriers admitted. Children's quiz/trail. Family activity packs. Family room with activities for children in Pavilion

Suitable for school groups. Education room/centre. Live interpretation. Hands-on activities. Adult study days. Details on www.cardingmillvalley.org.uk

Must be under control

On waymarked bridlepaths only

➡️ [137:SO443945] **Foot**: Jack Mytton Way; Shropshire Way. **Bus**: Whittle 435 Shrewsbury–Ludlow, alight Church Stretton, ½ml. NT shuttle bus service at weekends and BHols (Easter–Oct) connects Carding Mill Valley with Church Stretton station and other shuttles to Stiperstones, Discovery Centre and Bishop's Castle. **Station**: Church Stretton (U) 1m. **Road**: 15ml S of Shrewsbury, W of Church Stretton Valley and A49; approached from Church Stretton and, on W side, from Ratlinghope or Asterton

P Parking, 50yds (pay & display). Open daily all year. Parking £4 (March–Oct), £2.50 (Nov–Feb), 1 hr £2. Minibus £8, coach £10. Top car park closes at 7 (April–Oct), 4:15 (Nov–March). Opens at 9

NT properties nearby
Attingham Park, Berrington Hall, Croft Castle and Parkland, Powis Castle, Wenlock Edge, Wilderhope Manor

Charlecote Park

Warwick, Warwickshire CV35 9ER

1946 (4:K7)

Superb Tudor house and landscape deer park

The Tudor home of the Lucy family for more than 700 years, the mellow stonework and ornate chimneys of Charlecote sum up the very essence of Tudor England. There are strong associations with both Queen Elizabeth I and Shakespeare, who knew the house well – he is alleged to have been caught poaching the estate deer. The rich, early Victorian interior contains some important objects from Beckford's Fonthill Abbey. Landscaped by 'Capability' Brown, the balustraded formal garden opens on to a fine deer park on the River Avon.

What's new in 2008 Tours and talks, including gatehouse talk, outbuildings tour, park walks, costume talk. New park activities, including a family trail and a lifelong learning education service

Cleaning equipment in the tack room, Charlecote Park, Warwickshire

ℹ️ **T** 01789 470277
E charlecotepark@nationaltrust.org.uk

🏃 House tours 1 March–28 Oct, 11–12 on house open days

♿ 🚻 Building 🏢🔿 Grounds 🏢➡️

🏪 Shop located beyond Victorian kitchens

🍽️ The Orangery (licensed). Hot meals 12–2:30. Children's menu

👶 Baby-changing facilities. Hip-carrying infant seats for loan. Children's play area. Children's quiz/trail

🏫 Suitable for school groups. Education room/centre. Live interpretation

➡️ [151:SP263564] **Bus**: Stagecoach in Warwickshire 18/A 🚆 Leamington Spa–Stratford-upon-Avon. **Station**: Stratford-upon-Avon, 5½ml; Warwick 6ml; Leamington Spa 8ml. **Road**: 1ml W of Wellesbourne, 5ml E of Stratford-upon-Avon, 6ml S of Warwick on N side of B4086

🅿️ Free parking, 300yds

NT properties nearby
Baddesley Clinton, Coughton Court, Hidcote Manor Garden, Packwood House, Upton House and Gardens

Charlecote Park									
Park/gardens*			M	T	W	T	F	S	S
2 Feb–24 Feb	10:30–4		M	T			F	S	S
1 Mar–28 Oct	10:30–6		M	T			F	S	S
31 Oct–31 Jan 09	10:30–4		M	T			F	S	S
Restaurant									
2 Feb–24 Feb	11–4							S	S
1 Mar–28 Oct	10:30–5		M	T			F	S	S
1 Nov–21 Dec	11–4							S	S
House tours									
1 Mar–28 Oct	11–12		M	T			F	S	S
House									
1 Mar–28 Oct	12–5		M	T			F	S	S
6 Dec–21 Dec	12–4							S	S
Shop									
1 Mar–28 Oct	10:30–5:30		M	T			F	S	S
1 Nov–21 Dec	11–4							S	S

Park, gardens & restaurant open 11–17 Feb. Parts of the house only open Dec. *Restricted access to gardens Feb & Nov–Jan 09

Coughton Court

nr Alcester, Warwickshire B49 5JA

🏃 ⏱️ 1946 (4:K6)

Imposing Tudor house set in beautiful gardens with a fascinating collection of Catholic treasures

One of England's finest Tudor houses, Coughton Court has been the home of the Throckmorton family since 1409. The house has fine collections of furniture, porcelain and family portraits, and fascinating connections with the Gunpowder Plot. The family has created and developed the grounds over a number of years. Highlights include the walled garden and labyrinth, spectacular award-winning displays of roses, hot and cool herbaceous borders, bog garden and walks beside the river and lake.

What's new in 2008 New interpretation, events programme and second-hand books. Lady Lilian Throckmorton's room reopening during 2008

⭐ The Throckmorton family manages the gardens and plant sales. A charge applies for the walled garden for NT members

ℹ️ **T** 01789 762435 (Infoline), 01789 400777
E coughtoncourt@nationaltrust.org.uk

🏃 Free introductory talks, Gunpowder Plot tours and Catholic family tours upon request (charge applies)

🎭 Full programme of events and activities, including lecture lunches in Oct and Christmas events in Dec. Tel. for details

🏃 Riverside walk and bluebell wood in season

Coughton Court									
House			M	T	W	T	F	S	S
15 Mar–29 Jun	11–5				W	T	F	S	S
1 Jul–31 Aug	11–5			T	W	T	F	S	S
3 Sep–28 Sep	11–5				W	T	F	S	S
4 Oct–2 Nov	11–5							S	S
Garden/shop/restaurant									
As house	11–5:30								
Walled garden									
As house	11:30–4:45								

Closed Good Fri. Closed 14 June and 6 Sept. Admission by timed ticket on very busy days. Open BH Mons and Tues

Dogs assisting visitors with disabilities are always welcome

The Dining Room with 16th-century panelling at Coughton Court, Warwickshire

♿ 🚾 Building ♿ Grounds ♿ ➡️

🛍️ NT shop selling wide range of gifts and local produce. Plants for sale, cultivated by the family's gardeners, available from the Throckmorton family plant centre

☕ Licensed restaurant. Serves hot meals 12–2:30. Coach House selling light refreshments – open on busy days (licensed). Children's menu

🚼 Baby-changing and feeding facilities. Front-carrying baby slings and hip-carrying infant seats for loan. Children's play area. Children's quiz/trail

🎒 Suitable for school groups. Tudor connections, priest holes and interesting links with the Gunpowder Plot

➡️ [150:SP080604] **Cycle**: NCN5, ½ml. **Bus**: First 247 Redditch–Evesham (passing ➔ Redditch & close ➔ Evesham); Stagecoach in Warwickshire 25/6 from Stratford-upon-Avon (passing close ➔ Stratford-upon-Avon). **Station**: Redditch 6ml. **Road**: 2ml N of Alcester on A435

🅿️ Free parking, 150yds

NT properties nearby
Baddesley Clinton, Birmingham Back to Backs, Charlecote Park, Hanbury Hall, Hidcote Manor Garden, Packwood House, Upton House and Gardens

Croft Castle and Parkland

Yarpole, nr Leominster, Herefordshire HR6 9PW

1957 (4:H6)

Castellated manor house set in stunning countryside with panoramic views

Croft Castle is a late 17th-century house with fine Georgian interiors and a family connection dating back more than 1,000 years. There are restored walled gardens, stunning views over the Welsh Marches and miles of marked walks. It is renowned for its fine parkland, which contains more than 300 veteran trees – including a magnificent avenue of Spanish chestnuts. A walk through the woodlands reveals the Iron Age hill fort at Croft Ambrey, which commands views over fourteen of the old counties.

What's new in 2008 Children's play area. Tramper all-terrain buggy on new route in front of Castle

ℹ️ T 01568 780141 (Infoline), 01568 780246
E croftcastle@nationaltrust.org.uk

🎭 Introductory tours on castle open days March-Oct and Nov-Dec

🎭 Country fairs, open-air theatre, spooky Hallowe'en, family nature days, guided walks

Please remember – your membership card is always needed for free admission

- 🚶 Occasional guided walks to discover fungi, birds, gardens

- ♿ 🚻 🦽 P♿ D♿ 🏛 Building 🦽 ♿
- Grounds 🦽 ➡

- 🛍 Shop. Plant sales. Second-hand bookshop

- ☕ Carpenter's Shop tea-room. Open weekends during winter. Children's menu

- 👶 Hip-carrying infant seats for loan. Children's quiz/trail. Family activity packs. All-terrain pushchairs on loan. Children's play area. Dressing-up clothes

- 🎒 Suitable for school groups

- 🐕 On leads and only in parkland

- ➡ [137:SO455655] **Bus:** Lugg Valley/Whittle 492 Ludlow–Hereford (passing close ‡ Ludlow & Leominster), alight Gorbett Bank, 2¼ml. **Station:** Leominster (U) 7ml. **Road:** 5ml NW of Leominster, 9ml SW of Ludlow; approach from B4362, turning N at Cock Gate between Bircher and Mortimer's Cross; signposted from Ludlow–Leominster road (A49) and from A4110 at Mortimer's Cross

- P Parking, 100yds, out-of-hours £3

NT properties nearby
Berrington Hall, Brockhampton Estate, The Weir

Croft Castle and Parkland									
Parkland									
All year	8–9	M	T	W	T	F	S	S
Tea-room/picnic area/play area									
11 Feb–17 Feb	11–4	M	T	W	T	F	S	S
1 Mar–16 Mar	11–5	M	T	W	T	F	S	S
19 Mar–31 Oct	11–5	M	T	W	T	F	S	S
1 Nov–31 Jan 09	11–4	M	T	W	T	F	S	S
Castle									
1 Mar–16 Mar	1–5	M	T	W	T	F	S	S
19 Mar–31 Oct	1–5	M	T	W	T	F	S	S
1 Nov–21 Dec	1–4	M	T	W	T	F	S	S
Castle tours									
19 Mar–31 Oct	11–1	M	T	W	T	F	S	S
1 Nov–21 Dec	12–1	M	T	W	T	F	S	S
Garden/shop									
As castle	11–5							

Open BH Mons. Castle tours 11–1 & 12–1 in Nov–Dec. Park closes dusk if earlier

Croome Park

Croome D'Abitot, Worcestershire WR8 9DW

✚ ❄ ⚐ 🏕 🏠 ☕ 𝍖 🎋 🚩 ⚒
🦇 🚶 1996   **(4:J7)**

Magnificent landscape park restored to its former glory

Croome was 'Capability' Brown's first complete landscape, making his reputation and establishing a new style of garden design which became universally adopted over the next 50 years. The elegant park buildings and other structures are mostly by Robert Adam and James Wyatt. There are miles of walks through lakeside gardens, shrubberies and parkland.

What's new in 2008 Restored Second World War sick quarters. New reception, WCs, canteen and exhibition room. Several parkland structures will undergo restoration

- ⭐ Postal address: NT Estate Office, The Builders' Yard, High Green, Severn Stoke, Worcestershire WR8 9JS. The Trust acquired 270ha (670 acres) of the park in 1996 with substantial grant aid from the Heritage Lottery Fund and a generous donation from Royal & SunAlliance

- ℹ **T** 01905 371006
  E croomepark@nationaltrust.org.uk

- 😀 Contact for details

- 🚶 Walks available. Ask at reception

- ♿ 🚻 🖼 ∴ 🔍 P♿ Grounds 🦽 ➡ 🦽 ♿

- 🛍 NT shop. Plant sales

Croome Park									
1 Mar–30 Mar	10–5:30	M	T	W	T	F	S	S
31 Mar–31 Aug	10–5:30	M	T	W	T	F	S	S
3 Sep–26 Oct	10–5:30	M	T	W	T	F	S	S
1 Nov–21 Dec	10–4	M	T	W	T	F	S	S
26 Dec–1 Jan 09	10–4	M	T	W	T	F	S	S
3 Jan–31 Jan 09	10–4	M	T	W	T	F	S	S
Tea-room/shop									
As park									

Open BH Mons. Croome church open in association with The Churches Conservation Trust (which owns it). Last admission 45mins before closing

🍴 1940s-style canteen in restored wartime buildings

👶 Baby-changing facilities. Pushchairs admitted

▓ Hands-on activities

🐕 On leads in garden. Under close control in wider parkland

➔ [150:SO878448] **Bus**: Aston's 382 Worcester–Pershore, alight Ladywood Rd/Rebecca Rd crossroads, 2ml. **Station**: Pershore 7ml. **Road**: 9ml S of Worcester and E of M5. Signposted from A38 and B4084

P Free parking, 200yds

NT properties nearby
Brockhampton Estate, The Fleece Inn, The Greyfriars, Hanbury Hall, Middle Littleton Tithe Barn, Snowshill Manor

Cwmmau Farmhouse

Brilley, Whitney-on-Wye, Herefordshire HR3 6JP

🏠🔒🏠💷🏃🌳👶 1965   (4:G7)

Superb early 17th-century farmhouse

★ Open eight afternoons a year. At other times the farmhouse is available as holiday accommodation (tel: 0870 458 4411 for NT Holiday Cottages information)

i **T** 01981 590509
E cwmmaufarmhouse@nationaltrust.org.uk

➔ 4ml SW of Kington between A4111 and A438. From Kington take Brilley road at junction opposite church, 4ml. Turn left at NT signpost. From A438 between Rhydspence and Whitney on Wye take Brilley road at junction, 2ml. Turn right at NT signpost. Farmhouse is approx. 1ml down a 'no through road'

Cwmmau Farmhouse									
17 May–18 May	2–5	M	T	W	T	F	**S**	**S**
14 Jun–15 Jun	2–5	M	T	W	T	F	**S**	**S**
27 Sep–28 Sep	2–5	M	T	W	T	F	**S**	**S**
20 Dec–21 Dec	1–4	M	T	W	T	F	**S**	**S**

Dudmaston

Quatt, nr Bridgnorth, Shropshire WV15 6QN

🏠✳️♿🎣🏠🏠💷🏃🌳🛡️👶
▓ 🏃 1978   (4:I5)

Late 17th-century mansion with art collection, lakeside garden and estate

The house, with its intimate family rooms, contains fine furniture and Dutch flower paintings, as well as one of Britain's most important public collections of modern art in a classic country house setting. The lakeside gardens are a mass of colour in spring and visitors can enjoy walks in the Dingle, a wooded valley, or the popular 'Big Pool' walk. There are also estate walks to and from Hampton Loade. Dudmaston is the home of Colonel and Mrs Hamilton-Russell.

i **T** 01746 780866
E dudmaston@nationaltrust.org.uk

🏃 Guided tours of the house, garden and wider estate available throughout the season. See the board at the property for details

🛡️ Including snowdrop walks (2, 3, 9 & 10 Feb) and Christmas activities. Please send sae for full programme

🏃 Walks leaflet available. Please send sae and £1

♿ 🚾♿♿♿👁️👁️🅿️ **Building** ♿♿
Grounds ♿➡️♿

🏠 NT shop. Plant sales

💷 Tea-room in Orchard car park. Light lunches. Note: tea-room is open to the general public and not restricted to visitors to house or garden. Children's menu. Ice-cream kiosk

👶 Baby-changing facilities. Front-carrying baby slings and hip-carrying infant seats for loan. Children's quiz/trail. Family activity room in Hall

Dudmaston contains one of Britain's most important collections of contemporary art in a country house setting

Dudmaston

House									
23 Mar – 30 Sep	2–5:30	M	**T**	**W**	T	F	S	**S**
Garden									
23 Mar – 30 Sep	12–6	**M**	**T**	**W**	T	F	S	**S**
Shop									
23 Mar – 30 Sep	1–5:30	M	**T**	**W**	T	F	S	**S**
Tea-room									
23 Mar – 30 Sep	11:30–5:30	**M**	**T**	**W**	T	F	S	**S**

Open BH Mons. St Andrew's Church, Quatt, open same time as house. Snowdrop walks 2, 3, 9 & 10 Feb

Suitable for school groups. Hands-on activities. Adult study days

On leads only and keep to footpaths. Not in gardens immediately surrounding house

→ [138:SO746887] **Foot**: NT walks from Hampton Loade car park to the property. **Ferry**: from Severn Valley Railway via river ferry and walk from Hampton Loade. **Bus**: Whittle 297 Bridgnorth–Kidderminster (passing close ➡ Kidderminster). **Station**: Hampton Loade (Severn Valley Rly) 1½ml; Kidderminster 10ml. **Road**: 4ml SE of Bridgnorth on A442

P Free parking, 100yds in Orchard car park. Also parking in Hampton Loade (pay & display)

NT properties nearby
Attingham Park, Benthall Hall, Berrington Hall, Kinver Edge and the Rock Houses, Sunnycroft, Wightwick Manor

Farnborough Hall

Farnborough, nr Banbury, Oxfordshire OX17 1DU

 1960 (4:L7)

Honey-coloured stone house with exquisite plasterwork and fine landscaped garden

⭐ Farnborough Hall is occupied and administered by the Holbech family

i **T** 01295 690002 (Infoline)
E farnboroughhall@nationaltrust.org.uk

→ 6ml N of Banbury, ½ml W of A423

Farnborough Hall

2 Apr – 27 Sep	2–5:30	M	T	**W**	T	**F**	**S**	S
4 May – 5 May	2–5:30	**M**	T	W	T	F	S	**S**

Terrace walk open as house

The Fleece Inn

Bretforton, nr Evesham, Worcestershire WR11 7JE

🔲 🍴 🍺 🎭 🔔 🍸 1978 (4:K7)

An unspoilt English pub

The Fleece Inn is a half-timbered medieval farmhouse which originally sheltered a farmer and his stock. The Inn first became a licensed house in 1848. Fully restored to its former glory, with the witch circles and precious pewter collection, it has developed a reputation for traditional folk music and morris dancing. The Fleece provides top-quality cask ales, ciders, wines and a mouth-watering menu using local produce.

What's new in 2008 Thatched Barn is available for hire for functions, and has a civil-ceremony wedding licence. Hosts the Vale of Evesham Asparagus Festival

i **T** 01386 831173
E fleeceinn@nationaltrust.org.uk

🎭 Vale of Evesham Asparagus Festival, May BHol. Music and morris dancing throughout the year. Vintage and classic car events during the summer

♿ 🚽 📷 **Building** 🪜

🍺 Top quality cask ales, ciders, wines and home-cooked food using local produce. Asparagus special menu in May/June

→ [150:SP093437] At the village square in the heart of Bretforton. **Bus**: Henshaws 554 from Evesham–Chipping Campden. **Station**: Evesham 2½ml. **Road**: 4ml E of Evesham, on B4035

P Parking (not NT) in village square only

NT properties nearby
Croome Park, Dover's Hill, Hidcote Manor Garden, Middle Littleton Tithe Barn, Snowshill Manor

The Fleece Inn

All year	11–11	**M**	**T**	**W**	**T**	**F**	**S**	S
All year	12–10:30	M	T	W	T	F	S	**S**

Closed weekdays 3–6, Feb–mid June & mid Sept–Jan 09

For general and membership enquiries, please telephone 0844 800 1895

The Greyfriars

Friar Street, Worcester, Worcestershire WR1 2LZ

 **1966**　　　(4:J7)

15th-century merchant's house in Worcester city centre

Built in 1480, with early 17th- and 18th-century additions, this fine timber-framed house was rescued from demolition after the Second World War and has been carefully restored and refurbished. An archway leads through to a delightful walled garden.

⭐ No WC, nearest at Corn Market 200yds

ℹ **T** 01905 23571
　E greyfriars@nationaltrust.org.uk

🎫 Guided tours by appointment

🛡 Send sae for details

♿ 🔍 ⠿ Grounds ♿

📷 Plants grown at nearby Hanbury Hall

🍽 Kiosk in garden open weekends and fine weather

👪 Children's guide

🏫 Suitable for school groups. Hands-on activities

➡ [150:SO852546] In centre of Worcester on Friar Street. **Bus**: from surrounding areas. **Station**: Worcester Foregate Street ½ml

🅿 No parking on site. Pay & display car parks at Corn Market and St Martin's Gate

NT properties nearby

Brockhampton Estate, Croome Park, Hanbury Hall

The Greyfriars									
5 Mar–28 Jun	1–5	M	T	W	T	F	S	S
2 Jul–31 Aug	1–5	M	T	W	T	F	S	S
3 Sep–13 Dec	1–5	M	T	W	T	F	S	S
Admission by timed ticket on Sats & BHols. Open BH Mons. Closes dusk if earlier									

If the variety at Hanbury Hall has stimulated you, you'll find even more curiosities at Upton House and Gardens

Hanbury Hall

School Road, Hanbury, Droitwich Spa, Worcestershire WR9 7EA

 **1953**　　　(4:J6)

Early 18th-century country house, garden and park

Completed in 1701, this homely William and Mary-style house is famed for its fine painted ceilings and staircase by master-painter Sir James Thornhill. The stunning 8-hectare (20-acre) garden, recreated in keeping with the period of the house, is surrounded by 160 hectares (395 acres) of park, with beautiful views over the surrounding countryside. Fascinating features within the garden include an orangery, ice house, 18th-century bowling green and working mushroom house.

What's new in 2008 Improved visitor facilities in stableyard, including new catering outlet and extended shop. Extensive re-roofing project until autumn

⭐ Recreated 18th-century crown bowling green available to play on during normal opening hours. Private groups may book it at other times

ℹ **T** 01527 821214
　E hanburyhall@nationaltrust.org.uk

🎫 Guided tours 11–1, Sat–Wed when house open

Hanbury Hall									
Garden/park/tea-room/shop*									
1 Mar–16 Mar	11–5:30	M	T	W	T	F	S	S
17 Mar–30 Jun	11–5:30	M	T	W	T	F	S	S
1 Jul–31 Aug	11–5:30	M	T	W	T	F	S	S
1 Sep–29 Oct	11–5:30	M	T	W	T	F	S	S
1 Nov–31 Jan 09	11–5:30	M	T	W	T	F	S	S
26 Dec–1 Jan 09	11–5:30	M	T	W	T	F	S	S
House tours									
As house	11–1								
House									
1 Mar–16 Mar	1–5	M	T	W	T	F	S	S
17 Mar–29 Oct	1–5	M	T	W	T	F	S	S
Admission by timed ticket on BHols. Open Good Fri. Closes dusk if earlier. *Shop & tea-room close at 5. Garden, park, tea-room & shop open seven days a week during Easter school holidays, 26–30 May & 27–31 Oct. House open 6 & 7, 13 & 14 Dec 11–4									

For information regarding prices, see page 10

The Library at Hanbury Hall, a homely William and Mary-style house

🛡 Send sae for details

🚶 Details of circular park walk in welcome leaflet

♿ 🚻 👓 Ⓐ 🅿 🅳 ♨ **Building** 🔆 ♿

Grounds 🔆 ➡ ♿

📷 NT shop. Plant sales

🍽 Licensed tea-room in the hall, serving light lunches and refreshments. Group bookings by arrangement. Children's menu. Kiosk in stableyard

👶 Baby-changing facilities. Hip-carrying infant seats for loan. Children's play area. Children's quiz/trail

🏫 Suitable for school groups. Live interpretation. Hands-on activities

🐕 On leads in park on footpaths, not in garden. Dog-friendly circular walk

➡ [150:SO943637] **Foot**: a number of public footpaths cross the park. **Bus**: First 144 Worcester–Birmingham (passing close ≋ Droitwich Spa), alight Wychbold, 2½ml. **Station**: Droitwich Spa 4ml. **Road**: from M5 exit 5 follow A38 to Droitwich. From Droitwich 4½ml along B4090

🅿 Free parking, 150yds

NT properties nearby
Clent Hills, Coughton Court, Croome Park, The Greyfriars, Rosedene

Hawford Dovecote

Hawford, Worcestershire WR3 7SG

🏠 1973 (4:J6)

16th-century dovecote

The recently restored half-timbered dovecote is what remains of a former monastic grange.

⭐ No WC

ℹ **T** 01527 821214
E hawforddovecote@nationaltrust.org.uk

♿ **Building** 🔆

➡ [150:SO846607] **Bus**: First 303 Worcester–Kidderminster (passing ≋ Worcester Foregate Street & Kidderminster), alight Hawford Lodge, ¼ml. **Station**: Worcester Foregate Street 3ml; Worcester Shrub Hill 3½ml. **Road**: 3ml N of Worcester, ½ml E of A449

🅿 Parking, 50yds. Access is on foot via the drive of the adjoining house

NT properties nearby
The Greyfriars, Hanbury Hall, Wichenford Dovecote

Hawford Dovecote								
1 Mar–31 Oct		9–6	M	T	W	T	F	S S
Closes sunset if earlier. Other times by appointment								

Many Trust properties are offering Gift Aid on Entry for non-members, see page 10

Kinver Edge and the Rock Houses

The Warden's Lodge, Comber Road, Kinver, nr Stourbridge, Staffordshire DY7 6HU

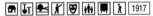 1917   (4:I5)

High sandstone ridge with fascinating rock houses

Kinver's woodland sandstone ridge offers dramatic views across surrounding counties and miles of heathland walking country. The famous Holy Austin rock houses, which were inhabited until the 1950s, have now been restored and are open to visitors at selected times.

⭐ No WC

ℹ️ **T** 01384 872553
   E kinveredge@nationaltrust.org.uk

🏃 Lower rock houses: out-of-hours tours by arrangement

🎭 Easter Egg trail on Easter Monday

🏃 Walks leaflet for sale at Lower Rock House

♿ **Grounds** 📷

👫 Easter Egg trail on Easter Monday

▦ Suitable for school groups

🐕 On leads within grounds of rock houses

➡️ [138:SO836836] **Bus**: Hansons 227/8
   ⬛ Stourbridge–Kinver. **Station**: Stourbridge Town 5ml. **Road**: 4ml W of Stourbridge, 4ml N of Kidderminster. 1½ml W of A449

🅿️ Free parking at Warden's lodge and on Compton Road for Rock Houses

NT properties nearby
Clent Hills, Dudmaston

Kinver Edge and the Rock Houses								
Kinver Edge								
All year		M	T	W	T	F	S	S
House grounds								
1 Feb–31 Jan 09	10–4	M	T	W	T	F	S	S
Lower rock houses, upper terrace								
1 Mar–30 Nov	2–4	M	T	W	T	F	S	S

Open BH Mons. Please note that the rock houses will be closed on the Kinver Fête day (date in May to be confirmed). Lower rock houses open for guided tours at other times (between Mar & Nov), by arrangement

Kinwarton Dovecote

Kinwarton, nr Alcester, Warwickshire B49 6HB

🏠 1958   (4:K7)

Circular 14th-century dovecote

The building is a fine example of a 14th-century circular stone dovecote – one of the few in this country. It is the only relic of a moated grange belonging to the Abbey of Evesham, situated to the north-west of the dovecote. The walls are more than a metre thick and inside are hundreds of nesting holes which could be reached by a potence (ladder) rotating around a central pivot.

⭐ No WC

ℹ️ **T** 01789 400777
   E kinwartondovecote@nationaltrust.org.uk

♿ **Building** 📷

➡️ [150:SP106585] **Cycle**: NCN5.
   Bus: Stagecoach in Warwickshire 25/6 from Stratford-upon-Avon; otherwise as for Coughton Court, but alight Alcester, 1½ml.
   Station: Wilmcote (U), 5ml; Wootton Wawen (U), not Sun, 5ml. **Road**: 1½ml NE of Alcester, just S of B4089

🅿️ Limited parking (not NT)

NT properties nearby
Charlecote Park, Coughton Court, Hanbury Hall

Kinwarton Dovecote								
1 Mar–31 Oct	9–6	M	T	W	T	F	S	S

Closed Good Fri. Closes dusk if earlier. Other times by appointment

Letocetum Roman Baths

Watling Street, Wall, nr Lichfield, Staffordshire WS14 0AW

🏛️ 🎭 👫 ▦ 1934   (4:K5)

Excavated Roman bathhouse and remains of buildings

Letocetum was an important staging post on the Roman military road to North Wales. Foundations of a *mansio* (Roman inn) and bathhouse can be seen.

⭐ Letocetum is in the guardianship of English Heritage. No WC

T 0121 625 6820
E letocetum@nationaltrust.org.uk

Grounds

Pushchairs and baby back-carriers admitted

Suitable for school groups

On leads only

→ [139:SK099067] **Cycle**: NCN5, 2¼ml. **Station**: Shenstone 1½ml. **Road**: on N side of A5 at Wall, near Lichfield

P Free parking (not NT), 50yds. Limited spaces

NT properties nearby
Moseley Old Hall, Shugborough Estate

Letocetum Roman Baths
Open all reasonable times

Middle Littleton Tithe Barn

Middle Littleton, Evesham, Worcestershire WR11 5LN

1975 **(4:K7)**

13th-century tithe barn, one of the largest and finest in the country

No WC

T 01905 371006
E middlelittleton@nationaltrust.org.uk

Building

Pushchairs and baby back-carriers admitted

→ [150:SP080471] **Bus**: First 247 Evesham–Redditch (passing close Evesham), alight Middle Littleton School Lane, ½ml. **Station**: Honeybourne (U) 3½ml; Evesham 4½ml. **Road**: 3ml NE of Evesham, E of B4085

P Parking

NT properties nearby
Charlecote Park, Croome Park, The Fleece Inn, Hidcote Manor Garden, Snowshill Manor

Middle Littleton Tithe Barn

1 Apr–2 Nov	2–5	M	T	W	T	F	S	S

Directions for access on barn door

Morville Hall

nr Bridgnorth, Shropshire WV16 5NB

1965 **(4:I5)**

Stone-built house of Elizabethan origin

All visits by guided tour. No WC

T 01746 780838
E morvillehall@nationaltrust.org.uk

Morville Hall
Admission by guided tour. By written appointment only with the tenants, Dr & Mrs C. Douglas

Moseley Old Hall

Moseley Old Hall Lane, Fordhouses, Wolverhampton, Staffordshire WV10 7HY

1962 **(4:J5)**

Elizabethan house, famous for its association with Charles II

The richly panelled walls of Moseley Old Hall conceal ingenious secret hiding places designed for Catholic priests. One of these cramped priest holes saved Charles II when he hid here after the Battle of Worcester in 1651, and the bed where he slept is on view. An exhibition in the barn tells the story of the King's dramatic escape from Cromwell's troops. The house underwent various alterations in the 19th century. The garden has a fantastic variety of herbs and plants and was recreated in 17th-century style with a formal knot garden, arbour and nut walk.

T 01902 782808
E moseleyoldhall@nationaltrust.org.uk

Entry, 12–1, by guided tour only. Free-flow through house from 1 (optional tours available). Last guided tour 3:30. Out-of-hours tours

Moseley Old Hall

		M	T	W	T	F	S	S
1 Mar–2 Nov	12–5			W			S	S
22 Jul–9 Sep	12–5		T	W			S	S
9 Nov–21 Dec	12–4							S

Open BH Mons (11–5) and following Tues (except 6 May). Entry, 12–1, by guided tour only (free-flow from 1). 9 Nov–21 Dec: guided tour only. Christmas events 23 & 30 Nov, 7 Dec

Charges for National Trust members apply on some special event days

The formal knot garden at Moseley Old Hall in Staffordshire

⚇ Send sae for details

♿ 🚻 ⚙ ⚙ ⠿ 🅐 P♿ D♿ **Building** ♿ ♿
Grounds ♿

🏪 NT shop. Plant sales

🍽 Tea-room on first floor of 18th-century coach house. Two tables at ground floor level. Children's menu

👪 Baby-changing facilities. Baby back-carriers admitted. Front-carrying baby slings and hip-carrying infant seats for loan. Children's quiz/trail

🏛 Suitable for school groups. Live interpretation. Hands-on activities

🐕 On leads only in grounds

➔ [127:SJ932044] **Bus**: Arriva/Central Connect 870 Wolverhampton–Cannock, alight Bognop Road, ¾ml; Choice Travel 613 from Wolverhampton, thence ¾ml (all pass close ⮨ Wolverhampton). **Station**: Wolverhampton 4ml. **Road**: 4ml N of Wolverhampton; S of M54 between A449 and A460; traffic from N on M6 leave at exit 11, then A460; traffic from S on M6 & M54 take exit 1; coaches must approach via A460 to avoid low bridge

P Free parking, 50yds. Dropping-off place for coaches, but no on-site parking. Narrow lanes and tight corners

NT properties nearby
Attingham Park, Benthall Hall, Letocetum Roman Baths, Shugborough Estate, Sunnycroft, Wightwick Manor

Packwood House

Lapworth, Solihull, West Midlands B94 6AT

🏠 ❀ ♣ 🏠 🍴 🎭 ☺ 👪 🏛 🚶 1941 (4:K6)

Much-restored Tudor house, park and garden with notable topiary

The house is originally 16th century, yet its interiors were extensively restored between the World Wars by Graham Baron Ash to create a fascinating 20th-century evocation of domestic Tudor architecture. Packwood contains a fine collection of 16th-century textiles and furniture and the gardens have renowned herbaceous borders and a famous collection of yews.

ℹ **T** 01564 783294
  E packwood@nationaltrust.org.uk

🍴 Out-of-hours tours by written arrangement

⚇ Easter trail for families. Meet the gardener. Open-air theatre

🚶 Lakeside walk

♿ 🚻 ⠿ P♿ D♿ **Building** ♿ ♿ **Grounds** ♿
🏪 NT shop. Plant sales

Packwood House								
Park								
All year			M	T	W	T	F	S	S
House/garden/shop								
9 Feb–2 Nov	11–5		M	T	**W**	**T**	**F**	**S**	**S**
Admission by timed ticket to house at busy times. Open BH Mons								

Parking in National Trust car parks is free for members displaying stickers

🍵 Cold drinks and ice-cream sold in the shop. Vending machine for hot drinks & soup

👶 Baby-changing facilities. Front-carrying baby slings and hip-carrying infant seats for loan. Children's guide. Children's quiz/trail. Family Easter trail

🎒 Suitable for school groups. Live interpretation

➜ [139:SP174723] **Bus**: Stagecoach in Warwickshire X20 Birmingham–Stratford-upon-Avon, alight Hockley Heath, 1¾ml. **Station**: Lapworth (U) 1½ml; Birmingham International 8ml. **Road**: 2ml E of Hockley Heath (on A3400), 11ml SE of central Birmingham

🅿 Free parking, 70yds

NT properties nearby
Baddesley Clinton, Birmingham Back to Backs, Charlecote Park, Clent Hills, Hanbury Hall

Rosedene

Victoria Road, Dodford, nr Bromsgrove, Worcestershire B61 9BU

🏠 ❄ 🚶 🎒 1997 (4:J6)

Mid-19th-century Chartist cottage

ℹ️ **T** 01527 821214
   E rosedene@nationaltrust.org.uk

➜ Follow signs for Dodford off A448, left into Priory Road, left into Church Road, then left into Victoria Road

---
Rosedene
Admission by guided tour. Suns April–Sept. Booking essential. Limited group visits at other times by arrangement

---

Shugborough Estate

Milford, nr Stafford, Staffordshire ST17 0XB

🏠 🐕 🧺 📷 ❄ 🌳 🍴 🎫 🛏 💷 🚶 🎠
🎭 🚻 🔔 👤 🔔 🌲 1966 (4:J4)

Rare survival of a complete estate, with all major buildings including mansion house, servants' quarters, model farm and walled garden

This historic estate is the home of the Earls of Lichfield. Visitors can view the entire estate, including all its major working historic buildings, set in their original parkland with several historic landscape monuments. Follow the story of food production on the estate – from its growth in the 1805 walled garden, its processing in the 1805 farm, its preparation in the multi-period servants' quarters, and finally its consumption in the fine dining room of the house. Some of the rooms contain artefacts from Admiral Anson's epic circumnavigation of the globe in the 1740s. Each part of this story is told by 'first person' guides, who work on a range of tasks using original equipment. Each day, visitors can see traditional methods being used – whether it is in the walled garden, at the mill, cheese-making in the dairy, cooking and baking, washing and ironing or even brewing (and you can sample the brewer's work). There are also guides in the house, who are 'modern'. After all that, there are the beautiful riverside gardens to enjoy.

What's new in 2008 Patrick Lichfield's arboretum now open, with stunning views of the house from across the river

Rosedene: a Chartist cottage restored to reflect the conditions in which the early Chartists lived

★ Shugborough is wholly financed, administered and maintained by Staffordshire County Council. Access to the house and gardens is free to NT members and to experience the whole estate a greatly reduced price all-sites ticket is available. Admission charges apply when special events are held. Please tel. or visit www.shugborough.org.uk

ℹ **T** 01889 881388
  E shugborough.promotions@staffordshire.gov.uk

🏃 Wide range of tours and activities

🎧 Available in the mansion house

🎪 Easter and May BHol events. Open-air concerts, craft fairs and spectacular Christmas evenings

🚶 Walks and trails suitable for all abilities

♿ 🚻🔤🔍🎨👓📷🅿🚌 Building 🔼🔽
Grounds 🔼➡️🚗

🍽️ Lady Walk Tea-room (not NT) (licensed) in the Midden Courtyard. Menus based on Mrs Stearn's historically inspired recipes using local, organic ingredients. Hot meals 12–2:30, light refreshments 11–4:45. Children's menu. Granary Tea-room (not NT). Open during school hols and weekends 11–4:30, serving drinks and home-made cakes. Garden room available for parties and group lunches

👶 Baby-changing and feeding facilities. Hip-carrying infant seats for loan. Children's play area. Children's guide. Children's quiz/trail. Farm gives children chance to see domestic and rare breeds of animals. Games gallery in corn mill. Pushchairs admitted to farm

🎒 Suitable for school groups. Education room/centre. Live interpretation. Hands-on activities

🐕 On leads and only in parkland and gardens

Shugborough Estate									
House/farm/servants' quarters/grounds/tea-room									
14 Mar–31 Oct	11–5	**M**	**T**	**W**	**T**	**F**	**S**	**S**	
Shop									
14 Mar–31 Oct	11–5	**M**	**T**	**W**	**T**	**F**	**S**	**S**	
1 Nov–23 Dec	11–4	**M**	**T**	**W**	**T**	**F**	**S**	**S**	
Opening times and prices may vary when special events held. Tel. or see website									

➡️ [127:SJ992225] **Foot**: pedestrian access from E, from the canal/Great Haywood side of the estate. Estate walks link to towpaths along Trent & Mersey Canal and Staffs & Worcs Canal and to Cannock Chase trails. Lies on Staffordshire Way. **Bus**: Arriva 825 🚃 Stafford–Lichfield (passing close 🚃 Lichfield City). **Station**: Rugeley Town 5ml; Rugeley Trent Valley 5ml; Stafford 6ml. **Road**: signposted from M6 exit 13; 6ml E of Stafford on A513; entrance at Milford.

🅿 Parking, £3 (pay & display). Refunded on purchase of an all-sites ticket

NT properties nearby
Attingham Park, Biddulph Grange Garden, Little Moreton Hall, Moseley Old Hall

Sunnycroft

200 Holyhead Road, Wellington, Telford, Shropshire TF1 2DR

🏠🐴❄️🍽️🏃🎪👓👶🎒 1999   (4:14)

Edwardian gentleman's suburban villa

The house is typical of the many thousands that were built for prosperous business and professional people on the fringes of Victorian towns and cities. Sunnycroft is one of the very few – perhaps the only one – to have survived largely unaltered and with a remarkable range of its contents remaining. The grounds amount to a 'mini-estate', with pigsties, stables, kitchen garden, orchards, conservatory, flower garden and superb Wellingtonia avenue.

What's new in 2008 House open on Saturdays from mid March to October. Small tea-room, serving cakes, ice-cream and drinks, open Friday to Monday 1–5, from mid March to October

ℹ **T** 01952 242884
  E sunnycroft@nationaltrust.org.uk

Sunnycroft									
14 Mar–26 Oct	1–5	**M**	T	W	T	**F**	**S**	**S**	
13 Dec–21 Dec	1–5	M	T	W	T	F	**S**	**S**	
Open Good Fri and BH Mons (free flow through house). Admission by timed ticket (advanced booking not possible) and guided tour only. Last admission 1hr before closing									

The Staircase Hall at Sunnycroft, Wellington, Shropshire

🎭 Volunteer guided tours focusing on the Landers' family history

👹 Including annual garden fête, Michaelmas Fair and Christmas opening, 13, 14, 20 & 21 Dec

♿ 🚽♿ P♿ D♿ Building 🦽 Grounds 🦽 ➡

🍴 Tea, coffee, cakes and ice-cream

👪 Children's quiz/trail

🏫 Suitable for school groups

🐕 In grounds only

➡ [127:SJ652109] **Cycle**: NCN81, 1ml. **Bus**: Arriva 66 from Telford (passing 🚂 Wellington Telford West). **Station**: Wellington Telford West ½ml. **Road**: M54 exit 7, follow B5061 towards Wellington

🅿 Free parking, 150yds in orchard. Not suitable for coaches. Additional free parking (not NT) in Wrekin Road car park

NT properties nearby
Attingham Park, Attingham Park Estate: Cronkhill, Benthall Hall, Carding Mill Valley and the Shropshire Hills, Dudmaston, Morville Hall, Moseley Old Hall, Wenlock Edge

Town Walls Tower

Shrewsbury, Shropshire SY1 1TN

🏠 1930   **(4:H4)**

Shrewsbury's last remaining watchtower

⭐ No WC

ℹ **T** 01743 708162
   E townwallstower@nationaltrust.org.uk

➡ Close to town centre near Welsh bridge, on S of town wall

Town Walls Tower

By written appointment only with the tenant, Mr A. A. Hector, Tower House, 26a Town Walls, Shrewsbury SY1 1TN

If you loved the authentic taste of a past way of living at Sunnycroft, come and see how others lived at the Birmingham Back to Backs

Unless indicated, last admission is always 30mins before closing time

Upton House and Gardens

nr Banbury, Warwickshire OX15 6HT

🏠✳️🏘️🏛️☕🍴🎭🌳🛡️♿🎭

🔔⏲️ 1948   (4:L7)

Outstanding art and porcelain collections in a 17th-century mansion, with superb terraced gardens

One of the National Trust's most important art collections can be found in this house, built in 1695 of mellow local stone, then purchased and remodelled in 1927–29 by Walter Samuel, 2nd Viscount Bearsted (Chairman of Shell, 1921–46, and son of the company's founder). Upton contains his outstanding collection of English and Continental Old Master paintings over three floors, including works by Hogarth, Stubbs, Romney, Canaletto, Brueghel and El Greco; Brussels tapestries; French Sèvres porcelain; Chelsea and Derby figures, and 18th-century furniture. There is an exhibition of paintings and publicity posters commissioned by Shell during Viscount Bearsted's chairmanship; also Lady Bearsted's restored bedroom and Art Deco bathroom. The garden is very fine, with lawns, terraces, orchard, herbaceous borders, kitchen

The Long Gallery, Upton House, Warwickshire

Upton House and Gardens									
Garden*/restaurant/shop/plant centre		M	T	W	T	F	S	S	
1 Mar–2 Nov	11–5	M	T	W	T	F	S	S	
17 Mar–30 Mar	11–5	M	T	W	T	F	S	S	
21 Jul–31 Aug	11–5	M	T	W	T	F	S	S	
3 Nov–21 Dec	12–4	M	T	W	T	F	S	S	
26 Dec–4 Jan 09	12–4	M	T	W	T	F	S	S	
House tours									
1 Mar–2 Nov	11–1	M	T	W	T	F	S	S	
17 Mar–30 Mar	11–1	M	T	W	T	F	S	S	
21 Jul–31 Aug	11–1	M	T	W	T	F	S	S	
House									
1 Mar–2 Nov	1–5	M	T	W	T	F	S	S	
17 Mar–30 Mar	1–5	M	T	W	T	F	S	S	
21 Jul–31 Aug	1–5	M	T	W	T	F	S	S	
8 Nov–21 Dec	12–4	M	T	W	T	F	S	S	

House admission from 11 on BHols by timed ticket, but visitors may then stay until 5. Ground floor open only in house 8 Nov–21 Dec. *Garden winter route only Nov–Jan 09. Open from 10 on 26 Dec

garden, ornamental pools and an interesting 1930s water garden, together with the National Collection of Asters.

What's new in 2008 New shop and plant centre. Newly opened Lord Bearsted's Dressing Room. 'Hogarth in Focus' picture display. New period advertising posters on show in Shell Exhibition Room. New winter/wet weather route through garden. Old Squash Court Exhibition Area due to open in the autumn

⭐ For safety some areas of the gardens may be closed during bad weather

ℹ️ **T** 01295 670266
E uptonhouse@nationaltrust.org.uk

🎭 Free house taster tours, garden tour and introductory talks when available. Private house and garden tours by written arrangement

🎭 Family activities, fine arts study tours, 1920s days, jazz concerts, classic car days, Civil War re-enactments, conservation displays, workshops and lecture lunches

♿ 🚻 🔵 👁️ 📷 🅿️ 🚌 ♿ Building 🦽♿ Grounds 🦽➡️

🏠 NT shop. Plant sales. Kitchen garden produce for sale when in season

■ Pavilion Restaurant (licensed). Open-air seating available. Children's menu. Summer ice-cream kiosk

♦ Baby-changing and feeding facilities. Front-carrying baby slings and hip-carrying infant seats for loan. Children's quiz/trail

■ Suitable for school groups. Adult study days

➔ [151:SP371461] On the edge of the Cotswolds, between Banbury and Stratford-upon-Avon. **Foot**: footpath SM177 runs adjacent to property, Centenary Way ½ml, Macmillan Way 1ml. **Cycle**: NCN5, 5ml. Oxfordshire Cycle Way 1½ml. **Station**: Banbury 7ml. **Road**: on A422, 7ml N of Banbury, 12ml SE of Stratford-upon-Avon. Signed from exit 12 of M40

P Free parking, 300yds. Parking is on grass with hard-standing for coaches

NT properties nearby
Canons Ashby House, Charlecote Park, • Chastleton House, Dover's Hill, Farnborough Hall, Hidcote Manor Garden

The Weir

Swainshill, nr Hereford, Herefordshire HR4 7QF

🏛 ❖ 𝕂 🎢 🎭 ♦ 🏃 1959   (4:H7)

Informal 1920s riverside garden with fine views

An unusual and dramatic garden of 4 hectares (10 acres) with stunning views along the River Wye and across the Herefordshire countryside. The Weir is managed to create a varied habitat for a wide range of wildlife and is spectacular all year round, with drifts of early spring bulbs giving way to a succession of wild flowers, followed by a final flourish of autumn colour – courtesy of the mature trees. The river provides a sense of movement and change and is the perfect backdrop for a tranquil walk.

The Weir									
1 Feb–29 Feb	11–4	M	T	W	T	F	S	S
1 Mar–5 May	11–5	M	T	W	T	F	S	S
7 May–26 Oct	11–5	M	T	W	T	F	S	S
24 Jan–31 Jan 09	11–4	M	T	W	T	F	S	S
Open BH Mons. Last admission 45mins before closing									

★ Due to the nature of the paths and steps, sturdy footwear is recommended

i **T** 01981 590509
E theweir@nationaltrust.org.uk

𝕂 Tours by arrangement

🎭 Including annual open-air concert

🏃 Conservation and archaeological interest walks

♿ 🚻 **Grounds** 🏛

♦ Baby-changing facilities. Pushchairs and baby back-carriers admitted

➔ [149:SO438418] **Bus**: to Hereford and then taxi. **Station**: Hereford 5ml. **Road**: 5ml W of Hereford on A438

P Free parking

NT properties nearby
Berrington Hall, Brockhampton Estate, Croft Castle and Parkland, Cwmmau Farmhouse

Wichenford Dovecote

Wichenford, Worcestershire

📷 1965   (4:I7)

17th-century half-timbered black-and-white dovecote

★ No WC

i **T** 01527 821214
E wichenforddovecote@nationaltrust.org.uk

♿ **Building** 🏛

➔ [150:SO788598] **Bus**: Bromyard 308, 310 from Worcester (passing close ≄ Worcester Foregate Street), alight Wichenford, ½ml. **Station**: Worcester Foregate Street 7ml; Worcester Shrub Hill 7½ml. **Road**: 5½ml NW of Worcester, N of B4204

P Free parking, 50yds

NT properties nearby
The Greyfriars, Hanbury Hall, Hawford Dovecote

Wichenford Dovecote									
1 Mar–31 Oct	9–6	M	T	W	T	F	S	S
Open other times by appointment									

For general and membership enquiries, please telephone 0844 800 1895

Wightwick Manor

Wightwick Bank, Wolverhampton, West Midlands WV6 8EE

🎦 1937 (4:J5)

Victorian manor house with William Morris interiors and colourful garden

Wightwick Manor is one of only a few surviving examples of a house built and furnished under the influence of the Arts & Crafts Movement. The many original William Morris wallpapers and fabrics, Pre-Raphaelite paintings, Kempe glass and de Morgan ware help conjure up the spirit of the time. An attractive 7-hectare (17-acre) garden reflects the style and character of the house.

What's new in 2008 Second-hand bookshop. Wightwick Nature Rooms open as garden. Extended William Morris gift shop. Restoration of the Victorian kitchen garden continues

ℹ️ **T** 01902 761400
E wightwickmanor@nationaltrust.org.uk

🎭 Guided tours run every open day. Taster tours 11–12:30. First Thur & Sat of each month free-flow through house

😃 Children's activity days Weds in Aug

🚶 7 hectares (17 acres) of beautiful gardens provide the perfect setting for a picturesque afternoon stroll

♿ 🅿️ 🔍 ∷ 🔍 🅿️ Building ♿
Grounds 🏞️ ▶️

🛍️ William Morris shop and tea-room open to the public

☕ Tea-room. Limited seating. Children's menu

Wightwick Manor									
1 Mar–2 Aug	11–5	M	T	W	T	F	S	S
3 Aug–31 Aug	11–5	M	T	W	T	F	S	S
1 Sep–20 Dec	11–5	M	T	W	T	F	S	S

Garden closes at 6. Shop opens at 12. Admission by timed ticket and guided tour only available from visitor reception. Taster tours 11–12:30. First Thur & Sat of each month, free-flow through house. House open BH Suns & Mons (ground floor only), 11–5. Many of the contents are fragile and some rooms cannot always be shown so tours vary

The night nursery, Wightwick Manor, West Midlands

👶 Baby-changing facilities. Hip-carrying infant seats for loan. Children's quiz/trail. Children's activity days Weds in Aug

🎭 Suitable for school groups. Live interpretation. Hands-on activities

🐕 On leads and only in garden

➡️ [139:SO869985] **Bus**: Arriva 890 Wolverhampton–Bridgnorth, Choice Travel 516 Wolverhampton–Pattingham (both passing close ≥ Wolverhampton). **Station**: Wolverhampton 3ml. **Road**: 3ml W of Wolverhampton, up Wightwick Bank (off A454 beside Mermaid Inn)

🅿️ Free parking, 120yds. Located at bottom of Wightwick Bank (please do not park in Elmsdale opposite the property)

NT properties nearby
Benthall Hall, Dudmaston, Moseley Old Hall

Wilderhope Manor

Longville, Much Wenlock, Shropshire TF13 6EG

🎦 🏇 🍽️ 📷 ☕ 🏠 👶 🎭 🚶 1971 (4:H5)

Elizabethan gabled manor house, unfurnished but with fine interior architectural features

⭐ The manor is used as a youth hostel so access to some occupied rooms may be restricted

ℹ️ **T** 0870 770 6090 (Hostel Warden YHA)
E wilderhope@nationaltrust.org.uk

➡️ 7ml SW of Much Wenlock, 7ml E of Church Stretton, ½ml S of B4371

Wilderhope Manor									
2 Apr–28 Sep	2–4:30	M	T	W	T	F	S	S
5 Oct–25 Jan 09	2–4:30	M	T	W	T	F	S	S

For information regarding prices, see page 10

North West

Imagine some of Britain's most impressive scenery, stunning houses, fascinating industrial heritage, not to mention delicious local food, and you have the North West of England. To the north, the dramatic, internationally-renowned beauty of the Lake District proves irresistible to all those keen on physical, mental or spiritual refreshment. To the south, the urban centres of Manchester and Liverpool are surrounded by countryside and parkland, which offer a 'green lung' for their communities and visitors.

The National Trust looks after one quarter of the Lake District National Park, including England's highest mountain, Scafell Pike; our deepest lake, Wastwater; and 90 farms. Almost all the central fell area and major valley heads are owned or leased by the Trust, together with 24 lakes and tarns.

Beatrix Potter's love of the area is well known, and she gave 1,600 hectares (4,000 acres) and fourteen farms to the Trust on her death in 1943. This great estate – purchased piece by piece, beginning in 1902 with Brandlehow Park on the shore of Derwentwater – is one of the Trust's most important acquisitions.

Fun and games, or peace and quiet – you choose – but there is something for everyone here in the North West.

We believe our local food is second to none. Don't miss the Chorley cakes at Rufford Old Hall, made with fruit from the orchards. Also be sure to sample some of the meats of the region – such as venison from the parks at Dunham and Lyme; Herdwick lamb from various Trust farms

in Cumbria; or organic beef from farms in Silverdale, Coniston or Cheshire.

If you prefer cheese, you will be spoilt for choice. Low Sizergh Farm produces many award-winning cheeses, including Kendal Organic Crumbly, and there are delicious blue and red cheeses at Little Moreton Hall. At Rufford, the Lancashire ploughman's lunches are made using local creamy Garstang Blue and other Lancashire cheeses.

Many Trust farms have B&Bs or tea-rooms serving delicious home-made and locally produced food. Taste Herdwick stew and other traditional Cumbrian fare at Yew Tree Farm, Borrowdale, or at the walkers' tea-room at Yew Tree Farm, Coniston.

Above: local produce
Left: Belted Galloways Below: Brandlehow Park
Right: Alderley Edge
Bottom right: steam yacht *Gondola*
Far right: shelduck drake

Previous page: the garden at Hill Top, Cumbria (6:D8)

In West Cheshire the Trust cares for part of the very special Sandstone Ridge. Enjoy extensive walks through this historic landscape, with splendid views of the Cheshire Plain and Welsh Mountains from Alderley Edge, Bickerton Hill and nearby Bulkeley Hill Wood; while Helsby Hill has views across the Mersey Estuary to Liverpool. Both Bickerton and Helsby have Bronze Age forts at their summits. Bulkeley, part of the Peckforton range of hills, has the Sandstone Trail running along its length and is home to 5 hectares (12 acres) of semi-natural ancient woodland.

Views of the Peak District and Welsh Mountains, with wide expanses of the great Cheshire Plain stretching in between, can be seen from The Cloud, a great rocky heathland 343 metres high near Timbersbrook in Cheshire.

Further south the Victorian folly of Mow Cop stands in romantic ruin, while to the west of the county the site of Lewis Carroll's birthplace near Daresbury, kindly donated to the Trust by the Lewis Carroll Birthplace Trust, offers visitors the chance to muse on this famous children's author. The site bears the footprint of Daresbury Parsonage, in which Carroll was born in 1832 and where he

entertained his ten brothers and sisters with his stories. Nearby Daresbury Church features a memorial to Carroll and his Wonderland characters in a stained glass window.

Arnside Knott in Cumbria and Eaves and Waterslack Woods in Lancashire are home to a fantastic variety of wild flowers and butterflies. Also important for wildlife are the Stubbins Estate and Holcombe Moor, north of Manchester.

Another place where you can get close to wildlife is at Formby Sands. Here you can enjoy the wonderful nature reserve, which stretches for miles along unspoilt coastline and includes one of the country's largest areas of sand dunes as well as one of the few remaining red squirrel colonies left in Britain today.

A rich variety of birds, including shelduck, eider duck, goldeneye and plovers, can be spotted around Sandscale Haws, where the high, grass-covered sand dunes are perfect for a day's exploring. Natterjack toads, a nationally rare species, have made themselves at home in a specially-constructed pool, where visitors can hear their extraordinary mating calls on May and June evenings.

In Cumbria, Coniston Water is home to a wealth of flora and fauna, including wetland plants, meadow flowers and the rare small-leaved lime. Arthur Ransome got his inspiration here, as did Donald Campbell. On Saturdays, from April to October, steam yacht *Gondola* sails to the northern end of Coniston Water, where you can follow a self-guided trail through Monk Coniston to the iconic landscape of Tarn Hows.

The Trust manages three Lake District camp sites in the most spectacular locations: Wasdale, Great Langdale and Low Wray. Go to www.ntlakescampsites.org.uk

In Borrowdale, you are surrounded by rugged crags, dramatic fells, old mine workings and wooded valleys. Here can be found fine sessile oak woodlands and thriving colonies of internationally important lichens, mosses and insects.

Wildfowl and waders nest along the shores of Derwentwater, and Friar's Crag, one of the Lakes' most famous viewpoints, sits at the north end of the lake near the handsome town of Keswick. There is wheelchair access to the Crag; other sites with access include Tarn Hows and Harrowslack, near Hawkshead.

Above and left: **Wasdale**

Scafell Pike, England's highest mountain, is one of a dramatic horseshoe of peaks rising around the head of Wasdale. Recently voted on ITV 'Britain's Favourite View', this remote and quiet valley is one of the wildest areas of the Lake District. At the foot of the slopes lies Wastwater, the area's deepest lake, where Arctic char survive in the pure water. Traditional thick drystone walls make a striking pattern at Wasdale Head, while the impressive scree slopes of Whin Rigg and Illgill Head provide ideal conditions for rare mountain plants.

Car parks in the Lake District

The National Trust is an independent charity which protects about one quarter of the Lake District National Park. All income from National Trust pay & display car parks supports landscape conservation work in the valleys where the car parks are located.

Lanthwaite Wood	NY 149 215	Wasdale Head	NY 182 074
Buttermere	NY 172 173	Old Dungeon Ghyll	NY 285 062
Honister Pass	NY 225 135	Stickle Ghyll	NY 295 064
Seatoller	NY 246 137	Elterwater	NY 329 047
Rosthwaite	NY 257 148	Tarn Hows	SD 326 995
Bowderstone	NY 254 167	Ash Landing	SD 388 955
Watendlath	NY 276 164	Sandscale Haws	SD 199 758
Kettlewell	NY 269 196	Blea Tarn	NY 296 044
Great Wood	NY 272 213	Harrowslack	SD 388 960
Aira Force	NY 401 201	Red Nab	SD 385 995
Glencoyne Bay	NY 387 188	Glen Mary	SD 321 998

Acorn Bank Garden and Watermill

Temple Sowerby, nr Penrith, Cumbria CA10 1SP

⚒ ⚓ 🐱 🏠 🏛 💼 🎋 🛡 👫 🛏

🚶 | 1950 | **(6:E7)**

Delightful garden renowned for its herbs and old English fruit; with superb tea-room and woodland walks

This tranquil garden, sheltered by ancient oaks and soft terracotta brick walls, is a haven for wildlife. The herb garden is nationally renowned – with 250 medicinal and culinary herbs – and the orchards are packed with traditional fruit varieties. Wander along the Crowdundle Beck to the partially restored watermill, then enjoy the magnificent backdrop of the rose-pink sandstone house (which, although not open to the public, adds to the wonderful setting). Taste local produce at the tea-room or stay a while longer in a holiday cottage.

ℹ️ **T** 017683 61893
   E acornbank@nationaltrust.org.uk

🛡 Newt watching in early summer. Apple Day in mid Oct (charge inc. NT members)

🚶 Through woodland, beside beck and pond to the watermill

♿ 🚾 ♿ ♿ ♿ •• ⬛ P♿ Building ♿♿
Grounds ♿♿ ➡️

Acorn Bank Garden and Watermill										
Woodland walks										
1 Mar – 9 Mar	11–4	M	T	W	T	F	**S**	**S**
15 Mar – 2 Nov	10–5	M	T	**W**	**T**	**F**	**S**	**S**
Garden/shop										
15 Mar – 2 Nov	10–5	M	T	**W**	**T**	**F**	**S**	**S**
Tea-room										
1 Mar – 9 Mar	11–4	M	T	W	T	F	**S**	**S**
15 Mar – 2 Nov	11–4:30	M	T	**W**	**T**	**F**	**S**	**S**
Open BH Mons: 10–5										

🏪 NT shop. Plant sales

☕ Restaurant. Children's menu

👫 Baby-changing facilities. Pushchairs and baby back-carriers admitted. Children's guide

🏛 Suitable for school groups. Adult study days

🐾 On leads on woodland walk

➡️ [91:NY612281] **Cycle**: NCN7, 6ml.
   Bus: Grand Prix 563 Penrith–Kirkby Stephen, to within 1ml (passes close ≋ Penrith & ≋ Appleby). **Station**: Langwathby (U) 5ml; Penrith 6ml. **Road**: just N of Temple Sowerby, 6ml E of Penrith on A66

🅿️ Free parking, 80yds. Tight access for coaches. Recommended route map available when booking

NT properties nearby
Ullswater and Aira Force, Wordsworth House

Acorn Bank Garden is renowned for its herbs

Unless indicated, last admission is always 30mins before closing time

Alderley Edge

c/o Cheshire Countryside Office, Nether Alderley, Macclesfield, Cheshire SK10 4UB

 1946   (5:D8)

Dramatic red sandstone escarpment, with impressive views

Alderley Edge is designated an SSSI for its geological interest. It has a long history of copper mining, going back to Bronze Age and Roman times. The mines are open twice a year, organised by the Derbyshire Caving Club. There are views across Cheshire and the Peak District and numerous paths through the oak and beech woodlands, including a link to Hare Hill.

⭐ Tea-room (not NT) may be closed for part of the year during refurbishment

ℹ️ **T** 01625 584412
E alderleyedge@nationaltrust.org.uk

🚶 Guided walks programme, April to Sept

🐃 Mines open days

🚶 Hare Hill 2ml. Alderley Edge walks leaflet available

🔋 Grounds ➡️

🖤 Tea-room (not NT). May be closed for part of the year during refurbishment

👪 Children's quiz/trail

🎭 Suitable for school groups

🐕 Under close control; on leads in fields

Alderley Edge									
All year	8–5:30	M	T	W	T	F	S	S
1 Jun–30 Sep	8–6	M	T	W	T	F	S	S
1 Oct–31 Oct	8–5:30	M	T	W	T	F	S	S
1 Nov–31 Jan 09	8–5	M	T	W	T	F	S	S
Tea-room									
All year	10–5*	M	T	W	T	F	**S**	**S**

*Tea-room also open BHols but closed 24 & 25 Dec

➡️ [118:SJ860776] **Station**: Alderley Edge 1½ml. **Road**: 1½ml east of Alderley village on B5087 Macclesfield road

🅿️ Parking (pay & display). Closing time displayed at entrance

NT properties nearby
Dunham Massey, Hare Hill, Lyme Park, Quarry Bank Mill and Styal Estate, Tatton Park

Beatrix Potter Gallery

Main Street, Hawkshead, Cumbria LA22 0NS

 1944   (6:D8)

17th-century solicitor's office, now home to the original watercolours and sketches of Beatrix Potter

Enjoy a new exhibition of Beatrix Potter's original artworks in this charming 17th-century building (previously the office of her husband, William Heelis). Many of these pictures are not displayed anywhere else. Learn about how

Alderley Edge, a designated SSSI, offers spectacular views

Hill Top was re-created for the *Miss Potter* film and more about Beatrix as a farmer and early supporter of the National Trust. Children's trail based on the display.

What's new in 2008 Exhibition featuring original watercolours used to illustrate *The Tale of Jemima Puddle-Duck* and *The Tale of Samuel Whiskers* (both celebrating their 100th birthdays)

★ No WC, public WC 200 yards away in main village car park

ℹ️ **T** 015394 36355, 015394 36471 (shop)
E beatrixpottergallery@nationaltrust.org.uk

🎭 Easter trail, book fair, occasional storytelling

♿ 🏷️🖼️⊡📁🖼️ **Building** 🏛️

🏪 50yds away in the square

👶 Hip-carrying infant seats for loan. Children's quiz/trail

🏫 Suitable for school groups

➔ [96:SD352982] In Main Street, Hawkshead village, next to Red Lion pub. **Bus**: Stagecoach in Cumbria 505 ➔ Windermere–Coniston. **Station**: Windermere 6½ml via ferry. **Road**: B5286 from Ambleside (4ml); B5285 from Coniston (5ml)

🅿 Parking (not NT), 200yds (pay & display)

NT properties nearby
Coniston and Tarn Hows, Fell Foot Park, *Gondola*, Hawkshead and Claife, Hill Top, Stagshaw Garden, Townend

Beatrix Potter Gallery									
Gallery									
15 Mar–2 Nov	10:30–4:30	M	T	W	T		S	S	
Shop									
9 Feb–24 Feb	10–4	M	T	W	T	F	S	S	
25 Feb–14 Mar	10–4			W	T	F	S	S	
15 Mar–2 Nov	10–5	M	T	W	T	F	S	S	
3 Nov–24 Dec	10–4			W	T	F	S	S	
27 Dec–31 Dec	10–4	M	T	W			S	S	

Admission by timed ticket issued on arrival to all visitors. Open Good Fri. Shop is open occasional extra days in winter. Please enquire before making a special journey

Borrowdale

Bowe Barn, Borrowdale Road, Keswick, Cumbria CA12 5UP

🏛️🔧🍴🏠📁🖼️🎒🎭
👶🏫🚶♿ [1902] (6:D7)

Spectacular and varied landscape around Derwentwater

This is the location of the National Trust's first acquisition in the Lake District – Brandelhow Woods, on the lakeshore. The Trust now protects 11,806 hectares (29,173 acres), including eleven farms, half of Derwentwater (including the main islands), the hamlet of Watendlath and sites with literary or historical interest such as the Bowder Stone, Friar's Crag, Ashness Bridge and Castlerigg Stone Circle, a free-standing megalithic monument of 38 stones near Keswick.

ℹ️ **T** 017687 74649
E borrowdale@nationaltrust.org.uk

🎭 Programme of events, including Easter Egg trail

🚶 Popular walks from NT car parks. See local guides and maps

♿ 🚻 **Grounds** 🏛️

🏪 Shop and information centre at Keswick lakeside

☕ Tea-rooms at Caffle House, Watendlath; at the Flock-In, Rosthwaite; at Knotts View, Stonethwaite; and at Seathwaite – properties owned, but not managed, by NT

👶 Baby-changing facilities (Watendlath WC). Easter Egg trail

🏫 Suitable for school groups. Farm tours by arrangement

🐕 Under close control. Stock grazing

🚲 Several cycle routes throughout the valley

Borrowdale								
All year		M	T	W	T	F	S	S
Shop/info centre								
9 Mar–28 Oct	10–5	M	T	W	T	F	S	S

Shop/information centre closes later on summer evenings, tel. for details

Fold Head Farm, Watendlath in Borrowdale, Cumbria

[90:NY266228] **Cycle**: NCN71 (C2C). **Ferry**: Derwentwater launch service to various NT properties around lake, tel. 017687 72263. **Bus**: to information centre: Stagecoach in Cumbria X4/5 Penrith–Workington, 555/6 Lancaster–Keswick (pass close Lancaster, Kendal & Windermere). **Road**: B5289 runs S from Keswick along Borrowdale

NT car parks at Great Wood, Watendlath, Kettlewell, Bowderstone, Rosthwaite, Seatoller and Honister (pay & display). None suitable for coaches

NT properties nearby
Acorn Bank Garden and Watermill, Borrowdale: Force Crag Mine, Derwent Island House, Wordsworth House

Borrowdale: Force Crag Mine

Head of Coledale, above Braithwaite, Keswick, Cumbria

1979 **(6:D7)**

Last mineral mine processing mill to operate in the Lake District

Borrowdale: Force Crag Mine
Admission by guided tour. Last admission 1hr before closing. Tours take place hourly throughout the day on: Thur 27 Mar, Thur 8 May, Thur 24 Jul, Sat 23 Aug, Sat 4 Oct

For information regarding prices, see page 10

Admission into mine building via booked tours only (charge inc. NT members). NB: no access to the mine itself. Not suitable for children under 10yrs. Tel. for booking and details. WC not always available. Portaloo only on public open days. Site accessible via public footpaths

T 017687 74649
E forcecragmine@nationaltrust.org.uk

From Braithwaite west of Keswick off A66 walk or cycle approx. 2¾ml up to mine buildings or catch minibus from Noble Knott Forestry car park opposite the Bassenthwaite Lake viewpoint, which is approx. ½ml from Braithwaite climbing up Whinlatter Pass towards Lorton

Buttermere and Ennerdale

Unit 16, Leconfield Industrial Estate, Cleator Moor, Cumbria CA25 5QB

1935 **(6:C7)**

Tranquil area of dramatic fells, farms and woodland, encompassing three lakes

This area of 3,588 hectares (8,866 acres) of fell and commonland includes the lakes of Buttermere, Crummock and Loweswater, seven farms and woodland, as well as lakeshore access to Ennerdale Water. The famous Pillar Rock can be found in the high fells to the south, and there are extensive prehistoric settlements on the fells south of Ennerdale. Fishing and boats are available on Crummock Water and Loweswater.

WC in Buttermere village (not NT)

T 01946 816940
E buttermere@nationaltrust.org.uk

Family events, such as pond-dipping and craft workshops

Grounds

Family events

Suitable for school groups. Education room/centre. Hands-on activities. Adult study days

Buttermere and Ennerdale	
All year	M T W T F S S

➡️ [89:NY180150] 8ml S of Cockermouth.
Bus: services from 🚃 Penrith, Whitehaven,
🚃 St Bees & Keswick and Cockermouth,
inc. Honister Rambler

🅿️ Parking (pay & display) at Honister Pass,
Buttermere village, Lanthwaite Wood
(Crummock Water)

NT properties nearby
Wordsworth House

Cartmel Priory Gatehouse

The Square, Cartmel, Grange-over-Sands,
Cumbria LA11 6QB

🏠 1946   **(6:D9)**

14th-century gatehouse of medieval priory

⭐ Most of the Gatehouse and the adjoining
cottage have been returned to private
residential use. The Great Room is expected
to be open to the public several days a year.
Tel. for details

ℹ️ **T** 01524 701178
  E cartpriorygatehouse@nationaltrust.org.uk

➡️ In the square in village centre

Cartmel Priory Gatehouse
Tel. property or visit NT website for information

Great family walking around Tarn Hows

Coniston and Tarn Hows

Boon Crag, Coniston, Cumbria LA21 8AQ

🏠 ♿ 🍽️ 👤 🔄 📷 🚶 🚴 1930   **(6:D8)**

**Landscape of fell, meadow and woodland
around Coniston Water**

The area looked after by the National Trust
covers some 2,695 hectares (6,660 acres),
including eleven farms and the well-known Tarn
Hows beauty spot, with its magnificent mountain
views. There is access to the shore of Coniston
Water. The valley of Little Langdale shows
several signs of early settlement, including a
Norse meeting place, Ting Mound. Blea Tarn,
with spectacular views of the Langdale Pikes, is
readily accessible and there are wonderful walks
to be enjoyed throughout the area.

What's new in 2008 Permitted paths through
the grounds of Monk Coniston Hall, linking
Coniston Water with Tarn Hows. Walks leaflet,
information shelter and WCs

ℹ️ **T** 015394 41197
  E coniston@nationaltrust.org.uk

👤 Guided tours by arrangement.
  Tel. 015394 41951

Coniston and Tarn Hows						
All year	M	T	W	T	F	S	S

🎧 Audio guide to Tarn Hows

🚶 Popular walks for all abilities, see local guides and maps

♿ 🅿 Grounds 🔲 ➡

🍵 Walkers' tea-room at Yew Tree Farm, Coniston (NT but privately run)

🏫 Suitable for school groups

🐕 On leads please

🚲 Cycle tracks along Coniston lakeshore (west), Yewdale and in woodland south of Tarn Hows. Many off-road routes

➡ [SD325995] Tarn Hows 2ml NE of Coniston. Blea Tarn in Little Langdale, 5ml N of Coniston. **Bus**: Cross Lakes Experience Stagecoach in Cumbria 525 Coniston–Bowness Pier 3 via Lake Windermere (April–Sept only plus weekends in Oct). Tel. 01539 445161 for complete ferry & bus timetable

🅿 Car parks, pay & display, not suitable for coaches. Located at Tarn Hows, Glen Mary and Blea Tarn

NT properties nearby
Beatrix Potter Gallery, *Gondola*, Hill Top

Dalton Castle

Market Place, Dalton-in-Furness, Cumbria LA15 8AX

🏠 👥 🐾 1965 **(6:D9)**

14th-century tower built to assert the authority of the Abbot of Furness Abbey

⭐ Opened on behalf of the Trust by the Friends of Dalton Castle

ℹ **T** 01524 701178
E daltoncastle@nationaltrust.org.uk

➡ In market place at top of main street of Dalton

Dalton Castle									
22 Mar–27 Sep	2–5	M	T	W	T	F	**S**	S

If you enjoyed Dunham Massey, you will be fascinated by Speke Hall, Garden and Estate

Derwent Island House

Derwent Island, Lake Road, Keswick, Cumbria CA12 5DJ

🏠 ❄ 📷 1951 **(6:D7)**

Intriguing 18th-century house on an idyllic wooded island in Derwentwater

⭐ Private residence, accessed by private boats, open to public subject to lake levels and weather conditions. No WC, nearest WC at lakeside car park (not NT)

ℹ **T** 017687 73780
E borrowdale@nationaltrust.org.uk

➡ In Derwentwater, Keswick

Derwent Island House
Admission by timed ticket. Tickets only bookable three days prior to open days being advertised – see website Tel. Keswick shop/info centre to book tickets and check cancellations due to lake levels

Dunham Massey

Altrincham, Cheshire WA14 4SJ

🏠 🏠 ✝ ✖ ❄ 🍴 🏠 🍵 🍴 🏠 🎭
👥 🏫 🚶 🍴 1976 **(5:D8)**

Mansion with important collections and fascinating 'below stairs' area, set in a large country estate and deer park, with a rich and varied garden

Visit this elegant Georgian mansion, filled with fabulous collections of paintings, furniture and Huguenot silver, and be captivated by tales of family scandal and romance in the sumptuously decorated hall. Go 'below stairs' to the service wing and discover how the running of a country house took place. Enjoy the great plantsman's garden full of native favourites and exotic treasures, then discover the rare Victorian bark house and Georgian orangery. Wander around the beautiful avenues and ponds in the ancient park and spot the fallow deer and many rare birds. Finally make your way to the sawmill, where the giant waterwheel has been restored to full working order, then treat yourself to one of Dunham's renowned cream teas and the generous range of dishes made from fresh, local ingredients.

Dunham Massey garden is full of native favourites and exotic treasures

What's new in 2008 Exhibition of toys from Dunham's hidden collection

⭐ Extensive building works to improve car parking facilities being undertaken. Parking may be restricted at times. We apologise for any inconvenience

ℹ️ **T** 0161 941 1025
E dunhammassey@nationaltrust.org.uk

🏃 House tours most afternoons. Garden tours Mon and Wed. Free

🎭 Including open-air theatre, Boredom Busters and family activities

🚶 Guided deer park walks Mon, Wed, Fri throughout year at 1:30. Free walks leaflet

♿ 🚻 ♿ 🔊 ⠿ 🔍 🅿 🅳 🚌 **Building** ♿ ♿ **Grounds** ♿ ➡️ ♿

🛍️ NT shop. Plant sales in garden

☕ Stables Restaurant (licensed) on first floor of old stables. Open for corporate and private bookings outside normal hours, groups only. Children's menu. Kiosk in car park

👶 Baby-changing facilities. Pushchairs admitted. Front-carrying baby slings and hip-carrying infant seats for loan. Children's quiz/trail. Boredom Busters and family activities

🏛️ Suitable for school groups. Education room/centre. Live interpretation. Hands-on activities. Adult study days

Dunham Massey										
House										
8 Mar–2 Nov	12–5	M	T	W	T		F		S	S
Garden										
8 Mar–2 Nov	11–5:30	M	T	W	T	F		S	S	
Park										
8 Mar–2 Nov	9–7:30	M	T	W	T	F		S	S	
3 Nov–31 Jan 09	9–5	M	T	W	T	F		S	S	
Restaurant/shop										
8 Mar–2 Nov	10:30–5	M	T	W	T	F		S	S	
3 Nov–31 Jan 09	10:30–4	M	T	W	T	F		S	S	
Mill										
8 Mar–2 Nov	12–4	M	T	W	T		F		S	S

House open Good Fri and BH Suns & Mons 11–5. Property closed, including park, 25 Dec. Also closed 27 Feb & 19 Nov for staff training

Charges for National Trust members apply on some special event days

🐕 Good walks around estate. On leads in deer park

➡ [109:SJ735874] **Foot**: close to Trans-Pennine Trail and Bridgewater Canal. **Cycle**: NCN62, 1ml. **Bus**: Arriva/Warrington Transport 38 ⊟ Altrincham Interchange–Warrington. **Station**: Altrincham 3ml; Hale 3ml. **Road**: 3ml SW of Altrincham off A56: M6 exit 19; M56 exit 7

P Parking 200yds. £4 car, £1 motorbike, £10 coach/minibus. Shuttle service operates between car park and visitor facilities when the house is open

NT properties nearby
Hare Hill, Lyme Park, Quarry Bank Mill and Styal Estate, Tatton Park

Dunham Massey: White Cottage

Park Lane, Little Bollington, Altrincham, Cheshire WA14 4TJ

🏠 🚶 1976   **(5:D8)**

Timber-framed cottage, built c.1500

⭐ All visits must be booked through the NT Altrincham office

ℹ **T** 0161 928 0075
   E dunmasswhite@nationaltrust.org.uk

➡ 3ml SW of Altrincham off A56: M6 exit 19; M56 exit 7

White Cottage		M T W T F S **S**
30 Mar–26 Oct	2–5	M T W T F S **S**
Open last Sun of each month only		

Fell Foot Park

Newby Bridge, Ulverston, Cumbria LA12 8NN

🅿 🏠 🍽 🎫 ⛴ 👪 🖼 🍴 1948   **(6:D9)**

Country park beside Lake Windermere

As you walk down from the car park the view of Lake Windermere below you is breathtaking. The Victorian lawns and garden sweep away to fine picnic areas and numerous waterside spots. The Victorian boathouses are now home to a

cosy tea-room, shop, ice-cream kiosk and rowing boat hire, and there are tables outside where you can enjoy the magnificent views of the lake and mountains beyond. In spring and early summer there are daffodils and rhododendrons in full bloom. Or visit in autumn or winter and enjoy the changing seasons.

⭐ No launching or landing of speedboats or jet-skis

ℹ **T** 015395 31273
   E fellfootpark@nationaltrust.org.uk

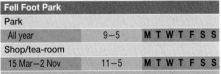
♿ 🚻 ♿ 🔊 ⠿ Ⓐ ♿ ♿ **Grounds** ♿ ♿

🍽 Tea-room at lakeshore. Trusty the Hedgehog lunch boxes

👪 Pushchairs and baby back-carriers admitted. Children's play area. Children's quiz/trail. Family activity packs

🖼 Suitable for school groups. Hands-on activities. 100 bird and bat boxes around the park relay live pictures to wildlife room

View from the lakeshore at Fell Foot Park

Fell Foot Park			
Park			
All year	9–5		M T W T F S S
Shop/tea-room			
15 Mar–2 Nov	11–5		M T W T F S S

Site closed 25 & 26 Dec. Closes dusk if earlier. Facilities, eg rowing boat hire (buoyancy aids available), 1 April–28 Oct: daily 11–4 (last boat), must be returned by 4:30

Parking in National Trust car parks is free for members displaying stickers

On leads only

→ [96/97:SD381869] **Ferry**: seasonal ferry links Fell Foot to Lakeside (southern terminus of main Windermere cruise ferries).
Bus: Stagecoach in Cumbria 618 Ambleside–Barrow-in-Furness (connections from ▆ Windermere). **Station**: Grange-over-Sands 6ml; Windermere 8ml. **Road**: at the extreme S end of Lake Windermere on E shore, entrance from A592

P Parking (pay & display). Access difficult for coaches, which must book in advance

NT properties nearby
Sizergh Castle and Garden

Formby

Victoria Road, Freshfield, Formby, Liverpool L37 1LJ

🛏️🏰🍦🎧🎪👫🎒🚶 1967   (5:B7)

Large area of beach, sand dunes and pine woods

This wonderful stretch of unspoilt coastline set between the sea and Formby town offers miles of walks through the woods and dunes. There are interesting plants and birds to be found, and this is one of the last places in England where visitors may catch a glimpse of the rare red squirrel.

What's new in 2008 Attractive new route for the Sefton Coastal Footpath

⭐ WCs close at 5:30 in summer, 4 in winter. Coach parking is restricted and must be booked. Address for correspondence: Countryside Office, Blundell Avenue, Freshfield, Formby L37 1PH

ℹ️ **T** 01704 878591
E formby@nationaltrust.org.uk

🎧 Audio guides available from entrance kiosk, £2. Last issue 3 in summer, 1:30 in winter. A deposit and ID are required

🚶 Send sae for details

♿ 🚾 ⠿ 🅿️ 🅿️ **Grounds** ♿ ➡️

Formby		
All year	Dawn–dusk	**M T W T F S S**
Closed 25 Dec		

💧 Ice-cream and soft drinks available

👫 Baby-changing facilities. Children's quiz/trail

🎦 Suitable for school groups, booking essential. Environmental education activities

Under close control; on leads around the squirrel walk

→ [108:SD275080] **Foot**: Sefton Coastal Footpath traverses the property.
Cycle: NCN62, 3ml. **Bus**: Cumfy Coaches 160/1/4, ▆ Formby–▆ Freshfield, to within ½ml. **Station**: Freshfield 1ml. **Road**: 15ml N of Liverpool, 2ml W of Formby, 2ml off A565. 6ml S of Southport. Follow brown signs from roundabout at N end of Formby bypass

P Cars £3.70, minibuses £10, coaches £25 – booking essential. Dune car park closes 5:30 April–Oct and 4 Nov–March. Note width restriction 3yds

NT properties nearby
20 Forthlin Road, Mr Hardman's Photographic Studio, Mendips, Rufford Old Hall, Speke Hall, Garden and Estate

Examining prehistoric footprints at Formby, Liverpool

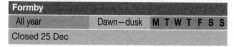

Dogs assisting visitors with disabilities are always welcome

20 Forthlin Road, Allerton

Allerton, Liverpool L24 1YP

 1995 (5:B8)

The childhood home of music icon Sir Paul McCartney

A little terrace house in Liverpool is where the Beatles met, rehearsed and wrote many of their songs. Join our characterful custodian on a trip around the McCartney family home and hear stories from one of the most exciting times in music history. Enjoy contemporary photos by Michael McCartney and original early Beatles memorabilia. Hear Michael's and Paul's reminiscences on the audio tour.

What's new in 2008 Online booking service available. Visit www.nationaltrust.org.uk/beatles Extended open season. This year Liverpool is European Capital of Culture 2008 – for details visit www.liverpool08.com

★ **There is no direct access by car or on foot**. Visits are by combined minibus tour only with Mendips, the childhood home of John Lennon (charge inc. NT members). Any photography inside 20 Forthlin Road or duplication of audio tour material is strictly prohibited. You will be asked to deposit handbags, cameras and recording equipment at the entrance to the house

ℹ️ **T** 0844 800 4791 (Infoline)
   E 20forthlinroad@nationaltrust.org.uk

The kitchen at 20 Forthlin Road, Paul McCartney's childhood home in Liverpool

20 Forthlin Road							
1 Mar – 30 Nov	M	T	**W**	**T**	**F**	**S**	**S**

Admission by guided tour only, up to four tours depart on days open to the public. To guarantee a place on the tour visitors are advised to book in advance, at www.nationaltrust.org.uk/beatles, or tel. Infoline. Tours depart by minibus from city centre in the morning and Speke Hall in the afternoon. Open BHol Mons

🎧 Audio tour features contributions from both Michael and Sir Paul McCartney

♿ Building

🛍️ At nearby Speke Hall

👪 Pushchairs admitted. Children's quiz/trail

🏫 Suitable for school groups

➡️ [108:SJ403862] Access is via minibus from Liverpool city centre or Speke Hall

🅿️ No parking on site. Nearest car park at Speke Hall

NT properties nearby
Formby, Mr Hardman's Photographic Studio, Mendips, Rufford Old Hall, Speke Hall, Garden and Estate

Gawthorpe Hall

Padiham, nr Burnley, Lancashire BB12 8UA

1972 (5:D6)

Elizabethan house with rich interiors and an important textile collection

This imposing house, set in tranquil grounds in the heart of urban Lancashire, resembles the great Hardwick Hall and is very probably by the same architect, Robert Smythson. In the middle of the 19th century Sir Charles Barry was commissioned to restore the house, thereby creating the opulent interiors we see today. The Long Gallery is hung with portraits of society figures from the 17th century, some of which are

Gawthorpe Hall								
Hall/tea-room								
1 Apr – 29 Oct	1–5	M	**T**	**W**	**T**	F	**S**	**S**
Garden								
All year	10–6	**M**	**T**	**W**	**T**	**F**	**S**	**S**
Tea-room opens 12:30. Open BH Mons and Good Fri								

on loan from the National Portrait Gallery, London. Several rooms display part of the international collection of needlework, lace and costume assembled by the last family member to live here, Rachel Kay-Shuttleworth. The wooded park and riverside location offer wonderful walks.

⭐ Gawthorpe Hall is financed and run by Lancashire County Council. The NT only maintains a small administration office and a tea-room/shop. Please note that opening times and prices are controlled by Lancashire County Council and subject to change. Please tel. to confirm. The Great Barn, an unusual aisled threshing barn with a cathedral-like atmosphere, is available for private hire and licensed for weddings

ⓘ **T** 01282 771004
E gawthorpehall@nationaltrust.org.uk

🔥 🚻 🔊 📷 📷 **Building** 🏞 **Grounds** 📷

📷 Coach House tea-room in the courtyard

🚼 Baby-changing facilities. Children's quiz/trail

📷 Suitable for school groups. Live interpretation. Hands-on activities. Adult study days

🐕 In grounds only and under close control

➔ [103:SD806340] **Foot**: pleasant walk by the River Calder from Padiham, ½ml; on route of Brontë Way public footpath. **Bus**: frequent services from Burnley. All pass close 🚉 Burnley Barracks & Burnley Manchester Road. **Station**: Rose Grove (U) 2ml. **Road**: on E outskirts of Padiham; ¾ml drive to house on N of A671; M65 exit 8 towards Clitheroe, then signposted from second traffic light junction to Padiham

🅿 Free parking, 150yds. Tight access to site. Tight turning facilities

NT properties nearby
East Riddlesden Hall, Rufford Old Hall, Stubbins Estate

Why not go for a sail on the steam yacht *Gondola*?

Gondola

Pier Cottage, Coniston, Cumbria LA21 8AJ

📷 📷 📷 🚻 📷 📷 1980   **(6:D8)**

Rebuilt Victorian steam-powered yacht on Coniston Water

The original steam yacht *Gondola* was first launched in 1859 and now, completely rebuilt by the Trust, gives passengers the chance to sail in her sumptuous, upholstered saloons. This is the perfect way to view Coniston's spectacular scenery.

What's new in 2008 *Gondola* will be calling at Monk Coniston jetty on certain days, enabling visitors easy access to the recently opened footpaths through the Monk Coniston Estate, linking Coniston Water to Tarn Hows. See website for details of guided walks combined with a cruise on *Gondola*

⭐ Charge inc. NT members. All sailings are weather permitting. No WC on board, nearest WC at Coniston Pier

ⓘ **T** 015394 41288
E gondola@nationaltrust.org.uk

🎭 Cruising the route of the original *Gondola* to Lake Bank. Campbell/*Bluebird* talks. Cruise on *Gondola* and guided walk of Monk Coniston Estate

🔥 🚻 📷 📷 📷 🏞 **Gangway** 📷

📷 Guidebook and *Gondola* souvenirs available on board

🚼 Pushchairs and baby back-carriers admitted

📷 Suitable for school groups

🐕 Dogs in outside areas only

Gondola							
20 Mar—31 Oct		**M**	**T**	**W**	**T**	**F**	**S** **S**

Steam yacht *Gondola* sails from Coniston Pier daily, weather permitting. Last sailing at 4. The National Trust reserves the right to cancel sailings and special charters in the event of high winds. In the event of cancellation due to adverse weather conditions, private charters or unforeseen operational difficulties, every reasonable effort will be made to inform the public. Piers at Coniston and Brantwood (not NT)

→ [96:SD307970] Sails from Coniston Pier (½ml from Coniston village). **Cycle**: no cycle parking. **Bus**: Stagecoach in Cumbria 505 from ⊒ Windermere. **Station**: Foxfield (U), not Sun, 10ml; Windermere 10ml via vehicle ferry. **Road**: A593 from Ambleside. Pier is at end of Lake Road, turn immediately left after petrol station if travelling S from centre of Coniston village

P Parking (not NT), 50yds, £2.20 (pay & display) at Coniston Pier. Two free coach parking spaces for booked groups

NT properties nearby
Beatrix Potter Gallery, Hill Top, Tarn Hows

Grasmere and Great Langdale

High Close, Loughrigg, Ambleside, Cumbria LA22 9HH

 1925   (6:D8)

Picturesque and varied landscape with Wordsworth connections

The protected area of 4,925 hectares (12,170 acres) includes ten farms and the famous Langdale Pikes. It also encompasses the glaciated valley of Mickleden, a Victorian garden at High Close and dramatic Dungeon Ghyll, as well as the bed of Grasmere lake and part of Rydal Water.

Great Langdale, Cumbria

Grasmere and Great Langdale		
All year		M T W T F S S

★ There is a spectacularly located NT campsite at Great Langdale, open all year [NY288057], charge (inc. NT members): tel. 015394 37668 or visit **www.langdalecampsite.org.uk**

i **T** 015394 37663
E grasmere@nationaltrust.org.uk

♿ 🚻 Pᴅ **Grounds** ♿

🏫 Suitable for school groups

🚴 Cycling on quiet roads and bridleways

→ [89/90:NY290060] Great Langdale valley starts 4ml W of Ambleside. **Bus**: to Grasmere information centre: Stagecoach in Cumbria 555/6, 599 from ⊒ Windermere. To Langdale Campsite: Stagecoach in Cumbria 516 from Ambleside. **Station**: Windermere 8ml

P Parking (pay & display). Three car parks in the two valleys, but none in Grasmere village

NT properties nearby
Beatrix Potter Gallery, Hill Top, Stagshaw Garden, Townend

Mr Hardman's Photographic Studio

59 Rodney Street, Liverpool L1 9EX

🏠 🗄 🛡 🚻 🏫 2003   (5:B8)

Beautiful Georgian terraced house – the former studio and home of the renowned local photographer E. Chambré Hardman

Situated just below the Anglican Cathedral in the centre of Liverpool is this fascinating house, home between 1947 and 1988 to Edward Chambré Hardman and his wife Margaret. The house contains a selection of photographs, the studio where most were taken, the darkroom where they were developed and printed, the business records and the Hardmans' living quarters – complete with all the ephemera of post-war daily life. The subject matter of the photographs – portraits of the people in Liverpool, their city and the landscapes of the surrounding countryside – provide a record of a more prosperous time when Liverpool was the

59 Rodney Street: the studio of E. Chambré Hardman

gateway to the British Empire and the world. Parallel to this is the quality of Hardman's work and his standing as a photographer.

What's new in 2008 New and improved selection of original Hardman photographs on display. Handling collection. Special costume and photographic tours. Focus on family days. Community Arts Project activities. Extended open season. This year Liverpool is European Capital of Culture 2008 – for details visit www.liverpool08.com

⭐ Admission by guided tour (booking not required). Group size restricted to avoid overcrowding and to preserve the fragile contents

ℹ **T** 0151 709 6261
E 59rodneystreet@nationaltrust.org.uk

📷 Range of events, from family summer holiday activities to specialist evening tours

♿ 🚻 🔍 🎨 ⠿ 📷 💷 **Building** ♿

📷 Guidebooks, prints and postcards on sale

👪 Pushchairs admitted. Hip-carrying infant seats for loan. Children's quiz/trail. Family days

Mr Hardman's Photographic Studio										
15 Mar–2 Nov	11–4:15	M	T	**W**	**T**	**F**	**S**	**S**
8 Nov–21 Dec	11–4:15	M	T	W	T	F	**S**	**S**

Admission by timed ticket only, inc. NT members. Open BH Mons. Visitors are advised to book in advance by tel. or email to property. Tickets on the day subject to availability

🔲 Suitable for school groups

➡ [108:SJ355895] Short walk north of Liverpool city centre. Rodney St is off Hardman St and Upper Duke St. Follow finger posts. **Ferry**: Mersey Ferry 1ml. **Bus**: frequent from surrounding areas. **Station**: Liverpool Lime St ½ml. **Underground**: Liverpool Central ½ml

🅿 No parking on site. Off-site parking most days near Anglican Cathedral (pay & display). Slater St NCP. Limited parking Rodney St and Pilgrim St (pay & display)

NT properties nearby
Formby, 20 Forthlin Road, Mendips, Rufford Old Hall, Speke Hall, Garden and Estate

Hare Hill

Over Alderley, Macclesfield, Cheshire SK10 4QB

🔲 📷 🏠 👤 1978 (5:D8)

Charming wooded and walled garden

This tranquil woodland garden, especially spectacular in early summer, includes more than 70 varieties of rhododendrons, plus azaleas, hollies and hostas. At its heart is a delightful walled area with a pergola and wire sculptures. The surrounding parkland has an attractive permitted link path to nearby Alderley Edge.

⭐ Car park closes at 5

ℹ **T** 01625 584412
E harehill@nationaltrust.org.uk

👤 To Alderley Edge 2ml

♿ 🚻 ⠿ 🔍 **Grounds** ♿

🐕 On leads at all times on estate. Not in garden

➡ [118:SJ875765] **Station**: Alderley Edge 2½ml; Prestbury 2½ml. **Road**: between Alderley Edge and Macclesfield (B5087). Turn off N on to Prestbury Road, continue ¾ml, entrance on the left. From Prestbury take Chelford Road 1½ml, entrance on right

Hare Hill									
22 Mar–11 May	10–5	M	T	**W**	T	**F**	**S**	**S**
12 May–1 Jun	10–5	**M**	**T**	**W**	**T**	**F**	**S**	**S**
2 Jun–30 Oct	10–5	M	T	**W**	**T**	F	**S**	**S**

Open BH Mons and Good Fri. Last admission 1hr before closing

P Parking, £1.90 (refunded on admission). Not suitable for coaches

NT properties nearby
Alderley Edge, Dunham Massey, Lyme Park, Nether Alderley Mill, Quarry Bank Mill and Styal Estate, Tatton Park

Hawkshead and Claife

c/o Hill Top, Near Sawrey, Ambleside, Cumbria LA22 0LF

🏠 🐾 📷 🏛 🎦 🚶 🐕 🦮 🚵 1929   **(6:D8)**

Classic south Lakeland countryside with views of the fells and lakes and picturesque buildings

Hawkshead village, home to the Beatrix Potter Gallery, is surrounded by beautiful scenery, much of which is owned by the National Trust, some bequeathed by Beatrix Potter. This includes 4 miles of access along Windermere lakeshore from Ash Landing to Low Wray Bay. Claife Woodlands and the low-lying small farms between Hawkshead and Lake Windermere are typical of the area. Just north of the village is the Courthouse, which dates from the 15th century and is all that remains of the village manorial buildings (once held by Furness Abbey). Claife Station, on the west bank of Windermere, is a late 18th-century viewing station with glimpses of the lake. At Wray Castle there is access to the grounds and limited access to the castle.

⭐ There is a NT campsite in a superb location on the lakeshore at Low Wray [NY372012], check website for opening times and prices

ℹ️ **T** 015394 36269
E hawkshead@nationaltrust.org.uk

🚶 Occasional warden-led walks

Hawkshead and Claife									
Countryside									
All year			M	T	W	T	F	S	S
Courthouse									
15 Mar–2 Nov	11–4		M	T	W	T	F	S	S

Hawkshead Courthouse: access by key from NT shop, The Square, Hawkshead or Beatrix Potter Gallery ticket office; free admission, but no parking facilities. Approx. ½ml walk from village

♿ **Grounds** 🏔️

📷 See Beatrix Potter Gallery

🎦 Suitable for school groups

🚵 Lakeshore track for mountain bikes from Harrowslack (SD388960) to St Margaret's Church (NY374006) along Windermere lakeshore (west)

➡️ [96/97:SD352982] Hawkshead is 6ml SW of Ambleside. **Foot**: off-road path from Windermere ferry to Sawrey; many footpaths in the area. **Ferry**: Windermere ferry. **Bus**: Stagecoach in Cumbria 505 🚌 Windermere–Coniston. **Station**: Windermere 6ml via vehicle ferry

P Pay & display car parks at Ash Landing (close to ferry) and Harrowslack; free car parks at Red Nab and Wray Castle. All close to Lake Windermere. Pay & display car parks (not NT) in Hawkshead village

NT properties nearby
Beatrix Potter Gallery, Coniston and Tarn Hows, Fell Foot Park, *Gondola*, Hill Top

Hill Top

Near Sawrey, Hawkshead, Ambleside, Cumbria LA22 0LF

🏠 ✣ 🍴 📷 🛡 🚶 1944   **(6:D8)**

Delightful small 17th-century farmhouse where Beatrix Potter wrote many of her famous children's stories

Enjoy the tale of Beatrix Potter – Hill Top is a time-capsule of this amazing woman's life. Packed full of her favourite things, the house appears as if Beatrix had just stepped out for a walk. Every room contains a reference to a

Hill Top									
House									
15 Mar–2 Nov	10:30–4:30		M	T	W	T	F	S	S
Shop/garden									
9 Feb–24 Feb	10–4		M	T	W	T	F	S	S
1 Mar–14 Mar	10–4		M	T	W	T	F	S	S
15 Mar–2 Nov	10:30–5		M	T	W	T	F	S	S
3 Nov–24 Dec	10–4		M	T	W	T	F	S	S

Last entry at 4. Limited number of timed tickets available daily

For information regarding prices, see page 10

The lovely garden at Hill Top in Cumbria

picture in a 'tale', as do the garden, village and surrounding countryside. The lovely cottage garden is a haphazard mix of flowers, herbs, fruit and vegetables, just as Beatrix used to plant. Her original watercolours are on display at the nearby Beatrix Potter Gallery.

What's new in 2008 Come and visit the house which was recreated for the film *Miss Potter*. Hill Top characters Jemima Puddle-Duck and Samuel Whiskers celebrate their 100th birthdays this year

⭐ Hill Top is a small house and a timed entry system is in operation to avoid overcrowding and to protect the fragile interior. As this can be a very busy property, visitors may sometimes have to wait to enter the house and early sell-outs are possible, especially at holiday times. Tickets cannot be booked in advance. Access to the garden and shop is always possible during opening hours

ℹ️ **T** 015394 36269
E hilltop@nationaltrust.org.uk

👹 Easter trail

🚶 Occasional Beatrix Potter-themed guided walks in surrounding countryside with NT Warden

♿ 🖼️ ⋮ 🔊 **Building** 🏞️ **Grounds** 🏞️

📷 Specialises in Beatrix Potter-related items; mail-order available all year from the online shop www.hilltopshop.co.uk

🍴 Drinks and treats available from shop. The Tower Bank Arms (NT-owned and let to tenant) serves traditional Cumbrian dishes using local produce, 12–2, 6–9; serves light refreshments at other times

➡️ [96/97:SD370955] 2ml S of Hawkshead, in hamlet of Near Sawrey; 3ml from Bowness via ferry. **Foot**: off-road path from ferry (2ml), marked. **Bus**: Cross Lakes Experience from Bowness Pier 3 across Lake Windermere on to Stagecoach in Cumbria 525; also 505 from 🚆 Windermere changing at Hawkshead (April–Sept only, plus weekends in Oct). Tel. 01539 445161 for complete ferry & bus timetable. **Station**: Windermere 4½ml via vehicle ferry. **Road**: B5286 and B5285 from Ambleside (6ml), B5285 from Coniston (7ml)

🅿️ Free parking, 150yds. Not suitable for coaches. The roads are narrow and can be very busy, please allow extra time to park during peak times such as summer hols

NT properties nearby
Beatrix Potter Gallery, Coniston and Tarn Hows, Fell Foot Park, *Gondola*, Hawkshead and Claife, Townend

Little Moreton Hall

Congleton, Cheshire CW12 4SD

🏠 ✝️ 🎎 📷 🍴 🚶 🎍 👹 🚻
🖼️ 🍷 1938 **(5:D9)**

Cheshire's most iconic black-and-white house – Tudor skill and craftsmanship at its finest

Gaze at the drunkenly reeling South Range, cross the moat into the cobbled courtyard and enter a Hall full of surprises. The skill of the craftsmen fascinates, as you climb the stairs to the Long Gallery – imagine life here in Tudor times. The various delights of wall paintings, WCs over the moat, the Knot Garden, as well as colourful tales of the Moreton family and this iconic building itself, are revealed to you by our guided tours. Delicious home-baked local food and a visit to the shop complete your day.

Little Moreton Hall									
1 Mar–16 Mar	11:30–4	M	T	W	T	F	**S**	**S**
19 Mar–2 Nov	11:30–5	M	T	**W**	**T**	**F**	**S**	**S**
8 Nov–21 Dec	11:30–4	M	T	W	T	F	**S**	**S**

Open BH Mons. Closes dusk if earlier. Access during Yuletide celebrations restricted to ground floor, garden, shop and restaurant. Special openings at other times for booked groups

Many Trust properties are offering Gift Aid on Entry for non-members, see page 10

Little Moreton Hall: Cheshire's most iconic black-and-white house

What's new in 2008 Joint ticket with Biddulph Grange Garden (6ml). New bus service

ⓘ **T** 01260 272018
  E littlemoretonhall@nationaltrust.org.uk

🏃 Free guided tours when open, 1 March–30 Nov

🎭 Open-air theatre and regular events, including live interpretation and music. Chapel service Suns between 23 March and 2 Nov

♿ 🚻 ♿ ♿ ♿ ♿ ♿ Ⓟ Ⓓ **Building** ♿ ♿ **Grounds** ♿ ➡

🛍 NT shop. Plant sales

🍽 Licensed restaurant. Home-cooked food with a regional and historic theme. Children's menu. Kiosk serving ice-cream, cold drinks, cakes and biscuits. Cold drinks in shop

👶 Baby-changing facilities. Front-carrying baby sling and hip-carrying infant seats for loan. Children's guide. Children's quiz/trail

🏫 Suitable for school groups. Education room/ centre. Live interpretation. Hands-on activities

🐕 On leads and only in car park

➡ [118:SJ832589] **Bus:** Stanways 315
  🚂 Alsager–Congleton. **Station:** Kidsgrove 3ml; Congleton 4½ml. **Road:** 4ml SW of Congleton, on E side of A34. From M6 jnct 17 & 18 follow A34 S

🅿 Parking, 100yds

NT properties nearby
Alderley Edge, Biddulph Grange Garden, Quarry Bank Mill and Styal Estate

Lyme Park

Disley, Stockport, Cheshire SK12 2NX

🏛 🏠 ✝ ♿ ♥ 🏠 🛍 🍽 🏃 🏠
🎭 🚻 🏫 🐕 ♿ 🍽 1947   **(5:E8)**

Glorious mansion house, surrounded by stunning gardens, moorland and ancient deer park

The mile-long drive to Lyme Park creates a real sense of anticipation, which the house more than matches up to. Originally Tudor, it now resembles a fabulous Italianate palace. Inside there are incredible Mortlake tapestries, an important collection of clocks, beautifully furnished rooms, along with a colourful family history. Stroll through the opulent Victorian garden, with its sunken parterre, or the Edwardian rose garden. Enjoy the luxurious Jekyll-style borders and Wyatt-designed Orangery, sit on the grass, or wander lazily by the lake (where Darcy and Elizabeth meet at 'Pemberley'), then venture beyond the garden, where the medieval deer park stretches into the distance; the vast moors and parkland are home to fallow and red deer. Seek out The Cage, an 18th-century hunting tower, or explore the woods and discover the lantern folly, with its breathtaking views. Delicious food, including venison from the park, is prepared in the Lyme kitchens; and with retail therapy at hand, Lyme really is a glorious day out.

What's new in 2008 Children's activity packs and pest detective quiz in house. Now available for wedding receptions

For details of events go to www.nationaltrust.org.uk/events

⭐ Lyme Park is owned and managed by the NT and partly financed by Stockport Metropolitan Borough Council

ℹ️ **T** 01663 766492 (Infoline), 01663 762023
E lymepark@nationaltrust.org.uk

🏃 Conservation-in-action tours, 1st & 2nd weekend in March, 11–5 (restricted numbers); house tours, 15 March–2 Nov, 11–1 (restricted numbers). Out-of-hours tours at extra charge, tel. for details

📧 Send sae for details

🚶 Walks leaflets in information centre

♿ 🚻 ♿ ♿ ♿ ♿ ♿ ♿ Building ♿ ♿
Grounds ♿

🛍️ Shops in The Timber Yard and house courtyard

☕ Licensed restaurant in house. Children's menu. Coffee shop in The Timber Yard. Children's menu. Refreshment kiosk in main car park

👶 Baby-changing facilities. Front-carrying baby slings and hip-carrying infant seats for loan. Children's play area. Children's quiz/trail. Children's activity packs. Bottle-warming facilities

The Dining Room at Lyme Park laid out in style

Lyme Park									
House/restaurant/shop									
1 Mar–9 Mar	11–5	M	T	W	T	F	S	S	
15 Mar–2 Nov	11–5	**M**	**T**	W	T	**F**	**S**	**S**	
Park									
1 Apr–12 Oct	8–8:30	**M**	**T**	**W**	**T**	**F**	**S**	**S**	
13 Oct–31 Jan 09	8–6	**M**	**T**	**W**	**T**	**F**	**S**	**S**	
Garden									
1 Mar–9 Mar	11–5	M	T	W	T	F	**S**	**S**	
15 Mar–2 Nov	11–5	**M**	**T**	**W**	**T**	**F**	**S**	**S**	
8 Nov–21 Dec	12–3	M	T	W	T	F	**S**	**S**	
Timber Yard plant sales/shop									
1 Mar–9 Mar	11–4	M	T	W	T	F	**S**	**S**	
15 Mar–2 Nov	10:30–5	M	**T**	**W**	**T**	**F**	**S**	**S**	
3 Nov–30 Nov	11–4	M	T	W	T	F	**S**	**S**	
1 Dec–4 Jan 09	11–4	M	T	**W**	**T**	**F**	**S**	**S**	
5 Jan–31 Jan 09	11–4	M	T	W	T	F	**S**	**S**	
Timber Yard coffee shop									
1 Mar–14 Mar	11–4	**M**	**T**	**W**	**T**	**F**	**S**	**S**	
15 Mar–2 Nov	10:30–5	**M**	**T**	**W**	**T**	**F**	**S**	**S**	
3 Nov–31 Jan 09	11–4	**M**	**T**	**W**	**T**	**F**	**S**	**S**	

Closed Christmas Day. 1st & 2nd weekend in March: Conservation-in-action tours (restricted numbers) 11–5. 15 March–2 Nov: house tours (restricted numbers) 11–1

📷 Suitable for school groups. Education room/centre

🐕 Under close control and only in park (in areas where livestock present on leads only)

🚲 Off-road cycling on the Knott area and hard surface roads only

➡️ [109:SJ965825] **Foot**: northern end of Gritstone Trail; paths to Macclesfield Canal, Poynton Marina 1ml and Peak Forest Canal 2½ml. **Bus**: TrentBarton 199 Buxton–Manchester Airport, to park entrance. **Station**: Disley, ½ml from park entrance. NT courtesy bus from park admission kiosk to house for pedestrians on days house is open, tel. property for details. **Road**: entrance on A6, 6½ml SE of Stockport (M60 exit 1), 12ml NW of Buxton (house and car park 1ml from entrance)

🅿️ Parking £4.60 (£2 motorbike), £12 coach, £6 minibus. Coaches bringing booked groups to house and garden admitted free to park

NT properties nearby
Alderley Edge, Dunham Massey, High Peak Estate, Quarry Bank Mill and Styal Estate

Charges for National Trust members apply on some special event days

Mendips

Woolton, Liverpool

 2002 (5:C8)

Childhood home of 20th-century icon John Lennon

Imagine walking through the back door into the kitchen where John Lennon's Aunt Mimi would have cooked him his tea. Join our fascinating Custodian on a trip down memory lane to life here where John's passion for music began, and where many early songs were written. Original photographs and other memorabilia are also on display. John's bedroom is a very atmospheric place in which to take a moment with your own thoughts about this incredible individual.

What's new in 2008 Extended open period. Reserve your place on the tour at www.nationaltrust.org.uk/beatles. This year Liverpool is European Capital of Culture 2008 – for details visit www.liverpool08.com

⭐ No WC. **There is no direct access by car or on foot**. Visits are by combined minibus tour only with 20 Forthlin Road, the childhood home of Paul McCartney (charge inc. NT members). Any photography inside Mendips or duplication of audio tour material is strictly prohibited. You will be asked to deposit all handbags, cameras and recording equipment at the entrance to the house

ℹ️ **T** 0844 800 4791 (Infoline)
   E mendips@nationaltrust.org.uk

🎧 Listen to extracts from interviews of former student lodgers who lived at Mendips

♿ 🚾 📷 ⊙ 📷 Building 🔓

📷 At nearby Speke Hall

🧑‍🧒 Pushchairs admitted. Children's quiz/trail

📷 Suitable for school groups

Mendips							
1 Mar–30 Nov		M	T	**W**	**T**	**F**	**S** **S**

Open BH Mons. Admission by guided tour only; up to four tours depart on days open to the public. Tours depart by minibus from city centre in the morning and Speke Hall in the afternoon. To guarantee a place on the tour visitors are advised to book. Tel. Infoline or visit www.nationaltrust.org.uk/beatles

John Lennon's bedroom at Mendips, Liverpool

➡️ [108:SJ422855] Access is via minibus from Liverpool city centre or Speke Hall

🅿️ No parking on site. Nearest car park at Speke Hall

NT properties nearby
Formby, 20 Forthlin Road, Mr Hardman's Photographic Studio, Rufford Old Hall, Speke Hall, Garden and Estate

Nether Alderley Mill

Congleton Road, Nether Alderley, Macclesfield, Cheshire SK10 4TW

🍴 🚻 🚻 📷 1950 (5:D8)

15th-century mill beside a tranquil mill pool

With its heavy oak framework, low beams and floors connected by wooden ladders set beneath an enormous sloping stone roof, this charming rustic mill is one of only four virtually complete corn mills in Cheshire.

⭐ The property can only be visited by booked groups, tel. for details. No WC

ℹ️ **T** 01625 527468
   E quarrybankmill@nationaltrust.org.uk

Parking in National Trust car parks is free for members displaying stickers

♭ Building

■ Suitable for school groups

→ [118:SJ844763] **Bus**: Arriva 130 Manchester–Macclesfield (passing ⊠ Alderley Edge). **Station**: Alderley Edge 2ml. **Road**: 1½ml S of Alderley Edge, on E side of A34

P Free limited NT parking. Space for one coach at a time, booking essential

NT properties nearby
Alderley Edge, Dunham Massey, Hare Hill, Quarry Bank Mill and Styal Estate, Tatton Park

Quarry Bank Mill and Styal Estate

Styal, Wilmslow, Cheshire SK9 4LA

🏠❌🔧❄🔌📷🍽🎪😊♿🔫
🚶🔔🍸 1939   (5:D8)

One of Britain's greatest industrial heritage sites, including cotton mill with working machinery, restored Apprentice House, mill workers' village and country estate set in the valley of the River Bollin

Quarry Bank, lying in the Bollin Valley, overflows with the atmosphere of the Industrial Revolution. Experience life as a mill worker – a visit to the cotton mill, powered by Europe's most powerful working waterwheel, will certainly stimulate your senses. The clatter of machinery and hiss of steam engines are astonishing. Take a tour of the Apprentice House, led by a costumed guide, and discover how – for food, clothing and lodgings – pauper children were expected to work in the mill. See the traditional vegetables, fruit and herbs still grown in the Apprentice House garden using organic methods and visit the newly opened 3-hectare (8-acre) 'Secret Garden' – the Greg family's stunningly picturesque valley retreat adjoining the mill and open to the public for the first time. Stroll to Styal village – built by the Greg family to house the mill workers and still a thriving community, with two chapels, allotments and cottages. Or walk through woods along the River Bollin. Finally enjoy delicious local produce in our restaurant.

Quarry Bank Mill and Styal Estate									
Mill/shop									
1 Mar–31 Oct	11–5		M	T	W	T	F	S	S
1 Nov–31 Jan 09	11–4		M	T	W	T	F	S	S
Apprentice House									
1 Mar–31 Oct	See note		M	T	W	T	F	S	S
1 Nov–31 Jan 09	See note		M	T	W	T	F	S	S
Garden									
21 Mar–31 Oct	11–5		M	T	W	T	F	S	S
Estate									
All year	7–6		M	T	W	T	F	S	S
Restaurant									
1 Mar–31 Oct	11–5		M	T	W	T	F	S	S
1 Nov–31 Jan 09	11–4		M	T	W	T	F	S	S

Open BH Mons, Boxing Day & New Year's Day. Closed 24/25 Dec. Mill: last admission 1hr before closing. Apprentice House: limited availability – timed tickets only, available from Mill on early arrival. Garden: timed tickets may be introduced during busy periods also Apprentice House closed 17 March

What's new in 2008 'Secret Garden', the Greg family's picturesque valley retreat adjoining the mill, is open for the first time

⭐ Allow 1½hrs minimum to visit Mill, 2½hrs to visit Mill and Apprentice House or Mill and Quarry Bank House Garden

i **T** 01625 445896 (Infoline), 01625 527468 **E** quarrybankmill@nationaltrust.org.uk

🛡 See website or tel. for leaflet

🚶 Guided walk of woodlands and village every second Sun in month at 2. Additional historical and nature walks

Mill worker at Quarry Bank Mill

Dogs assisting visitors with disabilities are always welcome

Building

Grounds

🎁 Selling souvenirs unique to the Mill together with a wide range of other gifts

🍽 Mill Restaurant (licensed) off mill yard. Children's menu during school holidays. Mill Pantry serves snacks and ice-cream

👶 Baby-changing facilities. Baby back-carriers admitted. Front-carrying baby slings and hip-carrying infant seats for loan. Children's play area. Children's trail

▣ Suitable for school groups. Live interpretation. Hands-on activities

🐕 Under close control on estate. On lead only in mill yard

➜ [109:SJ835835] **Bus**: Styal Shuttle 200 ✈ Manchester Airport–Wilmslow. **Station**: Styal, ½ml (not Sun); Manchester Airport 2ml; Wilmslow 2½ml. **Road**: 1½ml N of Wilmslow off B5166, 2ml from M56, exit 5, 10ml S of Manchester. Heritage signs from A34 and M56

P Parking, 200yds. Cars £3.60, motorcycles £2, coaches £15 unless booked

NT properties nearby
Alderley Edge, Dunham Massey, Lyme Park, Tatton Park

Rufford Old Hall

200 Liverpool Road, Rufford, nr Ormskirk, Lancashire L40 1SG

⊤ 1936   (5:C6)

One of Lancashire's finest 16th-century Tudor buildings

Step back in time at one of Lancashire's finest 16th-century Tudor buildings, where a young Will Shakespeare once performed. His stage, the Great Hall, is as spectacular today as when the Bard was performing for the owner, Sir Thomas Hesketh, and his raucous guests. Wander around the house and marvel over the fine collections of furniture, arms, armour and tapestries. Then step outside and soak up the gardens, topiary and sculpture and enjoy a walk in the woodlands, alongside the canal. Complete your visit with some delicious, freshly prepared local food in the cosy tea-room.

⭐ An admission charge may apply to NT members for special events

ℹ️ **T** 01704 821254
E ruffordoldhall@nationaltrust.org.uk

🚶 By arrangement

The Study at Rufford Old Hall

Please remember – your membership card is always needed for free admission

Rufford Old Hall

Garden/shop/restaurant			M	T	W	T	F	S	S
1 Mar–9 Mar	12–4							**S**	**S**
House									
15 Mar–2 Nov	1–5		**M**	**T**	**W**	T	F	**S**	**S**
Garden									
15 Mar–2 Nov	11–5:30		**M**	**T**	**W**	T	F	**S**	**S**
Shop/restaurant									
15 Mar–2 Nov	11–5		**M**	**T**	**W**	T	F	**S**	**S**
Garden/shop/restaurant									
7 Nov–21 Dec	12–4		M	T	W	T	**F**	**S**	**S**

Open Good Fri. Christmas gifts available Weds & Thurs in Dec 12–4

Indoor and open-air plays and concerts. Victorian Christmas fair. Children's activities, inc. crafts and world-famous gnome hunt

Short canal and woodland walk

Building Grounds

The Old Kitchen Tea-room (licensed). Winter opening and Christmas dinners, tel. for details. Children's menu

Baby-changing facilities. Front-carrying baby slings for loan. Children's guide. Children's quiz/trail. Bottle-warming service. Early learning toys

Suitable for school groups. Education room/ centre. Hands-on activities. Adult study days

On leads and only in grounds, not in formal gardens

→ [108:SD462161] **Foot**: adjoins towpath of Rufford extension of Leeds–Liverpool Canal. **Bus**: Stagecoach in Lancashire 101 Preston–Ormskirk, Suns only; otherwise J & S 347 Southport–Chorley. **Station**: Rufford (U), not Sun, ½ml; Burscough Bridge 2½ml. **Road**: 7ml N of Ormskirk, in village of Rufford on E side of A59. From M6 exit 27, follow signs for Parbold then Rufford

P Free parking, 10yds. Car park can be very busy on summer days. Limited coach parking

NT properties nearby
Formby, Gawthorpe Hall, Speke Hall, Garden and Estate

Sizergh Castle and Garden

Sizergh, nr Kendal, Cumbria LA8 8AE

1950 (6:E8)

Beautiful medieval house, extended in Elizabethan times, surrounded by rich gardens and estate in Cumbria's special limestone country

This imposing house, at the gateway to the Lake District, stands proud in a rich and beautiful garden with a pond, a lake, an important collection of hardy ferns and a superb limestone rock garden. The estate is crossed with footpaths, giving stunning views over Morecambe Bay and the Lakeland hills. Still lived in by the Strickland family, Sizergh has many tales to tell, showing centuries-old portraits, fine furniture and ceramics collections alongside modern-day family photos – it certainly feels lived in! The exceptional wood panelling culminates in the Inlaid Chamber, previously at the Victoria & Albert, and returned here in 1999. Take time to explore the house and garden, sample fine local produce in our contemporary café: then follow one of our trail leaflets around the estate.

i **T** 015395 60951
E sizergh@nationaltrust.org.uk

See website for details

Country walks on estate. Leaflets available from reception, shop and castle

Building Grounds

Sizergh Castle and Garden

Castle			M	T	W	T	F	S	S
17 Mar–2 Nov	1–5		**M**	**T**	**W**	**T**	F	S	**S**
Garden									
17 Mar–2 Nov	11–5		**M**	**T**	**W**	**T**	F	S	**S**
Café/shop									
1 Feb–16 Mar	11–4		M	T	W	T	F	**S**	**S**
17 Mar–2 Nov	11–5		**M**	**T**	**W**	**T**	F	S	**S**
8 Nov–21 Dec	11–4		M	T	W	T	F	**S**	**S**

Café/shop (only) open daily Feb 08 half-term, 9–24 Feb, and 26 Dec–2 Jan 09, 11–4. Also open Sat/Sun in Jan 09

Unless indicated, last admission is always 30mins before closing time

Herbaceous border in the garden at Sizergh Castle

[📦] NT shop. Plant sales

[☕] Café

[👶] Baby-changing facilities. Front-carrying baby slings and hip-carrying infant seats for loan. Children's guide. Children's quiz/trail

[📷] Suitable for school groups. Adult study days

[🐕] On public footpaths, not in garden

[→] [97:SD498878] 3½ml S of Kendal.
Foot: footpaths 530002 and 530003 pass by Sizergh Castle. **Cycle**: NCN6, 1½ml. Regional route 20 passes main gate. **Bus**: Stagecoach in Cumbria 555/6 Keswick–Lancaster (passing close ▣ Lancaster); 552/3 Kendal–Arnside (passing ▣ Arnside). All pass ▣ Kendal. **Station**: Oxenholme 3ml.
Road: M6 exit 36 then A590 towards Kendal, take Barrow-in-Furness turning and follow brown signs. From Lake District take A591 S then A590 towards Barrow-in-Furness

[P] Parking, 250yds

NT properties nearby
Arnside, including Arnside Knott, Heathwaite and Red Hills Wood, Fell Foot Park, Townend

Speke Hall, Garden and Estate

The Walk, Liverpool L24 1XD

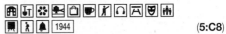 **1944** (5:C8)

Superb Tudor house with rich interiors, along with fine gardens and estate. Close to Liverpool City Centre – but with room to breathe

This rambling, atmospheric house spans the centuries – with a fine Great Hall and priest hole from the 16th century and an Oak Parlour and smaller cosy rooms from the Victorian era. Jacobean plasterwork and intricately carved furniture complete the picture. The fully equipped Victorian kitchen and servants' hall give a fascinating 'below stairs' experience. A lively trail and Tracker Packs, along with objects from the Dairy to be picked up and wondered over, mean children will be entertained. While the 21st-century Podcast tours will delight you, and perhaps even your teenagers. Wander through the garden for all seasons and enjoy spring bulbs, roses, summer borders, a delightful stream and autumn colour.

Speke Hall, Garden and Estate

House		M	T	W	T	F	S	S
15 Mar–2 Nov	1–5:30	M	T	**W**	**T**	**F**	**S**	**S**
8 Nov–14 Dec	1–4:30	M	T	W	T	F	**S**	**S**
Grounds								
15 Mar–2 Nov	11–5:30	M	**T**	**W**	**T**	**F**	**S**	**S**
4 Nov–31 Jan 09	11–dusk	M	**T**	**W**	**T**	**F**	**S**	**S**
Home Farm/restaurant/shop								
15 Mar–13 Jul	11–5	M	T	**W**	**T**	**F**	**S**	**S**
15 Jul–14 Sep	11–5	M	**T**	**W**	**T**	**F**	**S**	**S**
17 Sep–2 Nov	11–5	M	T	**W**	**T**	**F**	**S**	**S**
8 Nov–14 Dec	11–4:30	M	T	W	T	F	**S**	**S**

Open BH Mons. Grounds (garden and estate) closed
24–26 Dec, 31 Dec, 1 Jan 09

Woodland walks give fabulous views of the
North Wales hills and Mersey basin, while Home
Farm, a model Victorian farm building, houses
our shop and restaurant serving local food.
There is also an orchard and children's play area.

What's new in 2008 Children's Tracker Packs
and new house and garden trails. Behind-the-
scenes tours. Podcast tours of the house on MP3
players, narrated by local young adults. This
year Liverpool is European Capital of Culture
2008. For details visit www.liverpool08.com

⭐ Speke Hall is administered and financed by
the NT with the help of a grant from the
National Museums Liverpool

ℹ️ **T** 0844 800 4799 (Infoline), 0151 427 7231
E spekehall@nationaltrust.org.uk

🚶 Tudor tours by costumed guides when house
open, £1. Tours of the roof space, £3 (£2 NT
members). Victorian taster tours of the house
before we open to the public, £3, child £2
(NT members £2, child £1)

🎧 Podcast tours, available on MP3 players

🎭 Including Easter trails, Hallowe'en and
Christmas family events. Open-air theatre and
living history

🚶 Walks on The Bund and elsewhere on the
estate. Leaflet guide. Family estate trail
available at reception

♿ 🚻 🅰️ 🔦 🐕 📷 📷 📷 🅿️ 🅳 🚼
Building ♿ ♿ **Grounds** ♿ ➡️

📷 At Home Farm

🍴 Home Farm Restaurant 500yds from house.
Locally sourced produce. Children's menu

👶 Baby-changing and feeding facilities. Front-
carrying baby slings and hip-carrying infant
seats for loan. Children's play area. Children's
guide. Children's quiz/trail. Tracker Packs and
MP3 audio tours of the house for loan.
Pushchairs and back-carriers admitted at the
Home Farm centre only. Family estate trail

🖼️ Suitable for school groups. Education room/
centre. Live interpretation. Hands-on activities

🐕 On leads on woodland and signed estate walks

➡️ [108:SJ419825] **Cycle**: NCN62, 1¾ml.
Bus: Arriva 80A, Liverpool Great Charlotte
Street–Liverpool Airport (passing 🚆 Liverpool
South Parkway) and close Liverpool Lime
Street); 500 🚆 Liverpool Lime Street–Liverpool
Airport; Supertravel 886 🚆 Liverpool South
Parkway–Liverpool Airport. All to within ½ml.
Station: Liverpool South Parkway 2ml; Hunt's
Cross 2ml. **Road**: on N bank of Mersey, 1ml
off A561 W Liverpool Airport. Follow airport
signs from M62 exit 6, A5300; M56 exit 12

🅿️ Free parking, 100yds

NT properties nearby
Formby, 20 Forthlin Road, Mr Hardman's
Photographic Studio, Mendips, Rufford Old Hall

The rambling, atmospheric Speke Hall

Stagshaw Garden

Ambleside, Cumbria LA22 0HE

1957 **(6:D8)**

Steep woodland garden, noted for its flowering shrubs

The garden was created by the late Cubby Acland, Regional Agent for the Trust. It contains a fine collection of shrubs, including rhododendrons, azaleas and camellias. Adjacent to the garden are Skelghyll Woods, which offer delightful walks and access to the fells beyond.

No WC

T 015394 46027
E stagshaw@nationaltrust.org.uk

Grounds

Pushchairs admitted. Steep paths in places, with steps

[90:NY380029] **Ferry**: landing at Waterhead ½ml. **Bus**: Stagecoach in Cumbria 555/6, 599 from Windermere. **Station**: Windermere 4ml. **Road**: ½ml S of Ambleside on A591

Free parking. Not suitable for coaches. Very limited; access dangerous due to poor visibility; further pay & display parking for cars and coaches (not NT) ½ml at Waterhead

NT properties nearby
Ambleside, Townend, Windermere and Troutbeck

Stagshaw Garden		
1 Apr–30 Jun	10–6:30	M T W T F S S
July to end Oct: by appointment, send sae to Property Office, St Catherine's, Patterdale Road, Windermere LA23 1NH		

Tatton Park

Knutsford, Cheshire WA16 6QN

1960 **(5:D8)**

Award-winning estate with neo-classical mansion, 20 hectares (50 acres) of gardens, working farm, set in 400-hectare (1,000-acre) deer park

This is one of the most complete historic estates open to visitors. The early 19th-century Wyatt house sits amid a landscaped deer park and is opulently decorated, providing a fine setting for the Egerton family's collections of pictures, books, china, glass, silver and specially commissioned Gillows furniture. The theme of Victorian grandeur extends into the garden, with its Fernery, Orangery, Rose Garden, Tower Garden, Pinetum, and Italian and Japanese gardens. The restored Walled Garden includes a Kitchen Garden and magnificent glasshouses, where traditional methods of gardening are used. Other features include a 1930s working rare breeds farm, a children's play area, speciality shops and 400-hectare (1,000-acre) deer park.

What's new in 2008 Fully restored Pinery Vinery in the Walled Garden. Changing exhibitions in the mansion exhibition rooms

Tatton Park is financed, administered and maintained by Cheshire County Council. Without this commitment the Trust would not have been able to acquire this property. Members have free admission to the house and gardens only, except during special events, and half-price entry to the farm. Members must pay car entry charges, and full admission to any special events, such as the RHS Flower Show on 23–27 July

T 01625 374435 (Infoline), 01625 374400
E tatton@cheshire.gov.uk

The heather-thatched African hut at Tatton Park

For information regarding prices, see page 10

Tatton Park

House									
15 Mar–28 Sep	1–5	M	**T**	**W**	**T**	**F**	**S**	**S**

Gardens/shop									
15 Mar–28 Sep*	10–6	M	**T**	**W**	**T**	**F**	**S**	**S**
30 Sep–31 Jan 09	11–4	M	**T**	**W**	**T**	**F**	**S**	**S**

Restaurant									
15 Mar–28 Sep	10–6	**M**	**T**	**W**	**T**	**F**	**S**	**S**
30 Sep–31 Jan 09	11–4	M	**T**	**W**	**T**	**F**	**S**	**S**

Open BH Mons. *Shop open 10:30–5, 15 Mar–28 Sept. Park closes 1hr later than garden. Last admission 1hr before closing. House: special opening Oct half-term and Christmas events in Dec. Guided tours Tues–Sun 12 by timed ticket (available from garden entrance after 10:30) on first-come, first-served basis. Limited number of tickets. For prices and opening times for other attractions please contact Tatton Park. Tel. 01625 374400 or visit www.tattonpark.org.uk. Closed 25 Dec

🎭 Guided tours of mansion and Tudor Old Hall (booked groups only). Tours of the Japanese Garden on Weds and Sats

🎭 RHS Flower Show in July and Hallé concert in Aug. Open-air theatre and concerts throughout the season. Antique fairs, car shows, family events at the farm and historical festivals. Christmas events. See website for details

🚶 Some waymarked walks. Walks leaflets available

♿ 🚻🔊📷📹 Building 🏛♿ Grounds 🏛➡️♿

🏠 Tatton Gifts (not NT). Award-winning, expanded Housekeeper's Store selling estate and local food produce. Garden shop selling plants, gifts and seasonal produce from the Kitchen Garden

🍴 Stables Restaurant (not NT) (licensed) in stableyard. Serves hot and cold food throughout the day from quality local ingredients. Children's menu. Tuck shop adjacent to restaurant selling ice-creams and snacks in high season

👪 Baby-changing facilities. Front-carrying baby slings for loan. Children's play area. Children's quiz/trail

🏫 Suitable for school groups. Education room/centre. Live interpretation. Hands-on activities. Adult study days

🐕 On leads at farm and under close control in park. Not in gardens

🚲 Cycle hire available from stableyard. Tel. 01827 284646

➔ [109/118:SJ745815] **Cycle**: Cheshire Cycleway passes property. **Bus**: Bakers 27 from Macclesfield (passing close ➤ Macclesfield) weekends only; Big House Bus Chester–Manchester Airport, Suns April–Sept only; otherwise from surrounding areas to Knutsford, then 2ml. **Station**: Knutsford 2ml. **Road**: 2ml N of Knutsford, 4ml S of Altrincham, 5ml from M6, exit 19; 3ml from M56, exit 7, well signposted on A556; entrance on Ashley Road, 1½ml NE of junction A5034 with A50

🅿 Parking £4.50 (disabled £2.50), charge inc. NT members

NT properties nearby
Alderley Edge, Dunham Massey, Little Moreton Hall, Lyme Park, Quarry Bank Mill and Styal Estate

Townend

Troutbeck, Windermere, Cumbria LA23 1LB

🏠 🌸 🛡 👪 🏫 1948   **(6:D8)**

17th-century Lake District stone and slate house, former home of a wealthy farming family

A real Lakeland hidden treasure set in the beautiful village of Troutbeck, this 17th-century solid stone and slate house sits imposingly on the hillside, its huge chimneys typical of the area. The Brownes lived here for generations, a wealthy, hardworking family, who loved wood carving, books and furniture, and collected them in this homely place. See fascinating kitchen and domestic tools, along with period clothing and the cosy servants' rooms. Our children's trail brings it all to life. A real fire in the 'down house' most days makes this a 'must do' visit when in the Lake District.

Townend									
15 Mar–30 Mar	1–4	M	T	**W**	**T**	**F**	**S**	**S**
2 Apr–26 Oct	1–5	M	T	**W**	**T**	**F**	**S**	**S**
29 Oct–2 Nov	1–4	M	T	**W**	**T**	**F**	**S**	**S**

Open BH Mons. May close early due to poor light

Many Trust properties are offering Gift Aid on Entry for non-members, see page 10

Townend at Troutbeck, Cumbria

[i] **T** 015394 32628
E townend@nationaltrust.org.uk

[icon] Conservation demonstrations. Living history, 1st and 3rd Sat of each month and Thurs during local school hols

[icons] **Building** [icon] **Grounds** [icon]

[icon] Hip-carrying infant seats for loan. Children's quiz/trail

[icon] Suitable for school groups. Live interpretation. Hands-on activities

[→] [90:NY407023] 3ml SE of Ambleside at S end of Troutbeck village. **Bus**: Stagecoach in Cumbria 555/6, 599 from [rail] Windermere, alight Troutbeck Bridge, then 1½ml. **Station**: Windermere 2½ml. **Road**: off A591 or A592

[P] Free parking, 300yds. Coaches must apply to Cumbria Highways Department for permission to use a restricted road if visiting Townend. Tel. property for guidance. Minibuses can access Townend, and this may be a preferable option for groups

NT properties nearby
Fell Foot Park, Stagshaw Garden, Windermere and Troutbeck

Ullswater and Aira Force

Tower Buildings, Watermillock, Penrith, Cumbria
CA11 0JS

[icons] 1906   (6:D7)

Beautiful lake winding through a glaciated valley, and an impressive waterfall

Dramatic walks around Aira Force waterfall, renowned in Victorian times as a beauty spot, provides one of the highlights of the Trust's

---

Ullswater and Aira Force							
All year	M	T	W	T	F	S	S

ownership in the valley. This totals 5,242 hectares (13,000 acres) of fell and woodland, and four farms (including Glencoyne, the largest). There is access to parts of Brotherswater and Ullswater, site of Wordsworth's famous daffodils.

[i] **T** 017684 82067
E ullswater@nationaltrust.org.uk

[icons] **Grounds** [icons]

[icon] Tea-room (not NT) at Aira Force. Tel. 017684 82881. Tea-room (not NT) at Side Farm, Patterdale. Tel. 017684 82337 (walkers only, no parking)

[icon] Steps and slopes to waterfall at Aira Force, difficult for pushchairs

[icon] Suitable for school groups

[→] [90:NY401203] 7ml S of Penrith. **Cycle**: NCN71, 2ml. **Bus**: Stagecoach in Cumbria 108 [rail] Penrith–Patterdale. **Station**: Penrith 10ml

[P] Parking. Two pay & display car parks at Aira Force and Glencoyne Bay. NT members must display cards. Coaches by arrangement

NT properties nearby
Acorn Bank Garden and Watermill, Townend

Wasdale, Eskdale and Duddon

The Lodge, Wasdale Hall, Wasdale, Cumbria
CA20 1ET

[icons] 1929   (6:C8)

Vast area of open country – valleys, mountains, rivers and lake – from wild Wasdale to the Duddon Estuary

In Wasdale the Trust owns England's highest mountain, Scafell Pike (978m), and deepest lake, Wastwater, which has impressive scree slopes. The six valley farms are also owned by the Trust, as are the surrounding mountains – including Great Gable and the famous historic

Wasdale, Eskdale and Duddon							
All year	M	T	W	T	F	S	S

wall patterns at the valley head. Lower down the valley is the wooded and tranquil 600-hectare (1,482-acre) Nether Wasdale Estate with six farms. Over 5,000 hectares (12,300 acres) and eleven farms are protected in neighbouring Eskdale, with extensive areas of fell, six farms and Hardknott Roman Fort. In the beautiful and quiet Duddon Valley the Trust cares for 3,300 hectares (8,000 acres) and nine farms.

★ The stunningly located NT campsite at Wasdale Head (with WC for the less able) and shop are open Easter to end Oct (and Nov to Easter 2009 with limited facilities) [NY183076]; charge (inc. NT members). Tel. or visit www.wasdalecampsite.org.uk for details

i T 019467 26064
E wasdale@nationaltrust.org.uk

♿ Grounds 🪑

▥ Suitable for school groups

➜ [NY152055] Wasdale–Wastwater: 5ml E of A595 Cumbrian coast road from Barrow to Whitehaven, turning at Gosforth. Also from Santon Bridge. Eskdale [NY177013]–Boot: 6ml E of A595, turning at Eskdale Green. Also from Santon Bridge. Duddon [NY196932]–Ulpha: 3ml N of A595, turning at Duddon Bridge near Broughton-in-Furness. **Station**: Drigg 8ml; Dalegarth (Ravenglass & Eskdale Rly) ¼ml from Eskdale; Foxfield 8ml from Duddon; Seascale 8ml from Wasdale

P Parking (NT pay & display) at Wasdale Head

NT properties nearby
Dalton Castle, Sandscale Haws

Wasdale Head and Illgill Head

Windermere and Troutbeck (including Bridge House)

St Catherine's, Patterdale Road, Windermere, Cumbria LA23 1NH

🏠 🏛 🍽 🏚 🛡 ▥ ♿ 🐕 1927   **(6:D8)**

Fine varied walking country around popular Lake Windermere

This property includes the beautiful and secluded head of the Troutbeck Valley, as well as several sites next to Windermere and eleven farms. One of these, Troutbeck Park, was once owned by Beatrix Potter and was her largest farm. Ambleside Roman Fort, tiny Bridge House in Ambleside and Cockshott Point on the lake at Bowness-on-Windermere are all popular places to visit. Footpaths lead from Ambleside over Wansfell to the Troutbeck Valley and offer high-level views and contrasting valley landscapes. A Community Learning Officer is based at the property and educational group visits and other activities can be arranged.

What's new in 2008 Exciting education programme for school groups

★ No WC
i T 015394 46027
E windermere@nationaltrust.org.uk

🛡 Annual out-and-about events

♿ Grounds 🪑 ➡

▥ Suitable for school groups. New 'Footprint' learning centre available by arrangement

➜ [90:NY407023] **Bus**: Stagecoach in Cumbria 555/6, 599 from ⛳ Windermere, alight Troutbeck Bridge, then 1½ml walk. **Station**: Windermere 2½ml. **Road**: Troutbeck is signposted E of A591 Windermere to Ambleside road

P Car parks (not NT)

NT properties nearby
Fell Foot Park, Stagshaw Garden, Townend

Windermere and Troutbeck							
All year	M	T	W	T	F	S	S

Charges for National Trust members apply on some special event days

Wordsworth House

Main Street, Cockermouth, Cumbria CA13 9RX

🏠 ✴ 🏛 👕 🎋 🎭 👬 🖼 1938   **(6:C7)**

Birthplace and childhood home of William Wordsworth – a 'living' 1770s townhouse

Step back to the 1770s and experience life as William and his sister Dorothy might have done. Meet and talk to the household staff as you explore this award-winning property. Many of the rooms are there for you to enjoy as if you were a guest of the Wordsworth family – there are even toys for the children to play with and books to read. The maid will show you the Georgian kitchen and you can enjoy tastings of recipes popular at the time (18th-century Cumberland food is cooked in the kitchen daily). You may meet the clerk in the office used by William's father and test your writing skill with quill pen and ink; you may also hear music from the harpsichord drifting through the house. William loved his home, and refers to the views and the River Derwent in his poem *The Prelude*. The peaceful walled garden grows flowers, fruit, herbs and vegetables of the period – all of which are used in the house. The Discovery Room has interactive touch screens and fascinating research material. For a preview go to www.wordsworthhouse.org.uk then come and visit us in person.

A maid in the kitchen at Wordsworth House

Wordsworth House									
House									
12 Mar–1 Nov	11–4:30	**M**	**T**	**W**	**T**	**F**	**S**	S
Shop									
5 Mar–23 Dec	10–5	**M**	**T**	**W**	**T**	**F**	**S**	S
2 Jan–26 Jan 09	10–4	M	T	**W**	**T**	**F**	**S**	S

Admission by timed ticket available from visitor reception. Open BH Mons: 11–4:30. Education groups: 27 March–27 Oct: Tues, Wed & Thur 9:30–11 and at other times by arrangement. Booking essential

What's new in 2008 More to see and do in the Discovery Room. Regular harpsichord recitals, please check website for details

ℹ️ **T** 01900 820884 (Infoline), 01900 824805
E wordsworthhouse@nationaltrust.org.uk

🎭 Family activities in school holidays: trails, art and craft activities and games. Talks in the garden and the house. Regular cooking and harpsichord demonstrations. Georgian Fair on 3 May and local Cockermouth festival in the summer. Evening events and study days

♿ 🚻 🦽 ⠿ 📷 📖 Building 🦽 ↕

Grounds 🦽

🍽 Refreshments available at nearby cafés

👶 Baby-changing facilities

🖼 Suitable for school groups. Education room/centre. Live interpretation. Hands-on activities. Adult study days

🐕 On leads in front garden only

➡️ [89:NY118307] **Foot**: close to all town car parks and bus stop. **Cycle**: NCN71 (C2C), 7ml. NCN10 (Reivers) passes door. **Bus**: Stagecoach in Cumbria X4/5 🚂 Penrith–Workington; AA/Hoban/Reay's 35/6 Workington–Cockermouth. All pass close 🚂 Workington. **Station**: Workington 8ml, Maryport 6½ml. **Road**: just off A66, in Cockermouth town centre

🅿 No parking on site. Parking in town centre car parks. Long stay car park (not NT) 300yds on Wakefield Road, walk back over footbridge to house

NT properties nearby
Borrowdale: Force Crag Mine, Buttermere and Ennerdale, Derwent Island House

Parking in National Trust car parks is free for members displaying stickers

Yorkshire is world renowned for the beauty and scale of its scenery, and many of the county's most outstanding stretches of coast and countryside are in the care of the National Trust.

The Malham Tarn Estate and Upper Wharfedale contain some of the finest upland landscapes in the Yorkshire Dales, with limestone pavements, waterfalls, and flower-rich hay meadows criss-crossed with stone walls and studded with traditional field barns.

Caring for nearly 3,000 hectares (7,500 acres) in Malhamdale, the National Trust has waymarked walks and trails throughout the Dales. From Malham Cove to Fountains Fell, go for a ramble, a circular walk or follow a trail across the ancient limestone pavements. Take a route around Malham Tarn which, with adjacent areas of raised bog, fen and woodland, is protected as a National Nature Reserve.

This special area is home to a unique community of rare plants and animals, as well as being the focal point of an outstanding area of classic upland limestone country.

The limestone pavements in the Dales are a unique and irreplaceable habitat that has formed as a result of erosion by water over the centuries. Today it supports unusual and diverse plant communities. Visitors can discover more by joining one of the summer wildflower walks in Malhamdale or Upper Wharfedale hosted by the Trust.

There are many hidden delights on the edge of Hebden Bridge, including upland hay meadows, woodland walks and, in the spring, swathes of bluebells. Hardcastle Crags has a spectacular landscape. Formed by nature and shaped by man, it provides many varied wildlife habitats and so is home to an abundance of flora and fauna. There are waymarked walks and footpaths to follow across the estate for all to explore.

There is also a strong industrial past to the property, for at its heart sits 19th-century Gibson Mill, a former cotton mill and entertainments emporium. Now the mill is a flagship example of sustainable tourism, as it operates solely on green energies. The mill has no mains electricity, gas or water, and the only outside service is a telephone line.

Above: **limestone pavement, Darnbrook** Bottom: **Hardcastle Crags**

Previous page: enjoying the view from Buckstones Moss, on the Marsden Moor Estate (5:E7)

Right: **Brimham Rocks** Below: **Runswick Bay** Bottom: **Ravenscar**

Come and learn more about our social heritage and use our hands-on activities and displays to discover how we can all do more to make our homes green.

From amazing Jurassic rock formations to ancient woodland dating  from the last Ice Age, the Bridestones Estate on the North Yorkshire Moors is the perfect family retreat.

The landscape offers stunning views – panoramic from the summit of Blakey Topping – and the estate holds regular wildlife walks in the summer for visitors of all ages. These offer a fun way of learning more about life in the countryside. Whether you are interested in moths and butterflies or minibeasts and birds, there will be something to capture your interest – be it bug-hunting or stream-dipping. Just remember, wellies are a must.

Over near Pateley Bridge is Brimham Rocks, a remarkable location that includes strange and fantastic geological rock formations. Explore by foot and discover the Flower Pot, the Turtle, Lover's Leap, the Anvil, the Druid's Writing Desk and the Castle Rock – you can even see a Dancing Bear!

Formed by millions of years of geological movement, ice ages and the erosive effects of the sun, wind and rain, these marvellous natural structures stand at a height of nearly 300 metres.

Many of Yorkshire's finest stretches of coastline are in the care of the National Trust. From Runswick Bay and Port Mulgrave, down past Ravenscar, Staithes to Cayton Bay and Newbiggin cliffs, the beaches of the east coast take you back to a time when dinosaurs roamed the Earth. With a wealth of rock pools, they also provide an opportunity to search for marine minibeasts of all shapes and sizes.

www.nationaltrust.org.uk/coastandcountryside

At the Old Coastguard Station in Robin Hood's Bay explore the hidden depths of the marine aquarium and, using the interactive exhibitions, discover the story of the cliffs, the power of the weather and witness the immense force of the tide.

To really get away from it all take a walk on Marsden Moor. This windswept landscape appears bleak and inhospitable, but provides grazing for cattle and sheep and is home to birds such as golden plover, red grouse, curlew, snipe and the diminutive twite – so much so that the estate is designated as an international Special Protection Area for birds.

Footpaths across the moor sometimes follow ancient packhorse routes, from where it is possible to glimpse evidence of the estate's industrial past. Come and stand high on the open moor, with the mist swirling round, and thoughts of man's first contact with the area thousands of years ago come flooding to mind.

It is easy to imagine the Mesolithic hunters huddled around their camp fire, and you can almost hear the chink of

Above: **Marsden Moor** Right: grouse Below: **Robin Hood's Bay**

armour of the Roman centurions, who marched from Chester to York. More recently the moors would have echoed with the rattle made by the pack horses' harness and the clatter of the workers' clogs.

Walking at Marsden is not always for the faint-hearted – join one of many guided walks with our volunteers and discover stunning views, inspiring history and a rich variety of moorland.

Beningbrough Hall and Gardens

Beningbrough, York, North Yorkshire YO30 1DD

1958 (5:G4)

18th-century house with interactive galleries and National Portrait Gallery paintings. Grounds and working walled garden

A grand 1716 Georgian mansion with an impressive baroque interior, set in a park and gardens. There are more than 100 18th-century portraits and seven interpretation galleries, designed in partnership with the National Portrait Gallery. There is a fully equipped Victorian laundry, with wet and dry rooms, and a delightful walled garden which supplies The Walled Garden Restaurant. There are many family facilities, including a wilderness play area.

What's new in 2008 New visiting portrait exhibition from the National Portrait Gallery's collection, together with innovative hands-on activities in seven interpretation galleries, designed to enhance the visitor's understanding and enjoyment of portraiture. A recently installed

Vaulted corridor on the first floor at Beningbrough Hall, North Yorkshire

lift gives access to all floors. The House Galleries (top floor), garden and grounds, shop and restaurant are now open winter weekends (except Christmas and New Year)

⭐ Some ground and first-floor rooms have no electric light. Visitors wishing to make a close study of the interior and portraits should avoid dull days early and late in the season

ℹ **T** 01904 472027
E beningbrough@nationaltrust.org.uk

Garden walks most weekends. 'Living history with the Victorian laundry maid' (usually last Sat in month)

Free audio guides for the house, including programme for visually impaired people

Programme of events, summer concerts and themed restaurant evenings

Public footpath along the River Ouse. Permitted walk through the Pike Pond Woods

Building [symbols] **Grounds** [symbol]

NT shop and small plant centre, second-hand bookshop and artworks for sale

Beningbrough Hall and Gardens									
Grounds/shop/restaurant		M	T	W	T	F	S	S
2 Feb–3 Feb	11–3:30						S	S
9 Feb–17 Feb	11–3:30	M	T	W			S	S
23 Feb–24 Feb	11–3:30						S	S
1 Mar–30 Jun	11–5:30	M	T	W			S	S
1 Jul–31 Aug	11–5:30	M	T	W	T	F	S	S
1 Sep–29 Oct	11–5:30	M	T	W			S	S
1 Nov–21 Dec	11–3:30						S	S
10 Jan–31 Jan 09	11–3:30						S	S
House								
1 Mar–30 Jun	12–5	M	T	W			S	S
1 Jul–31 Aug	12–5	M	T	W	T	F	S	S
1 Sep–29 Oct	12–5	M	T	W			S	S
Galleries only								
2 Feb–3 Feb	11–3:30						S	S
9 Feb–17 Feb	11–3:30	M	T	W			S	S
23 Feb–24 Feb	11–3:30						S	S
1 Nov–21 Dec	11–3:30						S	S
10 Jan–31 Jan 09	11–3:30						S	S
Open Good Fri. Closed 27, 28 Dec & 3, 4 Jan 09									

Unless indicated, last admission is always 30mins before closing time

☕ Walled Garden Restaurant (licensed). Hot lunches 12–2. Gluten-free and vegan lunch options available (30mins notice required). Children's menu. Kiosk in the garden open on busy days. Special themed evening functions. Restaurant uses produce from the walled garden and mainly local and organic suppliers

♿ Baby-changing facilities. Hip-carrying infant seats for loan. Wilderness play area including large fort. Children's art activities. Children's activities linked to the portraits in the house

▣ Suitable for school groups. Education room/centre. Live interpretation (Victorian below stairs). Portrait-themed art activities. Hands-on interpretation. Outreach programme for rural schools. Community groups welcome

🚲 2ml of NT-permitted cycle path through parkland. NT-Sustrans leaflet available

➡ [105:SE516586] **Foot**: footpath from York, along R. Ouse, 10ml. **Cycle**: NCN65. **Bus**: Stephensons/Hutchinson 31/A/X York–Easingwold. **Station**: York 8ml. **Road**: 8ml NW of York, 2ml W of Shipton, 2ml SE of Linton-on-Ouse (A19)

🅿 Free parking, 100yds. Coaches must come via A19 and use coach entrance. No coach access from the west via Aldwark toll bridge

NT properties nearby
Fountains Abbey and Studley Royal, Nunnington Hall, Rievaulx Terrace and Temples, Treasurer's House

Braithwaite Hall

East Witton, Leyburn, North Yorkshire DL8 4SY

🏠 1941 (5:E3)

17th-century farmhouse in beautiful Coverdale

★ No WC

ℹ **T** 01969 640287
E braithwaitehall@nationaltrust.org.uk

➡ 1½ml SW of Middleham, 2ml W of East Witton (A6108). Narrow approach road

Braithwaite Hall
1st & 3rd Wed April–Sept, 2–5. Tel. the tenant, Mrs Duffus, in advance

Bridestones, Crosscliff and Blakey Topping

c/o Peakside, Ravenscar, Scarborough, North Yorkshire YO13 0NE

1944 (5:I3)

Moorland nature reserve with peculiar rock formations

The Bridestones and Crosscliff Estate covers an area of 488 hectares (1,205 acres) and is a mixture of farmland, open moorland and woodland. Bridestones Moor – named after its peculiar rock formations created from sandstone laid down under the sea during the Jurassic period – is a SSSI and nature reserve with typical moorland vegetation, including three species of heather, an ancient woodland estimated to date from the end of the last Ice Age, and herb-rich meadows. The Bridestones Nature Trail is approximately 1½ miles long and leads visitors through a range of habitats. Blakey Topping at the northern end of Crosscliff Moor is the result of massive erosion by glacial meltwater and now gives a superb 360° view from its summit.

★ Access by car is via Forest Enterprise's Forest Drive: toll payable (inc. NT members). WC at Staindale Lake car park

ℹ **T** 01723 870423
E bridestones@nationaltrust.org.uk

🎪 Children's events during summer hols

♿ Grounds

♿ Children's events during summer hols

▣ Suitable for school groups. Hands-on activities. Adult study days

🐕 On leads only

➡ [94:SE877906] In North York Moors National Park. **Foot**: from Hole of Horcum via Old Wives' Way. **Cycle**: along Forest Drive. **Bus**: to Bridestones: Moorsbus from Thornton le Dale (connections from York and Scarborough), Sun, April–Oct and daily in Aug; otherwise Yorkshire Coastline 840 Leeds–Whitby (passing ✇ York) to within 2¼ml.

Bridestones
All year M T W T F S S

To Blakey Topping: Yorkshire Coastliner as above, but to within 1½ml. **Road**: 3½ml along Dalby Forest Drive (toll payable) which starts 2½ml N of Thornton-le-Dale NE of Pickering

P Free parking (not NT), 100yds. Further parking at Staindale Lake, Crosscliff Viewpoint or Hole of Horcum (for Blakey Topping)

NT properties nearby
Nunnington Hall, Ormesby Hall, Rievaulx Terrace and Temples, Yorkshire Coast

Brimham Rocks									
All year	8−dusk	**M**	**T**	**W**	**T**	**F**	**S**	**S**
Shop/exhibition/kiosk									
9 Feb−17 Feb	11−5	**M**	**T**	**W**	**T**	**F**	**S**	**S**
15 Mar−18 May	11−5	M	T	W	T	**F**	**S**	**S**
24 May−5 Oct	11−5	**M**	**T**	**W**	**T**	**F**	**S**	**S**
11 Oct−2 Nov	11−5	M	T	W	T	**F**	**S**	**S**
9 Nov−21 Dec	11−dusk	M	T	W	T	F	**S**	**S**

Facilities may close in bad weather. Shop, kiosk and exhibition room open daily during local school holidays, also BHols, 26 Dec & 1 Jan 09, weather permitting

Brimham Rocks

Summerbridge, Harrogate, North Yorkshire
HG3 4DW

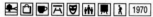 1970   (5:F4)

Dramatic moorland rock formations

At a height of nearly 300 metres, Brimham Rocks enjoy spectacular views over the surrounding countryside. Set within the Nidderdale Area of Outstanding Natural Beauty, this fascinating moorland is filled with strange and fantastic rock formations and is rich in wildlife.

Brimham Rocks, North Yorkshire

★ The property can be extremely busy on fine weekends, particularly from June to August, and Bank Holidays. Car parking is limited and queuing may be necessary. No barbecues please

i **T** 01423 780688
E brimhamrocks@nationaltrust.org.uk

🚶 Guided walks throughout year

♿ 🚻 📷 ⋮⋮ ⌾ 🅳 Building 🔼 🔽
Grounds 🔼

☕ Kiosk near Brimham House. Serves light refreshments

👶 Baby-changing facilities

🎒 Suitable for school groups

🐕 Under strict control at all times and on leads during April, May & June (ground-nesting birds)

→ [99:SE206650] 10ml SW of Ripon.
Foot: Nidderdale Way passes through.
Bus: Arriva 802 Wakefield-Richmond (Suns, May–Sept only) to within 1ml; otherwise Harrogate & District 24 ⊠ Harrogate–Pateley Bridge, alight Summerbridge, 2ml.
Road: 11ml NW of Harrogate off B6165, 10ml SW of Ripon, 4ml E of Pateley Bridge off B6265

P Parking (pay & display). £3.50 up to 4 hrs, £4.50 over 4hrs; motorcycle free; minibus £7 all day; coach £12 all day. Pay machines only accept coins. Coaches cannot be accepted on busy days

NT properties nearby
East Riddlesden Hall, Fountains Abbey and Studley Royal

East Riddlesden Hall

Bradford Road, Keighley, West Yorkshire BD20 5EL

🏰 🏠 ✂️ 🏛️ 🍽️ 🎭 🏕️ 🎭 👪 🖼️ 🚶

🔊 ☕ 1934   (5:E5)

East Riddlesden Hall			
House/shop/tea-room			
15 Mar–2 Nov	12–5		M **T W** T **F S S**

Open Good Fri. Tea-room open from 11 on Suns.
Shop and tea-room may open weekends in Nov/Dec.
Tel. for details

17th-century West Riding manor house with formal and wild gardens, duckpond and grounds

Every time that you stand in the gardens at East Riddlesden you will experience something new – the pink cherry trees, clematis, borders, daffodils and soothing lavender beds all create a sense of tranquillity far removed from the bustle of modern life. The house is a hidden gem above the Aire Valley, where visitors enjoy a picnic and children play. This air of peace is far removed from the Hall's tumultuous past, which includes tales of dastardly deeds that the dark sandstone of the Hall can only hint at on approach. Going into the Hall feels like walking through someone's home, it has a cosy lived-in feel, and creates a relaxing atmosphere where visitors can feel at ease examining the exquisite embroideries and blackwork, oak furniture and pewter.

ℹ️ **T** 01535 607075
E eastriddlesden@nationaltrust.org.uk

🎭 Costumed tours, specialist tours, spooky tours and evening tours available for private groups, subject to availability

🎭 Open-air theatre, children's events and open-air concerts

🚶 A permissive path runs alongside the river

♿ 🚻 🔍 📷 P♿ D♿ Building 🔊 ♿
Grounds 🔊

🛍️ NT shop. Plant sales

☕ Tea-room on first floor of bothy. Children's menu

👪 Baby-changing facilities. Hip-carrying infant seats for loan. Children's play area. Grass maze. Children's events

🖼️ Suitable for school groups. Hands-on activities. Live interpretation in July and Aug on Sun, Mon and Tues

🐕 On leads and only in grounds, not garden

➡️ [104:SE079421] **Bus**: Keighley & District 662 ⏃ Bradford Interchange–Keighley, alight Granby Lane. **Station**: Keighley 1½ml. **Road**: 1ml NE of Keighley on S side of the Bradford Road in Riddlesden, close to Leeds & Liverpool Canal. A629 relief road from Shipley and Skipton signed for East Riddlesden Hall

P Free parking, 100yds. Parking for one coach. Narrow entrance to property. No double-decker coaches

NT properties nearby
Fountains Abbey and Studley Royal, Gawthorpe Hall, Hardcastle Crags, Malham Tarn Estate

East Riddlesden Hall had a tumultuous past but is now a haven of tranquillity

For information regarding prices, see page 10

Ruins of the 12th-century Fountains Abbey, with the Half Moon Pond and weir in the foreground

Fountains Abbey and Studley Royal Water Garden

Fountains, Ripon, North Yorkshire HG4 3DY

🏠 🏚 ✝ 🍴 ♿ 🌳 🏛 📷 🍷 🎫 🎧
🏞 🛡 👪 📷 🚶 ♿ 🔔 🍸 1983   **(5:F4)**

Yorkshire's first World Heritage Site. Cistercian abbey, elegant Georgian water garden and medieval deer park

Set in the beautiful Skell Valley, this World Heritage Site offers a great day out for all the family. Lose yourself in the passages, staircases and towers of the largest monastic ruins in the country and marvel at a unique relic of ancient craftsmanship. Then explore the 12th-century abbey ruins, Elizabethan mansion (three rooms open to the public), medieval deer park and one of England's most spectacular Georgian water gardens – complete with neo-classical statues, follies and breathtaking surprise views. And, if this were not enough, there is also the only surviving 12th-century Cistercian corn mill in Britain, with interactive displays and an exhibition of artefacts from the abbey.

What's new in 2008 Abbey audio tour

⭐ The NT works in partnership with English Heritage to care for this site. EH maintains the Abbey (owned by the NT) and owns St Mary's Church (managed by the NT). Major restoration of Studley Lake

ℹ️ **T** 01765 608888
E fountainsenquiries@nationaltrust.org.uk

🎫 Free volunteer-led guided tours of abbey, deer park and water garden, April–Oct, plus extended tours of complete estate throughout the year. Special Christmas and winter tours

Fountains Abbey and Studley Royal										
Abbey/garden/visitor centre/mill										
1 Mar–31 Oct	10–5	M	T	W	T	F	S	S		
1 Nov–31 Jan 09	10–4	M	T	W	T	F	S	S		
Restaurant										
1 Feb–30 Apr	10–4	M	T	W	T	F	S	S		
1 May–31 Oct	10–5	M	T	W	T	F	S	S		
1 Nov–31 Jan 09	10–4	M	T	W	T	F	S	S		
St Mary's										
1 Apr–30 Sep	12–4	M	T	W	T	F	S	S		
Deer park										
All year	Dawn–dusk	M	T	W	T	F	S	S		

Please note: whole estate closed 24/25 Dec & on Fri in Nov, Dec, Jan 09. Estate open on Fri in Feb. Studley Royal shop and tea-room: opening times vary, check at property

Many Trust properties are offering Gift Aid on Entry for non-members, see page 10

🎧 Available from admissions, £2

🎭 Open-air theatre, inc. Shakespeare and children's classics. Autumn concerts in abbey. Medieval re-enactments. Autumn drive-in. Christmas entertainment. Religious services. Children's trails and craft workshops in school hols

🚶 Walking trails leaflet listing five walks, £1.50 from admissions and shops. Wildlife walks. Guided historical tours. Children's school holiday trails

♿ 🚻 ♿ ♿ ♿ ♿ Grounds ♿ ➡ ♿ ♿

🛍 Two shops, at visitor centre and at entrance to water garden. Plant sales (herbs & flowers)

🍽 Fountains Restaurant (licensed) at visitor centre. Children's menu. Licensed tea-room at entrance to water garden. Kiosk at Fountains Mill (ice-cream and beverages, limited opening)

👶 Baby-changing and feeding facilities. Pushchairs and baby back-carriers admitted. Children's quiz/trail. Children's activities in school holidays. Play area near visitor centre

🎒 Suitable for school groups. Education room/centre

🐕 On short leads only. Enclosed dog walk/WC at visitor centre

🚲 Cycling allowed through the deer park

➡ [99:SE271683] **Foot**: 4ml from Ripon via public footpaths and bridleways. **Cycle**: signed on-road cycle loop. **Bus**: 'Ripon Roweller' 139 from Ripon (with connections from 🚂 Harrogate on Harrogate & District 36); also Hutchinson 812 from 🚂 York, Suns, May–Sep only; Arriva 802 from Leeds, Suns, May–Sept only. **Road**: 4ml W of Ripon off B6265 to Pateley Bridge, signposted from A1, 12ml N of Harrogate (A61)

🅿 Free parking at visitor centre car park. Open March–Oct daily, 9–6:30; Nov–Feb daily except Fri, 9–5:30. Parking at Studley Royal deer park £3 (pay & display). Open March–Oct daily, 9–6; Nov–Feb daily, 9–6. Coach parking at visitor centre only. Access off B6265

NT properties nearby
Beningbrough Hall, Brimham Rocks, East Riddlesden Hall

Goddards Garden

27 Tadcaster Road, York, North Yorkshire
YO24 1GG

🆒 🚶 🖼 👶 [1983]   (5:H5)

Formal and informal gardens with a variety of features

Former home of Noel Goddard Terry of the famous York chocolate-making firm, the house (the Yorkshire office of the NT and not open to the public) was designed in 1927 by Walter Brierley. The garden, designed by George Dillistone, features terraces, a rockery, ponds, borders and a fine collection of shrubs.

What's new in 2008 Plant of the month. New interpretation featuring biography of designer. History of Richardsons of Darlington on display, the company which created the greenhouse

⭐ House not open to public (used as office space)

ℹ **T** 01904 702021
E goddardsgarden@nationaltrust.org.uk

🚶 Tours by arrangement

♿ Grounds ♿ ➡

👶 Pushchairs admitted

🐕 On leads

➡ [105:SE884498] **Bus**: First York 4, 12, 13; Yorkshire Coastliner 840, 842, 843, 845, X44 from 🚂 York. **Station**: 🚂 York 1½ml. **Road**: follow York outer ring road (A1237/A64), turn on to A1036 Tadcaster Road, signed to York racecourse, past York College, then turn right after St Edward's church, through brick gatehouse arch

🅿 Free parking. Not suitable for coaches

NT properties nearby
Beningbrough Hall, Treasurer's House

Goddards Garden								
17 Mar–31 Oct		11–4:30	**M**	**T**	**W**	**T**	**F**	S S
Closed 30 June for special event. Last admission 1hr before closing								

Hardcastle Crags

Hollin Hall, Crimsworth Dean, Hebden Bridge,
West Yorkshire HX7 7AP

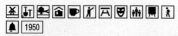

| 1950 |

(5:E6)

Beautiful wooded valley with 19th-century Gibson Mill at its heart, an exemplar of sustainable energy

A hidden beauty spot in the South Pennines with more than 160 hectares (400 acres) of unspoilt woodland. As well as being the home of the northern hairy wood ant, there are tumbling streams, glorious waterfalls and stacks of millstone grit, all crisscrossed by more than eighteen miles of footpaths. At its heart is Gibson Mill, a family-oriented visitor centre with hand-operated interactive displays, dressing up, dancing and exhibitions. With no link to the national grid, the mill is unique in the UK and the National Trust's flagship sustainable building.

What's new in 2008 Hardcastle Crags Tracker Packs. Gibson Mill Art Exhibition Centre (March–Oct)

★ Visitors are encouraged to come on foot, by cycle or public transport. Car parking and cycle racks available at Clough Hole car park on Widdop Road and Midgehole car park on Midgehole Road. During busy times limited car parking leads to heavy congestion. There are steep drops and water hazards throughout the property. Gibson Mill has narrow and low doorways and uneven floors. Gibson Mill may be closed if there is insufficient power. WC not always available, WCs at Gibson Mill (only when mill open)

Gibson Mill at the heart of Hardcastle Crags

Hardcastle Crags		M	T	W	T	F	S	S
Hardcastle Crags								
All year		**M**	**T**	**W**	**T**	**F**	**S**	**S**
Gibson Mill as a minimum								
1 Mar–6 Apr	11–4:30	M	T	W	T	F	**S**	**S**
7 Apr–31 Oct	11–4:30	M	T	**W**	T	F	**S**	**S**
1 Nov–31 Jan 09	11–3:30	M	T	W	T	F	**S**	**S**
Muddy Boots Café								
1 Mar–6 Apr	11–4:30	M	T	W	T	F	**S**	**S**
7 Apr–30 Apr	11–4:30	M	**T**	**W**	T	F	**S**	**S**
1 May–30 Sep	11–5:30	M	**T**	**W**	T	F	**S**	**S**
1 Oct–31 Oct	11–4:30	M	**T**	**W**	T	F	**S**	**S**
1 Nov–31 Jan 09	11–3:30	M	T	W	T	F	**S**	**S**

Also open Good Fri & 26 Dec. If limited power, café or parts of mill may close. Mill also open Mon–Thurs during local school hols

ℹ **T** 01422 844518
E hardcastlecrags@nationaltrust.org.uk

🏃 Guided walks throughout the year. Send sae for details. Orienteering course, technical tours and members' tours of Gibson Mill by arrangement

🎭 Send sae for details

♿ 🔤 ♿ ⠿ **Building** ♿ **Grounds** ♿

🍴 Muddy Boots Café. Light refreshments and snacks only

🚼 Baby-changing facilities. Pushchairs and baby back-carriers admitted

🏫 Suitable for school groups. Education room/centre. Hands-on activities

🐕 Under control at all times

➡ [103:SD988291] **Foot**: access on foot via riverside walk from Hebden Bridge. Pennine Bridleway passes property. **Bus**: Hebden Bridger A & B and First 593 from ✦ Hebden Bridge to within 1ml. **Station**: Hebden Bridge 2ml. **Road**: at end of Midgehole Road, 1½ml NE of Hebden Bridge off the A6033 Keighley road

🅿 Parking (pay & display). Midweek £3, weekend £4, weekend half day £2.50; motorcycle £1; minibus £5. NT members free

NT properties nearby
East Riddlesden Hall, Gawthorpe Hall, Marsden Moor Estate

Charges for National Trust members apply on some special event days

Maister House

160 High Street, Hull, East Yorkshire HU1 1NL

🏠 1966 **(5:J6)**

18th-century merchant's house

Rebuilt in 1743 during Hull's heyday as an affluent trading centre, this house is a typical but rare survivor of a merchant's residence of that period. The restrained exterior belies the spectacular plasterwork staircase inside. The house is now let as offices.

⭐ Staircase and entrance hall only on show. No WC

ℹ️ **T** 01723 870423
E maisterhouse@nationaltrust.org.uk

♿ Building 🦽

➡️ [107:TA102287] In Hull city centre.
Cycle: NCN65. **Bus:** local services to within 100yds. **Station:** Hull ¾ml

🅿️ No parking on site

NT properties nearby
Treasurer's House, Yorkshire Coast

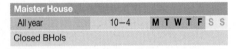

Maister House								
All year	10–4	**M**	**T**	**W**	**T**	**F**	S	S
Closed BHols								

Malham Tarn Estate

Yorkshire Dales Estate Office, Waterhouses, Settle, North Yorkshire BD24 9PT

🏕️🚶🏠🎫🖼️🚶🚴 1946 **(5:D4)**

High moorland landscape with dramatic limestone features

This outstanding area of 2,900 hectares (7,200 acres) of upland limestone country consists of six farms, many flower-rich hay meadows and limestone pavements. The National Nature Reserve at Malham Tarn is home to a unique community of rare plants and animals; the bird hide provides excellent views of the Tarn's varied birdlife.

What's new in 2008 Recently revamped farming exhibition at Town Head Barn in Malham. Includes interactive and audio displays, plus puzzles and activities for children

Malham Tarn Estate								
Estate								
All year		**M**	**T**	**W**	**T**	**F**	**S**	**S**
Town Head Barn								
3 Feb–16 Mar	10–4	M	T	W	T	F	S	**S**
23 Mar–26 Oct	10–4	M	**T**	**W**	**T**	**F**	**S**	**S**
2 Nov–14 Dec	10–4	M	T	W	T	F	S	**S**
4 Jan–25 Jan 09	10–4	M	T	W	T	F	S	**S**

⭐ WC available at the National Park car park in Malham

ℹ️ **T** 01729 830416
E malhamtarn@nationaltrust.org.uk

🚶 A selection of walks on the estate are included in walks leaflets, available from the National Park centre or Town Head Barn in Malham

♿ Grounds 🦽

🖼️ Farming exhibition in Town Head Barn, Malham

🚴 Off-road cycling permitted on bridleways

➡️ [98:SD890660] Estate extends from Malham village, 19ml NW of Skipton, N past Malham Tarn. **Foot:** 6ml of Pennine Way & ⅔ml of Pennine Bridleway on property. **Bus:** Pennine 210 from Skipton (passing 🚃 Skipton). Also Jacksons 809 from Settle, weekends April–Sept only (passing close 🚃 Settle). **Station:** Settle 7ml

🅿️ Parking (not NT) in Malham village (pay & display)

NT properties nearby
Brimham Rocks, East Riddlesden Hall, Fountains Abbey and Studley Royal, Upper Wharfedale

New House Farm, Malham Tarn, North Yorkshire

Marsden Moor Estate

Estate Office, The Old Goods Yard, Station Road, Marsden, Huddersfield, West Yorkshire HD7 6DH

🏠 🎫 ♿ 🐕 📷 🎦 🚻 🖼 🚶 🚲 1955 **(5:E7)**

Huge area of peak and moorland

The Estate, covering nearly 2,429 hectares (5,685 acres) of unenclosed common moorland and almost surrounding the village of Marsden, takes in the northern part of the Peak District National Park, with valleys, reservoirs, peaks and crags, as well as archaeological remains dating from pre-Roman times to the great engineering structures of the canal and railway ages. The landscape supports large numbers of moorland birds, such as golden plover, red grouse, curlew and diminutive twite. The Estate is a designated SSSI, forms part of an international Special Protection Area and is a candidate Special Area of Conservation.

⭐ Public WC in Marsden village. The 'Welcome to Marsden' exhibition at the NT Estate Office gives a good insight into the area

ℹ️ **T** 01484 847016
E marsdenmoor@nationaltrust.org.uk

🚶 Send sae to Estate Office for events and guided walks leaflet – a pocket guide to Marsden, including six self-guided walks and a heritage trail covering Tunnel End and Marsden village

♿ **Grounds** 🏔

🛍 Plant sales at events and some weekends at Estate Office

🖼 Suitable for school groups

Buckstones Moss, part of the Marsden Moor Estate

🐕 On leads only

🚲 Two bridleways cross the property. Also possible to undertake circular rides using these together with quiet roads

➡️ [109:SE025100] **Foot**: Kirklees Way and Pennine Way pass through the property. Huddersfield Narrow Canal towpath nearby. **Bus**: First 184, 350-2 from Huddersfield. **Station**: Marsden (adjacent to estate office). **Road**: estate covers area around Marsden village, between A640 and A635

🅿️ Free parking areas around the Estate, inc. in Marsden village (not NT) and at Buckstones and Wessenden Head (NT)

NT properties nearby
East Riddlesden Hall, Hardcastle Crags, High Peak Estate, Lyme Park, Nostell Priory and Parkland

Marsden Moor Estate								
Estate								
All year			M	T	W	T	F	S	S
Exhibition								
All year	9–5		M	T	W	T	F	S	S

Moulton Hall

Moulton, Richmond, North Yorkshire DL10 6QH

🏛 🚶 1966 **(5:F2)**

17th-century manor house

ℹ️ **T** 01325 377227
E moultonhall@nationaltrust.org.uk

➡️ 5ml E of Richmond; turn off A1, ½ml S of Scotch Corner

Moulton Hall
By arrangement with the tenant, Viscount Eccles

Dogs assisting visitors with disabilities are always welcome

Mount Grace Priory

Staddle Bridge, Northallerton, North Yorkshire
DL6 3JG

⊞ ⌂ 🗂 😀 🚻 📷 🧍 1953   **(5:G3)**

Ruin of a 14th-century Carthusian priory

This is England's most important Carthusian ruin. The individual cells reflect the hermit-like isolation of the monks; a reconstruction enables visitors to see the austere and simple furnishings. There is a small herb garden.

⭐ The priory is financed, administered and maintained by English Heritage. Please contact property to check details before your visit

ℹ️ **T** 01609 883494
    E mountgracepriory@nationaltrust.org.uk

♿ 🚻 📷 🅿 📀 **Building** 🏛️ **Grounds** 🏛️

📷 Shop. Herbs for sale May–Aug

☕ Hot drinks machine, cold drinks & snacks from shop (EH)

🚻 Baby-changing facilities. Pushchairs and baby back-carriers admitted. Children's quiz/trail. Family activity packs

📷 Suitable for school groups

➡️ [99:SE449985] **Foot**: Cleveland Way within ⅔ml. **Cycle**: NCN65, 2¼ml. **Bus**: Abbott 80, 89 🚉 Northallerton–Stokesley, alight Priory Road End, ½ml. **Station**: Northallerton 6ml. **Road**: 6ml NE of Northallerton, ½ml E of A19 and ½ml S of its junction with A172

🅿️ Free parking

NT properties nearby
Fountains Abbey and Studley Royal, Nunnington Hall, Ormesby Hall, Rievaulx Terrace and Temples

Mount Grace Priory									
21 Mar–30 Sep	10–6	M	T	W	**T**	**F**	**S**	**S**	
2 Oct–31 Jan 09	10–4	M	T	W	**T**	**F**	**S**	**S**	
Closed 24–26 Dec & 1 Jan 09									

If you enjoyed catching up with friends at Nostell Priory, why not make your next rendezvous at Treasurer's House

Nostell Priory and Parkland

Doncaster Road, Nostell, nr Wakefield, West Yorkshire WF4 1QE

🏛️ ⊞ 🎎 ⌂ 📷 🍴 🗂 😀 🚻 📷 🧍
🚴 🔔 🍽️ 1954   **(5:G6)**

18th-century architectural masterpiece with Adam interiors, Chippendale furniture, fine collections and landscape park and gardens

Nostell Priory was built by James Paine on the site of a medieval priory for Sir Rowland Winn, 4th Baronet, in 1733. Later Robert Adam was commissioned to complete the state rooms, which are among the finest examples of his interiors. The Priory houses England's best documented collections of Chippendale furniture, designed especially for the house by the great cabinetmaker. Other treasures include an outstanding art collection, with works by Pieter Brueghel the Younger and Angelica Kauffmann, the remarkable 18th-century doll's-house (with its original fittings and Chippendale-style furniture), one of the finest libraries in the National Trust's portfolio and the John Harrison long-case clock with its extremely rare movement made of wood. In the grounds are wonderful lakeside walks with a stunning collection of rhododendrons, azaleas and a delightful magnolia avenue in spring. More than 121 hectares (300 acres) of parkland are open to the public.

Nostell Priory and Parkland									
House									
15 Mar–2 Nov	1–5	M	T	**W**	**T**	**F**	**S**	**S**	
6 Dec–14 Dec	12–4	M	T	**W**	**T**	**F**	**S**	**S**	
Grounds/shop/tea-room									
1 Mar–2 Nov	11–5:30	M	T	**W**	**T**	**F**	**S**	**S**	
8 Nov–30 Nov	11–4:30	M	T	W	T	**F**	**S**	**S**	
6 Dec–14 Dec	11–4:30	**M**	**T**	**W**	**T**	**F**	**S**	**S**	
Parkland									
All year	9–7	**M**	**T**	**W**	**T**	**F**	**S**	**S**	

Open BH Mons: house 1–5; gardens, shop & tea-room 11–5:30, parkland closes dusk if earlier. Rose garden may be closed on occasions for private functions. Open local Feb half-term. Tel. for details of possible extra openings 26 Dec–2 Jan 09

Please remember – your membership card is always needed for free admission

Chippendale furniture in the State Dressing Room, Nostell Priory, West Yorkshire

What's new in 2008 New parkland paths and lakeside walk. New children's adventure play area. Exhibitions and trails telling the story of the house and Winn family through the ages. Annually changing exhibitions in the museum room

⭐ The Angelica Kauffmann painting is on loan to the Royal Academy

ℹ️ **T** 01924 863892
E nostellpriory@nationaltrust.org.uk

🎟️ Including free introductory talks in house. Occasional conservation tours (booking required). Behind-the-scenes tours (booking required)

🎭 Craft and country fairs, open-air theatre and jazz and other musical spectaculars. Children's events every Thurs in Aug. Licensed for civil weddings. Cabinets and commodes open Sats & Suns in Sept. Every weekday: 'Object of desire'. Family croquet, giant chess set. Send sae for details

🚶 Walks from the front of the house, 10:30 Thurs & Fri

♿ 🦽🦼📷🔇📹👓🔊♿🅿️🎶
Building 🦽⬆️🦽 **Grounds** 🦽➡️♿

🏪 NT shop. Plant sales

🍽️ Stables tea-room. Serving lunches and refreshments. Children's menu

👶 Baby-changing and feeding facilities. Front-carrying baby slings and hip-carrying infant seats for loan. Children's play area. Children's quiz/trail. Family activity packs. Family area in tea-room. Children's events every Thurs in Aug. Family croquet

🏫 Suitable for school groups. Education room/centre. Adult study days

🐕 On leads only in park

🚲 Permitted in the park

➡️ [111:SE407172] **Cycle**: NCN67, 3ml. **Bus**: Arriva 496 Wakefield–Doncaster; also Arriva 485, B Line 123, 223, 244 from Wakefield. **Station**: Fitzwilliam 1½ml. **Road**: on A638 5ml SE of Wakefield towards Doncaster

🅿️ Parking, £2 (refunded on purchase of adult house or garden ticket)

NT properties nearby
Clumber Park, East Riddlesden Hall, Hardcastle Crags, Marsden Moor Estate, Mr Straw's House

Nunnington Hall

Nunnington, nr York, North Yorkshire YO62 5UY

🏛️❄️🏠🍽️🎫🛡️👶🏫 1953 (5:H4)

Picturesque Yorkshire manor house with organic garden and exciting programme of exhibitions

The sheltered walled garden, with spring-flowering organic meadows, orchards and flamboyant peacocks, complements this beautiful Yorkshire house, nestling on the quiet banks of the River Rye. Take the afternoon to enjoy and absorb the atmosphere of this former family home. Explore period rooms while hearing the Hall's many tales and then discover one of the world's finest collections of miniature rooms in the attic. The Hall also holds a series of important art and photography exhibitions during the year. Why not make a day of it? Its close proximity to Rievaulx Terrace makes it an ideal afternoon visit after a walk at Rievaulx Terrace in the morning.

ℹ️ **T** 01439 748283
E nunningtonhall@nationaltrust.org.uk

🎭 Full events list available

Unless indicated, last admission is always 30mins before closing time

Nunnington Hall: this picturesque Yorkshire manor house hosts many important exhibitions

🖐️ 🚻 🏠 Building 🛗 ♿

Grounds 🚶

🛍️ NT shop. Plant sales

🍽️ Restaurant within historic building. Children's menu

🏼 Baby-changing and feeding facilities. Hip-carrying infant seats for loan. Children's quiz/trail. Children's activity packs

🔲 Suitable for school groups

➡️ [100:SE670795] **Bus**: Hutchinson 195 Hovingham–Helmsley with connections from 🚉 Malton on Stephensons 194; Moorsbus M4 from Helmsley, Suns April–Oct plus Mon–Sat in Aug. **Road**: in Ryedale, 4½ml SE of Helmsley (A170) Helmsley–Pickering road; 1½ml N of B1257 Malton–Helmsley road; 21ml N of York, B1363. Nunnington Hall is 7½ml SE of the NT Rievaulx Terrace and Temples

🅿️ Free parking, 50yds

NT properties nearby
Beningbrough Hall, Bridestones, Ormesby Hall, Rievaulx Terrace and Temples, Treasurer's House

Nunnington Hall									
15 Mar–31 May	12–5	M	T	W	T	F	S	S
1 Jun–31 Aug	12–5:30	M	T	W	T	F	S	S
1 Sep–2 Nov	12–5	M	T	W	T	F	S	S

Hall opens 1. Open BH Mons. Winter weekend opening. See website or tel. for details

Ormesby Hall

Church Lane, Ormesby, nr Middlesbrough, Redcar & Cleveland TS7 9AS

🏠 🚗 ♿ 🌳 🍽️ 🎭 🏛️ 🛡️ 🏼 🔲 🚶 🔔 🍴

1962   (5:G2)

The Pennyman family's intimate 18th-century mansion

Ormesby Hall is an intimate home lived in by the Pennyman family for more than 300 years, with fine plasterwork, carved wood decoration and fascinating portraits. The Victorian laundry and kitchen with scullery and game larder are worth exploring, and there is a beautiful stable block (let to the Cleveland Mounted Police) that can be seen from the Hall. Ormesby has the only National Trust model railway layouts on permanent display. There is also an attractive garden.

What's new in 2008 Expanded programme of events and activities, some on weekdays

⭐ Parts of the house may occasionally be closed for private functions

ℹ️ **T** 01642 324188
E ormesbyhall@nationaltrust.org.uk

Ormesby Hall									
15 Mar–2 Nov	1:30–5	M	T	W	T	F	S	S

Open BH Mons and Good Fri. Closed 5/6 July for special event

For further information go to www.nationaltrust.org.uk

The Laundry at Ormesby Hall, Middlesbrough

🏃 Guided tours of hall and garden part of events programme

🎭 Send sae or see website for details

🏃 Orienteering route through estate – information available at property. Guided tours of garden part of events programme

♿ 🚾 🦽 🔲 📷 P♿ D♿ Building ♿🦽
Grounds 🦽➡

🍽 Tea-room

👶 Baby-changing facilities. Front-carrying baby slings for loan. Children's quiz/trail. Family activity packs

🏫 Suitable for school groups. Education room/centre. Living history programmes. Community activities

🐕 On leads only in park

➜ [93:NZ530167] **Cycle**: NCN65, 2¼ml.
Bus: from Middlesbrough (passing close
🚉 Middlesbrough). **Station**: Marton (U) 1½ml;
Middlesbrough 3ml. **Road**: 3ml SE of
Middlesbrough, W of A171. From A19 take
A174 to A172. Follow signs for Ormesby Hall.
Car entrance on Ladgate Lane (B1380)

P Free parking, 100yds

NT properties nearby
Mount Grace Priory, Nunnington Hall, Rievaulx
Terrace and Temples, Roseberry Topping, Souter
Lighthouse, Washington Old Hall

Rievaulx Terrace and Temples

Rievaulx, Helmsley, North Yorkshire YO62 5LJ

🏠 ❄ 🎣 🔲 🛏 🎭 🚻 🖼 1972   **(5:H3)**

One of Yorkshire's finest 18th-century landscape gardens, containing two temples

Discover one of Ryedale's true gems – the 18th-century landscape of Rievaulx Terrace. Stroll through woods then out on to the grass terrace, with its stunning views down over the Cistercian ruin of Rievaulx Abbey. In spring the bank between the temples is awash with wild flowers, in summer the lawns are the perfect spot for a picnic, while in autumn the beechwoods are a mass of rich autumnal hues. Step back into the 18th century as you gaze up at the wonderful painted ceiling of the Ionic Temple. Being so close to Nunnington Hall, the Terrace makes an ideal morning visit before discovering Nunnington in the afternoon.

⭐ No access to Rievaulx Abbey from Terrace

ℹ **T** 01439 798340 (summer), 01439 748283 (winter) **E** rievaulxterrace@nationaltrust.org.uk

🎭 For details contact Nunnington Hall

♿ 🚾 🦽 ∷ P♿ D♿ Building 🦽
Grounds 🦽➡🚵

🛍 NT shop

☕ Ice-cream, coffee/tea machine and cold drinks

👶 Baby-changing facilities. Pushchairs and baby back-carriers admitted. Children's quiz/trail. Children's activity packs

🏫 Suitable for school groups

🐕 On leads only

➜ [100:SE579848] **Foot**: Cleveland Way within
⅔ml. **Bus**: Hutchinson 198, Moorsbus M8 from
Helmsley (connections on Scarborough &
District 128 from 🚉 Scarborough), Tues & Thur
& Sat all year, Mon–Sat June–Sept, Suns, April–
Oct. **Road**: 2½ml NW of Helmsley on B1257

Rievaulx Terrace and Temples									
15 Mar–30 Sep	11–6	M	T	W	T	F	S	S
1 Oct–2 Nov	11–5	M	T	W	T	F	S	S

Last admission 1hr before closing. Ionic Temple closed 1–2

The Ionic Temple at Rievaulx Terrace, North Yorkshire

P Free parking, 100yds. Unsuitable for trailer caravans. Cars park beside visitor centre, coaches a short walk away. Tight corners and no turning space beyond coach park

NT properties nearby
Beningbrough Hall, Bridestones, Nunnington Hall, Ormesby Hall, Treasurer's House

Roseberry Topping

Newton-under-Roseberry, North Yorkshire
1985   (5:G2)

Distinctive hill with fine views across Yorkshire

The peculiar shape of this hill is due to a geological fault and a mining collapse early in the 20th century. From the summit at 320 metres there is a magnificent 360° view and, on a clear day, visitors can see as far as Teesside in one direction and the Yorkshire Dales in another. Newton and Cliff Ridge Woods skirt the northern edge of the property and Cliff Rigg quarry still retains evidence of the extraction of whinstone, once used for road-building. The area is rich in wildlife, particularly moorland birds. A spur of the Cleveland Way National Trail runs up to the summit.

Roseberry Topping		
All year		M T W T F S S

For information regarding prices, see page 10

★ Address for correspondence: Peakside, Ravenscar, Scarborough, North Yorkshire YO13 0NE. WC at Ayton car park

i T 01642 328901
E roseberrytopping@nationaltrust.org.uk

→ [93:NZ575126] **Foot**: Cleveland Way passes property. **Bus**: Arriva North East 81, 781 Redcar–Stokesley, alight Newton-under-Roseberry, then ½ml. **Station**: Great Ayton (U) 1½ml. **Road**: 1ml from Great Ayton next to Newton-under-Roseberry on A173 Great Ayton–Guisborough

P Parking (not NT), £2, at Newton-under-Roseberry

NT properties nearby
Bridestones, Nunnington Hall, Ormesby Hall, Rievaulx Terrace and Temples, Souter Lighthouse, Yorkshire Coast

Treasurer's House

Minster Yard, York, North Yorkshire YO1 7JL
1930 (5:H5)

Elegant town house dating from medieval times

Originally home to the treasurers of York Minster and built over a Roman road, the house is not all that it seems. Nestled behind the Minster, its size, splendour and contents are a constant surprise to visitors – as are the famous ghost stories. The house was carefully restored between 1897 and 1930 by one remarkable man, wealthy local industrialist Frank Green, with rooms presented in a variety of historic styles. Outside is an attractive formal sunken garden and herb garden.

What's new in 2008 Ghostly Myths tours, exploring the historical links between the five famous ghost stories and the people who lived here

Treasurer's House		
15 Mar–2 Nov	11–4:30	M T W T F S S
3 Nov–30 Nov	11–3	M T W T F S S

Nov opening: access by guided Ghostly Myths tour to selected rooms. Tea-room open

ⓘ **T** 01904 624247
E treasurershouse@nationaltrust.org.uk

🏃 Occasional garden tours; ghost cellar tours daily except Fri. Themed guided tours in Nov (charge, inc. NT members)

♿ 🚻 🖼️ ⁘ 🔊 🅿️ Building 🏞️
Grounds 🏔️ ➡️

🛍️ Small range of books, cards and souvenirs on sale at property

☕ Licensed tea-room. All food freshly prepared and baked on premises inc. traditional Yorkshire recipes. Special dietary requirements catered for. Children's menu

👶 Baby-changing and feeding facilities. Hip-carrying infant seats for loan. Children's guide. Children's quiz/trail. Interactive exhibition area for children

🖼️ Suitable for school groups

🐕 On leads and only in garden

➡️ [105:SE604523] In city centre adjacent to Minster (N side, at rear). **Cycle:** NCN65, ⅓ml. Close to city cycle routes. **Bus:** from surrounding areas. **Station:** York ½ml

🅿️ No parking on site. Public car park nearby in Lord Mayor's Walk. Park & ride service from city outskirts

NT properties nearby
Beningbrough Hall, Nunnington Hall

The West Sitting Room, Treasurer's House, York

Upper Wharfedale

Yorkshire Dales Estate Office, Waterhouses, Settle, North Yorkshire BD24 9PT

🏕️ 🏠 🏃 🖼️ 🚶 🚲 1989 **(5:E4)**

Area of classic Yorkshire Dales countryside

Amongst the 2,470 hectares (6,100 acres) of the Upper Wharfe Valley north of Kettlewell, the Trust owns nine farms and the hamlets of Yockenthwaite and Cray. The landscape incorporates the characteristic dry-stone walls and barns, important flower-rich hay meadows and valleyside woodland.

⭐ No WC, nearest at National Park car park in Buckden

ⓘ **T** 01729 830416
E upperwharfedale@nationaltrust.org.uk

🏃 Guided walks programme

🚶 A selection of the many walks in Upper Wharfedale are included in walks leaflets, available from the National Park centre or Townhead Barn, Buckden

♿ Grounds 🏔️

🖼️ Exhibition in Townhead Barn, Buckden

🚲 Off-road cycling permitted on bridleways

➡️ [98:SD935765] Upper Wharfedale extends from Kettlewell village (12ml N of Skipton) N to Beckermonds and Cray. **Bus:** Pride of the Dales 72 🚌 Skipton–Buckden; Arriva 800/5 from Leeds and 🚌 Ilkley (Suns only)

🅿️ Parking (not NT) in Kettlewell and Buckden (pay & display)

NT properties nearby
Brimham Rocks, East Riddlesden Hall, Fountains Abbey and Studley Royal, Malham Tarn Estate

Upper Wharfedale									
Estate									
All year			**M**	**T**	**W**	**T**	**F**	**S**	**S**
Townhead Barn									
2 Mar – 16 Mar	10–4		M	T	W	T	F	S	**S**
22 Mar – 25 Sep	10–4		**M**	**T**	**W**	**T**	F	S	**S**
28 Sep – 14 Dec	10–4		M	T	W	T	F	S	**S**
4 Jan – 25 Jan 09	10–4		M	T	W	T	F	S	**S**

Many Trust properties are offering Gift Aid on Entry for non-members, see page 10

Yorkshire Coast

Peakside, Ravenscar, Scarborough, North
Yorkshire YO13 0NE

(5:12)

Varied coastal area with natural history and industrial archaeology interest

This group of coastal properties extends more than 40 miles from Saltburn in the north to Filey in the south, centred on Robin Hood's Bay. The Cleveland Way National Trail follows the clifftop and gives splendid views. A wide range of habitats – meadow, woodland, coastal heath and cliff grassland – provides sanctuary to many forms of wildlife, from orchids to nesting birds. The area is rich in industrial archaeology, and the remains of the alum industry and jet and ironstone mining can be seen. The Old Coastguard Station in Robin Hood's Bay, an exciting exhibition and education centre, is run

Yorkshire Coast		M T W T F S S
All year		M T W T F S S
Coastguard Station		
9 Feb–24 Feb	10–4	M T W T F S S
25 Feb–16 Mar	10–4	M T W T F S S
22 Mar–6 Apr	10–5	M T W T F S S
7 Apr–2 May	10–5	M T W T F S S
3 May–31 Oct	10–5	M T W T F S S
1 Nov–28 Dec	10–5	M T W T F S S
29 Dec–31 Jan 09	11–4	M T W T F S S
Ravenscar		
22 Mar–18 Apr	10:30–5	M T W T F S S
19 Apr–23 May	10:30–5	M T W T F S S
24 May–5 Oct	10:30–5	M T W T F S S
Open BH Mons		

in partnership with the North York Moors National Park Authority. It shows how the elements have shaped this part of the coastline. At Ravenscar Coastal Centre an exhibition covers local history, including the story of alum production – Britain's first chemical industry.

[i] **T** 01723 870423, 01947 885900 (Old Coastguard Station)
E yorkshirecoast@nationaltrust.org.uk

Guided walks

Grounds

Shops in Old Coastguard Station and Ravenscar Coastal Centre

Suitable for school groups. Education room/centre. Hand-on activities (at Old Coastguard Station)

→ [94:NZ980025] **Foot**: Cleveland Way passes through property. **Cycle**: NCN1.
Bus: Scarborough & District 115 from Scarborough, Tues, Thur, Sat only, otherwise Arriva 93/A, X56 Scarborough–Whitby to within 3ml. **Station**: Scarborough 10ml. **Road**: Coastal Centre in Ravenscar village, signposted off A171 Scarborough–Whitby. Old Coastguard Station in Robin Hood's Bay

[P] Parking (not NT) (pay & display), charge inc. NT members at Old Coastguard Station. Free roadside parking at Ravenscar

NT properties nearby
Bridestones, Nunnington Hall, Ormesby Hall, Rievaulx Terrace and Temples

Cowbar Nab at Staithes, North Yorkshire

England's far north-eastern counties of Northumberland, Durham and Tyne & Wear offer magnificent scenery, with wide open stretches of unspoilt moorland and upland pasture, and a long and dramatic coastline, arguably one of the finest in Britain.

The National Trust cares for 16 miles of dunes, sandy beaches and tidal rock pools along the Northumberland coast, and 5 miles of the Durham coast. For many years, the Durham beaches were a dumping ground for the local collieries, but this unexpectedly beautiful area of coast now has Heritage Coast status.

In the south of the region, near Horden in County Durham, a piece of coast marks the 500th mile acquired through the Trust's Neptune Coastline Campaign. Once an industrial mining hotspot, this stretch of coastline has since been dramatically restored, and while even today it may take some time for the beaches to return to golden sands, the seeds have been sown for the future.

Inland are beautiful woodland walks, including one along the banks of the River Wear at Moorhouse Woods, north of Durham City, and another beside the Derwent at Ebchester.

Left: **Dunstanburgh**
Below: **puffin**
Bottom: **the Farne Islands**

Moving north, the spectacular coastline takes in the dramatic Souter Lighthouse and The Leas, with its famous seabird colony on Marsden Rock. Further north of the River Tyne and up the Northumberland coast is Druridge Bay, where the Trust owns a mile of coast backed by golden sand dunes.

From Craster, Trust ownership runs for 5 miles, including the brooding ruins of Dunstanburgh Castle (managed by English Heritage). Boats cross to the Farne Islands from Seahouses, allowing visitors the chance to see the homes of thousands of seabirds – including puffins, terns, kittiwakes and guillemots.

Previous page: Souter Lighthouse, Tyne & Wear (6:15)

Above: **Lindisfarne Castle** Right: **Housesteads Fort and Hadrian's Wall** Bottom: **Marsden Rock**

Once you've enjoyed the castle and garden take a stroll along the headland and explore Lindisfarne village – just remember to keep an eye on the tides which cover the causeway.

Along the Marsden coastline, just to the north of Sunderland is Souter Lighthouse. A beacon that warned boats of the lethal rocks below for more 100 years, it was the most technologically advanced lighthouse in the world and the first to be powered by electricity.

Now visitors can climb the 76 steps to the top of the tower and, on a clear day, see for miles out to sea. While at Souter, discover The Leas – a haven for flora and fauna, and enjoy a bracing walk along the clifftops.

Inland Northumberland offers the natural beauty and tranquillity of Allen Banks and Staward Gorge – a walking haven with many miles of footpaths. And both Ros Castle and the World Heritage Site of Hadrian's Wall boast breathtaking views.

Accessible by a causeway at low tide, Holy Island is an island treasure that has as its centrepiece Lindisfarne Castle. Once a Tudor fort, the castle sits on a rocky crag that can be seen for miles along the sweeping coastline.

Converted into a holiday home in 1903, be charmed by this enchanting place with its small rooms that are full of intimate decoration and design. Just below the castle is the lovely walled garden planned by Gertrude Jekyll and dating back to 1922.

One of the most rugged stretches of countryside in the North East is home to Hadrian's Wall. Snaking across the landscape, the wall was built around AD122 when the Roman Empire was at its most powerful. A World Heritage Site, it remains one of Britain's most impressive ruins. The Trust protects 6 miles of Hadrian's Wall, including Housesteads Fort, one of the best preserved sections of the ramparts and a place which conjures an evocative picture of Roman military life.

Allen Banks and Staward Gorge

Bardon Mill, Hexham, Northumberland NE47 7BU

🏠🏛️🎣🚶🏞️🚻🏭🚶 1942   (6:F5)

Wooded gorge of the River Allen

This extensive area of gorge and river scenery, including the 41-hectare (101-acre) Stawardpeel Site of Special Scientific Interest, has many miles of waymarked walks through ornamental and ancient woods. On a high promontory within Staward Wood are the remains of a medieval pele tower and at Allen Banks is a reconstructed Victorian summerhouse.

ℹ️ **T** 01434 344218
   E allenbanks@nationaltrust.org.uk

🚶 Free map and guide to four waymarked routes, available at the property

♿ 🚻 Grounds 🦽

👶 Baby-changing facilities. Family trail

🏭 Suitable for school groups. Visitor map and guides

🐾 Under close control

→ [86:NY799640] **Foot**: numerous public and permitted rights of way give access to walkers. **Cycle**: NCN72, 2½ml. **Bus**: Arriva/Stagecoach in Cumbria 685 Carlisle–Newcastle upon Tyne, to within ½ml. **Station**: Bardon Mill 1½ml. **Road**: 5½ml E of Haltwhistle, 3ml W of Haydon Bridge, ½ml S of A69, near meeting point of Tyne and Allen rivers

🅿️ Parking (pay & display) at Allen Banks. Cars £1.50 half day, £3 full day. Can accommodate two coaches at a time (all coaches must book). 3.3m (11ft) height restriction on approach road. Coaches £5 half day, £10 full day. NT members/Educational Group members free

NT properties nearby
Hadrian's Wall and Housesteads Fort

Allen Banks and Staward Gorge									
All year	Dawn–dusk	M	T	W	T	F	S	S	

Cherryburn

Station Bank, Mickley, nr Stocksfield, Northumberland NE43 7DD

🏠🏛️🚻🍴🎡🏠🍵🏞️🚩🚻 🏭🍽️ 1991   (6:G5)

Cottage and farmhouse, the birthplace of Thomas Bewick

Thomas Bewick (1753–1828), Northumberland's greatest artist, wood engraver and naturalist, was born in the cottage here. The nearby 19th-century farmhouse, the later home of the Bewick family, houses an exhibition on Bewick's life and work and a small shop selling books, gifts and prints from his original wood engravings. Occasional printing demonstrations take place in the adjoining barn. There are splendid views over the Tyne Valley. The south bank of the River Tyne, where Bewick spent much of his childhood, is a short walk away.

What's new in 2008 Extended portrait exhibition

ℹ️ **T** 01661 843276
   E cherryburn@nationaltrust.org.uk

🚩 Easter trail, Teddy Bears' Picnic. Folk in the Farmyard: traditional Northumbrian music, song or dance first Sun of every month. The 'Big Draw' in Oct. Concerts, lecture evenings and press room demonstrations

♿ 🚻 🖼️ 👓 🅿️ 🅳 Building 🦽 Grounds 🦽

🏠 Shop in farmhouse. Send sae for mail order Bewick print price list. Small selection of plants grown by Cherryburn volunteers, summer months only

🍵 Tea, coffee, soft drinks and snacks available

👶 Baby-changing facilities. Family guide. Children's quiz/trail. Children's toy corner. Farmyard animals usually include donkeys, poultry and lambs. Teddy Bears' Picnic

Cherryburn									
Public opening									
15 Mar–2 Nov	11–5	M	T	W	T	F	S	S	
Booked groups									
17 Mar–31 Oct	10–4	M	T	W	T	F	S	S	
3 Nov–31 Jan 09	10–3	M	T	W	T	F	S	S	

Shop open at other times by arrangement. Open Feb half-term, tel. for details

Please remember – your membership card is always needed for free admission

The Display Room at Cherryburn, Northumberland, with Thomas Bewick's portrait over his desk

📺 Suitable for school groups. Hands-on activities

➔ [88:NZ075627] Close to S bank of River Tyne. **Bus**: Arriva Northumbria 602 Newcastle–Hexham (passes ≊ Newcastle), alight Mickley Square ¼ml. **Station**: Stocksfield (U) 1½ml or Prudhoe (U) 1½ml. **Road**: 11ml W of Newcastle, 11ml E of Hexham; ¼ml N of Mickley Square (leave A695 at Mickley Square on to Riding Terrace leading to Station Bank)

P Free parking, 100yds

NT properties nearby
George Stephenson's Birthplace, Gibside

Cragside

Rothbury, Morpeth, Northumberland NE65 7PX

1977   **(6:G3)**

Extraordinary Victorian house, gardens and estate – the wonder of its age

The revolutionary home of Lord Armstrong, Victorian inventor and landscape genius, was a wonder of its age. Built on a rocky crag high above the Debdon Burn, Cragside is crammed with ingenious gadgets and was the first house in the world lit by hydroelectricity. Even the variety and scale of Cragside's gardens are incredible. Surrounding the house on all sides is one of the largest 'hand-made' rock gardens in Europe. In the Pinetum below, England's tallest

Douglas fir soars above other woodland giants. Across the valley, the Orchard House still produces fresh fruit of all varieties, from nectarines and apricots to grapes and strawberries. Today, Armstrong's amazing creation can be explored on foot and by car and provides one of the last shelters for the endangered red squirrel. The lakeside walks, adventure play area and labyrinth are all good reasons for children to visit Cragside again and again.

What's new in 2008 See the interactive engineering models at the Power House

⭐ Visitors may find the uneven ground, steep and slippery footpaths and distances between various parts of the property difficult. Stout footwear advisable. Pedestrians and vehicles share the same route in places, so please be vigilant. Work to restore the Iron Bridge will cause some disruption to access in the vicinity of the work. Estate will temporarily close when car parks are full. We do not have facilities to take credit/debit card payments at the admission point

ℹ️ **T** 01669 620333
E cragside@nationaltrust.org.uk

😃 Send sae for details

🚶 Leaflets for self-guided walks available

♿ 🚻🔡🈂️🖼️👓 P DJ **Building** ♿♿
Grounds ♿

🛍️ NT shop. Plant sales

🍴 Stables Restaurant (licensed) in visitor centre. Hot meals served 12–2. Children's menu. Kiosk in Crozier car park – mainly weekends and school hols (weather permitting)

Cragside									
House									
15 Mar–5 Oct	1–5:30	M	T	W	T	F	S	S
7 Oct–2 Nov	1–4:30	M	T	W	T	F	S	S
Gardens/estate/shop/restaurant									
15 Mar–2 Nov	10:30–5:30	M	T	W	T	F	S	S
5 Nov–21 Dec	11–4	M	T	W	T	F	S	S

Open BH Mons. On BHol weekends the property can be crowded. Last admission to house 1hr before closing. Gardens and estate close at 7 (dusk if earlier), last admission 5 (15 Mar–2 Nov), 3 (Nov–Dec). Last serving in restaurant 5

Unless indicated, last admission is always 30mins before closing time

The huge Drawing Room at Cragside was completed just before a royal visit in 1884

[icon] Baby-changing facilities. Front-carrying baby slings and hip-carrying infant seats for loan. Children's play area. Tracker Packs available during school holidays. Children's guide

[icon] Suitable for school groups. Education room/centre

[icon] On leads and only on estate

[icon] [81:NU073022] **Bus**: Arriva 508 from [rail] Newcastle, Sun only, June–Oct only; otherwise Northumbria Coaches/Arriva 416, 516 Morpeth–Thropton (all passing [rail] Morpeth) with connections from Newcastle (passing Tyne & Wear Metro Haymarket), alight Burnfoot, ¾ml. **Road**: 13ml SW of Alnwick (B6341) and 15ml NW of Morpeth on Wooler road (A697), turn left on to B6341 at Moorhouse Crossroads, entrance 1ml N of Rothbury

[P] Free parking in nine car parks throughout the estate. Coach parking 350yds from house, 150yds from visitor centre. Coaches cannot proceed beyond the coach park or tour estate as drive is too narrow in places

NT properties nearby
Wallington

Dunstanburgh Castle

Craster, Alnwick, Northumberland NE66 3TT

[icons] 1961   (6:H3)

Massive ruined castle in an impressive coastal setting

A magnificent ruin dominating a lonely stretch of Northumberland's beautiful coastline, Dunstanburgh must be reached on foot along paths following the rocky shore.

[icon] The castle is managed by English Heritage

[i] **T** 01665 576231
    E dunstanburghcastle@nationaltrust.org.uk

[icon] Small shop for postcards and souvenirs

[icon] Hot drinks and snacks

[icon] Suitable for school groups. Free school visits; book through EH

[icon] On leads only

Dunstanburgh Castle									
1 Apr–30 Sep	10–6	**M**	**T**	**W**	**T**		**F**	**S**	**S**
1 Oct–30 Oct	10–4	**M**	**T**	**W**	**T**		**F**	**S**	**S**
2 Nov–31 Jan 09	10–4	**M**	T	W	**T**		**F**	**S**	**S**

For further information go to www.nationaltrust.org.uk

→ [75:NU258220] 9ml NE of Alnwick, approached from Craster to the S or Embleton to the N (on foot only). **Cycle**: NCN1, ¾ml. **Bus**: Arriva 501 Alnwick–Bamburgh, with connections from ⇌ Berwick-upon-Tweed and Newcastle (passing ⇌ Tyne & Wear Metro Haymarket), alight Craster, 1½ml. **Station**: Chathill (U), not Sun, 5ml from Embleton, 7ml from castle; Alnmouth, 7ml from Craster, 8¼ml from castle

P Parking (not NT). Car parks at Craster and Embleton, 1½ml (no coaches at Embleton)

NT properties nearby
Craster, Embleton Links and Low Newton-by-the-Sea, Farne Islands, Lindisfarne Castle

Farne Islands

Northumberland

✚ 🏛 🐦 📷 🎦 | 1925   (6:H2)

Rocky islands, habitat for seals and many species of seabird

'Home' for more than 100,000 pairs of breeding seabirds, including 55,000 pairs of puffins, the Islands make up one of Europe's most important seabird reserves. Up to 21 to 23 species nest annually and many of the birds are very confiding, allowing excellent opportunities for study and photography. There is also a large grey seal colony, and the islands are interesting historically, having strong links with Celtic Christianity and, in particular, St Cuthbert.

★ Access by ferry (charge inc. NT members). WC on Inner Farne only

i **T** 01665 721099 (Infoline), 01665 720651 **E** farneislands@nationaltrust.org.uk

Farne Islands									
Both islands									
1 Apr–30 Apr	10:30–6	**M**	**T**	**W**	**T**	**F**	**S**	**S**	
Staple									
1 May–31 Jul	10:30–1:30	**M**	**T**	**W**	**T**	**F**	**S**	**S**	
Inner Farne									
1 May–31 Jul	1:30–5	**M**	**T**	**W**	**T**	**F**	**S**	**S**	
Both islands									
1 Aug–30 Sep	10:30–6	**M**	**T**	**W**	**T**	**F**	**S**	**S**	
Centre/shop									
22 Mar–30 Jun	10–5	**M**	**T**	**W**	**T**	**F**	**S**	**S**	
1 Jul–31 Aug	10–5:30	**M**	**T**	**W**	**T**	**F**	**S**	**S**	
1 Sep–30 Sep	10–5	**M**	**T**	**W**	**T**	**F**	**S**	**S**	
1 Oct–31 Oct	11–4	**M**	**T**	**W**	**T**	**F**	**S**	**S**	
1 Nov–21 Dec	11–4	M	T	**W**	**T**	**F**	**S**	**S**	
3 Jan–31 Jan 09	11–4	M	T	**W**	**T**	**F**	**S**	**S**	

Only Inner Farne and Staple Islands can be visited. Visitors to Inner Farne in June should wear hats! Information centre/shop open half-term hols 10–5

Puffins on Inner Farne, with the lighthouse in the background

♿ 🚾♿♿ **Grounds** ♿

📷 Information centre and shop at 16 Main Street, Seahouses

🏛 Suitable for school groups

➔ [75:NU230370] 2–5ml off the Northumberland coast, opposite Bamburgh. Trips every day from Seahouses harbour, weather permitting. **Cycle**: NCN1, ¾ml. From Seahouses harbour. **Bus**: Arriva 501 Alnwick–Bamburgh, with connections from ➔ Berwick-upon-Tweed and Newcastle (passing Tyne & Wear Metro Haymarket), alight Seahouses, 1½ml. **Station**: Chathill (U), not Sun, 4ml

🅿 Parking (not NT) in Seahouses, opposite harbour (pay & display)

NT properties nearby
Dunstanburgh Castle, Lindisfarne Castle, Northumberland Coast

George Stephenson's Birthplace

Wylam, Northumberland NE41 8BP

🏠♿♿♿♿♿♿♿🏛♿♿ 1949 (6:G5)

Birthplace of the world-famous railway engineer

This small stone tenement was built c.1760 to accommodate mining families. The furnishings reflect the year of Stephenson's birth here (1781), his whole family living in the one room.

What's new in 2008 Fully accessible WC

ℹ **T** 01661 853457
E georgestephensons@nationaltrust.org.uk

🎭 Geordie Food Day – June; Teddy Bears' Tea Party – Aug

♿ 🚾♿♿ **Building** ♿

🍵 Tea-room serving light refreshments

👪 Pushchairs admitted. Children's quiz/trail

🏛 Suitable for school groups

George Stephenson's Birthplace			
15 Mar–2 Nov	12–5	M T W **T F S S**	
Open BH Mons			

For information regarding prices, see page 10

➔ [88:NZ126650] **Foot**: access on foot (and cycle) through country park, ½ml E of Wylam. **Cycle**: NCN72. Easy (flat) ride beside River Tyne (approx. 5ml). **Bus**: Arriva 684 Newcastle–Ovington, alight Wylam, 1ml. **Station**: Wylam (U) ½ml. **Road**: 8ml W of Newcastle, 1½ml S of A69 at Wylam

🅿 Parking (not NT) by war memorial in Wylam village, ½ml (pay & display).

NT properties nearby
Cherryburn, Gibside

Gibside

nr Rowlands Gill, Burnopfield, Newcastle upon Tyne NE16 6BG

1974 (6:H5)

Stunning 18th-century landscape garden

The Column of Liberty, rising dramatically high above the treetops, is the first sight visitors have of this impressive landscape garden created by the Bowes family in the 18th century. Spanning 160 hectares (400 acres), Gibside is a 'grand design' of spectacular vistas, winding paths and grassy open spaces. At key points there are decorative garden buildings, such as the Palladian chapel, Georgian stables, greenhouse and the ruins of a bathhouse and hall. There is a wonderfully tranquil atmosphere, and visitors will feel themselves very close to nature as much of Gibside is a Site of Special Scientific Interest.

What's new in 2008 Wildlife hide. Audio guide

⭐ Chapel access restricted during weddings and on Fri 11 & Sat 12 July

ℹ **T** 01207 541820
E gibside@nationaltrust.org.uk

🏃 Guided tours and refreshments available by arrangement

🎧 New audio guide

🎭 Including concerts, theatre and family events. Weddings (Church of England ceremonies)

🏃 Free map of trails up to 4ml

♿ 🚾♿♿♿♿♿♿ **Chapel** ♿♿
Grounds ♿♿

Looking down the Grand Walk to Gibside Chapel, Newcastle upon Tyne

📷 Gift shop with regional products

☕ Tea-room serves light lunches. Children's menu. Kiosk serves ice-cream and snacks

👶 Baby-changing facilities. Pushchairs and baby back-carriers admitted. Family activity and Tracker Packs. Special family events

🏫 Suitable for school groups. Education room/centre. Hands-on activities. Adult study days

🐕 On leads and only in the grounds

➡ [88:NZ172583] **Foot**: ½ml from Derwent Walk, footpath/cycle track linking Swalwell and Consett. **Cycle**: NCN14, ½ml. **Bus**: Go North East 'The Red Kite' 45, 46/A from Newcastle (passing Newcastle ≋ and Metrocentre). On all, alight Rowlands Gill, ½ml. **Station**: Blaydon (U) 5ml; Metrocentre 5ml. **Road**: 6ml SW of Gateshead, 20ml NW of Durham; entrance on B6314 between Burnopfield and Rowlands Gill; from A1 take exit north of Metrocentre and follow brown signs

🅿 Free parking, 100yds. Limited coach parking

NT properties nearby
Cherryburn, George Stephenson's Birthplace, Souter Lighthouse, Washington Old Hall

Gibside									
Grounds									
1 Feb–9 Mar	10–4	M	T	W	T	F	S	S
10 Mar–2 Nov	10–6	M	T	W	T	F	S	S
3 Nov–31 Jan 09	10–4	M	T	W	T	F	S	S
Chapel									
15 Mar–2 Nov	11–4:30	M	T	W	T	F	S	S
Stables									
1 Feb–9 Mar	11–3:30	M	T	W	T	F	S	S
10 Mar–2 Nov	11–4:30	M	T	W	T	F	S	S
3 Nov–31 Jan 09	11–3:30	M	T	W	T	F	S	S
Shop/tea-room									
1 Feb–9 Mar	11–4	M	T	W	T	F	S	S
10 Mar–2 Nov	11–5	M	T	W	T	F	S	S
3 Nov–31 Jan 09	11–4	M	T	W	T	F	S	S

Closed 22–26 Dec and 29 Dec–2 Jan 09. Last admission times: 1 Feb–9 March 3:30; 10 March–2 Nov 4:30; 3 Nov–31 Jan 09 3:30. Shop and tea-room open 10 weekends. Last entry to tea-room 15mins before closing

Hadrian's Wall and Housesteads Fort

Bardon Mill, Hexham, Northumberland NE47 6NN

🏛 🌊 🏠 📷 ☕ 👶 🏫 1930 (6:F5)

Roman wall snaking across dramatic countryside

Running through an often wild landscape with vast panoramic views, the Wall was, for a long period, the Roman Empire's most northerly outpost. Built around AD122, it has sixteen permanent bases, of which Housesteads Fort is one of the best preserved, conjuring up an evocative picture of Roman military life.

⭐ The Trust owns approx. 6 miles of the Wall, running west from Housesteads Fort to Cawfields Quarry, and over 1,000ha (2,471 acres) of farmland. Access to the Wall and the public rights of way is from car parks operated by the Northumberland National Park Authority at Housesteads, Steel Rigg and Cawfields. Housesteads Fort is owned by the NT, and maintained and managed by English Heritage

Many Trust properties are offering Gift Aid on Entry for non-members, see page 10

Hadrian's Wall running through the wild Northumbrian countryside

ℹ️ **T** 01434 344363 (EH site staff)

♿ 🚻 **Building** 🏛️ **Grounds** 🏛️

🏪 Shop/information centre at Housesteads car park

🍴 Kiosk. Picnic tables outside information centre; seating inside. Children's lunch pack

🚼 Baby-changing facilities. Children's guide

🏫 Suitable for school groups. Education room/centre. Free school visits; book through EH

🐕 On leads only (sheep and ground-nesting birds)

➡️ [87:NY790688] **Foot**: 6ml of Hadrian's Wall Path & Pennine Way on property. **Bus**: Stagecoach in Cumbria AD122 Hadrian's Wall service, June–Sept & Suns in April & Oct, 🚃 Hexham–Carlisle (passing 🚃 Haltwhistle). **Station**: Bardon Mill (U) 4ml. **Road**: 6ml NE of Haltwhistle, ½ml N of B6318; best access from car parks at Housesteads, Cawfields and Steel Rigg

🅿️ Parking (not NT) (pay & display), charge inc. NT members. Car and coach parks (operated by National Park Authority) at Housesteads (½ml walk to the Fort), Steel Rigg and at Cawfields at the western end

NT properties nearby
Allen Banks and Staward Gorge, Bellister

Hadrian's Wall and Housesteads Fort									
1 Apr–30 Sep	10–6	**M**	**T**	**W**	**T**	**F**	**S**	**S**	
1 Oct–31 Jan 09	10–4	**M**	**T**	**W**	**T**	**F**	**S**	**S**	

Closed 24–26 Dec & 1 Jan 09. Opening times subject to confirmation by EH. Tel. for details or visit www.english-heritage.org.uk

Holy Jesus Hospital

City Road, Newcastle upon Tyne NE1 2AS

🏠 🍴 🚻 🍽️   (6:H5)

An extraordinary mix of architecture from over seven centuries of Newcastle upon Tyne's history

The Holy Jesus Hospital survives amid 1960s city centre developments, displaying features from all periods of its 700-year existence. There are remains of the 14th-century Augustinian friary, 16th-century fortifications connected with the Council of the North, a 17th-century almshouse built for the Freemen of the City and a 19th-century soup kitchen. The National Trust's Inner City Project is now based here, working to provide opportunities for modern inner-city dwellers to gain access to and enjoy the countryside on their doorstep. An exhibition room is open to visitors and guided tours of the whole site are offered once a month.

⭐ Holy Jesus Hospital is owned by Newcastle City Council and leased to the NT as the base for its Inner City Project. The building and arrangements for visiting are managed by the NT

ℹ️ **T** 0191 255 7610
E innercityproject@nationaltrust.org.uk

Holy Jesus Hospital									
4 Mar–26 Jun	12–4	M	**T**	**W**	**T**	F	S	S	
30 Jun–29 Aug	12–4	**M**	**T**	**W**	**T**	**F**	S	S	
2 Sep–11 Dec	12–4	M	**T**	**W**	**T**	F	S	S	
14 Jan–28 Jan 09	12–4	M	**T**	**W**	**T**	F	S	S	

Closed BH Mons and Good Fri. Guided tours first Sat of every month except Jan 09, 10–4

🏃 1st Sat of every month (except Jan) or by arrangement

♿ 🖼️ 🔍 📷 🔶 **Building** 🔷 ↕️

👶 Pushchairs and baby back-carriers admitted

➡️ [88:NZ253642] In centre of Newcastle upon Tyne. **Cycle**: close to riverside routes. **Bus**: from surrounding areas. **Station**: Newcastle ½ml. **Underground**: Tyne & Wear Metro-Manors, ¼ml. **Road**: close to Tyne Bridge and A167

🅿 No parking on site. City centre car parks nearby; pay & display 30yds

NT properties nearby
Cherryburn, George Stephenson's Birthplace, Gibside, Souter Lighthouse, Washington Old Hall

Lindisfarne Castle

Holy Island, Berwick-upon-Tweed,
Northumberland TD15 2SH

🏰 🐕 ⛵ ❄️ 🖼️ 🐑 🔶 🏠 📷 🏃 🎭 👶
🟥 🔷 🚲 🔔 1944   **(6:G1)**

Romantic 16th-century castle with spectacular views, transformed by Lutyens into an Edwardian holiday home

Dramatically perched on a rocky crag and accessible over a causeway at low tide only, the island castle presents an exciting and alluring aspect. Originally a Tudor fort, it was converted into a private house in 1903 by the young Edwin Lutyens. The small rooms are full of intimate decoration and design, with windows looking down upon the charming walled garden planned by Gertrude Jekyll. The property also has several extremely well-preserved 19th-century lime kilns.

⭐ Holy Island can only be reached by vehicle or on foot via a 3ml causeway, which is closed from 2 hours before high tide until 3 hours after. Tide tables are listed in local newspapers, on Northumberland County Council website and displayed at the causeway. To avoid disappointment check safe crossing times before making a long/special journey. No large bags, pushchairs or rucksacks in castle. Emergency WC only; otherwise nearest WC in village 1ml from castle

ℹ️ **T** 01289 389244
E lindisfarne@nationaltrust.org.uk

🏃 Guided tours by arrangement outside normal opening times

🎭 Gertrude Jekyll garden talks. Weddings

🚶 Headland walk around the castle

♿ 👓 📷 🔷 **Grounds** 🔶

📷 In main street on Holy Island showing a virtual tour of the castle. Occasional plant sales in Gertrude Jekyll garden

👶 Baby-changing and feeding facilities. Front-carrying baby slings and hip-carrying infant seats for loan. Children's quiz/trail

🟥 Suitable for school groups. Hands-on activities

🐕 On leads and only in field

🚲 Castle field is part of an island cycle route

➡️ [75:NU136417] **Foot**: castle is approached on foot from main Holy Island village and car park, 1ml from entrance. **Cycle**: NCN1. Coast & Castles cycle route. **Bus**: Travelsure 477 from 🚉 Berwick-upon-Tweed, with connecting buses at Beal to and from Newcastle. Times vary with tides. Also island minibus service from Holy Island car park to castle. **Station**: Berwick-upon-Tweed 10ml from causeway. **Road**: on Holy Island, 5ml E of A1 across causeway

🅿 Parking (not NT), 1,760yds (pay & display), charge inc. NT members

NT properties nearby
Dunstanburgh Castle, Farne Islands

Lindisfarne Castle								
16 Feb – 24 Feb	10–3	M	T	W	T	F	S	S
15 Mar – 2 Nov	Times vary	M	T	W	T	F	S	S
30 Dec – 2 Jan 09	10–3	M	T	W	T	F	S	S
Garden								
All year	10–dusk	M	T	W	T	F	S	S

Open BH Mons (inc. Scottish BHols). Lindisfarne is a tidal island accessed via a 3ml causeway at low tide. Therefore the castle opening times vary depending on the tides. On open days the castle will open for 5hrs, which will always include 12–3. It will open either 10–3 or 12–5. The NT flag will fly only when the castle is open. To obtain a copy of the tide tables and detailed opening times send sae to Lindisfarne Castle stating which month you wish to visit

Charges for National Trust members apply on some special event days

Souter Lighthouse

Coast Road, Whitburn, Sunderland, Tyne & Wear
SR6 7NH

🔳 👤 ⏛ 1990   (6:I5)

Striking Victorian lighthouse

Now boldly painted in red and white hoops,
Souter Lighthouse opened in 1871 and was the
first to use alternating electric current, the most
advanced lighthouse technology of its day. The
engine room, light tower and keeper's living
quarters are all on view, and there is a DVD,
model and information display. A ground-floor
closed-circuit TV shows views from the top for
those unable to climb. The Compass Room
contains hands-on exhibits for all visitors,
covering storms at sea, communication from
ship to shore, pirates and smugglers, lighthouse
life, lighting the seas and shipwreck. Immediately
to the north is The Leas, 2½ miles of beach, cliff
and grassland with spectacular views, flora and
fauna, and to the south, Whitburn Coastal Park,
with coastal walks to the Whitburn Point Local
Nature Reserve.

ℹ️ **T** 01670 773966 (Infoline),
0191 529 3161
E souter@nationaltrust.org.uk

🏃 Tel. for details of tower tours

🎭 Festivals, themed evenings, Christmas
lunches and talks

🚶 Rockpool rambles and coastal walks

♿ 🚾 ♿ ♿ ♿ •• ♿ Dₐ Building ♿ ♿
Grounds ♿

🏠 NT shop

🍵 Tea-room. Home-made food (special dietary
requirements catered for), inc. seasonal
vegetables and fruit grown in lighthouse
grounds. Children's menu. Paint Store Pantry
in Foghorn Field, within lighthouse grounds.
Open weekends throughout season and other
days, weather permitting. Children's menu.
Coffee shop by shop

Souter Lighthouse							
15 Mar–2 Nov	11–5	**M T W T** F **S S**
Open Good Fri		

👶 Baby-changing facilities. Pushchairs admitted.
Hip-carrying infant seats for loan. Children's
play area. Family guide. Children's quiz/trail.
Family activity packs. Families welcome but
for safety reasons back-carriers are not
permitted inside. At busy times it may not be
possible to allow small children up steep
tower staircase

🔳 Suitable for school groups. Education
room/centre. Hands-on activities.
Interpretation panels along coastal path

🐕 On leads and only in grounds

➡️ [88:NZ408641] **Foot**: South Tyneside
Heritage Trail; 'Walking Works Wonders' local
trail. **Cycle**: NCN1, adjacent to property.
Bus: Stagecoach in South Shields E1
🚈 Sunderland–South Shields (passes
🚈 Sunderland & Tyne & Wear Metro South
Shields). **Station**: East Boldon (Tyne & Wear
Metro) 3ml. **Road**: 2½ml S of South Shields
and 5ml N of Sunderland on A183 coast road

🅿️ Free parking, 100yds. Car-park barrier locked
at set times in the evening – please see
notices at entrance

NT properties nearby
Gibside, Ormesby Hall, Penshaw Monument,
Washington Old Hall

Wallington

Cambo, Morpeth, Northumberland NE61 4AR

👶 🔳 🚶 🔔 1941   (6:G4)

**Magnificent mansion with fine interiors
and collections, set in an extensive garden
and parkland**

Dating from 1688, the house was home to many
generations of the Blackett and Trevelyan
families, who all left their mark. The restrained
Palladian exterior gives way to the magnificent
rococo plasterwork of the interior, which houses
fine ceramics, paintings, needlework and a
collection of doll's-houses. The Central Hall was
decorated to look like an Italian courtyard,
heavily influenced by the Pre-Raphaelites, with
a series of scenes of Northumbrian history by
William Bell Scott. The original formality of
Sir Walter Blackett's 18th-century landscape,

influenced by 'Capability' Brown, who went to school in the estate village, underlies the present surroundings. There are walks through a variety of lawns, shrubberies and woodland, enlivened with water features, lakes, buildings, sculpture and a wildlife hide. The beautiful walled garden has varied collections of plants and a well-stocked conservatory. Longer estate walks encompass wooded valleys and high moorland, including land around the recently reacquired Folly at Rothley Castle.

What's new in 2008 The Estate is taking the lead in finding ways to reduce its environmental impact through the Wallington Carbon Footprint project. This is a pilot project for other Trust properties across the country to follow

⭐ The walled garden, grounds and farm shop are open all year in support of the estate's farm tenants and other regional suppliers

ℹ️ **T** 01670 773967 (Infoline), 01670 773600
E wallington@nationaltrust.org.uk

🏃 Out-of-hours house and garden tours by arrangement

🎭 Year-round programme, open-air theatre, tours and talks, music, dancing, family fun day. Tel. or see website for details

🚶 Leaflets for self-guided walks available

♿ ♿🚻 ... ... P♿ **Building** ... ...
Grounds ... ➡️ ...

🛍️ NT shop. Plant sales and farm shop

Wallington		M	T	W	T	F	S	S
House								
15 Mar–30 Sep	1–5:30	M		W	T	F	S	S
1 Oct–2 Nov	1–4:30	M		W	T	F	S	S
Walled garden								
1 Feb–31 Mar	10–4	M	T	W	T	F	S	S
1 Apr–30 Sep	10–7	M	T	W	T	F	S	S
1 Oct–31 Oct	10–6	M	T	W	T	F	S	S
1 Nov–31 Jan 09	10–4	M	T	W	T	F	S	S
Shop/restaurant								
1 Feb–15 Feb	10:30–4:30			W	T	F	S	S
16 Feb–25 May	10:30–5:30	M		W	T	F	S	S
26 May–30 Sep	10:30–5:30	M	T	W	T	F	S	S
1 Oct–2 Nov	10:30–4:30	M		W	T	F	S	S
3 Nov–31 Jan 09	10:30–4:30			W	T	F	S	S
Farm shop								
1 Feb–15 Feb	10:30–4	M	T	W	T	F	S	S
16 Feb–30 Sep	10:30–5	M	T	W	T	F	S	S
1 Oct–31 Jan 09	10:30–4	M	T	W	T	F	S	S
Grounds								
All year	Dawn–dusk	M	T	W	T	F	S	S

Last admission to house 1hr before closing, restaurant 30mins. Shop and restaurant closed 22 Dec–2 Jan 09 inc. Farm shop open limited hours on Christmas Eve and New Year's Eve, closed 25/26 Dec and 1/2 Jan 09

☕ Restaurant. May be limited off-season. Children's menu

👪 Baby-changing facilities. Front-carrying baby slings and hip-carrying infant seats for loan. Children's play area. Children's quiz/trail. Tracker Packs

Stunning colour in the cut-flower garden, Wallington, Northumberland

Dogs assisting visitors with disabilities are always welcome

■ Suitable for school groups. Hands-on activities

🐕 On leads only in grounds and walled garden

➔ [81:NZ030843] **Foot**: Public transport limited, tel. property for details. **Bus**: Snaith's 419 from Morpeth, Wed, Fri only (passing close ⊞ Morpeth); Arriva 508 from ⊞ Newcastle, Sun, June–Oct only. **Road**: A1 N to Newcastle then 20ml NW (A696, airport/Ponteland road), and turn off on B6342 to Cambo. A1 S to Morpeth then 12ml W (B6343)

P Free parking, 200yds

NT properties nearby
Cragside

Intricate topiary at the 17th-century Washington Old Hall

Washington Old Hall

The Avenue, Washington Village, Washington, Tyne & Wear NE38 7LE

 1956 (6:H5)

Manor house associated with the family of George Washington

Washington Old Hall is a delightful stone-built 17th-century manor house, which incorporates parts of the original medieval home of George Washington's direct ancestors. It is from here that the family took their surname of 'Washington'. There are displays on George Washington, and the recent history of the Hall. There is also a fine collection of oil paintings, delftware and heavily carved oak furniture, giving an authentic impression of gentry life following the turbulence of the English Civil War. The tranquil Jacobean garden leads to the Nuttery, a wildflower nut orchard.

ℹ️ **T** 0191 416 6879
   E washingtonoldhall@nationaltrust.org.uk

🎭 4 July Independence Day celebrations. Lunchtime lectures

♿ 🚾🅰️.:.📷P📷 Building 🦽♿
Grounds 🦽

🗄️ Souvenir desk in entrance hall

🍽️ Tea-room (not NT) on first floor. Serving light refreshments (run by Friends of Washington Old Hall)

👶 Hip-carrying infant seats for loan. Children's quiz/trail. Pushchairs admitted (ground floor only)

■ Suitable for school groups. Education room/centre

🐕 On leads only in garden

➔ [88:NZ312566] In Washington Village next to church on the hill. **Cycle**: NCN7, 1ml. **Bus**: Go North East M1-3 from Tyne & Wear Metro Heworth, X2, X88 from ⊞ Sunderland, all go to Galleries bus station then W6 to Hall. **Station**: Heworth (Tyne & Wear Metro) 4ml; Newcastle 7ml. **Road**: 7ml S of Newcastle, 5ml from The Angel of the North. From A1 exit Jct 64 and follow brown signs. From A19 join A1231 and follow brown signs. From all other routes, join A1231 and follow brown signs

P Free parking in small car park beside Old Hall. Otherwise unrestricted parking on The Avenue. Coaches must park on The Avenue

NT properties nearby
Gibside, Ormesby Hall, Penshaw Monument, Souter Lighthouse

Washington Old Hall									
House									
16 Mar–2 Nov	11–5	M	T	W	T	F	S	S
Garden									
As house	10–5	M	T	W	T	F	S	S
Tea-room									
As house	11–4	M	T	W	T	F	S	S
Open Good Fri and Easter Sat									

Please remember – your membership card is always needed for free admission

Wales is a land of myth and legend. Enjoy walking miles of rugged coastline – you may even be lucky enough to catch a glimpse of new-born seals or dolphins riding the waves. Or why not take to the mountains and explore some of the highest peaks in Britain? By following one of the hundreds of footpaths you'll be guaranteed a breathtaking view of some of the most dramatic and iconic landscapes in Wales.

Pembrokeshire

Pembrokeshire is famed for its superb scenically and geologically varied coastline, more than 60 miles of which is cared for by the National Trust. Legends of Celtic saints will take you on a mythical journey into the past.

When following the coastal footpath it's hard not to notice that it is studded with Iron Age promontory forts. There are fine examples at Greenala and Fishpond Camp on the Stackpole Estate, and Porth y Rhaw near Solva. St David's Head is a classic prehistoric landscape complete with chambered graves.

Explorers are very well catered for, with hundreds of miles of coastal and inland footpaths. Fine circular walks can be found at Stackpole (lakes and cliffs), Marloes, St David's Head, Dinas Island near Fishguard, Little Milford and Lawrenny Woods on the secluded River Cleddau.

Porthdinllaen

Llŷn Peninsula

The Llŷn Peninsula is one of the jewels of Wales. Multicoloured beach huts provide a vibrant backdrop to the long, sweeping beach at Llanbedrog. In the sheltered bay at Porthor the sand famously whistles underfoot, due to the unique shape of the grains. The fishing village of Porthdinllaen is picture-postcard perfect. An exhibition about its history and traditions is open throughout the season.

For one of the best views in Wales stroll to the Coastguard's Hut on top of Mynydd Mawr – you may even see Ireland on a clear day. Look out for rare choughs flying overhead, dolphins swimming in the bay and seals basking in the sun. A coastal path has recently been opened around the whole peninsula.

Further south, Llandanwg is well worth a visit. Its beautiful, sandy beach has views across to the Llŷn Peninsula and a medieval church half buried in sand. Egryn, a site of continuous habitation for more than 5,000 years, is only a stone's throw away. The Medieval Hall House and outbuildings are being restored and will be open on certain days later this year.

Marloes Sands, Pembrokeshire

Previous page: a corner of Lord Anglesey's Bedroom, Plas Newydd, Anglesey (4:D2)

Tryfan, with Glyder Fawr, Snowdonia

Snowdonia

Snowdonia is a land of legend, majesty and breathtaking beauty. The National Trust cares for eleven of its peaks, as well as miles of footpaths. A wheelchair-accessible, riverside path in the village of Beddgelert leads to the grave of the legendary faithful hound, Gelert, mistakenly killed by his master after saving the life of the Prince's young baby.

At Craflwyn there are woodland walks meandering past waterfalls and streams. For the more adventurous, the Watkin Path is a spectacular route from Hafod y Llan Farm to Snowdon summit. Along the way you will see where the National Trust is grazing Welsh black cattle to conserve the flora and fauna of this world-famous landscape.

Glyn Tarell in the Brecon Beacons

Carmarthenshire

The Dinefwr Historic Parkland in Carmarthenshire was recently designated a National Nature Reserve. A landscape restoration project is transforming the historic landscape and buildings, as well as improving access and facilities. New walks have been developed through the 'Capability' Brown-inspired landscape. Much of the project is focused on returning it to its former 18th-century glory. This is being done by replacing modern fencing with traditional styles, approximately 2 miles of cleft-oak fencing is being built, walls are being repaired, and plantations of poplars and conifers are being replaced with 6,000 oak saplings.

Why not enjoy an historic walk with stunning views towards the castle, house and along the Tywi Valley? You may even see some resident fallow deer or some of the stunning white park cattle that have been in Dinefwr for more than 1,000 years.

Brecon Beacons

With its spectacular combination of sensational valleys, distinctive flat-topped summits, craggy slopes, tumbling streams and wildlife-rich moorland, the Brecon Beacons, is home to some of Wales' most iconic and dramatic landscapes.

The National Trust cares for more 5,000 hectares (12,400 acres) of the Brecon Beacons, about four per cent of the National Park, including some of its most popular gems – Pen y Fan, Sugarloaf, Skirrid and Henrhyd Falls.

The picturesque beauty spot of Henrhyd Falls on the Nant Llech boasts the impressive title of the highest waterfall in South Wales. The waterfall lies on the boundary of the Carboniferous coal and sandstone. It is only one of a series of beautiful waterfalls produced by the narrow, steep-sided gorges which exist throughout the area at the head of the Neath and Tawe rivers.

www.nationaltrust.org.uk/coastandcountryside

Anglesey

The lagoon at Cemlyn is a haven for wildlife and nesting birds. During the winter it is a great place to come and watch the wildfowl, while the late spring sees the return of a colony of Arctic and common terns for their nesting season. A selection of walks leaflets is available to help guide you on the circular routes along the coast and inland, through farmland and small fields with their typical 'cloddiau' drystone walls. The rocky sea cliffs here are among the oldest in Britain, with some being more than 1,000 million years old.

Rhossili, on the tip of the Gower Peninsula

Ceredigion

The coast of Ceredigion has an unspoilt and intimate charm, and is nationally important as a conservation resource. The gently rolling coastline, with occasional striking rocky outcrops and steep wooded river valleys which run inland, is a valuable example of man's long-term relationship with his environment.

Mwnt is a small horseshoe-shaped bay with steep cliffs that run south from the beach. The site is of great historical importance – it was a 13th-century battlefield against the invading Flemish, who left their mark on many place names in the area. This is probably the best place in Ceredigion to spot a bottlenose dolphin.

A few miles north is Penbryn – a golden beach which is a safe and popular magnet to families. The wooded Hoffnant Valley, also known locally as 'Cwm Lladron' (the Robber's Valley), was a well-known destination for illicit Irish cargoes during the 18th century.

Cwmtudu, another tiny cove famed for smuggling, is also well worth a visit. You can walk for several hours in a tranquil atmosphere through the beautiful coastline to New Quay. The area is rich in legend, and resonates with a distinctive Welsh cultural identity.

Gower

One of Gower's most iconic beauty spots is, undoubtedly, the spectacular Rhossili. The 3-mile long, sweeping bay is on the very tip of the Gower Peninsula. To add to the drama, wooden ribs of the *Helvetia*, shipwrecked in 1887, protrude from the sand at low tide. There are fabulous walks along the clifftop towards the tidal island of Worm's Head and the old coastguard lookout.

The area has a highly valued and wide range of important habitats and species. Among its gems are the black bog ant, chough, rare marsh fritillary butterfly and brown hare. Gower also reflects a broad timeline – there are at least 1,200 archaeological sites within this Area of Outstanding Natural Beauty of different periods and types. These include caves, Iron Age forts, Bronze Age burial cairns, Neolithic chambered tombs, medieval castles

and churches. There are also many remnants of industrial archaeology, such as a lighthouse, a 19th-century silver lead mine, quarries and traces of the 19th-century lime industry, as well as a Second World War radar station.

Below: Llanerchaeron, Ceredigion Right: brown hare

Aberconwy House

Castle Street, Conwy LL32 8AY

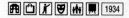 1934 **(4:E2)**

14th-century merchant's house

This is the only medieval merchant's house in Conwy to have survived the turbulent history of the walled town over nearly six centuries. Furnished rooms and an audio-visual presentation show daily life from different periods in its history.

⭐ The house has limited electric lighting and is therefore dark on dull days. No WC, nearest 50yds on quay

ℹ️ **T** 01492 592246
E aberconwyhouse@nationaltrust.org.uk

🎭 Various musical events

♿ **Building** 🔾

👪 Family guide. Children's quiz/trail

▣ Suitable for school groups

➡️ [115:SH781777] At junction of Castle Street and High Street. **Cycle**: NCN5. **Bus**: from surrounding areas. **Station**: Conwy 300yds

🅿️ No parking on site

NT properties nearby
Bodnant Garden, Conwy Suspension Bridge, Penrhyn Castle

Aberconwy House								
House								
20 Mar–2 Nov	11–5	M	T	W	T	F	S	S
Shop								
1 Mar–24 Mar	10–5	M	T	W	T	F	S	S
25 Mar–29 Oct	10–5:30	M	T	W	T	F	S	S
30 Oct–31 Dec	10–5	M	T	W	T	F	S	S
2 Jan–31 Jan 09	11–5	M	T	W	T	F	S	S

Shop closed 25, 26 Dec. Shop opens at 11 on Suns

If you enjoyed discovering Aberdulais Falls, you might like to try searching for gold at Dolaucothi Gold Mines

Aberdeunant

Taliaris, Llandeilo, Carmarthenshire SA19 6DL

1996 **(4:E8)**

Traditional Carmarthenshire farmhouse in an unspoilt setting

⭐ As the property is extremely small, visitor access is limited to no more than six people at a time. The property is administered and maintained on the Trust's behalf by a resident tenant. The gegin fawr (farm kitchen) and one bedroom are shown to visitors. No WC

ℹ️ **T** 01558 650177 (Dolaucothi Gold Mines)
E aberdeunant@nationaltrust.org.uk

➡️ Full details are sent on booking

Aberdeunant
Admission by guided tour and appointment only. Tours take place April to Sept: first Sat & Sun of each month 12–5. Tel. Dolaucothi Gold Mines to book. Last booking taken at 5 on Fri prior to opening

Aberdulais Falls

Aberdulais, nr Neath, Neath & Port Talbot SA10 8EU

1980 **(4:E9)**

Famous waterfalls and fascinating industrial site with tin workers' exhibition

For more than 400 years the Falls provided the energy to drive the wheels of industry. In 1584 a copper-smelting furnace was established and the remains of the only survivor of a small water-powered tin works can be seen. It has also been visited by famous artists, such as Turner in 1796. The site today houses a unique hydroelectric scheme which has been developed to harness the waters of the River Dulais. The Turbine House provides access to an interactive computer, fish pass, observation window and display panels. Special lifts allow disabled visitors access to the upper levels, which afford excellent views of the Falls. The waterwheel is the largest currently used in Europe to generate electricity, which makes Aberdulais Falls self-sufficient in environmentally friendly energy. The new visitor building has an air heat recovery unit to heat the building – the first commercial one in the UK.

Unless indicated, last admission is always 30mins before closing time

What's new in 2008 Exciting new exhibition and interpretation project shows how Aberdulais Falls played an important role in the industrialisation of South Wales. Visitor centre and exhibition on tin men and their contribution to an expanding world. Tourism information centre for the Neath Valley and industrial heritage sites

⭐ The operation of the fish pass, waterwheel and turbine is subject to water levels and maintenance

ℹ️ **T** 01639 636674
E aberdulais@nationaltrust.org.uk

🚶 Guided tours by arrangement

♿ 🚻 🦽 🅿️ 🚗 Building ♿ ⬍ 🔉
Grounds ♿ ➡️

🍴 The Friends of Aberdulais Falls serve light refreshments in the Old Works Library and Victorian schoolroom; other times by arrangement. Bar meals and limited car-parking at Dulais Rock Inn (not NT)

🚼 Baby-changing facilities. Pushchairs and baby back-carriers admitted. Children's quiz/trail

🏫 Suitable for school groups. Education room/centre. Adult study days. Artists' days

🐕 On leads only

➡️ [170:SS772995] **Foot**: via Neath–Aberdulais Canal footpath. **Cycle**: NCN47 passes property. Access near B&Q Neath to Neath Canal towpath and Aberdulais Canal Basin. **Bus**: First 158 Swansea–Banwen, 154/8, 161 from Neath; Veolia 63 Brecon–Swansea; 60:60 Coaches 68 to Neath. **Station**: Neath 3ml. **Road**: on A4109, 3ml NE of Neath. 4ml from M4 exit 43 at Llandarcy, take A465 signposted Vale of Neath

🅿️ Parking outside and on opposite side of road

NT properties nearby
Dinefwr Park and Castle, Henrhyd Falls, Rhossili Visitor Centre

Aberdulais Falls									
1 Feb–16 Mar	11–4	M	T	W	T	F	**S**	**S**
17 Mar–2 Nov*	10–5	**M**	**T**	**W**	**T**	**F**	S	S
7 Nov–21 Dec	11–4	M	T	W	T	**F**	**S**	**S**
3 Jan–31 Jan 09	11–4	M	T	W	T	F	**S**	**S**
Open BH Mons and Good Fri: 11–6. *BHols and Sat/Sun open 11–6									

Aberdulais Falls' waterwheel still generates electricity

Bodnant Garden

Tal-y-Cafn, Colwyn Bay, Conwy LL28 5RE

🏠 ✳️ 🍴 🌳 🚻 🔔 1949   (4:F2)

World-famous garden noted for its botanical collections

One of the world's most spectacular gardens, Bodnant Garden is situated above the River Conwy, with stunning views across Snowdonia. Begun in 1875, Bodnant Garden is the creation of four generations of Aberconways and features huge Italianate terraces and formal lawns on its upper level, with a wooded valley, stream and wild garden below. There are dramatic colours throughout the season, with fine collections of rhododendrons, magnolias and camellias in early spring, and the spectacular laburnum arch, a 55-yard tunnel of golden blooms from mid May to early June. Herbaceous borders, roses, hydrangeas, water lilies and clematis delight throughout the summer, with superb autumn colours during October.

What's new in 2008 Entrance is now via a ramp and underpass beneath the road. New visitor reception. Round Garden completely replanted with box hedging, scented plants and herbs

⭐ The Garden and Pavilion Tea-room are managed on behalf of the Trust by the Hon. Michael McLaren QC. Picnics on grass in car park area only

For further information go to www.nationaltrust.org.uk

Bodnant Garden									
Garden									
8 Mar–2 Nov	10–5	M	T	W	T	F	S	S	
Plant centre									
All year	10–5	M	T	W	T	F	S	S	
Tea-room									
As garden	10–5								
RHS members free									

ℹ️ **T** 01492 650460
E bodnantgarden@nationaltrust.org.uk

🎭 Occasional open-air evening events

♿ 🚾 ♿ 🅿️ **Grounds** ♿ ➡️

🏪 Shop (not NT). Plant sales, gift shop, art and craft studios. Tel: 01492 650731

🍴 Bodnant Pavilion Tea-room (licensed) in car park. Serving a wide range of home-produced food. Morning coffee, lunches and afternoon teas

👶 Baby-changing facilities. Pushchairs and baby back-carriers admitted. Front-carrying baby slings for loan

The laburnum arch at Bodnant Garden, Conwy

➡️ [115/116:SH801723] **Bus**: Arriva 25, 84 from Llandudno (passing ☰ Llandudno Junction). **Station**: Tal-y-Cafn (U) 2ml. **Road**: 8ml S of Llandudno and Colwyn Bay off A470, entrance ½ml along the Eglwysbach road. Signposted from A55, exit 19

🅿️ Free parking, 50yds. Tight turning circle for coach access

NT properties nearby
Aberconwy House, Conwy Suspension Bridge, Penrhyn Castle, Tŷ Mawr Wybrnant

Chirk Castle

Chirk, Wrexham LL14 5AF

🏰 ✝️ ♣️ 🌳 🏠 🏠 🖥️ 🎿 🎡 🛡️ 👫
🎦 🚶 🔔 🍷 1981   **(4:G3)**

Magnificent medieval fortress of the Welsh Marches

Completed in 1310, Chirk is the last Welsh castle from the reign of Edward I still lived in today. Features from its 700 years include the medieval tower and dungeon, 18th-century servants' hall and 20th-century laundry. There is also a 17th-century Long Gallery and grand 18th-century state apartments, with elaborate plasterwork, Adam-style furniture, tapestries and portraits. In the award-winning gardens are clipped yews, herbaceous borders and a stunning shrub garden, with many rare varieties. Other areas are more informal, with a thatched 'Hawk House' and rock garden. A terrace with stunning views looks out over the Cheshire and Salop plains and leads to a classical pavilion and 17th-century lime tree avenue. The 18th-century parkland provides a habitat for rare invertebrates and contains many mature trees and also some splendid wrought-iron gates, made in 1719 by the Davies brothers.

What's new in 2008 Conservation in action and roof-top guided tours. Victorian and medieval family activity rooms with costumes and games. Bird hide on woodland walk. Restored farm buildings and pigsties, complete with first residents for 50 years. Forge Tea-room at Home Farm Visitor Centre

⭐ All visitors, including members, need to obtain tickets from Home Farm Visitor Centre before going up to castle

Chirk Castle: a magnificent medieval fortress

🖵 Licensed restaurant in castle courtyard. Children's menu. Refreshment kiosk and Forge Tea-room at Home Farm Visitor Centre

👫 Baby-changing and feeding facilities. Front carrying baby slings and hip-carrying infant seats for loan. Family activity rooms. Children's play area. Children's quiz/trail. Children's Tracker Packs for woodland walk

📖 Suitable for school groups. Education room/centre. Live interpretation. Hands-on activities. Adult study days

🐕 On leads and only in car park and on estate walks (closed Nov–Jan 09 inc.)

→ [126:SJ275388] **Foot**: permitted footpaths from Chirk and Offa's Dyke Path open April–Sept. Entrance and exit drives during season 1½ml to visitor centre and castle. 1½ml from Llangollen Canal–moor near Chirk Tunnel. **Bus**: Arriva 2/A Wrexham–Oswestry. **Station**: Chirk (U) ¼ml to gates, 1½ml to castle. **Road**: entrance 1ml off A5, 2ml W of Chirk village; 7ml S of Wrexham, signposted off A483

🅿 Free parking, 50yds to visitor centre, 200yds to castle. Short, steep hill from Visitor Centre to castle and garden

NT properties nearby
Attingham Park, Erddig, Powis Castle

ℹ **T** 01691 777701
E chirkcastle@nationaltrust.org.uk

👟 Special interest tours by arrangement (15+), Wed–Fri am only. Connoisseurs' tour, veteran trees, Head Gardener tour, historic laundry tour. Conservation in action and roof-top tours daily from 11, 15 March–2 Nov. Sunrise beind-the-scene tours, 2–17 Feb on open days

🛡 Including medieval festival, craft fairs, living history, children's events and family Thursdays in summer school holidays. Snowdrop walks in February. 'Victorian Christmas at the Castle' in December. Send sae for details

🚶 Circular 1¼ml walk through historic parkland, with ancient trees and wild flowers

♿ 🚻 ♿ 🎧 👓 🅿 Dₗ 🖼 Building ♿ ♿
Grounds ♿

🏠 NT gift shop. Farm shop with local and estate produce. Plant sales, including plants from garden. Second-hand bookshop

Chirk Castle									
Castle									
2 Feb–10 Feb	11–4	M	T	W	T	F	**S**	**S**
13 Feb–17 Feb	11–4	M	T	**W**	**T**	**F**	**S**	**S**
15 Mar–30 Jun	11–5	M	T	**W**	**T**	**F**	**S**	**S**
1 Jul–31 Aug	11–5	M	**T**	**W**	**T**	**F**	**S**	**S**
1 Sep–30 Sep	11–5	M	T	**W**	**T**	**F**	**S**	**S**
1 Oct–2 Nov	11–4	M	T	**W**	**T**	**F**	**S**	**S**
6 Dec–14 Dec	11–5	M	T	W	T	F	**S**	**S**
Garden/estate									
As castle*	10–6**								
NT shop/farm shop									
As castle	10–5***								
Tea-room/restaurant									
As castle	10–5***								

Open BH Mons. Last admission to garden 1hr before closing. *Not open during Dec. **Closes 5 in Oct. ***Closes 4 in Feb & Oct. Estate not open Feb/Dec

Unless indicated, last admission is always 30mins before closing time

Cilgerran Castle

nr Cardigan, Pembrokeshire SA43 2SF

🏰 📷 1938   **(4:C7)**

Striking 13th-century ruined castle

The remains of the castle are perched overlooking the spectacular Teifi Gorge and have inspired many artists, including Turner.

⭐ Cilgerran Castle is in the guardianship of Cadw: Welsh Historic Monuments

ℹ️ **T** 01239 621339
E cilgerrancastle@nationaltrust.org.uk

➡️ [145:SN195431] **Bus**: Richards 430, Midway 431 from Cardigan; otherwise First/Richards 460/1 🚋 Carmarthen–Cardigan, alight Llechryd, 1½ml by footpath. **Road**: on rock above left bank of the Teifi, 3ml SE of Cardigan, 1½ml E of A478

Cilgerran Castle		M	T	W	T	F	S	S
1 Feb–20 Mar	9:30–4	M	T	W	T	F	S	S
21 Mar–31 Oct	9:30–6	M	T	W	T	F	S	S
1 Nov–31 Jan 09	9:30–4	M	T	W	T	F	S	S

Rhododendrons in Colby Woodland Garden. Just a part of the year-round colour

Colby Woodland Garden

Amroth, Narberth, Pembrokeshire SA67 8PP

❄️ 🌷 🛠️ 🏞️ 🏠 📷 ☕ 🎪 🎭 🚼 🏫
🚶 1980   **(4:C8)**

Beautiful woodland garden with year-round interest

The 3.25-hectare (8-acre) garden has a fine display of colour in spring – with rhododendrons, magnolias, azaleas and camellias, underplanted with bluebells. Later highlights are the summer hydrangeas and autumn foliage. Open and wooded pathways through the estate offer a variety of lovely walks.

What's new in 2008 Ongoing opening of new vistas and pathways along with widespread new planting for greater access and enjoyment. New map of estate woodland walks

⭐ The early 19th-century house is not open; Mr & Mrs A. Scourfield Lewis kindly allow access to the walled garden during opening hours

ℹ️ **T** 01834 811885 **E** colby@nationaltrust.org.uk

🎭 Including guided walks and lunch with Head Gardener, guided history tours and lunch, family fun days, Easter trails and art days

🚶 Beautiful walks through the wooded valleys of the Colby Estate and down to the sea

♿ 🚾 🏠 📷 ⬤⬤ ♿ **Grounds** 🏠 ➡️ ♿

📷 NT gift shop and gallery displaying work of Pembrokeshire artists and craftspeople. Plants from local peat-free nurseries

☕ Bothy tea-rooms (NT-approved concession) (licensed). Serves freshly prepared food using local produce. Children's menu

🚼 Baby-changing facilities. Pushchairs and baby back-carriers admitted. Hip-carrying infant seats for loan. Children's quiz/trail

🏫 Suitable for school groups

🐕 On leads, but not in walled garden

Colby Woodland Garden		M	T	W	T	F	S	S
Woodland garden/shop/gallery/tea-room								
15 Mar–2 Nov	10–5	M	T	W	T	F	S	S
Walled garden								
15 Mar–2 Nov	11–5	M	T	W	T	F	S	S

Many Trust properties are offering Gift Aid on Entry for non-members, see page 10

➜ [158:SN155080] **Foot**: from beach via public footpath in Amroth (beside Amroth Arms). **Bus**: Silcox 350/1 from Tenby (passing ☒ Kilgetty). **Station**: Kilgetty (U) 2½ml. **Road**: 1½ml inland from Amroth beside Carmarthen Bay. Follow brown signs from A477 Tenby-Carmarthen road or off coast road at Amroth Castle

P Free parking, 100yds. Contact property for route map for coaches and cars

NT properties nearby
Stackpole Estate, Tudor Merchant's House

Conwy Suspension Bridge

Conwy LL32 8LD

🔲🔲🔲🔲🔲🔲🔲 1965   **(4:E2)**

Elegant suspension bridge and toll-keeper's house

See how trade and travel brought Conwy to life and discover how a husband and wife kept Thomas Telford's bridge open every day of the year, whatever the weather.

What's new in 2008 Guidebook exploring the story of this fascinating bridge and town

⭐ No WC

i **T** 01492 573282
E conwybridge@nationaltrust.org.uk

♿ **Building** 🔲

🔲 NT shop 600yds from bridge

👫 Family guide

🔲 Suitable for school groups

➜ [115:SH785775] 100yds from town centre, adjacent to Conwy Castle. **Cycle**: NCN5. **Bus**: from surrounding areas. **Station**: Conwy ¼ml; Llandudno Junction ½ml

P No parking on site

NT properties nearby
Aberconwy House, Bodnant Garden, Penrhyn Castle

Dinefwr Park and Castle

Llandeilo, Carmarthenshire SA19 6RT

🔲🔲🔲🔲🔲🔲🔲🔲🔲🔲🔲
🔲🔲🔲🔲 1990   **(4:E8)**

12th-century Welsh castle and 18th-century landscape park, enclosing a medieval deer park

Dinefwr Park and Castle is home to more than 100 fallow deer and a small herd of Dinefwr White Park cattle. A number of scenic walks include access to Dinefwr Castle, with fine views across the Towy Valley. There is also a wooded boardwalk, particularly suitable for families and wheelchair users. Newton House, built in 1660, but now with a Victorian façade and a fountain garden, is at the heart of the site. The basement and ground floor are furnished c.1912 and new exhibition rooms on the first floor tell the story of this land of power and influence.

What's new in 2008 Exhibition on the first floor of Newton House tells the story of the history and landscape of Dinefwr. NT gift shop

i **T** 01558 824512
E dinefwr@nationaltrust.org.uk

🔲 Guided tours of Newton House and the deer park by arrangement (additional charge). Badger watches can be booked

🔲 Food and Country Festival, inc. world sheep dog trials, 11–14 Sept. Admission charge

🔲 Five walks leaflets

🔲🔲🔲🔲🔲🔲 **Building** 🔲🔲
Grounds 🔲

🔲 New NT gift shop

🔲 Tea-room (not NT). Children's menu

👫 Baby-changing and feeding facilities. Pushchairs admitted. Children's quiz/trail

🔲 Suitable for school groups. Education room/centre

🔲 On leads and only in outer park

Conwy Suspension Bridge									
20 Mar–2 Nov	11–5	**M**	**T**	**W**	**T**	**F**	**S**	**S**	

Dinefwr Park and Castle									
15 Mar–2 Nov	11–5	**M**	**T**	**W**	**T**	**F**	**S**	**S**
7 Nov–21 Dec	11–5	M	T	W	T	**F**	**S**	**S**

Newton House, at the heart of Dinefwr Park, has a Victorian façade but was built in 1660

➡ [159:SN625225] **Bus**: from surrounding areas to Llandeilo, then 1ml. **Station**: Llandeilo ½ml. **Road**: on W outskirts of Llandeilo A40(T); from Swansea take M4 to Pont Abraham, then A48(T) to Cross Hands and A476 to Llandeilo; entrance by police station

🅿 Parking, 50yds. Narrow access

NT properties nearby
Aberdeunant, Aberdulais Falls, Dolaucothi Gold Mines, Paxton's Tower

Dolaucothi Gold Mines

Pumsaint, Llanwrda, Carmarthenshire SA19 8US

🏛 ⚒ 🦮 🏠 👜 🎻 🖼 🎭 👫 🚌 🚶

🚲 1941 (4:E7)

Gold mines in use from Roman times to the 20th century

These unique gold mines are set amid wooded hillsides overlooking the beautiful Cothi Valley. The Romans who exploited the site almost 2,000 years ago left behind a complex of pits, channels, adits and tanks. Mining resumed in the 19th century and continued through the 20th century, reaching a peak in 1938. Guided tours take visitors through the Roman and the more recent underground workings. The main mine yard contains a collection of 1930s mining machinery, an exhibition about the history of gold and gold mining, video and interpretation. Gold panning gives visitors the opportunity to experience the frustrations of the search for gold. Other attractions include waymarked walks and picnic areas. There is fishing and accommodation on the estate, including a 35-pitch touring caravan site.

⭐ Underground tour (charge inc. NT members). Stout footwear essential. Younger children may not be carried on the tours. Pushchairs may be taken on the Long Adit tour, but children must wear a correctly fitting hard hat. Please tel. for advice

ℹ **T** 01558 825146 (Infoline), 01558 650177 **E** dolaucothi@nationaltrust.org.uk

🎭 Roman weekends, vintage machinery day, spooky Hallowe'en tours, Easter trails

Dolaucothi Gold Mines									
Mines									
15 Mar–2 Nov	10–5	M	T	W	T	F	S	S
Shop									
15 Mar–2 Nov	10–5	M	T	W	T	F	S	S
Christmas shop									
5 Nov–21 Dec	11–5	M	T	W	T	F	S	S
Tea-room									
15 Mar–2 Nov	10–5	M	T	W	T	F	S	S

Groups can be booked at other times. Pumsaint Information Centre and estate walks open all year. Underground tours last about 1hr and involve hillside walking, so stout footwear is essential; helmets with lights are provided. Smaller children will be allowed on the tours only at the discretion of the property staff. Please tel. for advice

Charges for National Trust members apply on some special event days

🚶 Leaflet showing walks around the 1,000ha (2,500-acre) Dolaucothi Estate

♿ 🏫🏫⚬⚬🅿 **Building** 🏛

🏺 Welsh gold for sale (including by mail order)

🍴 Tea-room

👶 Baby-changing and feeding facilities. Pushchairs admitted. Children's quiz/trail. Children's parties (booking essential)

🏫 Suitable for school groups. Education room/centre

🐕 On leads only. May go on guided Roman tour

🚲 2½ml of NT permitted cycle route

➡ [146:SN662403] **Bus:** Morris 289 from Lampeter. **Station:** Llanwrda (U), 8ml. **Road:** between Lampeter and Llanwrda on A482

🅿 Free parking. Overflow car park available across road from main entrance

NT properties nearby
Aberdeunant, Dinefwr Park and Castle, Llanerchaeron

The well-stocked kitchen at Erddig, Wrexham

Erddig

Wrexham LL13 0YT

🏠🏠✝❄🏵🐑🏠☕🖌🎧🎵🎋
🎭👥🚪🚶🚲🍴 1973   **(4:H3)**

Atmospheric house and estate, vividly evoking its family and servants

Erddig is one of the most fascinating houses in Britain, not least because of the unusually close relationship that existed between the family of the house and their servants. The beautiful and extensive range of outbuildings includes kitchen, laundry, bakehouse, stables, sawmill, smithy and joiner's shop, while the stunning state rooms display most of their original 18th- and 19th-century furniture and furnishings, including some exquisite Chinese wallpaper. The large walled garden has been restored to its 18th-century formal design and has a Victorian parterre and yew walk. It also contains the National Collection of Ivies. There is an extensive park with woodland walks. Horse-drawn carriage rides are available.

Erddig

House

15 Mar–31 Mar	12–4	M	T	W	T	F	S	S
1 Apr–30 Jun	12–5	M	T	W	T	F	S	S
1 Jul–31 Aug	12–5	M	T	W	T	F	S	S
1 Sep–30 Sep	12–5	M	T	W	T	F	S	S
1 Oct–2 Nov	12–4	M	T	W	T	F	S	S
8 Nov–21 Dec	12–4	M	T	W	T	F	S	S

Garden/restaurant/shop

9 Feb–9 Mar	11–4	M	T	W	T	F	S	S
15 Mar–31 Mar	11–5	M	T	W	T	F	S	S
1 Apr–30 Jun	11–6	M	T	W	T	F	S	S
1 Jul–31 Aug	10–6	M	T	W	T	F	S	S
1 Sep–30 Sep	11–6	M	T	W	T	F	S	S
1 Oct–2 Nov	11–5	M	T	W	T	F	S	S
8 Nov–21 Dec	11–4	M	T	W	T	F	S	S

Restaurant & shop close 1hr earlier 15 Mar–2 Nov. Open Good Fri. Last admission 1hr before closing. Guided tours of the house are conducted every Thurs in July and Aug. Limited access Nov/Dec

What's new in 2008 Bicycles available for hire. Virtual tour. Baby food warming facilities

★ Most rooms have no electric light; visitors wishing to make a close study of pictures and textiles should avoid dull days. The Small Chinese Room is open Wednesday and Saturday on application

ℹ **T** 01978 315151 (Infoline), 01978 355314 **E** erddig@nationaltrust.org.uk

Three different walks

Building Grounds

NT shop. Plant sales. Second-hand bookshop. Christmas opening

Licensed restaurant. Children's menu. Tea-room

Baby changing facilities. Baby food warming facilities. Front-carrying baby slings and hip-carrying infant seats for loan. Children's quiz. Garden adventure trail. Garden Tracker Packs. Garden Art Packs. Family events all year

Suitable for school groups. Education room/centre. Hands-on activities

On leads and only in car park and country park

Bridleway crosses estate giving cyclists shared access. Cycle hire

→ [117:SJ326482] **Bus**: from surrounding areas. Alight Felin Puleston, 1ml walk through the country park. **Station**: Wrexham Central (U) 2½ml, Wrexham General 3½ml via Erddig Rd & footpath. **Road**: 2ml S of Wrexham, signposted A525 Whitchurch road, or A483/A5152 Oswestry/Chester road

P Free parking, 200yds. Passing bays on access drive

NT properties nearby
Chirk Castle

The Kymin

Monmouth, Monmouthshire NP25 3SE

1902 (4:H8)

Landmark hill topped by two interesting Georgian buildings

Set in 4 hectares (9 acres) of woods and pleasure grounds, this property encompasses a small two-storey circular banqueting house and naval temple, a monument dedicated to the glories of the British Navy. Nelson visited the site in 1802. The grounds afford spectacular views of the surrounding countryside.

★ A croquet set is available for hire. WC not always available

ℹ **T** 01600 719241 **E** kymin@nationaltrust.org.uk

Offa's Dyke footpath and Wysis Way footpath run through the land

Building Grounds

Children's quiz/trail

In grounds only

The Kymin

Round House

21 Mar–26 Oct	11–4	M	T	W	T	F	S	S

Temple/grounds

All year		M	T	W	T	F	S	S

Open Good Fri. Round House: last entry 3:45

Dogs assisting visitors with disabilities are always welcome

→ [162:SO528125] **Foot**: Offa's Dyke Path runs through the property. **Bus**: H & H 60 from Newport (passing close ▣ Newport), Drake 83 from Abergavenny (passing close ▣ Abergavenny), Stagecoach in Wye & Dean 416 from ▣ Hereford, Classic 65 from Chepstow (passing close ▣ Chepstow), Stagecoach in Wye & Dean 34 from Ross-on-Wye. On all alight Monmouth, then 1½ml. Also H & H/Stagecoach in South Wales 69 from Chepstow (passing close ▣ Chepstow), alight Wyesham, then 1ml. **Road**: 2ml E of Monmouth and signposted off A4136

P Free parking, 300yds. Not suitable for coaches. Steep narrow road with hairpin bends from junction with A4136

NT properties nearby
Skenfrith Castle, Skirrid Fawr, The Weir, Westbury Court Garden

Llanerchaeron

Ciliau Aeron, nr Aberaeron, Ceredigion SA48 8DG

1989   (4:D6)

18th-century Welsh gentry estate – a rare survival

Mr J. P. Ponsonby Lewes, last of the ten generations of the family to have lived here, bequeathed Llanerchaeron to the National Trust in 1989. This rare example of a self-sufficient 18th-century Welsh minor gentry estate has survived virtually unaltered. The villa, designed in the 1790s, is the most complete example of the early work of John Nash. It has its own service courtyard with dairy, laundry, brewery and salting house, and walled kitchen gardens producing fruit, vegetables, herbs and plants, all now on sale in season. The pleasure grounds with ornamental lake provide wonderful peaceful walks. The Home Farm complex has an impressive range of traditional and atmospheric outbuildings and is now a working organic farm with Welsh Black cattle, Llanwenog sheep and rare Welsh pigs. Visitors can see farming activities in progress, such as lambing, shearing and hay-making. Beyond, the wide expanse of parkland offers breathtaking walks through the beautiful Aeron Valley.

Llanerchaeron									
15 Mar–20 Jul	11:30–4	M	T	**W**	**T**	**W**	**T**	**F**	**S** **S**
22 Jul–31 Aug	11:30–4	M	**T**	**W**	**T**	**W**	**T**	**F**	**S** **S**
3 Sep–2 Nov	11:30–4	M	T	**W**	**T**	**W**	**T**	**F**	**S** **S**

Open BH Mons. Farm and garden open at 11 & close at 5. Car park closes at 5:30

What's new in 2008 Restored lake and waterwheel. Check website for regular farming activities

ℹ️ **T** 01545 570200, 01545 573024 (Visitor Services Manager)
E llanerchaeron@nationaltrust.org.uk

🏃 Guided tours of the garden and Home Farm start 1:30 every Thur, June to end Sept. £1, inc. NT members. Mobile induction loop will be available on request

🎭 Daffodil days, Easter trail, plant fair, shearing day, brewing weekend, children's activity days, learn-about-farming day, apple week

🚶 Five walks leaflets (50p each)

♿ **Building** **Grounds**

🛍️ Shop area in visitor building selling local jams, chutneys and beer, Llanerchaeron farm meat (pork, beef and lamb) and fresh produce and plants from the walled garden. Range of NT gifts and books available

The well-stocked herb garden in the East Walled Garden at Llanerchaeron, Ceredigion

Please remember – your membership card is always needed for free admission

- 🍵 Tea-room (NT-approved concession) in visitor building. Light lunches and teas using local produce
- 👪 Baby-changing and feeding facilities. Hip-carrying infant seats for loan. Children's guide. Children's quiz/trail. Easter trail, children's activity days, learn-about-farming day
- 🎒 Suitable for school groups. Education room/centre. Adult study days
- 🚲 Lane from Llanerchaeron links with the cycle track to Aberaeron
- ➡ [146:SN480602] **Foot**: 2½ml foot/cycle track from Aberaeron to property along old railway track. **Bus**: Arriva/First X40 ➡ Aberystwyth–➡ Carmarthen. **Road**: 2½ml E of Aberaeron off A482
- 🅿 Free parking, 50yds

NT properties nearby
Dinefwr Park and Castle, Dolaucothi Gold Mines, Mwnt, Penbryn

Penrhyn Castle

Bangor, Gwynedd LL57 4HN

🏯✝⚒♣🏠🍵🗝🎧🎭👪
🎒🍷 1951   (4:E2)

19th-century fantasy castle with spectacular contents and grounds

This enormous neo-Norman castle sits between Snowdonia and the Menai Strait. Built by Thomas Hopper between 1820 and 1845 for the wealthy Pennant family, who made their fortune from Jamaican sugar and Welsh slate, the castle is crammed with fascinating things such as a 1-ton slate bed made for Queen Victoria. Hopper also designed the castle's interior with

Penrhyn Castle: a 19th-century fantasy castle

elaborate carvings, plasterwork and mock-Norman furniture. The castle contains an outstanding collection of paintings. The Victorian kitchen and other servants' rooms, including scullery, larders and chef's sitting room, have been restored to reveal the preparations for the banquet for the Prince of Wales' visit in 1894. The stable block houses an industrial railway museum, a model railway museum and a superb dolls' museum displaying a large collection of 19th- and 20th-century dolls. The 24.3 hectares (60 acres) of grounds include parkland, an extensive exotic tree and shrub collection and a Victorian walled garden.

- ℹ **T** 01248 371337 (Infoline), 01248 353084
  E penrhyncastle@nationaltrust.org.uk
- 🗝 Specialist guided tours
- 🎧 Adult's and child's, in English and Welsh, £1

 Building 🦽🦽
Grounds 🦽

- 🍵 Licensed tea-room. Children's menu. Kiosk in grounds

Penrhyn Castle								
Castle								
19 Mar–30 Jun	12–5	M	T	W	T	F	S	S
1 Jul–31 Aug	11–5	M	T	W	T	F	S	S
1 Sep–2 Nov	12–5	M	T	W	T	F	S	S
Shop/museum								
19 Mar–2 Nov	11–5	M	T	W	T	F	S	S

Grounds and tea-room as castle but open 1hr earlier. Victorian kitchen: as castle but last admission 4:45. Last audio tour 4

Unless indicated, last admission is always 30mins before closing time

Redesigned in the 18th century, Plas Newydd is an elegant house in a stunning setting

🛉 Baby-changing and feeding facilities. Front-carrying baby slings and hip-carrying infant seats for loan. Children's play area. Children's guide. Children's quiz/trail. Model railway museum and dolls' museum

▥ Suitable for school groups. Education room/centre. Hands-on activities. Adult study days

🐕 On leads and only in grounds

➔ [115:SH602720] **Cycle**: NCN5, 1¼ml. **Bus**: Arriva 5/5X Caernarfon-Llandudno, KMP 9 Llandudno–Llangefni, 9A/B Llandudno–Llanberis, Silver Star 6, Arriva 7, 67 Bangor–Bethesda; 66 Bangor–Gerlan. All pass close ≋ Bangor and end of drive to castle. **Station**: Bangor 3ml. **Road**: 1ml E of Bangor, at Llandygai on A5122. Signposted from junction 11 of A55 and A5

🅿 Free parking, 500yds

NT properties nearby
Aberconwy House, Conwy Suspension Bridge, Glan Faenol, Plas Newydd, Plas yn Rhiw, Tŷ Mawr Wybrnant

Plas Newydd

Llanfairpwll, Anglesey LL61 6DQ

🏠 ❄ 🦆 🏭 🏚 ☕ 🛒 🎿 🎴 🎭 🛉 🏮
🚶 🔔 🍷 1976   (4:D2)

Home of the Marquess of Anglesey, with spectacular views of Snowdonia

Set amidst breathtakingly beautiful scenery on the banks of the Menai Strait, this elegant house was redesigned by James Wyatt in the 18th century and is an interesting mixture of classical and Gothic. The comfortable interior, restyled in the 1930s, is famous for its association with Rex Whistler, whose largest painting is here. There is also an exhibition about his work. A military museum contains campaign relics of the 1st Marquess of Anglesey, who commanded the cavalry at the Battle of Waterloo. There is a fine spring garden and Australasian arboretum with an understorey of shrubs and wild flowers, as well as a summer terrace and, later, massed hydrangeas and autumn colour. A woodland walk gives access to a marine walk on the Menai Strait.

For further information go to www.nationaltrust.org.uk

★ Historical cruises – boat trips on the Menai Strait – operate from the property, weather and tide permitting (additional charge). House is accessible to manual wheelchairs only

ℹ️ **T** 01248 715272 (Infoline), 01248 714795 **E** plasnewydd@nationaltrust.org.uk

🎫 Connoisseurs' and garden tours

🛡️ Send sae for details

🚶 Woodland & marine walk (leaflet available)

♿ 🚻 ⬚ ⬚ ⬚ 📷 P🅿 D🅿 **Building** ⬚ ⬚ **Grounds** ⬚

📖 Second-hand bookshop

☕ Tea-room and coffee shop (licensed). Home-cooked food using local produce whenever possible. Seasonal menu in Nov & Dec. Children's menu

🚼 Baby-changing facilities. Front-carrying baby slings and hip-carrying infant seats for loan. Children's play area. Family guide. High chairs in tea-room

🏫 Suitable for school groups

➡️ [114/115:SH521696] **Cycle**: NCN8, ¼ml. **Bus**: Arriva 42 Bangor–Llangefni (passing ≋ Bangor & close ≋ Llanfairpwll). **Station**: Llanfairpwll (U), 1¾ml. **Road**: 2ml SW of Llanfairpwll A55 junctions 7 and 8a, or A4080 to Brynsiencyn; turn off A5 at W end of Britannia Bridge

🅿️ Free parking, 400yds

NT properties nearby
Penrhyn Castle

Plas Newydd									
House/coffee shop/bookshop									
1 Mar–12 Mar	12–4*	**M**	**T**	**W**	T	F	**S**	**S**
15 Mar–29 Oct	12–5*	**M**	**T**	**W**	T	F	**S**	**S**
Garden/walks									
1 Mar–12 Mar	11–4	M	T	W	T	F	**S**	**S**
15 Mar–29 Oct	11–5:30	**M**	**T**	**W**	T	F	**S**	**S**
Shop/tea-room									
1 Mar–12 Mar	10:30–4	M	T	W	T	F	**S**	**S**
15 Mar–29 Oct	10:30–5:30	**M**	**T**	**W**	T	F	**S**	**S**
1 Nov–14 Dec	11–4	M	T	W	T	F	**S**	**S**

Open Good Fri. *Coffee shop and bookshop as house but opens 11:30. Rhododendron garden open early April–early June, 11–5:30

Plas yn Rhiw

Rhiw, Pwllheli, Gwynedd LL53 8AB

🏠 ❄️ 🚻 🏠 ⬚ ☕ 🎫 🎭 🎭 🚼
🏫 1952 **(4:C4)**

Delightful manor house with ornamental garden and wonderful views

The house was rescued from neglect and lovingly restored by the three Keating sisters, who bought it in 1938. The views from the grounds and gardens across Cardigan Bay are among the most spectacular in Britain. The house is 16th century with Georgian additions, and the garden contains many beautiful flowering trees and shrubs, with beds framed by box hedges and grass paths. Stunning whatever the season.

ℹ️ **T** 01758 780219 **E** plasynrhiw@nationaltrust.org.uk

🎫 Specialist guided tours by arrangement

🛡️ Plant sales. Easter egg hunt

♿ 🚻 ⬚ ⬚ D🅿 **Building** ⬚ **Grounds** ⬚

☕ Hot and cold drinks available in shop

🚼 Baby-changing facilities. Easter egg hunt

🏫 Suitable for school groups

🐕 On leads and only on the woodland walk

➡️ [123:SH237282] **Bus**: Arriva 17B, Nefyn 8B from Pwllheli (passing ≋ Pwllheli) to Rhiw village, 1ml from property. **Station**: Pwllheli 10ml. **Road**: 12ml SW of Pwllheli. Follow signs to Plas yn Rhiw. B4413 to Aberdaron (drive gates at bottom Rhiw Hill)

🅿️ Free parking, 80yds. Narrow lanes

NT properties nearby
Llanbedrog Beach, Penrhyn Castle, Porthdinllaen, Porthor

Plas yn Rhiw									
20 Mar–30 Apr	12–5	M	T	W	**T**	**F**	**S**	**S**
1 May–30 Jun	12–5	**M**	T	W	**T**	**F**	**S**	**S**
1 Jul–31 Aug	12–5	**M**	T	**W**	**T**	**F**	**S**	**S**
1 Sep–30 Sep	12–5	**M**	T	W	**T**	**F**	**S**	**S**
1 Oct–2 Nov	12–4	M	T	W	**T**	**F**	**S**	**S**

Open BHols. Garden and snowdrop wood open occasionally at weekends in Jan & Feb; tel. for details

Powis Castle and Garden

Welshpool, Powys SY21 8RF

| 1952 | | (4:G5) |

Medieval castle rising dramatically above the celebrated garden

The world-famous garden, overhung with enormous clipped yews, shelters tender plants and sumptuous herbaceous borders. Laid out under the influence of Italian and French styles, it retains its original lead statues, an orangery and an aviary on the terraces. In the 18th century an informal woodland wilderness was created on the opposite ridge. High on a rock above the terraces, the castle, originally built c.1200, began life as a fortress of the Welsh Princes of Powys and commands magnificent views towards England. Remodelled and embellished over more than 400 years, it reflects the changing needs and ambitions of the Herbert family, each generation adding to the magnificent collection of paintings, sculpture, furniture and tapestries. A superb collection of treasures from India is displayed in the Clive Museum. Edward, the son of Robert Clive, the conqueror of India, married Lady Henrietta Herbert in 1784, uniting the Powis and Clive estates. The 19th-century State Coach and Livery, the finest in the ownership of the National Trust, is on display in the coach house.

Powis Castle

Garden/restaurant/shop		M	T	W	T	F	S	S
1 Mar–9 Mar	11–4:30	M	T	W	T	F	**S**	**S**
13 Mar–30 Jun	11–5:30	**M**	T	W	**T**	**F**	**S**	**S**
2 Jul–31 Aug	11–5:30	**M**	T	**W**	**T**	**F**	**S**	**S**
1 Sep–21 Sep	11–5:30	**M**	T	W	**T**	**F**	**S**	**S**
25 Sep–2 Nov*	11–5	**M**	T	W	**T**	**F**	**S**	**S**
8 Nov–29 Nov	10–3	M	T	W	T	F	**S**	**S**
Castle/museum								
13 Mar–30 Jun	1–5	**M**	T	W	**T**	**F**	**S**	**S**
2 Jul–31 Aug	1–5	**M**	T	**W**	**T**	**F**	**S**	**S**
1 Sep–21 Sep	1–5	**M**	T	W	**T**	**F**	**S**	**S**
25 Sep–2 Nov	1–4	**M**	T	W	**T**	**F**	**S**	**S**

Last admission to castle 45mins before closing.
*Garden closes 30mins earlier

What's new in 2008 Visitors can now gain access to the east front, the original grand entrance into the castle

★ All visitors (inc. NT members) need to obtain a ticket from visitor reception in the main car park on arrival. Please note: dogs not allowed at the property or deer park

ℹ **T** 01938 551944 (Infoline), 01938 551929
E powiscastle@nationaltrust.org.uk

Guided tours of castle and/or garden by arrangement

Building Grounds

Powis Castle contains a magnificent collection of paintings, sculpture, furniture and tapestries

For information regarding prices, see page 10

📷 NT shop. Plant sales

🍴 Licensed restaurant. Serves home-made seasonal menu with fresh local ingredients. Children's menu. Garden tea-room

👶 Baby-changing and feeding facilities. Front-carrying baby slings and hip-carrying infant seats for loan. Children's quiz/trail

🏛 Suitable for school groups

➡ [126:SJ216064] **Foot**: 1ml walk from Park Lane, off Broad St in Welshpool. **Bus**: Tanant Valley D71 Oswestry–Welshpool; X75 Shrewsbury–Llanidloes. On both alight High Street, 1ml. **Station**: Welshpool 1¼ml from town on footpath. **Road**: 1ml S of Welshpool; pedestrian access from High Street (A490); vehicle route signed from main road to Newtown (A483); enter by first drive gate on right

🅿 Free parking. Tel. for advice on coach parking

NT properties nearby
Attingham Park, Chirk Castle, Erddig

Rhossili, Worm's Head and Visitor Centre, Gower

Coastguard Cottages, Rhossili, Gower SA3 1PR

🛏 🚗 🏠 📷 🏛 🚶 🚲 1933   **(4:D9)**

Visitor Centre in area of spectacular countryside and coast with lovely beaches

Rhossili is the ideal location from which to walk along the south Gower coast and discover its rare wildlife, archaeology, unspoilt cliffs and beaches. Rhossili Bay stretches for three miles, behind it the 200-metre climb to Rhossili Down allows you to appreciate the spectacular tidal island of Worm's Head and intricate medieval open-field system of The Vile. It is this patchwork of important landscape features which ensured Gower's status as the first Area of Outstanding Natural Beauty in 1956. The Visitor Centre includes a shop, exhibition and information about the area. The Trust cares for 75% of Gower's beautiful coastline and 2,226 hectares (5,500 acres) of its countryside.

⭐ No WC, nearest at Rhossili car park

ℹ **T** 01792 390707
 E rhossili@nationaltrust.org.uk

Rhossili Visitor Centre								
Coastline								
All year		M	T	W	T	F	S	S
Centre/shop								
1 Feb – 29 Feb	11 – 4	M	T	**W**	**T**	**F**	**S**	**S**
1 Mar – 15 Mar	10:30 – 5*	M	T	**W**	**T**	**F**	**S**	**S**
16 Mar – 2 Nov	10:30 – 5*	**M**	**T**	**W**	**T**	**F**	**S**	**S**
3 Nov – 21 Dec	11 – 4	M	T	**W**	**T**	**F**	**S**	**S**
3 Jan – 31 Jan 09	11 – 4	M	T	**W**	**T**	**F**	**S**	**S**

*Closes 6 on Sat/Sun

♿ 🅿 ⊙ 📷 📷 Building 🏔 Grounds 🏔

🏛 Suitable for school groups. Hands-on activities. Booking essential

🐕 Must be under control and on leads only at lambing time; not in Visitor Centre or shop

🚲 Cycling on bridleways

➡ [159:SS418883] **Bus**: Pullman 118/9 from Swansea (passing close ⊞ Swansea). **Road**: SW tip of Gower Peninsula, approached from Swansea via A4118 and then B4247

🅿 Parking (not NT), 50yds. Charge inc. NT members

NT properties nearby
Aberdulais Falls, Brecon Beacons, Dinefwr Park and Castle

St David's Visitor Centre and Shop

Captains House, High Street, St David's, Haverfordwest, Pembrokeshire SA62 6SD

🛏 🚗 📷 🚶 1974   **(4:A8)**

Visitor Centre on the beautiful Pembrokeshire coast

The National Trust owns and protects much of the picturesque St David's Head and surrounding coastline. The Visitor Centre is conveniently situated in the centre of St David's, Wales' smallest historic city, opposite The Cross (owned by the NT). Using interactive technology the centre offers a complete guide to the National Trust in Pembrokeshire, its properties, beaches and walks.

⭐ No WC

Many Trust properties are offering Gift Aid on Entry for non-members, see page 10

St David's Visitor Centre and Shop

		M	T	W	T	F	S	S
1 Feb–15 Mar	10–4	M	T	W	T	F	S	S
16 Mar–9 Nov	10–5:30	M	T	W	T	F	S	S
16 Mar–9 Nov	10–4:30	M	T	W	T	F	S	S
10 Nov–31 Dec	10–4	M	T	W	T	F	S	S
2 Jan–31 Jan 09	10–4	M	T	W	T	F	S	S
Closed 25–26 Dec & 1 Jan 09								

ℹ️ **T** 01437 720385
E stdavids@nationaltrust.org.uk

🚶 Local walks leaflets available

♿ **Building** ♿

➡️ [115:SM753253] In the centre of St David's.
Foot: Pembrokeshire Coast Path within 1ml.
Bus: Richards 411 from ▣ Haverfordwest.
Celtic Coaster & Puffin Shuttle during main
holiday season

🅿️ No parking on site

NT properties nearby
St David's Head, Porthclais Harbour

Segontium

Caernarfon, Gwynedd

🏛️ 🅿️ 👪 ▣ 1937   **(4:D2)**

Remains of a Roman fort

The fort was built to defend the Roman Empire
against rebellious tribes and later plundered to
provide stone for Edward I's castle at Caernarfon.
There is a museum containing relics found
on-site (not NT).

⭐ Segontium is in the guardianship of Cadw:
Welsh Historic Monuments. The museum is
not NT and is managed by a local trust on
behalf of the National Museums and Galleries
of Wales, c/o Institute Building, Pavilion Hill,
Caernarfon, Gwynedd LL55 1AS. WC not
always available

ℹ️ **T** 01286 675625
E segontium@nationaltrust.org.uk

Segontium

		M	T	W	T	F	S	S
All year	10:30–4:30	M	T	W	T	F	S	S

Open BH Mons. Opening times may vary. Tel. for
details. Closed 24–26 Dec & 1 Jan 09. Museum
(not NT) open 12:30–4:30, Tues–Sun. See
www.segontium.org.uk

♿ **Grounds** ♿

👪 Pushchairs and baby back-carriers admitted

▣ Occasional educational activities

➡️ [115:SH485624] **Cycle**: NCN8, ½ml.
Bus: from surrounding areas to Caernarfon
(KMP S4 and Express Motors 93 pass
museum, on others ½ml walk to fort).
Station: Bangor 9ml. **Road**: on Beddgelert
road, A4085, on SE outskirts of Caernarfon,
500yds from town centre

🅿️ No parking on site

NT properties nearby
Glan Faenol, Penrhyn Castle, Plas Newydd,
Plas yn Rhiw

Skenfrith Castle

Skenfrith, nr Abergavenny, Monmouthshire
NP7 8UH

🏛️ 🅿️ 🚶 🐾 1936   **(4:H8)**

Remains of an early 13th-century fortress

The castle was built beside the River Monnow to
command one of the main routes between
England and Wales at a time when the two
nations were involved in a long drawn-out
conflict following the Norman Conquest. A keep
and the curtain wall with towers have survived.

⭐ Skenfrith Castle is in the guardianship of
Cadw: Welsh Historic Monuments

ℹ️ **T** 01874 625515
E skenfrithcastle@nationaltrust.org.uk

🚶 Skenfith is part of the Three Castles Trail

♿ **Building** ♿

➡️ [161:SO456203] **Cycle**: local Three Castles
cycle trail starts at nearby Abergavenny
castle. **Road**: 6ml NW of Monmouth, 12ml
NE of Abergavenny, on N side of the Ross
road (B4521)

🅿️ Free parking (not NT)

NT properties nearby
The Kymin, Skirrid Fawr, Sugar Loaf, Westbury
Court Garden

Skenfrith Castle

		M	T	W	T	F	S	S
All year	Dawn–dusk	M	T	W	T	F	S	S

Stackpole Estate

Old Home Farm Yard, Stackpole, nr Pembroke, Pembrokeshire SA71 5DQ

(4:B9)

Beautiful and varied stretch of the Pembrokeshire coast

This extensive estate is a coastal property of great contrast, including eight miles of cliff, headlands, beaches and sand dunes, elongated freshwater lakes bordered by trees, sheltered bays and mature woodlands. The Bosherston Lakes and Stackpole Warren are part of Stackpole National Nature Reserve, managed by the National Trust in partnership with the Countryside Council for Wales. Lake wildlife includes otters, herons, wintering wildfowl and more than twenty species of dragonfly. The cliffs are an important site for breeding seabirds and the resident chough. There are eleven species of bat on the Stackpole Estate, some of which live in the outbuildings of the former mansion of Stackpole Court, which was demolished in 1963 – about which there is an exhibition in the old game larder. There is an excellent bathing beach at Broadhaven South. At Barafundle Bay golden sands are backed by dunes and ringed by trees. The beautiful bay is so secluded that it can only be accessed from Stackpole Quay by walking along the cliff path, followed by a steep descent to the beach.

What's new in 2008 Upgraded facilities for anglers at Bosherston Lakes. Fishing allowed from marked pegs in eastern and western arms (charged). Two angling points for wheelchair users. Closed season 15 March–15 June inclusive. Lakes being improved, with silt being removed

ℹ️ **T** 01646 661359
   E stackpole@nationaltrust.org.uk

🚶 Guided walks. Tel. for details

🚶 18½ml of footpaths. Map leaflets available

♿ 🚻 Ｐ Building 🔽 Grounds 🔼 ▶

🍴 Boathouse Tea-room (NT-approved concession) (licensed) at Stackpole Quay

🎭 Suitable for school groups. Stackpole for Outdoor Learning runs week-long residential environmental courses for schools and groups. The Stackpole Centre offers accommodation for education groups and others

➡️ [158:SR992958] 6ml S of Pembroke. **Foot**: via Pembrokeshire Coast Path. **Bus**: Silcox 387 Coastal Cruiser from 🚉 Pembroke. **Station**: Pembroke 5ml. **Road**: B4319 from Pembroke to Stackpole and Bosherston (various entry points on to estate)

Ｐ Three car parks, cars £3 (NT members display card) at Stackpole Quay & Broadhaven South. Bosherston Lily Ponds free (Easter–Sept). Access via narrow lanes with passing places

NT properties nearby
Colby Woodland Garden, Tudor Merchant's House

Tudor Merchant's House

Quay Hill, Tenby, Pembrokeshire SA70 7BX

🏠 🚶 🐕 😷 👥 🖼️ 1937

(4:C9)

Late 15th-century town house

Located near the harbour in this historic walled town, the three-storey house is characteristic of the area at the time when Tenby was a thriving trading port. On the ground floor at the rear of the house is a fine example of a 'Flemish' round chimney, and the original scarfed roof-trusses survive. The remains of 18th-century secco paintings can be seen on three interior walls, and the house is furnished to recreate family life from the Tudor period onwards. There is access to the small herb garden, weather permitting.

What's new in 2008 Tudor costumes for children to try on and a collection of toys typical of the Tudor period

⭐ No WC

ℹ️ **T** 01834 842279
   E tudormerchantshouse@nationaltrust.org.uk

🚶 Special out-of-hours tours by arrangement (charged)

Stackpole Estate							
All year	M	T	W	T	F	S	S

Tudor Merchant's House								
17 Mar–2 Nov	11–5	M	T	W	T	F	S	S
Open Sats on BH weekends 11–5								

Charges for National Trust members apply on some special event days

The Tudor Merchant's House in Tenby, Pembrokeshire

Tŷ Mawr Wybrnant

Penmachno, Betws-y-Coed, Conwy LL25 0HJ

🏠 🚲 🍴 🏠 🎭 👫 🎞 🚶 🚲 1951 **(4:E3)**

Traditional stone-built upland 16th-century farmhouse

Explore centuries of Welsh living in this traditional stone-built upland farmhouse. Set in the heart of the beautiful Conwy Valley, Tŷ Mawr was the birthplace of Bishop William Morgan, the first translator of the Bible into Welsh. A footpath leads from the house through woodland and the surrounding traditionally managed fields.

⭐ No access for coaches. 33-seater minibuses welcome. Tel. to arrange access

ℹ **T** 01690 760213
  E tymawrwybrnant@nationaltrust.org.uk

🎭 Introductory talk

🚶 Leaflet available featuring walks around Tŷ Mawr and the Ysbyty Estate

♿ 🚻 🅿 Building 🏠 Grounds 🏠

👫 Pushchairs admitted. Children's guide. Children's quiz/trail

🎞 Suitable for school groups

🐕 Under close control

🚲 Newly constructed cycle path around the Penmachno area

➡ [115:SH770524] **Bus**: Jones 64 Llanrwst–Cwm Penmachno (passing ⟲ Betws-y-Coed), alight Penmachno, then 2ml walk. **Station**: Pont-y-pant (U) 1½ml. **Road**: at the head of the Wybrnant Valley. From A5 3ml S of Betws-y-Coed, take B4406 to Penmachno. House is 2½ml NW of Penmachno by forest road

🅿 Free parking, 500yds

NT properties nearby
Aberconwy House, Bodnant Garden, Conwy Suspension Bridge, Penrhyn Castle, Ysbyty Estate

🎭 Easter and Hallowe'en family events

♿ ⠿ Building 🏠

👫 Hip-carrying infant seats for loan. Children's quiz/trail. Easter and Hallowe'en family events

🎞 Suitable for school groups. Hands-on activities

➡ [158:SN135004] In the centre of Tenby off Tudor Square. **Foot**: Pembrokeshire Coast Path within ¼ml. **Bus**: from surrounding areas. **Station**: Tenby ½ml

🅿 Parking (not NT). Limited parking on town streets. Town is pedestrianised throughout July & Aug when parking is in pay & display car parks only or via park & ride

NT properties nearby
Colby Woodland Garden, Stackpole Estate

Ty'n-y-Coed Uchaf

Penmachno, Betws-y-Coed, Conwy LL24 0PS

Closed in 2008. Tel. 01492 860123 (NT Wales office) for further information

Tŷ Mawr Wybrnant									
20 Mar–28 Sep	12–5	M	T	W		**T**	**F**	**S**	**S**
2 Oct–2 Nov	12–4	M	T	W		**T**	**F**	**S**	**S**
Open BH Mons									

Parking in National Trust car parks is free for members displaying stickers

Northern Ireland

Northern Ireland is world renowned for its breathtaking natural beauty and sheer diversity of landscape. From the dramatic granite peaks of the Mourne Mountains and the bucolic wooded glens of Antrim to the legendary basalt columns of the Giant's Causeway, the pastoral drumlin landscape of Strangford Lough and the idyllic Fermanagh Lakeland – the spectacular scenery speaks for itself.

The National Trust plays a proactive role in protecting and managing some of Northern Ireland's most stunning coast and countryside, and provides public access to what are probably some of the UK's most special places for both wildlife and scenery.

Coastal treasures and bustling birdlife

Northern Ireland's iconic World Heritage Site, the celebrated Giant's Causeway, is the beating heart of the breathtaking North Antrim coast. Along the nearby shoreline are dotted some of the region's best-loved visitor attractions. Discover the historic ruins of Dunseverick Castle, or stroll along the majestic sweeping arc of White Park Bay. Brave the elements and cross Carrick-a-Rede rope bridge, or marvel at the bustling seabird colonies at Larrybane and the views beyond to Rathlin Island and the west coast of Scotland.

There are few better places to experience this diverse coastline, with splendid views, than along the rugged headlands stretching along County Antrim's famous seashore, including Fair Head, Murlough Bay and Skernaghan Point.

Other coastal treasures include the fragile 6,000-year-old sand dunes of Murlough National Nature Reserve, near Newcastle, and the inspirational views across to the Scottish Islands and Mull

of Kintyre – which can be seen from the waymarked path through Ballyconagan on unspoilt Rathlin Island. Some of the finest examples of coastal saltmarsh can be explored at Strangford Lough, the Bann Estuary and along the picturesque Dundrum coastal path.

Marvel at the spectacular birdlife along the muddy sand and saltmarshes at Barmouth on the Bann Estuary. These rich feeding grounds for waders, wildfowl and nesting birds can be viewed from a purpose-built hide on the west side of the River Bann.

Rathlin Island is home to noisy nesting colonies of puffins, guillemots and razorbills, in fact the north coast is also Northern Ireland's only breeding site for the chough. Further south is Strangford Lough, Britain's largest sea lough and one of Europe's key wildlife habitats. The Trust's Wildlife Scheme manages the entire foreshore of the Lough, as well as some 50 islands, and provides access to 6,070 hectares (15,000 acres) of this wild and naturally diverse site.

Above: **Giant's Causeway** Below: **White Park Bay**

Wild countryside

Why not escape to some of Northern Ireland's best 'off-the-beaten track' experiences?

Just a stone's throw from the region's capital In the heart of the Belfast Hills, the heathland-rich Divis and the Black Mountain provide the stunning backdrop to the city's skyline and a perfect haven for those in search of wild countryside.

Other rural escapes in the Belfast area well worth exploring include the hidden woodland paths of Collin Glen and the fine riverbank and meadows of Minnowburn, as well as the wonderful waterfalls at Lisnabreeny.

To the west of the region idyllic County Fermanagh is perfect walking country, boasting a kaleidoscope of tranquil landscapes to discover; including the woodland and wetlands of Crom on the serene shores of Lough Erne. Visitors to Crom can experience a time-honoured boat trip on the lough in a traditional 'cot'. Cut and shaped from Crom oak more than 100 years ago, this unique boat is still being enjoyed today.

Or for a real walk on the wild side, the Trust's Mourne Mountain paths allow

Right: Ballyquintin Farm on the Ards Peninsula *Below:* Lough Erne *Bottom:* Divis and the Black Mountain

hikers to enjoy the dramatic scenery of Northern Ireland's highest mountain, the majestic Slieve Donard, as well as neighbouring Slieve Commedagh. Visitors to Ballyquintin Farm, on the Ards Peninsula, can enjoy stunning views of Strangford Lough and learn how this critical site is managed for wildlife and conservation.

Meanwhile, along the geologically rich coastline to the south-east lies the delightful seaside village of Cushendun and the ecologically important raised blanket peat bog at Cushleake Mountain.

From enticing open spaces to exhilarating challenges and serenely tranquil getaways, there is something for everyone to explore and enjoy throughout the year at the National Trust gems across Northern Ireland.

Discover things you never knew and be captivated by places you've never ventured to before. Whether in search of bracing mountain walks, exciting family fun days, attention-grabbing storytelling, garden walks, boat trips or open-air theatre, there are amazing days out to suit every taste.

Page 351: entrance to the Walled Garden at Rowallane Garden, Co. Down (7:E7)

The wildly beautiful Strangford Lough is Britain's largest sea inlet and one of Europe's key wildlife habitats. It is an area where visitors can enjoy bracing coastal walks among delicate wild flowers and butterflies, or explore the many rock pools bursting with marine life. There is also some of the best birdwatching in the UK and Ireland.

Covering a total area of 58 square miles the scenery is astonishingly diverse. The landscape ranges from vast northern sandflats to the fast-flowing tidal channel of the Strangford Narrows, where it connects to the Irish Sea. Further inland the waters are more sheltered and are surrounded by soft, rolling hills – many of which are partially submerged, forming more than 70 islands and countless smaller rocky outcrops.

Above: **Brent geese**
Left: **drumlins at Strangford Lough**
Below: **birdwatching**

Strangford Lough is one of the most important breeding sites in Ireland for the common seal, and you might even be lucky enough to catch a glimpse of porpoises, otters or the occasional basking shark.

One of the best spectacles at Strangford has to be the arrival of thousands of migrant birds that flock here every autumn. Large flocks of knot, dunlin, curlew, redshank, oystercatcher, plover and godwits arrive from their Arctic breeding grounds. Thousands of birds perform spectacular aerobatics, forming twisting, swirling clouds while wildfowl such as wigeon, teal, pintail and shelduck march across the sandflats. The highlight of the autumn is the arrival of 75 per cent of the world's population of pale-bellied Brent geese from Arctic Canada.

As the winter visitors depart, the summer ones arrive. More than 4,000 sandwich, common and Arctic terns (a third of the entire Irish population) form noisy breeding colonies. A great example is Swan Island, easily seen from the Strangford to Portaferry ferry. Gulls, cormorants, oystercatchers, ringed plovers, mergansers, eiders, mallards and tufted ducks also breed here.

For everything you want to know about Strangford Lough, come to the Wildlife Centre at Castle Ward, where knowledgeable wardens will answer questions, introduce interpretative displays and informative wildlife videos, as well as providing useful leaflets on the area.

■ Craig McCoy, Strangford Lough Warden

Further information

- ■ Euro notes are accepted by the Trust's Northern Ireland properties.

- ■ Under the National Trust Ulster Gardens Scheme, a number of private gardens are generously opened to the public in order to provide income for Trust gardens in Northern Ireland. For the 2008 programme tel. 028 9751 0721.

- ■ To find out what is happening in the region this year, see our 2008 *Events Guide*.

Ardress House

64 Ardress Road, Annaghmore, Portadown,
Co. Armagh BT62 1SQ

 `1959` **(7:D7)**

**17th-century house with elegant 18th-century
decoration and a traditional farmyard**

i **T** 028 8778 4753
E ardress@nationaltrust.org.uk

Ardress House									
15 Mar–28 Sep	2–6	M	T	W	T	F	**S**	**S**

Admission by guided tour. Open BH Mons and all
other public hols in N Ireland **inc. 17 March**. Grounds
('My Lady's Mile') open daily all year, dawn to dusk

The Argory

144 Derrycaw Road, Moy, Dungannon,
Co. Armagh BT71 6NA

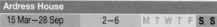
`1979` **(7:C7)**

**Atmospheric Irish gentry house and
wooded riverside estate**

Built in the 1820s, this handsome Irish gentry
house is surrounded by its 130-hectare (320-
acre) wooded riverside estate. The former home
of the Bond family, a tour of this neo-classical
masterpiece reveals it is unchanged since 1900
– the eclectic interior still evoking the family's
Edwardian tastes and interests. Outside there
are sweeping vistas, superb spring bulbs, scenic
walks and fascinating courtyard displays. A
second-hand bookshop, adventure playground
and Lady Ada's award-winning tea-room
provide retreats for children and adults alike.

★ House is due to reopen in 2008 following
extensive reservicing work. Please contact
property for opening times. Tea-room, shop,
grounds and education programme will also
be open for group visits

i **T** 028 8778 4753
E argory@nationaltrust.org.uk

Craft fairs, walks and family days

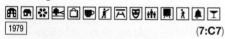 Grounds

Lady Ada's Tea-room. Afternoon teas.
All produce baked on the premises

The Argory: a neo-classical masterpiece with an
eclectic interior

Baby-changing facilities. Hip-carrying infant
seats for loan. Children's play area. Children's
quiz/trail

Suitable for school groups. Education
room/centre. Live interpretation. Hands-on
activities. Adult study days

On leads and only in grounds and garden

→ [H418640] **Cycle:** NCN95, 7ml.
Bus: Ulsterbus 67 Portadown–Dungannon
(both pass close ≋ Portadown), alight
Charlemont, 2½ml walk. **Road:** 4ml from
Charlemont, 3ml from M1, exit 13 or 14
(signposted). NB: coaches must use exit 13;
weight restrictions at Bond's Bridge

P Parking, 100yds

NT properties nearby
Ardress House, Derrymore House

The Argory									
House									
3 May–29 Jun	2–5:30	M	T	W	T	F	**S**	**S**
1 Jul–31 Aug	2–5:30	**M**	**T**	**W**	**T**	**F**	**S**	**S**
6 Sep–28 Sep	2–5:30	M	T	W	T	F	**S**	**S**
Grounds									
1 Feb–30 Apr	10–4	**M**	**T**	**W**	**T**	**F**	**S**	**S**
1 May–30 Sep	10–6	**M**	**T**	**W**	**T**	**F**	**S**	**S**
1 Oct–31 Jan 09	10–4	**M**	**T**	**W**	**T**	**F**	**S**	**S**
Tea-room/shop									
15 Mar–29 Jun	2–5:30	M	T	W	T	F	**S**	**S**
22 Mar–30 Mar*	2–5:30	**M**	**T**	**W**	**T**	**F**	**S**	**S**
1 Jul–31 Aug	2–5:30	**M**	**T**	**W**	**T**	**F**	**S**	**S**
6 Sep–28 Sep	2–5:30	M	T	W	T	F	**S**	**S**

Admission by guided tour. Open BH Mons and all
other public hols in N Ireland. Conservation work will
affect house opening times in March/April. Tel. for
details. Grounds open 2–6 on event days. Last
admission 1hr before closing. ***Easter week**

Unless indicated, last admission is always 30mins before closing time

Carrick-a-Rede

119a Whitepark Road, Ballintoy, Co. Antrim
BT54 6LS

 1967   (7:D3)

Rocky island connected to the cliffs by a rope bridge

Take the exhilarating rope bridge challenge to Carrick-a-Rede island and enjoy a truly clifftop experience. Near the North Antrim Coast Road, amid unrivalled coastal scenery, the 30-metre deep and 20-metre wide chasm is traversed by a rope bridge that was traditionally erected by salmon fishermen. Visitors bold enough to cross from the cliffs to the rocky island (which is a Site of Special Scientific Interest) are rewarded with splendid uninterrupted views to Rathlin, the Scottish islands and fantastic birdwatching.

What's new in 2008 Tea-room now NT. Children's Discovery Trail for 8–14 year olds. Binoculars for hire. Disposable raincoats for sale

⭐ Maximum of eight people on bridge at any one time. Suitable outdoor clothing and footwear is recommended

ℹ️ **T** 028 2076 9839
   E carrickarede@nationaltrust.org.uk

Putting up the bridge, Feb

Grounds

Tea-room

Carrick-a-Rede		
Rope bridge		
1 Mar–25 May	10–6	M T W T F S S
26 May–31 Aug	10–7	M T W T F S S
1 Sep–2 Nov	10–6	M T W T F S S

Bridge open weather permitting, final access to rope bridge 45mins before closing. Car park and North Antrim Coastal Path open all year

👶 Baby-changing facilities. Baby back-carriers admitted. Pushchairs not permitted over rope bridge. Children's discovery trail

📖 Suitable for school groups

🐕 On leads, not permitted to cross rope bridge

➔ [D062450] **Foot**: on North Antrim Coastal Path and road, 7ml from Giant's Causeway, ½ml from Ballintoy village and 1½ml from Ballintoy Church on Harbour Rd. **Cycle**: NCN93, 5ml. **Bus**: Ulsterbus 172, 177. Causeway Rambler bus (Ulsterbus 376) between Bushmills and Carrick-a-Rede operates in summer; or Ulsterbus 252 is a circular route via the Antrim Glens from Belfast. Both stop at Carrick-a-Rede. **Road**: on B15, 7ml E of Bushmills, 5ml W of Ballycastle. Giant's Causeway 7ml

P Free parking. Access all year

NT properties nearby
Cushendun, Giant's Causeway, Hezlett House, Mussenden Temple and Downhill Demesne, Portstewart Strand, White Park Bay

The famous Carrick-a-Rede rope bridge connects a rocky island with the mainland cliffs

Castle Coole

Enniskillen, Co. Fermanagh BT74 6JY

1951   (7:A7)

Magnificent 18th-century mansion and landscape park

Savour the exquisite stately grandeur of this stunning 18th-century mansion set in an historic wooded landscape park – ideal for family walks. Castle Coole is one of Ireland's finest neo-classical houses, and the sumptuous Regency interior, boasting an especially fine State Bedroom prepared for George IV, provides a rare treat for visitors, allowing them to glimpse what life was like in the home of the Earls of Belmore.

The front façade of Castle Coole with wildflower meadows in the foreground

What's new in 2008 Licensed for civil weddings. Guided tours of historic basement on Bank Holidays

i **T** 028 6632 2690
E castlecoole@nationaltrust.org.uk

Classical and popular music events, including opera and jazz

Off the Beaten Track walks series

Building
Grounds

Tea-room (NT-approved concession) in Tallow House

Baby-changing facilities. Baby back-carriers admitted. Front-carrying baby slings for loan. Children's play area

Suitable for school groups

On leads and only in grounds

[H378788] **Cycle**: NCN91. Property entrance lies on the Kingfisher Trail, Ireland's first long-distance trail covering approx. 300ml. **Bus**: Ulsterbus 95, Enniskillen–Clones (connections from Belfast). **Road**: 1½ml SE of Enniskillen on Belfast–Enniskillen road (A4)

P Walkers' car park. Main car park, 150yds. 'Honesty box' for car parking charge

NT properties nearby
Crom, Florence Court

Castle Ward

Strangford, Downpatrick, Co. Down BT30 7LS

1953   (7:F7)

Interesting 18th-century mansion, famed for its mixture of architectural styles

Explore this exceptional 332-hectare (820-acre) walled demesne dramatically set overlooking Strangford Lough and marvel at the quirky mid-Georgian mansion, home of the Ward family since the 16th century. An architectural curiosity, it is built inside and out in the distinctly different styles of classical and gothic. Children can dress up and play with period toys in the Victorian Past Times Centre or learn about local wildlife at the Strangford Lough Wildlife Centre. Winding woodland, lakeside and parkland walks afford amazing unexpected vistas. Stay at the caravan site or holiday cottage and you'll have longer to explore.

What's new in 2008 Pirate's Picnic in July

Castle Coole									
Grounds									
1 Feb–31 Mar	10–4	M	T	W	T	F	S	S
1 Apr–30 Sep	10–8	M	T	W	T	F	S	S
1 Oct–31 Jan 09	10–4	M	T	W	T	F	S	S
House									
15 Mar–17 Mar	1–6	M	T	W	T	F	S	S
21 Mar–30 Mar*	1–6	M	T	W	T	F	S	S
5 Apr–31 May	1–6	M	T	W	T	F	S	S
1 Jun–30 Jun	1–6	M	T	W	T	F	S	S
1 Jul–31 Aug	12–6	M	T	W	T	F	S	S
6 Sep–28 Sep	1–6	M	T	W	T	F	S	S

Admission by guided tour. Open BH Mons and all other public hols in N Ireland **inc. 17 March**. Last tour 1hr before closing. Tea-room & shop open as house, but close at 5:30. *Easter week

ℹ️ **T** 028 4488 1204
E castleward@nationaltrust.org.uk

🏃 Guided and specialist behind-the-scenes house tours, morning and evening by prior arrangement

🎭 Shakespeare in the park, jazz in the garden, murder mystery theatre, opera, Pumpkinfest, book fair, dinner and a movie, craft fairs, Santa's house

🚶 Free trail maps from leaflet dispensers in car park area, visitor reception and gift shop. All walks are moderate

♿ 🚻 ♿ ♿ ♿ Pₐ Dₐ Building ♿ ♿ Grounds ♿ ➡️

🛍️ Gift shop and second-hand bookshop in stableyard

☕ Tea-room. Children's menu

👶 Baby-changing and feeding facilities. Hip-carrying infant seats for loan. Family guide. Children's quiz/trail. Children's activity packs. Children's play area (adventure playground in woodland). Victorian Past Times Centre; toys & dressing up

📖 Suitable for school groups. Education room/centre. Live interpretation. Hands-on activities. Adult study days

🐕 On leads and only in grounds

Castle Ward		M	T	W	T	F	S	S
Grounds								
1 Feb–31 Mar	10–4	M	T	W	T	F	S	S
1 Apr–30 Sep	10–8	M	T	W	T	F	S	S
1 Oct–31 Jan 09	10–4	M	T	W	T	F	S	S
House								
15 Mar–17 Mar	1–6	M	T	W	T	F	S	S
22 Mar–30 Mar*	1–6	M	T	W	T	F	S	S
5 Apr–29 Jun	1–6	M	T	W	T	F	S	S
1 Jul–31 Aug	1–6	M	T	W	T	F	S	S
6 Sep–28 Sep	1–6	M	T	W	T	F	S	S
Shop/tea-room								
As house	12–5							

Admission by guided tour. Open BH Mons and all other public hols in N Ireland **inc. 17 March.** Last house tour 4:30. Corn mill operates on Suns during open season. For Strangford Lough Wildlife Centre opening times contact 028 4488 1411. *Easter week

For information regarding prices, see page 10

The Gothic Boudoir, Castle Ward, County Down

🚲 Free trail maps from leaflet dispensers in car park area, visitor reception and gift shop

➡️ [J752494] **Foot:** on Lecale Way. **Ferry:** from Portaferry. **Bus:** Ulsterbus 16E Downpatrick–Strangford, with connections from Belfast (passing close 🚉 Belfast Great Victoria Street); bus stop at gates. Ulsterbus Lecale Rambler (Sat, Sun only) in summer. **Road:** 7ml NE of Downpatrick, 1½ml W of Strangford village on A25, on S shore of Strangford Lough, entrance by Ballyculter Lodge

🅿️ Free parking, 250yds

NT properties nearby
Mount Stewart, Murlough National Nature Reserve, Rowallane Garden

Crom

Upper Lough Erne, Newtownbutler,
Co. Fermanagh BT92 8AP

🏠 🌳 🛶 🏆 🏠 🏛️ 🎯 🏃 🎪 🎭 👶
📖 🚶 🚲 🔔 🍽️ 1987   (7:A8)

Romantic and tranquil landscape of islands, woodland and historical ruins

Escape to this breathtaking 810-hectare (2,000-acre) demesne, set amid the romantic and tranquil landscape of Upper Lough Erne. One of Ireland's most important nature conservation areas, Crom's ancient woodland

Crom

Grounds								
15 Mar–30 May	10–6	M	T	W	T	F	S	S
1 Jun–31 Aug	10–7	M	T	W	T	F	S	S
1 Sep–2 Nov	10–6	M	T	W	T	F	S	S
Visitor centre								
15 Mar–30 Mar	10–6	M	T	W	T	F	S	S
5 Apr–27 Apr	10–6	M	T	W	T	F	S	S
1 May–14 Sep	10–6	M	T	W	T	F	S	S
15 Sep–12 Oct	10–6	M	T	W	T	F	S	S
13 Oct–2 Nov	10–5	M	T	W	T	F	S	S

Open BH Mons and all other public hols in N Ireland **inc. 17 March**. Last admission 1hr before closing. Tel. for tea-room opening arrangements

and picturesque islands are home to many rare species, including the elusive pine marten. The award-winning visitor centre offers a huge range of exciting activities and adventures for all the family – from boating and coarse angling to inspirational nature trails. There are also fascinating wildlife exhibitions. Stay for longer in the award-winning holiday cottages or campsite.

What's new in 2008 Licensed for civil weddings in function rooms and ruins of Old Crom Castle

★ The 19th-century castle is private and not open to the public. WC available only when visitor centre open. Showers available for campsite users

ℹ️ **T** 028 6773 8118
E crom@nationaltrust.org.uk

🎭 Family days, bat nights, history and nature walks

🚶 Guided walks to discover wildlife and social history

♿ 🚻 Building
Grounds

📷 In visitor centre

☕ Little Orchard Tea-room in visitor centre

👶 Baby-changing facilities. Pushchairs and baby back-carriers admitted. Hip-carrying infant seats for loan. Children's play area. Family activity packs. Family days

🎒 Suitable for school groups

🐕 On leads only

🚲 2ml of NCN91, designated as the Kingfisher Trail, runs through the property

➡️ [H455655] **Cycle**: NCN91. **Ferry**: ferry from Derryvore Church must be booked 24hrs in advance, tel. for details. **Bus**: Ulsterbus 95 Enniskillen–Clones (connections from Belfast), alight Newtownbutler, 3ml. **Road**: 3ml W of Newtownbutler, on Newtownbutler–Crom road, or follow signs from Lisnaskea (7ml). Crom is next to the Shannon–Erne waterway. Public jetty at visitor centre

🅿️ Parking, 100yds

NT properties nearby
Castle Coole, Florence Court

Ruins of historic Crom Castle with Crichton Tower on Gad Island in the distance

The Crown Bar

46 Great Victoria Street, Belfast, Co. Antrim
BT2 7BA

 1978   (7:E6)

The most famous pub in Belfast

With its brightly coloured ornate tile-and-glass
interior, period gas lighting and cosy snugs, this
atmospheric hostelry is one of the finest
examples of a High Victorian saloon still in
existence in the UK.

What's new in 2008 Interior has been restored
to its former glory

- i **T** 028 9027 9901 **E** info@crownbar.com
- Traditional, home-cooked lunch menu
- → [J336736] **Cycle**: NCN9, ½ml. **Bus**: opposite
  Europa Buscentre. **Station**: opposite Great
  Victoria Street
- P Street parking only

NT properties nearby

Divis and the Black Mountain, Mount Stewart,
Patterson's Spade Mill, Rowallane Garden

The Crown Bar		M	T	W	T	F	S	S
All year	11:30–11	**M**	**T**	**W**	**T**	**F**	**S**	S
All year	12:30–10	M	T	W	T	F	S	**S**

Derrymore House

Bessbrook, Newry, Co. Armagh BT35 7EF

🏚 🚶 👫 🚶 🚲 1953   (7:D8)

Late 18th-century thatched house in gentrified vernacular style

This elegant 18th-century thatched cottage with
its peculiar gentrified vernacular style, rests
peacefully in a pleasant landscape demesne.
It has a rich history, being built by Isaac Corry,
who represented Newry in the Irish House of
Commons for 30 years from 1776. The pretty
parkland has fine views and boasts impressive
spring bulbs.

What's new in 2008 Treaty Room due to reopen
in July and August following conservation work

- ★ No WC. House due to open July and August
- i **T** 028 8778 4753
  E derrymore@nationaltrust.org.uk
- 👨‍🦽 P♿ **Grounds** ➡
- 👫 Pushchairs admitted
- 🐕 On leads and only in grounds
- 🚲 NCN9 passes through estate

Exterior of the elegant 18th-century Derrymore House
with spring bulbs in the foreground

Derrymore House

Grounds										
1 Feb−30 Apr	10−4	M	T	W	T	F	S	S		
1 May−30 Sep	10−6	M	T	W	T	F	S	S		
1 Oct−31 Jan 09	10−4	M	T	W	T	F	S	S		
Treaty Room										
5 Jul−31 Aug*	2−5:30	M	T	W	T	F	**S**	**S**		

*Open BH Mons and all other public hols in N Ireland **inc. 17 March**

→ [J056280] **Cycle**: NCN9. **Bus**: Ulsterbus 42, 44, 341C from Newry (passing close ⮞ Newry). **Station**: Newry 2ml. **Road**: on A25 off the Newry–Camlough road at Bessbrook, 1½ml from Newry

P Free parking, 30yds

NT properties nearby
Ardress House, The Argory

Florence Court

Enniskillen, Co. Fermanagh BT92 1DB

 1954 **(7:A7)**

Splendid 18th-century house and demesne

There is something for all the family at the warm and welcoming 18th-century former home of the Earls of Enniskillen. The house enjoys a peaceful setting in west Fermanagh, with a startlingly beautiful backdrop of mountains and forests. There are many glorious walks to enjoy, as well as fine vistas and play areas in the outstanding grounds. There is even a charming walled garden. Every aspect of life in this imposing classical Irish house, with its fine interiors and exquisite decoration, are brought to life on the fascinating guided tours. Outside there are numerous unusual places to explore, including a sawmill, ice house and the thatched Heather House.

What's new in 2008 Tours of the Carpenter's Workshop on selected days

i **T** 028 6634 8249
E florencecourt@nationaltrust.org.uk

🏃 'Living History' tours, Suns in July & Aug

🎭 Events include Easter Egg trails, family fun days, craft fairs, Hallowe'en and Christmas activities. Annual Country Fair on Sun 25 May

The warm and welcoming hall at Florence Court

🚹 WC ♿ ♿ ⦂⦂ 📷 Pⅉ Dⅉ Building 🔍 ♿
Grounds 🏔 ➡ 🚲

🍽 Stables Restaurant (NT-approved concession)

👶 Baby-changing facilities. Baby back-carriers admitted. Front-carrying baby slings for loan. Children's play area. Children's quiz/trail

🏫 Suitable for school groups. Education room/ centre. Live interpretation. Hands-on activities

🐕 On leads and only in garden and grounds

→ [H175344] **Cycle**: NCN91. Property entrance lies on Kingfisher Trail. **Bus**: Ulsterbus 192 Enniskillen–Swanlinbar, alight Creamery Cross, 2ml walk. **Road**: 8ml SW of Enniskillen via A4 Sligo road and A32 Swanlinbar road, 4ml from Marble Arch Caves

P Parking, 200yds

NT properties nearby
Castle Coole, Crom

Florence Court

Grounds									
1 Feb−31 Mar	10−4	M	T	W	T	F	S	S	
1 Apr−30 Sep	10−8	M	T	W	T	F	S	S	
1 Oct−31 Jan 09	10−4	M	T	W	T	F	S	S	
House									
15 Mar−17 Mar	1−6	M	T	W	T	F	**S**	**S**	
21 Mar−30 Mar*	1−6	M	T	W	T	F	S	S	
5 Apr−31 May	1−6	M	T	W	T	F	**S**	**S**	
1 Jun−30 Jun	1−6	M	T	**W**	**T**	F	S	S	
1 Jul−31 Aug	12−6	M	T	W	T	F	S	S	
6 Sep−28 Sep	1−6	M	T	W	T	F	**S**	**S**	
Tea-room/shop									
As house		Close 5:30							

Admission by guided tour to house. Open BH Mons and all other public hols in N Ireland **inc. 17 March**. Last admission 1hr before closing. *Easter week

Charges for National Trust members apply on some special event days

Giant's Causeway

44a Causeway Road, Bushmills, Co. Antrim
BT57 8SU

 1962   **(7:D3)**

Famous geological World Heritage Site on the North Antrim Coast

Northern Ireland's iconic World Heritage Site is steeped in a wealth of history and legend. All the family will enjoy exploring the renowned amphitheatres of layered basalt stone columns left by volcanic eruptions 60 million years ago, and searching for the distinctive stone formations fancifully named the wishing chair, camel, harp and organ. The centrepiece of an internationally important designated Area of Outstanding Natural Beauty, the Causeway is home to a wealth of local and natural history.

⭐ The car park and tourist information centre are owned and operated by Moyle District Council

ℹ️ **T** 028 2073 1582
E giantscauseway@nationaltrust.org.uk

🧍 Sensible outdoor footwear recommended

♿ 🚾 ♿ ♿ 🅿️ Building 🏛️ ♿
Grounds 🏛️ ➡️

🍽️ Tea-room. Children's menu

👶 Baby-changing facilities. Pushchairs and baby back-carriers admitted

🏫 Suitable for school groups

🐕 On leads only

➡️ [C952452] **Foot**: path from Portballintrae alongside steam railway and from Dunservick Castle (4½ml). **Cycle**: NCN93. **Bus**: Ulsterbus 172, 177. Causeway Coaster minibus from visitor centre to stones (NT members free). Causeway Rambler bus (Ulsterbus 376) between Bushmills and Carrick-a-Rede operates in summer; Ulsterbus 252 is a circular route via the Antrim Glens from Belfast. Both stop at the Causeway. **Station**: Coleraine 10ml or Portrush 8ml. Giant's Causeway & Bushmills Steam Railway, 200yds. Tel. 028 2073 2844. **Road**: on B146 Causeway–Dunseverick road 2ml E of Bushmills

Giant's Causeway		
All year		**M T W T F S S**

Shop & tea-room: tel. for opening arrangements. Open all year, except 25/26 Dec

🅿️ Parking (not NT), 100yds. Charge includes NT members

NT properties nearby
Carrick-a-Rede, Hezlett House, Mussenden Temple and Downhill Demesne, Portstewart Strand, White Park Bay

Gray's Printing Press

49 Main Street, Strabane, Co. Tyrone BT82 8AU

🖼️ 🖼️ 🖼️ 🖼️ 🖼️ 1966   **(7:B5)**

18th-century printing press

Take a step back in time and discover a treasure trove of ink, galleys and presses hidden behind an 18th-century shop front in the heart of Strabane, once the leading printing town in Ulster. See the 18th-century printing press where John Dunlap, printer of the American Declaration of Independence, and James Wilson, grandfather of President Woodrow Wilson, learnt their trade, and hear the story of printing and emigration.

⭐ For opening dates and times tel. Property Manager, 028 8674 8210

Demonstration of printing techniques at the 18th-century Gray's Printing Press

Hezlett House: rare 17th-century survivor, simply furnished in mid-Victorian style

i **T** 028 7188 0055
E grays@nationaltrust.org.uk

Building

Suitable for school groups. Live interpretation

→ [H345977] **Cycle:** NCN92. **Bus:** Ulsterbus Express 273 Belfast–Derry City, alight Strabane centre; few mins walk.
Road: situated close to the Omagh road on the main street in the centre of Strabane

P Parking (not NT), 100yds (pay & display)

NT properties nearby
Mussenden Temple and Downhill Demesne, Springhill, Wellbrook Beetling Mill

Admission by guided tour. Last admission 45mins before closing. For opening dates and times tel. Property Manager, 028 8674 8210

Hezlett House

107 Sea Road, Castlerock, Coleraine,
Co. Londonderry BT51 4TW

〔icons〕 1976 **(7:C4)**

17th-century thatched house and garden

Learn about the reality of life in a rural 17th-century Irish thatched cottage told through the experiences of the people who once lived in one of Northern Ireland's oldest surviving buildings. Hezlett's quaint exterior, with its elegant Georgian windows, hides a curious early timber frame dating from 1690, and the cosy interior is simply furnished in mid-Victorian style. Guided tours offer an enthralling afternoon treat for all the family. Hezlett House is also home to the Downhill Marbles collection from the Bishop of Derry's Demesne at Downhill.

What's new in 2008 Refreshments available in visitor reception. Roof rethatched and walls limewashed

i **T** 028 2073 1582
E hezletthouse@nationaltrust.org.uk

Building Grounds

Light refreshments

Baby-changing facilities

Suitable for school groups

On leads and only in grounds

→ [C772349] **Cycle:** NCN93. **Bus:** Ulsterbus 134 Coleraine–Londonderry, alight crossroads, few mins walk. **Station:** Castlerock ¾ml.
Road: 4ml W of Coleraine on Coleraine–Downhill coast road, A2. Beside Castlerock turn-off at crossroads

P Free parking

NT properties nearby
Carrick-a-Rede, Giant's Causeway, Mussenden Temple and Downhill Demesne, Portstewart Strand, White Park Bay

Admission by guided tour. Tel. property for opening arrangements

Dogs assisting visitors with disabilities are always welcome

Looking across the colourful Italian Garden to the house at Mount Stewart

Mount Stewart House, Garden and Temple of the Winds

Portaferry Road, Newtownards, Co. Down
BT22 2AD

🏠 🐾 ❀ 🏛 ☕ 🍴 🎭 🍲 👪 🖼 🚶

🔔 🍷 1976   (7:F6)

Neo-classical house and celebrated gardens

The exotic luxuriance of Mount Stewart's celebrated gardens, created in the 1920s by Edith, Lady Londonderry, has helped make it one of Northern Ireland's most popular Trust properties with all the family. Nominated as a World Heritage Site, the impressive landscaped garden makes the most of the unique microclimate of the Ards Peninsula and boasts magnificent views across Strangford Lough from the romantically idyllic Temple of the Winds. Engaging tours of the opulent house reveal its fascinating heritage and historic world-famous artefacts and artwork.

What's new in 2008 Open-air theatre. Wedding Fair and Harvest Food Fayre. Candle shop

ℹ️ **T** 028 4278 8387
   E mountstewart@nationaltrust.org.uk

🚶 Special behind-the-scenes tours for groups. Available to smaller parties for a higher charge (booking essential)

🎭 Drama, music and craft events, Easter Egg trails, half-term activities for families. Grand Garden and Craft Fair, 17/18 May

🚶 Programme of specialised garden walks and talks conducted by a member of the garden team throughout the year (some include supper)

♿ 🚾 ♿ 🅿️ 🅿️ **Building** ♿ ♿
Grounds ♿ ➡️ ♿

Mount Stewart									
Lakeside gardens									
1 Feb−31 Jan 09	10−sunset	**M**	**T**	**W**	**T**	**F**	**S**	**S**	
Formal gardens									
8 Mar−31 Mar	10−4	**M**	**T**	**W**	**T**	**F**	**S**	**S**	
1 Apr−30 Apr	10−6	**M**	**T**	**W**	**T**	**F**	**S**	**S**	
1 May−30 Sep	10−8	**M**	**T**	**W**	**T**	**F**	**S**	**S**	
1 Oct−31 Oct	10−6	**M**	**T**	**W**	**T**	**F**	**S**	**S**	
House									
8 Mar−17 Mar	12−6	M	T	W	T	F	**S**	**S**	
21 Mar−30 Mar*	12−6	**M**	**T**	**W**	**T**	**F**	**S**	**S**	
5 Apr−27 Apr	12−6	M	T	W	T	F	**S**	**S**	
1 May−31 May	1−6	**M**	T	**W**	**T**	**F**	**S**	**S**	
1 Jun−30 Jun	1−6	**M**	**T**	**W**	**T**	**F**	**S**	**S**	
1 Jul−31 Aug	12−6	**M**	**T**	**W**	**T**	**F**	**S**	**S**	
1 Sep−30 Sep	12−6	**M**	T	**W**	**T**	**F**	**S**	**S**	
4 Oct−2 Nov	12−6	M	T	W	T	F	**S**	**S**	
Temple of the Winds									
23 Mar−25 Mar*	2−5	**M**	T	W	T	F	**S**	**S**	
5 Apr−26 Oct	2−5	M	T	W	T	F	**S**	**S**	

Admission by guided tour to house. Open BH Mons and all other public hols in N Ireland **inc. 17 March.** Last admission 1hr before closing. **NB: house opens at 12 every weekend.** House and formal gardens closed Nov–Jan 09. Lakeside gardens closed 25 Dec. Tel. for shop and restaurant opening times. *Easter week

Please remember – your membership card is always needed for free admission

NT shop selling quality local gifts. Plant sales

Bay Restaurant (licensed). Serving main and light meals using finest local ingredients. Catering available outside normal hours by arrangement. Special events: gourmet evenings and summer safaris. Children's menu

Baby-changing facilities. Pushchairs and baby back-carriers admitted. Hip-carrying infant seats for loan. Children's quiz/trail. Family activity packs. Easter egg trails. Family half-term activities. Big draw event in October. Children's winter trails

Suitable for school groups. Education room/centre. Live interpretation. Hands-on activities

On leads only and in grounds and garden

→ [J553695] **Bus**: Ulsterbus 10 Belfast–Portaferry, bus stop at gates. **Station**: Bangor 10ml. **Road**: 15ml SE of Belfast on Newtownards–Portaferry road, A20, 5ml SE of Newtownards

P Free parking, 100yds

NT properties nearby
Castle Ward, Divis and the Black Mountain, Patterson's Spade Mill, Rowallane Garden

Mussenden Temple and Downhill Demesne

Mussenden Road, Castlerock, Co. Londonderry
BT51 4RP

[icons] 1949   (7:C3)

Landscaped demesne and romantic temple in a dramatic coastal setting

Take a stroll around the stunning landscape park of Downhill Demesne, with its beautiful sheltered gardens and magnificent clifftop walks affording rugged headland views across the awe-inspiring north coast. Discover the striking 18th-century mansion of the eccentric Earl Bishop that now lies in ruin, then explore the romantic Mussenden Temple, precariously perched on the cliff edge.

What's new in 2008 Licensed for civil weddings in Mussenden Temple

Mussenden Temple and Downhill Demesne									
Grounds									
All year	Dawn–dusk	M	T	W	T	F	S	S	
Facilities									
15 Mar–17 Mar	10–5	M	T	W	T	F	S	S	
22 Mar–30 Mar	10–5	M	T	W	T	F	S	S	
5 Apr–29 Jun	10–5	M	T	W	T	F	S	S	
1 Jul–31 Aug	10–5	M	T	W	T	F	S	S	
6 Sep–2 Nov	10–5	M	T	W	T	F	S	S	

Open BH Mons and all other public hols in N Ireland
inc. 17 March

★ Admission charge at both the Lion's Gate and Bishop's Gate entrances

i **T** 028 2073 1582
E downhilldemesne@nationaltrust.org.uk

Midsummer concerts

[icons] **Building** [icon] **Grounds** [icon]

Baby-changing facilities. Pushchairs admitted. Family guide. Children's quiz/trail. Family activity packs

Suitable for school groups

On leads only

The Mussenden Temple, Downhill, County Londonderry

➔ [C757357] **Cycle**: NCN93, borders property. **Ferry**: Magilligan–Greencastle Ferry (8ml). **Bus**: Ulsterbus 134 Coleraine–Londonderry. **Station**: Castlerock ½ml. **Road**: 1ml W of Castlerock and 5ml W of Coleraine on Coleraine–Downhill coast road (A2)

P Parking (pay & display) at Lion's Gate where information, WCs and picnic tables are provided. Not suitable for 50-seater coaches. Alternative parking for coaches at Bishop's Gate entrance, ½ml from Temple

NT properties nearby
Carrick-a-Rede, Giant's Causeway, Hezlett House, Portstewart Strand

Patterson's Spade Mill

751 Antrim Road, Templepatrick, Co. Antrim
BT39 0AP

🏠 🍴 ⬆️ 🎭 🚗 🐄 👪 🎦 🐕 🔔
☂ 1991   (7:E6)

The last working water-driven spade mill in daily use in the British Isles

See history literally forged in steel at the last working water-driven spade mill in daily use in the British Isles. Hear the hammers, smell the grit and feel the heat of traditional spade-making. Guided tours vividly capture life during the Industrial Revolution and dig up the history and culture of the humble spade. Then take home one of only 150 hand-made spades produced each year that are on sale.

What's new in 2008 Licensed for weddings

Spade-maker at work in the finishing room

Patterson's Spade Mill									
15 Mar–17 Mar	2–6	**M**	T	W	T	F	**S**	**S**
22 Mar–30 Mar*	2–6	**M**	**T**	**W**	**T**	F	**S**	**S**
5 Apr–29 Jun	2–6	M	T	W	T	F	**S**	**S**
2 Jul–31 Aug	2–6	**M**	T	**W**	**T**	F	**S**	**S**
6 Sep–28 Sep	2–6	M	T	W	T	F	**S**	**S**

Admission by guided tour. Open BH Mons and all other public hols in N Ireland **inc. 17 March**. Last admission 1hr before closing. *Easter week

i **T** 028 9443 3619
E pattersons@nationaltrust.org.uk

🎭 Guided tour with the Spade-maker

🎭 'Farming in the 40s' and steam working day

♿ 🚻 P♿ D♿ Building 🏛♿ Grounds 🏛

🛍 No shop but spades for sale

👪 Pushchairs and baby back-carriers admitted. Children's guide

🎦 Suitable for school groups. Live interpretation. Hands-on activities

➔ [J263856] **Bus**: Ulsterbus 110 & 120, bus stop at gates. **Station**: Antrim 8ml. **Road**: 2ml NE of Templepatrick on Antrim–Belfast road, A6; M2 exit 4

P Free parking, 50yds

NT properties nearby
Divis and the Black Mountain, Mount Stewart, Rowallane Garden, Springhill, Wellbrook Beetling Mill

Portstewart Strand

Strand Road, Portstewart, Co. Londonderry
BT55 7PG

🅿 🚗 🐕 🛍 ☕ 🎭 👪 1981   (7:C3)

Miles of golden sand

The magnificent two-mile Strand of glistening golden sand is one of Northern Ireland's finest and most popular Blue Flag beaches with all ages. It is the perfect spot to spend lazy summer days, have fun family picnics and take long walks into the sand dunes, which are a haven for wild flowers and butterflies. New environmentally friendly visitor facilities are open at the beach and include WCs, showers, catering and retail, and a visitor services area with interpretation.

Rowallane Garden

Saintfield, Co. Down BT24 7LH

🏵 🏠 🍽 🍴 🎋 🎭 👫 🚶 | 1956 | (7:E7)

A true plantsman's garden in an informal style – with trees, shrubs and plants from around the world

Be inspired by this enchanting garden's dazzling array of exotic species from the four corners of the globe. Created in the mid 1860s by the Reverend John Moore, this informal plantsman's garden reflects the beautiful natural landscape of the surrounding area. There are spectacular displays of shrubs, superb spring bulbs and several areas managed as wildflower meadows. It is also home to a notable natural Rock Garden Wood with shade-loving plants. The outstanding Walled Garden includes the colourful National Collection of Penstemons.

What's new in 2008 Two new walks, the Farmland Walk and Woodland Walk, allow visitors to explore Rowallane Garden further

⭐ Tea-room is not open the same hours as the property

ℹ️ **T** 028 9751 0131
   E rowallane@nationaltrust.org.uk

🎋 By arrangement

🎭 Easter trail, plant fairs, craft fairs and musical events

🚶 Two new walks, Farmland Walk and Woodland Walk

♿ 🚻 🅿️ **Grounds** ♿ ♿

🏠 Plant sales from spring to autumn

🍽 Tea-room (NT-approved concession)

👫 Pushchairs admitted. Children's quiz/trail

🐕 On leads only

Sunset at Portstewart Strand, County Londonderry

What's new in 2008 Environmentally friendly visitor facilities, with WCs, showers, catering and retail and a visitor services area

ℹ️ **T** 028 2073 1582
   E portstewart@nationaltrust.org.uk

🛡 Family fun days, 5 July and 16 Aug

🏠 Shop in new visitor facility

🍽 Refreshments in new visitor facility

👫 Baby-changing facilities. Family Fun days

🐕 Dogs on leads. Dog litter area

➡️ [C720360] On S side of River Bann, 1½ml E of Castlerock and 5ml NW of Coleraine. **Cycle**: NCN93 runs nearby. **Bus**: Ulsterbus 218 from Belfast terminates in Portstewart. **Station**: Coleraine

🅿️ Parking on beach

NT properties nearby
Carrick-a-Rede, Giant's Causeway, Hezlett House, Mussenden Temple and Downhill Demesne

Portstewart Strand									
All year		M	T	W	T	F	S	S
Facilities								
1 Mar–27 Apr	10–6	M	T	W	T	F	S	S
28 Apr–1 Jun	10–8	M	T	W	T	F	S	S
2 Jun–31 Aug	10–9	M	T	W	T	F	S	S
1 Sep–30 Sep	10–8	M	T	W	T	F	S	S
1 Oct–2 Nov	10–6	M	T	W	T	F	S	S

Rowallane Garden									
1 Feb–11 Apr	10–4	M	T	W	T	F	S	S
12 Apr–14 Sep	10–8	M	T	W	T	F	S	S
15 Sep–31 Jan 09	10–4	M	T	W	T	F	S	S
Closed 25/26 Dec & 1 Jan 09. Tel. for tea-room opening times									

Rowallane Garden: a true plantsman's garden – with trees, shrubs and plants from around the world

→ [J412581] **Foot**: ¾ml from Saintfield village centre. **Bus**: Ulsterbus 15 Belfast–Downpatrick (passing ⊠ Belfast Great Victoria Street). **Road**: 11ml SE of Belfast, 1ml S of Saintfield, on road to Downpatrick (A7)

P Free parking

NT properties nearby
Castle Ward, Divis and the Black Mountain, Mount Stewart, Patterson's Spade Mill

Springhill

20 Springhill Road, Moneymore, Magherafelt, Co. Londonderry BT45 7NQ

[icons] [icons] 1957 **(7:C6)**

Pretty 17th-century 'Plantation' home with a significant costume collection

Experience the beguiling spirit of this inimitable 17th-century 'Plantation' home, with its walled gardens and parkland, full of tempting waymarked paths. Informative 'Living History' tours breathe life into the fascinating past of this welcoming family home. There are ten generations of Lenox-Conyngham family tales to enthrall you, as well as numerous portraits and much furniture to admire – not forgetting Ireland's best-documented ghost, Olivia. The old laundry houses the celebrated Costume Collection, which features some fine 18th- to 20th-century pieces that highlight its welcoming charm and fascinating past.

What's new in 2008 Outstanding new Costume Museum exhibition

i **T** 028 8674 8210
E springhill@nationaltrust.org.uk

🧒 Out-of-hours tours by arrangement

😊 Family days at Easter and Teddy Bears' Picnic in June. Living History presentations. 'Clueso for Kids'

🚶 Woodland walk

Springhill										
15 Mar–17 Mar	1–6	**M**	**T**	W	T	F	**S**	**S**
22 Mar–25 Mar*	1–6	**M**	**T**	W	T	F	**S**	**S**
29 Mar–29 Jun	1–6	M	T	W	T	F	**S**	**S**
1 Jul–31 Aug	1–6	**M**	**T**	**W**	**T**	F	**S**	**S**
6 Sep–28 Sep	1–6	M	T	W	T	F	**S**	**S**

Admission by guided tour to house. Open BH Mons and all other public hols in N Ireland **inc. 17 March**. Last admission 1hr before closing. Tel. property for shop and tea-room opening arrangements.
***Easter week**

For information regarding prices, see page 10

🦽 🚻 🖼️ ⋯ ♿ Building 🪜 ♿

🏪 NT shop. Plant sales

🍽️ Tea-room in Servants' Hall serving light refreshments

👶 Baby-changing facilities. Pushchairs and baby back-carriers admitted. Hip-carrying infant seats for loan. Children's play area. Children's quiz/trail. Family days at Easter. Teddy Bears' Picnic. 'Clueso for Kids'

🖼️ Suitable for school groups. Education room/centre. Live interpretation. Hands-on activities. Adult study days

🐕 On leads and only in grounds

➡️ [H866828] **Foot**: from Moneymore village, 1ml. **Cycle**: NCN94/95, 5ml. **Bus**: Ulsterbus 210 & 110 Belfast–Cookstown, alight Moneymore village, 1ml. **Road**: 1ml from Moneymore on Moneymore–Coagh road, B18

🅿️ Parking, 50yds

NT properties nearby
Gray's Printing Press, Wellbrook Beetling Mill

Wellbrook Beetling Mill

20 Wellbrook Road, Corkhill, Cookstown, Co. Tyrone BT80 9RY

🖼️🔧🍽️🏪🎭🎪🛡️👶🖼️🚶 1968   (7:C6)

Working water-powered mill used in the manufacture of linen

Nestling in an idyllic wooded glen full of lovely walks and picnic spots, the last working water-powered linen beetling mill in Northern Ireland offers a unique experience for all the family. Try some scutching, hackling and weaving with costumed guides at a hands-on demonstration, then, against the thundering cacophony of beetling engines, learn of the importance of the linen industry to 19th-century Ireland.

ℹ️ **T** 028 8675 1735
   E wellbrook@nationaltrust.org.uk

🎭 Out-of-hours tours by arrangment

🛡️ Living History days

🦽 🚻 ⋯ Building 🪜 Grounds 🪜
🏪 Selection of Irish linen

Wellbrook Beetling Mill		M	T	W	T	F	S	S
15 Mar–17 Mar	2–6	**M**	T	W	T	F	**S**	**S**
22 Mar–25 Mar*	2–6	**M**	**T**	W	T	F	**S**	**S**
29 Mar–29 Jun	2–6	M	T	W	T	F	**S**	**S**
1 Jul–31 Aug	2–6	**M**	**T**	**W**	**T**	F	**S**	**S**
6 Sep–28 Sep	2–6	M	T	W	T	F	**S**	**S**

Admission by guided tour. Open BH Mons and all other public hols in N Ireland **inc. 17 March.** Last admission 1hr before closing. Tel. property for shop opening arrangements. ***Easter week**

👶 Pushchairs and baby back-carriers admitted

🖼️ Suitable for school groups. Live interpretation. Hands-on activities

🐕 On leads only in grounds

➡️ [H750792] **Cycle**: NCN95. **Bus**: Ulsterbus 90 from Cookstown, with connections from Belfast. ½ml walk to mill. **Road**: 4ml W of Cookstown, ½ml off Cookstown–Omagh road (A505): from Cookstown turn right at Kildress Parish Church or follow Orritor Road (A53) to avoid town centre

🅿️ Free parking, 10yds

NT properties nearby
Gray's Printing Press, Springhill

The Beetling Mill at Wellbrook, County Tyrone

Many Trust properties are offering Gift Aid on Entry for non-members, see page 10

This section of the *Handbook* provides a range of information that will help you make the most of your visits to our properties. Please also see the questions and answers on p.387, as these contain important information.

Admission fees and opening arrangements

Members of the National Trust are admitted free to virtually all properties (see special information about National Trust membership, p.384). Admission fees include VAT and are liable to change if the VAT rate is altered.
The prices for many properties include a voluntary 10% donation under the Gift Aid on Entry scheme – see p.10 for full details. Current admission prices are given in full on our website **www.nationaltrust.org.uk** or are available from the Membership Department on 0844 800 1895.

Children: under 5s are free. Children aged 5–16 usually pay half the adult price. 17s and over pay the adult price. Children not accompanied by an adult are admitted at the Trust's discretion. Most properties offer discounted family tickets (usually covering 2 adults and up to 3 children, unless stated otherwise).

Concessions: as a registered charity which has to raise all its own funds, the National Trust cannot afford to offer concessions on admission fees.

Colourful border at Sizergh Castle Garden

Education groups: many properties offer educational facilities and programmes. Teachers are urged to make a free preliminary visit by prior arrangement with the property. We highly recommend our Educational Group membership (see p.384).

Group visits: groups are always welcome at our properties. All group visitors are required to book in advance and arrangements should be made direct with the property. Admission discounts are usually available for groups of more than 15 people, although this can vary and needs to be confirmed with the property when booking. The Travel Trade Office at NT Central Office (see p.382) can also provide general groups information and details on special interest tours and activities for groups. For further information visit **www.nationaltrust.org.uk/groups**

National Gardens Scheme open days: each year many of the National Trust's gardens are opened in support of the National Gardens Scheme (NGS). If this is on a day when the garden is not usually open, National Trust members will have to pay for entry. All money raised is donated by the NGS to support nurses' and garden charities, including the National Trust garden careership training scheme. In 2008, National Trust gardens with careership gardeners will open for the NGS on 19 July. The National Trust acknowledges with gratitude the generous and continuing support of the National Gardens Scheme Charitable Trust.

Busy properties: properties can be extremely popular on bank holidays and summer weekends. At some, timed tickets may be issued to smooth the flow of people entering (but not to limit the duration of a visit), and all visitors (including NT members) are required to use these tickets. This system aims to create better viewing conditions for visitors and to minimise wear and tear on historic interiors and gardens. On very rare occasions entry may not be possible on that day. If you are planning a long journey, please telephone the property in advance. At a few places special considerations apply and booking is essential, eg Red House, Mr Straw's House.

Please see p.385 for the application for membership form

The *Access Guide*, which contains detailed access information about our built properties, can be downloaded from www.nationaltrust.org.uk and is available from the Membership Department: tel. 0844 800 1895 or write to FREEPOST NAT9775, Warrington, WA5 7BR.
This book is also available in large print and on tape.

The National Trust Magazine is available free on tape to members, as are several regional newsletters.
If you wish to receive these regularly, please contact the **Access for All** office at our Central Office address (see p.382), email accessforall@nationaltrust.org.uk or tel. 01793 817634.

WCs

There is always one available, either at the property, when open, or nearby, unless the property entry specifically indicates 'no WC'.

𝐾 Guided tours

Most guided tours are for groups, so to avoid disappointment please telephone the property in advance or check the website.

Events

An incredible range of events takes place at National Trust properties throughout the year, from springtime estate and wildflower walks to family fun at Easter and Hallowe'en. There are live summer concerts, living history events, countryside open days and open-air theatre productions. In autumn lecture lunches and 'behind-the-scenes' tours look at the work of our gardeners and house staff. The year ends with Christmas craft fairs and carol concerts. Call 0844 800 1895 for a regional leaflet or visit **www.nationaltrust.org.uk/events**

Visitors with disabilities

Property entries will again be shown using symbols this year. For a key to the Access symbols please see the inside front cover.

The Trust continues to work with disability organisations to advance our Access for All work. After our success with the Hearing Dog Friendly Award in 2006, we continue to work closely with Hearing Dogs for Deaf People. In 2007, we were delighted to host events for this organisation at our properties to help celebrate its 25th anniversary. The Trust continues to welcome all assistance dogs at our properties.

The Trust was also an award-winner in 2007, when our central office, Heelis, obtained the RNID's 'Louder Than Words' Chartermark. Properties in our Thames and Solent region also received this award.

Our admission policy enables the necessary companion of a disabled visitor to be admitted free of charge, on request, while the normal charge applies to the disabled visitor. If you are disabled and would like an Admit One Card to save having to request the admission for your companion, please contact the Access for All office, details in the box above.

Our properties continue with their commitment to develop and promote inclusive access opportunities which are creative and sensitive to the surroundings. Many have made more areas of their property accessible by installing ramps, purchasing self-drive and wheelchair-accessible volunteer-driven powered vehicles and in some cases installing lifts.

Wherever possible, we admit users of powered wheelchairs and similar small vehicles to our buildings. This is subject to the physical limitations of the property and any other temporary constraints which may apply on the day.

Most properties offer Braille and large-print guides, and many are developing sensory information. Properties continue to develop virtual tours and more have been commissioned during the past year. Some properties are now offering BSL tours – places are limited on these tours and may need to be booked.

We recommend that if you need further information or wish to reserve a PMV, you contact the property direct.

🏠 🍴 Shopping and eating

All the Trust's shops and 150 restaurants, tea-rooms and coffee shops are managed by National Trust Enterprises. The profit they generate goes to support the work of the National Trust, and in 2006/2007 contributed £19.2 million to funds. Every purchase makes a vital contribution to the Trust's work.

Shops: many properties have shops offering a wide range of related merchandise, much of which is exclusive to the National Trust. These shops are indicated in relevant property entries by the shop symbol and their times given in the 'Opening arrangements' table. Many are open for Christmas shopping. The Trust also operates a number of shops in towns and cities, which are open during normal trading hours (see below). We also offer many National Trust gifts for sale online at
www.nationaltrust-shop.co.uk

Town shops: opening times vary, so please telephone for details if you are making a special journey.

Bath Marshall Wade's House, Abbey Churchyard BA1 1LY (tel. 01225 460249)

Cambridge 9 King's Parade CB2 1SJ (tel. 01223 311894)

Canterbury 24 Burgate CT1 2HA (tel. 01227 457120)

Chichester 92a East Street PO29 1HA (tel. 01243 773125)

Cirencester Tourist Information Centre, Cornhall, Market Place GL7 2NW (tel. 01285 654180)

Conwy Aberconwy House, Castle Street LL32 8AY (tel. 01492 592246)

Dartmouth 8 The Quay TQ6 9PS (tel. 01803 833694)

Hereford 7 Gomond Street HR1 2DP (tel. 01432 342297)

Hexham 25/26 Market Place NE46 3PB (tel. 01434 607654)

Kendal 16–20 Stricklandgate LA9 4ND (tel. 01539 736190)

London Blewcoat School, 23 Caxton Street, Victoria SW1H 0PY (tel. 020 7222 2877)

Monmouth 5 Church Street NP25 3BX (tel. 01600 713270)

St David's Visitor Centre & Shop, Captain's House, 6 High Street SA62 6SD (tel. 01437 720385)

Salisbury 41 High Street SP1 2PB (tel. 01722 331884)

Seahouses Information Centre & Shop, 16 Main Street NE68 7RQ (tel. 01665 721099)

Sidmouth Cosmopolitan House, Old Fore Street EX10 8LS (tel. 01395 578107)

Skipton 6 Sheep Street BD23 1JH (tel. 01756 799378)

Stratford-upon-Avon 45 Wood Street CV37 6JG (tel. 01789 262197)

Street Clark's Village, Farm Road BA16 0BB (tel. 01458 440578)

Swindon Heelis Café & Shop, Kemble Drive SN2 2NA (tel. 01793 817600: shop; 01793 817474: café)

Truro 9 River Street TR1 2SQ (tel. 01872 241464)

Wells 16 Market Place BA5 2RB (tel. 01749 677735)

York Shop & Tea-room, 32 Goodramgate YO1 7LG (tel. 01904 659050: shop; 01904 659282: tea-room)

Please remember – your membership card is always needed for free admission

Families can be sure
of a warm welcome at
National Trust
properties

Restaurants and tea-rooms: the National Trust operates more than 150 tea-rooms and restaurants, usually located in special old buildings – including castles, lighthouses, stables, and even hot-houses! We aim to offer a welcoming atmosphere, value for money and traditional home cooking. Many properties feature menus which reflect the changing seasons and use locally sourced products and local suppliers. Tea-rooms and restaurants are often open at times of the year when houses and gardens are closed and many offer programmes of events, such as lecture lunches, as well as festive meals in the run-up to Christmas.

The National Trust Home Collection:
National Trust Enterprises collaborates with leading British designers and manufacturers to create inspiring collections based on the Trust's historical properties, land and archives. Partners include Zoffany furnishings and wallpaper, Bylaw and Duresta furniture, Hypnos beds, The Medici Society greeting cards, Stevensons of Norwich plaster mouldings, Goodacres carpets, Alitex greenhouses, Marshalls paving, Scotts of Thrapston summerhouses, Vale Garden Houses, Museums and Galleries stationery and Richard Burbidge wood mouldings. You can also join the National Trust Wine Club. For further details tel. 01793 817509 or visit **www.nationaltrust.org.uk/homecollection**

Family facilities/activities

The National Trust welcomes families. Many properties organise activities specifically for families and family tickets are offered at most properties. Parking is made easy, and many places provide baby-feeding and baby-changing areas, sometimes in purpose-designed parent and baby rooms.

Our restaurants have highchairs, children's menus, colouring sheets and, at some properties, play areas. Staff are happy to advise you about what is on offer.

In historic buildings, visitors with smaller babies are welcome to use front slings, which are often available on loan, and hip-carrying infant seats or reins for toddlers can be borrowed at some places. There are usually arrangements for storing prams or pushchairs at the entrance, as it is not possible to take these into fragile interiors.

Some houses are able to admit baby back-carriers at all times; others may admit them on quiet days mid-week, at the discretion of staff. We realise that the restriction on back-carriers, prams and pushchairs may be awkward for those with older and/or heavier children, and as access arrangements vary at each property, we suggest that you telephone in advance to check whether there are any restrictions that will affect you.

For general and membership enquiries, please telephone 0844 800 1895

🪶 Learning and Discovery – when places come to life

The National Trust is committed to placing learning at the heart of the organisation. We provide a variety of experiences, which are inspiring, stimulating and fun. We encourage everyone – local communities, young people, families – to engage with us to develop their sense of discovery and their enthusiasm for sharing it.

Our properties welcome visitors from across the educational sector and from special interest groups. Many have an on-site learning officer and a programme of learning activities. For more information email **learning@nationaltrust.org.uk** or visit **www.nationaltrust.org.uk/learning**

Over 60 National Trust properties have guides for children and families, some have family activity rooms – and many more have trails, handling activities and other things to do for young visitors and families. Tracker Packs at some houses and gardens provide activities for the whole family as they explore the property. Trusty the Hedgehog, our own children's character, appears at events and has his own website: **www.trusty.org**

At **www.nationaltrust.org.uk/events** you can search by date or location for things to do especially suitable for children and families. Many more activities are arranged than may be listed, especially during weekends, bank holidays and school holidays, so do call individual properties for information. The Membership Department can send you appropriate regional events leaflets. Tel. 0844 800 1895 or email **enquiries@thenationaltrust.org.uk**

🐕 Dogs allowed

Dogs assisting visitors with disabilities are welcome inside our houses, gardens, restaurants and shops. The dog symbol is used in property entries to indicate places where dogs are allowed in the grounds or other specified areas. If a property does not show the dog symbol, there are no opportunities to take your dog on the visit. Only assistance dogs are allowed beyond the car park.

We endeavour to provide facilities for dogs, such as water for drinking bowls, advice on suitable areas to exercise dogs and shady spaces in car parks (though dogs should not be left alone in cars). These facilities vary from property to property and according to how busy it is on a particular day. The primary responsibility for the welfare of dogs remains, of course, with their owners.

Dogs are welcome at most countryside

Making discoveries on a minibeast safari at Wicken Fen, Cambridgeshire

Please remember – your membership card is always needed for free admission

sites, where they should be kept under close control at all times. Please observe local notices on the need to keep dogs on leads, particularly at sensitive times of year, eg during the breeding season for ground-nesting birds, at lambing time or when deer are calving. Dogs should be kept on a short lead on access land between 1 March and 31 July, and at any other time in the vicinity of livestock.

In some areas we have found it necessary to introduce restrictions, usually seasonal, and particularly on beaches, due to conflicts with other users. Where access for dogs is restricted, we attempt to identify suitable alternative locations nearby.

Clear up dog mess and dispose of it responsibly. Where dog waste bins are not provided, please take the waste away with you.

🔔🍷 Weddings and private functions

These symbols at the top of entries in this handbook indicate that the property is licensed for civil weddings (bell symbol) and/or available for private functions (glass symbol) such as wedding receptions, anniversaries, family celebrations and so on. For more information, contact the property, the Membership Department on 0844 800 1895 or visit **www.nationaltrust.org.uk/hiring**

Corporate hospitality and meetings

The National Trust's new portfolio of eight properties was launched last year and has since welcomed many top companies from Britain and overseas for events including grand dinners, elegant conferences, formal meetings, team-building and family fun days. Each property has been carefully prepared to offer a variety of facilities, striking settings and exclusivity for clients demanding something different. Entertaining is about attention to detail and making each event as individual as the company hosting it. For more information, email the Functions Team at **functions@nationaltrust.org.uk**, tel. 01494 755515 for functions at Basildon, Osterley, Mottisfont and Waddesdon and 01284 747574 for functions at Blickling, Wimpole, Sutton Hoo and Ickworth, or visit **www.nationaltrust.org.uk/hiring**

Your safety

We aim to provide a safe and healthy environment for visitors to our properties, and we take measures to ensure that the work of our staff, volunteers and contractors does not in any way jeopardise visitors' safety or health. You can help us by:

- observing all notices and signs during your visit;
- following any instructions and advice given by Trust staff;
- ensuring that children are properly supervised at all times;
- wearing appropriate clothing and footwear at countryside properties and in gardens.

At all our properties the responsibility for the safety of visitors should be seen as one that is shared between the Trust and the individual visitor. The Trust takes reasonable measures to minimise risks in ways that are compatible with our conservation objectives – but not necessarily to eliminate all risks. This is especially the case at our coastal and countryside properties. As the landscape becomes more rugged and remote, the balance of responsibility between the landowner and the visitor changes. There will be fewer safety measures and warning signs, and visitors will need to rely more on their own skills, knowledge, equipment and preparation. You can help to ensure your own safety by:

- taking note of weather conditions and forecasts and being properly equipped for changes in the weather;
- making sure you are properly prepared, equipped and clothed for the terrain and the activity in which you are participating;
- giving notice of your intended route and estimated time of return;
- making sure you have the necessary skills and fitness for the location and activity, and being aware of your own limitations.

→ How to get there

Each property entry includes its OS Landranger (or OSNI) series map number and grid reference, an indicator of its location and public transport/road access.

Car-free days out

Travelling on foot, by bike, bus, train or boat to National Trust properties can be an enjoyable and environmentally friendly way of visiting. In support of car-free travel, a growing number of properties offer incentives for visitors arriving without a car – from a discount on entry to a tea-room voucher. Visit www.nationaltrust.org.uk/carfreedaysout

Public transport

Details of access by public transport are correct as at July 2007. No indication of frequency of services is given so please check times before setting out.

The National Trust is very grateful to Barry Doe, a life member, for this travel information, which he has provided for the past 25 years. Barry retires this year – any Trust member who would like to continue his work should contact the Editor on lucy.peel@nationaltrust.org.uk

Ferry: some properties are best reached – or can only be reached – by boat.

Bus: unless otherwise stated, bus services pass the property entrance (although there may be a walk from the bus-stop). Many bus services connect properties with local train stations – 'passing ➔' indicates that the bus service passes the station entrance or approach road and 'passing close ➔' indicates that a walk is necessary.

Train/London Underground: the distance from the property to nearest railway stations is given. Unstaffed stations are indicated by (U).

🚲 Cycling

More than 200 National Trust properties are within $1\frac{1}{4}$ miles or 2km of the UK's 10,000-mile National Cycle Network (NCN). Combined with bridleways, byways and quiet roads, this provides many opportunities for cycling to your favourite places. We work closely with Sustrans, the sustainable transport charity, to promote cycling as a healthy, enjoyable and environmentally-friendly way of reaching our properties.

● Handbook property entries give information on the nearest NCN route. For example NCN4, 2ml denotes the property is 2 miles from NCN route number 4.

● Unless otherwise stated, most National Trust properties have cycle parking on site or nearby.

● The bicycle symbol shows cycling opportunities at the property itself.

Further information to help plan your journey

Transport Direct: plan how to get to our properties by public transport or car from any UK location or postcode using www.transportdirect.info

Sustrans: for NCN routes and cycling maps visit www.sustrans.org.uk or tel. 0117 929 0888.

Traveline: for bus routes and times for England, Wales and Scotland visit www.traveline.info or tel. 0871 200 2233.

National Rail Enquiries: for train times visit www.nationalrail.co.uk or tel. 08457 48 49 50.

Taxis from railway stations: www.traintaxi.co.uk

Public transport in Northern Ireland (train and bus): www.translink.co.uk or tel. 028 9066 6630.

Please remember – your membership card is always needed for free admission

♁ Walking

There is no better way to appreciate the variety of places cared for by the National Trust than by exploring on foot. Long-distance walking routes, including thirteen National Trails, link many Trust properties, on top of a scenic web of local paths and access land. We have promoted the freedom to roam over open country, coast and woods for more than a century and continue to work to improve access for all today.

Hundreds of guided walks take place at our properties each year. They are a great way to find out more about our conservation work, wildlife, history, farming and so much more, while enjoying a healthy stroll. Many properties also offer waymarked trails, leaflets and maps. Lots of walks sheets are available for free on the National Trust website to download, print and take on your day out. Visit **www.nationaltrust.org.uk/walking**

Handbook property entries give information on pedestrian access from the nearest town or railway station and details of routes passing through or nearby.

P Car parks

Visitors use car parks at National Trust properties entirely at their own risk. They are advised to secure their cars and not to leave any valuable items in them during their visit.

National Trust books, guidebooks and prints

The National Trust publishes a range of titles that promote its work and the great variety of properties and collections in its care. Books and guidebooks are available from most Trust shops or from all good bookshops. Details of new books can be found in the members' magazine and on the website under the 'shop' section. A range of guidebooks can be ordered through **www.tempus-publishing.com/nationaltrust.php** or via individual property pages on the website.

www.ntprints.com features carefully selected images available to purchase from the National Trust's very own photographic library. This collection of images vividly illustrates the rich diversity and historical range of properties and collections in the National Trust's care. Whatever the subject – wild moors, craggy cliffs, tranquil gardens, imposing country houses, breathtaking works of art or beautifully conserved interiors – our images have been created to capture the spirit of each location. Prints of the photos featured in the 2008 *Handbook* may be ordered direct.

Treasures from the
National Trust   £30
ISBN: 9781905400454

Great Family
Days Out 2008   £9.99
ISBN: 9781905400584

One of the extensive range
of National Trust property
guidebooks

For general and membership enquiries, please telephone 0844 800 1895

The National Trust has selected a group of leading specialist travel operators to offer a range of holidays with special appeal to members and supporters. Every booking made earns important income for the Trust.

The National Trust Holiday Cottages

More than 360 unique properties in outstanding locations make up the National Trust's Holiday Cottages Collection. From the really rural getaway to a city break, a coastal location to apartments in our great houses, this collection contains the widest choice that we have ever offered either as a main holiday or short break. Our cottages range from cosy hideaways for two, to large rambling farmhouses able to accommodate up to fourteen people for gatherings or to provide the setting to make a birthday or anniversary event special. For a brochure call 0844 800 2072, quoting ref. NT HBK. To book or check availability tel. 0844 800 2070 or visit www.nationaltrustcottages.co.uk

The National Trust European Self-Catering Collection

The properties in this programme have been picked to complement the Trust's own holiday cottage portfolio at home. Cottages in the Provençal countryside, beautifully renovated apartments in the Chianti hills of Tuscany, farmhouses in the meadows of Switzerland, a restored mill in southern Spain – these are just a few of the highlights of this European self-catering collection, operated for the Trust by Inntravel, one of the country's leading specialist travel companies. For a brochure tel. 0844 800 2076, quoting ref. NT HBK, email nationaltrust@inntravel.co.uk or visit www.nationaltrust.org.uk/europeancottages

The National Trust Active Holiday Collection

Discover the most beautiful regions of Europe, walking or cycling from village to village while your luggage is transported ahead. There are holidays for all levels, from easy coastal routes to mountain hikes, and you journey at your own pace, guided by detailed route notes which include information about the places of interest along the way. Stay in welcoming country inns and choose from a range of travel options. For a brochure tel. 0844 800 2076, quoting ref. NT HBK, or visit www.nationaltrust.org.uk/activeholidays

The National Trust Hotel Reservation Service

A comprehensive range of two to five star hotels across Britain, operated for the Trust by leading short break specialist Superbreak. The wide choice of locations makes it easy to get away and find hotels close to faraway Trust properties you've always wanted to visit. For a brochure tel. 0844 800 2076, quoting ref. NT HBK. To book visit www.nationaltrust.org.uk/hotels

Take a break at Ferris's Cottage, Trelissick Garden. Just one of many National Trust holiday cottages

Please remember – your membership card is always needed for free admission

Make friends and make a difference on a National Trust working holiday

The National Trust Escorted Tours and Cruise Collections

The cruises and tours in this programme are operated by Saga, with more than 50 years experience of organising holidays, providing the highest standards of service and unbeatable value for money with so much more included in the price. The exclusive cruises and tours have been developed to appeal to members and supporters of the Trust – from a cruise around Britain or exploring the vineyards of France and Iberia, to a tour of Madeira or Italy, there will be a holiday for you! For a brochure tel. 0844 800 2076, quoting reference NT HBK or visit **www.saga.co.uk/nationaltrust**

The National Trust Working Holidays

The National Trust Working Holidays programme provides great opportunities to make new friends, socialise and work together in a team. You can get away from the day-to-day distractions of modern living to achieve a worthwhile objective and make a significant difference to the preservation of our coast and countryside. They are a true learning experience, with activities ranging from hedge laying or drystone walling, to archaeological digs or dragonfly identification. For those of you who like your home comforts, premium holidays offer en-suite accommodation.

Also included are Youth Discovery holidays for 16–18 year olds. Young people wanting to know more about this or other opportunities should email **youth@nationaltrust.org.uk**

Each holiday is run by Trust staff and trained leaders, so experience is not necessary – just plenty of energy and enthusiasm! For a brochure tel. 0844 800 3099, email **working.holidays@nationaltrust.org.uk** or to book online visit **www.nationaltrust.org.uk/workingholidays**

Bed and Breakfast on National Trust Farms, Camping and Caravan Sites

Enjoy some of the best of our countryside and coastal areas by staying with National Trust tenant farmers or at one of our camping and caravan sites.

For brochures call our Membership Department (see p.382) or visit **www.nationaltrust.org.uk/holidays**

For general and membership enquiries, please telephone 0844 800 1895

As a charity we rely greatly upon additional support, beyond membership fees, to help us to protect and manage the coastline, countryside, historic buildings and gardens in our care. You can help us in several ways, such as making a donation or considering a gift to the National Trust in your Will.

Legacies

By making provision for the National Trust with a gift in your will, you would be providing a lasting gift for future generations, Every sum, whatever the size, will be put to good use and make a positive difference to our work across England, Wales and Northern Ireland in permanently safeguarding our natural and built heritage. We guarantee never to use a single penny on administration costs or overheads. Choose too where you would like your gift to be directed – the project, property or region which means most to you.

Find out more by requesting the free colour booklet entitled *Guide to Making and Updating your Will*, available from our Membership Department or visit us today at **www.nationaltrust.org.uk/legacies** Your gift is as special to us as the unique places it helps to protect.

Donations

The Trust organises several programmes to give donors the opportunity to see at first hand the work they support, such as the Benefactor and Patron programmes, which include special 'behind-the-scenes' events. You can help us by donating to our appeals, such as the Tyntesfield appeal, or other projects of special significance to you, or by buying raffle tickets at our properties.

For further information or to make a donation, please contact the Fundraising Department at our Swindon Central Office (see p.382).

How you can support the National Trust in the US – join The Royal Oak Foundation

More than 40,000 Americans belong to The Royal Oak Foundation, the National Trust's membership affiliate in the US. A not-for-profit organisation, The Royal Oak Foundation helps the National Trust through the generous tax-

Join a group

You can make more of your membership by joining a member or other supporter group. Member groups are known as associations, centres or clubs and by paying a small annual subscription you can:

- enjoy a programme of informative talks;
- take part in social and fundraising events;
- go on rambles, day trips, visits and holidays.

You could also join one of our many local Friends groups and advisory bodies, which work directly with some Trust houses and countryside properties providing practical assistance and valuable advice.

All our supporter groups offer great opportunities to get involved as a volunteer in all kinds of ways (see opposite). There are more than 40 National Trust Volunteer Groups which work with properties on conservation and environmental projects. Many of the members' groups also act as a focus for local volunteering, whether it is organising the group's programmes or directly working on volunteer activities at specific houses and countryside properties.

Want to know more about your local groups? Tel. 01793 817636 or visit **www.nationaltrust.org.uk/supportergroups**

deductible support of members and friends by making grants towards its work. Member benefits include *The National Trust Handbook*, three editions of *The National Trust Magazine*, the quarterly *Royal Oak Newsletter*, and free admission to properties of the National Trust and of the National Trust for Scotland. Royal Oak sponsors lectures, tours and events in the US, designed to inform Americans of the Trust's work, on topics related to English gardens, country house interior design, art, architecture and social history.

The Royal Oak Foundation, 26 Broadway, Suite 950, New York, NY 10004, USA tel. 001 212 480 2889, fax 001 212 785 7234 email **general@royal-oak.org** website **www.royal-oak.org**

Please remember – your membership card is always needed for free admission

Volunteering for a brighter future

The National Trust was formed by three volunteers and last year an incredible 49,000 people contributed more than 2.9 million hours of their time to support our work in over 200 different volunteer roles.

We would like you to volunteer with us. There are lots of roles available, from welcoming visitors to a built property to tackling countryside conservation tasks. Not to mention taking part in a working holiday (see p.379), joining a supporter group (see opposite) or taking part in our employee volunteering programme.

By volunteering with us you can: make new friends; gain work experience; use and develop old skills in new environments; see behind the scenes and make a difference.

To find out more contact your local property, tel. 01793 817632 or visit www.nationaltrust.org.uk/volunteering

Voluntary talks service

The National Trust has a group of enthusiastic and knowledgeable volunteer speakers available to give illustrated talks to groups of all sizes. Talks cover many aspects of the Trust's work, from the Neptune Coastline Campaign to garden history, conservation, individual properties and regional round-ups. Talks can also be tailored to meet your group's particular interests. To find out more, contact the Talks Service Co-ordinator at your local National Trust regional or country office (see p.383).

Heritage Lottery Fund

The Heritage Lottery Fund (HLF) enables communities to celebrate, look after and learn more about our diverse heritage. From museums and historic buildings, to parks and nature reserves to celebrating traditions, customs and history, the HLF has awarded more than £3.3 billion to projects that open up our nation's heritage for everyone to enjoy.

We have supported the following National Trust projects:

59 Rodney Street, Liverpool

Attingham Park, Shropshire

Beningbrough Hall, North Yorkshire

Biddulph Grange Garden, Staffordshire

Birmingham Back to Backs, West Midlands

Croome Park, Worcestershire

Dinefwr, Carmarthenshire

Divis & Black the Mountain, Belfast

Gibside, Newcastle upon Tyne

Glastonbury Tor, Somerset

Greenway, Devon

Hardcastle Crags and Gibson Mill, W. Yorkshire

Hardwick Hall, Derbyshire

Holy Jesus Hospital, Newcastle

Llanerchaeron, Ceredigion

Nostell Priory, West Yorkshire

Prior Park, Bath

Springhill, Co. Londonderry

Sudbury Museum of Childhood, Derbyshire

Tyntesfield, North Somerset

Wordsworth House, Cumbria

The Workhouse, Nottinghamshire

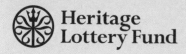

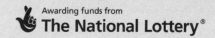

If you would like to find out more please visit **www.hlf.org.uk**

For general and membership enquiries, please telephone 0844 800 1895

The National Trust supports the National Code of Practice for Visitor Attractions.

We are very willing to answer questions and receive comments from members and visitors. Please speak to a member of staff in the first instance. Many properties provide their own comment cards and boxes. All comments will be noted, and action taken where necessary, but it is not possible to answer every comment or suggestion individually.

Enquiries by telephone, email or in writing should be made to the Trust's Membership Department (see below), open seven days a week (9–5:30 weekdays, 9–4 weekends and bank holidays). Detailed property enquiries, eg accessibility for wheelchairs, should be made to the individual property. Business callers should contact the appropriate regional or country office by telephone (0844 numbers are charged at 5p per minute from BT landlines, charges from mobiles and other operators may vary). You can also obtain information from our website, www.nationaltrust.org.uk

Central Office
The National Trust &
National Trust (Enterprises) Ltd
Heelis, Kemble Drive, Swindon,
Wiltshire SN2 2NA
Tel: 01793 817400
Fax: 01793 817401

National Trust Membership Department
PO Box 39, Warrington WA5 7WD
Tel: 0844 800 1895
Fax: 0844 800 4642
Minicom: 0844 800 4410
Email: **enquiries@thenationaltrust.org.uk**
for all general enquiries, including membership
and requests for information

National Trust Holiday Cottages
Tel: 0844 800 2072 for brochures
Tel: 0844 800 2070 for reservations

Heelis: our award-winning Central Office in Swindon

The National Trust online

You can find information about all the properties in this *Handbook* on our website at www.nationaltrust.org.uk Online property information is updated on a daily basis. Most properties show additional information about their history and features, to help you make the most of your visit. The website includes information about volunteering and learning opportunities, hiring a venue for corporate or private functions, events and regional news. We also have a dedicated holiday cottages website at www.nationaltrustcottages.co.uk and online gift shop at www.nationaltrust-shop.co.uk

For monthly National Trust news, events information, details of things to do and places to visit, updates on our work and suggestions of how you might get involved, sign up for your free email newsletter via www.nationaltrust.org.uk/email

This Handbook contains email addresses for those properties which can be contacted direct. General email enquiries should be sent to **enquiries@thenationaltrust.org.uk**

Please remember – your membership card is always needed for free admission

Regional contacts

Devon & Cornwall

(*Devon*)
Killerton House, Broadclyst, Exeter EX5 3LE
Tel: 01392 881691. Fax: 01392 881954
Email: dc.customerenquiries@nationaltrust.org.uk

(*Cornwall*)
Lanhydrock, Bodmin PL30 4DE
Tel: 01208 74281. Fax: 01208 77887
Email: dc.customerenquiries@nationaltrust.org.uk

Wessex

(*Bristol/Bath, Dorset, Gloucestershire,
Somerset & Wiltshire*)
Eastleigh Court, Bishopstrow,
Warminster, Wiltshire BA12 9HW
Tel: 01985 843600. Fax: 01985 843624
Email: wx.customerenquiries@nationaltrust.org.uk

Thames & Solent

(*Berkshire, Buckinghamshire, Hampshire,
part of Hertfordshire, Isle of Wight,
Greater London & Oxfordshire*)
Hughenden Manor, High Wycombe,
Bucks HP14 4LA
Tel: 01494 528051. Fax: 01494 463310
Email: ts.customerenquiries@nationaltrust.org.uk

South East

(*Kent, Surrey, East Sussex & West Sussex*)
Polesden Lacey, Dorking, Surrey RH5 6BD
Tel: 01372 453401. Fax: 01372 452023
Email: se.customerenquiries@nationaltrust.org.uk

East of England

(*Bedfordshire, Cambridgeshire, Essex, part of
Hertfordshire, Norfolk & Suffolk*)
Westley Bottom, Bury St Edmunds, Suffolk IP33 3WD
Tel: 01284 747500. Fax: 01284 747506

East Midlands

(*Derbyshire, Leicestershire, S. Lincolnshire,
Northamptonshire, Nottinghamshire & Rutland*)
Clumber Park Stableyard, Worksop, Notts S80 3BE
Tel: 01909 486411. Fax: 01909 486377
Email: em.customerenquiries@nationaltrust.org.uk

West Midlands

(*Birmingham, Herefordshire, Shropshire,
Staffordshire, Warwickshire & Worcestershire*)
Attingham Park, Shrewsbury, Shropshire SY4 4TP
Tel: 01743 708100. Fax: 01743 708150
Email: wm.customerenquiries@nationaltrust.org.uk

North West

(*Cumbria & Lancashire*)
The Hollens, Grasmere, Ambleside,
Cumbria LA22 9QZ
Tel: 015394 35599. Fax: 015394 35353
Email: nw.customerenquiries@nationaltrust.org.uk

(*Cheshire, Greater Manchester & Merseyside*)
18 High Street, Altrincham, Cheshire WA14 1PH
Tel: 0161 928 0075. Fax: 0161 929 6819
Email: nw.customerenquiries@nationaltrust.org.uk

Yorkshire & North East

(*Yorkshire, Teesside, N. Lincolnshire*)
Goddards, 27 Tadcaster Road, York YO24 1GG
Tel: 01904 702021. Fax: 01904 771970
Email: yne.customerenquiries@nationaltrust.org.uk

(*Co. Durham, Newcastle & Tyneside,
Northumberland*)
Scots' Gap, Morpeth, Northumberland NE61 4EG
Tel: 01670 774691. Fax: 01670 774317
Email: yne.customerenquiries@nationaltrust.org.uk

Wales

Trinity Square, Llandudno LL30 2DE
Tel: 01492 860123. Fax: 01492 860233
Email: wales.customerenquiries@nationaltrust.org.uk

Northern Ireland

Rowallane House, Saintfield, Ballynahinch,
Co. Down BT24 7LH
Tel: 028 9751 0721. Fax: 028 9751 1242
Email: enquiriesni@nationaltrust.org.uk

National Trust for Scotland

Wemyss House, 28 Charlotte Square,
Edinburgh EH2 4ET
Tel: 0131 243 9300
Email: information@nts.org.uk

For general and membership enquiries, please telephone 0844 800 1895

- Membership of the National Trust allows you free parking in Trust car parks and free entry to most Trust properties open to the public during normal opening times and under normal opening arrangements, provided you can present a valid membership card.

  Remember to display your car parking sticker.

- **Please check that you have your card with you before you set out on your journey. We very much regret that you cannot be admitted free of charge without it, nor can admission charges be refunded subsequently.**

- Membership cards are **not transferable**.

- If your card is lost or stolen, please contact the Membership Department (address on p.382), tel. 0844 800 1895.

- A replacement card can be sent quickly to a temporary address if you are on holiday. Donations to cover the administrative costs of a replacement card are always welcome.

- In some instances an entry fee may apply. Additional charges may be made:
  - when a special event is in progress at a property;
  - when a property is opened specially for a National Gardens Scheme open day;
  - where the management of a property is not under the National Trust's direct control, eg Tatton Park, Cheshire;
  - where special attractions are not an integral part of the property, eg steam yacht *Gondola* in Cumbria, Wimpole Hall Home Farm in Cambridgeshire, Dunster Watermill in Somerset, the model farm and museum at Shugborough in Staffordshire and the Tudor old hall and farm at Tatton Park in Cheshire;
  - where special access conditions apply, eg 20 Forthlin Road or Mendips in Liverpool, where access is only by minibus from Speke Hall and Liverpool city centre, and **all** visitors (including Trust members) pay a fare for the minibus journey.

- The National Trust encourages educational use of its properties. Our Educational Group membership is open to all non-profit-making educational groups whose members are in full-time education. Subscription rates are banded according to the number of pupils on roll. Tel. 0844 800 1895 for further details.

- Individual life members of the National Trust who enrolled as such before 1968 have cards which admit one person only. Members wishing to exchange these for 'admit two' cards, to include the guest facility, or those wishing to change from one category of life membership to another, should contact the Membership Department for the scale of charges.

- Entry to properties owned by the Trust but maintained and administered by English Heritage or Cadw (Welsh Historic Monuments) is free to members of the Trust, English Heritage and Cadw.

- Members of the National Trust are also admitted free of charge to properties of the National Trust for Scotland, a separate charity with similar responsibilities. NTS properties include the famous Inverewe Garden, Bannockburn, Culloden and Robert Adam's masterpiece, Culzean Castle. Full details are contained in *The National Trust for Scotland Guide to Properties* (priced £5, inc. p.&p.), which can be obtained by contacting the NTS Customer Service Centre, tel. 0131 243 9300. Information is also available at www.nts.org.uk

- Reciprocal visiting arrangements also exist with certain overseas National Trusts, including Australia, New Zealand, Barbados, Bermuda, Canada, Jersey, Guernsey and the Manx Museum and National Trust on the Isle of Man. During 2008 all National Trust members will receive free entry to properties belonging to the Italian National Trust (FAI). For a full list, contact our Membership Department.

- Trust members visiting properties owned by the National Trust for Scotland or overseas Trusts are only eligible for free entry **on presentation of a valid membership card.**

Application for membership

Twelve-month membership

☐ **Individual: £46**
and, for each additional member living at the same address, **£31**.
One card for each member.
Pensioner rate available to those who have held membership for at least five years, aged 60+ and retired. Available on request.
Tel. 0844 800 1895 for details.

☐ **Family group: £82**
for two adults, living at the same address, and their children or grandchildren under 18.
Please give names and dates of birth for all children. Two cards cover the family.

☐ **Family one adult: £62**
for one adult and his/her children under 18, living at the same address. Please give names and dates of birth for all children.
One card covers the family.

☐ **Child: £21**
Must be under 13 at time of joining.
Please give date of birth.

Rates valid from 1 March 2008 to 28 February 2009

☐ **Young person: £21**
Must be 13 to 25 at time of joining.
Please give date of birth.

☐ **Educational group membership:**
See opposite. Tel. 0844 800 1895 for details.

Life membership

☐ **Individual: £1,125**
(**£735** if aged 60 or over and retired). Please note CAF payments cannot be accepted for individual life membership. One card admits the named member and a guest.

☐ **Joint: £1,350**
for lifetime partners (**£890** if either partner is aged 60 or over and retired). Two cards, each admitting the named member.

☐ **Family joint: £1,550**
for two adults, living at the same address, and their children or grandchildren under 18.
Please give names and dates of birth for all children. Two cards cover the family.

Full address					
Postcode			Tel.		
Title	First name	Surname		Date of birth	Value £

'I would like the tax to be reclaimed on any eligible donations or membership subscriptions that I have ever made or will make to the National Trust until further notice. I confirm that I pay an amount of UK income or capital gains tax at least equal to the tax that the National Trust will reclaim.' ☐ *giftaid it*

Amount attached: £
Cheque/postal order
Delete as appropriate
Please allow up to 21 days for receipt of your membership card and new member's pack

Signature   Date

Credit/debit card/direct debit payments can be made by telephoning 0844 800 1895 (Minicom 0844 800 4410) in office hours, 7 days a week. Immediate membership can be obtained by joining at a National Trust property, shop or countryside information point, or you can join online at **www.nationaltrust.org.uk/join**

I am happy to be contacted by the National Trust by email and email newsletters about conservation, membership, fundraising and other activities. My email address is (please print).

National Trust Enterprises also works with carefully selected organisations and we may contact you by email and email newsletter with special offers from them that will benefit the National Trust. Please tick this box if you do want to receive these offers. ☐

The National Trust collects and processes personal information for the purposes of customer analysis and direct marketing so that we can contact you about our conservation, membership, fundraising and other activities. Please tick this box if you would prefer not to hear from the National Trust in this way. ☐

National Trust Enterprises also works with carefully selected organisations and we may contact you with special offers from them that will benefit the National Trust. Please tick this box if you would prefer not to receive these offers. ☐

Governance

A guide to the Trust's governance arrangements is available on our website **www.nationaltrust.org.uk** A paper copy is also available on request from the Secretary. Copies of our Annual Report and Accounts are also available; contact our Membership Department for more information or to request a copy.

Annual General Meeting

We believe that it is a crucial part of the governance of any large organisation such as the Trust that once a year the members have the chance to meet the officers and senior staff of the organisation at the Annual General Meeting (AGM). It is an opportunity for you to comment and make suggestions, to make your views known to the Trustees and the staff both through questions and through putting forward and debating resolutions of real interest to the organisation.

You will receive the formal papers for our AGM in the autumn magazine. The meeting is held in different towns or cities every year and we hope you will consider attending. However you don't need to come to the meeting to take part. You can listen to the meeting and take part in the debates on our webcast. You can also let us know your views by returning your voting papers ahead of the meeting.

In addition, you have the opportunity to elect members of our Council. The voting papers are distributed with the autumn edition of the magazine. The Council is made up of 52 members, 26 elected by you and 26 elected by organisations whose interests coincide in some way with those of the National Trust. This mix of elected and appointed members ensures that the Trust takes full account of the wider interests of the nation for whose benefit it exists. The breadth of experience and perspective which this brings also enables the Council to act as the Trust's conscience in delivering its statutory purposes.

Privacy Policy

The National Trust's Privacy Policy sets out the ways in which the National Trust processes personal data. This Privacy Policy only relates to personal data collected by the National Trust via our website, membership forms, fundraising responses, emails and telephone calls. The full Privacy Policy is available on our website **www.nationaltrust.org.uk**

The Data Protection Act 1998

The National Trust makes every effort to comply with the principles of the Data Protection Act 1998.

Use made of personal information

Personal information provided to the National Trust via our website, membership forms, fundraising responses, emails and telephone calls will be used for the purposes outlined at the time of collection or registration in accordance with the preferences you express.

Consent

By providing personal data to the National Trust you consent to the processing of such data by the National Trust as described in the full Privacy Policy. You can alter your preferences as follows.

Verifying, updating and amending your personal information

If, at any time, you want to verify, update or amend your personal data or preferences please write to:

The National Trust,
Membership Department,
PO Box 39,
Warrington WA5 7WD

Verification, updating or amendment of personal data will take place within 28 days of receipt of your request.

If subsequently you make a data protection instruction to the National Trust which contradicts a previous instruction (or instructions), then the National Trust will follow your most recent instruction.

Subject access requests

You have the right to ask the National Trust, in writing, for a copy of all the personal data held about you (this is known as a 'subject access request') upon payment of a fee of £15. If you would like to access your personal data held by the National Trust, please apply, in writing, to:

The Data Controller,
The National Trust,
Heelis,
Kemble Drive,
Swindon SN2 2NA

If you have any questions about our Privacy Policy please contact the National Trust on: 0844 800 1895.

Please remember – your membership card is always needed for free admission

May I use my mobile telephone?

The use of mobile telephones can interfere with the correct operation of sensitive electronic environmental monitoring equipment, and so visitors are asked to switch them off when entering houses and other buildings where such equipment is likely to be fitted.

Where can I picnic?

Many properties welcome picnics; some have a designated picnic area, a few cannot accommodate them (in which case the 'suitable for picnics' symbol ⊼ is not included in the property entry). Fires and barbecues are generally not allowed. If you are planning a picnic at a Trust property for the first time, please telephone in advance to check.

Is there somewhere to leave large or bulky bags?

At some properties visitors will be asked to leave behind large items of hand luggage while they make their visit. This is to avoid accidental damage and to improve security. This restriction includes rucksacks, large handbags, carrier bags, bulky shoulder bags and camera/camcorder bags. In most houses where the restriction applies (principally historic houses with vulnerable contents, fragile decorative surfaces or narrow visitor routes) it is possible to leave such items safely at the entrance. See the Family facilities/activities section on p.373 for additional information on back-carriers and pushchairs.

What types of footwear are restricted?

Any heel which covers an area smaller than a postage stamp can cause irreparable damage to floors, carpets and rush matting. We regret, therefore, that sharp-heeled shoes are not permitted. Plastic slippers are provided for visitors with unsuitable or muddy footwear, or alternative footwear is available for purchase.

Please remember that ridged soles trap grit and gravel, which scratch fine floors. Boot-scrapers and brushes are readily available. Overshoes may be provided at properties with vulnerable floors.

Where can I sit down?

Seats for visitors' use are provided at various points in all the Trust's historic houses and gardens. Watch out for clearly identifiable and adequate visitor seating at Trust properties being introduced this year. A new mechanism for distinguishing those chairs which are available for our visitors to use from those that form part of the historic collection, has been developed to make it easy for you to take a breather with confidence.

Why is it dark inside some houses?

To prevent deterioration of light-sensitive contents, especially textiles and watercolours, light levels are regularly monitored and carefully controlled using blinds and sun-curtains. We recommend that visitors allow time for their eyes to adapt to darker conditions in rooms where light levels are reduced to preserve vulnerable material.

Some historic houses offer special tours during the winter months, when house staff demonstrate traditional housekeeping practices. They explain why National Trust conservation policies require low light levels inside houses and closure to visitors during the winter. These 'Putting the House to Bed' events are advertised in the local press and in regional newsletters, or details can be obtained from the Membership Department (see p.382), or **www.nationaltrust.org.uk/events**

Where can I take photographs?

We welcome amateur photography out of doors at our properties. We regret that photography is not permitted indoors when houses are open to visitors. The use of mobile phones with built-in cameras is also not permitted indoors.

At most properties special arrangements can be made for interested amateurs (as well as voluntary National Trust speakers, research students and academics) to take interior photographs by appointment outside normal opening hours.

Requests to arrange a mutually convenient appointment must be made in writing to the property concerned. Not all properties are able to offer this facility and those that do may make an admission charge (including NT members).

All requests for commercial photography must be channelled through the Broadcast Media Liaison Officer: tel. 020 7799 4547.

THE NATIONAL TRUST
OUTDOOR PROGRAMME

Yorkshire Bank and Clydesdale Bank are the National Trust's new outdoor programme sponsor, providing funding to help the Trust maintain and develop its spectacular gardens that welcome over 11 million visitors a year.

Properties with no individual entries are shown in italics.
* Denotes properties shown only on maps.

England

Bath & NE Somerset

Bath Assembly Rooms (1:J4)   38
Bath Skyline (1:J4)   29
Prior Park Landscape Garden
(1:J4)   6, 90

Bedfordshire

Chilterns Gateway Centre
(3:E8)   189
Dunstable Downs
(3:E8)   182, 183, 189
Sharpenhoe Clappers (3:F8)   183
Whipsnade Estate (3:E8)   189
Whipsnade Tree Cathedral
(3:E8)   209
Willington Dovecote and
Stables (3:F7)   210

Berkshire

Ankerwycke (2:E5)   *14
Ashdown House (2:C5)   114
Basildon Park (2:D5)   115
Finchampstead Ridges (2:E5)   *14
The Holies (2:D5)   *14
Lardon Chase (2:D5)   *14
Lough Down (2:D5)   *14
*Maidenhead and Cookham
Commons (2:E5)*   *14

Birmingham

Birmingham Back to Backs
(4:J5)   243

Bristol

Blaise Hamlet (1:I3)   39
Leigh Woods (1:I4)   29
Westbury College Gatehouse
(1:I3)   106

Buckinghamshire

Ascott (2:E3)   113
Boarstall Duck Decoy
(2:D3)   111, 118
Boarstall Tower (2:D3)   111, 118
Bradenham Village (2:E4)   120
Buckingham Chantry Chapel
(2:D2)   121
Claydon House (2:D3)   127
Cliveden (2:E5)   128
Coombe Hill (2:E4)   *14
Dorneywood Garden (2:E5)   129
Hughenden Manor (2:E4)   134

King's Head (2:E3)   137
Long Crendon Courthouse
(2:D4)   *111, 139*
Pitstone Windmill (2:E3)   147
Stowe Landscape Gardens
(2:D2)   158
Waddesdon Manor (2:D3)   161
West Wycombe Park (2:E4)   164
West Wycombe Village
and Hill (2:E4)   165

Cambridgeshire

Anglesey Abbey,
Gardens (3:G7)   182, 185
Houghton Mill (3:F6)   182, 196
Lode Mill (3:G7)   185
Peckover House
and Garden (3:G5)   182, 203
Ramsey Abbey Gatehouse
(3:F6)   204
Wicken Fen National Nature
Reserve (3:G6)   183, 184, 209
Wimpole Hall
(3:G7)   182, 183, 210
Wimpole Home Farm
(3:G7)   184, 212

Cheshire

Alderley Edge (5:D8)   265, 268
Bickerton Hill (5:C9)   265
Bulkeley Hill Wood (5:C9)   265
Dunham Massey (5:D8)   272
Hare Hill (5:D8)   279
Helsby Hill (5:C8)   265
*Lewis Carroll's Birthplace
(5:C8)*   265
Little Moreton Hall (5:D9)   264, 281
Lyme Park (5:E8)   282
Nether Alderley Mill (5:D8)   284
Quarry Bank Mill (5:D8)   4, 6, 285
Styal Estate (5:D8)   285
Tatton Park (5:D8)   290
White Cottage (5:D8)   274

Cornwall

Antony (1:E8)   32
Barras Nose (1:D7)   31
Bedruthan Steps (1:C8)   26, 45
Bodigga Cliff (1:E8)   *12
Boscastle (1:D7)   39
Bosigran (1:B9)   28
Botallack Count House (1:A9)   27
Cape Cornwall (1:A9)   *12
Carnewas (1:C8)   26, 45
Chapel Porth (1:C9)   26, 28

Cornwall *(continued)*

Cornish Mines and Engines
(1:C9)   53
Cotehele (1:E8)   53
Cotehele Mill (1:E8)   54
Crackington Haven (1:D6)   *12
Crantock (1:C8)   26, 28
The Dodman (1:D9)   *12
Glendurgan Garden (1:C9)   60
Godolphin (1:B9)   61
Godrevy (1:B9)   26, 62
The Gribbin (1:D9)   27
Gunwalloe (1:B10)   26, 88
Holywell Bay (1:C8)   26
Kynance Cove (1:C10)   26, 28, 79
Lanhydrock (1:D8)   6, 28, 76
Lawrence House (1:E7)   77
Levant Mine and Beam
Engine (1:A9)   77
The Lizard (1:C10)   26, 28, 79
Lizard Point (1:C10)   28
Lizard Wireless Station (1:C10)   79
Loe Pool (1:B10)   29, 88
Marconi Centre (1:C10)   79
Mayon Cliff (1:A10)   27
Nare Head (1:C9)   *12
Park Head (1:C8)   *12
Penrose Estate (1:B10)   88
Pentire Point (1:D7)   31
Porthcurno (1:B10)   26
Port Quin (1:D7)   *12
Rough Tor (1:D7)   *12
The Rumps (1:D7)   31
St Anthony Head (1:C9)   27, 90
St Michael's Mount (1:B9)   91
Sandy Mouth (1:D6)   26
Tintagel Old Post Office (1:D7)   99
Trelissick Garden (1:C9)   101
Trengwainton Garden (1:B9)   102
Trerice (1:C8)   103
Zennor Head (1:B9)   28

Cumbria

Acorn Bank Garden and
Watermill (6:E7)   267
Aira Force (6:D7)   292
Arnside Knott (6:E9)   265
Beatrix Potter Gallery (6:D8)   268
Borrowdale (6:D7)   264, 266, 269
Brandlehow Park (6:D7)   264
Bridge House (6:D8)   293
Buttermere (6:C7)   270
Cartmel Priory Gatehouse
(6:D9)   271
Castlerigg Stone Circle (6:D7)   *22
Claife (6:D8)   280

Coniston **(6:D8)**   264, 265, 271
Dalton Castle **(6:D9)**   272
Derwent Island House **(6:D7)** 272
Derwentwater **(6:D7)**   264, 266
Duddon **(6:D8)**   292
Ennerdale **(6:C7)**   270
Eskdale **(6:C8)**   292
Fell Foot Park **(6:D9)**   274
Force Crag Mine **(6:D7)**   270
Friar's Crag **(6:D7)**   266
Gondola **(6:D8)**   265, 277
Grasmere **(6:D8)**   278
Great Langdale **(6:D8)**   266, 278
Hawkshead **(6:D8)**   280
Hill Top **(6:D8)**   280
Holme Park Fell **(6:E9)**   *22
Keld Chapel **(6:E7)**   *22
Sandscale Haws **(6:D9)**   265
Scafell Pike **(6:D8)**   264, 266
Sizergh Castle and Garden
  (6:E8)   5, 287
Stagshaw Garden **(6:D8)**   290
Tarn Hows **(6:D8)**   265, 266, 271
Townend **(6:D8)**   291
Troutbeck **(6:D8)**   293
Ullswater **(6:D7)**   292
Wasdale **(6:C8)**   266, 292
Wastwater **(6:D8)**   264, 266
Wetheral Woods **(6:E6)**   *22
Windermere **(6:D8)**   293
Wordsworth House **(6:C7)**   294

Derbyshire

Calke Abbey
  (3:C4)   214, 215, 217
Dovedale **(3:B3)**   214
Edale **(3:B2)**   *16
Hardwick Hall **(3:D3)** 4, 215, 221
High Peak Estate **(3:B2)** 214, 222
Ilam Park **(3:B3)**   223
Kedleston Hall **(3:C4)**   215, 224
Kinder Scout **(3:B2)**   214
Longshaw Estate **(3:C2)** 214, 225
Mam Tor **(3:B2)**   214
Milldale **(3:B3)**   *16
Museum of Childhood,
  Sudbury Hall **(3:B4)**   4, 229
The Old Manor **(3:B4)**   227
Riley Graves **(3:C2)**   *16
South Peak **(3:B3)**   214
Stainsby Mill, Hardwick
  Estate **(3:D3)**   227
Sudbury Hall and the National
  Trust Museum of Childhood
  (3:B4)   229
Winnats Pass **(3:B2)**   214
Winster Market House **(3:C3)** 232

Devon

A La Ronde **(1:G7)**   32
Abbotsham **(1:E5)**   *12
Arlington Court **(1:F5)** 28, 31, 33
Ashclyst Forest **(1:G7)**   28
Baggy Point **(1:E5)**   *12
Bolt Head **(1:F9)**   28, 31
Bolt Tail **(1:F9)**   28
Bradley **(1:G8)**   40
Branscombe **(1:H7)**   26, 29
Branscombe – The Old Bakery,
  Manor Mill and Forge **(1:H7)** 41
Buckland Abbey **(1:E8)**   43
Buck's Mills **(1:E6)**   *12
Budlake Old Post Office
  Room **(1:G7)**   70
Castle Drogo **(1:F7)**   45
The Church House **(1:F7)**   47
Clyston Mill **(1:G7)**   70
Coleton Fishacre **(1:G9)**   50
Compton Castle **(1:G8)**   51
Countisbury **(1:F5)**   *12
East Titchberry **(1:E5)**   *12
Finch Foundry **(1:F7)**   58
Gammon Head **(1:G9)**   *13
Greenway **(1:G8)**   63
Hembury Woods **(1:F8)**   28
Holne Woods **(1:F8)**   *12
Killerton **(1:G6)**   28, 68
Knightshayes Court **(1:G6)**   73
Little Dartmouth **(1:G9)**   *13
Loughwood Meeting
  House **(1:H7)**   80
Lundy **(1:D5)**   81
Lydford Gorge **(1:F7)**   28, 82
Lynmouth **(1:F5)**   *12
Marker's Cottage **(1:G7)**   71
Morte Point **(1:E5)**   31
National Trust's Carriage
  Collection **(1:F5)**   33
The Old Mill **(1:F9)**   87
Overbeck's **(1:F9)**   87
Parke Estate **(1:G7)**   *13
Plym Bridge Woods **(1:F8)**   28
Portlemouth Down **(1:F9)**   *12
Prawle Point **(1:G9)**   *13
Salcombe Hill **(1:H7)**   29
Saltram **(1:F8)**   92
Shute Barton **(1:H7)**   93
Soar Mill Cove **(1:F9)**   *12
South Hole **(1:E6)**   *12
Steps Bridge **(1:G7)**   *13
Teign Valley **(1:F7)**   *12
Trowlesworthy Warren **(1:F8)** *12
Watersmeet **(1:F5)**   105
Wembury Point **(1:F9)**   26
West Exmoor Coast **(1:F5)**   106

Wheal Coates **(1:C9)**   *12
Woolacombe **(1:E5)**   26

Dorset

Badbury Rings **(1:K6)**   *13
Brownsea Island **(1:K7)**   28, 42
Burton Bradstock **(1:I7)**   26
Cerne Giant **(1:J6)**   *13
Clouds Hill **(1:J7)**   49
Cogden Beach **(1:I7)**   *13
Coney's Castle **(1:I7)**   *13
Corfe Castle **(1:K7)**   28, 52
Creech Grange Arch **(1:J7)**   *13
Fontmell Down Estate **(1:K6)** 28
Golden Cap **(1:I7)**   26
Hardy Monument **(1:J7)**   65
Hardy's Cottage **(1:J7)**   65
Hartland Moor **(1:K7)**   *13
Hod Hill **(1:J6)**   27
Kingston Lacy **(1:K7)**   72
Lambert's Castle **(1:I7)**   27
Max Gate **(1:J7)**   84
Melbury Beacon **(1:K6)**   *13
Melbury Downs **(1:K6)**   28
Pilsdon Pen **(1:I6)**   *13
Spyway Farm **(1:K7)**   *13
Studland Beach and Nature
  Reserve **(1:K7)**   28, 98
Turnworth Down **(1:J6)**   *13
White Mill **(1:K6)**   108

County Durham

Beacon Hill (Durham) **(6:I6)**   *23
Ebchester **(6:G5)**   316
Hawthorn Dene **(6:I6)**   *23
Horden Beach **(6:I6)**   316
Moorhouse Woods **(6:H6)**   316
Penshaw Monument **(6:H6)**   *23
Warren House Gill **(6:I6)**   *23

East Sussex: see Sussex

East Yorkshire: see Yorkshire

Essex

Blake's Wood **(3:H9)**   184
Bourne Mill **(3:I8)**   188
Coggeshall Grange Barn **(3:I8)** 190
Copt Hall Marshes **(3:I9)**   183
Danbury Common **(3:H9)**   *17
Dedham Vale **(3:I8)**   182
Hatfield Forest **(3:G8)**   184, 194
Lingwood Common **(3:H9)**   *17
Northey Island **(3:I9)**   183
Paycocke's **(3:I8)**   203
Rayleigh Mount **(3:I10)**   204

Gloucestershire

Ashleworth Tithe Barn (1:J2) 34
Chedworth Roman Villa (1:K2) 47
Dover's Hill (1:K1) *13
Dyrham Park (1:J4) 57
Ebworth Estate (1:K2) *13
Hailes Abbey (1:K1) 65
Haresfield Beacon (1:J2) *13
Hidcote Manor Garden (1:L1) 66
Horton Court (1:J3) 68
Little Fleece Bookshop (1:J2) 78
Lodge Park (1:K2) 80
Minchinhampton Common
(1:J3) 28
Newark Park (1:J3) 86
Rodborough Common (1:J2) 28
Sherborne Estate (1:L2) 29, 80
Snowshill Manor (1:K1) 94
Westbury Court Garden (1:J2) 107
Woodchester Park (1:J3) 108

Hampshire

Bramshaw Commons (2:C7) *14
Curbridge Nature Reserve
(2:D8) *14
Hale Purlieu (2:B8) *14
Hinton Ampner (2:D7) 133
Ibsley Common (2:B8) *14
Ludshott Common (2:E7) *14
Mottisfont Abbey Garden,
House and Estate (2:C7) 140
Rockford Common (2:B8) *14
Sandham Memorial Chapel
(2:C6) 151
Selborne Hill and Common
(2:E7) *14
Speltham Down (2:D8) *14
Stockbridge Common Down
& Marsh (2:C7) *14
The Vyne (2:D6) 160
West Green House Garden
(2:D6) 164
Winchester City Mill (2:D7) 167

Herefordshire

Berrington Hall (4:H6) 241
Brockhampton Estate
(4:I7) 237, 244
Croft Castle and Parkland
(4:H6) 237, 248
Cwmmau Farmhouse (4:G7) 250
The Weir (4:H7) 261

Hertfordshire

Ashridge Estate (2:E3) 110, 114
Shaw's Corner (3:F9) 184, 205

Isle of Wight

Bembridge Windmill (2:D9) 117
Brighstone Shop and
Museum (2:C9) 120
Compton Bay (2:C9) *14
Mottistone Manor Garden
(2:C9) 141
The Needles Old Battery and
New Battery (2:C9) 142
Newtown Old Town Hall (2:C9) 143
Tennyson Down (2:C9) *14

Kent

Chartwell (2:G6) 123
Chiddingstone (2:H7) 111
Coldrum Long Barrow (2:H6) 112
Emmetts Garden (2:H6) 129
Ightham Mote (2:H6) 135
Knole (2:H6) 137
Old Soar Manor (2:H6) 145
Owletts (2:H5) 145
Quebec House (2:G6) 148
Royal Military Canal (2:J7) 110
St John's Jerusalem (2:H5) 151
Scotney Castle (2:I7) 151
Sissinghurst Castle Garden
(2:I7) 5, 154
Smallhythe Place (2:I7) 155
South Foreland Lighthouse
(2:K6) 111, 155
Sprivers Garden (2:H7) 156
Stoneacre (2:I6) 157
Toys Hill (2:G6) 111
The White Cliffs of Dover
(2:K7) 110, 111, 166

Lancashire

Eaves & Waterslack Woods
(6:E9) 265
Gawthorpe Hall (5:D6) 276
Heald Brow (6:E9) *22
Heysham (6:D10) *22
Holcombe Moor (5:D6) 265
Jack Scout (6:E9) *22
Rufford Old Hall (5:C6) 264, 286
Stubbins Estate (5:D6) 265

Leicestershire

Staunton Harold Church
(3:C4) 228
Ulverscroft Nature Reserve
(3:D5) 232

Lincolnshire

Belton House (3:E4) 214, 215, 216
Grantham House (3:E4) 220
Gunby Hall (3:G3) 220

Monksthorpe Chapel (3:G3) 221
Science Discovery Centre
(Woolsthorpe Manor) (3:E4) 232
Tattershall Castle (3:F3) 231
Woolsthorpe Manor (3:E4) 232

Liverpool/Merseyside

(inc. Sefton)

Caldy Hill (5:B8) *20
Formby (5:B7) 7, 265, 275
20 Forthlin Road, Allerton
(5:B8) 7, 276
Mr Hardman's Photographic
Studio (5:B8) 7, 278
Mendips (5:C8) 7, 284
Speke Hall, Garden
and Estate (5:C8) 7, 288
Thurstaston Common (5:B8) *20

London Boroughs:

Barking & Dagenham
Eastbury Manor House (2:G5) 172
Bexley
Red House (2:H5) 178
Camden
Fenton House (2:G4) 172
2 Willow Road (2:G5) 180
Croydon
Selsdon Wood (2:G6) *15
Hackney
Sutton House (2:G4) 170, 179
Havering
Rainham Hall (2:H5) 177
Hounslow
Osterley Park and House
(2:F5) 6, 170, 176
Kensington & Chelsea
Carlyle's House (2:F5) 171
Lindsey House (2:G5) 175
Merton
Morden Hall Park (2:G5) 170, 175
Watermeads (2:G6) *15
Richmond
East Sheen Common (2:F5) *14
Ham House and Garden (2:F5) 174
Southwark
George Inn (2:G5) 173
Westminster
Blewcoat School Gift Shop
(2:G5) 171
'Roman' Bath (2:G5) 179

Middlesbrough/Teeside

Ormesby Hall (5:G2) 310

Newcastle/Tyne & Wear

Gibside (6:H5)   322
Holy Jesus Hospital (6:H5)   324
The Leas (6:I5)   316, 317
Marsden Rock (6:I5)   316
Souter Lighthouse
  (6:I5)   316, 317, 326
Washington Old Hall (6:H5)   328

Norfolk

Beeston Regis Heath (3:J4)   *17
Blakeney National Nature
  Reserve (3:I3)   183, 186
Blickling Hall, Gardens
  and Park (3:J4)   183, 184, 187
Brancaster (3:H3)   184, 188
Darrow Wood (3:J6)   *17
Elizabethan House
  Museum (3:K5)   192
Felbrigg Hall, Garden and
  Park (3:J4)   182, 183, 192
Heigham Holmes (3:K5)   182
Horsey Mere (3:K4)   182
Horsey Windpump (3:K4)   196
Oxburgh Hall, Garden and
  Estate (3:H5)   182, 201
St George's Guildhall (3:H5)   205
Sheringham Park (3:J4)   182, 206
Stiffkey Marshes (3:I3)   *17
West Runton (3:J4)   182

Northamptonshire

Canons Ashby House (3:D7)   218
Lyveden New Bield (3:E6)   226
Priest's House, Easton (3:E5)   227

Northumberland

Allen Banks (6:F5)   317, 318
Bellister Estate (6:F5)   *22
Beadnell Harbour (6:H2)   *23
Cherryburn (6:G5)   318
Cragside (6:G3)   319
Craster (6:H3)   316
Druridge Bay (6:H3)   316
Dunstanburgh Castle
  (6:H3)   316, 320
Embleton Links (6:H3)   *23
Farne Islands (6:H2)   316, 321
George Stephenson's
  Birthplace (6:G5)   322
Hadrian's Wall (6:F5)   317, 323
Housesteads Fort (6:F5)   317, 323
Lady's Well (6:G3)   *23
Lindisfarne Castle (6:G1)   317, 325
Low Newton-by-Sea (6:H3)   *23
Newton Links & Point (6:H2)   *23

Ros Castle (6:G2)   317
St Aidan's Dunes (6:H2)   *23
St Cuthbert's Cave (6:G2)   *23
Seahouses (6:H2)   316
Staward Gorge (6:F5)   317, 318
Wallington (6:G4)   326

North Yorkshire:

see Yorkshire

Nottinghamshire

Clumber Park
  (3:D2)   5, 214, 215, 219
Mr Straw's House (3:D2)   228
The Workhouse, Southwell
  (3:D3)   4, 6, 234

Oxfordshire

Badbury Hill (2:C4)   *14
Buscot Estate (2:C4)   121
Buscot Old Parsonage (2:C4)   122
Buscot Park (2:B4)   122
Chastleton House (2:C3)   124
Coleshill Estate (2:B4)   121
Great Coxwell Barn (2:C4)   130
Greys Court (2:D5)   130
Priory Cottages (2:C5)   148
Watlington Hill (2:D4)   *14
White Horse Hill (2:C4)   112

Shropshire

Attingham Park (4:H4)   238, 239
Benthall Hall (4:I5)   241
Carding Mill Valley (4:H5)   245
Cronkhill (4:H5)   240
Dudmaston (4:I5)   250
Long Mynd (4:H5)   236
Morville Hall (4:I5)   255
Shropshire Hills
  (4:H5)   6, 236, 238, 245
Sunnycroft (4:I4)   258
Town Walls Tower (4:H4)   259
Wenlock Edge (4:I5)   236
Wilderhope Manor (4:H5)   262

Somerset

Barrington Court (1:I6)   37
Beacon Hill (Somerset) (1:H5)   *13
Bicknoller Hill (1:H5)   *13
Brean Down (1:H4)   27, 41
Cheddar Cliffs (1:I4)   27
Clevedon Court (1:I4)   48
Coleridge Cottage (1:H5)   49
Collard Hill (1:I5)   28
Crook Peak (1:I4)   *13
Dunster Castle (1:G5)   56
Dunster Working Watermill
  (1:G5)   57

Fyne Court (1:H5)   59
Glastonbury Tor (1:I5)   59
Holnicote Estate (1:G5)   28, 29, 67
King John's Hunting Lodge (1:I4)   71
Lytes Cary Manor (1:I5)   83
Middle Hope (1:I4)   *13
Montacute House (1:I6)   85
Priest's House, Muchelney (1:I6)   89
Sand Point (1:I4)   *13
Selworthy (1:G5)   *13
Shute Shelve Hill (1:I4)   *13
Stembridge Tower Mill (1:I5)   95
Stoke-sub-Hamdon Priory
  (1:I6)   95
Tintinhull Garden (1:I6)   100
Treasurer's House, Martock
  (1:I6)   100
Tyntesfield (1:I4)   104
Walton Hill (1:I5)   *13
Wellington Monument (1:H6)   *13
West Pennard Court Barn
  (1:I5)   106

Staffordshire

Biddulph Grange Garden
  (4:J2)   243
The Cloud (5:D9)   265
Downs Banks (4:J3)   237
Hawksmoor Nature Reserve
  (4:J3)   237
Kinver Edge and the Rock
  Houses (4:I5)   236, 254
Leek & Manifold Valley (4:K3)   214
Letocetum Roman Baths
  (4:K5)   254
Moseley Old Hall (4:J5)   255
Mow Cop (4:J3)   265
Rock Houses (4:I5)   254
Shugborough Estate (4:J4)   257

Suffolk

Dunwich Heath: Coastal Centre
  and Beach (3:K6)   183, 191
Flatford: Bridge Cottage
  (3:I8)   182, 194
Ickworth House, Park and
  Gardens (3:H7)   183, 184, 197
Kyson Hill (3:J7)   *17
Lavenham: The Guildhall of
  Corpus Christi (3:I7)   199
Melford Hall (3:I7)   184, 200
Orford Ness National Nature
  Reserve (3:K7)   183, 200
Pin Mill (3:J8)   *17
Sutton Hoo (3:J7)   6, 182, 184, 207
Theatre Royal,
  Bury St Edmunds (3:I7)   208
Thorington Hall (3:I8)   208

Surrey

Box Hill (2:F6) *110*, 119
Clandon Park (2:F6) 125
Claremont Landscape Garden
(2:F6) 126
Dapdune Wharf (2:E6) *110*, 149
The Devil's Punch Hole
Café (2:E7) *110*, 132
Frensham Common (2:E7) **14*
Hatchlands Park (2:F6) 131
Hindhead Commons (2:E7) 132
The Homewood (2:F6) 134
Leith Hill (2:F7) *110*, 139
Oakhurst Cottage (2:E7) 145
Polesden Lacey (2:F6) 147
Reigate Fort (1:F6) *112*
River Wey and Godalming
Navigations (2:F6) *110*, 149
Runnymede (2:F5) 150
Shalford Mill (2:E6) 152
Winkworth Arboretum (2:F7) 167
The Witley Centre (2:E7) 168

Sussex

(East Sussex and West Sussex)

Alfriston Clergy House (2:H8) 113
Bateman's (2:H7) 116
Birling Gap (2:H9) *111*
Black Down (2:E7) **14*
Bodiam Castle (2:I7) 118
Chyngton Farm (2:H9) **15*
Cissbury Ring (2:F8) *112*
Crowlink (2:H9) **15*
Devil's Dyke (2:G8) *110, 111*
East Head (2:E9) *111*
Frog Firle Farm (2:H8) **15*
Harting Down (2:E8) *111*
Lamb House (2:J8) 138
Monk's House (2:G8) 140
Nymans (2:G7) 143
Petworth House and Park
(2:E7) 146
Saddlescombe Farm (2:G8) *112*
Seven Sisters (2:H9) *110, 111*
Sheffield Park Garden (2:G7) 153
Slindon Estate (2:E8) *111*
Standen (2:G7) 156
Uppark House and
Garden (2:E8) 159
Wakehurst Place (2:G7) 163

Warwickshire

Baddesley Clinton (4:K6) 240
Charlecote Park (4:K7) 246
Coughton Court (4:K6) 247
Farnborough Hall (4:L7) 251
Kinwarton Dovecote (4:K7) 254

Packwood House (4:K6) 256
Upton House and Gardens
(4:L7) 260

West Midlands

Wightwick Manor (4:J5) 262

West Sussex: *see Sussex*

West Yorkshire:
see Yorkshire

Wiltshire

Avebury (1:K4) 35
Avebury Manor and Garden
(1:K4) 36
Cherhill Down (1:K4) *28*
Cley Hill (1:J5) **13*
The Courts Garden (1:J4) 55
Dinton Park (1:K5) 89
Figsbury Ring (1:L5) **13*
Fox Talbot Museum (1:K4) 74
Great Chalfield Manor
and Garden (1:J4) 62
Heelis (1:K3) 66
Lacock Abbey and Village
(1:K4) 74
Little Clarendon (1:K5) 78
Mompesson House (1:K5) 84
Pepperbox Hill (1:L5) **13*
Philipps House (1:K5) 89
Stonehenge Landscape (1:K5) 95
Stourhead (1:J5) *5*, 96
Westwood Manor (1:J4) 107
Win Green Hill (1:K6) **13*

Worcestershire

Bredon Barn (1:K1) 42
Clent Hills (4:J6) *236, 238*
Croome Park (4:J7) *238, 249*
The Fleece Inn (4:K7) 251
The Greyfriars (4:J7) 252
Hanbury Hall (4:J6) 252
Hawford Dovecote (4:J6) 253
Middle Littleton Tithe Barn
(4:K7) 255
Rosedene (4:J6) 257
Wichenford Dovecote (4:I7) 261

Yorkshire

*(East Yorkshire, North Yorkshire
inc. Middlesbrough, West
Yorkshire and York)*

Beningbrough Hall and
Gardens (5:G4) 299
Blakey Topping (5:I3) *297*, 300
Braithwaite Hall (5:E3) 300

Bridestones (5:I3) *297*, 300
Brimham Rocks (5:F4) *297*, 301
Cayton Bay (5:J3) *297*
Crosscliff (5:I3) 300
East Riddlesden Hall (5:E5) 302
Farndale (5:H3) **21*
Fountains Abbey (5:F4) 303
Gibson Mill (5:E6) *296*, 305
Goddards Garden (5:H5) 304
Hardcastle Crags
(5:E6) *6, 296*, 305
Hayburn Wyke (5:I3) **21*
Hudswell Woods (5:F3) **20*
Maister House (5:J6) 306
Malham Tarn Estate
(5:D4) *296*, 306
Marsden Moor Estate
(5:E7) *298*, 307
Moulton Hall (5:F2) 307
Mount Grace Priory (5:G3) 308
Newbiggin cliffs (5:J3) *297*
Nostell Priory and Parkland
(5:G6) 308
Nunnington Hall (5:H4) 309
Old Coastguard Station
(5:I2) *298, 314*
Ormesby Hall (5:G2) 310
Peak Alum Works (5:I3) **21*
Port Mulgrave (5:I2) *297*
Ravenscar Coastal
Centre (5:I3) *297*
Rievaulx Terrace and Temples
(5:H3) 311
Roseberry Topping (5:G2) 312
Runswick Bay (5:I2) *297*
Scarthwood Moor (5:G2) **21*
Studley Royal Water Garden
(5:F4) 303
Treasurer's House, York
(5:H5) *6*, 312
Upper Wharfedale (5:E4) *296*, 313
Yorkshire Coast (5:I2) 314

Wales

Anglesey

Cemlyn (4:D1) *332*
Plas Newydd (4:D2) 344

Carmarthenshire

Aberdeunant (4:E8) 333
Dinefwr Park and Castle
(4:E8) *331*, 338
Dolaucothi Gold Mines (4:E7) 339
Newton House (4:E8) 338
Paxton's Tower (4:D8) **18*
Ragwen Point (4:C8) **18*

Ceredigion
Llanerchaeron (4:D6) — 342
Mwnt (4:C7) — 332
Mynachdy'r Graig (4:E6) — *18
Penbryn (4:D7) — 332

Conwy
Aberconwy House (4:E2) — 333
Bodnant Garden (4:F2) — 334
Conwy Suspension Bridge (4:E2) — 338
Tŷ Mawr Wybrnant (4:E3) — 350
Ty'n-y-Coed Uchaf (4:E3) — 350

Vale of Glamorgan
Lanlay Meadows (4:G10) — *19

Gwynedd
Aberglaslyn (4:E3) — *18
Braich y Pwll (4:C4) — *18
Carneddau (4:E2) — *18
Craflwyn (4:E3) — 331
Cregennan (4:E4) — *18
Cwrt (4:C4) — *18
Dinas Oleu (4:E4) — *18
Dolmelynllyn Estate (4:E4) — *18
Glan Faenol (4:D2) — *18
Hafod y Llan (4:E3) — 331
Llanbedrog Beach (4:D4) — 330
Mynydd Bychestyn (4:C4) — *18
Penarfynydd (4:C4) — *18
Penrhyn Castle (4:E2) — 343
Plas yn Rhiw (4:C4) — 345
Porthdinllaen (4:D3) — 330
Porthor (4:C3) — *18
Segontium (4:D2) — 348
Ysbyty Estate (4:F3) — *18

Monmouthshire
Clytha (4:H8) — *19
The Kymin (4:H8) — 341
Skenfrith Castle (4:H8) — 348
Skirrid Fawr (4:H8) — 331
Sugarloaf (4:H8) — 331

Neath & Port Talbot
Aberdulais Falls (4:E9) — 333

Pembrokeshire
Barafundle Bay (4:B9) — *18
Broadhaven (4:B9) — *18
Cilgerran Castle (4:C7) — 337
Colby Woodland Garden (4:C8) — 337
Dinas Island (4:B7) — 330
Freshwater West (4:B9) — *18
Lydstep Headland (4:C9) — *18
Marloes Deer Park & Sands (4:B8) — 330
Martin's Haven (4:B8) — *18
Pen Anglas (4:B7) — *18
St Bride's Bay (4:B8) — *18
St David's Head (4:A8) — 330
St David's Visitor Centre and Shop (4:A8) — 347
Stackpole Estate (4:B9) — 330, 349
Tudor Merchant's House (4:C9) — 349
Ynys Barri (4:B7) — *18

Powys
Abergwesyn Common (4:F7) — *18
Brecon Beacons (4:F8) — 331
Corn Du (4:F8) — *18
Cribyn (4:F8) — *18
Henrhyd Falls (4:F8) — 331
Pen y Fan (4:F8) — 331
Powis Castle and Garden (4:G5) — 346

Swansea
Gower Peninsula (4:D9) — 332
Pennard Cliffs (4:E9) — *18
Rhossili, Worm's Head and Visitor Centre, Gower (4:D9) — 332, 347

Wrexham
Chirk Castle (4:G3) — 335
Erddig (4:H3) — 340

Northern Ireland

Co. Antrim
Ballyconagan (7:E3) — 352
Carrick-a-Rede (7:D3) — 352, 356
Cushendun (7:E4) — 353
Cushleake Mountain (7:E4) — 353
Dunseverick Castle (7:D3) — 352
Fair Head (7:E3) — 352
Giant's Causeway (7:D3) — 6, 352, 362
Glenoe (7:E5) — *24
The Gobbins (7:F5) — *24
Larrybane (7:D3) — 352
The Manor House, Rathlin Island (7:E3) — *24
Mullaghdoo & Ballykeel (7:F5) — *24
North Antrim Cliff Path (7:D3) — *24
Patterson's Spade Mill (7:E6) — 366
Portmuck (7:E5) — *24
Rathlin Island (7:E3) — 352
Skernaghan Point (7:E5) — 352
White Park Bay (7:D3) — 352

Co. Armagh
Ardress House (7:D7) — 355
The Argory (7:C7) — 355
Ballymoyer (7:C8) — *24
Derrymore House (7:D8) — 360

Belfast
Black Mountain (7:E6) — 353
Collin Glen (7:E6) — 353
The Crown Bar (7:E6) — 360
Divis Mountain (7:E6) — 353
Lisnabreeny (7:E6) — 353
Minnowburn (7:E6) — 353

Co. Down
Ballymacormick Point (7:F6) — *24
Ballyquintin Farm (7:F7) — 353
Blockhouse Island (7:E9) — *24
Castle Ward (7:F7) — 354, 357
Green Island (7:E9) — *24
Kearney (7:F7) — *24
Knockinelder (7:F7) — *24
Lighthouse Island (7:F6) — *24
Mount Stewart House, Garden and Temple of the Winds (7:F6) — 364
Mourne Coastal Path (7:E8) — 352, 353
Murlough Bay (7:E3) — 352
Murlough National Nature Reserve (7:E8) — 352
Orlock Point (7:F6) — *24
Rowallane Garden (7:E7) — 367
Slieve Donard (7:E8) — 353
Strangford Lough Wildlife Centre (7:F7) — 352, 354

Co. Fermanagh
Castle Coole (7:A7) — 356
Crom (7:A8) — 353, 358
Florence Court (7:A7) — 361

Co. Londonderry
Barmouth (7:C4) — 352
Downhill Demesne (7:C3) — 365
Grangemore Dunes (7:C4) — *24
Hezlett House (7:C4) — 363
Mussenden Temple (7:C3) — 365
Portstewart Strand (7:C3) — 366
Springhill (7:C6) — 368

Co. Tyrone
Gray's Printing Press (7:B5) — 362
Wellbrook Beetling Mill (7:C6) — 369

Properties with no individual entries are shown in italics.
* Denotes properties shown only on maps.

A La Ronde (1:G7) — 32
Abbotsham (1:E5) — *12
Aberconwy House (4:E2) — 333
Aberdeunant (4:E8) — 333
Aberdulais Falls (4:E9) — 333
Aberglaslyn (4:E3) — *18
Abergwesyn Common (4:F7) — *18
Access Guide — 371
Acorn Bank Garden and
    Watermill (6:E7) — 267
Aira Force (6:D7) — 292
Alderley Edge (5:D8) — 265, 268
Alfriston Clergy House (2:H8) — 113
Allen Banks (6:F5) — 317, 318
Anglesey Abbey,
    Gardens (3:G7) — 182, 185
Ankerwycke (2:E5) — *14
Antony (1:E8) — 32
Ardress House (7:D7) — 355
The Argory (7:C7) — 355
Arlington Court (1:F5) — 28, 31, 33
Arnside Knott (6:E9) — 265
Ascott (2:E3) — 113
Ashclyst Forest (1:G7) — 28
Ashdown House (2:C5) — 114
Ashleworth Tithe Barn (1:J2) — 34
Ashridge Estate (2:E3) — 110, 114
Associations and centres — 380
Attingham Park (4:H4) — 238, 239
Avebury (1:K4) — 35
Avebury Manor and Garden
    (1:K4) — 36

Badbury Hill (2:C4) — *14
Badbury Rings (1:K6) — *13
Baddesley Clinton (4:K6) — 240
Baggy Point (1:E5) — *12
Ballyconagan (7:E3) — 352
Ballymacormick Point (7:F6) — *24
Ballymoyer (7:C8) — *24
Ballyquintin Farrn (7:F7) — 353
Barafundle Bay (4:B9) — *18
Barmouth (7:C4) — 352
Barras Nose (1:D7) — 31
Barrington Court (1:I6) — 37
Basildon Park (2:D5) — 115
Bateman's (2:H7) — 116
Bath Assembly Rooms (1:J4) — 38
Bath Skyline (1:J4) — 29

Beacon Hill (Durham) (6:I6) — *23
Beacon Hill (Somerset) (1:H5) — *13
Beadnell Harbour (6:H2) — *23
Beatrix Potter Gallery (6:D8) — 268
Bedruthan Steps (1:C8) — 26, 45
Beeston Regis Heath (3:J4) — *17
Bellister Estate (6:F5) — *22
Belton House (3:E4) — 214, 215, 216
Bembridge Windmill (2:D9) — 117
Beningbrough Hall and
    Gardens (5:G4) — 299
Benthall Hall (4:I5) — 241
Berrington Hall (4:H6) — 241
Bickerton Hill (5:C9) — 265
Bicknoller Hill (1:H5) — *13
Biddulph Grange Garden
    (4:J2) — 243
Birling Gap (2:H9) — 111
Birmingham Back to Backs
    (4:J5) — 243
Black Down (2:E7) — *14
Black Mountain (7:E6) — 353
Blaise Hamlet (1:I3) — 39
Blake's Wood (3:H9) — 184
Blakeney National Nature
    Reserve (3:I3) — 183, 186
Blakey Topping (5:I3) — 297, 300
*Blewcoat School Gift Shop
    (2:G5)* — 171
Blickling Hall, Gardens
    and Park (3:J4) — 183, 184, 187
Blockhouse Island (7:E9) — *24
Boarstall Duck Decoy
    (2:D3) — 111, 118
Boarstall Tower (2:D3) — 111, 118
Bodiam Castle (2:I7) — 118
Bodigga Cliff (1:E8) — *12
Bodnant Garden (4:F2) — 334
Bolt Head (1:F9) — 28, 31
Bolt Tail (1:F9) — 28
Books — 377
Borrowdale (6:D7) — 264, 266, 269
Boscastle (1:D7) — 39
Bosigran (1:B9) — 28
Botallack Count House (1:A9) — 27
Bourne Mill (3:I8) — 188
Box Hill (2:F6) — 110, 119
Bradenham Village (2:E4) — 120
Bradley (1:G8) — 40

Braich y Pwll (4:C4) — *18
Braithwaite Hall (5:E3) — 300
Bramshaw Commons (2:C7) — *14
Brancaster (3:H3) — 184, 188
Brandlehow Park (6:D7) — 264
Branscombe – The Old Bakery,
    Manor Mill and Forge (1:H7) — 41
Branscombe (1:H7) — 26, 29
Brean Down (1:H4) — 27, 41
Brecon Beacons (4:F8) — 331
Bredon Barn (1:K1) — 42
Bridestones (5:I3) — 297, 300
Bridge House (6:D8) — 293
Brighstone Shop and
    Museum (2:C9) — 120
Brimham Rocks (5:F4) — 297, 301
Broadhaven (4:B9) — *18
Brockhampton Estate
    (4:I7) — 237, 244
Brownsea Island (1:K7) — 28, 42
Buck's Mills (1:E6) — *12
Buckingham Chantry Chapel
    (2:D2) — 121
Buckland Abbey (1:E8) — 43
Budlake Old Post Office
    Room (1:G7) — 70
Bulkeley Hill Wood (5:C9) — 265
Burton Bradstock (1:I7) — 26
Buscot Estate (2:C4) — 121
Buscot Old Parsonage (2:C4) — 122
Buscot Park (2:B4) — 122
Buttermere (6:C7) — 270

Caldy Hill (5:B8) — *20
Calke Abbey
    (3:C4) — 214, 215, 217
Canons Ashby House (3:D7) — 218
Cape Cornwall (1:A9) — *12
Car parking sticker — 10
Carding Mill Valley (4:H5) — 245
Carlyle's House (2:F5) — 171
Carneddau (4:E2) — *18
Carnewas (1:C8) — 26, 45
Carrick-a-Rede (7:D3) — 352, 356
Cartmel Priory Gatehouse
    (6:D9) — 271
Castle Coole (7:A7) — 356
Castle Drogo (1:F7) — 45
Castle Ward (7:F7) — 354, 357

Castlerigg Stone Circle (6:D7) *22
Cayton Bay (5:J3) 297
Cemlyn (4:D1) 332
Cerne Giant (1:J6) *13
Chapel Porth (1:C9) 26, 28
Charlecote Park (4:K7) 246
Chartwell (2:G6) 123
Chastleton House (2:C3) 124
Cheddar Cliffs (1:I4) 27
Chedworth Roman Villa (1:K2) 47
Cherhill Down (1:K4) 28
Cherryburn (6:G5) 318
Chiddingstone (2:H7) 111
Chilterns Gateway Centre
   (3:E8) 189
Chirk Castle (4:G3) 335
The Church House (1:F7) 47
Churchill, Winston 123
Chyngton Farm (2:H9) *15
Cilgerran Castle (4:C7) 337
Cissbury Ring (2:F8) 112
Claife (6:D8) 280
Clandon Park (2:F6) 125
Claremont Landscape Garden
   (2:F6) 126
Claydon House (2:D3) 127
Clent Hills (4:J6) 236, 238
Clevedon Court (1:I4) 48
Cley Hill (1:J5) *13
Cliveden (2:E5) 128
The Cloud (5:D9) 265
Clouds Hill (1:J7) 49
Clumber Park
   (3:D2) 5, 214, 215, 219
Clyston Mill (1:G7) 70
Clytha (4:H8) *19
Cogden Beach (1:I7) *13
Coggeshall Grange Barn (3:I8) 190
Colby Woodland Garden
   (4:C8) 337
Coldrum Long Barrow (2:H6) 112
Coleridge Cottage (1:H5) 49
Coleshill Estate (2:B4) 121
Coleton Fishacre (1:G9) 50
Collard Hill (1:I5) 28
Collin Glen (7:E6) 353
Compton Bay (2:C9) *14
Compton Castle (1:G8) 51
Coney's Castle (1:I7) *13
Coniston (6:D8) 264, 265, 271
Constable, John 194
Conwy Suspension Bridge
   (4:E2) 338

Coombe Hill (2:E4) *14
Copt Hall Marshes (3:I9) 183
Corfe Castle (1:K7) 28, 52
Corn Du (4:F8) *18
Cornish Mines and Engines
   (1:C9) 53
Cotehele (1:E8) 53
Cotehele Mill (1:E8) 54
Coughton Court (4:K6) 247
Countisbury (1:F5) *12
The Courts Garden (1:J4) 55
Crackington Haven (1:D6) *12
Craflwyn (4:E3) 331
Cragside (6:G3) 319
Crantock (1:C8) 26, 28
Craster (6:H3) 316
Creech Grange Arch (1:J7) *13
Cregennan (4:E4) *18
Cribyn (4:F8) *18
Croft Castle and Parkland
   (4:H6) 237, 248
Crom (7:A8) 353, 358
Cronkhill (4:H5) 240
Crook Peak (1:I4) *13
Croome Park (4:J7) 238, 249
Crosscliff (5:I3) 300
Crowlink (2:H9) *15
The Crown Bar (7:E6) 360
Curbridge Nature Reserve
   (2:D8) *14
Cushendun (7:E4) 353
Cushleake Mountain (7:E4) 353
Cwmmau Farmhouse (4:G7) 250
Cwrt (4:C4) *18
Cycling 376

Dalton Castle (6:D9) 272
Danbury Common (3:H9) *17
Dapdune Wharf (2:E6) 110, 149
Darrow Wood (3:J6) *17
Dedham Vale (3:I8) 182
Derrymore House (7:D8) 360
Derwent Island House (6:D7) 272
Derwentwater (6:D7) 264, 266
Devil's Dyke (2:G8) 110, 111
The Devil's Punch Bowl
   Café (2:E7) 110, 132
Dinas Island (4:B7) 330
Dinas Oleu (4:E4) *18
Dinefwr Park and Castle
   (4:E8) 331, 338
Dinton Park (1:K5) 89
Divis Mountain (7:E6) 353

The Dodman (1:D9) *12
Dogs 374
Dolaucothi Gold Mines (4:E7) 339
Dolmelynllyn Estate (4:E4) *18
Donations 380
Dorneywood Garden (2:E5) 129
Dovedale (3:B3) 214
Dover's Hill (1:K1) *13
Downhill Demesne (7:C3) 365
Downs Banks (4:J3) 237
Druridge Bay (6:H3) 316
Duddon (6:D8) 292
Dudmaston (4:I5) 250
Dunham Massey (5:D8) 272
Dunseverick Castle (7:D3) 352
Dunstable Downs
   (3:E8) 182, 183, 189
Dunstanburgh Castle
   (6:H3) 316, 320
Dunster Castle (1:G5) 56
Dunster Working Watermill
   (1:G5) 57
Dunwich Heath: Coastal Centre
   and Beach (3:K6) 183, 191
Dyrham Park (1:J4) 57

East Head (2:E9) 111
East Riddlesden Hall (5:E5) 302
East Sheen Common (2:F5) *14
East Titchberry (1:E5) *12
Eastbury Manor House (2:G5) 172
Eaves & Waterslack Woods
   (6:E9) 265
Ebchester (6:G5) 316
Ebworth Estate (1:K2) *13
Edale (3:B2) *16
Education groups 370
Elizabethan House
   Museum (3:K5) 192
Embleton Links (6:H3) *23
Emmetts Garden (2:H6) 129
Ennerdale (6:C7) 270
Erddig (4:H3) 340
Eskdale (6:C8) 292
Events 371

Fair Head (7:E3) 352
Families 373
Farnborough Hall (4:L7) 251
Farndale (5:H3) *21
Farne Islands (6:H2) 316, 321
Felbrigg Hall, Garden and
   Park (3:J4) 182, 183, 192

Fell Foot Park (6:D9) 274
Fenton House (2:G4) 172
Figsbury Ring (1:L5) *13
Finch Foundry (1:F7) 58
Finchampstead Ridges (2:E5) *14
Flatford: Bridge Cottage
  (3:I8) 182, 194
The Fleece Inn (4:K7) 251
Florence Court (7:A7) 361
Fontmell Down Estate (1:K6) 28
Force Crag Mine (6:D7) 270
Formby (5:B7) 7, 265, 275
20 Forthlin Road, Allerton
  (5:B8) 7, 276
Fountains Abbey (5:F4) 303
Fox Talbot Museum (1:K4) 74
Frensham Common (2:E7) *14
Freshwater West (4:B9) *18
Friar's Crag (6:D7) 266
Frog Firle Farm (2:H8) *15
Functions 375
Fyne Court (1:H5) 59

Gammon Head (1:G9) *13
Gawthorpe Hall (5:D6) 276
George Inn (2:G5) 173
George Stephenson's
  Birthplace (6:G5) 322
Giant's Causeway
  (7:D3) 6, 352, 362
Gibside (6:H5) 322
Gibson Mill (5:E6) 296, 305
Gift Aid on Entry 10
Glan Faenol (4:D2) *18
Glastonbury Tor (1:I5) 59
Glendurgan Garden (1:C9) 60
Glenoe (7:E5) *24
The Gobbins (7:F5) *24
Goddards Garden (5:H5) 304
Godolphin (1:B9) 61
Godrevy (1:B9) 26, 62
Golden Cap (1:I7) 26
Gondola (6:D8) 265, 277
Governance 386
Gower Peninsula (4:D9) 332
Grangemore Dunes (7:C4) *24
Grantham House (3:E4) 220
Grasmere (6:D8) 278
Gray's Printing Press (7:B5) 362
Great Chalfield Manor
  and Garden (1:J4) 62
Great Coxwell Barn (2:C4) 130
Great Langdale (6:D8) 266, 278

Green Island (7:E9) *24
Greenway (1:G8) 63
The Greyfriars (4:J7) 252
Greys Court (2:D5) 130
The Gribbin (1:D9) 27
Group visits 370
Gunby Hall (3:G3) 220
Gunwalloe (1:B10) 26, 88

Hadrian's Wall (6:F5) 317, 323
Hafod y Llan (4:E3) 331
Hailes Abbey (1:K1) 65
Hale Purlieu (2:B8) *14
Ham House and Garden
  (2:F5) 174
Hanbury Hall (4:J6) 252
Hardcastle Crags
  (5:E6) 6, 296, 305
Hardman, E. Chambré 7, 278
Hardwick Hall (3:D3) 4, 215, 221
Hardy Monument (1:J7) 65
Hardy, Thomas 65, 84
Hardy's Cottage (1:J7) 65
Hare Hill (5:D8) 279
Haresfield Beacon (1:J2) *13
Harting Down (2:E8) 111
Hartland Moor (1:K7) *13
Hatchlands Park (2:F6) 131
Hatfield Forest (3:G8) 184, 194
Hawford Dovecote (4:J6) 253
Hawkshead (6:D8) 280
Hawksmoor Nature Reserve
  (4:J3) 237
Hawthorn Dene (6:I6) *23
Hayburn Wyke (5:I3) *21
Heald Brow (6:E9) *22
Heelis (1:K3) 66
Heigham Holmes (3:K5) 182
Helsby Hill (5:C8) 265
Hembury Woods (1:F8) 28
Henrhyd Falls (4:F8) 331
Heritage Lottery Fund 381
Heysham (6:D10) *22
Hezlett House (7:C4) 363
Hidcote Manor Garden (1:L1) 66
High Peak Estate (3:B2) 214, 222
Highlights 4, 5, 6, 7
Hill Top (6:D8) 280
Hindhead Commons (2:E7) 132
Hinton Ampner (2:D7) 133
Hod Hill (1:J6) 27
Holcombe Moor (5:D6) 265
Holidays 378

The Holies (2:D5) *14
Holme Park Fell (6:E9) *22
Holne Woods (1:F8) *12
Holnicote Estate (1:G5) 28, 29, 67
Holy Jesus Hospital (6:H5) 324
Holywell Bay (1:C8) 26
The Homewood (2:F6) 134
Horden Beach (6:I6) 316
Horsey Mere (3:K4) 182
Horsey Windpump (3:K4) 196
Horton Court (1:J3) 68
Houghton Mill (3:F6) 182, 196
Housesteads Fort (6:F5) 317, 323
Hudswell Woods (5:F3) *20
Hughenden Manor (2:E4) 134

Ibsley Common (2:B8) *14
Ickworth House, Park and
  Gardens (3:H7) 183, 184, 197
Ightham Mote (2:H6) 135
Ilam Park (3:B3) 223

Jack Scout (6:E9) *22

Kearney (7:F7) *24
Kedleston Hall (3:C4) 215, 224
Keld Chapel (6:E7) *22
Killerton (1:G6) 28, 68
Kinder Scout (3:B2) 214
King John's Hunting Lodge
  (1:I4) 71
King's Head (2:E3) 137
Kingston Lacy (1:K7) 72
Kinver Edge and the Rock
  Houses (4:I5) 236, 254
Kinwarton Dovecote (4:K7) 254
Kipling, Rudyard 116
Knightshayes Court (1:G6) 73
Knockinelder (7:F7) *24
Knole (2:H6) 137
The Kymin (4:H8) 341
Kynance Cove (1:C10) 26, 28, 79
Kyson Hill (3:J7) *17

Lacock Abbey and Village
  (1:K4) 74
Lady's Well (6:G3) *23
Lamb House (2:J8) 138
Lambert's Castle (1:I7) 27
Lanhydrock (1:D8) 6, 28, 76
Lanlay Meadows (4:G10) *19
Lardon Chase (2:D5) *14
Larrybane (7:D3) 352

Lavenham: The Guildhall of
Corpus Christi **(3:I7)**   199
Lawrence House **(1:E7)**   77
Lawrence T. E.   49
Learning   374
The Leas **(6:I5)**   316, 317
Leek & Manifold Valley **(4:K3)**   214
Legacies   380
Leigh Woods **(1:I4)**   29
Leith Hill **(2:F7)**   110, 139
Lennon, John   284
Letocetum Roman Baths
(4:K5)   254
Levant Mine and Beam
Engine **(1:A9)**   77
Lewis Carroll's Birthplace
(5:C8)   265
Lighthouse Island **(7:F6)**   *24
Lindisfarne Castle **(6:G1)**   317, 325
Lindsey House **(2:G5)**   175
Lingwood Common **(3:H9)**   *17
Lisnabreeny **(7:E6)**   353
Little Clarendon **(1:K5)**   78
Little Dartmouth **(1:G9)**   *13
Little Fleece Bookshop **(1:J2)**   78
Little Moreton Hall **(5:D9)**   264, 281
Liverpool – European
Capital of Culture 2008   7
The Lizard **(1:C10)**   26, 28, 79
Lizard Point **(1:C10)**   28
Lizard Wireless Station **(1:C10)**   79
Llanbedrog Beach **(4:D4)**   330
Llanerchaeron **(4:D6)**   342
Lode Mill **(3:G7)**   185
Lodge Park **(1:K2)**   80
Loe Pool **(1:B10)**   29, 88
Long Crendon Courthouse
(2:D4)   111, 139
Long Mynd **(4:H5)**   236
Longshaw Estate **(3:C2)**   214, 225
Lough Down **(2:D5)**   *14
Loughwood Meeting
House **(1:H7)**   80
Low Newton-by-Sea **(6:H3)**   *23
Ludshott Common **(2:E7)**   *14
Lundy **(1:D5)**   81
Lydford Gorge **(1:F7)**   28, 82
Lydstep Headland **(4:C9)**   *18
Lyme Park **(5:E8)**   282
Lynmouth **(1:F5)**   *12
Lytes Cary Manor **(1:I5)**   83
Lyveden New Bield **(3:E6)**   226

Maidenhead and Cookham
Commons **(2:E5)**   *14
Maister House **(5:J6)**   306
Malham Tarn Estate
(5:D4)   296, 306
Mam Tor **(3:B2)**   214
The Manor House,
Rathlin Island **(7:E3)**   *24
Marconi Centre **(1:C10)**   79
Marker's Cottage **(1:G7)**   71
Marloes Deer Park & Sands
(4:B8)   330
Marsden Moor Estate
(5:E7)   298, 307
Marsden Rock **(6:I5)**   316
Martin's Haven **(4:B8)**   *18
Max Gate **(1:J7)**   84
Mayon Cliff **(1:A10)**   27
McCartney, Paul   276
Melbury Beacon **(1:K6)**   *13
Melbury Downs **(1:K6)**   28
Melford Hall **(3:I7)**   184, 200
Membership   384
Mendips **(5:C8)**   7, 284
Middle Hope **(1:I4)**   *13
Middle Littleton Tithe Barn
(4:K7)   255
Milldale **(3:B3)**   *16
Minchinhampton Common
(1:J3)   28
Minnowburn **(7:E6)**   353
Mompesson House **(1:K5)**   84
Monk's House **(2:G8)**   140
Monksthorpe Chapel **(3:G3)**   221
Montacute House **(1:I6)**   85
Moorhouse Woods **(6:H6)**   316
Morden Hall Park **(2:G5)**   170, 175
Morris, William   156, 178
Morston Marshes **(3:I4)**   *17
Morte Point **(1:E5)**   31
Morville Hall **(4:I5)**   255
Moseley Old Hall **(4:J5)**   255
Mottisfont Abbey Garden,
House and Estate **(2:C7)**   140
Mottistone Manor Garden
(2:C9)   141
Moulton Hall **(5:F2)**   307
Mount Grace Priory **(5:G3)**   308
Mount Stewart House,
Garden and Temple of
the Winds **(7:F6)**   364
Mourne Coastal Path
(7:E8)   352, 353

Mow Cop **(4:J3)**   265
Mr Hardman's Photographic
Studio **(5:B8)**   7, 278
Mr Straw's House **(3:D2)**   228
Mullaghdoo & Ballykeel **(7:F5)**   *24
Murlough Bay **(7:E3)**   352
Murlough National Nature
Reserve **(7:E8)**   352
Museum of Childhood,
Sudbury Hall **(3:B4)**   4, 229
Mussenden Temple **(7:C3)**   365
Mwnt **(4:C7)**   332
Mynachdy'r Graig **(4:E6)**   *18
Mynydd Bychestyn **(4:C4)**   *18

Nare Head **(1:C9)**   *12
National Gardens Scheme   370
National Trust for Scotland   383
National Trust's Carriage
Collection **(1:F5)**   33
The Needles Old Battery and
New Battery **(2:C9)**   142
Nether Alderley Mill **(5:D8)**   284
Newark Park **(1:J3)**   86
Newbiggin cliffs **(5:J3)**   297
Newton House **(4:E8)**   338
Newton Links & Point **(6:H2)**   *23
Newton, Isaac   232
Newtown Old Town Hall **(2:C9)**   143
North Antrim Cliff Path **(7:D3)**   *24
Northey Island **(3:I9)**   183
Nostell Priory and Parkland
(5:G6)   308
Nunnington Hall **(5:H4)**   309
Nymans **(2:G7)**   143

Oakhurst Cottage **(2:E7)**   145
Old Coastguard Station
(5:I2)   298, 314
The Old Manor **(3:B4)**   227
The Old Mill **(1:F9)**   87
Old Soar Manor **(2:H6)**   145
Orford Ness National Nature
Reserve **(3:K7)**   183, 200
Orlock Point **(7:F6)**   *24
Ormesby Hall **(5:G2)**   310
Ormesby Hall **(5:G2)**   310
Osterley Park and House
(2:F5)   6, 170, 176
Overbeck's **(1:F9)**   87
Owletts **(2:H5)**   145
Oxburgh Hall, Garden and
Estate **(3:H5)**   182, 201

Packwood House (4:K6)   256
Park Head (1:C8)   *12
Parke Estate (1:G7)   *13
Patterson's Spade Mill (7:E6)   366
Paxton's Tower (4:D8)   *18
Paycocke's (3:I8)   203
Peak Alum Works (5:I3)   *21
Peckover House
    and Garden (3:G5)   182, 203
Pen Anglas (4:B7)   *18
Pen y Fan (4:F8)   331
Penarfynydd (4:C4)   *18
Penbryn (4:D7)   332
Pennard Cliffs (4:E9)   *18
Penrhyn Castle (4:E2)   343
Penrose Estate (1:B10)   88
Penshaw Monument (6:H6)   *23
Pentire Point (1:D7)   31
Pepperbox Hill (1:L5)   *13
Petworth House and Park
    (2:E7)   146
Philipps House (1:K5)   89
Photography   387
Pilsdon Pen (1:I6)   *13
Pin Mill (3:J8)   *17
Pitstone Windmill (2:E3)   147
Plas Newydd (4:D2)   344
Plas yn Rhiw (4:C4)   345
Plym Bridge Woods (1:F8)   28
Polesden Lacey (2:F6)   147
Port Mulgrave (5:I2)   297
Port Quin (1:D7)   *12
Porthcurno (1:B10)   26
Porthdinllaen (4:D3)   330
Porthor (4:C3)   *18
Portlemouth Down (1:F9)   *12
Portmuck (7:E5)   *24
Portstewart Strand (7:C3)   366
Potter, Beatrix   264, 268, 280
Powis Castle and Garden
    (4:G5)   346
Prawle Point (1:G9)   *13
Priest's House, Easton (3:E5)   227
Priest's House, Muchelney
    (1:I6)   89
Prior Park Landscape Garden
    (1:J4)   6, 90
Priory Cottages (2:C5)   148
Privacy Policy   386
Public Transport   376

Quarry Bank Mill (5:D8)   4, 6, 285
Quebec House (2:G6)   148

Ragwen Point (4:C8)   *18
Rainham Hall (2:H5)   177
Ramsey Abbey Gatehouse
    (3:F6)   204
Rathlin Island (7:E3)   352
Ravenscar Coastal
    Centre (5:I3)   297
Rayleigh Mount (3:I10)   204
Red House (2:H5)   178
Regional Contacts   383
Reigate Fort (1:F6)   112
Restaurants and tea-rooms   373
Rhossili, Worm's Head and
    Visitor Centre, Gower
    (4:D9)   332, 347
Rievaulx Terrace and Temples
    (5:H3)   311
Riley Graves (3:C2)   *16
River Wey and Godalming
    Navigations (2:F6)   110, 149
Rock Houses (4:I5)   254
Rockford Common (2:B8)   *14
Rodborough Common (1:J2)   28
'Roman' Bath (2:G5)   179
Ros Castle (6:G2)   317
Roseberry Topping (5:G2)   312
Rosedene (4:J6)   257
Rough Tor (1:D7)   *12
Rowallane Garden (7:E7)   367
Royal Military Canal (2:J7)   110
Royal Oak Foundation   380
Rufford Old Hall (5:C6)   264, 286
The Rumps (1:D7)   31
Runnymede (2:F5)   150
Runswick Bay (5:I2)   297

Saddlescombe Farm (2:G8)   112
Salcombe Hill (1:H7)   29
Saltram (1:F8)   92
Sand Point (1:I4)   *13
Sandham Memorial Chapel
    (2:C6)   151
Sandscale Haws (6:D9)   265
Sandy Mouth (1:D6)   26
Scafell Pike (6:D8)   264, 266
Scarthwood Moor (5:G2)   *21
Science Discovery Centre
    (Woolsthorpe Manor) (3:E4)   232
Scotney Castle (2:I7)   151
Seahouses (6:H2)   316
Segontium (4:D2)   348
Selborne Hill and Common
    (2:E7)   *14

Selsdon Wood (2:G6)   *15
Selworthy (1:G5)   *13
Seven Sisters (2:H9)   110, 111
Shalford Mill (2:E6)   152
Sharpenhoe Clappers (3:F8)   183
Shaw G. B.   205
Shaw's Corner (3:F9)   184, 205
Sheffield Park Garden (2:G7)   153
Sherborne Estate (1:L2)   29, 80
Sheringham Park (3:J4)   182, 206
Shopping   372
Shropshire Hills
    (4:H5)   6, 236, 238, 245
Shugborough Estate (4:J4)   257
Shute Barton (1:H7)   93
Shute Shelve Hill (1:I4)   *13
Sissinghurst Castle Garden
    (2:I7)   5, 154
Sizergh Castle and Garden
    (6:E8)   5, 287
Skenfrith Castle (4:H8)   348
Skernaghan Point (7:E5)   352
Skirrid Fawr (4:H8)   331
Slieve Donard (7:E8)   353
Slindon Estate (2:E8)   111
Smallhythe Place (2:I7)   155
Snowshill Manor (1:K1)   94
Soar Mill Cove (1:F9)   *12
Souter Lighthouse
    (6:I5)   316, 317, 326
South Foreland Lighthouse
    (2:K6)   111, 155
South Hole (1:E6)   *12
South Peak (3:B3)   214
Speke Hall, Garden
    and Estate (5:C8)   7, 288
Speltham Down (2:D8)   *14
Spencer, Stanley   151
Springhill (7:C6)   368
Sprivers Garden (2:H7)   156
Spyway Farm (1:K7)   *13
St Aidan's Dunes (6:H2)   *23
St Anthony Head (1:C9)   27, 90
St Bride's Bay (4:B8)   *18
St Cuthbert's Cave (6:G2)   *23
St David's Head (4:A8)   330
St David's Visitor Centre
    and Shop (4:A8)   347
St George's Guildhall (3:H5)   205
St John's Jerusalem (2:H5)   151
St Michael's Mount (1:B9)   91
Stackpole Estate (4:B9)   330, 349
Stagshaw Garden (6:D8)   290

Stainsby Mill, Hardwick
 Estate **(3:D3)** 227
Standen **(2:G7)** 156
Staunton Harold Church
 (3:C4) 228
Staward Gorge **(6:F5)** *317*, *318*
Stembridge Tower Mill **(1:I5)** 95
Steps Bridge **(1:G7)** *13
Stiffkey Marshes **(3:I3)** *17
Stockbridge Common Down
 & Marsh **(2:C7)** *14
Stoke-sub-Hamdon Priory **(1:I6)** 95
Stoneacre **(2:I6)** 157
Stonehenge Landscape **(1:K5)** 95
Stourhead **(1:J5)** *5*, 96
Stowe Landscape Gardens
 (2:D2) 158
Strangford Lough Wildlife
 Centre **(7:F7)** *352*, *354*
Stubbins Estate **(5:D6)** 265
Studland Beach and Nature
 Reserve **(1:K7)** *28*, 98
Studley Royal Water Garden
 (5:F4) 303
Styal Estate **(5:D8)** 285
Sudbury Hall and the National
 Trust Museum of Childhood
 (3:B4) 229
Sugarloaf **(4:H8)** *331*
Sunnycroft **(4:I4)** 258
Sutton Hoo **(3:J7)**
 6, *182*, *184*, 207
Sutton House **(2:G4)** *170*, 179

Talks service *381*
Tarn Hows **(6:D8)** *265*, *266*, 271
Tattershall Castle **(3:F3)** 231
Tatton Park **(5:D8)** 290
Teign Valley **(1:F7)** *12
Tennyson Down **(2:C9)** *14
Terry, Ellen *155*
Theatre Royal,
 Bury St Edmunds **(3:I7)** 208
Thorington Hall **(3:I8)** 208
Thurstaston Common **(5:B8)** *20
Tintagel Old Post Office **(1:D7)** 99
Tintinhull Garden **(1:I6)** 100
Town Walls Tower **(4:H4)** 259
Townend **(6:D8)** 291
Toys Hill **(2:G6)** *111*
Treasurer's House, Martock
 (1:I6) 100

Treasurer's House, York
 (5:H5) *6*, 312
Trelissick Garden **(1:C9)** 101
Trengwainton Garden **(1:B9)** 102
Trerice **(1:C8)** 103
Troutbeck **(6:D8)** 293
Trowlesworthy Warren **(1:F8)** *12
Tudor Merchant's House
 (4:C9) 349
Turnworth Down **(1:J6)** *13
Tŷ Mawr Wybrnant **(4:E3)** 350
Ty'n-y-Coed Uchaf **(4:E3)** 350
Tyntesfield **(1:I4)** 104

Ullswater **(6:D7)** 292
Ulverscroft Nature Reserve
 (3:D5) 232
Uppark House and
 Garden **(2:E8)** 159
Upper Wharfedale **(5:E4)** *296*, 313
Upton House and Gardens
 (4:L7) 260

Volunteering *381*
The Vyne **(2:D6)** 160

Waddesdon Manor **(2:D3)** 161
Wakehurst Place **(2:G7)** 163
Walking *377*
Wallington **(6:G4)** 326
Walton Hill **(1:I5)** *13
Warren House Gill **(6:I6)** *23
Wasdale **(6:C8)** *266*, 292
Washington Old Hall **(6:H5)** 328
Wastwater **(6:D8)** *264*, *266*
Watermeads **(2:G6)** *15
Watermeet **(1:F5)** 105
Watlington Hill **(2:D4)** *14
Weddings *375*
The Weir **(4:H7)** 261
Wellbrook Beetling Mill **(7:C6)** 369
Wellington Monument **(1:H6)** *13
Wembury Point **(1:F9)** *26
Wenlock Edge **(4:I5)** *236*
West Exmoor Coast **(1:F5)** 106
West Green House Garden
 (2:D6) 164
West Pennard Court Barn
 (1:I5) 106
West Runton **(3:J4)** *182*
West Wycombe Park **(2:E4)** 164

West Wycombe Village
 and Hill **(2:E4)** 165
Westbury College Gatehouse
 (1:I3) 106
Westbury Court Garden **(1:J2)** 107
Westwood Manor **(1:J4)** 107
Wetheral Woods **(6:E6)** *22
Wheal Coates **(1:C9)** *12
Whipsnade Estate **(3:E8)** 189
Whipsnade Tree Cathedral
 (3:E8) 209
The White Cliffs of Dover
 (2:K7) *110*, *111*, 166
White Cottage **(5:D8)** 274
White Horse Hill **(2:C4)** *112*
White Mill **(1:K6)** 108
White Park Bay **(7:D3)** *352*
The Witley Centre **(2:E7)** 168
Wichenford Dovecote **(4:I7)** 261
Wicken Fen National Nature
 Reserve **(3:G6)** *183*, *184*, 209
Wightwick Manor **(4:J5)** 262
Wilderhope Manor **(4:H5)** 262
Willington Dovecote and
 Stables **(3:F7)** 210
2 Willow Road **(2:G5)** 180
Wimpole Hall
 (3:G7) *182*, *183*, 210
Wimpole Home Farm
 (3:G7) *184*, 212
Win Green Hill **(1:K6)** *13
Winchester City Mill **(2:D7)** 167
Windermere **(6:D8)** 293
Winkworth Arboretum **(2:F7)** 167
Winnats Pass **(3:B2)** *214*
Winster Market House **(3:C3)** 232
Wolfe, General James *148*
Woodchester Park **(1:J3)** 108
Woolacombe **(1:E5)** *26*
Woolf, Virginia *140*
Woolsthorpe Manor **(3:E4)** 232
Wordsworth House **(6:C7)** 294
The Workhouse, Southwell
 (3:D3) *4*, *6*, 234

Ynys Barri **(4:B7)** *18
Yorkshire Coast **(5:I2)** 314
Ysbyty Estate **(4:F3)** *18

Zennor Head **(1:B9)** 28